English

Based on Latest NCERT

Class 8

English

Based on Latest NCERT

Class 8

Authors
Srishti Agarwal
Wairakpam Chinglembi Chanu

ARIHANT PRAKASHAN
(School Division Series)

卐 **ADMINISTRATIVE & PRODUCTION OFFICES**

Regd. Office

'Ramchhaya' 4577/15, Agarwal Road, Darya Ganj, New Delhi -110002
Tele: 011- 47630600, 43518550; Fax: 011- 23280316

卐 **Head Office**

Kalindi, TP Nagar, Meerut (UP) - 250002, Tel: 0121-7156203, 7156204

卐 **SALES & SUPPORT OFFICES**

Agra, Ahmedabad, Bengaluru, Bareilly, Chennai, Delhi, Guwahati, Hyderabad, Jaipur, Jhansi, Kolkata, Lucknow, Nagpur & Pune.

PO No. : TXT-59-T065785-06-25

Published By Arihant Publications (India) Ltd.

For further information about the books published by Arihant, log on to www.arihantbooks.com or e-mail at info@arihantbooks.com

Follow us on  

卐 **PRICE** ₹ **365.00**

PRODUCTION TEAM

Publishing Managers
Mahendra Singh Rawat &
Keshav Mohan

Project Head
Ashwani

Cover Designer
Bilal Hashmi

Inner Designer
Ankit Tyagi

Page Layouting
Mayank Saini

Proof Readers
Mukul Kaushik
Manish Kumar

Inside the Book

Poetry

Supplementary Reader

All in One®

COMPLETE STUDY | COMPLETE PRACTICE | COMPLETE ASSESSMENT

SECTION A : READING SKILLS

Unseen Passages

Let's REVISE Reading Comprehension or Unseen Passages is a language activity that involves a thorough understanding of a given passage or poem consisting of one or more paragraphs. It tests the understanding powers and analytical skills of a student with questions that evaluate the reader's ability to

- find the main idea or a suitable title for the text.
- find information directly specified in the passage.
- draw conclusions from the given passage.
- determine the meaning of words used in the passage.
- determine the author's style, mood or point of view.

Types of Passages

There are many types of passages from which questions can be asked. They are

- **Factual Passages** These passages include a set of facts and descriptions which are provided in a clear and straightforward manner.
- **Discursive Passages** These passages include opinions, thoughts and comments that a reader interprets to form his/her own opinions.
- **Poetry** These include poems written by poets from all over the world.

Types of Questions

Two types of questions are asked from a reading comprehension

- Multiple Choice Questions
- Subjective Short Answer Type Questions

For a better understanding of the type of questions, we have divided the passages into these two categories.

Points to be Kept in Mind

- Read the passage carefully and thoroughly to understand its contents.
- Read all the questions given.
- Now, read the passage for the second time and underline the words, phrases and sentences which can be answers to the questions asked.
- **For subjective type questions**
  - (i) Write the answers in one or two sentences. Word count should not be more than 20 words.
  - (ii) Write your answers in the same tense in which the questions are asked.
  - (iii) Answer should be to-the-point and in your own words.
- **For MCQs**
  - (i) Read all the four options carefully.
  - (ii) Choose the answer that best connects with the question as per the passage.
- Underline the words you don't understand and try to guess their meaning from the meaning of the sentence. It will help you in answering vocabulary related questions.
- Read the passage again to counter check your answers.

SOLVED EXAMPLES

Objective Type Questions

Read the following passage and answer the questions that follow by choosing the correct option.

PASSAGE 1

No one can argue that acquiring knowledge is more fun and easier with computers. The mere act of touching and exploring this device constitutes an enjoyable activity for a child. This, along with a relaxed attitude and software interactivity, generally contributes to a better understanding of new knowledge. At the higher educational level, the availability of digital books, simulators and other academic materials provide the student with an always accessible source of information, which would otherwise not be at hand.

But in addition to the increasing complexity and behaviour of intelligent software, which is usually embedded in academic digital material, the need for human interaction in the learning process will always be present, at least in the near future. A human being is able to determine what each person's specific needs are. A computer, no matter how sophisticated its software, can hardly imitate a teacher's skill in how to explain and adapt complex concepts to different people.

Questions

1. According to the passage, what is the impact of computers on acquiring knowledge?

(a) It makes acquiring knowledge complex but entertaining.

(b) It makes acquiring knowledge more fun and easier.

(c) It makes acquiring knowledge repetitive and complex.

(d) It makes acquiring knowledge a scientific task.

2. What is the role of intelligent software in academic digital material, according to the passage?

(a) It replaces human interaction in the learning process.

(b) It helps students learn new knowledge more easily.

(c) It makes the learning process more complex and difficult.

(d) Both (a) and (b)

3. Why does the need for human interaction in the learning process still exist?

(a) Because computers are not sophisticated enough.

(b) Because each person's specific needs must be determined.

(c) Because computers are not always accessible.

(d) Because human interaction is a must for education.

4. What is the disadvantage of intelligent software, according to the passage?

(a) It is too expensive for educational institutions to afford.

(b) It requires too much effort from students to learn how to use it.

(c) It cannot adapt complex concepts to different people like a teacher can.

(d) It requires manpower to make sure that it is working correctly.

5. What does the word 'embedded' mean?

(a) Used (b) Joined (c) Inserted (d) Excluded

6. What can be an appropriate title for the passage?

(a) Can Computers Replace Teachers?

(b) Computers in Education

(c) What Computers Lack?

(d) The Generation of Computers

Answers

1. (b) It makes acquiring knowledge more fun and easier.
2. (d) Both (a) and (b)
3. (b) Because each person's specific needs must be determined.
4. (c) It cannot adapt complex concepts to different people like a teacher can.
5. (c) Inserted
6. (a) Can Computers Replace Teachers?

Subjective Type Questions

Read the following passage and answer the questions that follow.

PASSAGE 2

1. Yoga in India is considered to be around 5,000 years old mental, physical and spiritual practice. It originated in ancient times when people used to meditate to transform their body and mind. Launching and celebrating 21st June as Yoga Day was an initiative taken by the Indian Prime Minister in the United Nations General Assembly. From then, Yoga Day became a worldwide event celebrated by the people of all countries.

2. Yoga is essentially a spiritual discipline. It is the art and science of healthy living. It is a practice of controlled body part movements and control of breath. It is not just a physical practice but also a way to get control over mental, emotional and spiritual thoughts. It improves discipline and sense of power while providing a chance to live a healthy life without physical and mental problems.

3. Yoga is a very safe, easy and healthy way to remain fit without any problems. It can be practiced by people at any age-be it childhood, teenage, adult or old age irrespective of age, religion or health circumstances. It needs only safe, slow and controlled movements of body with controlled breathing. Regular practice of yoga regularises the connection between the body, mind and soul.
It enhances the functioning of all the body organs. By providing good health it fulfills our physical needs, through knowledge it fulfills our psychological needs and through inner peace it fulfills our spiritual needs. Thus, it helps in maintaining the harmony among all.

4. Regular practice of yoga in the morning provides outer and inner relief by keeping away from countless ailments at the physical and mental level. Practising postures or asana creates the feeling of well-being. It sharpens the human mind, improves intelligence and helps in achieving high level of concentration. Yoga is like a practical philosophy which develops self-discipline and self-awareness.

5. We cannot count the benefits of yoga; we can understand it only as a miracle which can be experienced by practice. It maintains physical fitness, reduces stress, controls emotions, feelings, controls negative thoughts, feelings of general well-being, improves mental clarity, enhances self-understanding and connects us to the nature.

Questions

1. What is the importance of asanas in yoga?
2. How does yoga fulfill our psychological needs?
3. Complete the given sentence with an appropriate inference with respect to the following.

   Yoga enables one to get control over ....
4. Is there any specificity in the age group for people who can practice yoga?
5. Substitute the underlined word in the given line with a word from the passage which means the opposite.

   The lights <u>diminishes</u> the ambience of the banquet.
6. What is meant by 'harmony' in the given passage?

Answers

1. Asanas in yoga create a feeling of well-being in a person. By practicing asanas, one can sharpen one's mind and improve one's intelligence and concentration.
2. Yoga fulfills our psychological needs by providing us knowledge.
3. our mental, emotional and spiritual thoughts
4. No, there is no specificity in the age group for people who can practice yoga. As per the writer, people from all walks of life can practice yoga.
5. Enhances
6. The word 'harmony' means 'balance' in the given passage.

REVIEW EXERCISE

Including Objective and Subjective Type Passages

Objective Type Questions

PASSAGE 1

Read the following passage and answer the questions that follow by choosing the correct option.

In a democratic setup, a consensual decision carries a special significance for any remarkable change. It reflects the collective spirit of the transformational journey. Recently, Bharat has witnessed historic decisions of global resonance — one is the building of consensus on the Delhi Declaration as part of the G20 presidency, the other is the passing of Nari Shakti Vandan Adhiniyam.

The first legislative agenda of the new Parliament building has set the tone for women-led development as a way forward for the nation. The Modi Government has shown great zeal to turn this sankalp into siddhi. This has been a 27-year-long journey to give women their due share in representative democracy. In a very simplistic manner, the existing minimal share of nari shakti, which constitutes half the population, was a lacuna. Social dynamics had made women a mere decision-adherer rather than a decision-maker to some extent. Numerous exceptions are there to counter this view: Women have broken the glass ceiling and have made the nation proud in every sphere. Now, the Narendra Modi Government has prioritised this moral choice and showcased a strong will to correct this historical lacuna. The gender justice proposed by the Nari Shakti Vandan Adhiniyam in the legislative domain will provide impetus to balanced policy formulation. It is a step to realise the spirit of one person, one vote and one value.

1. What is an important criterion for a remarkable change?
   (a) Consensual decision (b) Democratic set-up
   (c) Diversity (d) Both (a) and (b)
2. What does the phrase 'global resonance' indicate?
   (a) Prestige (b) Importance (c) Grace (d) Joy
3. What changed with the Nari Shakti Vandan Adhiniyam?
   (a) Women Empowerment became central.
   (b) Women were declared central to Make in India.
   (c) Women became decision makers.
   (d) Women representation increased.
4. The phrase 'glass ceilings' indicate ....
   (a) limitations (b) advantages
   (c) rights and duties (d) freedom
5. The word .... in the passage means 'gap'.
   (a) seal (b) lacuna (c) impetus (d) spirit
6. Which of the following is/are true for Nari Shakti Vandan Adhiniyam?
   (a) It tries to overcome the age old traditions that curb women's growth.
   (b) It was introduced in the G20 conference.
   (c) It was the first decision taken in the new Parliament Building.
   (d) All of the above

PASSAGE 2

Read the following passage and answer the questions that follow by choosing the correct option.

Manikarnika was born into a Maratha family. She was married to Raja Gangadhar Rao, the Maharaja of Jhansi and became the Rani of Jhansi. After her marriage, Manikarnika was named Lakshmibai. Before her marriage, she was known as Chabeeli (meaning 'jolly ways'). On the day before Raja's death in November 1853, he adopted his cousin's child. The Raja wrote a letter to the British Government of India requesting that his widow should be recognised as the ruler of Jhansi after his death during her lifetime. After the death of her husband, the British Government refused to allow her adopted son, Damodar Rao, to become Raja and rule Jhansi. They had a policy - if an Indian ruler died without a male child his adopted son would not succeed him. After all the British in Jhansi had been killed by Indian troops in June 1857, the Rani took over the administration provisionally. She had to form an army to defeat the invading forces of neighbours. British forces led by Sir Hugh Rose came to Jhansi to take back the city from Lakshmibai, who now wanted independence. Jhansi was taken after strong resistance. Many of the people of the city were killed in the battle. The Rani escaped to Kalpi and jointly with the Maratha general Tantya Tope held Gwalior. In the battle of Kotahki Serai their army was defeated, Rani Lakshmibai was wounded and died on 18th June, 1858.

Questions

1. What was Manikarnika known as before her marriage?

(a) Rani Lakshmibai (b) Rani of Jhansi
(c) Chabeeli (d) Jolly

2. Upon whose request was Manikarnika made the ruler of Jhansi?

(a) Raja Gangadhar Rao (b) Damodar Rao
(c) Her father (d) Britishers

3. Why couldn't Manikarnika's adopted son rule over Jhansi?

(a) Because the Britishers wanted to rule over Jhansi
(b) Because according to British law, adopted sons can't take over kingship
(c) Because the adopted son was deemed unfit by the Britishers
(d) Because the Britishers did not like the adopted son

4. Where did Manikarnika go after losing the battle to the Britishers?

(a) Gwalior (b) Maharastra
(c) Kalpi (d) All of these

5. What does the word 'provisionally mean'?

(a) Transitionally (b) Permanently
(c) Conditionally (d) Temporarily

6. Choose an antonym of 'resistance'.

(a) Opposition (b) Refusal
(c) Acceptance (d) Encouragement

PASSAGE 3

Read the following passage and answer the questions that follow by choosing the correct option.

The seasonal problem of water taps running dry is plaguing most of our major cities. With the bigger rivers flowing in trickles and ponds and wells reduced to clay-pits, village women in remote areas have to fetch every drop of water for drinking, cooking, washing and so on, across large distances. This has only worsened a perennial problem, that of widespread pollution of water, rendering it unfit for human consumption. The monsoons and the attendant floods will not solve this problem. The Delhi Administration is seriously worried about the threat to civic health posed by the polluted waters of the Yamuna. Two new tanks are to be set up to treat sewage. At present, only 60 per cent of the 200 million gallons of the city's sewage receives any kind of treatment before it is dumped into the river which supplies water not only to this city but to innumerable towns and villages downstream. The Ganga, the Yamuna, the Cauvery, in fact all our important rivers serving many urban conglomerations are fast becoming a major source of disease.

A comprehensive bill introduced in Parliament envisages the setting up of Central and State boards for the prevention and control of water pollution. But, it will obviously take some time before legislation is passed and effectively implemented. Meanwhile, the problem continues to swell.

According to a survey of eight developing countries conducted a couple of years ago, 90 per cent of all child deaths were due to water-borne diseases. It is the same unchanged story today. In a country like India, a burgeoning population continuing to use the open countryside as a lavatory means that with every dust storm and rain; human excreta laden with germs and parasite spores find their way to ponds, shallow wells and even the streams and rivers. Only 18 per cent of the rural folk have access to potable water.

Questions

1. What problem is being discussed in the passage?

(a) Lack of treatment of sewage water
(b) Water pollution
(c) Issues related with water
(d) The comprehensive bill related to water

2. What threat is Delhi facing?

(a) Civic health (b) Water scarcity
(c) Pollution of Yamuna (d) Children's deaths

3. What does the Comprehensive bill for water pollution call for?

(a) National boards to tackle the problem
(b) State boards to tackle the problem
(c) Law to impose fine on polluters
(d) Both (a) and (b)

4. What Indian problem related to water is mentioned in Para 4 of the passage?

(a) Lack of treatment (b) Open lavatories
(c) Lack of potable water (d) All of these

5. What does the word 'plaguing' mean?

(a) Suffering (b) Easing
(c) Torturing (d) Despairing

6. Which word from the passage means the same as 'a combination of businesses'?

(a) Conglomerates (b) Envisages
(c) Spores (d) Dumped

PASSAGE 4

Read the following passage and answer the questions that follow by choosing the correct option.

Skater Girl's set, which is now a public park in Khempur, is a training village for children to skate for free. This Desert Dolphin Skate Park is located in Khempur, which is about 40 km from Udaipur.

Film sets usually die soon after a movie has been wrapped up. The set of the Netflix original movie, Skater Girl (released on 11th June, 2021), has lived on and is producing sports stars. The movie revolves around a 16-year-old girl from a Rajasthan village who is introduced to skating through a chance encounter with a British-Indian woman in Khempur, a village about 40 km from Udaipur. The sport changes her life in the movie, and the park is changing the lives of many other children in the village.

Since the movie wrapped in 2019, the Desert Dolphin Skate Park has been the ground for training hundreds of village children to skate for free. Four kids from Khempur have gone on to represent Rajasthan in the National Skateboarding Championship in Chandigarh. A boy who was earlier considered 'slow' took part in the competition and topped his district in Sanskrit. "He's an expressive and creative child who just needed a catalyst to unleash his real talent and build his confidence. These kids who had never stepped on a skateboard before the skate park was made, are now in state jerseys travelling for the first time outside their villages to take part in a national level championship," says Manjari Makijany, the maker of Skater Girl and also the daughter of Mac Mohan, who played Sambha in the movie Sholay.

This Park sprawls across 14,500 sq. ft. and is open to all and has become a personal endeavour for Makijany and her producing partners. The family has set up a trust called 'The Living Grace Foundation' to support the project. The organisation has been providing skateboards, safety equipment and training for free to the children.

Zeroing on the location was no easy task. The filmmaker travelled thousands of kilometres through scorching summers to find the right location. While the vibrancy and picturesque backdrop of Rajasthan was one of the reasons they chose the state, they also wanted to pick a place where people would take to skating. "We had three prerequisites to lock a place: it had to have a rustic backdrop have concrete roads so kids could skate, and there had to be over a thousand kids in and around the village so the skate park could be beneficial to the local community after the film," says Makijany. Khempur checked all three boxes for them. "The children of Khempur were some of the most creative ones we met–they had made makeshift skateboards out of wood and scrap material. We feel incredibly proud of these kids and how they've excelled overall at school and in skating."

Diksha

Questions

1. Pick the option that suitably paraphrases the following excerpt from the text.

Film sets usually die soon after a movie has been wrapped up. The set of the Netflix original movie...has lived on...

(a) the personnel who worked on constructing the skate park shall continue to live in the memory of all.
(b) the skate park set continues to be used since it was not dismantled after the shooting of the movie.
(c) the shooting of the movie involved bringing a dead skate park to life and using it as a set.
(d) the villagers of the movie destination felt alive during the shooting of the movie.

2. One of the reasons why Makijany chose Khempur because she was aware that

(a) its summer would bring out the uncomfortable living conditions.
(b) the village had children who were creative and fit.
(c) lack of concrete roads would make village scenes seem authentic.
(d) a large number of children would eventually benefit from the created set.

3. Pick the feature of a dolphin that makes it an appropriate choice for being included in the name for the desert skate park at Khempur.

(a) Dolphins have a tapered streamlined body that's thick near the center and tapers down towards the ends.
(b) Dolphins communicate through clicks, whistles and also by slapping the water's surface with their tail or bodies.
(c) Dolphins are playful and are known, in part, for the aerial acrobatics they do out of the water.
(d) Dolphins must rise regularly to the surface to breathe.

4. What kind of people are Makijany and her producing partners, according to the lines given below?

This Park ... is open to all and has become a personal endeavour for Makijany and her producing partners.

(a) Philanthropists
(b) Stalwarts
(c) Consultants
(d) Socialites

5. Select the option with an appropriate Cause-Effect relationship, as per the text.

	Cause	Effect
(a)	Boy excelled overall at school	Skateboarding built confidence
(b)	Boy topped in Sanskrit	Creative and confident
(c)	Creative and confident	Boy excelled overall, at school
(d)	Skateboarding built confidence	Boy topped in Sanskrit

6. Which word from the passage means the same as 'release'?
   (a) Prerequisite (b) Unleashes
   (c) Catalyst (d) Endeavour

PASSAGE 5

Read the following passage and answer the questions that follow by choosing the correct option.

Many people think that dialects are distorted forms of language, spoken by ignorant people who make mistakes because they haven't learnt the correct grammar. This is not true at all. A standard language is not linguistically 'superior' to other dialects. It is only a dialect adopted for government and official purposes like education.

All English dialects have a long history, going back to "the distinct forms of speech of the Germanic and Scandinavian invaders who came from different parts of northern Europe to occupy Britain in the Middle Ages." And each of these dialects has a grammar that is as rich and systematic as Standard English.

Questions

1. What is the common misconception about dialects?
   (a) They are the only correct form of language
   (b) They are a distorted form of language spoken by ignorant people
   (c) They are only used for official government purposes
   (d) They are not important in language history
2. How far back does the history of English dialects go?
   (a) To the 18th century
   (b) To the Renaissance
   (c) To the Middle Ages
   (d) To the 20th century
3. What is the purpose of a standard language?
   (a) To be adopted for government and official purposes
   (b) To promote cultural diversity
   (c) To be linguistically superior to other dialects
   (d) To limit linguistic expression
4. What is the origin of English dialects?
   (a) They were created by language experts to enrich the English language
   (b) They were brought to England by French invaders
   (c) They were distinct forms of speech of Germanic and Scandinavian invaders
   (d) They evolved from Standard English over time
5. Why is it important to understand the value of dialects?
   (a) To promote a standardised form of language
   (b) To preserve cultural diversity and history
   (c) To limit linguistic expression
   (d) To prove the superiority of Standard English
6. What is the antonym of 'standard'?
   (a) Strange (b) Unusual (c) Great (d) Boring

PASSAGE 6

Read the following passage and answer the questions that follow by choosing the correct option.

If a country should have a message for its people, it should be a message of human dignity. The ideals of a nation should be freedom of thought, speech, press, right of assembly, and right of worship. A country should boldly declare to a world dominated by tyrants that "all men are created equal and endowed by their creator with certain unalienable rights" and "among them life, liberty and the pursuit of happiness". It should be the source of strength and power for a nation. If people have the freedom to live their lives with dignity, they can function with a sound mind and physical health.

A country's moral, political and economic status lies in the strength of its people. A nation should strive to become a more perfect, country where people are given commitment and hope in their hearts to work and cherish freedom, justice and opportunity. We don't always get what we want when we want it, but it's always good to believe that someday, somehow, we will get what we want.

Questions

1. What message should a country have for its people?
   (a) A message of power and strength
   (b) A message of superiority over other nations
   (c) A message of human dignity
   (d) A message of domination over other nations
2. What are the ideals of a nation, according to the passage?
   (a) Freedom of thought, speech, press, right of assembly, and right of worship
   (b) Authoritarianism, suppression of thought and speech, censorship, and forced religious adherence

(c) Monarchy, aristocracy, and theocracy
(d) Totalitarianism, fascism, and communism

3. What should a country declare to a world dominated by tyrants?
(a) That all men are created equal and endowed by their creator with certain unalienable rights
(b) That it is a superior nation with the right to dominate other nations
(c) That it is a weak and helpless nation that needs protection from other nations
(d) That it is a totalitarian state with no regard for individual rights

4. Where should a country's strength and power come from?
(a) From the freedom of its people to live their lives with dignity
(b) From its military might and aggression
(c) From its economic superiority over other nations
(d) From its political dominance over other nations

5. What lies in a country's moral, political, and economic status, according to the passage?
(a) The strength of its people
(b) The size of its military
(c) The amount of its natural resources
(d) The power of its political leaders

6. What should a nation strive to become, according to the passage?
(a) A country where people cherish freedom, justice, and opportunity
(b) A country that dominates other nations through military might
(c) A country that suppresses the rights of its people
(d) A country that follows the orders of its political leaders without question

PASSAGE 7

Read the following poem and answer the questions that follow by choosing the correct option.

Upon Westminster Bridge

Earth has not anything to show more fair:
Dull would he be of soul who could pass by
A sight so touching in its majesty:
This City now doth like a garment wear
The beauty of the morning; silent, bare,
Ships, towers, domes, theatres, and temples lie
Open unto the field, and to the sky;
All bright and glittering in the smokeless air.
Never did Sun more beautifully steep
In his first splendour valley, rock, or hill;
Ne'er saw I, never felt, a calm so deep!
The river glideth at his own sweet will:
Dear God! The very houses seem asleep;
And all that mighty heart is lying still!

by William Wordsworth

Questions

1. The narrator calls a person dull if he/she.
(a) Does not talk to him openly
(b) Does not know about romantic sites
(c) Passes by without experiencing the beauty of the morning
(d) Passes over the site and shouts loudly

2. The city of London appears as if it is ....
(a) covered with thick layer of smoke
(b) clad in attractive colourful clothing
(c) desolate and lonely
(d) sleeping beauty

3. The morning sight of the city bears a ....
(a) peaceful and serene look
(b) noisy and crowdy look
(c) dark and dreary scene
(d) enchanting and haunting appearance

4. 'All bright and glittering', all refers to ....
(a) residents of the city
(b) gardens of the city
(c) malls and multiplexes of the city
(d) ships, towers, domes, theatres, and temples

5. The movement of the river is ....
(a) rough and rumbling
(b) fast and gushing
(c) smooth and continuous
(d) dead slow and motionless

6. The word .... in the poem means the same as 'slide'.
(a) pass by (b) bare (c) unto (d) glideth

PASSAGE 8

Read the following poem and answer the questions that follow by choosing the correct option.

Oh! Defenders of borders
You are great sons of my land
When we are all asleep
You still hold on to your deed.
Windy season or snowy days
Or scorching sun's sweltering rays
You are there guarding all the time awake
Treading the lonely expanses as Yogis.
Climbing the heights or striding the valleys

Defending the deserts and guarding the marshes
Surveillance in seas and by securing the air
Prime of your youth given to the nation!!
Wind chimes of my land vibrate your feat
We pray for you brave men!! May the Lord bless you all!!

by Dr. APJ Abdul Kalam

Questions

1. What is the tone of the poem?
   (a) Soothing (b) Dedicative
   (c) Matter of fact (d) Happy
2. Pick the option that paraphrases the following lines.
   "Treading the lonely expanses as Yogis."
   (a) The soldiers take difficult journeys alone
   (b) The soldiers are as dedicated as Yogis
   (c) The soldiers hide in isolated places like Yogis
   (d) The soldiers are like yogis who have only one motive in mind
3. The word 'deed' in the given poem is a refers to
   (a) the position of soldiers (b) the act of safeguarding
   (c) the act of hiding (d) the dedication of soldiers
4. What qualities can be associated with soldiers on the basis of the poem?
   (a) Strong (b) Brave
   (c) High endurance (d) All of these
5. 'Wind chimes of my land vibrate your feat' can be best explained as appreciation for
   (a) the physical endurance of soldiers
   (b) the efforts and sacrifices of soldiers
   (c) bravery and strength of soldiers
   (d) Both (a) and (c)
6. Which word from the poem means the same as 'going through'?
   (a) sweltering (b) defending
   (c) treading (d) chimes

Subjective Type Questions

PASSAGE 1

Read the following passage and answer the questions that follow.

We've inherited a difficult Earth. It's not an extremely pleasant place to live in, and despite the jokes about Mars, we're limited to this world. It's made us angrier. We've grown up a wary, uncertain generation, bombarded with unprecedented amounts of information, most of which, at least in recent times, has been a sombre reminder of how terrible the world can be. We've grown up preparing ourselves for an inevitable war. Every generation has its conflicts, and we've had the dubious privilege of knowing that ours are vaster, deadlier, and more destructive than ever before. We are acutely aware of what's at stake, and crippled by this realisation as much as we are empowered by it.

In this flux, I have a small request for you. I implore you to chase beauty. Not in people, not in the ways the media tells you beauty manifests. No, I beg you to chase what calls to your heart, what makes your blood sing, what forces you to close your eyes and sigh softly because of the sheer impact it has on you. Chase colours that elude you. Hum half-remembered pieces of music till someone joins you in your search of the other half. Trace ink splatters again and again till they brand themselves into the muscles of your fingers.

You'll be told that this is a waste of time. That, in a world where people are dying, where you might be next, it's not wise to spend time looking at things, even creating things that can't double up as weapons. But please, all I ask of you is to pause.

To look at art, maybe, and sigh, not because of its historical value, but because it tugs at you. To read poetry and find it nestling in the crevices of your heart that need warmth. To smile, because you feel. Humanity has, since its inception, created art and revelled in it. It has, without fail, tried to seek out beauty, and has tried so hard to commemorate it. The world is very keen to make a hardened soldier out of you. Be soft, be receptive to love, to excitement, to joy. We've inherited a difficult Earth. But it's still Earth. It's still soil, fecund and fragrant, waiting for roots to wrap itself around. **Diksha**

Plant yourself. Breathe. Bloom.

Questions

1. This writer missed posting this piece of writing in a category and left it 'Uncategorised'.
   Which category from the given list would most likely categorise the given text?

Categories	
• architecture	• beauty and fashion
• dentistry	• education
• entertainment	• geography
• lifestyle and living	• music

2. State the correct sequence of the usage of the given words from the text to fill the given blanks.

(i) revelled	(ii) flux	(iii) dubious
(iv) unprecedented	(v) inception	

Meera never had a set routine. It was in a constant state of .... due to .... events that occurred frequently. Her father advised her to organise her schedule, to create a time-table, to do away with .... information about 'just chilling' and to reclaim the hours of the day. Meera is a changed person since the .... of this particular lifestyle advice. Good going Meera!

3. Why have we grown into a wary, uncertain generation?
4. What is the author's request in the passage?
5. For what reason do the people around you call chasing beauty a waste of time?
6. Which word in the passage is an antonym of 'end'?

PASSAGE 2

Read the following passage and answer the questions that follow.

Will anyone ever find Shackleton's lost ship?
by Jonathan Amos, Science correspondent

It's going to take a monumental effort to locate the iconic ship of Antarctic explorer Ernest Shackleton.

This is the conclusion of scientists who tried and failed last year to find the Endurance, which sank in 3,000m of water in the Weddell Sea in 1915. The team says the sea-ice in the area above the wreck site is nearly always thick and extensive. It means most expeditions would struggle even to get close enough to begin a search.

The Weddell Sea Expedition 2019 did amazingly well, reaching the recognised wreck location and launching an Autonomous Underwater Vehicle (AUV) to survey the ocean floor. But this robot broke communications with the expedition research vessel, SA Agulhas II, some 20 hours into its mapping operation and was never seen again.

What it might have detected, we'll never know. Encroaching sea-ice forced the team to abandon its AUV and to vacate the area. The expedition scientists have now written up an assessment of the local conditions in this unforgiving sector of the Antarctic. They've also provided some advice for anyone else who might want to search for Shackleton's polar yacht.

"To finally locate the Endurance on the seafloor would require favourable sea-ice conditions in the Central Western Weddell Sea, including the presence of wide (open water) leads," said Dr. Christine Batchelor from the Scott Polar Research Institute (SPRI) in Cambridge, UK.

"In addition, a two-ship operation may be needed to break ice and successfully launch and recover an autonomous underwater vehicle," she told BBC News.

Shackleton's story is one of the most extraordinary tales from the 'heroic age' of Antarctic exploration. Trapped in sea-ice for over 10 months, his Endurance ship drifted around the Weddell Sea until ultimately it was crushed by the floes and dropped to the deep. How Shackleton and his men then made their escape on foot and in lifeboats is the stuff of legend.

Diksha

Questions

1. How did Shackelton's men make their journey to safety?
2. According to scientists, what are the preliminary requirements for finding Shackelton's polar yacht?
3. State True or False.

   The Endurance sank in the year 1915.
4. Close to which continent did Shackleton's ship make its maiden voyage?
5. Complete the sentence appropriately.

   The expedition research vessel sent to look for Shackleton's ship was called ....
6. Which word from the passage means the same as 'expedition'?

PASSAGE 3

Read the following passage and answer the questions that follow.

Today's woman is a highly self-directed person, alive to the sense of her dignity and the importance of her functions in the private-domestic domain and the public domain of the world of work. Women are rational in approach, careful in handling situations and want to do things as best as possible. The Fourth World Conference of Women held in Beijing in September 1995 had emphasised that no enduring solution of society's most threatening social, economic and political problems could be found without the participation and empowerment of women. The 1995 World Summit for Social Development had also emphasised the pivotal role of women in eradicating poverty and mending the social fabric.

The Constitution of India has conferred on women equal rights and opportunities - political, social, educational and of employment-with men. Because of oppressive traditions, superstitions, exploitation and corruption, a majority of women are not allowed to enjoy the rights and opportunities bestowed on them. One of the major reasons for this state of affairs is the lack of literacy and awareness among women. Education is the main instrument through which we can narrow down the prevailing inequality and accelerate the process of economic and political change in the status of women.

The role of women in a society is very important. Women's education is the key to a better life in the future. A recent World Bank study says that educating girls is not a charity, it is good economics and if developing nations are to eradicate poverty, they must educate the girls. Society would progress only if the status of women is respected and the presence of an educated woman in the family would ensure education of the family itself.

Questions

1. What are the qualities that can be attached to the women of today?
2. What had the Fourth World Conference of Women said about the empowerment of women?
3. Why are women not allowed to enjoy the rights conferred upon them by the Constitution?
4. List the importance of education as stated in the passage.
5. How is educating women 'good economics'?
6. Which word from the passage means the same as 'remove'?

PASSAGE 4

Read the following passage and answer the questions that follow.

Street Art in India - The Rise of True Expressions

Modern and contemporary art involves creative thinking and originality of conception more importantly than fineness of execution. In this era of rapidly evolving mediums of expression, several artists have done the unconventional by choosing the 'concrete jungle', that is the city, as their canvas. In India, in particular, street or public art has gained a serious increase in stature owing to the fine artistry involved and the socially and psychologically relevant issues they depict. There has been a surge of street art all over the country but its presence is felt most strongly in the country's capital.

The rise of this subculture can be attributed to the Street Art Festival held in Delhi for the first time in the year 2013, bringing together the efforts of a grand community of artists to liven up the dilapidated walls and buildings.
In particular, the alleyways of Shahpur Jat and Shankar Market areas in Delhi serve as examples of stunning exhibitions of murals depicting human life and the animal world. Prominent among the artists are The U.F.O crew, ostensibly based in Gujarat, TYLER from Mumbai, YANTR from Assam, and Lucangelo CORV from Kolkata - who challenge conventional notions of street art by introducing a near professional standard of craftsmanship in their works.

In using the urban landscape as inspiration, the underground street artists' movement has seen a growth in the new emerging forms of public art that deviates from stickers and stencils such as mosaics and 3D art. What seems promising is the fact that the government has been openly supportive of street artists on several occasions in the past, which has given the movement the impetus it needed to become a mainstream art form.

In fact, instances of this are visible in the form of the magnificent mural of Mahatma Gandhi painted on the walls of the Delhi police headquarters - an initiative of Street Art India. Perhaps the only downside to this form of art is the lack of preservation of the artworks, but since the canvas is a swiftly developing one, it also gives the artist the opportunity to repaint and recreate their works from a new perspective.

Diksha

Questions

1. Complete the sentence appropriately.

   Some artists challenge conventional notions of street art. This means that some artists ....
2. State True or False.

   Gandhi's image is painted on Delhi Police Headquarters.
3. State the meaning of the 'impetus' as used in the passage.
4. According to the text, Street Art makes use of the urban landscape as inspiration. What comes under urban landscape?

   (1) Buildings
   (2) Railway stations
   (3) Lakes and streams
   (4) Community Parks
   (5) Parking lots
   (6) Farm
5. The medium of expression used by the street artists is impermanent. Give one reason how this is that an advantage for this art form.
6. What is the downside of street art?

PASSAGE 5

Read the following passage and answer the questions that follow.

Today there is a lot of talk about the environment. All nations are coming to an agreement to save planet Earth. We pollute the Earth, we pollute the water; we also pollute the subtle environment through our negative feelings and emotions. We have become a victim of our greed and needs. We are not in control of our mind. We hear a lot about other things in life but we spend very little time to hear about ourselves. How to handle our mind? How to be in the present moment? How to be happy and grateful? This we have not learnt. This is the most unfortunate thing.
Then what is the solution? This is where we are reminded of a very fundamental principle that governs our environment, our mind, our emotions and our life in general.

Our body has the capactiy to sustain much longer the vibration of bliss and peace than it does negative emotions because positivity is in the centre of our existence. As with the structure of atom, protons and neutrons are in the centre of the atom and electrons constitute only the periphery; the same is with our lives. The centre core of our existence is bliss, positivity and joy but it is surrounded by a cloud of negative ions. Through the help of the breath we can easily get over our negative emotions in a short period of time. Through meditation and certain breathing techniques, we can clear this negative cloud.

Everyone wants to be successful in life. But without knowing what success is, you want to be successful. What is the sign of success? Just having a lot of money, is that success? Why do you think money means success? Because money gives you freedom so that you can do whatever you want. You may have a big bank balance, but you have stomachaches, ulcers, you may have to go for bypass surgery, can't eat this, can't do this, can't do that. We expend half our health to gain wealth and then spend half our wealth to gain back the lost health. Is this success? Infact, it is very bad mathematics.

Then, what is the sign of success? It is confidence, compassion, generosity and a smile that none can snatch away, being really happy and being able to be more free.

Questions

1. What is the most unfortunate thing?
2. How can we get rid of our negative emotions?
3. What is 'Bad Mathematics', according to the passage?
4. What are the main signs of a successful person?
5. How are we not in control of our mind?
6. Find out a word from the passage which means 'the outer area'.

PASSAGE 6

Read the following passage and answer the questions that follow.

The test of a great book is whether we want to read it only once or more than once. A really great book is one which we want to read the second time even more than we wanted to read it the first time; and every additional time that we read it we find new meanings and new beauties in it. A book that a person of education and good taste does not care to read more than once is most probably not worth much. But we cannot consider the judgement of a single individual infallible.

The opinion that makes a book great must be the opinion of many, for even the greatest critics are apt to have certain dullness. Carlyle, for example, could not endure Browning; Byron could not endure some of the greatest of English poets. A man must be many-sided to utter a trustworthy estimate of many books.

The best of all libraries for a poor man would be a library entirely composed of such great works only, books which have passed the test of time. This then would be the most important guide for us in the choice of readings.
The second fact demanding attention is the general character of the value that lies hidden within all such great books. They never become old; their youth is immortal. A great book is not apt to be comprehended by a young person at the first reading except in a superficial way. Only the surface, the narrative, is absorbed and enjoyed. No young man can possibly see at first reading the qualities of a great book.

Questions

1. What is the quality of a great book?
2. What kind of understanding of a great book is a young person likely to have at the first reading of that book?
3. Whose work did Carlyle find difficult to appreciate?
4. What would a poor man's library contain?
5. Find from the passage the words which mean not 'capable of making mistakes'.
6. Which word is an antonym of 'delight'?

PASSAGE 7

Read the following poem and answer the questions that follow.

I was angry with my friend:
I told my wrath, my wrath did end.
I was angry with my foe:
I told it not, my wrath did grow.
And I watered it in fears,
Night and morning with my tears;
And I sunned it with smiles,
And with soft deceitful wiles.
And it grew both day and night,
Till it bore an apple bright.
And my foe beheld it shine.
And he knew that it was mine,
And into my garden stole
When the night had veiled the pole;
In the morning glad I see
My foe outstretched beneath the tree.

Questions

1. How does the poet's anger for his friend ends?
2. What happened to the anger for the poet's foe?
3. How does the poet's foe die?
4. How did the poet get the Poison tree to bear an apple?
5. Give the synonym of the word 'foe'.
6. Do you think that the poem follows a rhyme scheme? What is it?

PASSAGE 8

Read the following poem and answer the questions that follow.

The Last Will of the Tiger

1. When you have stolen my skin from my entity
and removed the roar from my life
O hunter wield that skinning knife
with some grace a little skill
for I too have hunted and killed
many many many times
but every kill
was a prayer in praise of the Creator
my movements were always quick, clean, merciful
Such is the way of true believers

2. But do you now skinner slice slash and cut clean
I pray only that you leave no part of me behind
to be eaten by the jackal and the hyena
for I have ruled this forest on behalf of the creator
himself and there is no honour in a king becoming
carrion …

3. Send my claws to the young of the rich and the highborn
to save them from their own nightmares
Send my teeth to Tibet that their aspirations for freedom find new teeth
Send my bones to China that they find a cure
for the fear that builds such great walls
Send my fat to Singapore
so they learn to make a balm for pain
that is mine not only in name
Send my waste to the alchemists
for that is the only substance they have not yet tried
in their efforts to invent gold.

4. Give my entrails to whoever shall take them
But hang on to my eyes you puny murderer
that your tribe might know that
you did not kill a creature beneath you
that I looked you in the eye and did not flinch when
you shot me

5. Instead I have turned away
released
from the cancer of your footprint

by Amit Dahiyabadshah

Questions

1. What is the advice given to the hunter?
2. How does the tiger want its bones to be used?
3. What is the tiger's wish for his eyes?
4. What was the beauty of every kill by the tiger?
5. Pick out the word from the passage which is similar in meaning to 'exert'.
6. Pick out the word from the passage which is similar in meaning to 'weak'.

ANSWERS (REVIEW EXERCISE)

Objective Type Questions

Passage 1

1. (d) Both (a) and (b) 2. (b) Importance
3. (c) Women became decision makers.
4. (a) limitations 5. (b) lacuna
6. (c) It was the first decision taken in the New Parliament Building.

Passage 2

1. (c) Chabeeli 2. (a) Raja Gangadhar Rao
3. (b) Because according to British law, adopted sons can't take over kingship.
4. (c) Kalpi 5. (d) Temporarily 6. (c) Acceptance

Passage 3

1. (b) Water pollution 2. (a) Civic health
3. (d) Both (a) and (b) 4. (b) Open lavatories
5. (c) Torturing 6. (a) Conglomerates

Passage 4

1. (b) the skate park set continues to be used since it was not dismantled after the shooting of the movie.
2. (d) a large number of children would eventually benefit from the created set.
3. (c) Dolphins are playful and are known, in part, for the aerial acrobatics they do out of the water.
4. (a) Philanthropists
5.

	Cause	Effect
(d)	Skateboarding built confidence	Boy topped in Sanskrit

6. (b) Unleash

Passage 5

1. (b) They are a distorted form of language spoken by ignorant people
2. (c) To the Middle Ages
3. (a) To be adopted for government and official purposes
4. (c) They were distinct forms of speech of Germanic and Scandinavian invaders
5. (b) To preserve cultural diversity and history
6. (b) Unusual

Passage 6

1. (c) A message of human dignity
2. (a) Freedom of thought, speech, press, right of assembly, and right of worship
3. (a) That all men are created equal and endowed by their creator with certain unalienable rights
4. (a) From the freedom of its people to live their lives with dignity
5. (a) The strength of its people
6. (a) A country where people cherish freedom, justice and opportunity

Passage 7

1. (c) Passes by without experiencing the beauty of the morning
2. (d) sleeping beauty
3. (a) peaceful and serene look
4. (d) ships, towers, domes, theatres and temples
5. (c) smooth and continuous
6. (d) glideth

Passage 8

1. (b) Dedicative
2. (a) The soldiers take difficult journeys alone
3. (b) the act of safeguarding 4. (d) All of these
5. (b) the efforts and sacrifices of soldiers
6. (c) treading

Subjective Type Questions

Passage 1

1. lifestyle and living 2. (ii), (iv), (iii), (v)
3. We have grown a wary, uncertain generation because we have been provided with huge amounts of information, most of which, has been a reminder of how difficult the world is or can be.
4. The author of the given passage wants us to chase beauty that is found in things that calls to our heart, that makes our blood sing, that forces us to close our eyes and sigh softly because of the sheer impact it has on us.
5. According to the author, the people around us call chasing beauty a waste of time as they think that it's not wise to spend time looking at things, even creating things, that can't double up as weapons.
6. Inception

Passage 2

1. Shackleton and his men made their escape on foot and in lifeboats.
2. According to Dr. Christine Batchelor from the Scott Polar Research Institute (SPRI) in Cambridge, UK, the preliminary requirements for finding Shackelton's polar yacht are favourable sea-ice conditions and a two-ship

operation that may be needed to break ice and successfully launch and recover an autonomous underwater vehicle.

3. True
4. According to the passage, Shackleton's ship made its maiden voyage close to Antarctica.
5. SA Agulhas II
6. journey

Passage 3

1. As per the passage, the qualities that can be attached to the women of today are self-direction, rationality, carefulness and perfectionism.
2. The Fourth World Conference of Women held in Beijing in September 1995 had emphasised that no enduring solution of society's most threatening social, economic and political problems could be found without the participation and empowerment of women.
3. Women are not allowed to enjoy the rights conferred upon them by the Constitution because of oppressive traditions, superstitions, exploitation and corruption.
4. According to the passage, education is the main instrument through which we can narrow down the prevailing inequality and accelerate the process of economic and political change in the status of women.
5. Educating girls is good economics as it nurtures developing nations to eradicate poverty as the presence of an educated woman in the family would ensure education of the family itself.
6. Eradicate

Passage 4

1. dispute the standard rules and procedures related to street art.
2. True
3. The word 'impetus' means something that makes a process or activity happen or happen more quickly.
4. Buildings, railway stations, community parks and parking lots are examples of urban landscape.
5. As the medium used in street art is the wall, it gives the artist the opportunity to repaint and recreate their works from a new perspective.
6. The only downside to street art is the lack of preservation of the artworks.

Passage 5

1. The most unfortunate thing as per the passage is that we have not learnt how to control our minds, how to be in the present moment and how to be happy and grateful.
2. We can get rid of negative emotions through meditation and certain breathing techniques as they rejuvenate your soul.
3. Bad Mathematics refers to the practice wherein people focus money on wealth instead of health. As a result, we expend half our health to gain wealth and then spend half our wealth to gain back the lost health.
4. The main signs of a successful person are confidence, compassion, generosity and a smile that none can snatch away, being really happy and being able to be more free.
5. We are not in control of our mind as we cannot get rid of negative emotions and thoughts. As a result, we pollute the Earth, become a victim of our greed and needs.
6. Periphery

Passage 6

1. A great book is one which we want to read another time even more than we wanted to read it the previous time; and every additional time that we read it we find new meanings in it.
2. A young person is likely to have a superficial understanding of a great books at its first reading.
3. Carlyle found Browning's works difficult to appreciate.
4. A poor man's library would be entirely composed of only the great works which have passed the test of time.
5. Infallible
6. Dullness

Passage 7

1. The poet checks his anger for his friend and thereby manages to control it.
2. The anger for the poet's foe grows as he nurtures it and does not stop it from growing.
3. The poet's foe dies by eating an apple from the poisoned tree that was nurtured by the poet's anger.
4. The poet nurtures the Poison tree to bear an apple. He waters it with his tears and fears and suns it with his deceitful smiles so that the tree finally bears a fruit.
5. Enemy
6. Yes, the poem follows a rhyme scheme. It is aabb.

Passage 8

1. The tiger advises the hunter to use some skill while skinning the tiger and to put all his body parts to good use.
2. The tiger wants its bone to be sent to China where it can be used to find a cure for the fear that led them to build great walls.
3. The tiger wishes that the hunter keeps its eyes so that he and his tribesman can remember that the tiger was not a creature beneath man. It fought for its life and was not afraid of dying.
4. The beauty in each of the tiger's kill was that it killed in praise of the creator and its movements were always quick, clean, and merciful.
5. Wield
6. Puny

SECTION B : WRITING
&
SECTION C : GRAMMAR

Notice Writing

A notice is a short piece of written communication issued by individuals and organisations to convey some important information to a large group of people. It is usually displayed by authorities. It is displayed on notice-boards of schools, colleges, organisations and government bodies where everybody can read it conveniently.

There are many types of notices that we write. However, in Class VIII, we will study the following notices

- Announcement of Competitions/Events
- Lost and found
- Information regarding meetings
- Appeals
- Call for Magazine submissions

Points to be Kept in Mind

- Language of the contents should be simple, correct and clear.
- Always put the notice in a **box**.
- Adhere to the word limit, if given in the question.
- A notice should/must include some **value points** (necessary details) in order to make it precise and effective.
- If the name of the school is not given, write XYZ Public School.
- Remember to read your notice to make sure that you have not made any mistake in it.

Format of a Notice

You are the Secretary of the Environment Club of Dharmik Sandhya Public School. Write a notice to invite students to the tree plantation drive organised by the Club on the World Environment Day.

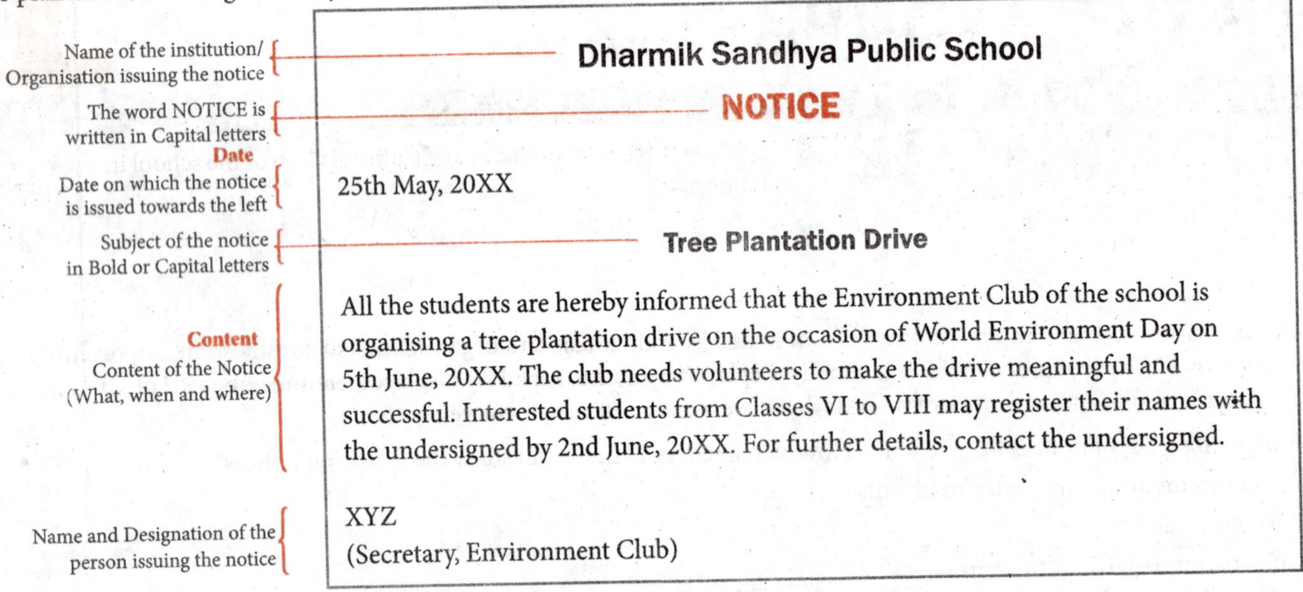

Dharmik Sandhya Public School

NOTICE

25th May, 20XX

Tree Plantation Drive

All the students are hereby informed that the Environment Club of the school is organising a tree plantation drive on the occasion of World Environment Day on 5th June, 20XX. The club needs volunteers to make the drive meaningful and successful. Interested students from Classes VI to VIII may register their names with the undersigned by 2nd June, 20XX. For further details, contact the undersigned.

XYZ
(Secretary, Environment Club)

SOLVED EXAMPLES

Notice For Events/Competition

A notice written for competitions gives us all the details required by the interested students. These include

- Name of the competition
- Time
- Venue
- For further details, contact info
- Date(s)
- Day
- Eligibility (if any)

1. You are Megha Gupta/Mehul Gupta, the Head Girl/Head Boy of St. Mary's School, Dehradun. Draft a notice, informing the students of Classes VI to VIII about a workshop on 'Understanding the New Education Policy' to be held in the school premises. Give all the necessary details.

Ans.

St Mary's School, Dehradun

NOTICE

20th October, 20XX

Understanding the New Education Policy

This is to inform all the students of Classes VI to VIII that our school is organising a workshop on 'Understanding the New Education Policy' on 25th October, 20XX (Wednesday) at 8:00 am in the school auditorium. It is mandatory for all the students to attend the workshop. For further details and other queries, please contact the undersigned.

Megha Gupta
(Head Girl)

2. **Write a notice for your school Notice Board about a charity show to be organised by your school in aid of cancer patients. You are Amar/Amrita, Secretary of Cultural Club of your school.**

Ans.

XYZ Public School

NOTICE

1st November, 20XX

Charity Show for Cancer Patients

This is to inform the students that a charity show will be organised by the Cultural Club of the school in aid of cancer patients. The details are as follows

Date 20th November, 20XX

Venue School Cultural Hall

Time 3:00 pm to 6:00 pm

All the interested students may give their names to their respective class teachers latest by 15th November, 20XX. Kindly cooperate and participate to make this show a great success. For any other details, you may contact the undersigned.

Amar

(Secretary, Cultural Club)

Notice for Lost and Found

A notice for Lost and Found includes details that would help the owner of the thing/finder of the thing recognise the lost/found item. The details include

- The location where the thing was lost or found
- A very clear description of the thing
- Contact information of the person who has lost/found the thing
- Mention of a reward for finders of the lost thing

1. **You lost your Titan wrist-watch in your school. Draft a notice, in not more than 50 words, to be placed on your school notice board. You are a student of Class VIII of Rani Ahalya Devi Senior Secondary School, Gwalior. Sign as Rani/Ram.**

Ans.

Rani Ahalya Devi Senior Secondary School, Gwalior

NOTICE

7th August, 20XX

Lost Wrist Watch

This is to inform all that I have lost a black strap, white dial Titan wrist-watch in the school playground during the 7th period yesterday. Anyone who finds it please contact the undersigned in Class VIII-A. Finder will be rewarded with a treat in the canteen.

Ram

(VIII-A)

2. **You have found a school bag in the school premises. Draft a notice in not more than 50 words for the school notice board. You are Rohan Saxena, School Head.**

Ans.

XYZ Public School, Delhi
NOTICE

7th August, 20XX

Found a Bag

This is to inform all students of our school that a blue coloured school bag has been found in the school premises. The bag contains some books, a lunchbox, a water bottle and a few other items. If anyone has lost their school bag, they can come to the school office and describe what was in your bag so that it can be returned to you.

Rohan Saxena
(School Head)

Notice for Meetings

While writing a notice for a meeting, details needed to be given include

- Who has called the meeting. Purpose or agenda of the meeting
- Date and time/duration of the meeting
- Details of persons to attend/departments to attend
- Venue, specific instructions for the persons called for the meeting
- If requiring further details, contact person with designation

1. **Chennai Book Society is going to organise a week-long book fair in the city. It has requested your school for volunteers to manage various counters. As Secretary, Cultural Club, Chennai Public School, write a notice in about 50 words informing all the members to join the meeting regarding the same.**

Ans.

Chennai Public School
NOTICE

20th April, 20XX

Meeting Regarding the Book Fair

All members of the Cultural Club are hereby informed to attend a meeting on 22nd April, 20XX at 4 pm in the Club Conference Room. The meeting will center around the organisation and management of volunteers for the week long book fair organised by the Chennai Book Society in the city. All the members are requested to come up with some ideas regarding the same.

XYZ
(Secretary, Cultural Club)

2. As the President of the Resident Welfare Organisation of the Mohan Kunj Apartments, write a notice to inform the members to attend the meeting regarding the problem of cleanliness faced by the society. Draft the notice in about 50 words giving all necessary details.

Ans.

Resident Welfare Organisation
Mohan Kunj Apartments
NOTICE

12th August, 20XX

Meeting Regarding Lack of Cleanliness

All members of the Resident Welfare Organisation are hereby informed to attend a meeting on 13th August, 20XX at 4 pm in the Community Hall. The meeting will be held to come up with a solution for the problem of lack of cleanliness in the society.

XYZ
President
(Resident Welfare Organisation)

Notice for Appeal

While writing a notice for an appeal, details needed to be given include

- Whom to appeal/warn
- Issuing authority (if different from the person signing the notice)
- Important instructions
- Name and designation of issuing person

1. You study in Lotus Public School, Delhi. Your school is holding a Cultural Fiesta for collecting funds for the flood victims of Bihar. Draft a notice for your School Notice Board giving details of the programme. Sign yourself as Ketan Mehta, Cultural Secretary.

Ans.

Lotus Public School, Delhi
NOTICE

15th September, 20XX

Appeal for Flood Victims

This is to inform the students of all the classes that a 'Cultural Fiesta' is being organised by the school. The money collected will go to the 'Prime Minister's Relief Fund' for the flood victims of Bihar. The programme is as follows

Date	21st September, 20XX
Time	4:00 pm
Venue	School Auditorium
Ticket	₹ 100 each
Chief Guest	Mr. SK Goswami (SSP, North Division)

For further details, contact the undersigned.

Ketan Mehta
(Cultural Secretary)

2. **Recently it was in the news that many people are dying of cold on the streets. You are Akansha, Head Girl of your school, draft a notice for the students and staff appealing for donations of relief products like clothes, money and other articles in not more than 50 words.**

Ans.

XYZ Public School, Delhi

NOTICE

8th December, 20XX

Appeal for Donations

This is to inform all that the Student Council of our school has organised a rehabilitation drive for the poor to help them face the severe cold. One can donate clothes, money and other articles like blanket, blazer, quilt, etc., to help those in need. By doing this, we will show our humanitarian nature. Certificates will be given to the major contributors. For other details, contact the undersigned.

Akansha
(Head Girl)

Notice for Submissions for Magazines

While writing a notice requesting submissions for magazines, details needed to be given include

- Name of the organisation whose magazine is to be published
- Request for articles, poems and other material
- Deadline of submission

1. **Write a notice to call for submission for the yearly school magazine. Provide all the necessary details in about 50 words. You are Monica, Head Girl of DLF International School.**

Ans.

DLF International School, Noida

NOTICE

18th August, 20XX

Call for Submission

This is to inform all that our school is yet again preparing to come out with its yearly magazine, Pramila. Interested students are requested to submit their creative articles including poems, short stories, essays etc., to their respective class teachers on or before 30th September, 20XX. It should be noted that the manuscripts must be written on one side of the paper and the writings must not exceed 50 words. Interested students may contact the undersigned for further details.

Monica
(Head Girl)

ASSESSMENT EXERCISE

1. You are Madhav/Madhavi of Fairfield Public School. You have found an VIII class Hindi textbook lying in the school auditorium. Draft a notice mentioning other relevant details of the book so as to find its owner.
2. You have lost your school identity card in the school playground. Write a notice mentioning other details about it and a suitable reward to be given to the finder.
3. You are Secretary of Sri Parthasarathy Sabha, Salem. Draft a notice in not more than 50 words to be sent to the members of the Sabha requesting them to attend an extraordinary meeting. Invent necessary details such as items on the agenda, date, time, etc. Sign as Kamal/Komal.
4. You are Tripti/Trilok Lahiri, Secretary, ABL School Cricket Association. It has been decided that a meeting of all the members of the school cricket team be held to discuss plans and strategies for the coming Zonal Tournament. Write a notice in not more than 50 words informing the members of the team about the meeting and requesting them to attend it.
5. An Inter Class Drama Competition is to be held in St. Stephen's School, Vishakapatanam. As Akash, Head Boy of the school, draft a notice informing the members of the Student Council as well as the Dramatics Club to attend a meeting to discuss the organisation of the same. Provide all necessary information in about 50 words.
6. Write a notice to be displayed on the school Notice Board regarding the Annual Day Event. Also, invite participants in not more than 50 words.
7. You are Vikram, School Captain of Krishna Public School, Shastri Market, Varanasi. Write a notice informing the students about a guest lecture by Mr. Rajiv, an environmentalist, on the topic 'The New Kind of Pollution : E-Waste'. Write the notice in not more than 50 words.
8. You are Smitha/Sunil, Secretary of AVM Housing Society. You are going to organise a Blood Donation Camp. Write a notice in not more than 50 words urging the members of your society to come in large numbers for this noble cause. Invent the necessary details.
9. Preeti, student of class VIII has lost her art file in the school field. She wants to put up a notice on the school Notice Board. Draft a notice in about 50 words.
10. You are Ramesh/Rekha, the Head Boy/Head Girl of St. Xavier's School, Patna. Prepare a notice in not more than 50 words for your school notice board asking the students to contribute to help the victims of the earthquake in Japan.
11. You are Srinivas/Srinidhi of D.P. Public School, Nagpur. As a student editor of your school magazine, draft a notice in not more than 50 words for your school notice board inviting articles/sketches from students of all classes.
12. An Inter School Kabaddi Competition is organised by your school. Write a notice, in not more than 50 words, requesting the students to be present at the venue to encourage the players. Invent the necessary details. You are Arjun, the Sports Captain of your school.

Message Writing

A message is a short, informal piece of writing conveying an important piece of information received over the telephone. It is written when the person to whom the message is to be given is not available to take the message. In such a case, the message is given to the person who picks up the telephone. This person, then, writes the message in clear and to the point manner.

We can face such situations almost daily. Hence, it is very important to know how to write a message properly.

Points to be Kept in Mind

- Take down the message carefully in a box.
- Always include the name of the caller in the message.
- Use simple and clear language in your message.
- Do not give unnecessary information in the message.
- Your message should not be in more than 50 words.
- Remember to read your message to make sure that you have not made any mistake in it.

Format of a Message

Below is a telephonic conversation between Mr. Kumar and Mr. Sharma.

Mr. Kumar	Hello, can I talk to Mr. Dua?
Mr. Sharma	He has gone out on business. Can I help you?
Mr. Kumar	I am Kumar from XYZ Enterprises. I had called to inform Mr. Dua that all the goods supplied by your firm were delivered. However, some flower vases were broken. Please ask him if they will be replaced. Also, tell him that I'll make the payment in two days' time.
Mr. Sharma	I will inform him when he comes back and will ask him to get back to you.
Mr. Kumar	Thank you.

As Mr. Sharma is leaving the shop early, he leaves a message for the manager Mr. Dua. Read the conversation and write the message.

The word MESSAGE is written in capital letters.	**MESSAGE**
Time is written towards the right.	11:00 am
Date is written towards the left	2nd March, 20XX
Name of the person to whom the message is written	Mr. Dua
Content of the message	There was a call from a customer, Mr. Kumar for you. He had called to inform you that all the goods supplied by us have been delivered. A few flower vases were found broken. Mr. Kumar has requested for their replacement. He will make the payment in two days' time.
Name of the person who writes the message	Sharma

SOLVED EXAMPLES

1. You are Rajat. You receive a phone call from your father's office in his absence and have the following conversation with the speaker. Write a message, for your father as you have to go for your tuitions. Put the message in a box.

Mr. Gupta	Hello, is this 252XXXX?
Yourself	Yes. May I know who's calling?
Mr. Gupta	I am Suresh Gupta. Can I talk to Mr. Mahajan?
Yourself	Hello Uncle! I am afraid Daddy is not at home. Do you have any message for him?
Mr. Gupta	Yes, please tell him that the meeting fixed for tomorrow i.e., 15th June has been cancelled.
Yourself	Ok, anything else?
Mr. Gupta	Please tell him that we shall let him know as and when the next date for the meeting is fixed.
Yourself	Ok Uncle, I shall tell Daddy when he comes back.

Ans.

> **MESSAGE**
>
> 14th June, 20XX — 7:30 pm
>
> Daddy
>
> Mr. Gupta called from your office stating that the meeting scheduled for tomorrow i.e. 15th June has been cancelled. He also informed that they would let you know as and when the next date is fixed for the meeting.
>
> Rajat

2. Koyal called Mrs. Grover, a furniture shop owner. Since she was not available, her Assistant, Vidhi answered. The following is a conversation between Koyal and Vidhi. As Vidhi was going out immediately afterwards, she left a message for Mrs. Grover. Read the conversation and write a message. Put your message in a box.

Koyal	Hello, is that Grand Furniture?
Vidhi	Yes.
Koyal	Could I speak to Mrs. Grover?
Vidhi	I am afraid she's not here at the moment.
Koyal	When will she be back?
Vidhi	Not before six in the evening. Can I take a message for her?
Koyal	Yes. Could you tell her that she has to deliver the furniture ordered by me for my new house on the 20th August and not on 14th August. Ask her to keep it ready by 9:00 am on the 20th of August. I will be sending a pick up van so she does not have to arrange for the same.
Vidhi	Ok, I will inform her.
Koyal	Thank you.

Ans.

> **MESSAGE**
>
> 10th August, 20XX — 5:00 pm
>
> Mrs. Grover
>
> Koyal, a customer, telephoned to inform you that the furniture ordered by her for her new house should be delivered on 20th August and not on 14th August. She wants the furniture to be ready by 9:00 am on the 20th August. She would be sending a van to pick up the furniture.
>
> Vidhi

3. You are Ramesh. Today you had the following conversation with Rajesh, a friend of your elder brother.

Rajesh Hello! Is it 991XXXXXXX?

Ramesh Yes. I'm Ramesh speaking. What can I do for you?

Rajesh Well, Ramesh! I'm Rajesh, your brother's friend.

Ramesh Oh, I see. Well, brother is not here now. How can I help you?

Rajesh Could you please convey a message to him that he should bring my practical book today in school as I need it in class today.

Ramesh That's fine. I'll do that.

As you are leaving for your school, write a message for your brother in about 50 words. Put your message in a box.

Ans.

MESSAGE

1st March, 20XX 7:00 am

Dear brother

Rajesh, your friend called in your absence. He wants you to bring his practical book to school today. He said it is urgent as he needs it.

Ramesh

4. Read this telephonic conversation between Shiksha and Mrs. Pandit.

Mrs. Pandit Hello!

Shiksha Hello! I'm Shiksha, Runa's friend. Can I speak with her, please?

Mrs. Pandit I'm Runa's mother. She is not at home. She has gone out with her father to buy some books.

Shiksha Oh! Aunty, would you please take a message for her?

Mrs. Pandit Sure, Shiksha.

Shiksha Okay, I had borrowed a novel from her and I was supposed to return it by the end of this week. But, it seems I would finish reading it only by next week. So, I will return the novel then. I'm sure she would understand.

Mrs. Pandit Yeah, that's okay. I'll give your message to her.

Shiksha Thank you so much, Aunty. Bye.

Mrs. Pandit Bye.

As Mrs. Pandit was going out herself, write the message for Runa.

Ans.

MESSAGE

9th September, 20XX 11:00 am

Runa

Shiksha called to inform you that she would be able to return the novel which she has borrowed from you only by next week instead of the end of this very week.

Mom

5. Read the following conversation over the phone between Sita and Geeta.

Sita Hello! Is it you, Geeta?

Geeta Yeah, it's me. And, it's Sita, right?

Sita Yeah, right. Well, would you come over to my house now? I'm all alone. My parents have gone out to buy some articles as we're leaving on a short trip to Manali this afternoon. I think we'll be back next week. And I would love to spend some time with my best friend before we leave on our vacation.

Geeta Sure, I'll be on my way right away. By the way, I am really very happy for you that you're going on a vacation.

Sita Great! I shall be waiting for you. Bye for now.

Geeta Yeah, bye.

Write the message Geeta will leave for her mother based on the telephonic conversation that just concluded.

Ans.

MESSAGE

11th October, 20XX 12:30 pm

Mom

I am going to Sita's house as she will be leaving for Manali this afternoon and return after a week. I will be back after seeing her off.

Geeta

ASSESSMENT EXERCISE

1. Read this telephonic conversation between Alisha and Mrs. Narang.

Mrs. Narang	Hello!
Alisha	Is it 25113079?
Mrs. Narang	Yes. May I know who is on the line please?
Alisha	I'm Alisha. Could I talk to Ankit?
Mrs. Narang	Ankit has a slight fever. I would have asked him to take the call but right now he's asleep.
Alisha	Was he absent from school because of the fever?
Mrs. Narang	Yes. Any message?
Alisha	He must be feeling worried about the Monday test. Tell him that it has been postponed till Friday. Monday has been declared a holiday on account of Eid.
Mrs. Narang	Good for Ankit! I'll tell him that.
Alisha	Ask him to take care of himself and give him my wishes.
Mrs. Narang	Thank you. Bye.
Alisha	Bye, Aunty.

Mrs. Narang was herself going out. So she left the following message for Ankit. Write the message.

2. Read the following telephonic conversation between Neeraj and the receptionist.

Neeraj	Hi! Is this Mr. Mittal's office?
Receptionist	Yes, it is. May I know who is speaking?
Neeraj	My name is Neeraj and I'm calling on behalf of the paper supplier. Can I have a word with Mr. Mittal please?
Receptionist	Mr. Neeraj, I'm afraid Mr. Mittal is not in the office at the moment. He would be back in an hour or so. But, I surely can take a message for him.
Neeraj	Okay. Basically, I've called to inquire about the bill for an order which he had placed with us and which we had executed last week. Would you please inform Mr. Mittal to give us a call as soon as possible with regard to this?
Receptionist	Sure, I'll give your message to Mr. Mittal.
Neeraj	Thanks.

Since the receptionist herself would be taking a break shortly, write a message for Mr. Mittal based on the just concluded telephonic conversation.

3. Read the following conversation.

Jatin	Hello, Is it 00000000077?
Rahul	Yes, it is.
Jatin	May I talk to Tina? I am Jatin, her classmate.
Rahul	She is not at home. You may leave a message for her.
Jatin	May I know who is speaking?
Rahul	I am Rahul, Tina's brother.
Jatin	Hi Rahul. Please tell Tina to bring ₹ 250 for the school trip as tomorrow is the last day to submit the fee.
Rahul	Ok, I will tell her.
Jatin	Thank you!

As Rahul had to leave for his coaching classes, he left this message for Tina. Write the message on his behalf in not more than 50 words. Put the message in a box.

4. Read the following conversation between Simmi and Shikha.

Simmi	Hello, is that Shikha?
Shikha	Yes, is that Simmi? When did you come to town?
Simmi	Just yesterday. In fact, I am leaving tomorrow and I would like to meet you today. Can you come over to my aunt's house in Patel Nagar, where I am staying.
Shikha	I am afraid I won't be able to come today as my mother has gone out and she doesn't have the keys.
Simmi	Why don't you leave the keys at your neighbour's house?
Shikha	Fine. That's a good idea. I will be at your town in 1 hour.

(Instruct) Shikha leaves the keys at her neighbour's house and leaves a message for her mother. Write the message in not more than 50 words. Put the message in a box.

5. Read the following conversation between Mrs. Neelam and Shrey.

Mrs. Neelam	Hello, is this 25268654?
Shrey	Yes.
Mrs. Neelam	I am Neelam, may I talk to Mrs. Sinha?
Shrey	I am afraid mom is not at home aunty.
Mrs. Neelam	When will she come back?
Shrey	Around 8:00 in the evening.
Mrs. Neelam	In that case, can you convey a message to her?
Shrey	Sure, I will.
Mrs. Neelam	Tell her that I have fixed a meeting with Mr. Ajay Kumar, the editor of the children's section of the newspaper 'The Hindustan Times'. The meeting is fixed for 10:00 am tomorrow. Also tell her that the office car will pick her up at 9:00 am and she should carry all the required documents with her.
Shrey	All right, Aunty. I will tell her.
Mrs. Neelam	Thank you, Bye.

Shrey has to leave for his tuitions and will not be home before late at night. Therefore, he decides to leave a message for his mother. Write the message and put in a box.

6. Read the following conversation carefully.

Rosy	Hello ! Is it 9035022565?
Rehana	Yes, please. Who's it there?
Rosy	I'm Rosy, a friend of Roma. Where is she?
Rehana	Oh! Sorry. Actually she has forgotten her mobile here. She has gone to the market. Can I help you, please?
Rosy	Oh, sure. In fact, I wanted to convey to her that today's music classes shall be suspended because the teacher is not well. Instead, it will be held on Sunday. So she should remember it. Could you please pass this message to her?
Rehana	Oh! Sure. Thank you.
Rosy	Thank you too.

As Rehana is going to her dance classes she needs to reproduce the message for Roma. Write the message on her behalf with every detail.

E-Mail Writing

In the present world, with improvement in internet and technology, e-mail has emerged as an easiest, fastest and important means of communication. It allows us to send, receive, store and forward messages to a number of persons simultaneously.

E-mails can be both formal and informal. However, they are most commonly used in formal communication. An e-mail generally comprises of many parts. They are

Parts of an E-mail

1. **Recipient's/Receiver's Address** The first thing you need to enter when composing an e-mail is the recipient's address. An example of e-mail address is: sakshiwrites@gmail.com When sending a message to multiple recipients, be sure to separate all addresses with a comma.
2. **Cc and Bcc** Another option when sending a message to multiple recipients is to use the Cc, or carbon copy, and Bcc or blind carbon copy fields. When using the Cc feature, all recipients can see the e-mail addresses of everyone the message was sent to. If you want your communication to be more private, choose the Bcc options and the identities of the other recipients will not be shown.
3. **Subject Line** The subject line is the first part of your e-mail that the recipient will see. When entering the subject line, write what the e-mail is about.
4. **Starting Salutation** Always address the recipient of the e-mail appropriately.
5. **Body** The body is where you actually write the message that you want to send.
6. **Attachments** Attachments are similar to enclosures in traditional mail. If you have files that you want to share with your recipient(s), you can include them as attachments in the e-mail.
7. **Complimentary Close and Signature** End your e-mail with a note of thanks, your name and designation. Some e-mail systems allow you to enter a signature that will appear automatically at the bottom of every mail you send. This feature is optional and can be turned off and on as needed.

E-mail Etiquettes

It refers to the do's and don'ts of the things to do while writing e-mails.

1. **Do not leave the Subject line blank** The subject of the e-mail states what your e-mail is about. So, it should be brief and accurate and must not be left blank.

   A few examples of a good subject line are

   (i) Assignment for Class VIII English (ii) Time Table for Class VIII B (iii) Subscription Enquiry

2. **Include Proper Salutation as per the E-mail type** One must include proper salutation before starting to write an e-mail.

   Examples

   Respected Sir/Ma'am
   Sir/Ma'am
   Dear Sir/Ma'am
3. **Avoid using Capital Letters** One should avoid using capital letters in an e-mail. Words written in capital letters are interpreted as if the sender is angry or shouting at the recipient(s).
4. **Use of Abbreviations and Acronyms** One should avoid using abbreviations and acronyms in formal e-mails.
5. **Add Appropriate Closing** One should use proper closing of the e-mail before hitting the send button. The closing of the e-mail should be appropriate.

   Examples

   Yours obediently
   Yours sincerely
   Yours faithfully

Points to be Kept in Mind

- The Subject of the e-mail should be short and concise.
- Do not use SMS language in an e-mail.
- Always write the e-mail in not more than 100 words.
- Use clear and easy language to write your message.
- Remember to read your e-mail to make sure that you have not made any error in it.

Format of an E-mail

Write an e-mail to the Principal of your school requesting him/her to grant you permission to conduct the event and inviting her/him to judge the competition.

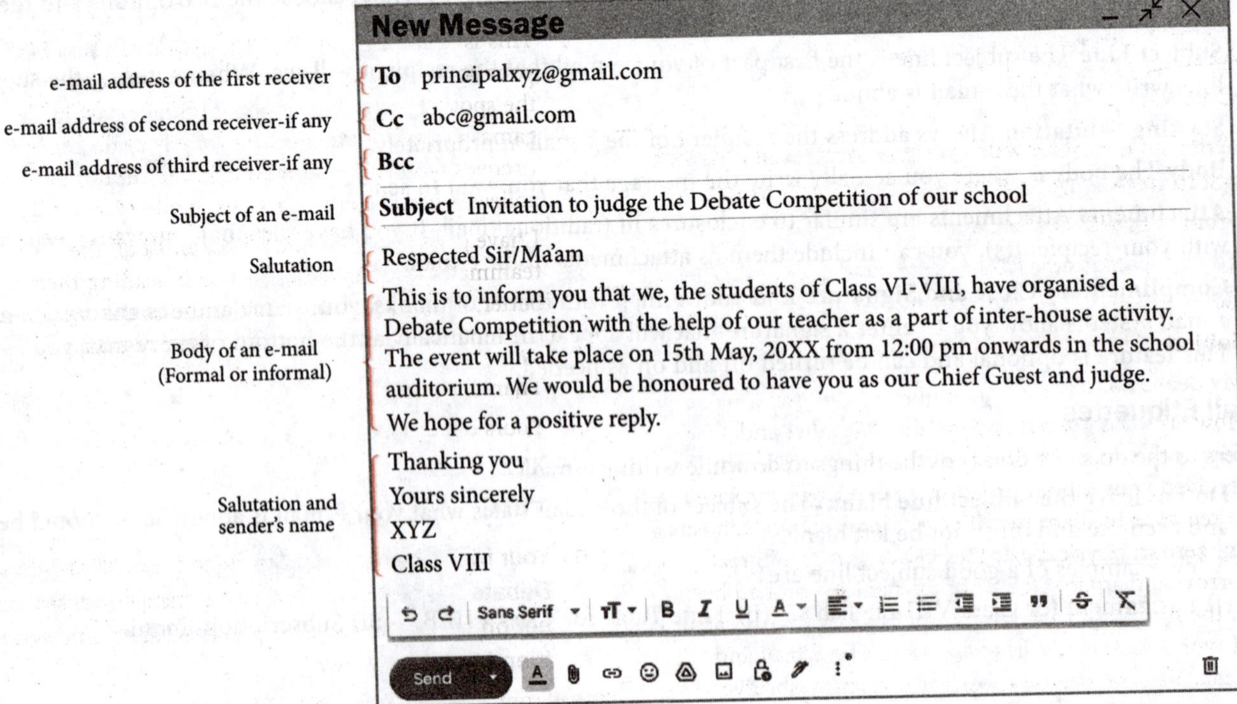

SOLVED EXAMPLES

1. Write an e-mail to the Principal of your school, requesting her or him to ask students to participate in the charity drive.

Ans. From students@gmail.com

To principalxyz@gmail.com

Cc abc@gmail.com

Subject Charity Drive on 22nd January, 20XX

Respected Sir/Ma'am

As you are already aware, we the members of the Nature Club, are organising a 'Charity Drive' in our school on the 22nd January, 20XX. It would be great help if you could make an announcement during the school assembly regarding the same.

The details of the charity drive are as follows : students are allowed to donate books, clothing, shoes, basic necessities which should be well within the expiration date, etc. All the items donated will be sent to non-profit organisations like Education for All, Life Foundation, etc. and they will further distribute it to the poor and needy.

We would be grateful if you could convince more students to participate in this drive for it to be a success.

Thanking you

Yours sincerely

XYZ

Class VIII

2. Write an e-mail to your younger brother asking him not to work very hard or tire himself too much.

Ans. From punit26@yahoo.com

To pankitindia@indiatimes.com

Cc

Subject Avoid overworking

My dear Pankit

How are you? I am doing good in Mumbai and hoping that you are doing good as well. I recently received your school progress report. I was surprised to see your brilliant performance in all school subjects but zero in physical exercise. It is a matter of great sorrow and anxiety for all of us. Pankit, you had been in the hospital for over a month just last year because of typhoid. As a result, you are extremely frail and weak. You are still on medicine and must observe precautions. It is said that prevention is better than cure.

You need not work and tire your feeble body as it will reflect upon your health. Your fever can relapse, you can fall prey to a serious illness. You should know that nothing is more important than life. If one is hale and hearty, one will enjoy all the blessings of life. But if one is ill, all the charm of life ends automatically. What is the use of being industrious and hardworking at the cost of losing one's health? Keep yourself free from strain and tension. Do not exert too much. Improve your health. Build your stamina. Acquire more and more physical resistance. Take plenty of exercise. Eat nourishing food. Next time when we meet, I want to see you healthy and glowing.

Your loving brother

Punit

3. Write an e-mail to your Games In-charge requesting him to nominate you as the captain of college football team.

Ans. From students@gmail.com

To principalxyz@gmail.com

Cc abc@gmail.com

Subject Request for nomination as captain of college football team

Respected Sir/Ma'am

This is to inform you that I am XYZ of Class VIII of your school. As you know, I am an active member of the sports team of the college and take part in the games actively. I am a good footballer and that's why I request you to nominate me as the captain of the college football team.

I have good coordination with almost all the teammates and this will help me in leading them better. I hope you will consider me as the captain of the football team. Anticipating your response.

Thanking you

Yours obediently

XYZ

VIII C

4. Your friend has received a prize in an Inter-School Debate Competition. Send an e-mail congratulating her on her achievement. You are Nisha and your friend is Anubha.

Ans. From nisha01@rediffmail.com

To anubhasc@gmail.com

Subject Congratulations and good wishes

Dear Anu

Congratulations! You did it buddy. I am so happy for you. May you go on adding more feathers in your cap! I wish you the best always!

I remember the last time when you had won, I was sitting right there in the front row. Honestly, you make me proud to be your friend. What a powerful speaker you are! And your arguments usually leave your opponents speechless. You deserve to win every time you are up on the stage. Well done, again!

If I'm not mistaken, you have now qualified for the state-level contest, haven't you? Well, you will beat them all again, I'm sure. But this level needs very serious preparation as it will be a contest among stalwarts and one cannot afford to take it easy.

My dad has been winning laurels for public speaking in his student days and after, and he'll be truly happy to hand you some valuable tips. Feel free to drop in whenever you wish to.

See you then.

Nisha

5. Write an e-mail to the President of the RWA of your locality, drawing his attention to the unkempt condition of the playground area.

Ans. From anurag99@yahoo.co.in

To xyz@gmail.com

Subject Complaint against the unkempt condition of playground

Sir/Ma'am

Through the medium of this mail, we, the children of PQR locality, would like to draw your kind attention to the unkempt condition of our locality's playground. The playground and the rides kept for the entertainment of children are in bad shape.

The playground is littered with garbage, the grass is overgrown and there are many water holes. Even the jungle jim and the other rides installed in the playground are worn down or broken. Thus, we cannot utilise the playground as it is unsafe for us. There is a gardener who comes to check the playground but he sits idly with other people and doesn't maintain the playground.

Therefore, we request you to maintain the playground so that we can play there safely. We hope that you would take immediate action and make the playground a safe place for us to enjoy our leisure time.

Thank you

Children of PQR, Block C

6. Write an e-mail to the Admission Officer of Ayra International Workshop Centre, asking him/her about the information on the admission process, fees, hostel facility, and eligibility criteria for a 2 month course in Computers.

Ans. From shreyakohli123@gmail.com

To admissionofficerAIWC@gmail.com

Subject Request for information on the admission process for the 2-month course in Computers

Respected Sir/Mam

This is to inform you that I am Shreya, a student of Class VIII. I have written this mail to request information on the admission process of your workshops. I am interested in pursuing the 2 month course in Computers from your reputed institution. Can you please provide me with information on the following

- Admission Process
- Eligibility Criteria
- Fees Structure
- Hostel Facility and Charges (including mess, dorm, sports charges)

Any information regarding these would be a great help from you. Looking forward to early action.

Thanks & Regards

Shreya Kohli

ASSESSMENT EXERCISE

1. You have planned to go abroad for further studies, as education in India involves a lot of stress. Write an e-mail to your cousin telling why you have made this decision.

   Hints
   - Indian education system - stressful
   - More opportunities abroad
   - Better facilities are offered abroad
   - Quality of living is better in foreign countries

2. Last week you attended an Adventure Camp. Write an e-mail to a friend mentioning various activities of the camp. You may take help of the hints given below

   Hints
   - Paragliding
   - Parasailing
   - Water Rafting
   - Full of adventure and thrill
   - Increased confidence

3. Write an e-mail to the Principal of your school complaining against insufficient supply of water in your school.

4. Write an e-mail to the Principal of your school, requesting her or him to ask students to participate in the Annual Christmas Fest.

5. Write an email to the Principal of your school requesting him to issue your Transfer Certificate and Character Certificate as your father has been transferred to another city and you have to go along and join another institution.

6. You had gone for a vacation to Kashmir and stayed in the 'Lake View Hotel'. When you returned you realised that you have forgotten some important documents in your hotel room (number 1022). Write an e-mail to the manager of the hotel, asking him to send you the documents.

7. As a member of your residential society, write an e-mail to the Inspector of Local Police Station, Mr. Sharma, informing him about miscreants who ride their bikes rashly every evening outside your society.

8. As a former student, write an e-mail to your professor, Mr. Mathur, thanking him for teaching and guidance that contributed to your overall development.

9. Write an e-mail to an English Daily requesting them to sponsor the Debating Competition to be held at your school. You are Jeevan/Jasper of Class VIII, Air Force School.

10. You purchased a pair of shoes from an outlet of a well-known brand. The sole of the shoes cracked within a month of your using them. Write an e-mail to Customer Care Department of the company asking them to replace your shoes.

Diary Entry

A diary entry is an informal and a personal account of an event of significance that took place on a given day in the life of an individual. It is essentially a first person narrative wherein a person writes about his/her feelings, emotions, thoughts, ideas, memories, activities, and daily life incidents. It is quite like talking to a close friend and helps the writer to connect with his/her inner feelings and analyse them. Such a piece of writing allows free expression of feelings that the writer may be unwilling or unable to share with anyone else.

Keeping a diary has been a regular practice with many great people in the past. One of the most famous of diary entries was written by Anne Frank.

Points to be Kept in Mind

- A diary is intimate and personal in tone and style. They are generally written at night before bed.
- Use personal pronouns in your entry.
- Always write the **day**, **date** and **time** of the entry.
- Use clear and simple language.
- Always include your own feeling in your entry.
- Do not exceed the limit of 150 words.
- Remember to read your diary entry to make sure there are no grammatical or punctuation errors in it.

Format of a Diary Entry

Imagine yourself to be Poonam. Write a diary entry describing the surprise gift given to you by your parents on Diwali.

Day and Date towards the left side Time towards the right side	Saturday, 18th October, 20XX 9:30 pm
Greetings (Optional)	Dear diary
Contains a personal account of the happenings of the day. The language is informal.	Today was a very eventful day as my parents gave me a surprise. They gave me a Diwali gift. It is the best gift that I have received so far, can you guess what is it? Well, it is an i-phone. Now, I can play my favourite games. I can also talk to my best friend, Alka, without any hassle. It has a very good camera and I am sure it will provide an excellent social networking experience through Whatsapp, Facebook etc. I dont have words to thank my parents.
(Optional)	Goodnight diary
First name	Poonam

SOLVED EXAMPLES

1. Today was your first day in your new school. Write about your experiences and feelings about the new school in your diary.

Ans. Wednesday, 1st July, 20XX 8:00 pm

Dear diary

Today, I joined my new school. It was very nice and exciting. My class teacher was very kind to me. She introduced me to the entire class who were as kind as her. I sat with Neha, the monitor of the class. She helped me in every way possible. She gave me her notebooks, shared her lunch with me and never made me feel alone. She even helped me with my classwork and introduced me to her group of friends.

The best thing I liked about the school was the library. It was big and spacious. I am a passionate reader and I found many books of my favourite authors. The computer lab was also well equipped with the latest models of computers.

I look forward to going to school tomorrow. I am still missing my old friends and school. However, it is not as bad as before. I think I will like it here. Now, I am going to sleep as I have to get up early in the morning to get ready for my second day at my new school.

Babli

2. You visited the old age home in Delhi. You met old people who were lonely and sick. When you talked to them, you felt bad about the fact that they were not living with their children. Write about your experiences in your diary.

Ans. Friday, 30th November, 20XX 7:30 pm

Dear diary

Today, I was sad and depressed. I had visited an old age home and was surprised to see so many old people there. Even though the medical facilities and food were good, it was disheartening to see that most of them were abandoned by their children in their time of need.

When I talked to them, my heart was filled with sympathy. What could I do to make them happy? I told them some jokes and riddles which made them laugh and smile. Their faces did not display their sorrow or hurt on being away from their family. I spent some time with them and promised myself that I will look after my parents when I grow up. I will never leave them like this.

I wondered why people misbehave with their parents like this. Parents should be respected and loved because parents are the best people in this world. I just can't think about doing such a thing to my parents.

Shubham

3. It was the happiest day of your life when your class teacher informed you that you have been selected as the 'Best Sportsman of the Year'. You are thrilled as now you will receive the award at the Annual Day Celebrations. Make a diary entry recording your feelings in it.

Ans. Thursday, 10th November, 20XX 9:00 pm

Dear diary

Today was the best day of my life. Guess why? Sumati ma'am told me that I have been selected as the 'Best Sportsman of the Year'. I am so happy that all the hard work that I had done, paid back today. I can never forget how much I had toiled in the field during the summer camp to get into the school football team. My coach had appreciated my efforts. My parents will be so proud of me when I will receive the trophy for the 'Best Sportsman' from the Chief Guest infront of so many people. All the parents and teachers will clap for me. I will feel like a hero at that moment.

And I completely forget to tell you that I have also been selected to represent the team for the School Nationals to be held next month.

God, please give me strength and endurance to live up to the expectations of my coach and my parents.

Piyush

4. Today you went for a trip to the zoo which made you upset about the condition of the caged birds and animals. Write a diary entry in about 100-120 words expressing your feelings.

Ans. Wednesday, 27th October, 20XX 10:00 pm

Dear diary

Today turned from excitement to disappointment for me. I went to my favourite place in the world. Yes! I went to the zoo with my family. It is not hidden from people who know me that I am very fond of birds and animals. However, contrary to my expectations, it turned out to be a sad experience. I did see many birds and animals in the zoo. However, they did not look happy at all in their confined spaces. Even though they were well-fed, they looked angry.

I think that they were missing the blue skies and the freedom to run around in the vast forest land. Not to forget, the constant poking humans must have irritated them. Sure, they are cared for and receive regular health check-ups but I can't overlook how tired and angry they seemed. I guess that is a result of their inactive life.

I don't think zoos are bad as they protect many endangered species. Still, it hurts to see the animals and birds being kept that way. I don't think I can visit a zoo again.

Ayana

5. Today you saw a bunch of poor children on the street who are unable to go to school which made you upset about them. Write a diary entry in about 100-120 words expressing your feelings. Suggest some ways as to how you can help them.

Ans. Friday, 15th February, 20XX 11:08 pm

Dear diary,

I feel very unhappy today. Why has God not given equal opportunity to all? Why are some kids so poor that they cannot even go to school? It pains my heart to think about what will these children, who beg around and do not learn any skill, do later in life. Will they go on to become criminals?

I am completely terrified at the thought.

The children I saw on the street today looked hungry and unhappy. They were wearing tatters for clothes in this severe winter. At that moment, I wanted to share my food, my clothes, my books and even my toys with them. I want to teach them to be clean and to live a hygienic life. Perhaps, there is no one to guide them.

There are so many poor children who are forced to stay out of school by their own parents.

I have decided that tomorrow evening, instead of playing with my friends, I will go with them to the slums next to our housing society and start the work of helping these underprivileged children.

I am very hopeful that all my friends will fully cooperate in this endeavour.

Goodnight!

Mayank

ASSESSMENT EXERCISE

1. You attended your friend's birthday party. She took everybody out to see a movie. Later, she treated you to snacks in a restaurant. Make a diary entry recording the fun that you had and the gifts that she received.
2. You have been made the monitor of your class. You are thrilled at being appointed the monitor as you have been waiting for a long time to become one. Make a diary entry of your feelings about being given such a responsible position.
3. You visited a blind school with some volunteers of your school. You felt bad for the blind people as they were helpless and dependent. Make a diary entry recording your experiences. Suggest some ways as to how you can help them.
4. You had a quarrel with your best friend. She had been your friend for the past 3 years. Record your feelings in your diary and the reason for your quarrel.
5. While returning home from school, you encountered a young boy who was serving the customers in a tea shop. You felt that it was wrong and got worried about the child. Write a diary entry in about 100-120 words describing the incident and your opinion on it.
6. Your class was taken to a barren land in the vicinity to participate in a green drive under which school children planted saplings. Make a diary entry, in about 100 words, recording your feeling regarding the events of the day.
7. The school children of your housing society came together to pick up brooms and clean the locality. This initiative would shame the residents into giving up their habit of littering and dumping kitchen waste all around. Make a diary entry about the event.
8. You went to the Book Fair held in your city. You loved the experience and bought many books. You also got a chance to talk to your favourite author. Make a diary event recording your feelings about the day.
9. You met your old friend in the market today after five years. Write a diary entry expressing your thoughts and emotions on the meeting.
10. You had to leave your ancestral home today for its renovation. You were extremely emotional about it even if the relocation is just for a few months. Write a diary entry expressing your thoughts and emotions.

Paragraph Writing

A paragraph is a short composition that revolves around a specific idea or topic. It generally comprises of a group of sentences that are organised in a meaningful order and united by its central theme. A paragraph might describe a place, character, or process; narrate a series of events and ask you to analyse a given data or chart. In Class VIII, we will specifically cover Constructive Paragraph Writing and Analytical Paragraph Writing.

A paragraph should always include

- **Introduction** It is an introductory line that addresses what the main idea of the paragraph is going to be. It can be a famous quote or a proverb or just a general statement about the topic.
- **Body** The paragraph should contain 8-10 sentence related to the topic in a meaningful order.
- **Conclusion** The last sentence of the paragraph should be the concluding sentence. It should tie the supporting thoughts together.

Points to be Kept in Mind

- Use simple and easy language to present your ideas.
- Take care of the tenses. Present tense is used when we describe something and past tense is used to talk about an event that has already taken place.
- If a word limit has been mentioned, do not exceed it.
- Remember to read your paragraph to make sure there are no grammatical or punctuation errors in it.

SOLVED EXAMPLES

Constructive Paragraph Writing

Constructive Paragraph Writing is a composition that generally involves imagination. In the questions from this type of paragraph writing, students have to think about a situation, person or thing and what they think about it.

1. On the occasion of Teacher's Day in your school, all the students are asked to give their opinion about their teachers so that the management can finalise a teacher for the 'Best Teacher Award'. They are asked to write a paragraph about the teacher they like the best and why.

Ans. It is common knowledge that all the teachers in my school are highly qualified. They are competent, dedicated, and sincere in their work. However, out of all my teachers, I like Ms. Mousami the most.

Ms. Mousami teaches us English in a very interesting manner. I like her because she is very friendly with the students and makes learning fun. Most of all, she explains everything very well and with her guidance we are able to understand English Grammar almost perfectly. She has an incredible knowledge of her subject and enthusiasm for teaching. She is passionate about teaching and working with children. She has a strong rapport with the students and has established trusting relationships with them. Even though she is friendly, she maintains discipline in class. She is ever ready to help us with our problems even after school hours. Above all, she is caring and compassionate. She goes the extra mile to make sure that each child is successful. Everybody respects her but I have special regard for her. She is an inspiration for me and I wish that she teaches me in my next class also.

2. You were elated when you visited the Taj Mahal in the summer vacations. Write a paragraph on your visit to the Taj Mahal.

Ans. My happiness knew no bounds when during summer vacations, my family arranged a visit to the Taj Mahal. I had wanted to visit this World Heritage Site since childhood. Now, I had the opportunity to do so.
We went to Agra by bus and reached our destination by the afternoon. We could see the marble glory within a few feet's distance. The Taj Mahal is a magnificent monument made of white marble. It is situated on the banks of Yamuna river. This architectural beauty was built by Emperor Shah Jahan in memory of his beloved wife, Mumtaz Mahal. Twenty thousand labourers worked for twenty-two years to build it. The monument depicts nothing but grace and magnificence. The Taj Mahal looks beautiful at all times but at night it becomes a wonderful sight to behold. It glitters in the moonlight and looks like a palace of silver. The Taj Mahal is, indeed, the loveliest work of art in the whole world and is rightfully one of the Seven Wonders of the World.

3. Write a paragraph on 'Morning Assembly in My School'.

Ans. We have always heard that we should start off our day on a positive note. Hence, it is no surprise that our school followed the principle and hosted morning assemblies. Our school starts the morning assembly at 8:30 am every day after the students have arrived and settled in their classes. Before 8:30, all the teachers, students, and helping staff gather together in the field for the choir team's prayer. The assembly starts with a prayer started by the music teacher. After the prayer, students from the designated class present important news, word of the day and the thought of the day. After this small introduction, special events on a theme are presented. These events include–plays, dance performance, singing, speeches and even quizzes. The entire assembly is only 30 minutes long which refreshes us for a productive start of the day.

4. Write a paragraph on 'If I were a Bird....'.

Ans. If I were a bird, life would be so beautiful. I would be free–free to soar high above the world, embracing the skies as my kingdom. With wings outstretched, I would navigate the winds, exploring the Earth's vast landscapes and witness its beauty from a unique perspective.
The ability to travel across forests, coastlines and mountains would be a privilege, granting me the chance to witness nature's marvels from close. Sitting amidst the trees or on high cliffs, I would sing melodies that would be heard through the air, celebrating the dawn and bidding farewell to the setting Sun.
I would travel continents, experiencing diverse cultures and terrains, from bustling cities to serene wilderness. Life would be much more different from now. There would be no school, no homework, and a complete vacation from everything in my life. If I were a bird, the world would be an endless canvas, and the sky, my limitless playground, would grant me the liberty to explore and appreciate the magnificence of our planet.

5. Write a paragraph on 'A Day without Internet'.

Ans. The modern world is the world of internet. Almost everything today runs with the help of internet. It has changed the world and has made such a huge impact on everyone that a life without the internet is pretty hard to even think about. Hence, if internet stops for a day, the world would become miserable. It would be a lot harder to talk to near and dear ones. An individual would have to go to a shop and buy all the required things. Without it, we would rely on TV programmes and newspapers for all news and information. In a day without internet, we would be back to a standard cheque book and calling our bank to find out balance. It also means paying bills would take much longer, as banks would also be less connected. Additionally, global commerce would be impressively slow and tedious on that day. Communication on the day without internet would be almost zero. We would need to send letters to far-away friends or rely on in-person interactions. So, a day without internet is not going to be entirely depressing as one might think.

Analytical Paragraph

An analytical paragraph is a small composition based on the analysis of a data. It basically explains your arguments regarding a subject with evidence. In other words, an analytical paragraph does not just describe the data but also points out some specific parts from it to justify your statement.

For writing an analytical paragraph, the following strategies need to be kept in mind

- Read the data carefully
- Understand the topic on which analytical paragraph is to be written
- Carefully study the trends, figures and information given for analysis
- Use the trends as an evidence to support your statement
- Give a clear introduction and conclusion
- Try to avoid the repetition of information

1. Gautam was alarmed to see the graph that tracked the rising levels of carbon dioxide in the air of his city, Nagpur. He decided to write a paragraph on the data to show his alarm and painted the present picture in order to caution people against environmental pollution. Write an analytical paragraph for Gautam.

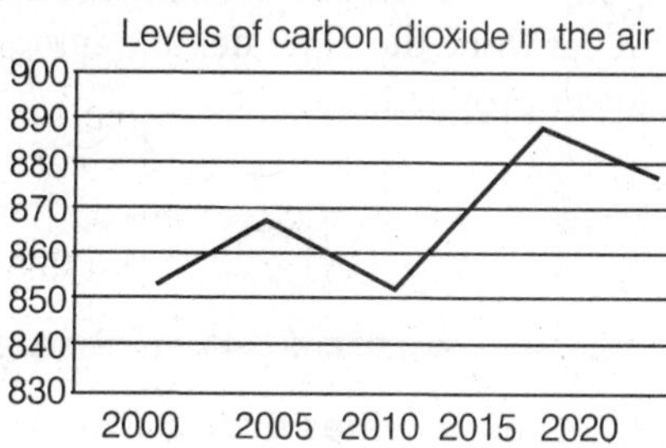

Ans. Air Pollution-Deadly Air in Nagpur

Air Pollution is a serious issue affecting our planet today yet many people continue to turn a blind eye thinking that it's not that serious. The given graph shows how alarming the issue of air pollution is, specifically in this city, Nagpur. Data very evidently shows a significant increase in the air pollution levels of the city. No doubt, people of Nagpur have been suffering from many respiratory diseases. While in 2000, the air pollution levels were not very low, the quality of air then was way better than the air the subsequent generations are inhaling. The years after 2005 leading to 2010 saw a decrease in the levels of carbon dioxide in the air. But suddenly after 2010, there was drastic change. The quality of air was constantly declining and the percentage of carbon dioxide was on a rise. The level of the gas reached from about 855 to 890. After that, the level of carbon dioxide has seen a slow decline.
This decline indicates that there are still a lot of changes that need to be implemented to make our environment pollution free.

2. You asked people what they thought was the most valuable thing. The given pie chart shows the analytics of the different answers you received. Write an analytical paragraph for a research project.

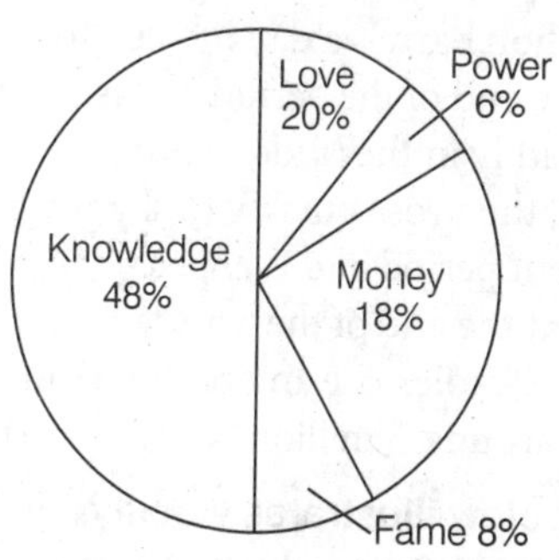

Ans. The pie chart in question offers a visual representation of people's views of what constitutes the most valuable entity in life. This chart is sliced into five distinct categories, each representing a different element deemed as most precious by the people. Notably, 'Knowledge' emerges as the main value, claiming a 48% majority of the chart. This illustrates a significant preference towards intellectual assets over materialistic or social standings. In stark contrast, 'Power' appears to be the least favoured and 'Fame' treads closely behind 'Power'. 'Love' and 'Money' demonstrate a near equal distribution, capturing 20% and 18% respectively. This balance suggests that emotional fulfillment and financial security are nearly equally significant yet fall behind the intellectual prowess represented by 'Knowledge'. In essence, the chart paints a picture of a society that places the highest worth on enlightenment and understanding, and a moderate valuation of emotional and monetary fulfillment.

3. The chart given below compares the oil consumption of 4 regions. Write a paragraph analysing the given information.

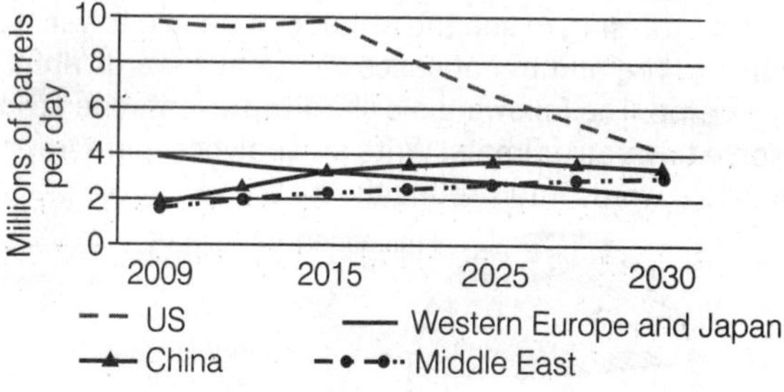

Ans. The line chart presents oil consumption in 4 major regions of the world the US, China, the Middle East, and Western Europe and Japan between 2009 and 2030. Looking from an overall perspective, it is apparent that despite the US consuming the most oil throughout, this is projected to fall dramatically.
Its consumption began by coming at just under 10 million from 2009 to 2015, though a fall is forecast to just over 4 million by 2030. Western Europe and Japan's numbers will continue to decline starting at

under 4 million barrels a day in 2009 to become the lowest by the end of the period. Consumption will increase steadily in the Middle East and China. The former, then rose quickly to slightly below 4 million by the present period and is expected to decline marginally at the end of the time surveyed. The latter will undertake a steadier rise and both regions will likely intersect at around 3 million barrels by 2030.

4. The table below illustrates weekly consumption by age groups of dairy products. Write a paragraph analysing the given information.

	AGES			
	<25	26 - 45	45 - 65	65+
Milk	1200 ml	1650 ml	1670 ml	1900 ml
Full fat	59%	20%	45%	30%
Low fat	41%	80%	55%	70%
Butter	12g	19g	60g	30g
Full fat	60%	38%	50%	49%
Low fat	40%	62%	50%	51%

Ans. The table illustrates weekly consumption of dairy products by age groups. The data clearly indicates that younger people tend to consume less milk and butter with high fat content, especially those under 25. While the oldest group drinks the largest amount of low fat milk, those in 45-65 age group eats highest quantity of butter. Milk consumption for the under 25 group is lowest at 1,200 ml, of which 59% is full fat and 41% low fat. This pattern is generally reversed for older people with individuals drinking 1,650ml, 1,670ml, and 1,900ml, respectively. The fat content is also lower at 20% for 26-45, 45% for 45-65, and 30% for the oldest age bracket. In terms of butter, younger people also use the least at just 12g, in contrast to 19g for those 26-45, and 60g and 30g for the two older groups. Younger individuals similarly opt for more fat while the older demographics have much lower proportions here.

ASSESSMENT EXERCISE

1. India is a country of varied festivals. Festivals signify celebration, joy, happiness and unity. Write a paragraph on 'My Favourite Festival'.
2. Write a paragraph on 'My First Day in My Dance Class'.
3. Write a paragraph on 'How I Celebrated My Birthday'.
4. Write a paragraph on 'If I were a President'.
5. Write a paragraph on 'My Favourite Sport'.
6. Write a paragraph on 'My Visit to a Museum'.
7. Write a paragraph on 'A Day I would Like to Forget'.
8. It is distressing to see the attitude of people towards animals. The number of cases of cruelty towards animals is increasing. The following pie chart represents the attitude of people towards animals. Write an analytical paragraph in 100-120 words interpreting the data given in the pie chart.

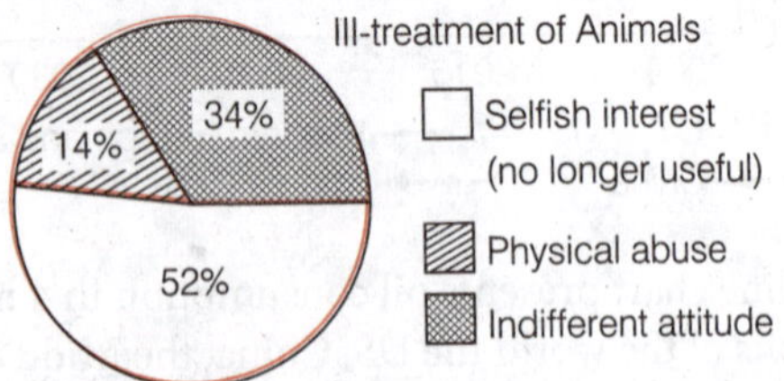

9. The chart below gives the percentage of social media users by age in India in 2020. Write a paragraph analysing the given information in 100-120 words.

Internet Activities by Age Group

	Age Group						
Activity %	Teens	20s	30s	40s	50s	60s	70+
Get news	76	73	76	75	71	74	70
Online games	81	54	37	29	25	25	32
Downloads	52	46	27	15	13	8	6
Product research	0	79	80	83	79	74	70
Buying a product	43	68	69	68	67	65	41
Searching for people	5	31	23	23	24	29	27

10. Look at the given data and write a paragraph analysing the given information in 100-120 words.

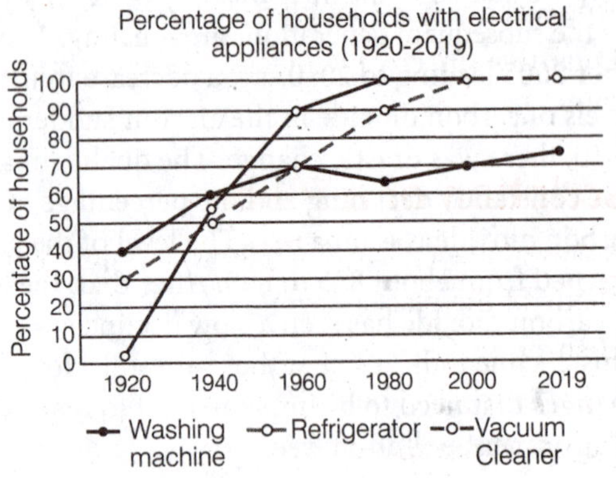

Description Writing

CHAPTER 6

A description is a detailed account of some salient aspects, characteristics or features of a person, place, thing or process etc. It is a short composition which is objective and factual. The word limit should not exceed 100-120 words.
The sentences used in it are short and sharp. These sentences are placed in a proper sequence to create the unity in thought.

Personal opinions, philosophical expressions and elaborate style should not be included while giving a description of a person, situation or event.

A descriptive paragraph is of four types

(i) Description of a person
(ii) Description of a place
(iii) Description of an event
(iv) Description of an object

Description of a Person

Description of a person includes his/her physical appearance, habits, profession, intellectual and emotional qualities, special traits, social status or role in the society, his/her influence on the society (if he/she is a famous personality).

You can use the following words to describe a person

- **Height** tall, short, medium height
- **Build** thin, underweight, plump, strong, sturdy, fat, overweight
- **Hair** long, short, curly, black, brown, grey
- **Eyes** dark, brown, big, small
- **Other features** beard, moustache, bushy eyebrows, broken teeth, broad chin, thick lips, long face
- **Appearance** good looking, charming, ugly, smart, handsome, beautiful
- **Qualities** sincere, intelligent, diligent, warm, patient, soft spoken, selfish, kind, honest, innovative, confident, punctual

Description of a Place

While describing a place, the following points should be taken into consideration

- Name of the place
- Location
- History
- What does it look like (size, appearance, atmosphere)?
- What is special about the place?
- What do you like there?
- Do you recommend other people to visit it?

Description of an Event

While describing an event, the following points should be taken into consideration

- Name of the event
- When did it happen?
- What happened (Give details)?
- Who were the people involved?
- Why was the event important?

Description of an Object

Describing an object encourages students to expand their observation skills and thought process as they start thinking about an object as a whole.

Describing an object can include

- What category is the object in?
- What does the object do?
- What does it look like?
- What color is it?
- What size is it?
- What does it smell/taste like?
- What sound does it make?
- What is it made of?
- What parts does it have?
- What shape is it?
- Where can you find it?
- Anything else you know about it

Points to be Kept in Mind

- It should give complete details about the person, place or thing being described in it.
- One should use simple language and short sentences in writing the description.
- The word limit of 100-120 words should be strictly adhered to.
- The visual and verbal clues given in the question can be used in constructing the description.
- It should not include the opinion of the writer, personal comments or recommendations about the person, place or event being described.

SOLVED EXAMPLES

1. Recently a new Principal joined your school. Your friends ask you to describe him. Write a description of your new Principal.

Ans. Mr. Rakesh Chopra, our new Principal, is a tall, fair young man. He has a moustache and is very handsome. He is highly qualified, kind and polite. Yet, he is a strict disciplinarian. He is punctual and diligent and inspires us to be fit and smart. He has a good command over the students and punishes habitual latecomers and indisciplined children. He is very kind as he helps the poor, needy children by distributing books, notebooks and other stationery material, free of cost. He is a big fitness enthusiast as he makes sure that every child in the school spends half an hour exercising. He also encourages all children to participate in an extracurricular activity. No doubt, he is liked and respected by all.

2. Look at the following visual and write a paragraph on the famous personality.

Narendra Modi

Ans. Narendra Modi, born on 17th September, 1950 in Vadnagar (Gujarat), is an Indian politician and government official who rose to become a senior leader of the BJP in 2014. He led his party to victory in elections to the Lok Sabha, after which he was sworn in as the Prime Minister of India. Prior to that he had served (2001-2014) as the Chief Minister (Head of Government) of Gujarat, in Western India. During his time as head of the Gujarat Government, Modi established a formidable reputation as an able administrator and he was given credit for the rapid growth of the state's economy. In June 2013, Modi was chosen the leader of the BJP's campaign for the 2014 elections to the Lok Sabha. After a vigorous campaign in which Modi portrayed himself as an efficient candidate who could turn around India's underperforming economy- he and the party were victorious, with the BJP winning a clear majority of seats in the assembly. Modi was sworn in as Prime Minister on 26th May, 2014 and since then, has taken India to new heights.

3. Write a descriptive paragraph on your role model based on the clues given below.

Name of the role model - why do you admire him/her- his/her qualities that appeal to you the most - his/her, traits, achievements etc.

Ans. My father is my role model. He is the person I admire the most in my life. It is because he is a very hardworking and down to Earth person. Although he was born in a very poor family, he defied (successfully overcome) all odds and became an engineer through his sheer hard work and will power. It is due to his efforts that I am able to live a comfortable life.

He never boasts of his success and keeps working hard. The other quality that I like about him is that he treats everyone with respect, be it his superiors or subordinates, young or old, rich or poor. He is also calm and composed in times of difficulties and never feels down due to them. He is not only a father but also a friend to me. It is he who I consult first whenever I need any help or suggestion in my life. I believe on living life to his ideal which is 'Simple living and High thinking'.

4. Describe a calculator in your own words.

Ans. Mathematical calculations have become easy with the help of a device known as a Calculator.
A calculator is, essentially, an electronic device used for doing calculations. These days we have all kinds of calculators in the market. The ordinary calculators perform simple arithmetical operations. Addition, subtraction, multiplication and division are used for basic calculations. Human minds can err but not calculators. Speed and accuracy are the watchwords of a calculator. A calculator looks like a small plastic box. The board contains numbers from 0 to 9 and +, -, x, ÷ marks. The pushbuttons carrying these numbers and signs are pressed to do the required calculations. Besides simple calculators, there are also sophisticated calculators to perform more complex operations. There are scientific calculators also which can perform various scientific functions. Calculators are mostly operated by battery cells. Electrical and solar calculators are also available in the market.

5. A Book Fair was organised in your city in the month of August. Describe the fair using the following hints

Time and place - purpose of the fair - arrangements - participants - number of people who attended the fair - what was special about it.

Ans. A Book Fair was organised at Pragati Maidan, Delhi in the month of August. People from Delhi and neighbouring cities came to attend this fair. The theme of the book fair was 'Role of Books in Revolutionising the World.' It was a rare opportunity for book lovers as there was a variety of books from different publishers all under one roof.

The fair with all the books, authors, quirky stationary and many other things was not only amazing but also very safe. People had to pass through metal detector to reach the different halls. Each hall was segmented into many stalls. There were local, national and international publishers. The stalls were attractively decorated. There were also stalls that sold unique stationary items. Food stalls and ice-cream parlours were also set up to facilitate the visitors. The book fair was a grand success.

6. Write a description of the garden you could never forget.

Ans. One of the most beautiful gardens that I have visited in my life is my grandma's garden. My grandma's house has been in Dehradun for 40 years now. Her house has an enormous garden with all the kinds of fruits you desire to eat. When you first go into the house the fragrance and the beauty of the flowers will take you to paradise. The beautiful colours, shapes and sizes of flowers leaves you mesmerised. You can sit there and talk to the flowers and you will feel like that they are listening to you. As you touch the flowers, you will feel safe and comfortable. They have as many different colours as a rainbow in the sky after a heavy rain.

ASSESSMENT EXERCISE

1. Describe your grandfather.
2. Describe a hill station which you visited during your summer vacations.
3. Describe a mall that you often go to with your friends. You can use the following hints

   Hints
   - Big building
   - Lifts and escalators
   - Eating joints
   - Play house for children
   - Many variety of shops
   - What attracted you most
4. A science fair was organised in your school. Describe it using the following hints

   Hints
   - When was it organised
   - Which classes participated
   - Models on different topics
   - Innovative ideas (working models)
   - Fair inaugurated by the Chairman
   - Arrangements
   - Most interesting model
5. Describe a gift you have received that was important to you.
6. Describe an object/category of objects whose invention you think is useful to people.
7. Write a descriptive paragraph on a social figure you admire the most based on the clues given below. (100-120 words)

   Name of personality - physical features - birth place/date - reason for being famous - his/her struggles - major achievements - qualities that you admire most about him/her.
8. Write a descriptive paragraph about your favourite cartoon character based on the hints given below.

   Name of the character - description - qualities - what you like the most about it.
9. Describe your mother to your school friends using the information given below.

   Age-40 years, height-tall, complexion-fair, appearance-beautiful, build-plump, education-post graduate, qualities-soft spoken, patient, understanding and kind. You can add other details if necessary.
10. Describe the Annual Day celebrations in your school in about 150 words. Use the following hints

    Date and Time - 22nd April, 2020 at 6:00 pm

    Place - School Auditorium

    Chief Guest - Mr. Ravindra Gupta, District Magistrate

    Activities - Annual Report Presentation, prize distribution, cultural programmes, speech by the chief guest, vote of thanks

Dialogue Writing

Dialogues are a form of communication between two or more people. They are generally spoken but are widely used in writing fiction, poems and dramas, generally to convey the view point of the characters.

Knowing how to write dialogues is an important skill as it helps students to develop communication skills, understand different perspectives and express themselves better.

A dialogue or conversation may be formal or informal, depending on the following factors

1. Relationship between the speakers
2. The topic of conversation
3. The situation in which the speakers are placed

Points to be Kept in Mind

- Always use the correct punctuation marks in your dialogue.
- Separate the dialogue from the speaker by using a hypen (-) or colon (:).
- Put the dialogue in double inverted commas.
- Use simple and clear language in the dialogue.
- Understand the situation for which you have to write a dialogue clearly.
- Re-read your conversation to make sure you have not made any grammatical or punctuation error in it.

SOLVED EXAMPLES

1. Write a dialogue between you and your teacher about which course to study during vacations.

Ans. Student : Good morning Sir, how are you?

Teacher : I am completely fine. What about you?

Student : I am great too. I came to ask you about something.

Teacher : Oh, please tell me what I can help you with?

Student : I was wondering which course to learn during my vacation.

Teacher : It can be confusing with so many options online. You should make a list and narrow it down as per your interest.

Student : I have tried that but still I am left with three options–Fine Arts, Computer language or Robotics.

Teacher : Well! All of them are very interesting courses but as far as I remember, you have always been interested in Robotics.

Student : Yes! I am because I feel it is our future.

Teacher : Well then, it's no harm in pursuing it and later if you find it less interesting you can always switch.

Student : Yes, it sounds like a great idea. Thanks!

2. The customer realises that the shopkeeper is being unfair to him. Write the dialogue between the two in which the customer makes the shopkeeper realise his mistake.

Ans. Customer : What is the rate of Kaju Burfi?

Shopkeeper : ₹ 600 per kg, Sir.

Customer : Pack half a kg for me.

Shopkeeper : In a minute, Sir.

Customer : But you have weighed less than half a kg.

Shopkeeper : Don't worry sir, you'll have less weight to carry.

Customer : Oh! Thank you for a good piece of advice.

Shopkeeper : Well! I am here to do good to my customers, Sir.

Customer : Here's your money.

Shopkeeper : But it's less money, Sir.

Customer : Don't worry, you'll have to count less money.

Shopkeeper : But that's not fair.

Customer : I'm simply following your advice, Sir.

Shopkeeper : I know what you are doing and I am sorry for trying to cheat you. Here, give that back to me. I will give you the correct quantity.

Customer : Thank you!

3. Rohit calls up Rajat to make a plan for the weekend. Write the dialogue between Rohit and Rajat.

Ans. Rohit : Hey Rajat! Are you free this weekend?

Rajat : Hi Rohit. I don't have any special plan.

Rohit : How do you like the idea of going to the zoo?

Rajat : That sounds good but I have to take my parent's permission.

Rohit : I'll come to your house this evening and request your parents to allow you to join me to see the zoo.

Rajat : Ok. I have no problem then.

Rohit : Will they be home in the evening?

Rajat : Yes. They will be at home.

Rohit : Then I'll surely come.

4. Sarita is being interviewed for the job of a teacher in a school. Write a dialogue between the interviewer and Sarita.

Ans. Interviewer : Hi Sarita, how are you?

Sarita : I am doing good. How are you doing?

Interviewer : I am fine too. So, Sarita why do you think you are suitable for the job?

Sarita : Ma'am, I am qualified for the job and I have a passion for children and teaching.

Interviewer : Can you speak any foreign language?

Sarita : Yes, I can speak and write German.

Interviewer : Do you have any prior experience?

Sarita : Yes, I have a teaching experience of 5 years in a public school.

Interviewer : Okay, Sarita. We will inform you if you are selected for the job.

5. Nirmal had gone to a family vacation where he sat across a trekking guide. He struck a conversation with him about trekking. Write a dialogue for the same.

Ans. Nirmal : I find trekking very exciting. Tell me something about it.

Guide : Well, trekking is the best form of adventure. Why don't you try it sometime?

Nirmal : Hmm! I want to try it. But I do not know who to contact for it.

Guide : Touring companies organise treks. You can contact them if you like.

Nirmal : Yes, I will.

Guide : Remember to carry essential things with you. They are a must or you will not enjoy the trek.

Nirmal : What are the essential things that I must carry?

Guide : Sleeping bag, tent, water bottles, a compass, a torch and packed food are a must.

Nirmal : Thanks for your precious advice.

Guide : You are most welcome.

6. Write a dialogue between Aarush and his friend, Ravish, two working adults who are making vacation plans.

Ans. Aarush : Hi Ravish. How are you doing? I have been waiting for an hour for you. Where have you been?

Ravish : Hey! I am fine, and I'm so sorry. I got a little late because of the jam-packed road.

Aarush : Never mind. Tell me how everything at the office is?

Ravish : Oh yes! Thanks for reminding me. Well, I am not very happy doing this job. They make me work a lot and do not pay on time. I feel so tired.

Aarush : I guess this is the same for each one of us. Deadlines are short, and payment is late. I feel like going away from this boring and bustling life.

Ravish : I feel the same to be honest. Oh! I have an idea!

Aarush : What is it? You sound very happy.

Ravish : We are going to get a week off this month. So why don't we plan a vacation?

Aarush : This sounds superb. We can probably ask Muskan, Avi and Tanya too. All of us can go on a trip and enjoy it together.

Ravish : I am in! Let us fix it as soon as possible so that we can book the tickets for the destination and hotels too.

Aarush : Let's go home and do a conference call with the others.

Ravish : Perfect! See you then.

Aarush : See you, friend.

ASSESSMENT EXERCISE

1. Write dialogues between three friends who are talking about the teachers at their school.
2. Write a dialogue between Amina and her brother, talking about the merits and demerits of online exams.
3. Vijay and Mina are discussing the use of crackers in spite of ban in Delhi. Write a dialogue between them.
4. Ashu and his mother are fighting over the advantages and disadvantages of social media. Write a dialogue between them.
5. Write an imaginary dialogue between Prime Minister Mr. Narendra Modi and yourself regarding the Swachh Bharat Abhiyaan.
6. Write an imaginary dialogue between a teacher and a student. Suppose that the teacher finds out the student hasn't done her homework. The student tries to make excuses for not doing the homework on time. She promises the teacher that she would submit the homework the next day.
7. One of the two friends is leaving the school in the middle of the semester as his father is getting transferred to another state. Frame a dialogue between the two friends.
8. A boy wants to buy a new cell phone. However, his father is not in favour of a new cell phone as the old one is functioning perfectly. Write a dialogue between the father and the son.
9. You had gone to the World Book Fair held in Delhi with your father. You bought many books and talked to some authors too. You are telling this to your friend. Write a dialogue for the same.
10. You are planning a surprise birthday party for your mother along with your cousin. Write a dialogue discussing the details of the party.

CHAPTER 8

Story Writing

A story is a record of an event which can be true or imaginary. It can impart a moral, capture a moment, event or someone's life to inculcate values and be there just for entertainment. Story Writing is a language skill that tests the student's creativity and writing skills.

Main Elements of a Short Story

1. **Theme** It is the main idea or message of the story.
2. **Plot** It is the logical connection among all parts of the story. A proper beginning, a middle and an end are essential components of a good plot.
3. **Setting** It is the time, location and the background suitable to work out the theme.
4. **Characters** The people, animals or other living creatures of the story are its characters. A short story has one main character and very few minor characters to support the plot.

Points to be Kept in Mind

- Always use past tense while writing a story.
- Consequences/Climax of the story should be clear and satisfying.
- Make simple and innovative use of language.
- Make sure that the story has a moral/message, if it requires one.
- A title may be given to the story if the question requires it; otherwise it is optional.

SOLVED EXAMPLES

1. Given below is an outline of the story given in the form of phrases. Using it, write a short story.

Rich man.........plans to give a feast to his friends......all dishes are prepared except fish as it is unavailable.......declares reward for anyone who would get fish.....poor fisherman catches a big fish and brings it........gatekeeper refuses to let him enter the house unless he agrees to give him half the reward......fisherman thinks of a plan........instead of the reward he asks the rich man for 100 lashes on his back......gives 50 lashes to the gatekeeper......moral.

Ans. **A Greedy Gatekeeper**

Once, there was a rich man who wanted to give a grand feast to his friends. He got all kinds of dishes prepared but was unable to get fish. So, he offered a reward to the man who would bring him a fish for his feast. A poor fisherman heard about the reward and caught a big fish for the rich man. He reached the rich man's house. However, the gatekeeper wouldn't let him in till he promised to give him half of the reward. The fisherman did not agree and was so irritated by the gatekeeper that he thought of teaching the greedy man a lesson. With a plan in his mind, the fisherman agreed to give half of his reward to the gatekeeper. When the fisherman gave the fish to the rich man, he was highly pleased and wanted to reward him with 100 coins but the fisherman refused to take it. Instead, he demanded a hundred lashes on his back. Everybody was surprised and tried to dissuade him. But the fisherman did not agree.

At last, the rich man ordered a servant to give him a hundred lashes. When the fisherman had received fifty, he asked them to stop as he had a partner in the business. The gatekeeper received the remaining 50 lashes. He had to suffer because of his greed. The rich man understood the whole situation and after giving the gatekeeper fifty lashes he dismissed him from service. The rich man then, gave the fisherman a handsome reward.

Moral Too much greed becomes the reason for your downfall.

2. Given below is an outline of the story given in the form of phrases. Using it, write a short story.

Lily found a key.....thought it was important..... searched the house and backyard...nobody knew where the key belonged.....determined....rememberd the old door in the attic...opened the door...found a treasure chest....everyone happy....informed the authorities....lost treasure...Lily awarded

Ans. **The Lost Key**

Once upon a time, there was a girl named Lily. One day, she found an old key in her backyard. She didn't know what the key was for but she thought it was important. Lily searched the house and the backyard, trying to find the lock that the key would fit into.

She asked her parents and her friends but nobody knew where the key belonged. However, Lily was determined to find the lock that the key belonged to. She spent every spare moment searching the door which could be opened with the key. Suddenly, she remembered an old door in the attic that she had never been able to open. She rushed up to the attic and tried the key in the lock. It turned and the door opened. Inside, Lily found a treasure chest filled with gold coins and precious jewels. She couldn't believe her luck. Lily's parents were thrilled with the discovery, and they praised her for her determination and perseverance. After carefully taking out the treasure, Lily's parents informed the authorities. The authority came and found that it was a lost treasure of an ancient king. Then, they took the treasure with themselves and rewarded Lily with some coins and some jewels as keepsake.

3. Given below is an outline of the story given in the form of phrases. Using it, write a short story.

Famine in a city...scarcity of food...hungry children....kind nobleman...invited children....put loaves of bread in a huge basket...asked children to take a loaf....children fought and struggled for the largest loaf...one girl waited aside.....took the last and smallest loaf....thanked the nobleman...at home she cut the loaf.....found silver pieces......returned to the nobleman's house...reward for patience and courteous behaviour.

Ans. **Sweet is the Fruit of Patience**

Once, a city was struck by famine and there was an acute scarcity of food. The poor children were hungry and were looking around for someone who could give them food or money to buy food. A kind nobleman, who lived nearby, took pity on them and invited them to his home. He put loaves of bread in a large basket and asked the children to take a loaf each.

The children rushed to the basket and started fighting with one another. Each one of them wanted to grab the largest loaf. After taking their loaves, they started eating their breads greedily and did not even thank the nobleman. All this time, a little girl stood patiently on one side. At last, she took the last small loaf that was left in the basket. She thanked the nobleman for his generosity and went home. Just as she cut the loaf into two to share it with her mother, she was amazed to find pieces of silver in it. The girl ran back to the nobleman's house to return the silver pieces. The nobleman smiled and said it was a reward for her patience and courteous nature.

4. Given below is an outline of the story given in the form of phrases. Using it, write a short story.

Two men...one cheerful...no worries...believed all would be well:....the other full of worries.....worried about old age...not able to work.....no money.....may have to beg...might go blind.....wants to know what blindness would be like...walks with eyes shut...does not see purse full of gold...companion spots it...picks up.....thanks God.

Ans. **The Result of Worry**

Two men were walking along a road together. One of them was a cheerful, happy-go-lucky fellow who had no worries. He believed if he worked as well as he could, all would turn out well in the future. However, the other man always saw the dark side of things.

He was worried about what would happen to him in old age when he would not be able to work anymore. He feared he would be in need of money and perhaps have to beg for a living. He began to fear that he might even go blind in his eyes. To try what blindness would be like, he started walking with his eyes shut. While he was doing this, he missed seeing a purse full of gold coins lying on the road. His companion, who was walking happily along with no worries, spotted the purse and picked it up. He thanked God for taking care of his future!

5. Given below is an outline of the story given in the form of phrases. Using it, write a short story.

Celebrated archer Guru Dronacharya taught archery.....selected a tree in forest.......placed a wooden bird on a bare branch.......were to hit the bird in the eye......Yudhisthir stepped forward........ "Can you see me?" asked Dronacharya. 'Yes' replied Yudhisthir......asked him to put down the bow...........each prince replied the same.......asked to retire from the competition......finally came Arjuna .... "Arjuna, do you see me?" asked Dronacharya. "I see only my target," said Arjuna ...Arjuna hit the bird's eye.

Ans. **Arjuna: The Most Accomplished Marksman**

The celebrated archer Guru Dronacharya taught the royal princes the finer points of archery. One day, he wanted to test the archery skills of his pupils. So, he brought his students to a forest and chose a tree standing in the open. He placed a wooden bird on a bare branch of that tree. The princes were asked to stand 200 yards away and aim at their target one by one. They were asked to hit the eye of the bird. Yudhisthir was first to start the competition. He took his bow and looked at his target. 'Can you see me?' asked Dronacharya. 'Yes sir!' replied Yudhisthir. 'Put down your bow,' asked the Guru. The disappointed prince retired from the contest. The same question was asked and all of them gave the same reply. Hence, all of them were asked to retire from the competition. Finally, it was Arjuna's turn. 'Arjuna do you see me?' asked the Guru. 'I see nothing but my target, the eye of the bird,' replied Arjuna. 'Good Arjuna, shoot now,' asked Dronacharya. Arjuna released the arrow aiming at his target. The arrow hit the eye of the wooden bird and was adjudged as the most accomplished marksman.

6. Look at the given images and write a story relating to it.

Ans. **The Lost Wallet**

Kabir was too excited to go snowboarding. It was his first time going to the mountains alone. He could go alone as he was an adult now. However, his parents were not easily convinced to let him go alone. They had wanted to come with him. However, Kabir told them that he had wanted to go alone and to convince them, he showed them every booking that he had made. Finally, his parents agreed. He had smoothly taken his flight and reached his destination high up in the mountains. From there, he took the tram to the snowboarding centre. He rented the snowboard for which he had to pre-pay ₹ 200 and the rest after he returned the board. The payment was decided according to the number of hours he used the board for. After happily paying his money, he took his blue coloured board and enjoyed snowboarding for a few hours. It was difficult at first but soon he successfully snowboarded. It was 4 pm when he decided to return. As he gave his board back and moved his hand towards his pocket, he found out that he had lost his wallet. For a moment, he panicked and told the cashier that he could not find his wallet. The cashier informed him that he had just received a wallet that a couple had found. He showed the wallet to Kabir. Much to his relief, it was his wallet. He then, quickly paid the due amount and left for his hotel.

7. Look at the given image and write a story titled 'In the Land of Lilliputians' in 150-200 words.

Ans. My boat had overturned in the water and as I woke up, I knew that I was in the realm of God. It was a pleasant scene. I was at a beach with clear blue water on one side and lush green forest on the other. However, when I tried to get up, I couldn't stand. I found my arms and legs tied down to the ground with strings. I could also hear the whispers around me. They seemed to be faint human voices. Then, I felt something moving on my body. It came near my face. He was a tiny little man of 3 inches height. He was dressed like a soldier.

As I looked behind him, I saw that forty more followed him. I was amazed to see such tiny men. I couldn't understand what they wanted to do with me. Then, I felt as if a thousand needles were pricking my body. The little men were shooting arrows at me. Then, I lay still without moving. One of the elders, perhaps their leader, stood on a raised platform near me.

I indicated for food and water. He seemed to understand me. He sent hundreds of men up to my face to feed me. When I asked him about where I was, I found out that I was alive and on the land of Lilliputians.

ASSESSMENT EXERCISE

1. Given below is an outline of the story given in the form of phrases. Using it, write a short story.

Raghu and Raj were two friends and neighbours.....Raghu-servant named Ramu....Raj's servant was Shammu...Both servants foolish.......who is more foolish?.......decided to give a test..........Raghu told Ramu "Run back to my house to find out if I am there or not".......Raj told Shammu.......''Go to your room and find out if you are there or not." Ramu and Shammu returned ....Ramu complained........wasted time.........master could have phoned to find himself.....Shammu reported........he was not in the room.......nothing to choose between them.

2. Given below is an outline of the story given in the form of phrases. Using it, write a short story.

An old lady becomes blind................calls in a doctor.................agrees to pay large fees if cured...............doctor comes daily................starts stealing one piece of furniture daily...............delays the cure.................at last cures her.................demands his fees.........lady refuses to pay, saying cure is not complete................doctor objects, lady says sight not restored as she cannot see all her furniture.................moral.

3. Given below is an outline of the story given in the form of phrases. Using it, write a short story.

God's promise to a disciple to visit her.........disciple cleans her house and waits for God.........poor old lady knocks her door.............disciple doesn't help her...............tells her not to waste her time ....next, beggar comes at her door step.................she doesn't entertain him either...........Finally a child knocks her door.........she sends him away too..........dreams of God that night...........God tells him that he had come thrice at her door step, but she didn't bother..........lady disappointed...........moral.

4. Given below is an outline of the story given in the form of phrases. Using it, write a short story.

Seema............working as maid...............eager to go to school.............unable to do so...............family responsibilities....................I lent a hand to support ....soon pass high school exams..........can teach her own children now, life changed.

5. Given below is an outline of the story given in the form of phrases. Using it, write a short story.

A king upset...........people in his kingdom, lazy...........decides to teach them a lesson...........he has a big stone put in the middle of the road...........next day whoever passes that stone goes round it...........nobody bothers to remove the stone...........all curse and blame the government for it...........at last a young man removes the stone...........under it was an iron box marked, "For the man who moves away the stone"...........inside the box were gold coins...........the people were ashamed.

6. Look at the given image and write a story relating to it.

7. Look at the given image and write a story relating to it.

8. Look at the given image and write a story relating to it.

9. Look at the given images and write a story titled 'Learning to Become Eco-friendly'.

10. Look at the given image and write a story titled 'How I Won the Relay Race'.

11. Look at the given image and write a story relating to it.

12. Look at the given image and write a story relating to it.

Article Writing

An article is a piece of writing that is written to inform, to persuade, to entertain or to convince the reader of something. It essentially has several paragraphs containing a distinct beginning, a middle and a conclusion.

Writing an article is a very challenging task for anyone. It requires a high degree of creativity, a good vocabulary and a thorough knowledge of the subject. Hence, knowing the elements and the format of article is very important.

Elements of an Article

1. **Title/Heading** There are no rules as such but it may comprise a single word, a phrase or a sentence of 4-6 words. The title should be thought-provoking and catchy, and should highlight the theme.
2. **Name of the Writer** Write your name immediately after the heading in the form of a byline.
3. **Introduction** Keep the topic in perspective. Write an interesting introduction. Keep the reader's interest intact by providing some surprising information or interesting facts related to the context.
4. **Description of the Topic** Highlight various facts of the topic like the causes and effects, advantages and disadvantages, etc.
5. **Ending** Wind up your article with your own views - criticism, suggestions etc.
6. **Conclusion** End the article with a desire, an appeal or a warning.

Points to be Kept in Mind

- Understand carefully the hints/information given in the verbal or visual input.
- Arrange all the hints/information in an order in which you want them to develop.
- Divide your article into several paragraphs when necessary. All the sentences in the paragraphs should be related to the main ideas of the topic.
- Use simple and straightforward language.
- Avoid the use of personal pronouns.
- Remember to re-read your article to make sure that there are no grammatical or punctuation error in it.

Format of an Article

Recently you read about an incident in a newspaper in which a child tried to imitate the stunts shown on television and sustained serious injuries. Write an article in 120-150 words on the hazards of unsupervised television viewing by kids and how parents should guide them in this matter.

Clues

- TV for overall well-being of children
- Ruin eyesight-lack of concentration
- Attracts mind-effect greater than ever
- Bad habits- copy actors-hero worship

Ans.

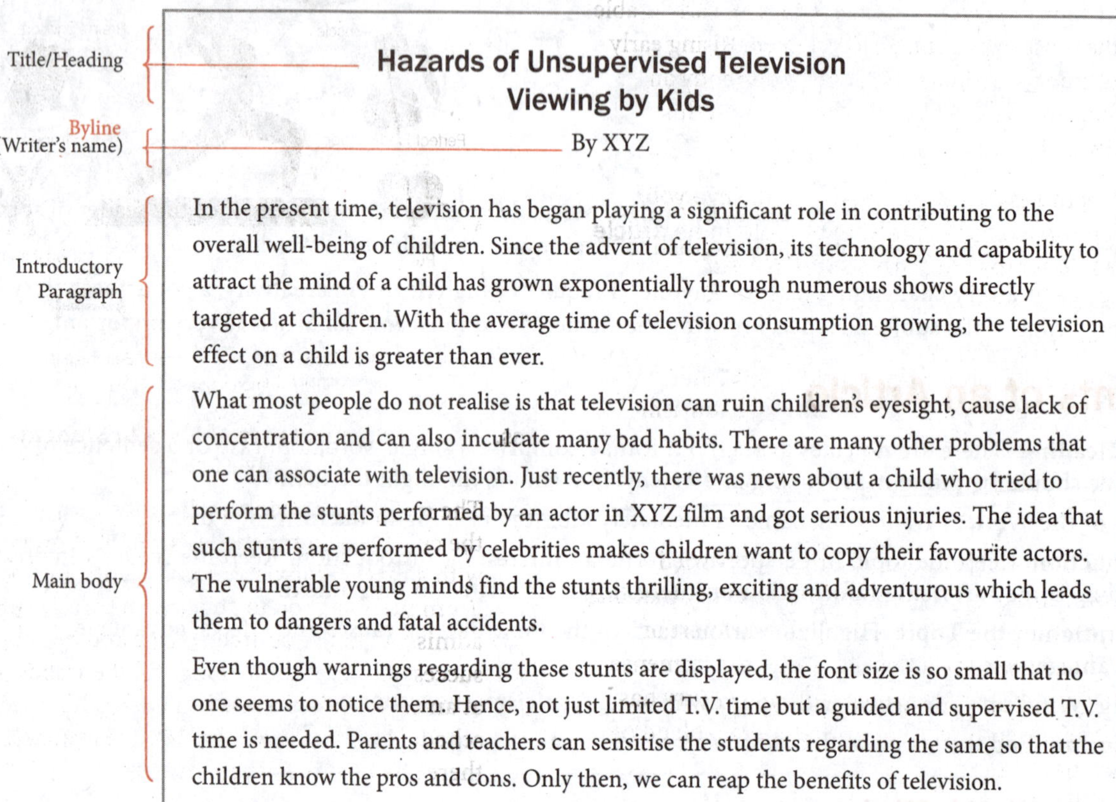

Hazards of Unsupervised Television Viewing by Kids

By XYZ

In the present time, television has began playing a significant role in contributing to the overall well-being of children. Since the advent of television, its technology and capability to attract the mind of a child has grown exponentially through numerous shows directly targeted at children. With the average time of television consumption growing, the television effect on a child is greater than ever.

What most people do not realise is that television can ruin children's eyesight, cause lack of concentration and can also inculcate many bad habits. There are many other problems that one can associate with television. Just recently, there was news about a child who tried to perform the stunts performed by an actor in XYZ film and got serious injuries. The idea that such stunts are performed by celebrities makes children want to copy their favourite actors. The vulnerable young minds find the stunts thrilling, exciting and adventurous which leads them to dangers and fatal accidents.

Even though warnings regarding these stunts are displayed, the font size is so small that no one seems to notice them. Hence, not just limited T.V. time but a guided and supervised T.V. time is needed. Parents and teachers can sensitise the students regarding the same so that the children know the pros and cons. Only then, we can reap the benefits of television.

SOLVED EXAMPLES

1. Write an article on 'The Benefits of Rising Early' in about 120-150 words. Use the following clues to frame your article.

Benefits of early rising

- Early morning hours are so peaceful and quiet.
- Rise early and you actually have time for breakfast.
- Easier to exercise exercising right after work is liable to be cancelled because of other things that come up.

Ans. **Benefits of Early Rising**

By XYZ

The benefits of early rising have been put into our minds from the time we are very young. As young children, we are taught by our elders that sleeping late and rising late is a bad habit. We all have heard the old proverb 'Early to bed, early to rise, makes a man healthy, wealthy and wise'. Rising early has always been associated with numerous scientifically proven benefits.

When we rise early we get those some extra hours during which we can work to keep our mind and body fit. This is a time when our minds are most receptive and hence, you may have heard people getting up early to study and do all kinds of important work.

During these early hours, there are less distractions and hence our productivity increases immensely. Rising early enables us to be on time. By beginning our day early, we are able to manage our work properly leading to better time management. One who rises early is able to get the most sound and peaceful sleep. Rising early gives us time to meditate which gives our body an energising and positive start to the day. And this positivity is the key to a stress free life.

2. India is a tourist's dream destination. Give your views on the tourism potential of India in an article in 120-150 words. You are Navtej/Navita.

- Places of worship-religious tourism
- Foreigners-places of historical interest
- The rich-hill stations during summers, the Sun-kissed beaches in winters, leisure tourism
- Medical tourism-world class hospitals

Ans.

Tourism Potential of India

By Navtej

India has been so blessed with a rich and varied geographical, cultural and linguistic diversity that one needs a lifetime to explore each and every part of India. Thus, it is no wonder that India has immense potential in the tourism industry. Each century has brought a new culture to India leading to a blend of cultures that has shaped modern India.

Well known for its ancient civilisation and the artifacts recovered and being excavated till today, India proves the genuineness of its claims. The ancient history of our culture has left behind exquisite monuments and temples which can amaze the tourist to no extent. From the mosques to the temples and churches, India is a living testament to its vast and varied heritage. For those, looking to just get away from the madding crowd, hill stations during summers, the sun-kissed beaches in winter and leisure tourism are the go-to options that cater to one and all in India.

Moreover, India is among the top three medical tourism destinations in Asia with world-class hospitals, quality and low-cost treatment and highly skilled doctors. The options enumerated so far are just some instances of India's diversified tourist potential. There is so much more waiting to be explored in what can truly be the dream destination for tourists.

3. Write an article on 'Importance of Yoga' in about 120-150 words. Use the following image to frame your answer.

Ans.

Importance of Yoga to Students

By Karuna

The modern lifestyle, the disorderly eating habits, and the cut-throat competition have filled each one of us with stress and anxiety. For students, it is much more. From scoring good to choosing a career, getting admission in the desired college and becoming successful–all of these things fill the minds of students at an early age. As a result, students fill up their entire schedule as they know that for one available seat, there are hundreds of applicants.

Such a situation makes the life of students very stressful. They do not get any time for relaxation which is as essential as other goals. Experts believe that a physically healthy body has a clear mind, better focus and low level of stress. And the best way to relax and feel rejuvenated is to practice yoga every day. Yoga not only keeps one physically fit but it also improves concentration as it calms the mind and keeps it healthy. Stress, more often than not, leads to behavioural problems, such as irritable mood, insomnia, sudden growth or loss of appetite, etc. and in severe cases, depression. Practicing yoga every day reduces such behavioural problems, decreases physical ailments and improves interpersonal relationships. It purifies the body and distresses the mind. It not only improves the body posture but also strengthens the muscles and improves the immune system.

So let us take small steps to keep ourselves healthy-mentally, physically and spiritually.

4. Increase in the number of private vehicles has caused problems like rising air pollution, traffic jams, lack of parking space, road rage etc. The solution lies in the use of public transport. Write an article on 'The Importance of Public Transport'. You are Karan/Karuna.

Ans. **The Importance of Public Transport**

By Karan

Transport is responsible for a substantial and growing proportion of air pollution in Indian cities besides causing traffic jams, parking space problems and road rage. This calls for a greater share of public transport in meeting mobility needs. Public transport has many advantages. The first is that it saves fuel, reduces an individual's carbon footprint and reduces congestion.

Public vehicles move people efficiently while producing significantly less air pollution to move one passenger one mile. It is easier to implement the usage of eco-friendly fuels in public transportation systems. A bus with 7-8 passengers is more fuel efficient than an average single occupant car. It not only saves fuel but also money and energy.

Understanding the need of the hour, the government is introducing many rules so that people start using public vehicles. The odd-even rule, started by Chief Minister of Delhi, was initiated to encourage the use of public transport and thereby reduce pollution caused by traffic. The authorities are working hard to make public aware of how useful, efficient and less damaging to the environment the use of public transport is.

5. To have a fair complexion is an obsession in our society. Demand for fair brides to matrimonial columns and sale of fairness creams are evidence enough. Write an article giving your views on 'Beautiful Mind, Better than a Fair Complexion'. You are Natwar/Nimmi. Use the following clues

Clues

- The West people like to be tanned
- Fair complexion only skin deep
- Beautiful mind
- Attitude to life
- Behaviour in society etc.

Ans. **Beautiful Mind, Better than a Fair Complexion**

By Natwar

If we look at the many matrimonial columns in the leading dailies, we observe great demand for fair brides and ads for sale of fairness creams. It implies that to have a fair complexion is an obsession in our society.

Our people, especially women, are immensely influenced by the West. They tend to follow Western culture and enrich facial beauty. However, we tend to forget the same Western people spend a lot of money to get tanned. Virtually, this facial make-up is only skin - deep and represents only external beauty of a person. It is absolutely temporary and only gives us sensual pleasure.

A fair complexioned person may or may not possess a beautiful mind. It all depends on his/her thoughts, deeds and behaviour that reveal what his/her persona is. Beauty of mind leads to a pretty mind, a kind heart and a beautiful soul. These qualities change one's attitude to life and add to make for a social behaviour. Those who possess these qualities do beautiful deeds such as Helen Keller, Vivekananda, B.T. Washington and many more. Beauty lies not in the face, but in the heart. Thus, a beautiful mind is better than a fair complexion.

6. Look at the given poster.

You read the poster with an article on 'Children and Smartphones' in a reputed magazine. Now, write an article for your school magazine expressing your views about the same. You are Ajeet/Akshara. You can use the following clues

Clues

- Smartphones in vogue and ubiquitous
- Become a necessity
- Maturity and understanding
- Personal data and life on public display
- Need for parental supervision
- Knowledge of advantages as well as misuse

Ans.

Children and Smartphones

By Akshara, XII A

Children today live in a world where smartphones are in vogue and ubiquitous (found everywhere). For them, it has become a necessity and they are eager to have their own smartphone as soon as possible. This fact has led many discussions about the ideal age for children to have their first smartphone.

Many experts agree on the need for children to be mature and understand the disadvantages of what they have in their hand. They must be able to understand the dangers of sharing too many details of their personal life on the internet. They have to be aware that any information shared on the internet remains publicly available and can be easily misused. Last but not the least, they need to understand that keeping manners matters. In other words, what in the online world is known as Netiquette (internet etiquettes) is important.

Mobiles will require parental supervision to protect children, to teach them how to properly use smartphones, to avoid possible problems and finally to take responsibility for their misuse. Children must know that although the smartphone is a great resource of knowledge and information, it also brings many ill-habits. So, they must know how to take advantage of mobile phones while avoiding its misuse.

ASSESSMENT EXERCISE

1. Write an article on the 'Role of Youth in National Development' using the following clues in about 150-200 words.
- Make innovation for development of the country
- Extricating society from age-old stigmas
- Preserve cultural heritage and infuse the spirit of patriotism
- Unite the people and create a feeling of brotherhood
- Reservoirs of unbounded energy and enthusiasm

2. Write an article on the 'Importance of Reading' on the basis of the given image.

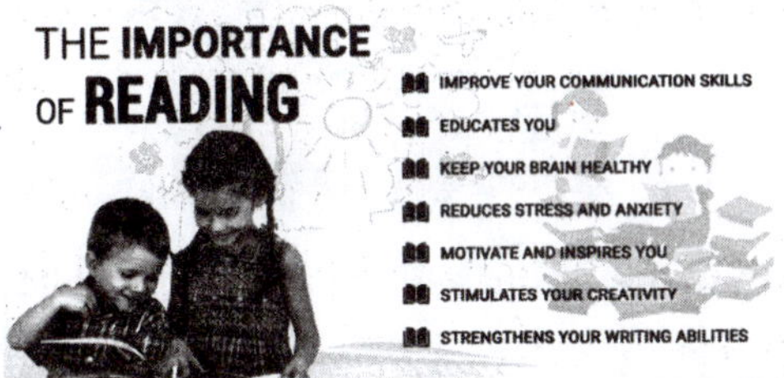

3. Write an article in 150-200 words on 'Festivals of India'. You are Karuna/Karan.

4. Hard work and punctuality are essential for a happy and successful life. They help in meeting the desired targets of our life. You are Kavya/Kanha. Write an article highlighting the importance of hard work and punctuality in a student's life.

5. The word 'father' is synonymous with strict discipline etc. but it is not completely true. The father fulfills his responsibilities affectionately for the family. Write an article on the topic, 'Role of Father in the Family'. You can use the following clues

Role of father-traditional image-teacher-counsellor-promoting equality-influence decisions-prepare for reality-providers and protectors-fulfill necessities-strict-enforce discipline-pillar of strength

6. Parents today are facing a major problem with their children. They waste most of their time on Facebook and other social networking sites with the result that their studies and other important activities are neglected. Write an article on this issue taking ideas from the hints given below

Hints

Pros include fast spread of information, source of news, solves crimes, helps students with academic work, improves relationships

Cons include spread of false information, students waste time, leads to stress, misunderstandings and arguments, children develop self centered personalities, leads to loneliness and depression

7. Looking at the increasing obesity among school children, write an article on the topic in taking help from the hints given below.

Hints
- Problem of being overweight in common in children
- Sedentary lifestyle, watch television, waste time on social networking sites, very little physical exercise
- Eat junk food and drink aerated drinks instead of balanced diet
- Should be encouraged to do more of physical exercise

8. You find it disturbing that despite a ban on the use of polythene bags, its use is rampant in the city. Write an article expressing your concern about the apathy of people towards environmental degradation. Also suggest ways to mobilise city dwellers for the cause of safe environment. You can use the following clues

9. The sports field is said to be a minifield of life. Whatever we experience or learn here serves as an invaluable experience for life. Write an article on 'More Lessons are Learnt on the Sports Field than in the Classroom' in 120-150 words. You are Sarika/Sandeep. You can use the following clues

Clues

- Cooperation, teamwork, leadership
- Tolerance and understanding
- No caste and religious prejudice
- Healthy life

10. Students are required to cope with a lot of pressure in today's competitive environment. Write an article highlighting the increasing stress faced by students and suggest ways to combat the same.

Speech Writing

A speech is an effective way of communicating a message to a large audience. It is one of the ways of spreading awareness regarding social issues or giving information regarding other important issues.

As a form of writing, a speech is similar to an article except that it begins with a formal address to the audience, is more conversational in tone and concludes with a 'Thank you'.

Components of a Speech

Introduction It begins with greeting the chief guest/principal/teachers and other listeners. It may include a striking statement, a saying or anything else which will immediately make the audience interested.

Elaboration of the Topic It will include a sequence of ideas to build up to the summing up and conclusion. You may include examples, evidence or data to support the ideas.

Summing up Summarise the most important points in your speech but do not repeat them.

Conclusion Depending on the purpose of your speech, conclude with a call for an action, an appeal, a warning, a request and an expression of thanks.

Points to be Kept in Mind

- Do not forget to write the introduction to the speech with a formal address to the audience.
- Use simple and clear language to make the speech understandable.
- Remember to end the speech with a thankyou.
- Always re-read your speech to make sure that there is no grammatical or punctuation error in it.

Format of a Speech

You have to write a speech to be delivered in the Inter School Speech Competition on the topic 'Obesity among School Children'.

Heading or Title (Optional-not to be spoken)	**Obesity among School Children**
Formal address	Respected Principal, teachers and dear friends. Today, I am standing before you to express my views on the topic 'Obesity among School Children'.
Content	Obesity has become a cause of concern for one and all. With the entry of companies like McDonalds, Dominoes, Pizza Huts, etc., the concept of fast food has spread like a wild fire. More and more school children have taken to chocolates and soft drinks without worrying about calories. The result is obesity increasing by leaps and bounds among school children. 'Junk food' appeals to our taste buds but our digestive system repels it. Oil and extra fat harm our liver. We put on flesh and increase our weight. Fresh home cooked meals are hygienic, better and full of vitamins as well as minerals that are easily digested. Our food should consist of coarse cereals, green and leafy vegetables, fruits, and pulses, etc. To keep ourselves agile, energetic and robust, we must do physical exercises and also play games like football, badminton, kabaddi, volleyball, etc. By eating healthy food and doing regular physical activities, not only will our body be healthy and toned but also our minds would remain active. I hope you all will give some consideration to my suggestion and try to instill it in your daily routine.
Formal thanks to audience	Thank you!

SOLVED EXAMPLES

1. On the occasion of 'World Environment Day', you have decided to speak on the topic, "How to Avoid the Use of Plastic in Everyday Life". Prepare your speech using the given clues

Plastic is relatively cheap- durable and versatile-many years to decompose-contaminate soil-water pollution- hamper aquatic life-damaging our planet- strict action against polluters-alternate to plastics

Ans. Good morning respected Principal Sir, teachers and my dear friends.

Today, we are here to celebrate World Environment Day and talk about the better ways in which we can avoid the use of plastic in everyday life. Plastics are used in almost all areas of everyday living.
It carries our drinks, holds our shampoos and keeps our vegetables fresh. Plastic is relatively cheap and makes our life easier. However, it is a great source of pollution.

Due to non-biodegradable nature of plastics, they take many years to decompose and damage our environment. Plastic contaminates the soil which makes it less fertile and stops the growth of plants.
It also causes water pollution as plastic bags which are thrown carelessly are carried away by winds into the water bodies. These plastic bags go deep into the water and hamper aquatic life. Hence, it is time for us to stop using plastic completely.

Though it may be difficult to avoid the plastic bags at first, it needs to be done for the greater good.
The government has banned the use of plastic bags but people continue to use it. In order to implement these laws strictly, the government must take strict action against the ones using it. Moreover, each of us must come forward to practice this ban. We must carry our own cloth or paper bags for shopping.
Try to pack your food in steel or aluminium containers instead of plastic ones. We must encourage people to avoid the use of plastic bags. Never throw away the

plastic on roads, as animals die after consuming it. We must come together to initiate a ban on plastic and make the world safer and healthier.

Thank you!

2. You are Ram/Rajani an academic counsellor. You have been invited to speak on the topic, 'Books are Our Best Friends'. Prepare a speech, giving your views on books, how they can be our best friends and how they happen to be better than real human friends and how they can lead us to the great hobby of reading.

Ans. Man is a social animal. Therefore, it is natural for him to need friends that he loves most. There are some who love the company of nature. There are also those who love the company of books.

Honourable Principal, Respected teachers and my dear students. Today, I will tell you about how 'Books are Our Best Friends'.

A book is the map of man's life. Every page of a great book is a storehouse of man's best and noblest thoughts. In a library, you meet all these mighty minds of the whole world. If you are feeling alone or have been betrayed by human friends, get in a friendship with books; they'll never leave you, they'll never betray you. Instead, they will always add something to your knowledge and will make you a successful person. Books make you laugh, make you cry and let you find the real meaning of life. In addition, reading books regularly develops our reading hobby. Books provide us good thoughts, fill our minds with knowledge and awaken our souls. The knowledge provided by the books is food for our minds. Reading good books daily is an excellent exercise as it refreshes our mind, provides us the solutions to our problems and makes us mentally strong.

Hence, I would like to conclude with a quote by C.W. Eliot: "Books are the quietest and most constant of friends; they are the most accessible and wisest of counsellors and the most patient of teachers."

Thank you!

3. Food wastage is a crime against humanity. Write a speech stressing the need of reducing food wastage.

Food equivalent to God - inequality in society - wastage in Indian wedding - wastage of resources - many sleep hungry - don't waste food.

Ans. Good morning everyone, today I, PQR want to discuss with you all the need of reducing food wastage.

According to Indian philosophy, food is equal to God. However, we do not give any respect to food these days. We fail to realise that millions of poor people are dying due to hunger when millions of tonnes of food is being thrown away and wasted for no good reason. Food wastage in Indian weddings is an eye opener. Extra food has to be prepared inspite of its expected wastage. While this is a direct consequence of the inequality that exists between people throughout the world, the situation is made a lot worse by the huge amounts of food that goes to waste each day due to improper management and disposal of leftovers.

The issue of food wastage is of high importance to fight hunger, raise income and improve food security in India. Each time food goes unconsumed, all the resources that went into producing, processing, packing and transporting the food are wasted. Food wastage is morally wrong because there are many people who are hungry or dying, simply because they have no food.

Gandhiji once told that if God were to appear to the millions of hungry people, it would be in the form of food.

So, please don't waste food.

Thank you!

4. Write a speech on the topic, 'Library Plays an Important Role at School' to be delivered in the morning assembly. You are Karuna/Karan, Head Girl/Head Boy.

Ans. The school library is central to learning and plays a key role in encouraging innovation and problem-solving.

Good morning, Respected Principal Sir, teachers and my dear friends. I have come before you all to speak on the topic, 'Library Plays an Important Role at School'.

Libraries make a difference to students' understanding and achievement. They provide support to both students and teachers. The presence of the school library ensures that each student has equal access to academic resources, books, and reading material. It also provides teachers full access to relevant curriculum, books, reference material, etc. The library not only promotes inquiry learning but also builds knowledge and confidence in seeking and processing information. It is a fundamental resource for supporting students' learning and encourages collaborative learning and sharing of ideas.

Students who regularly visit a library develop questioning skills and become creative and critical thinkers. It is in the library where students become active seekers and users of information. The school library thus, aims to give every student the opportunity to learn, to enjoy reading and to enhance their knowledge and understanding.

Thank You!

5. Peer pressure is useful for the development of an individual. If there is no peer pressure at all then there would be no goal or aim to succeed. Write a speech on the topic - 'Is Peer Pressure Beneficial or Not?' to be delivered on account of Children's Day celebration in your school.

Ans. Respected Principal Sir, honourable teachers and my dear friends, on the occasion of Children's Day, I am going to present my views on the topic 'Is Peer Pressure Beneficial or Not?'

Peer pressure is beneficial as long as we know our limits. It is all upto us to be so strong, firm, unshakable and filled with conviction to not go on the wrong track. Peer pressure is not always bad. Peers may teach you good habits and encourage you to follow them. Looking at what others do can help you bring a positive change in your way of thinking. Your peers, their choices and ways of life give you a glimpse of the world outside the four walls of your house. What they think about things in life, how they perceive situations, how they react in different circumstances can actually expose you to the world around. Being part of a larger group of peers exposes you to the diversity in human behaviour. This makes you reflect on your behaviour and know where you stand. Peer pressure can lead you to make the right choices in life.

Your peers can thus, influence the shaping of your personality in a positive way. Moreover, it's not pressure every time, sometimes it's inspiration changes you for good.

Thank you!

ASSESSMENT EXERCISE

1. Man's use of fossil fuels - coal, oil, and natural gas - together with deforestation has increased the concentration of atmospheric carbon dioxide, and heat-trapping greenhouse gas has begun the process of climate change. Higher temperatures are an indication of dangerous consequences: drought, disease, floods, and lost ecosystems.

Using the information given above and your own ideas, write a speech expressing your concerns about the rapidly increasing global warming and its consequences, giving your suggestions to improve the situation.

2. Write a speech on 'Laughter is the Best Medicine' using the following clues

Scientifically proven benefits-charm-motivation-positive emotional and physical changes-strengthens relationships-more spontaneous

3. Junk food can be very appealing to children, but they cause more harm to them than they can imagine. Prepare a speech, to be delivered in the school assembly on, 'The Harmful Effects of Junk Food on School Children'. Use the hints given below

Hints

- Proves to be harmful
- Addictive
- Obesity, chronic illness, low self esteem, depression
- Decreases concentration level
- High calorie, fats, carbohydrates and added sugars
- Creates deficiency of nutrients
- Diabetes, blood pressure, stroke
- Slow poison

4. Discipline leads to harmony in life whereas indiscipline leads to confusion. Prepare a speech on the topic 'Importance of Discipline in Life', to be delivered in the School Assembly. Use the following hints

Hints

- Discipline leads to harmony.
- Indiscipline leads to confusion and disorder.
- Discipline is required in all walks of life at school, at home and on the road.
- There is no place on heaven and Earth where discipline is not required.
- Discipline is the key to success.
- Self discipline is most important.

5. Games play an important role in our lives. They are not only the means of entertainment but also keep us physically fit. Some like indoor games and others outdoor. Write a speech in 120-150 words for your school's Morning Assembly on the topic 'The Importance of Games in Our Lives'.

6. Write a speech in 150 - 200 words on the topic, 'A Student Must Know How to Manage His Time'. It is to be delivered in the Morning Assembly. You are Karan/Karuna, Head Boy/Head Girl of the school.

Letter Writing

Letter writing is one of the most effective ways of communication. Today, although telephone, fax and e-mail have replaced personal (informal) letters, formal letters are still used for communication. Trade, official correspondence, public representation, complaints and other dealings, transactions and communication with people are still conducted through formal letters. Therefore, one must cultivate the art and skill of letter writing.

Types of Letters

We write two kinds of letters which are discussed below

1. **Informal Letters** An informal letter is a letter that we usually use to write to our friends, family or relatives. These letters are personal letters that are not used for official purposes. Hence, they use a very informal and simple language.
2. **Formal Letters** These letters are generally written to officials regarding serious issues. They have set patterns and are written using a crisp and clear language in a matter-of-fact style. The language should be kept simple without including any unnecessary expressions.

Main Elements of a Letter

- **Sender's Address** According to the latest format, sender's address is written at the top along with the pin code. Do not write sender's name with the address.

  e.g. K-127, Ashok Nagar
  New Delhi-110092

- **Date** It appears directly below the sender's address, after leaving a one line space. It is advisable to always write the full date in the following format.

  e.g. 25th December, 20XX

- **Receiver's Address** It appears directly below the date and comprises the receiver's designation and the complete address.

  e.g. The Editor
  The Hindustan Times
  47/1567, Daryaganj
  Delhi - 110002

Note It While writing the address (both sender's and receiver's), one must not use 'comma' at the end of each line. If the address is not provided in the question, then you may create a fictitious address but writing an address is mandatory.

- **Subject** Subject is written in a formal letter. It can be written after the receiver's address or after the salutation. It should be short and to the point.

  e.g. **Subject** Application for the Post of Content Writer

- **Salutation** This consists of words of greeting and is written on the left hand side of the page just below the subject after leaving a line. The form of greeting depends upon your relation to the person to whom the letter is being written.
  - In case of informal letters, you use Dear Rohan, Dear Mummy, etc.
  - In case of formal letters, you use only Sir/Ma'am.
- **The Body** The body is the main part of any letter. This is written in response to the given topic, in a simple and direct language.

  The body includes three main parts

  (i) **Introductory paragraph/sentence** States the purpose of writing the letter

  (ii) **Informative paragraphs** Details about the subject of the letter. It includes arguments related to the theme of the letter written in a simple and organised manner.

  (iii) **Concluding paragraph/sentence** The closure of the letter/conclusion stating hope, request or comment.
- **Complimentary Close** It is a courteous way of ending the letter. The expression used must match the salutation.
  - In case of informal letter, we use Yours friendly/Yours lovingly.
  - In case of formal letter, we use Yours sincerely/Yours faithfully/Yours truly.
- **Signature, Name and Position** It is written just below the 'complimentary close' and includes the sender's name and designation (if applicable).

  e.g. Ankita Chakravarti
  Editor

Points to be Kept in Mind

- The subject line should match with what is asked in the question. It should be short and to the point.
- Get right to the purpose of the letter in polite and formal language (formal letter).
- Be clear, concise and to the point. Stick to the word limit of 100-120 words.
- Use simple language so that the letter is easy to understand.
- Re-read your letter to check the format and to make sure that there are no grammatical errors in it.

1. Informal Letters

Format of an Informal Letters

Write a letter to your friend Rama/Raman requesting him/her to spend the summer holidays with you.

Sender's address	100, Old Lake Town Kolkata-26
Date	16th December, 20XX
Salutation	Dear Rama
Body of the letter	It's been a long time since we met. How are you? I hope you are doing well and this letter finds you in good health. As you know that summer vacation has already started, I was thinking of spending the vacations together in Mumbai. I want to take you out on the city tour as well as introduce my friends and family to you. I would love to go out and have street food with you. We can enjoy some time near Marine Drive. We can also visit Goa and Pune while here. I am just excited at the thought of me and you spending the vacations together. I just hope your parents agree for sending you here to spend the vacations with me. Let me know if it is possible for you to come to my place. Give my respect to uncle and aunty and love to your sister.
	With lots of love
Complimentary Close	Yours lovingly
Name and Signaure	Sakshi

SOLVED EXAMPLES

1. Write a letter to your friend generally asking him/her about how he/she and his/her family are doing.

Ans. 13 AK Street
Pitampura
Delhi

12th September, 20XX

Dear Pakhi

Hope you are safe and protected. It's been a long time since we last met. I have been quite busy recently. I had a day off from school today and so decided to write a letter to you asking about you and your family.

I am fine here. I have recently started learning French and have completed few modules. Next week, I have my last exam and hope to pass with flying colours. I also started cooking due to the lockdown and have attached few pictures of the dishes I learnt to cook. Mom and dad are fine and they quite often miss you.

How are uncle and aunty doing? I remember you had your exams last time we had a conversation. Are the results out? What are you planning to do next? I will be waiting for your reply. Please take care of yourself, uncle and aunty.

Lots of love
Yours friendly
Samar

2. Write a letter to your friend congratulating her/him for topping the examinations.

Ans. 96, Green Park
Rohini, New Delhi

16th January, 20XX

Dear Khushi

I am so excited to know that you have topped your examinations. It's been a long time since we met and I so wish that I could congratulate you in person.

Your result has proved how much effort, hard work, and dedication you have given to your exams. I am not shocked by this news because I have known since we were in Class 2. You have always been a sincere and hardworking girl. I knew that you are a bit nervous but then I was sure that you will score brilliantly. The only thing I regret is that I couldn't be there with you at the celebration party because I was having my exams then.

Hope to meet you as soon as possible. My parents and grandparents have congratulated you on your success!

With lots of love
Yours lovingly
Anaya

3. Write a letter to your cousin enquring about her first visit to paris.

Ans. 46, Park Avenue
Mumbai

24th September, 20XX

Dear Tanmayi

How are you? I am good here and hope the same for you. I was so glad to hear from my mother that you are back home from the trip. Hope you had a safe and enjoyable trip. I have been waiting to hear all about the trip from you.

Since this was the first time you have been to a foreign land, I guess every little bit of the trip was as exciting as you expected it to be. I have heard from my friends residing there that the place is extremely beautiful and that the people there are very endearing. I also know that you would have thoroughly enjoyed shopping from big brands.

I saw your pictures on instagram as well. I can't wait to meet you and hear all your stories. Waiting eagerly for your reply.

Your loving cousin,
Purvi

4. Your Uncle has presented a book to you on your birthday. It is related with the art of photography. Write a letter in about 100 words thanking you uncle for sending this valuable gift. You are Navin/Nalini living at 250, Rcydhani Enclave Baroda.

Ans. 250, Rajdhani Enclave
Baroda

2nd March, 20XX

My dear Uncle

How are you? I am good here and hope that you are healthy. It is always a pleasure to hear from you. Last Friday was my birthday and the same day I received your gift of the instax camera that I had been wanting for so long along with your blessings.

Thank you very much for this valuable gift. I have not yet used the camera for the fear of breaking it. However, I am planning to use it on the trip to Chandigarh that our school had planned for next month. I thank you once again for the nice birthday gift.

Yours affectionately
Navin

2. Formal Letter

There are many kinds of formal letters. However, in Class VIII, we will focus on

- Letter to the Editor
- Complaint letters
- Application to the Principal

Format of a Formal Letter

Auto rickshaws playing loud music while driving, is a common sight in cities. This is not only highly irritating but also dangerous as safe driving requires total concentration. Write a letter to the editor of a local newspaper drawing attention of the authorities to the problem and requesting them to take appropriate action. You are Raj/Rajani, 2, Isha Nagar, Delhi.

Sender's address	2, Isha Nagar Delhi
Date	14th November, 20XX
Receiver's address	The Editor The Times of India New Delhi
Subject of the letter	**Subject** The problem of people listening to music while driving
Salutation	Sir/Ma'am
Body of the letter	Through the columns of your esteemed newspaper, I would like to draw the attention of the people of my nation towards the problem of people listening to music using LEDs while driving. We all are aware of the various accidents that are continuously taking place because of the carelessness of people who use their phones while walking on the road or while driving. Today, we can see auto rickshaws playing loud music while driving, almost everywhere in cities. Sometimes the music is so loud that it causes discomfort to other people. Such loud music is not only highly irritating but also dangerous as safe driving requires total concentration. As the person's attention is not completely on the road, the situation becomes very dangerous for not only the driver and the passenger but also for those who are walking along the road. It is now the time to come up with strict laws against loud music from any vehicle. Violators should be fined and awareness regarding the problem can help to improve the situation. I hope this letter will elicit suitable action from the concerned authorities.
Complementary Close	Thanking you Yours truly
Name and Signaure	Navtej (Concerned citizen)

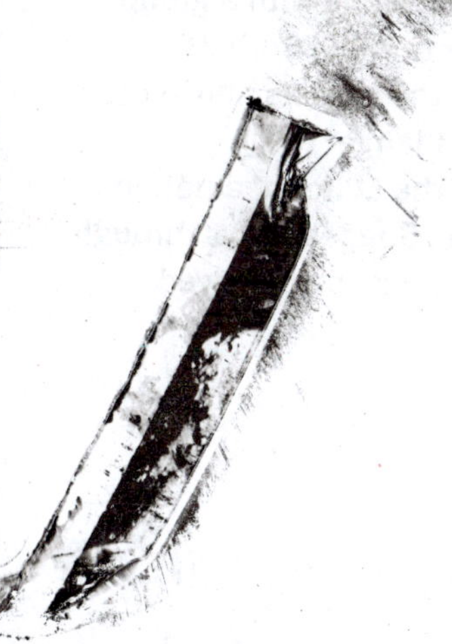

SOLVED EXAMPLES

Letter to the Editor

1. Write a letter to the Editor telling him about the need to take effective measures after the recent floods that have created havoc in the low lying areas of the city.

Ans. XYZ Colony
Kolkata
9th March, 20XX

The Editor
The Harbinger
New Delhi

Subject The need to take effective measures after the recent floods that have created havoc in the low lying areas of the city.

Sir/Ma'am

Through the columns of your esteemed newspaper, I would like to divert the attention of the concerned authorities towards the need to take effective measures after the recent floods that have created havoc in the low lying areas of the city.

The drainage system of Kolkata has yet again caused us a lot of trouble. Just like last year, the entire city is flooded which is adversely affecting the lives of people living in the low lying areas of the city. Innumerable people are losing their lives, livelihoods and even their homes because of the lack of measures that could have prevented their utter ruin.

Now that the floods are reducing, it is high time to take certain measures to help those affected people. Help in the form of jobs, money, clothes, food and so on should be collected for these people. The government should ensure that the people living in the low lying areas are properly evacuated to safe regions just as the warnings of the flood are issued. With certain steps we can help those affected to restart their life and further make arrangements that reduces any such losses in the future.

Thanking you

Yours sincerely
PQR

2. You are Sahil/Sahira, resident of 12, Mall Road, Kanpur. You recently visited an orphanage and saw many children living in poor conditions. You feel sympathy for them. They should get good food, healthy living conditions and proper education. Write a letter to the Editor of a national daily requesting the authorities to take proper care of these helpless children.

Ans. 12, Mall Road
Kanpur
14th November, 20XX

The Editor
The Times of India
New Delhi

Subject The miserable conditions of children living in the orphanages

Sir/Ma'am

Through the column of your esteemed newspaper, I want to throw light on a disheartening visit to the orphanage today.

Recently, I went to ABC Orphanage and saw that the condition of the children was very miserable. They lack even the basic necessities for healthy living like clean, hygienic and nutritious food, decent clothing and good education. I felt so sympathetic for these innocent children who are already lacking parental love and affection.

From what I understand, the orphanage gets good donations but it is not reaching the children due to inefficient management. Through your newspaper, I request the concerned authorities to take care of the children of orphanages. They deserve better!

Thanking you

Yours sincerely
Sahira
Concerned citizen

3. You are Navtej/Navita, Secretary, Environment Club, Akash Public School, Agra. You, along with a group of students, went on a 3-day tour through Corbett National Park. You found how the tourists abuse the available facilities and thus endanger the environment. Write a letter to the Editor of a national daily highlighting the situation. Suggest ways through which the environment of the park can be saved.

Ans. Akash Public School
Agra

14th November, 20XX

The Editor
The Times of India
New Delhi

Subject Environment of National Parks requires protection from tourists

Sir/Ma'am

Through the columns of your esteemed newspaper, I would like to draw the attention of concerned authorities towards the tourists who abuse the facilities provided in National Parks, endangering the environment there.

Recently, our school organised a 3 day trip to Jim Corbett National Park for the students who were members of the school's Environment Club. We were appalled to find that tourists were throwing their waste items all over the park instead of using the waste bins provided. Further, they were offering the animals cooked food to eat, although offering food to the animals in the park is prohibited.

Such activities of tourists should be stopped by increasing the number of forest guards with a power to fine the tourists on finding them indulging in such practices. Further, CCTV cameras should be installed in places much visited by tourists so that they can be prosecuted even later on. I hope this letter will elicit suitable action from the park management.

Thanking you

Yours sincerely
Navtej
Secretary, Environment Club

4. You have noticed many stray animals on the road during the busy hours of the day. These animals cause traffic jams as well as accidents. You have already written to the concerned authorities but no action has been taken so far. Write a letter to the Editor, The Hindu, drawing attention of the Municipal Commissioner, Chennai. You are Shantha/Suresh, 12 MG Road, Chennai.

Clues

- Causes traffic jams and accidents
- Concerned authorities should take strict action
- Becoming a nuisance
- Problem need to be rectified as soon as possible

Ans. 12, MG Road,
Chennai-600001

9th March, 20XX

The Editor
The Hindu
Chennai-600001

Subject Problems caused by stray animals

Sir/Ma'am

Through the columns of your esteemed daily, I would like to draw the attention of the Municipal Commissioner to the problems caused by stray animals on city roads. Not a single day passes when we don't witness traffic jams on the roads. The reasons of these jams are not heavy traffic movement but stray animals roaming about on the roads.

These animals not only cause traffic jams but also lead to severe accidents. Just three days ago, I witnessed a biker being chased by dogs. He tried to drive away, in the process jumping a red light and meeting with an accident. Yesterday, a bull hurt a person so badly that he needed to be admitted to a hospital.

Despite many complaints to the concerned authorities, no action has been taken so far. These stray animals are becoming a nuisance. They are a danger to not only us but to themselves also. It is my request to the Municipal Commissioner to please take a note of the situation and rectify it as soon as possible.

Thanking you

Yours sincerely
Suresh

Letters of Complaint

1. You placed an order with Regent Computer Accessories House for the supply of laptop tables, computer stationery, etc. However, you felt disappointed when you opened the consignment. Two out of the eight tables ordered have wobbly legs and two reams of paper contain defective sheets. Write a letter to the manager requesting him to replace the defective supplies. You are Sudha/Sudhir, Manager, Communication Services Centre, Paschim Vihar, Delhi.

Ans. Communication Services Center
Paschim Vihar, Delhi

20th February, 20XX

The Manager
Regent Computer Accessories House
Raja Garden, Delhi

Subject Complaint about supply of defective items

Sir/Ma'am

This is with reference to the order made on 10th February, 20XX *via*. order no XX239. I regret to inform you that the consignment received by me contains some defective items. I had placed an order to your company for the supply of laptop tables and computer stationery. Two tables out of eight have unsteady and wobbly legs. They are unfit and cannot be used. Moreover, two reams of computer paper is full of defective sheets which cannot be used either.

It is requested, therefore, that the defective items be replaced before I settle the final payment of the bill. Kindly take immediate action and get the defective pieces replaced at the earliest. An early response will be highly appreciated.

Thanking you

Yours truly
Sudhir
(Manager)

2. You are Arun/Arti 12, Raja Road, Kanpur. You had ordered Ram Book Depot, 4 Mall Road, Delhi for the supply of two books. You wanted to give them as a gift to a friend of yours. On receiving them you were disappointed to find that the books were damaged. Write a complaint letter to the Manager, about your problem.

Ans. 12, Raja Road
Kanpur

26th April, 20XX

The Manager
Ram Book Depot
4, Mall Road, Delhi

Subject Complaint against receiving damaged books

Sir/Ma'am

With reference to receipt number 456CVX dated 14th April, I would like to bring to your notice a complaint regarding the receiving of damaged books. I had ordered the Hunger Games series from your store, the payment for which I had made by an e-commerce website Paytm. I wanted to gift these books to my friend. On receiving the books yesterday, I was extremely disappointed to see their pathetic condition. The cover pages of the books were damaged and the pages were torn, crumpled and untidy. Because of its pathetic condition, I cannot present these damaged books to her.

So, I request you to send me the new pack of the books before 30th April. I am sending back the damaged books with the hope of receiving the new set of books by time. Awaiting a favourable response and prompt delivery.

Yours sincerely
Arti

Application to the Principal

1. Write an application to the Principal of your school requesting a fee concession.

Ans. To
The Principal
PQR school
Delhi

Subject Application for fee concession

Sir/Ma'am

This is to inform you that I am, Pankaj Soni, a student of your prestigious school. The purpose of writing this letter is to request you for a full fee concession so that I can continue my studies further.

I would like to inform you that I belong to a weaker section of the society. Thus, it becomes quite difficult for me to afford the tuition fees along with the study material. I had joined the institution earlier on a 2 year complete scholarship offer by the PQR NGO. I would like to mention here that I am a good student and have always scored high percentage of marks in all subjects. I am very hardworking and dedicated student. All the teachers appreciate me.

Therefore, I request you to kindly waive the fees and grant me scholarship. I am sure you will find me the most deserving. I am confident you would certainly be kind enough to grant me scholarship. I will be thankful to you. Hoping for a positive response.

Yours obediently

Pankaj Soni
(Student)

2. Write an application to the librarian of your school informing him that you have lost the book issued to you last week.

Ans. To

The Librarian
XYZ, school
Kanpur, UP

12th December, 20XX

Subject Information about lost of the issued book

Sir/Ma'am

This is to inform you that I am, PQR, a student of Class VIII D. I have written this letter to tell you that I got a book issued from the library last week which was to be returned tomorrow on 13th December. Unfortunately, I had lost the book and would like to apologise for it.

I also request you to kindly let me know the price of the book so that I may make the payment to compensate it.

Thanking you

Yours obediently

PQR

ASSESSMENT EXERCISE

1. Taking help from the information given below, write a letter to your younger brother advising him to give up the bad company in which he seems to have fallen.

   Hints
   - Letter from the Principal
   - Irregular in doing homework
   - Friendship with decent and intelligent children

2. Write a letter to your friend Rakesh/Rakhi inviting him to attend your sister's marriage.
3. Write a letter to the Editor of a local newspaper expressing your concern about the problems that the neglect of parks has created and suggest measures to reclaim them for children. You are Gautam/Gauri 2, Gobind Enclave, Meerut.
4. Write a letter to your cousin living in a distant city wishing him a speedy recovery from an accident.
5. Write a letter to your father requesting him to increase your pocket money.
6. Write a letter to the Principal of your school to request him/her to introduce co-curricular activities at regular intervals.
7. You are Ravikant, sports teacher of Sunshine Public School, Karol Bagh, Delhi. A month ago, you placed an order for the supply of a few sports goods. So far you have not received the goods. Write a letter in 120-150 words to the Sales Manager, Olympic Sports F-12 Darya Ganj, Delhi requesting a speedy delivery of the goods.
8. Last month you purchased a T.V. set from Ram Electronics, Pushp Vihar, Ambala. It is not working properly (imagine a few defects). Write a letter of complaint in 120-150 words to the Manager asking for repair or replacement. You are Amar/Amrita, M114 Model Town, Ambala.
9. You are Amit Kapoor, resident of 43/9, Shyam Enclave, Delhi. You visited Manali with your family during the summer vacation. You had two double suites at Lake View resort. Your stay at the hotel fell far short of the description in the brochure. Write a letter of complaint to the Customer Service Department to refund for your hotel stay.
10. Write an application to your games teacher requesting him to issue new sports kit for the students.
11. You are Shubha/Krushna Mohanty, residing in Subhadra Apartments, Bhubaneswar, Orissa. You have observed, that garbage collection continues to be done without segregation in your neighbourhood. Write a letter to the Editor of The Real Times, Bhubaneswar, explaining your concern along with the rationale behind the importance of garbage segregation.

How to manage waste at home?

12. Write a letter to the Editor about how reality T.V. ruins childhood.

Clues

- A mushrooming of 'Reality Shows' featuring children
- Lure for money
- Parents should be counselled
- Neglect of studies
- Loss of innocence
- Lot of inconvenience and overstraining

13. Write a letter to the editor of an English daily making a plea to the common people to switch over to solar energy to conserve electricity and limit electricity bills.

14. There is a flood of advertisements on television channels these days. Useless products are promoted through glamorous and exaggerated presentations. Write a letter to the Editor, Indian Express regarding the same using the clues given below. You are Sunita/Sunil of Mayur Vihar, Kanpur.

Clues

- Flood of advertisements
- Hide the realities of the products
- Lack in quality of the products
- Boring, too long and too dull
- In-between movies

15. You feel that the Right to Education is going to help India rise above the narrow boundaries of prejudices of caste, colour, creed and corruption. Write a letter to the Editor of The Times of India, reflecting your views on the subject. Sign yourself as Nandita/Naveen of Paschim Vihar, Delhi.

Sentences

1.1 Definition of Sentence

A Sentence is a group of words which is arranged in a meaningful manner that makes complete sense in itself.

e.g.
- Peehu has asked for her permission to go out.
- We won the match today!
- Do you go out for a walk daily?

Parts of a Sentence

A sentence can be divided into two parts - a Subject and a Predicate.

(i) **Subject** It is the part of a sentence which tells us who or what the sentence is about. It is either a noun or a pronoun.

(ii) **Predicate** It is the part of a sentence which tells us something about the subject.

e.g.
- **Ananya** *drives a scooter to work every day.*
- *The food was eaten by the* **kitten**.
- *In winters, only some* **lilies** bloom.

In the given examples the words in bold are the subjects of the sentences and the expressions in italics are predicates of the sentences.

1.2 Kinds of Sentences

On the basis of their usage, sentences can be divided into four types. These are discussed below

Assertive/Declarative Sentences

Sentences that are used to make a general statement to provide some information are called Assertive or Declarative sentences. These sentences always end with a full stop (.).

e.g.
- I will go to the stadium to watch the tournament tomorrow.
- He is my best friend's brother.
- The G20 conference was held in Delhi in 2023.

Assertive sentences can be divided into Affirmative (Positive) sentences or Negative sentences.

e.g.
- Raj and I are going to see the birds. *(Positive)*
- Raj and I are not going to see the birds. *(Negative)*

Interrogative Sentences

Sentences that are used to ask questions are called Interrogative Sentences. These sentences always end with a question mark (?).

e.g.
- Who is in-charge of cleaning the blackboard today?
- Did you clean your room?
- He called you, didn't he?

An Interrogative sentence can be of three types

(i) **Yes and No Questions** Such questions start with helping verbs (is/am/are/was/were/has/have/had/do/does/did). These questions can be answered in 'yes' or 'no'.

e.g.
- **Are you** going to complete the work today?
- **Have you** practiced your dance routine?
- **Was he** present when the announcement was made?

(ii) **Wh-Questions** Such questions start with the following words- 'Who', 'Whose', 'When' and 'Where'.

e.g.
- **When** does the train arrive?
- **Whose** pen is this?
- **Where** is Mehek going at this time?

(iii) **Question Tags** Question tags are short questions found at the end of assertive sentences. We generally use question tags to convert a sentence into a question.

e.g.
- The Godavari is the longest river in India, **isn't it**?
- Rose doesn't top her class every year, **does she**?
- He was found guilty, **wasn't he**?

When we use question tags, we need to remember that

(i) If the statement is positive, the question tag should be negative.

e.g. You are free, aren't you?

(ii) If the statement is negative, the question tag should be positive.

e.g. You aren't busy, are you?

Note it Question tags never contain nouns. They are always formed with pronouns for the nouns used in the assertive sentence.

Imperative Sentences

Sentences that are used to give a command, advice, suggestion, request or warning are called Imperative Sentences. They generally end with a full stop (.).

e.g. • Wash your hands now. *(Command)*
• Be nice to your friends. *(Advice)*
• Go to the doctor. *(Suggestion)*
• Please pass me the salt. *(Request)*
• Don't come near me. *(Warning)*

Exclamatory Sentences

Sentences that are used to express a strong emotion or feeling are called **Exclamatory Sentences**. These sentences always end with an exclamation mark (!).

e.g. • What a pleasant day it is!
• That birthday cake was so good!
• I'm so excited to watch this movie!

Note it We also use some words to express strong emotions. These words also end with exclamation marks and are called Interjections. Example of such words are-Hurrah!, Alas!, Ouch!, Great!.

REVIEW EXERCISE

Objective and Subjective Questions

1. Identify the type of sentences given below.

(i) What a clever boy he is!
(a) Assertive (b) Interrogative
(c) Imperative (d) Exclamatory

(ii) It is a very dirty room.
(a) Assertive (b) Interrogative
(c) Imperative (d) Exclamatory

(iii) Have some mercy upon us.
(a) Assertive (b) Interrogative
(c) Imperative (d) Exclamatory

(iv) What is the departure time for your flight?
(a) Assertive (b) Interrogative
(c) Imperative (d) Exclamatory

(v) How wonderful do the snow-clad mountains look!
(a) Assertive (b) Interrogative
(c) Imperative (d) Exclamatory

(vi) You must eat fruits daily.
(a) Assertive (b) Interrogative
(c) Imperative (d) Exclamatory

(vii) She is from New Delhi, isn't she?
(a) Assertive (b) Interrogative
(c) Imperative (d) Exclamatory

(viii) What a time to be alive!
(a) Assertive (b) Interrogative
(c) Imperative (d) Exclamatory

2. Choose the correct interjections to complete the sentences.

(i) .... Thank God!
(a) Wow (b) Oh
(c) Woah (d) Finally

(ii) .... I didn't see you were hiding here.
(a) Hey! (b) No!
(c) Oops! (d) Oh no!

(iii) .... I'll help you.
(a) Of course! (b) Fie!
(c) What! (d) Shhh!

(iv) .... We have won the match.
(a) Well done! (b) Woohoo!
(c) Ha ha! (d) Alas!

(v) .... I felt bad hearing that.
(a) Bah! (b) Alas! (c) Aww! (d) Oh!

(vi) .... Now that's what I call a good shot.
(a) Well, (b) Ouch!
(c) Woah! (d) Yeah!

(vii) .... That show was so gory.
(a) Hey! (b) Ewww!
(c) Help! (d) Yes!

(viii) .... Don't make noise.
(a) Shhh! (b) Hey!
(c) Hark! (d) Ha!

3. Separate the subject and predicate in the following sentences.

(i) No man can serve two masters.
(ii) The sea has many varieties of fishes.
(iii) My brother works for Acme Building Company.
(iv) The alligator was captured by the young boy.
(v) Here comes the jury!
(vi) The big, hungry, green crocodile dragged a deer from the river bank.
(vii) Many large trees are cut down to make buildings.
(viii) The girl with the long black hair lives in front of my house.

4. Complete the sentences using suitable subject.

(i) .... is good for health.
(ii) .... show me how to do it.
(iii) .... is the capital of Australia.
(iv) .... never fit well.
(v) .... was not built in a day.

5. Complete the sentences using suitable predicate.

(i) Delhi ....
(ii) The flower ....
(iii) Akbar ....
(iv) He ....
(v) There is a beggar ....

6. Fill in the blanks with appropriate question tags.

(i) She works here, ... ?
(ii) You knew him, ...?
(iii) She did not sent you a letter, ...?
(iv) You were going to work yesterday, ...?
(v) You have not seen something here, ...?
(vi) Sameer does not want to be an architect, ...?
(vii) Sumayya is not a teacher, ...?
(viii) You will pass the exams with good score, ...?

ANSWERS

1. (i) (d) Exclamatory (ii) (a) Assertive
(iii) (c) Imperative (iv) (b) Interrogative
(v) (d) Exclamatory (vi) (c) Imperative
(vii) (b) Interrogative (viii) (d) Exclamatory

2. (i) (b) Oh (ii) (c) Oops!
(iii) (a) Of course! (iv) (b) Woohoo!
(v) (d) Oh! (vi) (c) Woah!
(vii) (b) Ewww! (viii) (a) Shhh!

3. (i) **S** No man
P can serve two masters.
(ii) **S** The sea
P has many varieties of fishes.
(iii) **S** My brother
P works for Acme Building Company.
(iv) **S** The alligator
P was captured by the young boy.
(v) **S** the jury
P Here comes
(vi) **S** The big, hungry, green crocodile
P dragged a deer from the river bank.
(vii) **S** Many large trees
P are cut down to make buildings.
(viii) **S** The girl with the long black hair
P lives in front of my house.

4. Students can fill the given blanks as per their own understanding. An example for correctly filling the sentences is given below.
(i) Green leafy vegetables
(ii) Taran has decided to
(iii) Cranberra
(iv) The colours
(v) The ancient city of Rome

5. Students can fill the given blanks as per their own understanding. An example for correctly filling the sentences is given below.
(i) is the capital of India
(ii) blooms every year for only one night
(iii) had a trusted minister in Birbal
(iv) did not want to go for the movie
(v) who is dancing down that street

6. (i) doesn't she (ii) didn't you
(iii) did she (iv) weren't you
(v) have you (vi) does he
(vii) is she (viii) won't you

CHAPTER 2

Noun

2.1 Definition of Noun

A noun is defined as the name that is given to any person, place, animal, thing, feeling or an idea.

e.g.
- The **girls** are painting their **nails**.
- The **puppies** were found on the **street**.
- **Sonam** believes in **honesty**.
- **Russia** is the largest **country** in the **world**.

2.2 Kinds of Noun

Nouns can be categorised into various kinds. They are discussed below

Proper Noun

A proper noun is the unique name given to a particular person or a place. It always begins with capital letter.

e.g.
- **Varnita** will visit **Kashmir** soon.
- Those **pineapples** are very sour in taste.

Common Noun

A common noun is a general or common name given to all persons, places, animals or things of the same kind.

e.g.
- The **girl** is playing with her **doll**.
- Let us go to a **park**.

Collective Noun

A collective noun is the name that is given to a group/number of persons, animals or things.

e.g.
- A **priddlefdfowsod**
- A **troupe** of dancers

Abstract Noun

An abstract noun is the name of a feeling, state, idea or quality which we cannot see or touch.

e.g.
- The two groups have deep **love** for each other. (Feelings)
- The best phase of life is **childhood**. (State)
- **Freedom** is the birthright of all living beings. (Idea)
- The **beauty** of the waterfall cannot be described in words. (Quality)

Material Noun

Material nouns are names of substances of which things are made.

e.g.
- This ring is made of **gold**.
- The bat is made of **wood** from that tree.

Compound Noun

A compound noun is a noun that is formed by joining a noun with another noun, verb or adjective. Such nouns can be written as a single unit, as multiple words or as words connected by hyphens.

e.g.WatGreenkouse
- X-ray

2.3 Number Nouns

All nouns can be categorised into two categories on the basis of whether they can be counted or not. These nouns are discussed below

Countable Noun

It is the name of anything that can be counted in numbers.

e.g.
- We have 10 **balls** in the box.
- There are 12 **pencils** in the pen-stand.

Countable nouns can be further categorised into

(i) **Singular Nouns** Nouns that are one in number are Singular nouns.

e.g.
- The garden has a tall **tree**.
- I am taking a **pen** from your bag.

(ii) **Plural Nouns** Nouns that are more than one in number are Plural nouns.

e.g.
- The garden has tall **trees**.
- I am taking 10 **pens** from your bag.

Uncountable Nouns

It is the name of substances or concepts that cannot be counted in numbers.

e.g. • Raghav, eat the toast and **cheese** on your plate.

Note it The quantity of uncountable nouns can be indicated by words suggesting amount, size or portion. e.g. a kilo of sugar, cup of tea, two bags of grains, etc.

2.4 Gender Nouns

All nouns can be classified into four geners. They are discussed below

Masculine Gender Nouns It refers to a male person or animal.

e.g. boys, lion, man, king, etc.

Feminine Gender Nouns It refers to a female person or animal.

e.g. woman, lioness, aunt, queen, maid, etc.

Common Gender Nouns It refers to both male and female person or animal.

e.g. doctor, lawyer, parent, child, teacher, etc.

Neuter Gender Nouns It doesn't denote either male or female gender. It is used for non-living things.

e.g. tables, chairs, mobiles, box, etc.

REVIEW EXERCISE

Objective and Subjective Questions

1. Fill in the blanks with the correct option.

(i) The man in black thought that he was .... selected for the team to play at the National level.

(a) one of the player (b) one of the players
(c) is one player (d) the player of the team

(ii) The first film on Tagore was such a success that now they are going to make as ....

(a) serial (b) sequence
(c) sequel (d) sequential

(iii) The .... of cotton is very heavy.

(a) bald (b) bail
(c) bale (d) band

(iv) The .... were arrested for illegally hunting the bears.

(a) poachers (b) rangers
(c) soldiers (d) villagers

(v) She remained a .... all her life.

(a) spinster (b) bachelor
(c) unmarried (d) single

(vi) The .... of our civilisation from an agricultural society to today's complex industrial world was accompanied by war.

(a) adjustment (b) migration
(c) route (d) metamorphosis

(vii) Mahesh showed an .... for sports at a very early stage.

(a) attitude (b) aptitude
(c) imagination (d) intuition

(viii) If .... permits, we will go out for a walk.

(a) climate (b) whether
(c) weather (d) whither

(ix) A .... of Japanese artists stepped off the coach amidst a warm welcome.

(a) troop (b) troupe
(c) band (d) gang

(x) For all his .... he is a ....

(a) wealth, miser (b) health, player
(c) tricks, cheat (d) stupidity, fool

2. Choose the correct Abstract Noun from the following options.

(i) (a) Determination (b) Distracted
(c) Mysterious (d) Reliably

(ii) (a) Beneficial (b) Significantly
(c) Magnificent (d) Disbelief

(iii) (a) Differentiate (b) Justifiable
(c) Fascination (d) Aimless

(iv) (a) Zealous (b) Sophistication
(c) Strengthen (d) Obnoxious

(v) (a) Brilliance (b) Thoughtless
(c) Materialistic (d) Embarrassed

3. Pick out the correct sentence from the following.

(i) (a) All news were sad. (b) All newses were sad.
(c) All the news was sad. (d) Every news were sad.

(ii) (a) Richard gifted her three gold jewellery.
(b) Richard gifted her three gold jewelleries.

(c) Richard gifted her three items of gold jewellery.
(d) Richard gifted her three items of gold jewelleries.

(iii) (a) The people of India are peace loving.
(b) The peoples of India is peace loving.
(c) The peoples of India are peace loving.
(d) The people of India is peace loving.

(iv) (a) Riya has four pencil.
(b) Riya has four sticks of pencil.
(c) Riya has four sticks of pencils.
(d) Riya has four pencils.

(v) (a) You need a lost of patience.
(b) You needs a lot of patience.
(c) You need a lot of patience.
(d) You need a lot of patiences.

(vi) (a) The old woman lifted the woods.
(b) The old woman lifted the bunch of wood.
(c) The old woman lifted the bunch of woods.
(d) The old woman lifted the bunches of woods.

(vii) (a) I purchased the crockery for two thousand rupees.
(b) I purchased the crockeries for two thousand rupees.
(c) I purchased the crockery for two thousands rupee.
(d) I purchased the crockeries for two thousand rupee.

(viii) (a) Vibha is ten year old.
(b) Vibha is ten years old.
(c) Vibha was ten year old.
(d) Vibha were ten years old.

(ix) (a) The tree women are sister.
(b) The three woman are sisters.
(c) The three woman is sisters.
(d) The three women are sisters.

(x) (a) Abhi and Aryan are her brother-in-laws.
(b) Abhi and Aryan are hers brother in law.
(c) Abhi and Aryan are her brothers-in-law.
(d) Abhi and Aryan are her brother-in-laws.

4. Fill in the blanks with appropriate nouns.

(i) Kalidasa is often called the 'Shakespeare of ....'.
(ii) When we were on our trip, we saw a .... of ships in the harbor.
(iii) She went to .... for her summer vacation last year.
(iv) I often think back to the happy .... of childhood.
(v) My friends went to watch .... in a live concert.
(vi) I attended the .... when I was young.
(vii) The ...... of thieves ran when they heard the police.
(viii) Ruchi saw a .... of singers singing in the woods.
(ix) The toys made of .... were scattered all over the living room.
(x) My purse is made of ....
(xi) Our school's Principal gave a grand .... before the Annual Function began.
(xii) When I heard Harsh was coming, I started baking .... for him.
(xiii) His house was situated on top of a ....
(xiv) An .... of her poems was published soon after her demise.
(xv) In the future, I hope to visit the .... to see the fish.

5. Convert the given Verbs/Adjectives/Common nouns into abstract nouns.

Verb	Abstract Noun	Adjective	Abstract Noun	Common Noun	Abstract Noun
Enter	....	Curious	....	Infant	....
Know	....	Hot	....	Owner	....
Protect	....	Intelligent	....	Hero	....
Agree	....	Kind	....	Scholar	....
Grow	....	Real	....	King	....
Invite	....	Different	....	Member	....
Collect	....	Able	....	Priest	....

ANSWERS

1. (i) (b) one of the players (ii) (c) sequel
   (iii) (c) bale (iv) (a) poachers
   (v) (a) spinster (vi) (d) metamorphosis
   (vii) (b) aptitude (viii) (c) weather
   (ix) (b) troupe (x) (a) wealth, miser

2. (i) (a) Determination (ii) (d) Disbelief
   (iii) (c) Fascination (iv) (b) Sophistication
   (v) (a) Brilliance

3. (i) (c) All the news was sad.
   (ii) (c) Richard gifted her three items of gold jewellery.
   (iii) (a) The people of India are peace loving.
   (iv) (d) Riya has four pencils.
   (v) (c) You need a lot of patience.
   (vi) (b) The old woman lifted the bunch of wood.
   (vii) (a) I purchased the crockery for two thousand rupees.
   (viii) (b) Vibha is ten years old.
   (ix) (d) The three women are sisters.
   (x) (c) Abhi and Aryan are her brothers-in-law.

4. (i) India (ii) fleet
   (iii) Australia (iv) memories
   (v) Kailash Kher (vi) funeral
   (vii) gang (viii) choir
   (ix) plastic (x) leather
   (xi) speech (xii) muffins
   (xiii) hill (xiv) anthology
   (xv) aquarium

5.

Verb	Abstract Noun	Adjective	Abstract Noun	Common Noun	Abstract Noun
Enter	Entrance	Curious	Curiosity	Infant	Infancy
Know	Knowledge	Hot	Heat	Owner	Ownership
Protect	Protection	Intelligent	Intelligence	Hero	Heroism
Agree	Agreement	Kind	Kindness	Scholar	Scholarship
Grow	Growth	Real	Reality	King	Kingship
Invite	Invitation	Different	Difference	Member	Membership
Collect	Collection	Able	Ability	Priest	Priesthood

CHAPTER 3

Pronoun

3.1 Definition of Pronoun

A pronoun is a word that replaces a noun or a noun phrase.

e.g. • **He** didn't buy a new bicycle.
• Jiya said that the bangle was **hers.**
• The brothers are not talking to **each other.**

3.2 Kinds of Pronoun

Pronouns can be divided into various kinds as discussed below

Personal Pronouns

A personal pronoun is a word used in place of a person or a thing. It must agree with the gender and the number of the noun it replaces.

e.g. • **I** like having coffee in the morning.
• **She** will go to the market after cooking food for **us.**

Personal pronouns are of two types

(i) **Subject Pronoun** If the personal pronoun is the performer of the action or the subject of the sentence, it is called a subject pronoun.

e.g. • **I** like to watch TV but **he** does not.
• **She** needs to study hard to pass the exam.

(ii) **Object Pronoun** If the personal pronoun is the receiver of the action done by the subject, it is called an Object pronoun.

e.g. • Miracles happen to those who believe in **them.**
• This pencil box is **his.**

Personal pronouns also differ in their forms according to persons. These are discussed below

(i) **First Person Pronoun** It refers to the person speaking.

e.g. • **I** am writing this note.
• The dogs were running behind **us.**

(ii) **Second Person Pronoun** It refers to the person spoken to.

e.g. • **You** will learn swimming.
• I don't want to see **you.**

(iii) **Third Person Pronoun** It refers to the person being spoken of.

e.g. • **They** are Indians.
• **They** are also invited to the dinner.

Various Forms of Personal Pronouns

Person	Subject Pronouns		Object Pronouns	
	Singular	Plural	Singular	Plural
First person (speaker)	I	we	me	us
Second person (person spoken to)	you		you	
Third person (person spoken about)	he, she, it	they	him, her, it	them

Possessive Pronouns

A possessive pronoun shows ownership or possession. They are generally put at the end of a sentence. They are mine, yours, his, hers, ours, yours and theirs.

e.g. • These books are **mine.**
• I didn't have an umbrella so Maria lent me **hers.**

Demonstrative Pronouns

A demonstrative pronoun is used to point to a particular person or thing. There are four demonstrative pronouns- This, That, These and Those.

e.g. • **This** is the dress that's made of imported fabric.
• **That** is the boy who is an amazing mimic artist.
• **These** are the donated books.
• **Those** are the mangoes kept for the children.

Distributive Pronouns

A distributive pronoun is used to refer members of a group individually. Common distributive pronouns include each, either and neither.

e.g.
- I may buy **either** of these two mobile phones.
- **Each** of the students gets a certificate.
- **Neither** of those two students can secure first position.

Indefinite Pronouns

Indefinite pronoun does not refer to a particular person or thing.

e.g.
- **Anybody** can write an essay; it is an easy task.
- I will try to think of **somebody** who can help you.

Relative Pronouns

A relative pronoun refers to the noun mentioned before it. It helps in joining clauses or sentences.

e.g.
- The girl **who** I met yesterday is my cousin.
- Ms. Rachna is the teacher **whom** everybody adores.

Interrogative Pronouns

An interrogative pronoun is used while asking questions. The interrogative pronouns are used depending upon their usage as a 'subject' or an 'object'.

	Subject	Object
Person	Who	Whom
Thing		What
Person/Thing		Which
Person		Whose

e.g.
- **Who** told you?
  James told you.
- **Whom** did you tell?
  I told Radhika.
- **What** is this?
  This is a book.
- **Which** student came first?
  Ram came first.
- **Which** is your favourite car?
  The Porsche 911 is my favourite car.
- **Whose** key did you find?
  I found John's key.

Reciprocal Pronouns

A reciprocal pronoun is used to express a mutual action or a relationship. There are only two reciprocal pronouns 'each other' and 'one another'.

e.g.
- Tommy and Jane hate **each other.**
- Our two dogs and your cat love **one another.**

Note it Use 'each other' when we refer to two nouns/pronouns. Use 'one another when we refer to three or more than three nouns/pronouns.

Reflexive Pronouns

A reflexive pronoun is used to refer back to the subject in a sentence.

e.g.
- He is going to complete his project by **himself.**
- They need to solve the problem **themselves.**

Note it It is important to note that in sentences that use reflexive pronoun, the subject and the object refer to the same person. A reflexive pronoun can only be used as the object. It is not used as the subject in a sentence.

Emphatic Pronouns

An emphatic pronoun is used to emphasise the noun they refer. These are same pronoun which are classified as reflexive pronouns, but differ from them in usage.

e.g.
- We ourselves can plan and sponsor this party.
- She **herself** found the solution.

REVIEW EXERCISE

Objective and Subjective Questions

1. Fill in the blanks with appropriate pronoun.

(i) Are those chocolates ...., Kriti?
(a) yours (b) them (c) my (d) yourself

(ii) .... is the book I was looking for.
(a) That (b) Those (c) Either (d) These

(iii) The teacher gave .... their answer sheets.
(a) I (b) me (c) mine (d) myself

(iv) .... must answer your paper carefully.
(a) We (b) They (c) You (d) It

(v) The sister followed her brother everywhere .... went.
(a) they (b) him (c) his (d) he

(vi) .... are silly excuses for not doing your work.
(a) This (b) That
(c) Those (d) It

(vii) The purse was returned to its owner by ....
(a) him (b) me
(c) her (d) All of these

(viii) The priest .... delivered the sermon this Sunday.
(a) himself (b) themselves
(c) whom (d) who

(ix) You can take .... of the two books.
(a) each (b) them (c) both (d) either

(x) Both of them were fighting with .... about who broke the laptop.
(a) one another (b) each other
(c) themselves (d) them

2. Identify the kind of pronoun for the underlined words in the following sentences.

(i) <u>She</u> often reads books.
(a) Reflexive pronoun (b) Personal pronoun
(c) Possessive pronoun (d) Interrogative pronoun

(ii) <u>These</u> would go on the wall.
(a) Demonstrative pronoun
(b) Possessive pronoun
(c) Reflexive pronoun
(d) Personal pronoun

(iii) <u>Who</u> is the boy Rohan is fighting?
(a) Interrogative pronoun
(b) Emphatic pronoun
(c) Reflexive pronoun
(d) Demonstrative pronoun

(iv) You <u>yourself</u> need to ask him that.
(a) Reflexive pronoun (b) Emphatic pronoun
(c) Possessive pronoun (d) Interrogative pronoun

(v) Those grapes kept in the freezer are <u>mine</u>.
(a) Reflexive pronoun (b) Personal pronoun
(c) Possessive pronoun (d) Emphatic pronoun

(vi) Sophie <u>herself</u> told me that she was going abroad.
(a) Demonstrative pronoun
(b) Personal pronoun
(c) Possessive pronoun
(d) Emphatic pronoun

(vii) <u>Either</u> will do the job.
(a) Reflexive pronoun (b) Emphatic pronoun
(c) Distributive pronoun (d) Personal pronoun

(viii) The boy <u>who</u> you met yesterday is my nephew.
(a) Interrogative pronoun
(b) Relative pronoun
(c) Possessive pronoun
(d) Reflexive pronoun

(ix) <u>He</u> has climbed to the top of that tree.
(a) Reflexive pronoun (b) Personal pronoun
(c) Possessive pronoun (d) Emphatic pronoun

(x) Rita enjoyed <u>herself</u>.
(a) Reflexive pronoun (b) Personal pronoun
(c) Possessive pronoun (d) Interrogative pronoun

3. Write the correct form of pronoun in the following blanks.

(i) Be sure that everyone brings .... own book.

(ii) Mark and .... have been very good friends for years.

(iii) If .... calls, tell them that .... will be back in an hour.

(iv) Did you see Tom and .... at the match?

(v) Between you and ...., a politician cannot be trusted.

(vi) Each person in the room turned .... head to the front when the teacher entered.

(vii) The local government plans to cut .... budget for recreation.

(viii) .... who purchased one of the paintings was pleased.

(ix) Christopher and .... want to travel to the far East someday.

(x) The cost of the repairs shocked both of my brother and ....

4. In the following sentences use pronouns in place of noun wherever you can.

(i) John gave John's pen to James and James lent the pen to John to write John's copy with the pen.

(ii) Rama had taken Rama's watch out of his pocket and was looking at the watch uneasily, shaking the watch every now and then and holding the watch to his ear.

(iii) Atul loved Sandeep's sweater and asked Sandeep from where Sandeep had bought the sweater.

(iv) Sita informed Rama that Rama's cab was late in arriving and therefore, Rama might go home with Sita.

(v) Lata found Lata's books torn by Lata's brother.

5. Join together each of the following pairs of sentences by the means of a connective.

(i) I know lady. The lady has been to London.

(ii) I saw a girl. She was singing.

(iii) I met a boy. He was very cruel.

(iv) The child is dead. I saw the child last week.

(v) The horse was lame. We saw the horse.

(vi) She is a rouge. No one trusts her.

(vii) He does his best. He should be praised.

(viii) MF Hussain is famous. He made some famous paintings.

(ix) We met a boy. The boy had lost his way.

(x) The lady is honest. The lady is trusted.

6. Identify the pronouns in the following sentences and categorise them as relative and interrogative pronouns.

(i) Which of these brands is trustworthy?

(ii) The boy who gave the interview is my friend.

(iii) The coffee that we had in the morning was refreshing.

(iv) Whom did you call for the party?

(v) The dog which hurt its leg was taken to the hospital.

(vi) The shops that had shut down due to lockdown opened again.

(vii) Whoever has the courage to say such a thing in the class?

(viii) The scientist who created this vaccine was awarded a Nobel Prize.

(ix) Who drew this beautiful picture?

(x) What did he say to make her smile like that?

7. Some pronouns are underlined in the given sentences. Identify their type.

(i) <u>Whose</u> is this raincoat?

(ii) Where was the book? I have been looking for <u>it</u> everywhere.

(iii) The book <u>that</u> was kept on the table got wet in the rain.

(iv) She <u>herself</u> is clueless about what to order for dinner.

(v) <u>That</u> is the boy who asked me to talk to you.

(vi) We will manage to reach the venue <u>ourselves</u>.

(vii) <u>That</u> is my book on the top shelf.

(viii) The hospital <u>which</u> is near your house is not open anymore.

(ix) I told <u>her</u> to meet me at the party yesterday.

(x) Minali <u>herself</u> took the initiative to lead the class.

ANSWERS

1. (i) (a) yours (ii) (a) That
(iii) (b) me (iv) (c) You
(v) (d) he (vi) (c) Those
(vii) (d) All of these (viii) (a) himself
(ix) (d) either (x) (b) each other

2. (i) (b) Personal pronoun
(ii) (a) Demonstrative pronoun
(iii) (a) Interrogative pronoun
(iv) (b) Emphatic pronoun
(v) (c) Possessive pronoun
(vi) (d) Emphatic pronoun
(vii) (c) Distributive pronoun
(viii) (b) Relative pronoun
(ix) (b) Personal pronoun
(x) (a) Reflexive pronoun

3. (i) his or her (ii) I (iii) anyone, I
(iv) him (v) me (vi) his
(vii) its (viii) Everyone (ix) I
(x) me

4. (i) John gave his pen to James and James lent it to John to write his copy with the pen.

(ii) Rama had taken his watch out of his pocket and was looking at it uneasily, shaking it every now and then and holding it to his ear.
(iii) Atul loved Sandeep's sweater and asked him from where he had bought it.
(iv) Sita informed Rama that her cab was late in arriving and therefore, she might go home with her.
(v) Lata found her books torn by her brother.

5. (i) I know the lady who has been to London.
(ii) I saw the girl who was singing.
(iii) I met the boy who was very cruel.
(iv) The child whom I saw last week is dead.
(v) The horse that we saw was lame.
(vi) She whom no one trusts is a rouge.
(vii) He who does his best should be praised.
(viii) MF Hussain, who made some famous paintings, is famous.
(ix) We met the boy who had lost his way.
(x) The lady who is honest is trusted.

6. (i) **which** Interrogative pronoun
(ii) **who** Relative pronoun
(iii) **that** Relative pronoun
(iv) **whom** Interrogative pronoun
(v) **which** Relative pronoun
(vi) **that** Relative pronoun
(vii) **whoever** Interrogative pronoun
(viii) **who** Relative pronoun
(ix) **who** Interrogative pronoun
(x) **what** Interrogative pronoun

7. (i) Interrogative pronoun
(ii) Personal pronoun
(iii) Relative pronoun
(iv) Emphatic pronoun
(v) Demonstrative pronoun
(vi) Reflexive pronoun
(vii) Demonstrative pronoun
(viii) Relative pronoun
(ix) Personal pronoun
(x) Emphatic pronoun

Adjective

4.1 Definition of an Adjective

Adjectives are words that modify a noun or a pronoun in a sentence.

e.g.
- My friend Dustin has a **beautiful black** cat.
- **Ancient, precious** coins are exhibited in this museum.

4.2 Kinds of Adjectives

Adjectives can be categorised into eight kinds. They are discussed below

Descriptive Adjective/Adjective of Quality

A descriptive adjective is a word that describes the quality of the noun or the pronoun in a sentence. It answers the question 'of what kind?'.

e.g.
- Candies and cakes are extremely **sweet** in taste.
- This is a very **ancient** book.

Quantitative Adjective/Adjective of Quantity

A quantitative adjective is a word that describes the quantity of the noun or the pronoun in a sentence. It answers the question 'how much?'.

e.g.
- There is **a lot of** confusion regarding the exam procedure.
- There are **enough** meals for the children.

Numeral Adjective/Adjective of Numbers

A numeral adjective is a word that tells exactly how many or how much quantity of noun and the position order of a noun in specific numbers. It answers the question 'how many' and is used with countable nouns.

e.g.
- There are **six** things in my basket.
- The **fifth** seat from the back is mine.

Adjective of number can be further categorised into three kinds. They are

(i) **Definite Adjectives of Number** These adjectives tell us the exact number of the noun.

e.g. • I have **two** brothers and **one** sister.
• He is the **first** to join army in our family.

Definite adjectives of number are of two types

(a) **Cardinals** which state the number of people or things. e.g. one, two, thousand, lakhs, etc.

(b) **Ordinals** which state the order of people or things in a series. e.g. first, second, third etc.

(ii) **Indefinite Adjectives of Number** These adjectives are used to refer to an indefinite amount of a countable noun.

e.g. • It will take me **some** time to recall your number.
• There are **many** customers standing outside the shop.

Note it When the noun is uncountable, these indefinite adjectives of number work as adjectives of quantity.

(iii) **Distributive Adjectives of Number** These are adjectives that refer to one or a part out of a group of people, places or things. They are, either, neither, each, every.

e.g. • **Each** person must bring their own essentials.
• **Neither** of these boys went there.

Demonstrative Adjectives

A demonstrative adjective is a word that is used to identify or express the relative position of a noun in time or space. They are this, that, these, those.

e.g. • **These** mangoes that you brought are ripe.
• **This** pen write smother than that pen.

Possessive Adjectives

A possessive adjective is a word that is used to indicate ownership or possession. They are his, her, my, your, its, their, and our.

e.g. • **Her** father is working as a software engineer in Bangalore.
• She took **my** bag and went to **her** school.

Interrogative Adjectives

An interrogative adjective is a word that is used to ask questions about the noun in a sentence. They are which, whose, what.

e.g. • **Which** box did you lend to our neighbour, Yamini?
• Do you know **whose** books these are?

Remember

- The words that form Distributive, Demonstrative, Possessive and Interrogative Adjectives are same as Distributive, Demonstrative, Possessive and Interrogative Pronouns. Hence, it is important to remember that difference between them.
- The Distributive, Demonstrative, Possessive and Interrogative Adjectives are always followed by a noun while the pronouns are used in place of the nouns.

Proper Adjectives

A proper adjective is a word that is formed by proper nouns.

e.g. • I am going to make a **Spanish** omlette for breakfast.
• **African** drums are lots of fun to play.

Emphasising Adjectives

Emphasising adjectives are words that emphasise the noun and show strong emotions or feelings. These adjectives specifically lay stress on the noun or the subject of the sentence. Common emphasising adjectives include very, own, absolute, utter, total and complete.

e.g. • I am in **complete** shock at the news.
• Why can't you write in your **own** book?

Order of Adjectives

When more than one adjective comes before a noun to describe it, the adjectives are normally used in a particular order.

Study the table given below

Order	Relating to	Examples
1.	Quantity	Three, Four, Five
2.	Opinion	Unusual, Lovely, Beautiful
3.	Size	Big, Small, Tall
4.	Physical Quality	Thin, Rough, Untidy
5.	Shape	Round, Square, Rectangular
6.	Age	Young, Old, Youthful
7.	Colour	Blue, Red, Pink
8.	Origin	Dutch, Japanese, Turkish
9.	Material	Metal, Wood, Plastic
10.	Type	General-Purpose, Four-S9ded, U-Shaped

e.g. • My sister bought a **big white** house.
• This is an **old black leather** jacket.

4.2 Degrees of Comparison

Adjectives are not only used to describe a noun but also to make a comparison between two or more nouns. When we use an adjective to compare the qualities of two or more nouns, we use Degrees of Comparison.

There are three degrees of adjectives. They are

(i) **Positive Degree of Adjective** The Positive Degree of an Adjective is the adjective in its simple form. It is used when no comparison is made.

e.g. • Rita is an **intelligent** woman.

(ii) **Comparative Degree of Adjective** The Comparative Degree of an Adjective denotes a higher degree of the quality than the Positive, and is used when two things (or sets of things) are compared.

e.g. • Rita is **more intelligent** than **Ron.**

(iii) **Superlative Degree of Adjective** The Superlative Degree of an Adjective denotes the highest degree of the quality, and is used when more than two things (or sets of things) are compared.

e.g. • Rita is the **most intelligent** in her office.

REVIEW EXERCISE

Objective and Subjective Questions

1. Fill in the blanks with suitable adjective.

(i) Make sure you wear a scarf because the weather outside is quite ....

(a) windy (b) humid (c) hot (d) rainy

(ii) My new bed not only looks good but is also very ....

(a) heavy (b) ugly
(c) comfortable (d) stiff

(iii) The .... little kitten climbed up the curtains and spilled her milk.

(a) naughty (b) lazy (c) old (d) fat

(iv) We sat and watched as the setting Sun created a .... sky.

(a) dull (b) clear (c) gorgeous (d) dark

(v) I will be performing in front of a large audience tomorrow, so I am feeling ....

(a) angry (b) anxious (c) jealous (d) sleepy

(vi) The younger sister felt .... as the elder one was being showered with presents on her birthday.

(a) foolish (b) wise (c) jealous (d) poor

(vii) Helping my mother with the chores seemed fun at first, but soon it became ....

(a) relaxed (b) tedious
(c) exciting (d) happening

(viii) She is too .... to learn the error of her ways.

(a) arrogant (b) hardworking
(c) disciplined (d) wise

(ix) She was .... to receive the bad news.

(a) happy (b) excited (c) shocked (d) elated

(x) It was so .... of you to offer them help.

(a) rude (b) horrible (c) kind (d) terrible

2. In the following questions, select the option which is the correct form of the sentence. If you think none of the options is correct, your answer is 'd'.

(i) Harish is senior than you.

(a) Harish is more senior than you.
(b) Harish is more senior to you.
(c) Harish is senior to you.
(d) None of the above

(ii) My shirt is more superior than yours.

(a) My shirt is superior to yours.
(b) My shirt is superior than yours.
(c) My shirt is more superior to yours.
(d) None of the above

(iii) Sangeeta is more wiser than Sunita.

(a) Sangeeta is wise than Sunita.
(b) Sangeeta is more much wiser than Sunita.
(c) Sangeeta is wiser than Sunita.
(d) None of the above

(iv) It is the most impossible to stay in the flames of fire for a long time.

(a) It is the more impossible to stay in the flames of fire for a long time.
(b) It is impossible to stay in the flames of fire for a long time.
(c) It is more impossible in the flames of fire for a long time.
(d) None of the above

(v) Tony is the most happiest boy in the world.

(a) Tony is most happiest boy in the world.
(b) Tony is the happiest boy in the world.
(c) Tony is the most happy boy in the world.
(d) None of the above

(vi) Sonu is more cleverer than industrious.

(a) Sonu is more cleverer to industrious.

(b) Sonu is more clever to industrious.

(c) Sonu is more clever than industrious.

(d) None of the above

(vii) Surjeet is better than any player in the team.

(a) Surjeet is better than any other player in the team.

(b) Surjeet is more better than any other player in the team.

(c) Surjeet is better than any players in the team.

(d) None of the above

(viii) Rohit is my oldest son.

(a) Rohit is my most oldest son.

(b) Rohit is my eldest son.

(c) Rohit is my most eldest son.

(d) None of the above

(ix) These sort of people are not liked by me.

(a) This sort of people are not liked by me.

(b) These sorts of people are not liked by me.

(c) This sort of peoples are not liked by me.

(d) None of the above

(x) I sat nearest to her.

(a) I sat nearer to her.

(b) I sat more nearer to her.

(c) I sat next to her.

(d) None of the above

3. Complete the following sentences using the correct degree of suitable adjective.

(i) The boys eat .... than girls.

(ii) A group of individuals is .... than a single individual.

(iii) She is the .... cunning lady of the whole group.

(iv) It is always good to work for a .... cause.

(v) Milk is .... diet.

(vi) This road is the .... one in the town.

(vii) Black is the .... colour.

(viii) Birbal was a .... man.

(ix) I can run .... than she.

(x) This is the .... gift I have ever received.

4. Complete the following table.

Positive	Comparative	Superlative
Good		
Smart		
	Stronger	
Helpful		
		Bravest
Many		
Old		
	More Beautiful	
		Richest
	Wealthier	

5. Fill in the blanks with the correct form of degree of the adjectives given in brackets.

(i) Nadira was the most .... girl that Salim had ever seen. (beautiful)

(ii) I have not seen any child that is .... than Sharvilak. (naughty)

(iii) To preach is .... than to practise. (easy)

(iv) These lights are .... than those ones. (bright)

(v) Hollywood movies are grory but not as .... Bollywood movies. (interesting)

(vi) Mumbai is much .... than any other city in Maharashtra. (busy)

(vii) Who is the .... actress according to you? (pretty)

(viii) I think, this cloth is .... than the one we purchased earlier. (fine)

(ix) Autumn is the .... season that I have ever loved. (lovely)

(x) Living in Bangalore is .... than living in Hyderabad. (expensive)

6. Fill in the blank with the adjectives given in the bracket in the correct order. The first one has been done for you.

(i) She has .... hair. (green, straight)

(ii) Could you hand me my .... hat? (trendy, red, French)

(iii) Rupa gave me a .... dinner set for my birthday. (classy, glass)

(iv) They went to a .... (ancient, beautiful, Italian) cafe.

(v) Ratika had thrown a .... dance party last night. (bollywood, retro)

(vi) We have adopted a .... puppy. (brown, little, cute)

(vii) On our journey to Mumbai, we saw .... buildings. (numerous, red, little)

(viii) I am very jealous of her .... cottage. (three-storeyed, Elizabethan, wooden)

(ix) She has an .... vase that was a gift from her grandmother. (blue, porcelain, antique)

(x) Ritesh has bought a .... jacket. (rugged, black, Japanese)

ANSWERS

1. (i) (a) windy
(ii) (c) comfortable
(iii) (a) naughty
(iv) (c) gorgeous
(v) (b) anxious
(vi) (c) jealous
(vii) (b) tedious
(viii) (a) arrogant
(ix) (c) shocked
(x) (c) kind

2. (i) (c) Harish is senior to you.
(ii) (a) My shirt is superior to yours.
(iii) (c) Sangeeta is wiser than Sunita.
(iv) (b) It is impossible to stay in the flames of fire for a long time.
(v) (b) Tony is the happiest boy in the world.
(vi) (c) Sonu is more clever than industrious.
(vii) (a) Surjeet is better than any other player in the team.
(viii) (b) Rohit is my eldest son.
(ix) (b) These sorts of people are not liked by me.
(x) (c) I sat next to her.

3. (i) more (ii) stronger
(iii) most (iv) noble
(v) the best (vi) longest
(vii) darkest (viii) wise
(ix) faster (x) best

4.

Positive	Comparative	Superlative
Good	better	best
Smart	smarter	smartest
Strong	stronger	strongest
Helpful	more helpful	most helpful
Brave	braver	bravest
Many	more	most
Old	older	oldest
Beautiful	more beautiful	most beautiful
Rich	richer	richest
wealthy	wealthier	wealthiest

5. (i) beautiful (ii) naughtier
(ii) easier (iv) brighter
(v) interesting as (vi) busier
(vii) prettiest (viii) finer
(ix) loveliest (x) more expensive

6. (i) Straight green (ii) Trendy red French
(iii) Classy glass (iv) Beautiful ancient Italian
(v) Bollywood retro (vi) Cute little brown
(vii) Numerous little red
(viii) Three-storeyed Elizabethan wooden
(ix) Antique blue porcelain
(x) Rugged black Japanese

Verb

5.1 Definition of Verb

A verb is a word that expresses an action, possession or state of being in a sentence.

e.g. • Ramesh **works** hard at his job. (action)
• ...ama **has** the book. (possession)
• He **is** a ballet dancer. (state of being)

5.2 Types of Verbs : On the Basis of Use

On the basis of their use, verbs are of three kinds

Main Verb

Main Verbs are verbs that depict or denote the action performed by the subject. They are also called Action verbs.

e.g. • He **died** in an accident.
• The servant is **cleaning** the floor.

Main verbs can be further categorised into two kinds. They are discussed below

(i) **Transitive Verbs** They are verbs that require an object to complete their meaning.

e.g. • She **left** her book on the table. (Here, book is the object)
• Please **buy** me a dog. (Here, dog is the object)

(ii) **Intransitive Verbs** They are verbs that do not require an object to complete their meaning.

e.g. • Jiya **screamed** loudly.
• The rate of profit **has increased**.

Some transitive verbs can sometimes be used intransitively and vice-versa. e.g.

	Verbs used Transitively	Verbs used Intransitively
(i)	She sang a nice song.	She sang melodiously.
(ii)	Dr. Gupta runs an organisation for old people.	He runs very fast.
(iii)	Gauri is reading a comic.	Gauri is reading loudly.
(iv)	Deepanita wrote many articles.	Deepanita wrote very precisively.

Linking Verbs

Linking verb is a verb that serves as a connector between the subject and other words (object) in a sentence. There are only a few linking words in English. They are- am, is, are, was, were, has been, become, seem, look, smell, touch, appear, sound, taste, feel, act, grow, stay, appear, prove, turn, become, remain, and get.

e.g. • She **is** happy with her result.
• My eyes **feel** watery.

Helping Verbs

A helping verb or an auxiliary verb is not the main verb of a sentence. It is another verb which comes with the main verb to enhance its meaning.

e.g. • I **can** come to your house by 7 pm.
• You **should** see a doctor.

There are two types of helping verbs as discussed below

(i) **Primary Auxiliary Verbs** are used to make the sentence grammatically complete. It is the most commonly used verb and are commonly called Helping Verbs.

These verbs change their form according to the number and person of the subject as well as the time of the action.

e.g. • Raja **is** climbing the hill.
• They **had** planned for a trip.

Primary Auxiliary Verbs include to be, to have and to do verbs only.

Verb	Present	Past
To Be	is, am, are	was, were
To Have	has, have	did
To Do	has, have	had

(ii) **Modal Auxiliary Verbs** are used with the main verb to give us more information about the action. It tells us the 'manner' of the main verb and never changes its form. The main purpose of these verbs is that it tells us whether a sentence expresses a possibility, ability, a wish, a necessity, willingness, promise, request, etc.

There are 9 modal auxiliaries in total. These are Can, Could, Shall, Should, Will, Would, May, Might, Must.

5.3 Types of Verbs : On the Basis of Form

On the basis of whether they change their form or not, verbs are of two kinds

- Finite Verbs
- Non-Finite Verbs

Finite Verbs

Finite verbs change their forms when there is a change in the number and person of the subject and the tense of a sentence.

e.g. • He **has inspected** the bags of travellers already.
• They **have inspected** the bags of travellers every day.
• I **have been inspecting** the bags of travellers all day.
• She **will inspect** the bags of travellers tomorrow.

Conjugation of Verbs Verbs are used in different forms in different situations. These different forms of verbs are called conjugation of verbs.

There are primarily three forms of verbs

(i) Present (Original Form)
(ii) Past
(iii) Past Participle

Following is the list of verbs with their forms

Present Tense (V_1)	Past Tense (V_2)	Past Participle (V_3)
Add	Added	Added
Act	Acted	Acted
Bore	Bored	Bored
Borrow	Borrowed	Borrowed
Boil	Boiled	Boiled
Call	Called	Called
Carve	Carved	Carved
Dress	Dressed	Dressed
Earn	Earned	Earned
Adore	Adored	Adored
Adorn	Adorned	Adorned
Mark	Marked	Marked
Drill	Drilled	Drilled
Treat	Treated	Treated
Paint	Painted	Painted
Show	Showed	Showed
Become	Became	Became
Bend	Bent	Bent
Feed	Fed	Fed
Bring	Brought	Brought
Build	Built	Built
Burn	Burnt	Burnt
Catch	Caught	Caught
Dream	Dreamed/Dreamt	Dreamed/Dreamt
Keep	Kept	Kept
Make	Made	Made
Send	Sent	Sent
Shine	Shone	Shone
Sweep	Swept	Swept
Feel	Felt	Felt
Fight	Fought	Fought
Find	Found	Found
Meet	Met	Met
Begin	Began	Begun
Bite	Bit	Bitten
Blow	Blew	Blown
Choose	Chose	Chosen
Do	Did	Done
Draw	Drew	Drawn
Eat	Ate	Eaten
Fall	Fell	Fallen
Fly	Flew	Flown
Grow	Grew	Grown
Lie	Lay	Lain
Sink	Sank	Sunk
Sing	Sang	Sung
Speak	Spoke	Spoken
Spring	Sprang	Sprung
Take	Took	Taken
Write	Wrote	Written

All three forms are same in some verbs

Present Tense (V_1)	Past Tense (V_2)	Past Participle (V_3)
Bet	Bet	Bet
Burst	Burst	Burst
Cut	Cut	Cut
Hit	Hit	Hit
Hurt	Hurt	Hurt
Shut	Shut	Shut

Non-Finite Verbs

Non-finite verbs do not change their form when the number, person, and tense of the subject changes. In fact, such verbs often do not act as verbs in a sentence. They can act like a Noun, Adjective or an Adverb

e.g.
- I would like **to run** you today.
- They would like **to run** today.
- Let us go **to run** tomorrow morning.

There are three types of Non-Finite Verbs

(i) **Gerunds** Gerunds are verbs that act like nouns in a sentence. They use the -ing form of a verb.

e.g.
- **Dancing** is a hobby of mine.
- Aditi likes **painting**.

(ii) **Infinitives** An infinitive is a verb that does not play the role of a verb but has some other role to play in the sentence. It can act like a Noun, Adjective or an Adverb and is formed by adding 'to' before the verb.

e.g. • **To tell** the truth is the right way of life.

• Meera needs **to leave** soon.

(iii) **Participles** A Participle is a verb that functions as an adjective. It is formed by adding '-ing', '-ed', 't' or 'en' at the end of the verb.

e.g. • I met a **learned** man yesterday.

• The **speeding** car hurt the boy.

It is important to note here that depending upon the suffix they take; there are three kinds of participles.

(a) **Present Participle** have the form - verb + ing. They are used as

(i) As a verb in the beginning of the sentence

e.g. • **Seeing** that you are busy, I went to the other window.

(ii) As an adjective

e.g. • This is an **interesting** story.

(b) **Past Participle** have the form - verb + -d/-ed/-t/-en/-n. They are used as

(i) As a verb in the beginning of the sentence

e.g. • **Charmed** with her looks, Kunal tried to talk to her.

(ii) As an adjective

e.g. • The Marines saw a **dead** child at the bank of the river.

(c) **Perfect Participle** have the form - having + past participle form of the verb. It shows that the action is complete, either at some time in the past or at present.

e.g. • **Having walked** continuously, I am fully exhausted now.

• **Having lost** his wallet, he had to ask others for help.

REVIEW EXERCISE

Objective and Subjective Questions

1. Fill in the blanks with the correct form of action verb.

(i) My sister .... her homework late.

(a) submitted (b) submit (c) submits (d) submitting

(ii) My younger brother .... earlier in the night, even before his test.

(a) sleep (b) slept (c) sleeping (d) sleeps

(iii) The teachers .... us in all the remaining problems.

(a) guide (b) guides (c) guided (d) guiding

(iv) The Moon .... brightly at night.

(a) shining (b) shiny (c) shine (d) shines

(v) Manners .... a man.

(a) makes (b) make (c) made (d) making

(vi) My sister got me a ...... doll.

(a) danced (b) dances (c) dance (d) dancing

(vii) .... football is not only his hobby, but also his profession.

(a) Played (b) Play (c) Playing (d) Player

(viii) We .... home from the picnic with the setting Sun behind us.

(a) returned (b) returning (c) return (d) returns

(ix) In order to .... early in the morning, you must go to bed early at night.

(a) wakes (b) wake (c) waking (d) awaken

(x) We are encouraged .... our teeth after every meal.

(a) to brush (b) brush (c) brushing (d) brushed

(xi) I had a hard time staying .... during the boring speech.

(a) awoke (b) awake (c) awaken (d) awakened

(xii) Peter .... in China in 1965.

(a) lived (b) lives (c) living (d) life

(xiii) She goes .... every morning.

(a) run (b) running (c) ran (d) runs

(xiv) My father .... a newspaper every day.

(a) buy (b) bought (c) buys (d) buying

(xv) The universe is .... and has been so since its beginning.

(a) exposing (b) expanding (c) passing (d) questioning

2. **Choose the third form of the verbs given in capital letters below.**

(i) Arise
(a) Arose (b) Arosed (c) Arisen (d) Arised

(ii) Win
(a) Win (b) Won (c) Winner (d) Wins

(iii) Wear
(a) Wears (b) Wearn (c) Wore (d) Worn

(iv) Drink
(a) Drunk (b) Drank (c) Drink (d) Drinks

(v) Be
(a) Was (b) Were (c) Been (d) Be

(vi) Beat
(a) Beat (b) Beated (c) Beating (d) Beaten

(vii) Bite
(a) Bitten (b) Bit (c) Bite (d) Bited

(viii) Keep
(a) Kept (b) Keeping (c) Kepted (d) Keep

(ix) Send
(a) Sented (b) Sending (c) Sent (d) Sended

(x) Rise
(a) Rise (b) Rose (c) Rosen (d) Risen

3. **Identify the type of verb underlined in the given sentence.**

(i) The burglar disappeared with the cash.
(a) Transitive verb (b) Intransitive verb
(c) Linking verb (d) Auxiliary verb

(ii) The director told the actors, 'Do your best, and we'll be a hit.'
(a) Transitive verb (b) Intransitive verb
(c) Linking verb (d) Auxiliary verb

(iii) He would tell me if he thought we were in danger.
(a) Transitive verb (b) Intransitive verb
(c) Linking verb (d) Auxiliary verb

(iv) His ability to concentrate is legendary.
(a) Transitive verb (b) Intransitive verb
(c) Linking verb (d) Auxiliary verb

(v) The campers hid inside the cabin when they saw the bear.
(a) Transitive verb (b) Intransitive verb
(c) Linking verb (d) Auxiliary verb

(vi) Alexis is swimming in the state championship contest next week.
(a) Transitive verb (b) Intransitive verb
(c) Linking verb (d) Auxiliary verb

(vii) Frustrated with the official's call, Ethan kicked the bench.
(a) Transitive verb (b) Intransitive verb
(c) Linking verb (d) Auxiliary verb

(viii) The student procrastinated too long and failed to finish the project.
(a) Transitive verb
(b) Intransitive verb
(c) Linking verb
(d) Auxiliary verb

(ix) The vegetarian burger tasted like salted cardboard.
(a) Transitive verb (b) Intransitive verb
(c) Linking verb (d) Auxiliary verb

(x) Ellen nodded to the audience and sang her song.
(a) Transitive verb (b) Intransitive verb
(c) Linking verb (d) Auxiliary verb

4. **In each of the following sentences, the underlined verb may be inappropriately used. Choose the correct form of the verb from the options. If the verb has been used correctly, write your answer as 'No correction required'.**

(i) I have scrutinising the area thoroughly. There is no mischievous thing here.
(a) scrutinise (b) scrutinised
(c) was scrutinising (d) was scrutinised

(ii) How does a butterfly gets its colour?
(a) got (b) is getting
(c) getting (d) get

(iii) She thinking it would rather sound silly than defensive.
(a) think (b) thought
(c) was thought (d) has been thinking

(iv) This project has to work out very diligently.
(a) worked (b) been worked
(c) is working (d) working

(v) Asha Bhonsle was give life Time Achievement Award in IFFA 2014 in Dubai.
(a) given (b) gave
(c) been given (d) giving

(vi) Everybody is waiting for the arrival of the US President very eagerly.
(a) has been waiting (b) waited
(c) waiting (d) had waited

(vii) India winning the match against Pakistan by 76 runs.
(a) has winning (b) had won
(c) won (d) were winning

(viii) Their flight may taking off in around half an hour, weather permitted.
(a) took (b) take (c) is taking (d) was taken

(ix) I think, she has deliberately switch the mobile off.
(a) switches (b) switching
(c) switched (d) is switching

(x) **The entire audience <u>bursting</u> out in a hilarious laughter as she said the punchline.**
(a) burst (b) had burst
(c) is bursting (d) were bursting

5. Fill in the blanks with the correct forms of the verbs given in brackets.

(i) Riddhi ...... (start) her day with a prayer everyday.
(ii) The Sun ...... (shine) brightly today.
(iii) Ayushman has ...... (sing) a beautiful song in the movie.
(iv) The temperature .... (fluctuate) a lot yesterday.
(v) Tears ...... (roll) down his cheeks when he heard the story.
(vi) The officer offered to ...... (reiterate) the clauses so that the staff might understand them well.
(vii) We never had to ...... (nag) Sumedha to do anything. She herself was very active and careful too.
(viii) The lady often ...... (banter) easily with her men-coworkers.
(ix) How long have you been ...... (prepare) this material?
(x) The car suddenly ...... (stop) while we were ...... (drive) to Madurai.

6. Give the past and past participle forms of the following verbs.

(i) Worry (ii) Send
(iii) Remove (iv) Shake
(v) Survive (vi) Walk
(vii) Dwell (viii) Certify
(ix) Fly (x) Drink

7. In the given sentences, underline the action verb and identify if it is Transitive (T) or Intransitive (IT).

(i) As soon as the break was over, Rehman left.
(ii) The boy jumped.
(iii) The officer reminded me to pay the fine.
(iv) Ramesh cooks daily.
(v) The train arrived early.
(vi) She sang a beautiful melody.
(vii) The boatman rows the boat.
(viii) The light shines brightly.
(ix) The traveller packed some light snacks.
(x) Her mother came in quietly.

8. Fill in the blanks with suitable gerunds and infinitives.

(i) It takes a lot of hard work .... tennis well. (play)
(ii) We hope .... the game tonight. (watch)
(iii) .... on roads is a big fear for him. (drive)
(iv) I can't help but .... lonely. (feel)
(v) ...... is a good way to expand your worldview. (travel)
(vi) My passion is .... (read)
(vii) I will have .... my assignment today. (submit)
(viii) .... is an exchange of ideas. (write)
(ix) Her teacher encouraged her .... in the annual function. (participate)
(x) Ms. Smita taught us .... (dance)

ANSWERS

1. (i) (a) submitted (ii) (b) slept
(iii) (a) guide (iv) (d) shines
(v) (b) make (vi) (d) dancing
(vii) (c) Playing (viii) (a) returned
(ix) (b) wake (x) (a) to brush
(xi) (b) awake (xii) (a) lived
(xiii) (b) running (xiv) (c) buys
(xv) (b) expanding

2. (i) (c) Arisen (ii) (b) Won
(iii) (d) Worn (iv) (a) Drunk
(v) (c) Been (vi) (d) Beaten
(vii) (a) Bitten
(viii) (a) Kept
(ix) (c) Sent
(x) (d) Risen

3. (i) (a) Transitive verb (ii) (a) Transitive verb
(iii) (d) Auxiliary verb (iv) (c) Linking verb
(v) (a) Transitive verb (vi) (d) Auxiliary verb
(vii) (a) Transitive verb (viii) (b) Intransitive verb
(ix) (a) Transitive verb (x) (b) Intransitive verb

4. (i) (b) scrutinised (ii) (d) get
(iii) (b) thought (iv) (a) worked
(v) (a) given (vi) (a) has been waiting
(vii) (c) won (viii) (b) take
(ix) (c) switched (x) (a) burst

5. (i) starts (ii) is shining
(iii) sung (iv) fluctuated
(v) rolled (vi) reiterate
(vii) nag (viii) bantered
(ix) preparing (x) stopped, driving

6.

	Main Verb	Past Tense	Past Participle
(i)	Worry	Worried	Worried
(ii)	Send	Sent	Sent
(iii)	Remove	Removed	Removed
(iv)	Shake	Shook	Shaken
(v)	Survive	Survived	Survived
(vi)	Walk	Walked	Walked
(vii)	Dwell	Dwelled	Dwelled
(viii)	Certify	Certified	Certified
(ix)	Fly	Flew	Flown
(x)	Drink	Drank	Drunk

7. (i) left- Intransitive verb
(ii) jumped- intransitive verb
(iii) reminded- transitive verb
(iv) cooks- intransitive verb
(v) arrived- intransitive verb
(vi) sang- transitive verb
(vii) rows- transitive verb
(viii) shines- intransitive verb
(ix) packed- transitive verb
(x) came- intransitive verb

8. (i) to play (ii) to watch
(iii) Driving (iv) feel
(v) Travelling (vi) reading
(vii) to submit (viii) Writing
(ix) to participate (x) dancing

Adverb

6.1 Definition of Adverb

An adverb is a word that modifies the meaning of a verb or an adjective or another adverb.

e.g.
- Mandy is a **very** careful driver.
- Mandy drives **carefully.**
- Mandy drives **very** carefully.

In first sentence, the word 'very' modifies the meaning of the adjective 'careful'.

In second sentence, the word 'carefully' modifies the meaning of the verb 'drives'.

In third sentence, the word 'very' modifies the meaning of another adverb 'carefully'.

6.2 Types of Adverbs

Adverbs can be categorised into various kinds. They are discussed below

Adverbs of Time

They tell us when the action takes place. They answer the question 'when'.

e.g.
- I went for a movie **yesterday.**
- They will rehearse for the show **tonight.**

Adverbs of Frequency

They tell us how often an action takes place.

e.g.
- Jeet practices violin **regularly.**
- Neil **frequently** makes such a comment.

Adverbs of Place

They tell us where an action takes place. They answer the question 'where'.

e.g.
- Come **here** at once!
- She took the lady **inside.**

Adverbs of Manner

They tell us how or the manner in which an action takes place. They answer the question 'how'.

e.g.
- He is **persistently** making efforts to crack the exam.
- Amrita speaks English **fluently.**

Adverbs of Degree

They used to indicate the intensity or degree of a verb, an adverb or an adjective.

e.g. • The business is **entirely** out of money.

• The sea is **perfectly** calm.

Adverbs of degree should be used according to the intensity as follows

Low Degree

- The story you told is a **bit** disappointing.
- I am **least** interested in it. Tell it to the marines.
- The question is a **little** confusing.
- This is **slightly** tilted.

Medium Degree

- The sitting arrangement is **fairly** enough.
- This is **sufficiently** large.
- They performed **pretty** well.
- This book is **rather** nice.

High Degree

- This is **extremely** beautiful.
- I had done it **quite** before you asked.
- The speech was **fantastically** awesome.
- The man is **too** old.

Adverbs of Reason

They answer the question, 'why an action took place'.

e.g. (i) Sudha has been shortlisted. **Hence**, she has to prepare for the final round.

(ii) She has become weak. **So**, she should have a proper diet.

Interrogative Adverbs

The words used to ask questions are interrogative adverbs.

e.g. • **Where** do you live? (Place)

• **When** will Sara be back? (Time)

• **Why** were you absent? (Reason)

• **How** is she going to do this? (Manner)

• **How much** effort does it require? (Degree)

• **How many** siblings do you have? (Number)

Relative Adverbs

Adverbs that are used to join two sentences or two clauses. Relative adverbs indicate their antecedents in the process of joining.

e.g. • This is the place **where** he was born.

• Nobody knows the reason **why** Amit behaved that way.

REVIEW EXERCISE

Objective and Subjective Questions

1. Fill in the blanks with suitable adverb.

(i) ...., I met my childhood friend Meeta.

(a) Yesterday
(b) Today
(c) Tomorrow
(d) This sunday

(ii) You need to run .... to win this race.

(a) slow (b) steadily
(c) fast (d) lazily

(iii) I won't say it ....

(a) progressively (b) repeatedly
(c) necessarily (d) correctly

(iv) Speak ...., I cannot hear you.

(a) loudly
(b) slowly
(c) hardly
(d) quickly

(v) You should .... smoke as it is dangerous for your health.

(a) always (b) usually
(c) never (d) hardly

(vi) We searched ...... but we were unable to find her lost jewellery.

(a) nowhere (b) anywhere
(c) everywhere (d) all where

(vii) I hope to see you ....!

(a) soon
(b) never
(c) randomly
(d) occasionally

(viii) Deepak never dressed .... for work.

(a) formally
(b) coolly
(c) dirtily
(d) casually

(ix) **The manager looked at me .... when I reached late.**

(a) sadly (b) regretfully
(c) angrily (d) politely

(x) **Ranjit speaks .... good French, he can be of great help to you.**

(a) very (b) great
(c) quite (d) too

(xi) **He .... goes to office in the weekends as his office remains shut.**

(a) always (b) never
(c) often (d) sometime

(xii) **I believe in punctuality, so I go to work on time and .... come home by 8.**

(a) always (b) sometimes
(c) never (d) often

(xiii) **He has not .... applied for the job we told him about.**

(a) still (b) yet
(c) now (d) since

(xiv) **Tom is .... clever, but Peter is rather stupid.**

(a) fairly (b) rather
(c) almost (d) just

(xv) **Her case is so heavy that she can .... lift it.**

(a) hardly (b) have
(c) nearly (d) fairly

(xvi) **The ballerina moved .... as she danced.**

(a) softly (b) politely
(c) gracefully (d) None of these

(xvii) **He and his friends work ....**

(a) hardly (b) hard
(c) only (d) diligently

(xviii) **Sanjay is .... better today.**

(a) fairly (b) rather
(c) very (d) too

(xix) **We waited .... for the bus to arrive.**

(a) patiently (b) promptly
(c) punctually (d) gently

(xx) **If you do something you don't really want to do, you do it ....**

(a) eagerly (b) reluctantly
(c) accidently (d) exactly

2. In each of the following questions, a sentence is given which may or may not be correct. Select the option which is the correct form of the sentence.

(i) **My brother smokes seldom.**

(a) My brother smokes little.
(b) My brother seldom smokes.
(c) My brother smokes less.
(d) None of the above

(ii) **Tom is enough rich to help the poor.**

(a) Tom is rich enough to help the poor.
(b) Tom is enough rich than to help the poor.
(c) Tom is rich enough than to help the poor.
(d) None of the above

(iii) **It is nothing else than pride.**

(a) It is nothing else but pride.
(b) It is nothing else than a pride.
(c) It is nothing else but a pride.
(d) None of the above

(iv) **It is too cold today.**

(a) It is very cold today.
(b) It is much cold today.
(c) It is very a cold today.
(d) None of the above

(v) **I shall come back just now.**

(a) I shall come back just after.
(b) I shall come back in a few.
(c) I shall come back just then.
(d) None of the above

(vi) **She works quick than you.**

(a) She works quickly than you.
(b) She works more quickly than you.
(c) She works much more quick than you.
(d) None of the above

(vii) **You are so nice.**

(a) You are so a nice.
(b) You are much nice
(c) You are a very nice.
(d) None of the above

(viii) **My brother met me presently.**

(a) My brother met me just now.
(b) My brother met me now.
(c) My brother met me just.
(d) None of the above

(ix) **The almirah is too much heavy for me.**

(a) The almirah is too heavy for me.
(b) The almirah is too very heavy for me.
(c) The almirah is much heavy for me.
(d) None of the above

(x) **She only spent ten rupees.**

(a) She spent only ten rupees.
(b) She only spent a ten rupee notes.
(c) She only spent a ten rupee note.
(d) None of the above

3. Identify the adverb in each of the following sentences.

(i) They spoke loudly.

(ii) I am highly impressed with her presentation.

(iii) She looked quite nervous.

(iv) Radha works diligently in order to get promoted.

(v) Fox is often believed to be cunning animal.

(vi) Barking dogs seldom bite.

(vii) Earlier, they used to travel in their car.

(viii) The birds were chirping merrily.

(ix) I sometimes go for a walk in the park.

(x) He never came to my place to visit me.

4. Use appropriate adverbs of degree (a bit, a little, very, extremely or pretty) according to the context of the sentences given below.

(i) I am ..... tired. But I will definitely try to come with you.

(ii) I am not able to make out the answer. It is .... confusing.

(iii) The boy found the girl .... ugly and disagreed to marry her.

(iv) The arrangements of the birthday party were .... nice. One could not help, but appreciate them.

(v) We can think of some other place. This one is .... boring.

(vi) The paintings and carvings at Ajintha and Verul are .... beautiful.

(vii) The audience were .... spell bound. They liked the speech .... much.

(viii) He slowed down the speed .... so that he might not meet with an accident.

(ix) This building is .... old. It looks like a haunted place now.

(x) She sings .... well. She can try her hand at singing.

ANSWERS

1. (i) (a) Yesterday (ii) (c) fast
(iii) (b) repeatedly (iv) (a) loudly
(v) (c) never (vi) (c) everywhere
(vii) (a) soon (viii) (d) casually
(ix) (c) angrily (x) (c) quite
(xi) (b) never (xii) (a) always
(xiii) (b) yet (xiv) (a) fairly
(xv) (a) hardly (xvi) (c) gracefully
(xvii) (d) diligently (xviii) (b) rather
(xix) (a) patiently (xx) (b) reluctantly

2. (i) (b) My brother seldom smokes.
(ii) (a) Tom is rich enough to help the poor.
(iii) (a) It is nothing else but pride.
(iv) (a) It is very cold today.
(v) (b) I shall come back in a few.
(vi) (b) She works more quickly than you.
(vii) (d) None of the above
(viii) (a) My brother met me just now.
(ix) (a) The almirah is too heavy for me.
(x) (a) She spent only ten rupees.

3. (i) loudly (ii) highly
(iii) quite (iv) diligently
(v) often (vi) seldom
(vii) Earlier (viii) merrily
(ix) sometimes (x) never

4. (i) a little/a bit (ii) very
(iii) extremely (iv) extremely
(v) a little (vi) very/extremely
(vii) extremely, very (viii) a little
(ix) very (x) pretty

CHAPTER 7

Prepositions

7.1 Definition of Preposition

Prepositions are words that show relation between the nouns, pronouns or phrases to other words in a sentence.

e.g. • I always go **to** my office **by** metro train.
• The tournament was cancelled **after** the heavy rainfall.

7.2 Kinds of Preposition

On the basis of their function in a sentence, preposition can be categorised into three kinds which are discussed below

Preposition of Time

Preposition of time is used to denote when a person or thing performs an action.

e.g. • I will be home **by** seven o'clock in the evening.
• Automobiles and airplanes became very popular **in** the 20th century.

Preposition of Place

Preposition of place is used to denote the location at which someone or something is located.

e.g. • I kept my bag in the space **between** my friend and me.
• The sofa is more comfortable than sitting **on** the brown chair.

Preposition of Direction/Movement

Preposition of Direction/Movement is used to express motion or direction of someone or something from one place to another.

e.g. • I walked slowly **through** the crowd.
• He saw that I was running **towards** him and left.

Some common prepositions and their uses

Common Preposition	Their Uses	Examples
On	• To specify days and dates • To refer to a surface • To refer to devices	• I will come back from my trip on Tuesday. • My notebook is lying on the dining table. • I will watch a movie on my laptop tonight.
At	• To refer to a particular time • To indicate a part of a place	• My brother called and said that he'll be home at eight o'clock. • I am waiting for my family at home.
In	• To specify day, month, season, year • To refer to longer periods of time • To indicate a location like cities, states, streets, roads etc. • It is used with directions	• The winter vacations will start in December. • I met him in the month of June • My little sister stays in Delhi. • Kanyakumari is in the South of India.
To	• To refer to a period • To indicate direction	• I will be home from Friday to Sunday. • We are going to the New Delhi railway station.

Common Preposition	Their Uses	Examples
For	• To indicate the duration or unspecified time • To indicate the receiver of something or to get the benefit of it	• He has been ill for quite some time now. • I've brought a cup of tea for you.
By	• To indicate before the given time • To indicate proximity • To show means	• The meeting should have finished by 4:30 pm. • I live by the old building on the main street. • Little children go to school by bus.
Into	• To show a position in or inside something • To show the direction of something	• The thieves broke into the house. • He jumped into the river to save the little boy.
From	• To show the time period of action • To show how far apart two places are	• The doctor said, "I will see you from 12 to 1 pm tomorrow." • His house is around a kilometer from my house.
Before	• To refer to timed events • To refer to a place	• I will go for the class before the match. • Please drop me at the bus stop before the railway station.
After	• To refer to a 'later' time • To show 'next to' a place	• He will meet me day after tomorrow. • What do those letters after your name mean?
Since	• to specify the start of an action	• Annie has been sleeping since 4 o'clock.
Towards	• to denote direction	• This road goes towards the museum.
Across	• to denote expansion	• They spread their business across the country.
Behind	• to denote position at the back of something	• There is a mystery behind the door.
In front of	• To denote position at the front of something	• There is a mirror in front of my window.
Between	• Used for two persons or things	• Chintu is sitting between me and Vaishali.
Among	• Use for more than two persons or things	• Sania is the fastest among all girls.

Phrasal Prepositions

Phrasal prepositions are made of two or more words consisting of simple preposition(s). They also contain another word which can be an adverb, adjective, conjunction or noun. Some common phrasal prepositions are on behalf of, on account of, due to, in front of, in addition to, by means of, according to.

e.g. • I won't be available for the test **because** of my illness.
• Don't stand right **in front of** me; I can't see anything.

REVIEW EXERCISE

Objective and Subjective Questions

1. **Fill in the blanks with suitable preposition.**

(i) **In the month of December, the temperature falls .... 4°C.**

(a) from (b) below
(c) at (d) into

(ii) **A jeep hit him while he was going .... the main road.**

(a) on (b) across
(c) behind (d) through

(iii) **She is .... a noble family of Rajputs.**

(a) from (b) of (c) among (d) at

(iv) **The case was put .... the judge and the judge decided it within an year.**

(a) at (b) from
(c) before (d) of

(v) **The bridge .... this river was built in the year 1995.**

(a) at (b) over
(c) above (d) on

(vi) **She is suffering .... fever.**

(a) with (b) of
(c) through (d) from

(vii) We saw wounded tiger while passing .... the forest.

(a) from (b) through
(c) along (d) among

(viii) Chairs are made .... wood.

(a) of (b) from
(c) on (d) through

(ix) There are tall beautiful coconut trees .... the river.

(a) along (b) at
(c) into (d) over

(x) We are proud .... our children.

(a) on (b) at
(c) after (d) of

(xi) Mt Abu is about five thousand feet .... the sea-level.

(a) above (b) along
(c) after (d) behind

(xii) I shall always be indebted ... you for this timely help.

(a) from (b) of
(c) to (d) with

(xiii) He broke the jug ... hundred pieces.

(a) an (b) into
(c) at (d) of

(xiv) Do not cry ...... spilt milk.

(a) above (b) under
(c) over (d) on

(xv) He looked ...... his watch all around the house.

(a) of (b) for
(c) to (d) from

(xvi) I am fond ...... watching movies.

(a) from (b) for
(c) of (d) about

(xvii) Don't loiter ...... the street.

(a) onto (b) about
(c) on (d) into

(xviii) They will go to Bengaluru ...... plane.

(a) on (b) in
(c) by (d) from

(xix) He drained what was left ...... his drink.

(a) from (b) in
(c) of (d) off

(xx) It became clear that the strangers were heading ...... a serious disaster.

(a) along
(b) towards
(c) for
(d) into

2. Select the option which is the correct form of the sentence.

(i) I agreed to you.

(a) I agreed with you.
(b) I agreed for you.
(c) I agreed on you.
(d) None of these

(ii) Tony reached at the station in time.

(a) Tony reached on the station in time.
(b) Tony reached the station in time.
(c) Tony reached to the station in time.
(d) None of the above

(iii) A gang of robbers attacked on the bank manager.

(a) A gang of robbers attacked the bank manager.
(b) A gang of robbers attacked at the bank manager.
(c) A gang of robbers attacked to the bank manager.
(d) None of the above

(iv) He accompanied with us to Mumbai.

(a) He accompanied us to Mumbai.
(b) He accompanied to us to Mumbai.
(c) He accompanied on us to Mumbai.
(d) None of the above

(v) He was accused with murder.

(a) He was accused for murder.
(b) He was accused to murder.
(c) He was accused of murder.
(d) None of the above

(vi) He was accustomed on going for a walking in the morning.

(a) He was accustomed to going for a walk.
(b) He was accustomed for going for a walk.
(c) He was accustomed at going for a walk.
(d) None of the above

(vii) He achieved on A great success in life.

(a) He achieved A great success in life.
(b) He achieved to A great success in life.
(c) He achieved for A great success in life.
(d) None of the above

(viii) The jury acquitted Tony for murder.

(a) The jury acquitted Tony to murder.
(b) The jury acquitted Tony of murder.
(c) The jury acquitted Tony on murder.
(d) None of the above

(ix) Ajit was anxious on his mother's health.

(a) Ajit was anxious for his mother's health.
(b) Ajit was anxious about his mother's health.
(c) Ajit was anxious at his mother's health.
(d) None of the above

(x) **Rupesh applied for a Principal.**

(a) Rupesh applied to the post of a Principal.

(b) Rupesh applied for the post of a Principal.

(c) Rupesh applied on the post of a Principal.

(d) None of the above

3. Fill in the blanks with appropriate prepositions.

(i) The weather is not good here .... December.

(ii) The kids are hiding .... the table.

(iii) Jack and Jill went .... the hill.

(iv) Send a set of papers .... the cardboard.

(v) Are you going ...... the examination tomorrow?

(vi) Read the instructions .... the top.

(vii) The class is .... 9:00 am today.

(viii) The customer care can be contacted .... any queries.

(ix) As a young man, he travelled a lot and was always...... .

(x) Vishnu goes .... temple on Saturday.

(xi) Ice-cream is made .... milk and cream.

(xii) The artist is insulted .... the music director.

(xiii) This piece of land was a dispute .... the four boys.

(xiv) I purchased a book .... perfumes for my younger brother.

(xv) The patient had died .... the surgery was carried out.

4. Fill in the blanks with appropriate phrasal prepositions.

(i) .... making milkshakes, he made cold coffees for all of us.

(ii) .... him, he knows everything about science.

(iii) Please don't behave like an imbecile .... my parents.

(iv) I am declaring tomorrow as a holiday .... our boss.

(v) The company's financial losses were .... poor management.

(vi) .... the doctors, smoking can cause lung cancer.

(vii) The flight arrived a little late .... the heavy rainfall.

(viii) I stayed in bed all day .... going to work.

(ix) Thoughts are conveyed .... words.

(x) .... his own family, she teaches the children in her sister's family.

ANSWERS

1. (i) (b) below (ii) (b) across (iii) (a) from (iv) (c) before (v) (b) over (vi) (d) from (vii) (b) through (viii) (a) of (ix) (a) along (x) (d) of (xi) (a) above (xii) (c) to (xiii) (b) into (xiv) (c) over (xv) (b) for (xvi) (c) of (xvii) (c) on (xviii) (c) by (xix) (c) of (xx) (b) towards

2. (i) (a) I agreed with you.

(ii) (b) Tony reached the station in time.

(iii) (a) A gang of robbers attacked the bank manager.

(iv) (a) He accompanied us to Mumbai.

(v) (c) He was accused of murder.

(vi) (a) He was accustomed to going for a walk.

(vii) (a) He achieved great success in life.

(viii) (b) The jury acquitted Tony of murder.

(ix) (b) Ajit was anxious about his mother's health.

(x) (b) Rupesh applied for the post of a Principal.

3. (i) in (ii) under (iii) up (iv) with (v) to (vi) from (vii) at (viii) for (ix) out (x) to (xi) of (xii) by (xiii) among (xiv) about (xv) before

4. (i) In addition to

(ii) According to

(iii) in front of

(iv) on behalf of

(v) due to

(vi) According to

(vii) on account of

(viii) instead of

(ix) by means of

(x) According to

Conjunction (Connectors)

8.1 Definition of Conjunction

Conjunctions are words used to join words, phrases, clauses or sentences to form new sentences.

e.g.
- Please give me some juice **and** toast to eat.
- He goes to the library a lot **because** he loves to read.

8.2 Kinds of Conjunctions

Conjunctions can be categorised into three types. They are discussed below

Coordinating Conjunctions

Coordinating conjunctions are used to join two or more words, phrases and clauses of equal ranks.

The coordinating conjunctions include and, but, or, nor, for, yet, so.

e.g.
- He doesn't like you very much **but** is civil with you.
- Manvi loves to sing **and** dance.

Use of Coordinating Conjunctions

And It is used to combine similar facts or statements.

e.g.
- Monika likes to play badminton **and** chess.
- He eats cake, chocolate, pastry **and** chips.

But It is used to connect opposite or contrasting ideas/statements.

e.g.
- You can go for camping **but** are not allowed to go river rafting.
- I like to read poetry **but** sometimes I read gothic novels too.

Or It is used to express a choice between two things.

e.g.
- You can eat it with a fork **or** a spoon.
- Neetu could cook dinner for us **or** we could go out for dinner.

For It is used to show outcome or result for the previous statement/expression.

e.g.
- I cannot attend the meeting **for** I am unwell.
- He did not buy it **for** it was very expensive.

So It is used to show outcome, result or consequence of something.

e.g.
- Everyone was busy in work **so** I brought all the items myself.
- All the rooms of the hotel were occupied **so** I had to shift here.

Nor It is used to combine two words or ideas both of which are to be negated.

e.g.
- He doesn't eat cake, **nor** does he eat biscuits.
- I will not negotiate with you **nor** with Jane.

Yet It is used to express a contradictory or contrasting concept to an existing logical idea or point.

e.g.
- He's seventy-two, **yet** he still swims, runs and plays football regularly.
- She always seems to proofread the papers carefully, **yet** she never catches all the errors.

Correlative Conjunctions

Those conjunctions that are used in pairs to connect two words, phrases or sentences of equal importance are known as correlative conjunctions.

Correlative conjunctions are both-and, not only-but also, either-or, neither-nor, no sooner-than, hardly-when, such-that, whether-or

e.g.
- The company produces **both** shampoo **and** bath soaps.
- I will **either** eat salad **or** drink milk.

Use of Correlative Conjunctions

Either.....or It is used to show choice between two things.

e.g. • **Either** Max **or** James has taken the pen.
• I will drink **either** cold coffee **or** ice tea.

Neither.....nor It is used to negate both of the given choices.

e.g. • She is **neither** rich **nor** generous.
• **Neither** the blue one **nor** the red one is available in your size.

Both.....and It is used to combine two ideas.

e.g. • My brother is **both** smart **and** intelligent.
• I will eat **both** North Indian food **and** Chinese food.

Whether.....or It is used to express doubt or choice between two things.

e.g. • Tell me **whether** you will do it **or** not.
• Do you know **whether** it will rain today **or** not?

Not only......But also It is used to express the inclusion of more than one thing.

e.g. • She is **not only** a dancer **but also** a singer.
• We are **not only** composing the music for the film **but also** directing the film.

No sooner..... than It is used to show that one thing happens immediately after another thing.

e.g. • **No sooner** had I started mowing the lawn **than** it started raining.
• We had **no sooner** started cooking **than** there was a power cut.

Subordinating Conjunctions

Subordinating conjunctions are used to join subordinate clauses to main clauses.

e.g. • I am not talking to him **because** we had a fight.
• Naina met Yashika **when** they were in San Francisco.

Here is the list of the subordinating conjunction

after	if	though	although
if only	till	as	in order that
unless	as if	now that	until
as long as	once	when	as though
rather than	whenever	because	since
where	before	so that	whereas
even if	than	wherever	even though
that		while	

Use of Subordinating Conjunctions

After It is used to express the sequence of happening of two things.

e.g. • I will drink the milk **after** my brother drinks it.
• You could go and play **after** you have done the dishes.

If 'If' is used to express a condition in the clause.

e.g. • **If** you work hard, you will pass.
• She may look beautiful **if** she uses this cream.

Though, Although and Even though It is used to show a contrast between the two clauses.

e.g. • **Though** he is poor, he is honest.
• I am happy **although** I want to be more.
• **Although** they are good at it, they did mistakes.
• I was late to my work **even though** I helped the old lady.

If only It is used to show a specific condition stated in the clause.

e.g. • **If only** I would be a Prime Minister.
• I could get there, **if only** tomorrow.

Till/Until They are used to connect an action to a point in time.

e.g. • Let's wait here **till** the rain stops.
• I'll be here **until** 2 o'clock.

As It is used to show time, cause and reason in a sentence.

e.g. • **As** I left my home, I found a purse. (time)
• She is weak **as** she was ill. (cause)

Unless It shows the negativity stated in a condition.

e.g. • You will not pass **unless** you study.
• She will not stop crying **unless** she meets her father.

When It introduces adverbial clause expressing when an action takes place.

e.g. • **When** my sister called me, I was coming back home.
• She is aware **when** they could harm her.

Rather than This is used to show preferences or choices in a sentence.

e.g. • She would die **rather than** beg.
• I would live in Delhi **rather than** London.

Because It is used to express the reason of an action.

e.g. • I will eat a pizza **because** I am hungry.
• We have to clean the house **because** tomorrow is Diwali.

Since It is used to give reason for something.

e.g. • **Since** she was ill, we all postponed the party.
• She decided to walk **since** her house was near.

Before It is used to suggest that the second event happened soon after the first one.

e.g. • **Before** she left, she gave everyone a present.
• I need to tell her the truth **before** anyone else does.

Whereas It shows the contrast between the two clauses.

e.g. • She is intelligent **whereas** her brother is not.
• America is developed **whereas** India is developing.

While It is used to show that actions or events happen at the same time.

e.g. • I was reading **while** eating.
• She was talking **while** crossing the road.

Compound Conjunctions

Compound conjunctions are the groups of words (phrases) that are used as conjunction.

Use of Compound Conjunctions

In order that This conjunction is used to express purpose.

e.g. I took a leave **in order that** I could go to Agra.

On condition that It is used to express a condition which is a necessity for another action.

e.g. She accepted the invitation **on condition that** she brings the cake.

Even if It is used to express an action done in spite of a negative condition or an unfavourable situation.

e.g. I will go to the park **even if** it is raining.

So that This is used to express purpose just as 'in order that' is used.

e.g. He did the work **so that** I would not be burdened.

Provided that It is used to express a conditional statement which is either a warning or requirement for the other action.

e.g. Manya will do the task **provided that** she is given sufficient time.

As though/ As if 'As if' and 'as though' are used to express an imaginary situation.

e.g. Rajeev acted **as if/as though** he had won the debate.

As well as It is used to join two nouns (persons) or phrases of the same rank just as co-ordinating conjunction 'and' does.

e.g. Pramila **as well as** Urmila are coming to visit us.

As soon as It is used to join two actions which happen one after another.

e.g. He went inside **as soon as** he saw the dog.

REVIEW EXERCISE

Objective and Subjective Questions

1. Choose the appropriate conjunction from the options to fill in the given blanks.

(i) Either you .... your sister has done it.
(a) or (b) but
(c) nor (d) and

(ii) I waited for him .... the clock struck seven.
(a) until (b) unless (c) upto (d) as

(iii) Both Veena .... Meena are beautiful.
(a) also (b) and
(c) as well as (d) but

(iv) Make hay .... the Sun shines.
(a) but (b) or (c) while (d) when

(v) Believe in your mother .... do your duty.
(a) though (b) unless (c) and (d) because

(vi) Make haste .... you will be late.
(a) but (b) lest (c) else (d) as

(vii) He finished first .... he began late.
(a) but (b) though (c) since (d) yet

(viii) He behaved .... a brave man should do.
(a) that (b) lest (c) else (d) as

(ix) We all know .... sin and sorrow go together.
(a) that (b) lest (c) else (d) as

(x) Veena will succeed .... she is working hard.
(a) but (b) till (c) since (d) unless

(xi) .... my father is sick, he goes to the office
(a) If (b) Unless (c) Yet (d) Although

(xii) The sky is .... cloudy nor bright.
(a) neither (b) unless (c) either (d) though

(xiii) We eat .... we remain healthy.

(a) as soon as
(b) so that
(c) still
(d) otherwise

(xiv) .... she saw the tiger, she shouted.

(a) So that
(b) Still
(c) As soon as
(d) As well as

(xv) Thomas worked very hard, ... he did not stand first.

(a) therefore
(b) and
(c) still
(d) so that

(xvi) She must eat .... she will become ill. So, he .... his brother are trying to get her to eat.

(a) or, or
(b) so, as well as
(c) otherwise, and
(d) as soon as, and

(xvii) The box was heavy; .... he could not lift it.

(a) still
(b) so
(c) so that
(d) therefore

(xviii) He has been ill .... he reached Mumbai.

(a) since
(b) and
(c) therefore
(d) as soon as

(xix) I am not feeling well; ...., I will come to the party.

(a) because
(b) however
(c) since
(d) unless

(xx) .... I have had my lunch, my hunger has not gone.

(a) Although
(b) Moreover
(c) Finally
(d) Already

2. In each of the following questions, a sentence is given which may or may not be correct. Select the option which is the correct form of the sentence.

(i) Although he is poor but he is honest.

(a) Although he is a poor but he is a honest.
(b) Although he is poor yet he is honest.
(c) Although he is poor, he is honest.
(d) None of the above

(ii) No sooner I step out of the house when it started raining.

(a) No sooner had I stepped out of the house than it started raining.
(b) No sooner did I step out of the house when it started raining.
(c) No sooner did I stepped out of the house than it started raining.
(d) None of the above

(iii) I had scarcely opened the door then a cool breeze rushed in.

(a) I had scarcely open the door when a cool breeze rushed in.
(b) Scarcely had I opened the door when a cool breeze rushed in.
(c) Scarcely had I open the door then a cool breeze rushed in.
(d) None of the above

(iv) Tony is not only wise but honest.

(a) Tony is not only a wise boy but an honest boy.
(b) Tony is not only a wise boy but honest boy.
(c) Tony is not only wise but also honest.
(d) None of the above

(v) I and you am to blame.

(a) I not you am to blame.
(b) I as well as you are to blame.
(c) I along with you is to blame.
(d) None of the above

(vi) Unless you do not disclose the secret, I shall not let you go.

(a) Unless you do not disclose the secret, yet I shall not let you go.
(b) Unless you disclose the secret, I shall not let you go.
(c) Unless you disclose the secret yet I shall not let you go.
(d) None of the above

(vii) She is as happy like you.

(a) She is as happy as you are
(b) She is as happy like you are.
(c) She is as happy so like you.
(d) None of the above

(viii) This horse runs as fast like the tiger.

(a) This horse runs as fast as the tiger.
(b) This horse runs as fast as like the tiger.
(c) This horse runs as fast like as the tiger.
(d) None of the above

(ix) Wait until I do not return.

(a) Wait until I return.
(b) Wait until I am not return.
(c) Wait until I not return.
(d) None of the above

(x) Both Raju as well as Ravi are intelligent boys.

(a) Both Raju and Ravi are intelligent boys.
(b) Both Raju or Ravi are intelligent boys.
(c) Both Raju as well as Ravi are intelligent.
(d) None of the above

3. Fill in the blanks with appropriate connector.

(i) Susan is very fat .... very active.
(ii) A student must obey .... he may leave.
(iii) The bridge collapsed .... it was made of stones.
(iv) He will try .... he is forced to.
(v) The old man cared for the puppy .... it were his baby.
(vi) He is cheerful .... he has worked the whole day.
(vii) Lydia likes to sing .... dance when she is happy.

(viii) You will do well .... you study hard.

(ix) The show started .... the chief guest arrived.

(x) He was rowing the boat .... I slept.

(xi) Meena can ...... read ...... write in French.

(xii) He speaks ..... fast ...... no one can understand him.

(xiii) .... you like it ...... not, you have to do it.

(xiv) .... Vicky ...... Vijay stole my purse.

(xv) You can .... go out .... stay home and get bored.

(xvi) I am going to meet .... Mrinal .... Sona.

(xvii) .... had I gone to sleep ...... the alarm rang.

(xviii) .... you want to achieve something, ... you should try.

(xix) .... had he entered his room ...... he received a call to go back.

(xx) He is ...... a great batsman .... a very experienced coach.

4. Join the following sentences using appropriate conjunctions. Rewrite the sentence in the space that follows.

(i) Ruhi is very ill. The doctors don't expect her to recover.

(ii) He walked out of the room. He slammed the door angrily.

(iii) We waited for you to arrive. You did not turn up.

(iv) I had no money. I got admission in the college.

(v) Ajay tested positive for Covid-19. He could not go to work.

(vi) Shreyansh doesn't spend his money. He doesn't invest it.

(vii) Sheila is very pretty. She is very intelligent.

(viii) I wanted to go to picnic with my friends. My father would not let me go.

(ix) Her family got her the best treatment. They could not save her.

(x) He has already delivered an excellent performance. Nobody can question his eligibility.

ANSWERS

1. (i) (a) or
(ii) (a) until
(iii) (b) and
(iv) (c) while
(v) (c) and
(vi) (c) else
(vii) (b) though
(viii) (d) as
(ix) (a) that
(x) (c) since
(xi) (d) Although
(xii) (a) neither
(xiii) (b) so that
(xiv) (c) As soon as
(xv) (c) still
(xvi) (c) otherwise, and
(xvii) (b) so
(xviii) (a) since
(xix) (b) however
(xx) (a) Although

2. (i) (c) Although he is poor, he is honest.
(ii) (a) No sooner had I stepped out of the house than it started raining.
(iii) (b) Scarcely had I opened the door when a cool breeze rushed in.
(iv) (c) Tony is not only wise but also honest.
(v) (b) I as well as you are to blame.
(vi) (b) Unless you disclose the secret, I shall not let you go.
(vii) (a) She is as happy as you are.
(viii) (a) This horse runs as fast as the tiger.
(ix) (a) Wait until I return.
(x) (a) Both Raju and Ravi are intelligent boys.

3. (i) but
(ii) or
(iii) though
(iv) if
(v) as though
(vi) though
(vii) and
(viii) if
(ix) as soon as
(x) while
(xi) both, and
(xii) so, that
(xiii) Whether, or
(xiv) Neither, nor
(xv) either, or
(xvi) both, and
(xvii) Hardly, when
(xviii) If, then
(xix) No sooner, than
(xx) not only, but also

4. (i) Ruhi is so ill that the doctors don't expect her to recover.
(ii) He walked out of the room and slammed the door angrily.
(iii) We waited for you to arrive but you did not turn up.
(iv) I had no money yet I got admission in the college.
(v) Ajay tested positive for Covid-19 so he could not go to work.
(vi) Neither does Shreyansh spend his money nor he invests it.
(vii) Not only is Sheila very pretty but she is also very intelligent.
(viii) I wanted to go to picnic with my friends but my father would not let me go.
(ix) Even though her family got her the best treatment, they could not save her.
(x) Since he has already delivered an excellent performance, nobody can question his eligibility.

Tenses

9.1 Definition of Tenses

The tense of a verb in a sentence refers to when an action takes place.

e.g.
- I **carry** a bottle. (at present)
- I **carried** a bottle. (in the past)
- I will **carry** a bottle. (in future)

9.2 Kinds of Tenses

There are three basic kinds of tenses. They are

1. **Present tense** is used to denote an action that is happening at present.

   e.g. My brother **lives** in New Delhi.

2. **Past Tense** is used to denote an action that had already been completed in the past.

   e.g. They **went** to work early in the morning.

3. **Future Tense** is used to denote an action that will or expected to occur in the future.

   e.g. We **will go** to the concert tomorrow.

Each of these tenses can further be categorised into 4 categories namely

(i) Simple (ii) Continuous
(iii) Perfect (iv) Perfect Continuous

Present Tense

Simple Present Tense

The simple present tense is used in a sentence to represent an action or event that takes place or just happened at the present time. It is also called Present Indefinite Tense.

e.g. Aditi **goes** to the park daily.

Uses of Simple Present Tense

(i) To indicate universal/scientific facts.

e.g. Two and two **makes** four.

(ii) To show habitual actions.

e.g. My aunt **goes** to temple every morning.

(iii) To indicate schedules, timetables, itineraries and specific future actions.

e.g. She **leaves** for Jaipur by next bus.

(iv) For actions happening in near future,

e.g. Gargi **leaves** for Singapore next month.

(v) When the time of action is not definite.

e.g. My mother **cooks** desserts for the gala.

Sentence Structure

Type of Sentence	*Structure*	*Example*
Affirmative	Singular Subject + V1 + s/es + Object	She lives in Delhi.
	I/Plural Subject + V1 + Object	They live in Delhi.
Negative	Singular Subject + does not + V1 + Object	She does not live in Delhi.
	I/Plural Subject + do not + V1 + Object	They do not live in Delhi.
Interrogative	Does + Singular Subject + V1 + Object?	Does she live in Delhi?
	Do+ I/Plural Subject + V1 + Object?	Do they live in Delhi?

Present Continuous Tense

The present continuous tense is used for actions which are taking place at the time of speaking.

e.g. The boys **are climbing** the mango tree.

Uses of Present Continuous Tense

(i) To describe an action that is taking place but not at the exact moment of speech,

e.g. Soni is **working** in a multinational company.

(ii) To indicate an action that is certain to occur in the near future,

e.g. We are **meeting** tomorrow at 8 p.m.

Sentence Structure

Type of Sentence	*Structure*	*Example*
Affirmative	Singular Subject + is/am + V1 + -ing + Object	She is living in Delhi.
	Plural Subject + are + V1 + -ing + Object	They are living in Delhi.
Negative	Singular Subject + is/am + not + V1 + -ing + Object	She is not living in Delhi.
	Plural Subject + are + not + V1 + -ing + Object	They are not living in Delhi.
Interrogative	Is/Am + Singular Subject + V1 + -ing + Object?	Is she living in Delhi?
	Are + Plural Subject + V1 + -ing + Object?	Are they living in Delhi?

Present Perfect

The present perfect tense is used in a sentence to denote an action that has been completed in the recent past and still has its effect in the present.

e.g. He **has written** a letter.

Uses of Present Perfect

(i) To indicate an action whose time is not known or definite,

e.g. Sashrika **has gotten** a new job offer.

(ii) To indicate a continuing state of an action.

e.g. Varsha and **I have been** friends for seven years.

(iii) To express actions that are complete,

e.g. I **have just had** my lunch.

Sentence Structure

Type of Sentence	*Structure*	*Example*
Affirmative	Singular Subject + has + V3 + Object	She has lived in Delhi.
	I/Plural Subject + have + V3 + Object	They have lived in Delhi.
Negative	Singular Subject + has + not + V3 + Object	She has not lived in Delhi.
	I/Plural Subject + have + not + V3 + Object	They have not lived in Delhi.
Interrogative	Has + Singular Subject + V3 + Object?	Has she lived in Delhi?
	Have + I/Plural Subject + V3 + Object?	Have they lived in Delhi?

Present Perfect Continuous Tense

The present perfect continuous tense is used in a sentence to indicate that an action started in the recent past and is continuing in present.

e.g. The athletes **have been practicing** for four months.

Sentence Structure

Type of Sentence	Structure	Example
Affirmative	Singular Subject + has been + V1 + -ing + Object	She has been living in Delhi.
	I/Plural Subject + have been + V1 + -ing + Object	They have been living in Delhi.
Negative	Singular Subject + has + not + been + V1 + -ing + Object	She has not been living in Delhi.
	I/Plural Subject + have + not + been + V1 + -ing + Object	They have not been living in Delhi.
Interrogative	Has + Singular Subject + been + V1 + -ing + Object?	Has she been living in Delhi?
	Have + I/Plural Subject + been + V1 + -ing + Object?	Have they been living in Delhi?

Past Tense

Simple Past Tense

The simple past tense is used to indicate an action that happened in the past.

e.g. He **went** to Jaipur yesterday.

Uses of Simple Past Tense

(i) To indicate a habitual action in the past,

e.g. She **always drank** warm water in the morning.

(ii) Past habits,

e.g. Sanjana **rode** a motocycle during college days.

Sentence Structure

Type of Sentence	Structure	Example
Affirmative	Singular/Plural Subject + V2 + Object	She lived in Delhi.
Negative	Singular/Plural Subject + did not + V1 + Object	They did not live in Delhi.
Interrogative	Did + Singular/Plural Subject + V1 + Object?	Did they live in Delhi?

Past Continuous Tense

Past continuous tense denotes those actions that are happening for a particular time in the past.

e.g. I **was sleeping** when you got home late last night.

Uses of Past Continuous Tense

(i) To indicate an action in the past that was interrupted by another action,

e.g. Meena **was going** to market when the guests arrived.

(ii) To indicate a past action which was going on over a period of time,

e.g. The farmer **was working** in the field all afternoon.

Sentence Structure

Type of Sentence	Structure	Example
Affirmative	Singular Subject + was + V1 + -ing + Object	She was living in Delhi.
	Plural Subject + were + V1 + -ing + Object	They were living in Delhi.
Negative	Singular Subject + was + not + V1 + -ing + Object	She was not living in Delhi.
	Plural Subject + were + not + V1 + -ing + Object	They were not living in Delhi.
Interrogative	Was + Singular Subject + V1 + -ing + Object?	Was she living in Delhi?
	Were + Plural Subject + V1 + -ing + Object?	Were they living in Delhi?

Past Perfect Tense

The past perfect tense states that one action took place before another action in the past.

e.g. Srishti **had gone** out when her mother arrived.

Uses of Past Perfect Tense

To indicate a past hope or intention that has not yet been realised in the present,

e.g. I **had hoped** to win the lottery this year.

Sentence Structure

Type of Sentence	Structure	Example
Affirmative	Singular/Plural Subject + had + V3 + Object	They had lived in Delhi.

Negative	Singular/Plural Subject + had + not + V3 + Object	She had not lived in Delhi.
Interrogative	Had + Singular/Plural Subject + V3 + Object?	Had they lived in Delhi?

Past Perfect Continuous Tense

Past perfect continuous tense is used to indicate an action that began in the past, continued for some time and ended in the past.

e.g. The players **had been practising** for about two hours when it started to rain.

Sentence Structure

Type of Sentence	*Structure*	*Example*
Affirmative	Singular/Plural Subject + had been + V1 + -ing + Object	She had been living in Delhi.
Negative	Singular/Plural Subject + had + not + been + V1 + -ing + Object	They had not been living in Delhi.
Interrogative	Had + Singular/Plural Subject + been + V1 + -ing + Object?	Had they been living in Delhi?

Future Tense

Simple Future Tense

The simple future tense is used to represent an action that takes place in the future.

e.g. They **will do** this work tomorrow.

Uses of Simple Future Tense

(i) To predict a future event

e.g. It **will rain** tomorrow according to the weather predictions.

(ii) To make promises / requests / refusals / offers.

e.g. I **will call** you when I come back.

(iii) To ask for suggestions or advice,

e.g. **Will** you help me with this project?

Sentence Structure

Type of Sentence	*Structure*	*Example*
Affirmative	Singular/Plural Subject + will/shall + V1 + Object	She will live in Delhi.
Negative	Singular/Plural Subject + will/shall + not + V1 + Object	They will not live in Delhi.
Interrogative	Will/Shall + Singular/ Plural Subject + V1 + Object?	Will they live in Delhi?

Future Continuous Tense

The future continuous tense is used to represent an event or action that will be happening at a particular time in the future.

e.g. She **will be** staying here till Monday.

Uses of Future Continuous Tense

(i) To indicate an event that has been planned for future,

e.g. The Director **will be** finalising the cast in August next year.

Sentence Structure

Type of Sentence	*Structure*	*Example*
Affirmative	Singular/Plural Subject + will/shall be + V1 + -ing + Object	They will be living in Delhi.
Negative	Singular/Plural Subject + will/shall not be + V1 + -ing + Object	She will not be living in Delhi.
Interrogative	Will/Shall + Singular/Plural Subject + be + V1 + -ing + Object?	Will they be living in Delhi?

Future Perfect Tense

The future perfect tense is used to denote an action that will start and be completed at a certain time in the future.

e.g. By 3 o'clock tomorrow, I **will have taken off** for Manali.

Sentence Structure

Type of Sentence	*Structure*	*Example*
Affirmative	Singular/Plural Subject + will/shall have + V3 + Object	She will have lived in Delhi.
Negative	Singular/Plural Subject + will/shall + not + have + V3 + Object	They will not have lived in Delhi.
Interrogative	Will/shall + Singular/Plural Subject + have + V3 + Object?	Will she have lived in Delhi?

Future Perfect Continuous Tense

Future perfect continuous tense is used to denote an action that will begin before a given time in the future and that will be completed at sometime in future.

e.g. By the end of the month she **will have been** working here for seven years.

Sentence Structure

Type of Sentence	*Structure*	*Example*
Affirmative	Singular/Plural Subject + will/shall have been + V1 + -ing + Object	They will have been living in Delhi.
Negative	Singular/Plural Subject + will/shall + not + have been + V1 + -ing + Object	She will not have been living in Delhi.
Interrogative	Will/Shall + Singular/Plural Subject + have been + V1 + -ing + Object?	Will they have been living in Delhi?

REVIEW EXERCISE

Objective and Subjective Questions

1. Identify the tense underlined in the given sentence.

(i) I finished the book after I had returned from college.
(a) Past perfect
(b) Present perfect continuous
(c) Past indefinite
(d) Present perfect

(ii) Probably, it will be raining when you reach Bhopal.
(a) Present continuous
(b) Past continuous
(c) Future perfect continuous
(d) Future continuous

(iii) She has been suffering from fever for two days.
(a) Past continuous
(b) Present perfect continuous
(c) Future perfect continuous
(d) Past perfect continuous

(iv) He will have rung up his wife before he arrives.
(a) Present perfect
(b) Past perfect continuous
(c) Future perfect
(d) Future perfect continuous

(v) I asked her what she was doing next Sunday.
(a) Present continuous (b) Future continuous
(c) Past continuous (d) Simple past

(vi) He will be learning his lesson.
(a) Simple future (b) Future continuous
(c) Future perfect (d) None of these

(vii) She had written a novel.
(a) Simple past (b) Past continuous
(c) Past perfect (d) None of these

(viii) When I reached the bookstore, all the copies had already been sold.
(a) Past perfect tense (b) Past indefinite tense
(c) Present perfect tense (d) Present indefinite tense

(ix) We are going to reach the destination as scheduled.
(a) Present continuous tense
(b) Future perfect continuous tense
(c) Future continuous tense
(d) Present perfect continuous tense

(x) "Her brother will walk her down the aisle."
(a) Future indefinite tense (b) Future perfect tense
(c) Present indefinite tense (d) Present perfect tense

2. Fill in the blanks with appropriate tenses.

(i) Just as in a family, it is the willing cooperation of its members that .... happiness and contentment, so is it in the larger family of the nation.
(a) brought (b) will bring
(c) brings (d) bought

(ii) The old man could not remember where he .... his money.
(a) deposits (b) is depositing
(c) had deposited (d) will deposit

(iii) Hamid .... in Mumbai for three years when his parents came to visit.
(a) has lived (b) had lived
(c) was living (d) had been living

(iv) Two years have passed since he .... here.
(a) has come (b) come
(c) came (d) had come

(v) Will those of you who have objections to this proposal .... put up your hands, please?
(a) discussed (b) being discussed
(c) having discussed (d) discussing

(vi) She had frequent toothaches. So she decided to ....
(a) remove her teeth
(b) removing her teeth
(c) have her teeth removed
(d) having her teeth removed

(vii) The mechanic .... the vehicle since this morning.
(a) repaired (b) repairing
(c) has been repairing (d) will be repairing

(viii) If I had worked here, I .... very high marks in the examination.
(a) scored (b) would score
(c) could score (d) would have scored

(ix) I got used .... on the right when I was in the U.S. for two years.
(a) driving (b) to drive
(c) to driving (d) by driving

(x) Had you told me earlier I .... the meeting.
(a) had attended
(b) have attended
(c) attended
(d) would have attended

(xi) There will be a rush for seats when the train ....
(a) will arrive (b) arrived
(c) is arriving (d) arrives

(xii) By the time I reach America, it .... morning.
(a) is (b) will be (c) must be (d) was

(xiii) She feared that she ....
(a) will fail (b) may fail
(c) might have fail (d) would fail

(xiv) I was washing my face as the insect .... quietly into the bedroom.
(a) crept (b) creeps
(c) was creeping (d) has crept

(xv) During the recent floods, two thirds of our city .... in ruins.
(a) are (b) were
(c) is (d) was

(xvi) I have .... Lakshmi for the past twelve years.
(a) know (b) knew
(c) known (d) knows

(xvii) The engineers .... this bridge since last year.
(a) have repaired (b) had repaired
(c) have been repairing (d) are repairing

(xviii) If I had helped him, he ....
(a) will not be drowned
(b) would not be drowned
(c) will not have drowned
(d) would not have drowned

(xix) The lady .... cakes burning and ran to switch off the oven.
(a) smell (b) smells
(c) smelt (d) smelling

(xx) The farmers .... their farms, if they had known that a thunderstorm was approaching.
(a) will leave (b) would leave
(c) will have left (d) would have left

3. Change the tense of the following sentences as directed without changing their meaning.

(i) Change into Simple Present Tense.
Anand was breathing Oxygen from the cylinder.
(a) Anand breathe the oxygen from cylinder.
(b) Anand breaths the oxygen from cylinder.
(c) Anand is breathing the oxygen from cylinder.
(d) Anand took a breath of oxygen from the cylinder.

(ii) Change into Simple Past Tense.
But I have had my revenge at last.
(a) But I had have my revenge at last.
(b) But I had had my revenge at last.
(c) But I had my revenge at last.
(d) But I have my revenge at last.

(iii) Change into Future Perfect Continuous Tense.
I had been working for Anil.
(a) I will have worked for Anil.
(b) I will work for Anil.
(c) I will be working for Anil.
(d) I will have been working for Anil.

(iv) Change into Past Perfect Continuous Tense.
Dingko Singh had inspired many youngsters in Manipur.
(a) Dingko Singh did inspiring many youngsters in Manipur.
(b) Dingko Singh had been inspiring many youngsters in Manipur.
(c) Dingko Singh was being inspired many youngsters in Manipur.
(d) Dingko Singh was inspiring many youngsters in Manipur.

(v) **Change into Present Continuous Tense.**

Will you train your child to be a boxer as well?

(a) Are you training your child to be a boxer as well?

(b) Were you training your child to be a boxer as well?

(c) Will you have been training your child to be a boxer as well?

(d) Are you being trained to be a boxer as well?

4. Fill in the blanks with the correct tense of the verb given in the bracket.

(i) When the burglars broke into the house, everybody .... sound sleep. (have)

(ii) The milk ..... over as she went to see the crowd passing by with loud slogans. (spill)

(iii) If Shubham ..... any mistake, he will be rewarded. (not + make)

(iv) They were watching TV when they ..... a loud bang at the door. (hear)

(v) The bus ..... the stop before we could catch it. (leave)

(vi) Rounak ...... the same song for last three days. It has become boring now. (play)

(vii) Shamal ...... after we reach home. (call)

(viii) The show ...... its one thousand episodes by next month. (complete)

(ix) Don't worry, we will be ...... the airport in time. (reach)

(x) Arman has .... sick after eating some snacks at the street side shop. (fall)

(xi) The climate of the city .... mild and pleasant most of the time. (remain)

(xii) One day he .... into a hotel in Shillong, a beautiful city in Meghalaya. (book)

(xiii) You will certainly .... rewards for what you are doing. (get)

(xiv) Do you .... the day we moved the piano upstairs? (remember)

(xv) The rain completely .... our day. (spoil)

(xvi) Akbar .... the king at the age of fifteen after the sudden death of his father. (become)

(xvii) The criminal .... the place before the police could reach. (escape)

(xviii) They .... all the arrangements before the guest's arrival. (make)

(xix) She .... her job by tomorrow evening. (complete)

(xx) Aryan .... his mother in making rangoli in the yard for last one hour. (help)

5. Change the following sentences as directed. The first one has been done for you.

(i) She will be teaching her sister. (Present Continuous)

(ii) The baby cried again. (Future Continuous)

(iii) The Indian team will score two hundred runs. (Present Perfect)

(iv) Hamid is waiting in the lobby. (Past Perfect)

(v) He will dismiss them from service for carelessness. (Past Continuous)

(vi) The police has reached there. (Future Perfect)

(vii) My mother saw the Red Fort. (Simple Future)

(viii) Those boys made noise in the library. (Present Perfect Continuous)

(ix) They will go to meet her. (Simple Past)

(x) I was listening to the radio. (Future Continuous)

(xi) The artist has finished the painting. (Past Continuous)

(xii) The car splashed through the water. (Simple Present)

(xiii) The little baby clings to his mother. (Past Perfect)

(xiv) The children will blow up these balloons. (Future Continuous)

(xv) I am travelling by bus to my office. (Present Perfect)

ANSWERS

1. (i) (a) Past perfect
(ii) (d) Future continuous
(iii) (b) Present perfect continuous
(iv) (c) Future perfect
(v) (c) Past continuous
(vi) (b) Future continuous
(vii) (c) Past perfect
(viii) (a) Past perfect tense
(ix) (a) Present continuous tense
(x) (a) Future indefinite tense

2. (i) (c) brings (ii) (c) had deposited
(iii) (d) had been living (iv) (c) came
(v) (b) being discussed
(vi) (c) have her teeth removed
(vii) (c) has been repairing
(viii) (d) would have scored
(ix) (c) to driving
(x) (d) would have attended

(xi) (d) arrives
(xii) (b) will be
(xiii) (b) may fail
(xiv) (a) crept
(xv) (d) was
(xvi) (c) known
(xvii) (c) have been repairing
(xviii) (d) would not have drowned
(xix) (c) smelt
(xx) (d) would have left

3. (i) (b) Anand breaths the oxygen from cylinder.
(ii) (c) But I had my revenge at last.
(iii) (d) I will have been working for Anil.
(iv) (b) Dingko Singh had been inspiring many youngsters in Manipur.
(v) (a) Are you training your child to be a boxer as well?

4. (i) were having (ii) spilt
(iii) does not make (iv) heard
(v) had left (vi) has been playing
(vii) will call (viii) will have completed
(ix) reaching (x) fallen
(xi) remains (xii) booked
(xiii) be getting (xiv) remember
(xv) is spoiling (xvi) became
(xvii) had escaped (xviii) will have made
(xix) will have completed
(xx) has been helping

5. (i) She is teaching his sister.
(ii) The baby will be crying again.
(iii) The Indian team has scored two hundred runs.
(iv) Hamid had waited in the lobby.
(v) He was dismissing them from service for carelessness.
(vi) The police will have reached there.
(vii) My mother will see the Red Fort.
(viii) These boys have been making noise in the library.
(ix) They went to meet her.
(x) I will be listening to the radio.
(xi) The artist was finishing the painting.
(xii) The car splashes through the water.
(xiii) The little baby clung to his mother.
(xiv) The children will be blowing up these balloons.
(xv) I have travelled by bus to my office.

CHAPTER 10 Subject–Verb Agreement

Subject-verb agreement refers to a set of rules that suggests the subject and the verb present in the sentence should agree with each other for the sentence to be grammatically correct. In other words, the verb must agree with the subject in number and person

e.g. • **Ridhi** and **Sanvika** teach underprivileged kids.
• **Rajni** works at a paper company.

In the above sentences, for plural subjects 'Ridhi and Sanvika', the plural verb 'teach' is used and for singular subject 'Rajni', the singular verb 'works' is used.

Rules Involved in Subject-Verb Agreement

(i) If the subject is singular, it takes a singular verb and if the subject is plural, it takes a plural verb.

e.g. • Rohan **wakes** up early in the morning.
• These paintings **are** magnificient.

(ii) When two or more nouns are joined by the conjunction 'and', a plural verb is used.

e.g. • The doctors and Rani **are going** to attend the seminar.
• Rita and Shyama **were** best friends in school.

(iii) When there are two subjects but they refer to one idea, a singular verb is used.

e.g. • Peanut butter and jelly **is** my favourite breakfast. (Peanut Butter and jelly refers to a single food item)

• Time and tide **waits** for none. (Time and tide refers to the passing of time)

(iv) When there is one subject in the sentence and more than one verb, all the verbs must agree with the subject.

e.g. • Tom **likes** video games and **thinks** he can set up and run a gaming centre.

• Ruhaan **likes** jelly but **hates** mint chocolate ice-cream.

(v) When two or more singular nouns are joined by 'or' or 'nor', a singular verb is used.

e.g. • A pen or a pencil **is** mandatory to be carried into the seminar.

• My aunt nor my uncle **is coming** for my birthday next month.

(vi) Two singular subjects connected by either/or and neither/nor require a singular verb.

e.g. • Either Jane or Mary **is going** to qualify for the semi finals.

• Neither Rishi nor Mona **is coming** for the party tonight.

(vii) When a singular and plural subject are connected by either/or or neither/nor, the plural subject should be placed last and a plural verb should be used.

e.g. • Neither the diary nor the pens **are** on the rack.

• Neither he nor his friends **are playing** tonight.

(viii) When the subject has two nouns or pronouns joined by connectors like as well as, with, along with, in addition to and together with, etc. the verb agrees with the first one.

e.g. • Dairy milk as well as soy milk **is** good for health.

• The minister together with the governor **is** arriving for the protest.

(ix) Uncountable nouns take a singular verb.

e.g. • The time for the inauguration of the magazine **has come**.

• Water **flows** from high to low.

(x) Collective nouns take a singular verb.

e.g. • My team **has designed** the interior of this cafe.

• A flock of sheep **was cared** for by the shepherd.

However, when the units of the collective noun are separated into groups, a plural verb is used.

e.g. • The family members **are** in disagreement about where to go for the picnic.

• The jury members **have caused** delay in the verdict for his case.

(xi) We use plural verbs with quantifiers such as both, few and many. Much takes a singular verb.

e.g. • A few students **are** already in the hall.

• Both he and I **are visiting** the campus today.

(xii) A singular verb must be used with the singular indefinite pronouns each, neither, either, anyone, everyone, no one, someone, anybody, everybody, nobody, somebody, anything, everything, nothing, and something.

e.g. • Nobody **has brought** their car.

• Each of the boys **has come** home.

(xiii) When two subjects are joined by not only....but also, the verb agrees with the subject that is closest to it.

e.g. • Not only my friends but also my mother **was excited** for my admission.

• Not only my father but my cousins also **were overjoyed** at his selection.

(xiv) Titles of books, magazines and films take singular verbs, even if they contain plural nouns.

e.g. • The Birds **is** a movie from 1963.

• Harry Potter **is** my favourite book.

(xv) Some subjects might appear plural (eg. News, Gymnastics, Physics, Statistics etc.) but are actually singular in meaning and so take a singular verb.

e.g. • Measles **is** the only childhood disease I haven't had.

• Physics **was** always my favourite subject.

(xvi) A singular verb is generally used after words denoting an amount (time, money, measurement, weight, volume).

e.g. • 100 kilograms **is** an unhealthy weight for anybody.

• Twenty miles **is** not a long distance.

REVIEW EXERCISE

Objective and Subjective Questions

1. **Complete the following sentences with a verb form that agrees with the subject.**

   (i) The aims of the course .... me willing to begin.
   (a) makes (b) were made
   (c) make (d) making

   (ii) The children of the man who works with me .... broken the window this morning.
   (a) were (b) have
   (c) had (d) has

   (iii) The men of the community .... not support the leader.
   (a) does (b) have
   (c) has (d) do

   (iv) Neither the man nor his son .... convinced of the idea.
   (a) had (b) has
   (c) was (d) have

   (v) Although every student in my class .... the schedule, one of my students always .... late to the class.
   (a) know/come (b) knows/coming
   (c) knows/comes (d) knows/coming

   (vi) All the furniture I bought .... at my home now.
   (a) are (b) was (c) is (d) were

   (vii) Mathematics .... John's favorite subject, while Civics .... Andrea's favorite subject.
   (a) is, is (b) are, was
   (c) was, Are (d) has, had

   (viii) I have to .... the conference.
   (a) attends (b) attending
   (c) attend (d) attendance

   (ix) Only when each of the committee members .... reading the instructions then can you .... them to the hall.
   (a) would finish/took (b) is finishing/be taking
   (c) finish/take (d) finishes/take

   (x) Each candidate .... fill in these forms and sign them.
   (a) are to (b) have to
   (c) has to (d) were to

   (xi) One of my close friends .... us a question that neither of us .... able to answer.
   (a) have asked/are (b) has asked/is
   (c) had asked/are (d) have asked/is

   (xii) Every student .... going to be responsible for his chapters and each student .... bring his or her homework on the exam day.
   (a) are/will (b) are/has to
   (c) is/have to (d) is/has to

   (xiii) The grandchildren of the old man whom he told me about a great deal during the journey .... students at university now.
   (a) was (b) were
   (c) is (d) are

   (xiv) A number of my friends .... riding bicycles, but neither my brother nor my sister .... a bicycle. At 4 o'clock, either my mother or father .... coming to pick me up (in a car).
   (a) love/owns/is
   (b) loves/owns/are
   (c) loves/own/is
   (d) loved/owned/were

   (xv) Finding a job where you can learn new skills .... a lot of effort. I have been looking for six months. Six months .... a long time. Not even one company that I applied to .... responded.
   (a) take/is/has
   (b) takes/are/have
   (c) taken/are/had
   (d) takes/is/has

   (xvi) The truth about those two rival companies .... going to be exposed.
   (a) was (b) is
   (c) has (d) are

   (xvii) All precautions .... taken to prevent the river from bursting its bank.
   (a) has been (b) have been
   (c) had been (d) were

   (xviii) Second-hand furniture .... here at reasonable prices.
   (a) are sold (b) were selling
   (c) has sold (d) is sold

   (xix) Something .... wrong with my car. It just refuses to start.
   (a) are (b) is
   (c) was (d) were

   (xx) Sita told them that they .... wrong.
   (a) are (b) will be (c) were (d) can

2. In each of the following questions, a sentence is given which may or may not be correct. Select the option which is the correct form of the sentence. If you think none of the options is correct, your answer is 'D'.

(i) Slow and steady win the race.
(a) Slowly and steady wins the race.
(b) Slow and steady won the race.
(c) Slow and steady wins the race.
(d) None of the above

(ii) These news were broadcasted on Radio BBC.
(a) These news were broadcast on Radio BBC.
(b) This news was broadcast on Radio BBC.
(c) This news was broadcasted on Radio BBC.
(d) None of the above

(iii) Every boy and girl were given a prize
(a) Every boy and girl were given prizes.
(b) Every boy and girl was given prizes.
(c) Every boy and girl was given a prize.
(d) None of the above

(iv) Everyone of them were clapping at the performance of the clown.
(a) Everyone of them were clapping at the performance of the clowns.
(b) Everyone of them was clapping at the performance of the clowns.
(c) Everyone of them was clapping at the performances about the clowns.
(d) None of the above

(v) Law and order are to be maintained at all costs.
(a) Law and orders are to be maintained at all costs.
(b) Law and order is to be maintained at all costs.
(c) Laws and orders are to be maintained at all costs.
(d) None of the above

(vi) Five hundred rupees are a long sum.
(a) Five hundred rupee is a long sum.
(b) Five hundred rupee is a big sum.
(c) Five hundred rupees is a big sum.
(d) None of the above

(vii) Mohit not his friends are to blame.
(a) Mohit not his friends, is to blame.
(b) Mohit not his friend are to blame.
(c) Mohit not his friends is on to blame.
(d) None of the above

(viii) I as well as you was to blame.
(a) I as well as you is to blame.
(b) I as well as you are to blame.
(c) I as well as you am to blame.
(d) None of the above

(ix) You did not do so nor he did.
(a) You did not do so he nor did.
(b) You did not do so nor did he.
(c) You did not do so he did nor.
(d) None of the above

(x) Hardly I had opened the window when a stream of cool breeze started rushing in.
(a) Hardly I had opened the window then ....
(b) Hardly had I opened the window when ....
(c) Hardly had I opened the window then ....
(d) None of the above

3. Identify the sentence that follows the rules of Subject-Verb Agreement.

(i) (a) One of the state in which Satyagraha were offered was Rajkot, where he has spent his youth.
(b) The average age at which people begins to need eye-glasses are increasing.
(c) The increase in consumption is directly proportional to the increase in income.
(d) The government have many new schemes for people who want to start businesses in rural areas.

(ii) (a) A bouquet of flowers are required for the event.
(b) The Prime Minister, together with his wife, greet the press cordially.
(c) Everything work fine if it's done correctly.
(d) A mere amount of thousand rupees is all that he wants.

(iii) (a) Five years ago today, I am sitting in a small Japanese car, driving across Poland towards Berlin.
(b) You cannot forbid him to leave.
(c) 20 kms are not a great distance in these days of fast moving vehicles.
(d) But in all this cases conversion from scale are well-formulated.

(iv) (a) The doctoral student and the committee members writes every day.
(b) The members of the choir are very happy with the performance.
(c) The staff has gone their separate ways for the holidays.
(d) Diabetes affect many people around the world.

(v) (a) This singer, along with a few others, plays the harmonica on stage.
(b) Every one of the shirts have a green collar.
(c) Either Cassie or Marie pay the employees this afternoon.
(d) The president or the vice president are speaking today.

4. Identify the sentence that does not follow the rules of Subject-Verb Agreement.

(i) (a) How are the employees enjoying the new building?
(b) A bouquet of yellow roses lend color and fragrance to the room.
(c) The focus of the interviews was nine purposively selected participants.
(d) Locally produced goods have the advantage of shorter supply chains.

(ii) (a) My roommate stays in his bedroom from morning to night.
(b) The students or the teacher has to inform the principal.
(c) Either blue or green works for the wallpaper color.
(d) One of the world's leading scientists still have trouble speaking in public.

(iii) (a) The politician, along with the newsmen, are expected shortly.
(b) My aunt or my uncle is arriving by train today.
(c) Neither the serving bowl nor the plates go on that shelf.
(d) I, my dad, and my step-mom are going to the movies.

(iv) (a) The doctoral student and the committee members write every day.
(b) Interviews are one way to collect data and allow researchers to gain an in-depth understanding of participants.
(c) The chairperson or the CEO approves the proposal before proceeding.
(d) The information obtained from the business owners were relevant to include in the study.

(v) (a) The committee participates in various volunteer activities in their private lives.
(b) Locally produced goods has the advantage of shorter supply chains.
(c) The proceeds from the sale go to support the homeless population in the city.
(d) Strategies that the teacher uses to encourage classroom participation include using small groups and clarifying expectation.

5. Fill in the banks appropriately with correct verb.

(i) Each of the Girl Scouts .... a community project.
(ii) Everyone selected to serve on this jury .... to be willing to give up a lot of time.
(iii) Shivani Wangu together with her teammates, ... a formidable opponent on the cricket ground.
(iv) He seems to forget that there .... things to be done before he can graduate.
(v) Some of the grain .... to be contaminated.
(vi) A high percentage of the population .... voting for the new school.
(vii) Neither of the two boys .... done it.
(viii) Two hundred rupees .... a large amount fifty years ago.
(ix) The mother and not her children .... been arrested for committing the theft.
(x) Either he or you .... do the work.
(xi) The news .... by him.
(xii) The frogs at the cottage .... very loudly.
(xiii) Many a girl ....
(xiv) The man with the roses .... like your brother.
(xv) The football players .... five kilometres every day.
(xvi) That red-haired lady in the fur hat ...... across the street.
(xvii) Each of the girls .... good on stage.
(xviii) Everybody .... asked to remain quiet.
(xix) Neither of the men .... here yet.
(xx) Nobody in the class .... the answer.

6. Rewrite the sentences after correcting the sentences which have errors. If no error is present, write 'no error'.

(i) The members of the jury is in disagreement over the verdict.
(ii) Here are the proof that you wanted.
(iii) Something about this book are very special.
(iv) Not only do Vikas speak fluently, but he can also speak multiple languages.
(v) The album of *The Fault in Our Stars* are beautiful.
(vi) Much of my time get occupied by work.
(vii) Education are a fundamental right in India.
(viii) Vishnu says he don't want the car, but it seem like he does.
(ix) The concepts of physics together with the application of mathematics makes sums easier.
(x) The engineer and his associates were going to the canteen.
(xi) Olympics have included gymnastics in its list.
(xii) There has been many cases of Covid-19 till date.
(xiii) The committee have made its decision about the new park construction.
(xiv) The band members along with their lead singer is going to Kurukshetra Music Festival tomorrow.
(xv) A centennial are a long time to revoke regressive laws.

ANSWERS

1. (i) (c) make (ii) (b) have
(iii) (d) do (iv) (c) was
(v) (c) knows/comes (vi) (c) is
(vii) (a) is, is (viii) (c) attend
(ix) (d) finishes/take (x) (c) has to
(xi) (b) has asked/is (xii) (d) is/has to
(xiii) (b) were (xiv) (a) love/owns/is
(xv) (d) takes/is/has (xvi) (b) is
(xvii) (b) have been (xviii) (d) is sold
(xix) (b) is (xx) (c) were

2. (i) (c) Slow and steady wins the race.
(ii) (b) This news was broadcast on Radio BBC.
(iii) (c) Every boy and girl was given a prize.
(iv) (b) Everyone of them was clapping at the performance of the clowns.
(v) (b) Law and order is to be maintained at all costs.
(vi) (c) Five hundred rupees is a big sum.
(vii) (a) Mohit not his friends, is to blame.
(viii) (b) I as well as you are to blame.
(ix) (b) You did not do so nor did he.
(x) (b) Hardly had I opened the window when ....

3. (i) (c) The increase in consumption is directly proportional to the increase in income.
(ii) (d) A mere amount of thousand rupees is all that he wants.
(iii) (b) You cannot forbid him to leave.
(iv) (b) The member of the choir are very happy with the performance.
(v) (a) This singer, along with a few others, plays the harmonica on stage.

4. (i) (b) A bouquet of yellow roses lend color and fragrance to the room.
(ii) (d) One of the world's leading scientists still have trouble speaking in public.
(iii) (a) The politician, along with the newsmen, are expected shortly.
(iv) (d) The information obtained from the business owners were relevant to include in the study.
(v) (b) Locally produced goods has the advantage of shorter supply chains.

5. (i) does (ii) has
(iii) presented (iv) are
(v) appears (vi) is
(vii) has (viii) was
(ix) has (x) has to
(xi) was brought (xii) croak
(xiii) has seen this movie (xiv) looks
(xv) run (xvi) lives
(xvii) looks (xviii) was
(xix) is (xx) has

6. (i) The members of the jury **are** in disagreement over the verdict.
(ii) Here **is** the proof that you wanted.
(iii) Something about this book **is** very special.
(iv) Not only **does** Vikas speak fluently, but he can also speak multiple languages.
(v) The album of *The Fault in Our Stars* **is** beautiful.
(vi) Much of my time **gets** occupied by work.
(vii) Education **is** a fundamental right in India.
(viii) Vishnu says he **doesn't** want the car, but it seems like he does.
(ix) The concepts of physics together with the application of mathematics **make** sums easier.
(x) No error
(xi) Olympics **has** included gymnastics in its list.
(xii) There **have** been many cases of Covid-19 till date.
(xiii) The committee **has** made its decision about the new park construction.
(xiv) The band members along with their lead singer **are** going to Kurukshetra Music Festival tomorrow.
(xv) A centennial **is** a long time to revoke regressive laws.

Modals

11.1 Definition of Modal

Modals are verbs that are used to express the mood or attitude of the speaker. They are also called modal auxiliaries. They are used to convey certain ideas such as permission, duty, warning, obligation, promise, request etc.

e.g. • I **can** arrange your party tomorrow.
• **Will** you see Aanya when you go to Chennai?

Uses of Modals

Will

(i) To show promise, willingness, determination

e.g. • I **will** give you a gift of your choice. (promise)
• We **will** help you in the best possible way. (willingness)
• I **will** change the system of our organisation. (determination)

(ii) To express request, assumption, characteristic or habit

e.g. • **Will** you please help me? (request)
• She **will** be in the school during school hours. (assumption)
• The lion **will** kill the other animals. (characteristic/habit)

Would (Past form of 'Will')

(i) To express past habit

e.g. He **would** drink a cup of coffee in the morning.

(ii) To make a request

e.g. **Would** you please give me your bike?

(iii) To express wish

e.g. I wish she **would** be healthy.

Shall

(i) To ask for suggestion, request, advice with the first person (I, We) in the interrogative sentence

e.g. • **Shall** I proceed with this project? (advice)
• **Shall** I have a cup of coffee from your shop? (request)
• **Shall** we open a new shop? (suggestion)

(ii) In the second and third person to indicate threat, warning, command, promise, assurance and determination

e.g. • If you sit with bad boys, you **shall** be punished. (threat)
• You **shall** go now. (command)
• She **shall** get a bicycle. (promise)

Should (Past form of 'shall')

(i) To express duty or obligation

e.g. • I **should** help my friends. (duty)
• You **should** not be lazy. (obligation)

(ii) To give or take advice or suggestion

e.g. We should obey our elders.

Can

(i) To express an ability, capability, capacity or power

e.g. • I **can** lift 60 kg. (Ability)
• She **can** pass the MBA examination. (Capability)
• **Can** you understand the English language? (Capacity)
• I **can** grant you leave. (Power)

(ii) To show possibility

e.g. She **can** fall on the road as it is slippery.

(iii) To take or give permission

e.g. **Can** I sit here?

Could (Past form of 'can')

(i) To express ability/talent in the past

e.g. They **could** win the game a few years back.

(ii) To express polite request

e.g. **Could** I have your pen?

May

(i) To show possibility or probability

e.g. The inspector **may** attend the school today.

(ii) To give or take permission

e.g. **May** I come in?

(iii) To wish or pray

e.g. **May** you get well soon!

(iv) To show a purpose

e.g. He is working hard so that he **may** win.

Might (Past form of 'may')

(i) To express less possibility

e.g. He **might** help us.

(ii) For permission

e.g. **Might** I begin to reveal the truth?

(iii) To express a guess

e.g. That **might** be Rohit.

Must

(i) To express necessity or obligation

e.g. You **must** take part in the competition.

(ii) To indicate assumption or conclusion

e.g. She **must** be here in the evening.

(iii) In case of prohibition

e.g. You **must** not bunk school.

Ought to

(i) To express moral obligation or duty

e.g. You **ought to** respect your parents.

(ii) To give advice

e.g. You **ought to** study hard to achieve success.

Dare

(i) It is generally used in negative and interrogative sense.

e.g.
- Rani **dare** not cross me again. (Negative)
- Does he **dare** to oppose you?

(ii) It is used at places where we are to use courage.

e.g. **Dare** I cross my dad?

Used to

It is used to express past habits and existence.

e.g.
- Aadar **used to** be fond of the Beatles. (Past habit)
- I **used to** study with my cousin sister. (Existence)

REVIEW EXERCISE

Objective and Subjective Questions

1. Choose the correct option and fill the blanks with appropriate modal verb.

(i) .... I have more cheese on my sandwich?

(a) Must (b) Could
(c) Would (d) Have to

(ii) You .... eat more vegetables.

(a) should (b) might
(c) would (d) shall

(ii) I .... like to buy the same television for my house.

(a) could (b) must
(c) would (d) have to

(iv) .... I have coffee please?

(a) Must (b) Have to
(c) May (d) Would

(v) You .... smoke near children.

(a) have to
(b) may
(c) shouldn't
(d) would not

(vi) The passengers .... wear their seat belts at all times.

(a) could (b) must
(c) will (d) may

(vii) We .... go to the concert if the rain stops. We don't know for sure.

(a) mustn't (b) might
(c) have to (d) wouldn't

(viii) I .... do ice skating very well.

(a) can (b) may
(c) must (d) should

(ix) Our team .... easily defeat them.

(a) can (b) may
(c) has to (d) needs to

(x) The rock band .... play very well last year. Now they are much better.

(a) must (b) couldn't
(c) can (d) should

(xi) You .... be punctual.

(a) should (b) would
(c) shall (d) may

(xii) .... he live long!

(a) May (b) Might
(c) Will (d) Can

(xiii) Tom's teacher says that he .... play the violin pretty well in half a year.

(a) will (b) ought to
(c) will be able to (d) will have to

(xiv) Swimming in the sea in such rough conditions .... be difficult.

(a) must (b) shall
(c) has to (d) need to

(xv) I am sure Nira .... explain everything when she returns.

(a) will be able to (b) need to
(c) must (d) could have to

(xvi) My dog .... jump very high when he was younger.

(a) could (b) could have
(c) might (d) should

(xvii) One of the boys .... get out of the cave to call the villagers for help.

(a) could (b) had to
(c) was able to (d) have to

(xviii) Several criminals .... have managed to escape into the woods.

(a) should (b) might
(c) had to (d) ought to

(xix) I wanted to talk to you yesterday but .... get free time.

(a) can (b) couldn't
(c) wouldn't (d) might not

(xx) Anyone .... make a mistake.

(a) must (b) can
(c) should (d) has to

2. What does the underlined modal in the following sentences suggest?

(i) I promise that I will never repeat this mistake in future.

(a) Possibility (b) Promise
(c) Future (d) Voluntary action

(ii) I shall never forget the way you helped me.

(a) Possibility (b) Promise
(c) Future (d) Voluntary action

(iii) By now, they should have reached London.

(a) Possibility (b) Expectation
(c) Future (d) Voluntary action

(iv) You ought to stop drinking.

(a) Possibility (b) Suggestion
(c) Future (d) Voluntary action

(v) This must be the right ingredient for her dish!

(a) Possibility (b) Predestination
(c) Certainty (d) Voluntary action

3. Fill in the blank with the correct modal or semi-modal.

(i) Sheetal .... go for a run everyday before the Covid-19 pandemic.

(ii) You .... take your music lessons more seriously if you intend to be a singer.

(iii) Vimya asked her mother if she .... go on a trip with her cousins.

(iv) I .... not have been more careful with using the heater.

(v) You .... not stress over your marks if you have prepared honestly.

(vi) You .... be very pleased with yourself for achieving first rank in class.

(vii) .... you like some help?

(viii) It .... rain this Sunday.

(ix) If he wants, he .... borrow my car.

(x) I .... be submitting my resignation tomorrow.

(xi) Don't worry we, ... find a way.

(xii) When I was in Delhi I, ... walk to college.

(xiii) You .... eat green vegetables.

(xiv) .... I meddle with the laws of nature?

(xv) Vaccination .... be free for everyone.

4. Read the following sentences containing modals and state the function of the modal in the sentence. One has been done for you.

(i) Rimi can dance very well.

(ii) He might leave on Monday.

(iii) I shall be happy to meet you.

(iv) Would you please help me carry these things?

(v) When I was young, I could walk for hours.

(vi) You may go to the sleepover at your friend's house.

(vii) Kimmy might come for lunch.

(viii) You must respect your elders.

(ix) I will win the competition.

(x) My family can go to Vrindavan tomorrow.

5. In the given sentences, the modal verb may be correctly or incorrectly used. Underline the modal and write the correct modal in the given blank. If the modal is correctly used, write 'correct' in the blank.

(i) I might play the piano when I was younger.

(ii) It shall rain later so take an umbrella while going out.

(iii) You could get a haircut.

(iv) I will know my result tomorrow.

(v) We could visit the theatre next week.

(vi) Should you shut the window, please?

(vii) He must learn Japanese.

(viii) I wondered whether the news can be true.

(ix) The Principal will arrive here in an hour.

(x) The prices might fall down a little.

ANSWERS

1. (i) (b) Could (ii) (a) should (iii) (c) would (iv) (c) May (v) (c) shouldn't (vi) (b) must (vii) (b) might (viii) (a) can (ix) (a) can (x) (b) couldn't (xi) (a) should (xii) (a) May (xiii) (c) will be able to (xiv) (a) must (xv) (a) will be able to (xvi) (a) could (xvii) (a) could (xviii) (b) might (xix) (b) couldn't (xx) (b) can

2. (i) (b) Promise (ii) (b) Promise (iii) (b) Expectation (iv) (b) Suggestion (v) (c) Certainty

3. (i) used to (ii) should (iii) could (iv) could (v) should (vi) must (vii) Would (viii) might (ix) can (x) will (xi) will (xii) used to (xiii) ought to (xiv) Dare (xv) should

4. (i) Can ability
(ii) Might possibility
(iii) Shall expressing future action
(iv) Would ask a polite question
(v) Could ability in the past
(vi) May permission
(vii) Might possibility
(viii) Must obligation
(ix) Will expressing future event
(x) Can possibility

5. (i) Might–could (ii) Shall–might (iii) Could–should (iv) Will–correct (v) Could–will (vi) Should–can (vii) Must–should (viii) Can–might (ix) Will–correct (x) Might–correct

Determiners

12.1 Definition of Determiners

Determiners are words that can be used with nouns to modify their meaning. They function like adjectives and are also called 'fixing words'.

e.g. • It is **a** German Shepherd.
• **Some** people don't like getting wet in rain.

12.2 Kinds of Determiners

Determiner can be classified into

- Articles
- Demonstrative Adjectives
- Possessive Adjectives
- Distributive Adjectives
- Quantifiers

Note It You have already studied Demonstrative, Possessive and Distributive Adjectives in Ch-4 Adjectives.

Articles

An Article is a word that is used to modify a noun. It is used to point out the noun we are referring to in a sentence. It also tells us whether we are referring to a noun in general or a specific.

We know that there are only three articles

(i) A (ii) An (iii) The

These three articles can be categorised into two types

Definite and Indefinite articles.

(i) **Indefinite Articles** The words 'A' and 'An' are Indefinite articles. They do not refer to any specific or unique noun. They make the noun general and are used only with singular nouns.

e.g. • Can you please fill **a** glass of water for me?
• I have left the key in **an** envelope.

Use of Article 'A' and 'An'

(a) The article A is used with words that start with a consonant sound.

e.g. • I found **a** kitten in the garden.
• He wants to become **a** doctor.

However, in some cases, the article 'A' is used before words that start with a vowel letter. This is so because the words begin with a consonant sound.

e.g. • She is **a European.** (European starts with the sound of 'y')
• Please give me **a one-rupee note**. (One- rupee note starts with the sound of 'w')
• I want to go to **a university**. (University starts with the sound of 'y')

(b) The article 'An' is used with words that start with a vowel sound.

e.g. • My mother gave me **an** orange to eat.
• I should carry **an** umbrella as it is going to rain.

However, in some cases, the article 'An' is used before words that start with a consonant letter. This is so because the consonant letter is silent and the word starts with a vowel sound.

e.g. • Vishal will be late by **an hour**.
• My father is **an honest** man.

In these sentences, the sound of 'h' is silent. The words start with the sound of 'o'.

(ii) **Definite Article** 'The' is called the definite article. It is used to denote a specific noun or a noun that has already been referred to.

e.g. • I found my sister's pet puppy in **the** neighbour's garden.
• **The** United Nations is an organisation that aims to maintain global peace.

Use Article of 'The'

(i) Before a noun that has already been referred to before.

e.g. • Anima has adopted a dog. **The** dog is brown in colour.

(ii) When a singular noun represents a whole class.

e.g. • **The** horse is a royal animal.

(iii) Some proper nouns, such as

Proper Nouns	Examples
Name of oceans and seas	the Indian ocean, the Mediterranean sea
Name of rivers	the Ganga, the Thames
Name of canals	the Suez canal,
Name of deserts	the Thar desert, the Sahara desert
Name of groups of Islands	the West Indies,
Name of mountain ranges	the Himalayas, the Appalachians
Name of some countries	the Netherlands, the United States of America
Name of some famous monuments	the Qutub Minar, the India Gate
Name of holy and classical books	the Quran, the Puranas
Name of newspapers	The Times of India, The Hindustan Times
Name of organisations	the United Nations, the Red Cross Society
Name of geographical areas	the Middle East, the West Pacific
Name of unique things	the Sun, the Moon, the Earth
Name of Newspaper	The Hindu, The Deccan Herrald

(iv) Before the superlative degree of adjectives.

e.g. He is **the** best calligrapher in the class.

(v) Before the people mentioned by their professions.

e.g. **The** engineers are obliged to wear the yellow hat while on field.

(vi) With ordinal numbers (first, second, third and so on).

e.g. Armstrong was **the** first man to step on the moon.

(vii) Before the name of some musical instruments.

e.g. Bhavya plays **the** flute.

(viii) Names of decades, centuries and historic periods take the definite article.

e.g. **The** 1990s was a time of digital revolution.

(ix) With adjectives like poor, rich, elderly, unemployed, etc. to talk about groups of people.

e.g. Life is very easy for **the** rich.

Omission of Articles

Articles are not used

(i) Before plural countable nouns used in a general sense.

e.g. I do believe that **children** are the gift of god.

(ii) Before names of meals, diseases, months, festivals, etc.

e.g. • "**Breakfast** is ready," my mother said to my brother and me.
- A person suffering from **typhoid** has high fever.
- The festival of **Diwali** usually falls in the month of **October**.

(iii) Before languages.

e.g. My favourite language is **Russian** even though **French** is my mother tongue.

(iv) Before names of relations.

e.g. **Mother** is going to the market to buy groceries.

(v) Before proper nouns (like name of a person, name of a company etc.) except those mentioned in the list above.

e.g. **India** lies in the Southern part of Asia.

(vi) Before material nouns.

e.g. My sister bought a bracelet made of **gold**.

Quantifiers

A quantifier is a word or phrase which is used before a noun to indicate the amount or quantity. Types of quantifiers are as follows

(i) **Definite** One, two, hundred, ..., first, second, both, etc.

(ii) **Indefinite** Some, many, much, enough, few, a few, all, little, a little, several, most, etc.

(iii) **Difference** Another, other.

(iv) **Comparative** More, less, fewer.

Usage of quantifiers is as follows

Use of Little, a Little and the Little

(i) Little means 'hardly any' or the lack of something.

e.g. • We have **little** money right now.

(ii) A little signifies that even though it is not much, there is enough of an item.

e.g. • There's **a little** ice-cream left; who will eat it?

(iii) The little means 'not much but all that is'.

e.g. • The cat has knocked over **the little** milk in the jug.

Note it Both 'Little' and 'A little' mean the same thing. However, they are used in different contexts. 'Little' has negative implications while 'A little' has positive implications.

Use of Few, A Few and the Few

'Few', 'a few' and 'the few' have similar meanings as 'little', 'a little' and 'the little'. However, they are generally used with countable nouns.

e.g. • I have only **few** friends.
• **A few** suggestions wouldn't hurt you.
• There are refreshments for **the few** guests that stayed behind.

Use of Much and Many

We use **much** with singular uncountable nouns and **many** with plural nouns.

e.g. • I haven't got **much** change; I've only got a hundred rupee note.
• Are there **many** campsites near your place?

Uses of Some and Any

The words **some** and **any** are used with both countable and uncountable nouns when the exact number or amount of something is not known. The only difference between them is that 'Some' has a positive implication whereas 'any' has a negative implication.

e.g. • So you have **some** time for the meeting?
• She can come **any** minute now.

Use of More, Less and Fewer

(i) We use **more** or **less** before singular uncountable nouns by adding 'than' after it to indicate an additional or lesser quantity of something.

e.g. • I do **more** work than Suresh.
• Satish does **less** work than me.

(ii) We use **fewer** before plural countable nouns to refer to a group of things smaller than another.

e.g. **Fewer** students succeeded in passing than last year.

Use of Most and Several

(i) We usually use **most** with plural uncountable nouns to refer to a large quantity or number.

e.g. **Most** people here cannot be trusted.

(ii) We usually use **several** with plural nouns to refer to a number which is not very large

e.g. **Several** people were crushed in the stampede.

Use of Another and Other

We use **another** only with singular countable nouns, whereas **other** can be used with singular countable, plural countable or uncountable nouns.

e.g. • Bring me **another** knife, as this one is blunt.
• I would prefer the **other** house.

REVIEW EXERCISE

Objective and Subjective Questions

1. Fill in the given blanks with the correct determiner.

(i) Despite the material donations from the local shops, the school still needs .... more equipments.

(a) a few (b) many
(c) some (d) no

(ii) A colleague of mine has lent us .... holiday cottage for a week.

(a) him (b) his (c) its (d) them

(iii) I've seen .... of his work to know that he's ready for a promotion.

(a) a number (b) both
(c) a few (d) enough

(iv) .... of the area managers is going to report his total sales to head office .... two weeks.

(a) Each/every
(b) Both/another
(c) Any/all
(d) Every/several

(v) .... sheep escaped from Farmer Gile's field last week and so far, only .... of them has been found.

(a) Several/one (b) Many/a few
(c) More/each (d) Some/enough

(vi) Thank you for letting me know about this birthday wish of ....

(a) him (b) me
(c) your (d) his

(vii) Upon graduation, ... student is sent an information pack giving useful tips and information about finding suitable employment.

(a) all (b) each
(c) none (d) a few

(viii) Although we've already had .... volunteers, we're still looking for .... to help out at the school fete.

(a) plenty of/much
(b) several/much more
(c) a number of/a few more
(d) a lot of/a little more

(ix) If people showed .... concern for the environment, there wouldn't be .... pollution in the world.

(a) much/too many (b) enough/none
(c) less/several of (d) more/so much

(x) We had .... other choice apart from deciding to cease trading, or we would have gone bankrupt.

(a) some (b) no
(c) many (d) each

(xi) .... who enjoys jazz music will enjoy this festival, tickets for which can be bought at .... good music shop.

(a) Nobody/some (b) Anyone/several
(c) Everybody/all (d) Somebody/both

(xii) Slimming bars claim to provide .... the vitamins and minerals the body needs, but eating them cannot be as healthy as a meal containing plenty of fruit and vegetables, which can also supply .... nutrients required by the body.

(a) all/other (b) plenty of/another
(c) every/any (d) both/each

(xiii) .... bus we were travelling on stopped suddenly because .... tree had fallen across the road.

(a) A/the (b) The/-
(c) The/the (d) The/a

(xiv) When I woke up this morning, there was .... heavy dew covering .... long green summer grass in our garden.

(a) the/a (b) -/the
(c) some/a (d) the/-

(xv) Public transport is getting more and more unbearable in this city because there are .... people, but not .... vehicles.

(a) many more/much
(b) several/a little
(c) plenty of/a few
(d) too many/enough

(xvi) Last month we went to see .... National book fair with our teacher.

(a) some (b) the
(c) a (d) an

(xvii) We bought .... books.

(a) much (b) more
(c) any (d) many

(xviii) .... of them were story books, while the others were of General Knowledge.

(a) Much (b) Any
(c) Some (d) The little

(xix) I need a pencil. Please give me ....

(a) any (b) one
(c) some (d) a

(xx) Though they were sent last week .... of the parcels have not arrived yet.

(a) none (b) little (c) all (d) most

2. From the given options, choose the sentence that uses determiners correctly.

(i) (a) He was a first man to walk on the Moon.
(b) We still have few minutes left before the class gets over.
(c) We have little money right now; we should go out for dinner another day.
(d) I haven't got a lot of change; I've only got a hundred rupee note.

(ii) (a) These problem is much more difficult than that yet we have much less time to solve it.
(b) According to the studies, dolphins, whales and many other sea creatures use highly sophisticated navigation systems.
(c) We saw many of birds in the bird sanctuary and enjoyed the day thoroughly.
(d) I spoke to Alok, Shikha, Vishal and a few another friends.

(iii) (a) Today, the number of people who enjoy winter sports is bigger than that of twenty years ago.
(b) The dietary habits of a child often have most to do with that child's eating habits as an adult.
(c) In the United States of America, there are adult literacy classes for workers, much of whom never graduated from high school.
(d) In the first many months of life, an infant learns how to lift its head, how to smile and how to recognise its parents.

(iv) (a) After many terms in Congress, Shirley Chisholm became an important United States politician.
(b) Although the language learning abilities of apes have surprised much scientists.
(c) One of the students of the class writes the date on a black board every day.
(d) The Alps is the highest mountain range system in Europe.

(v) (a) There have been a few isolated incidents of violence, but majority of World Cup supporters have been well-behaved.
(b) Americans plays produced during the 19th century were mostly sensational melodrama and therefore of many literary importance.
(c) The different peoples in Africa every have its own myths about the creation of the world.
(d) Pasta, which literally means dough in Italian, is the Italian food now popular, in such forms as spaghetti, macaroni and ravioli all over the world.

3. From the given options, choose the sentence that uses determiners incorrectly.

(i) (a) I knew that his wife wasn't a good cook, so I doubted that she had cooked all the dishes she served us.
(b) Marketing research is a expensive undertaking and its costs are built into the prices of products.
(c) I listened to some news on the radio about the man arrested for embezzlement last Tuesday.
(d) I was thinking of buying a pregnancy dress myself, but I was given one as a present by my husband.

(ii) (a) One of the few things the warring factions have in common is their opposition to the US.
(b) A very close relative of me has just arrived from a trip during which he experienced many interesting adventures.
(c) American Indians often sold their land to white people or gave it away without realising that it would no longer be theirs.
(d) For the potable water system onboard the ship there are a number of standards, like the first one, that it be potable.

(iii) (a) Monkeys are famous for their eagerness to approach people and playfully interact with them especially in the circus.
(b) According to the schedule, the teachers have to come together every other week to discuss the problems of their students.
(c) High cholesterol is one of the three major risk factors for heart disease. Cigarette smoking and high blood pressure are another two.
(d) Despite the huge budget deficit, a great quantity of local government spending is directed towards the private sector.

(iv) (a) Laura has three pets, the one which is a Siamese cat that has just given birth to twin kittens and the others are male dogs that frequently fight.
(b) Every question in the test was checked in detail before given to the students and any including mistakes or causing ambiguity were corrected by the teachers.
(c) While there are many formidable women on the screen today, very few of them have involved themselves in the method school as part of their training.
(d) Astronomers suggest that there are two separate universes, one made out of matter, our own and each made out of antimatter.

(v) (a) With those scrutinising the election saying they found a little widespread evidence of vote-rigging, there would seem to be many chance of the result being reversed.
(b) How does one go about making sure adults discharge responsibilities when they are themselves unaware of what they can do?
(c) Rescue efforts resumed in Beichuan after the entire city was evacuated amid fears that it could be engulfed by a river bursting its banks.
(d) Both the Alliance elements in Afghanistan and the Shiite factions in Iraq had been recipients of Iranian support before the US interested itself in their causes.

4. Fill in the blanks of the sentences with the correct determiner.

(i) Harish and Neha settled abroad to give .... children a different lifestyle.
(ii) We are reaping the benefits of the labour of .... earlier generation.
(iii) Her brother had .... work.
(iv) Do you have .... idea of the trouble you have caused us?
(v) Shouldn't you do something about .... man standing near .... door?
(vi) Tomorrow morning the vehicle shall be at .... door.
(vii) I was wondering if I could get .... advance on the next month's salary?
(viii) How are so .... people asleep at this hour of the day?
(ix) .... rules make no sense to me.
(x) .... year has gone by since I last met him.
(xi) Her voice was shaking .... on the phone.
(xii) .... man walking on the Earth is mortal.
(xiii) .... banana seems to be fresh anymore.
(xiv) Could you please keep the guests in the living room for .... minutes?
(xv) The waffles are worth .... hundred rupees or more, I am not sure.
(xvi) She is going to the business convention to talk about .... start-up.
(xvii) It is a work of .... month.
(xviii) There are .... countries in the world where population is not growing fast.
(xix) .... money he had, was spent on his education.
(x) She showed .... concern for her step-daughter.

5. **Rewrite the sentences after rectifying the errors present in them. The errors can be of omission or wrong usage of determiners.**

(i) The letters that came from India did not brighten me neither.

(ii) Little years before, China had lost a war against England and France.

(iii) The three sisters sat on her heels, waiting for their brother to bring them little milk.

(iv) Steve Jobs is the founder of the Apple.

(v) These country is my homeland.

(vi) He wished he could have bought one of that fish for his family.

(vii) He looked for it eagerly, perhaps little anxiously, but saw only people, buildings and traffic, but heard only honking of horns.

(viii) People pushed past with there market bags, handbags and briefcases, grumbling loudly.

(ix) A sand was washed clean by last night's tide and no one had walked on it except the birds that fished along an coast.

(x) Iron is a most useful element.

(xi) His either novel, short story and essay has been read and enjoyed for decades.

(xii) I thought I could do it all following the plan that came to mine head on the spot.

(xiii) We went to Sahara Desert last year.

(xiv) Much debates have arisen from misunderstanding.

(xv) Either you nor he is suitable for a leadership position.

ANSWERS

1. (i) (c) some (ii) (b) his
(iii) (d) enough (iv) (a) Each/every
(v) (a) Several/one (vi) (d) his
(vii) (b) each
(viii) (c) a number of/a few more
(ix) (d) more/so much (x) (b) no
(xi) (b) Anyone/several (xii) (a) all/other
(xiii) (d) The/a (xiv) (b) -/the
(xv) (d) too many/enough
(xvi) (b) the
(xvii) (d) many
(xviii) (c) Some
(xix) (b) one
(xx) (d) most

2. (i) (c) We have little money right now; we should go out for dinner another day.
(ii) (b) According to the studies, dolphins, whales and many other sea creatures use highly sophisticated navigation systems.
(iii) (a) Today the number of people who enjoy winter sports is bigger than that of twenty years ago.
(iv) (d) The Alps is the highest mountain range system in Europe.
(v) (a) There have been a few isolated incidents of violence, but majority of World Cup supporters have been well-behaved.

3. (i) (a) I knew that his wife wasn't a good cook, so I doubted that she had cooked all the dishes she served us.
(ii) (b) A very close relative of me has just arrived from a trip during which he experienced many interesting adventures.
(iii) (c) High cholesterol is one of the three major risk factors for heart disease. Cigarette smoking and high blood pressure are another two.
(iv) (d) Astronomers suggest that there are two separate universes, one made out of matter, our own, and each made out of antimatter.
(v) (a) With those scrutinising the election saying they found a little widespread evidence of vote rigging, there would seem to be many chance of the result being reversed.

4. (i) their (ii) the
(iii) a lot of (iv) any
(v) the, that (vi) your
(vii) an (viii) many
(ix) These (x) This
(xi) a little (xii) Every
(xiii) Neither (xiv) a few
(xv) a (xvi) her
(xvii) a (xviii) many
(xix) The little (xx) little

5. (i) The letters that came from India did not brighten me **either**.
(ii) **Few** years before, China had lost a war against England and France.
(iii) The three sisters sat on their heels, waiting for their brother to bring them **some** milk.
(iv) Steve Jobs is the founder **of Apple**.
(v) **This** country is my homeland.
(vi) He wished he could have bought one of **those** fish for his family.

(vii) He looked for it eagerly, perhaps **a little** anxiously, but saw only people, buildings and traffic, but heard only honking of horns.

(viii) People pushed past with **their** market bags, handbags and briefcases, grumbling loudly.

(ix) **Sand** was washed clean by last night's tide and no one had walked on it except the birds that fished along **the** coast.

(x) Iron is **the** most useful element.

(xi) His **every** novel, short story and essay has been read and enjoyed for decades.

(xii) I thought I could do it all following the plan that came to **my** head on the spot.

(xiii) We went to **the** Sahara Desert last year.

(xiv) **Many** debates have arisen from misunderstanding.

(xv) Either you **or** he is suitable for a leadership position.

Active and Passive Voice

13.1 Definition of Active and Passive Voice

Active Voice When the action is performed by the subject, it is called **Active Voice.**

Sentence Structure Subject + Verb + Object
e.g. He will pay the fine.

Passive Voice When the action is received by the subject, it is called **Passive Voice.**

Sentence Structure Object + Verb + Subject
e.g. The fine will be paid by him.

General Rules for Changing Active Voice into Passive Voice

1. The subject of the verb in the active voice becomes the object in the passive voice sentence.
   e.g. • **Kanika** is cleaning the house. (Active)
   The house is being cleaned by **Kanika.** (Passive)
2. The third form of the verb, (the past participle form of the verb) is used in the passive voice.
   e.g. • Kanishk **buys** a pen every week. (Active)
   A pen is **bought** by Kanishk every week. (Passive)
3. Auxiliary verb 'be' (am, is are, was, were) is added before the past participle according to the tense of the verb.
   e.g. • The postman delivered the letters on time. (Active)
   The letters **were** delivered by the postman on time. (Passive)
4. Generally, 'by' is used before the object of the passive voice sentences.
   e.g. • The teachers are attending a meeting. (Active)
   A meeting is being attended **by** the teachers. (Passive)
5. The pronouns are changed into objective case while changing into passive voice.
   e.g. • I water my plants everyday. (Active)
   My plants are watered by **me** everyday. (Passive)

Change of Person

Active Voice	Passive Voice
I	me
We	us
You	you
She	her
He	him
They	them
Any name	Name remains as it is

13.2 Rules for Change in Tenses

1. Present Tense

Simple Present Tense

Active S + V_1 + O
Passive O + am/is/are + V_3 + by + S

e.g. • She plucks flowers from the plant. (Active)
Flowers are plucked from the plant by her. (Passive)

Present Continuous Tense

Active S + am/is/are/ + V_1 + ing + O
Passive O + am/is/are + being + V_3 + by + S

e.g. • Vaibhav is making a loud noise. (Active)
A loud noise **is being made** by Vaibhav. (Passive)

Present Perfect Tense

Active S + have/has + V_3 + O
Passive O + have/has + been + V_3 + by + S

e.g. • Arpita has forgotten his name. (Active)
His name **has been forgotten** by Arpita. (Passive)

2. Past Tense

Simple Past Tense

Active S + V_2 + O
Passive O + was/were + V_3 + by + S

e.g. • Nobody believed their fake stories. (Active)
Their fake stories **were believed** by nobody. (Passive)

Past Continuous Tense

Active S + was/were + V_1 + ing + O
Passive O + was/were + being + V_3 + by + S

e.g. • She was reading a novel written by Kate Thompson. (Active)
A novel written by Kate Thompson **was being read** by her. (Passive)

Past Perfect Tense

Active S + had + V_3 + O
Passive O + had been + V_3 + by + S

e.g. • I had watched the movie earlier. (Active)
The movie **had been watched** earlier by me. (Passive)

3. Future Tense

Simple Future Tense

Active S + shall/will + V_1 + O
Passive O + shall/will + be + V_3 + by + S

e.g. • Arjit will never forgive Rinnie for her blunder. (Active)
Rinnie **will** never **be forgiven** for her blunder by Arjit. (Passive)

Future Perfect Tense

Active S + shall/will + have + V_3 + O
Passive O + shall/will + have + been + V_3 + by + S

e.g. • Our scientists will have invented a device for artificial sleep in future. (Active)
A device for artificial sleep **will have been invented** in future by our scientists. (Passive)

Passive Voice with Modal Auxiliaries

When a sentence in active voice has a modal auxiliary (can, could, may, might, etc.), the modal verb does not change its form.

e.g. • Shaurya **can** cook many international cuisines. (Active)
Many international cuisines **can be** cooked by Shaurya. (Passive)

Changing Interrogative Sentences into Passive Voice

When an interrogative sentence is changed into passive voice, the sentence remains in the question form.
Interrogative sentences are of two types

1. Questions Words (Wh)
2. 'Yes/No' Questions

1. **Questions Words (Wh)** The question words such as 'what, why, when, where, which and how' do not change and remain at the starting position of the sentence.

   e.g. • **What** did you buy? (Active)
   What was bought by you? (Passive)

Note it Remember 'Who' is converted to 'By whom' in passive voice.

   e.g. • **Who** told you about tomorrow's holiday? (Active)
   By whom were you told about tomorrow's holiday? (Passive)

2. **'Yes/No' Questions** The questions that start with helping verbs do/ does/ did are changed into be verbs (is, am, are, was, were) in the passive voice.

   e.g. • **Do** they perform fine arts? (Active)
   Are fine arts performed by them? (Passive)

Changing Imperative Sentences into Passive Voice

Subject is usually not mentioned in the imperative sentences. Thus, they can be changed into passive voice in the following manner

(i) Sentences with suggestion, advised or request etc.

e.g. • **Do not** harm the animals. (Active)

The animals **should not be** harmed. (Passive)

OR Let the animals **not be** harmed. (Passive)

OR **You are advised** not to harm the animals. (Passive)

(ii) If the sentence starts with 'Let', change it into passive voice in the following manner

e.g. • **Let** him feed the dog. (Active)

• **Let** the dog **be** fed by him. (Passive)

REVIEW EXERCISE

Objective and Subjective Questions

1. Change the Active/Passive voice of the given sentence into Passive/Active voice.

(i) His hard work satisfied me.
(a) I was satisfied for his hard work.
(b) I was satisfied by his hard work.
(c) I was satisfied with his hard work.
(d) I was satisfied at his hard work.

(ii) I saved him from the clutches of pickpockets.
(a) He may have been saved by me from the clutches of pickpockets.
(b) He could be saved by me from the clutches of pickpockets.
(c) He was saved by me from the clutches of pickpockets.
(d) He has been saved by me from the clutches of pickpockets.

(iii) The news has been brought to us by him.
(a) He brought us the news.
(b) He has brought us the news.
(c) He was brought the news to us.
(d) We brought the news to him.

(iv) Who can count the stars in the sky?
(a) By whom can the stars in the sky be counted?
(b) By whom can be stars in the sky counted?
(c) By whom could the stars be counted in the sky?
(d) By whom could the stars in the sky be counted?

(v) Don't subject the animals to cruelty.
(a) The animals are not to be subjected to cruelty.
(b) The animals shall not be subjected to cruelty.
(c) The animals will not be subjected to cruelty.
(d) The animals should not be subjected to cruelty.

(vi) He was disgusted with the flattery of his assistant.
(a) The flattery of his assistant disgusted him.
(b) His assistants flattery had disgusted him.
(c) He was disgusted with his assistant for his flattery.
(d) The flattery of this assistant will disgust him.

(vii) Father called up Angela on her birthday.
(a) Angela called up her father on her birthday.
(b) Angela was called up by father on her birthday.
(c) Angela received a call from her father on her birthday.
(d) On her birthday Angela was called up by her father.

(viii) The child's shrill wail broke the silence.
(a) The silence was being broken by the child's shrill wail.
(b) The child's shrill wail was broken by the silence.
(c) The silence was broken by the child's shrill wail.
(d) The silence was being broken by the child's shrill wail.

(ix) The company paid her a meager salary.
(a) She was paid a meager salary by the company.
(b) A meager salary has been paid to her by the company.
(c) She was being paid a meager salary by the company.
(d) A meager salary was to be paid to her by the company.

(x) The packet has not been opened by someone.
(a) Anyone has not opened the packet.
(b) Someone has opened the packet.
(c) No one has not opened the packet.
(d) No one has been opening the packet.

(xi) The people couldn't move me to the hospital and the doctor operated on me at home.

(a) I couldn't be moved to the hospital and was operated on at home by the doctor.

(b) I couldn't be moved to the hospital and I had to be operated on at home.

(c) I couldn't be moved to the hospital and I was operated at home by the doctor.

(d) I couldn't be moved to the hospital by the people and operated on at home.

(xii) Lie face-down; stretch your arms in front.

(a) You are face down, arms are to be outstretched

(b) You should be lying face down, with arms outstretched.

(c) You should be lying face down; let arms stretch out.

(d) Let face be down; let arms be stretched out.

(xiii) The prisoner is known to have assaulted the warden earlier too.

(a) It is known that the warden has been assaulted by the prisoner earlier too.

(b) It is known that the warden has assaulted the prisoner earlier too.

(c) It is known that the prisoner has assaulted the warden earlier too.

(d) The warden was assaulted by the prisoner earlier too.

(xiv) Cacao is bitter when it is tasted.

(a) Cacao is bitter.

(b) Cacao tastes bitter.

(c) Cacao's taste is bitter

(d) Cacao tasted bitter.

(xv) Who was teaching him French?

(a) Whom was he being taught French?

(b) Who had he been taught French by?

(c) By whom was he being taught French?

(d) By whom was he been taught French?

(xvi) Was the latest technology mobile displayed by the show room?

(a) Is the latest technology mobile displayed by the show room?

(b) Does the showroom display the latest technology mobile?

(c) Did the showroom displayed the latest technology mobile?

(d) Did the showroom display the latest technology mobile?

(xvii) They created such a fuss over a trivial matter.

(a) Such a fuss is being created over a trivial matter.

(b) Such a fuss was created over a trivial matter.

(c) Such a fuss has been created over a trivial matter.

(d) By them such a fuss has been created over a trivial matter.

(xviii) We all know that there is only one God

(a) It is known to us all that there is only one God.

(b) We are all known that there is only one God.

(c) We have all known that there is only one God.

(d) Only one God is known by us all.

(xix) The schools take care of the overall needs of the students.

(a) The overall needs of the students are taken care of by the schools.

(b) The overall need of the students will be taken care of by the schools

(c) The overall needs of the students are taken care by the schools

(d) The overall needs of the students are to be taken care of by the school.

(xx) The scheme permits investors to buy the shares from foreign companies.

(a) Under the scheme the investors may be permitted to buy shares from foreign companies.

(b) Under the scheme the investors have been permitted to buy shares from foreign companies.

(c) Under the scheme the investors are permitted to buy shares from foreign companies.

(d) Under the scheme the investors were permitted to buy shares from foreign companies.

(xxi) Wearing the seat belt has been mandatory in all metros by the police.

(a) The Police have made wearing the seat belt mandatory in all metros.

(b) The Police have been made wearing the seat belt mandatory in all metros.

(c) The Police has make wearing the seat belt mandatory in all metros.

(d) The Police has made worn the seat belt mandatory in all metros.

(xxii) It is your duty to make tea at eleven o'clock.

(a) You are asked to make tea at eleven o'clock.

(b) You are supposed to make tea at eleven o'clock.

(c) You are expected to make tea at eleven o'clock.

(d) Tea is to be made by you at eleven o'clock.

(xxiii) Was Priya writing a book?

(a) Was the book being written by Priya?

(b) Had the book been written by Priya?

(c) Was the written by Priya?

(d) Was the book been written by Priya?

(xxiv) He neither questions nor understands them.

(a) They were neither questioned nor understood by him.

(b) They are neither questioned nor understood by him.

(c) They are neither questioned nor understood by him.
(d) They are neither questioned nor have been understood by him.

(xxv) When he left school, the textbooks were put aside by him and were never reopened.
(a) After he left school, he put aside his textbooks and they were never reopened.
(b) He put aside his textbooks when he left school and never reopened them.
(c) He put aside his textbooks when he left school and were never reopened by him.
(d) He put aside his textbooks as he left school and never reopened.

(xxvi) Our vehicle had been stolen from our garage by the same burglary team.
(a) The same burglary team had stolen our vehicle from our garage.
(b) The same burglary team has stolen our vehicle from our garage.
(c) The same burglary team is stealing our vehicle from our garage.
(d) The same burglary team will have stolen our vehicle from our garage.

(xxvii) Does your watch show right time?
(a) Is the right time shown in your watch?
(b) Is the right time shown your watch?
(c) Is the right time show by your watch?
(d) Is the right time shown by your watch?

(xxviii) Though foreigners praised Rabindranath's Gitanjali, Indian critics ignored it in the beginning.
(a) Though Rabindranath's Gitanjali is praised by foreigners, it was ignored by Indian critics in the beginning.
(b) Though Rabindranath's Gitanjali was praised by foreigners, it had been ignored by Indian critics in the beginning.
(c) Though Rabindranath's Gitanjali was praised by foreigners, it has been ignored by Indian critics in the beginning.
(d) Though Rabindranath's Gitanjali was praised by foreigners, it was ignored by Indian critics in the beginning.

(xxix) Not a word was spoken by the criminal in self-defence.
(a) The criminal spoke not a word in self-defence.
(b) The criminal in self-defence spoke no word.
(c) The criminal did not speak a word in self-defence.
(d) The criminal spoke in self-defence not a word.

(xxx) Bipin was not told about the meeting.
(a) Somebody did not tell Bipin about the meeting.
(b) There was nobody who could tell Bipin about the meeting.
(c) Nobody told Bipin about the meeting.
(d) The meeting was not told about to Bipin.

2. Read the instructions given below and complete the paragraph that follows.

(i)
- Cut a fresh onion into small pieces.
- Boil these pieces in 10 ml of distilled water for 3-4 min.
- Cool the solution.
- Filter the content to be used as food extract.
- Perform Benedict's test.
- The solution turns green, then orange and finally red.
- This confirms the presence of glucose in onion.

In order to test the presence of glucose in onions, the following experiment must be performed. First, the onion is cut into small pieces. Then these onion pieces .... for 3-4 minutes. The solution is allowed to cool. It is then .... Now .... on the content. You will observe that initially, the solution turns green, then orange and finally red. Thus, the presence of glucose in onion is confirmed.

(a) Are boiled in 10 ml of distilled water, filtered to be used as food extract, Benedict's test is performed.
(b) Are to be boiled in distilled water, is to be filtered to be used a food extract, the benedict test is to be performed.
(c) Is bought to boil in 10 ml of water, is filtered as food extract, benedict test are performed.
(d) Are to be boiled in distilled water, filtered to be used as food extract, Benedict's test is performed.

(ii)
- Obtain form from the bank
- Fill in the form with all the relevant details
- Ask an account-holder to countersign your form
- Submit two passport-size photographs
- Deposit the minimum amount required

First a form must be .... all relevant details .... The form must then .... Two passport-size photographs along with proof of residence .... Finally the minimum amount required is deposited.

(a) Obtained, is to be filled in the form, be countersigned by an account holder, is to be submitted
(b) Obtained, are to be filled in the form, needs to be countersigned by an account holder, is to be submitted.
(c) Obtained, are filled in the form, be countersigned by an account holder, are submitted
(d) Obtained, have been filled in the form, need be countersigned by a account holder, has to be submitted.

3. **Change the following sentences to passive voice.**
   (i) She sings a song.
   (ii) Help Suhani.
   (iii) Are you writing a letter?
   (iv) I will finish the task before the evening.
   (v) The boy killed the ant.
   (vi) They took all the necessary precautions.
   (vii) They have informed him of his mother's death.
   (viii) The students did some research on the topic.
   (ix) The car hit the dog.
   (x) The dolphins have learned many tricks.

4. **Change the following sentences to active voice.**
   (i) The guitar was played by Lisa.
   (ii) The book is being read by Mary.
   (iii) The rat is eaten by the cat.
   (iv) A washing machine has been bought by him.
   (v) The lucky draw will be won by him.
   (vi) A stone was being thrown by the man.
   (vii) The door had been locked by someone.
   (viii) A seat was offered to them by her.
   (ix) Some trees have been planted by the gardener.
   (x) Some advice will be given to you by the doctor.

5. **Read the instructions given below and complete the paragraph that follows.**
   - Wash the thermometer with fresh water thoroughly.
   - Shake it well to bring down the reading below 37°C.
   - Place the die bulb of the thermometer under the patient's tongue.
   - Ask the patient to keep the mouth closed.
   - Keep the thermometer under the patient's tongue for at least 2 minutes.
   - Take out the thermometer and read the temperature.

   The clinical thermometer .... with freshwater and the reading .... by shaking it well. Then the bulb of the thermometer .... under the patient's tongue and he is asked to keep the mouthclosed. The thermometer should be kept there for at least two minutes. It is then taken out and the temperature is read.

6. Stir together grated coconut mid condensed milk - cook on high in the microwave for 7 mins - switching off, opening and stirring every 30 seconds - add the almonds and cardamom in the hot and bubbling coconut mixture-pour the mixture into the prepared pan.

   To prepare 'coconut burfi' grated coconut and condensed milk are stirred together in a large microwave-safe bowl. Then, it .... on high in the microwave for 7 minutes. It .... opened and stirred every 30 seconds. When the coconut mixture is hot and bubbling, almonds and cardamom .... The mixture is poured into a prepared pan and after cooling, cut into small squares with a greased knife.

ANSWERS

1. (i) (c) I was satisfied with his hard work.
   (ii) (c) He was saved by me from the clutches of pickpockets.
   (iii) (b) He has brought us the news.
   (iv) (a) By whom can the stars in the sky be counted?
   (v) (d) The animals should not be subjected to cruelty.
   (vi) (a) The flattery of his assistant disgusted him.
   (vii) (b) Angela was called up by father on her birthday.
   (viii) (c) The silence was broken by the child's shrill wail.
   (ix) (a) She was paid a meager salary by the company.
   (x) (c) No one has opened the packet.
   (xi) (a) I couldn't be moved to the hospital and was operated on at home by the doctor.
   (xii) (d) Let face be down; let arms be stretched out.
   (xiii) (a) It is known that the warden has been assaulted by the prisoner earlier too.
   (xiv) (b) Cacao tastes bitter.
   (xv) (c) By whom was he being taught French?
   (xvi) (d) Did the showroom display the latest technology mobile?
   (xvii) (b) Such a fuss was created over a trivial matter.
   (xviii) (a) It is known to us all that there is only one God.
   (xix) (a) The overall needs of the students are taken care of by the schools.
   (xx) (c) Under the scheme the investors are permitted to buy shares from foreign companies.
   (xxi) (a) The Police have made wearing the seat belt mandatory in all metros.
   (xxii) (b) You are supposed to make tea at eleven o'clock.
   (xxiii) (a) Was the book being written by Priya?
   (xxiv) (c) They are neither questioned nor understood by him.
   (xxv) (b) He put aside his textbooks when he left school and never reopened them.

(xxvi) (a) The same burglary team had stolen our vehicle from our garage.
(xxvii) (d) Is the right time shown by your watch?
(xxviii) (d) Though Rabindranath's Gitanjali was praised by foreigners, it was ignored by Indian critics in the beginning.
(xxix) (c) The criminal did not speak a word in self-defence.
(xxx) (c) Nobody told Bipin about the meeting.

2. (i) (a) are boiled in 10 ml of distilled water, filtered to be used as food extract, Benedict's test is performed.
(ii) (c) Obtained, are filled in the form, be countersigned by an account holder, are submitted

3. (i) A song is sung by her.
(ii) Let Suhani be helped.
(iii) Is a letter being written by you?
(iv) The task will be finished before the evening.
(v) The ant was killed by the boy.
(vi) All the necessary precautions were taken by them.
(vii) He has been informed of his mother's death.
(viii) Some research on the topic was done by the students.
(ix) The dog was hit by the car.
(x) Many tricks have been learnt by the dolphins.

4. (i) Lisa played the guitar.
(ii) Mary is reading the book.
(iii) The cat eats the rat.
(iv) He has bought a washing machine.
(v) He will win the lucky draw.
(vi) The man was throwing a stone.
(vii) Someone had locked the door.
(viii) She offered them a seat.
(ix) The gardener has planted some trees.
(x) Doctor will give you some advice.

5. is washed, is brought down, is placed

6. is cooked, is switched off, are added

CHAPTER 14

Reported Speech

Reported Speech refers to the two ways in which we represent a speech or a spoken statement. The two ways are Direct and Indirect Speech.

14.1 Direct Speech

In direct speech, we reproduce the exact words of the speaker.

e.g. He said, "I have lost my books."

In a sentence in Direct Speech

- The exact words of the speaker is stated in double quotation marks ("")
- The direct speech of the speaker is separated from the introductory phrase using a comma (,)
- The exact words of the speaker start with a capital letter
- The punctuation mark of the exact words of a speaker like question mark (?), full stop (.), and exclamation mark (!) come before the closing quotation mark.

14.2 Indirect Speech

In indirect speech, we report the words of the speaker in our own words, without necessarily using the exact words of the speaker.

e.g. He said that he had lost his books.

In a sentence in Indirect Speech

- The comma and the double quotation marks are removed.
- The conjunction 'that' is used to join the introductory phrase and the speech.
- The punctuation marks like the question mark (?) and exclamation mark (!) are replaced by a full stop (.).
- The tenses, pronouns and possessive adjectives along with words indicating nearness of time and position are also changed.

General Rules for Changing Direct Speech into Indirect Speech

(i) The commas and the quotation marks are removed in indirect speech.

(ii) The conjunction 'That' is generally to join the two parts of the introductory part and the exact words of the speaker.

e.g. • The dwarf said, "We were wandering in the forest." (Direct speech)
The dwarf said that they were wandering in the forest. (Indirect speech)

Beside these changes, we change the tense, pronouns, modals and time and place expressions. These are discussed below

Change in Tense

When we convert a sentence from direct to indirect speech, the tense of the speech may or may not change depending on the reporting verb.

Note it The Reporting verb of the sentence is the verb that is placed before the Statement given in the inverted commas.
e.g. She **says**, "I am not going to the concert." (Herein 'says' is the reporting verb)

(i) If the reporting verb is in Present, the tense of the verbs in the introductory phrase and exact words of the speaker does not change.

e.g. • My mother **says**, "You **are not going** to the mall." (Direct speech)
My mother **says** that **I am not going** to the mall. (Indirect speech)
• The teacher **tells** the students, "Your exams **will begin** after the holidays." (Direct speech)
The teacher **tells** the students that their exams **will begin** after the holidays. (Indirect speech)

(ii) If the reporting verb is in Past Tense, the tense of the speech in double quotation marks undergoes a change as given in the table

Tenses	Present	Past	Future
Simple			
Direct	Ashima said, "I love my parents."	Keshav said to his father, "I wrote a poem for you".	She said, "I will live in Mumbai."
Indirect	Ashima said that she loved her parents.	Keshav told his father that had written a poem for him.	She said that she would live in Mumbai.
Continuous			
Direct	Arvind said, "I am watching a T.V. serial."	The tourist said to the guide, "I was going to buy some clothes."	Madhu said, "He will be buying a computer."
Indirect	Arvind said that he was watching a T.V. serial.	The tourist told the guide that he had been going to buy some clothes.	Madhu said that he would be buying a computer.
Perfect			
Direct	Kanika said to her mother, "They have reached the airport."	She said, "They had no choice but work for him."	He said, "I shall have gone abroad tomorrow."
Indirect	Kanika told her mother that they had reached the airport.	She said that they had no choice but work for him.	He said that he would have gone abroad the next day.
Perfect Continuous			
Direct	I said to my friend, "I have been sleeping since morning."	He said, "I had been cleaning the garden for two hours."	Mother said, "You shall have been dieting for three months tomorrow.
Indirect	I told my friend that I had been sleeping since morning.	He said that I had been cleaning the garden for two hours.	Mother said that I/you/she/he would have been dieting for three months the following day.

Exceptions

There are certain exception to the rules given above

(i) If there is a universal truth, a habitual fact or a historical fact in the direct speech, the tense of the main verb remains unchanged.

e.g. • My mother said, "The Earth rotates round its axis." (Universal fact) (Direct speech)
My mother said that the Earth rotates round its axis. (Indirect speech)

• Ajay said, "India got independence on 15th August, 1947." (Historical fact) (Direct speech)
Ajay said that India got independence on 15th August, 1947. (Indirect speech)

(ii) If the information is relevant at the time of its reporting, the tense of the main verb remains unchanged.

e.g. • My brother said, "I like to eat biscuits with coffee." (Direct speech)
My brother said that he likes to eat biscuits with coffee. (Indirect speech)

(iii) If the reported speech is about two simultaneously happening actions.

e.g. • Sahil said, "The dogs were barking while I was walking in the park". (Direct speech)
Sahil said the dogs were barking while he was walking in the park. (Indirect speech)

(iv) If the reported speech is about an imaginary sentence.

e.g. • Mohan said, "If I were a bird, I would fly everywhere". (Direct speech)
Mohan said (that) if he were a bird, he would fly everywhere. (Indirect speech)

Changes in Pronoun

(i) The pronoun in the indirect speech remains unchanged if the speaker is in first person.

e.g. • I said, "I will do my homework later." (Direct speech)
I said that I would do my homework later. (Indirect speech)

(ii) The pronoun in the indirect speech is changed to second person if the speaker is in second person.

e.g. • You said, "I am going to Mumbai." (Direct speech)
You said that you were going to Mumbai. (Indirect speech)

(iii) The pronoun in the indirect speech is changed to third person in accordance with the gender of the speaker, if the speaker is in third person.

e.g. • He said, "I adopted a puppy." (Direct speech)
He said that he had adopted a puppy. (Indirect speech)

Change in Modals

Modal verbs are changed in the following manner

- May - might
- Can - could
- Must - had to
- Ought to - ought to

Change in Time and Place Expressions

The words that indicate time or position also undergoes a change when we convert a direct speech into indirect speech.

Time Indicators

Direct Speech	Indirect Speech
Now	Then
Ago	Before
Today	That day
Tonight	That night
Yesterday	The previous day/the day before
Tomorrow	The next day/ the following day
In an hour	An hour later

Place Indicators

Direct Speech	Indirect Speech
Here	There
This	That
These	Those

Changes in Interrogative Sentences

When we have to change a direct question into indirect speech, we make the following changes

(i) The reporting verb 'said/ said to' is changed to 'asked/enquired/demanded'. The question form is converted to statement form.

(ii) If the question starts with helping verbs (is, were, have, does, etc.) or modal verbs (can, would, may, etc.), then they are replaced by conjunctions 'if' or 'whether'.

(iii) If the question starts with -wh words (why, when, what, which) or how, no conjunctions are used. Other changes are done according to rules mentioned above.

e.g. • Neha said to her teacher, "**Can** I come in Ma'am?" (Direct speech)
Neha asked her teacher **whether/if** she could come inside. (Indirect speech)

- Monika said to her younger sister, "**Which** dress do you want to buy?" (Direct speech)

  Monika asked her younger sister **which** dress she wanted to buy. (Indirect speech)

Changes in Imperative Sentences

If the direct speech contains a request or a command, the reporting verb changes to told, requested, ordered, commanded, suggested, advised, etc. according to the intent of the spoken words. Other changes are done according to the rules mentioned above.

e.g. • He **said** to me, "Go to school now." (Direct speech)

He **advised** me to go to school then. (Indirect speech)

Changes in Exclamatory Sentences

While changing exclamatory sentences into indirect speech, we make the following changes.

(i) The reporting verb 'said/said to' is changed to 'exclaimed'.

(ii) The exclamatory word (interjection) is replaced by 'exclaimed with joy/sorrow/regret/surprise/contempt, etc.' Other changes are done according to the rules mentioned above.

e.g. • The old man **said**, "**Alas**! Mr. Goel has lost his son." (Direct speech)

The old man **exclaimed with sorrow** that Mr. Goel had lost his son. (Indirect speech)

REVIEW EXERCISE

Objective and Subjective Questions

1. Change this given Direct/Indirect speech into Indirect/Direct speech and choose the correct answer.

(i) Nancy said, "I may leave tomorrow."

(a) Nancy said that she might leave the next day.
(b) Nancy said that she might leave tomorrow.
(c) Nancy asked if she should leave the next day.
(d) Nancy informed me to leave tomorrow.

(ii) I reiterated, "I don't care about the job."

(a) I reiterated that I did not care about the job.
(b) I repeatedly said that I cared about the job.
(c) I said again and again I didn't care about the job.
(d) I reiterated I didn't care about the job.

(iii) She said to me, "I took breakfast in the morning."

(a) She told me that she has taken breakfast in the morning.
(b) She said to me that she was taking breakfast in the morning.
(c) She told me that she had taken breakfast in the morning.
(d) She told me that she took breakfast in the morning.

(iv) Bala's mother: "Will you lock the door, Bala?"

(a) Bala's mother asked Bala if he would lock the door.
(b) Bala's mother asked Bala if he had locked the door.
(c) Balas mother said lock the door.
(d) Bala's mother told Bala that he need not lock the door.

(v) He said, "The Sun rises in the east."

(a) He said that the Sun will rise in the East.
(b) He said that the Sun may rise in the East.
(c) He said that the Sun rises in the East.
(d) He said that the Sun rised in the East.

(vi) He asked me why I did not come on time the previous day.

(a) He said to me, "Why didn't I come on time yesterday?"
(b) He asked me, "Why didn't I come on time the previous day?"
(c) He asked me, "Why you didn't come on time yesterday?"
(d) He said to me, "Why didn't you come on time yesterday?"

(vii) The kids yelled in a loud voice, "We love our family."

(a) The kids yelled in a loud voice that they loved our family.
(b) The kids were shouting loudly that they loved their family.
(c) The kids yelled in a loud voice that they loved their family.
(d) The kids yelled loudly that they love our family.

(viii) **He said that he had been waiting there for a long time.**
(a) He said "He has been waiting there for a long time."
(b) He said "I am waiting here for a longtime."
(c) He said "He has been waiting here for a long time."
(d) He said "I have been waiting here for a long time."

(ix) **Rahul said, "I will do it now or never".**
(a) Rahul said that he would do it then or never.
(b) Rahul said that he would now or never do it.
(c) Rahul said that he will now or never do it.
(d) Rahul said that he will do it now or never.

(x) **The teacher said, "You are suspended!"**
(a) The teacher exclaimed that I am suspended.
(b) The teacher exclaimed to me to suspend.
(c) The teacher informed me that I was suspended.
(d) The teacher exclaimed that I was suspended.

(xi) **"I am going out tonight." Manisha said.**
(a) Manisha said that she was going out tonight.
(b) Manisha said that she was going out that night.
(c) Manisha said she was going out that night.
(d) Manisha said that she will be going out that night.

(xii) **Kiara said that she had been planning for that for a while.**
(a) Kiara said, "I had a plan for this for a while."
(b) Kiara said, "I have planned for this for a while."
(c) Kiara said, "I have been planning for this for a while."
(d) Kiara said, "I planned this for a while."

(xiii) **The head said to the staff that they had thought of a solution.**
(a) The head said, "We have a solution."
(b) The head said to the staff, "We have thought of a solution!"
(c) The head said to the staff, "We have thought of a solution."
(d) The head said, "We have been thinking of a solution."

(xiv) **The coach asked us if we had any doubts.**
(a) The coach said to us, "Do you have any doubts?"
(b) The coach said, "Has anyone have doubts?"
(c) The coach said to us, "Any doubts?"
(d) The coach said, "Would you have doubts?"

(xv) **Anne said, "It is time to leave for the meeting."**
(a) Anne told that it is time to leave for the meeting.
(b) Anne said its time to leave for the meeting.
(c) Anne said that it was time for the meeting.
(d) Anne said that it was time to leave for the meeting.

(xvi) **George exclaimed with joy that he was happy with his result.**
(a) George said, "I am happy with my result."
(b) George said, "Alas! I am happy with the result."
(c) George said, "Hurrah! I am happy with my result."
(d) George said, "Happy with the result!"

(xvii) **The kids yelled in a loud voice, "We are going out."**
(a) The kids yelled in a loud voice that they went out.
(b) The kids yelled in a loud voice that they were going out.
(c) The kids yelled in a loud voice that they are going out.
(d) The kids yelled loudly that they went outside.

(xviii) **The King ordered that they should celebrate their victory.**
(a) The King said, "We should celebrate our victory."
(b) The King said, "One should celebrate their victory."
(c) The King said, "I order everyone to celebrate."
(d) The King said, "We may celebrate."

(xix) **I said to the boy, "Will you step with me into the garden?"**
(a) I asked the boy if he would step with me into the garden.
(b) I said to the boy if he would step with me in the garden.
(c) I said the boy if he would like to step with me into the garden.
(d) I requested the boy to step with me into the garden.

(xx) **Mr. Steven said that that explanation was easier.**
(a) Mr. Steven said, "That explanation is easier!"
(b) Mr. Steven said, "This explanation was easier."
(c) Mr. Steven said, "This explanation could be easier."
(d) Mr. Steven said, "This explanation is easier."

2. Read the conversation given below and complete the paragraph that follows.

Rajan Where can we meet tomorrow?
Raashi I may not be able to meet you tomorrow.
Rajan Are you going to be busy?
Raashi Yes, I will be traveling tomorrow.

Rajan asked Raashi .... .Raashi replied .... Rajan asked if he was going to be busy. Raashi said that he ....

(a) About the place where they will meet tomorrow, that he will not be able to meet him, has to travel tomorrow.
(b) where they could meet the following day, he might not be able to meet him, would be traveling the next day.
(c) Where they will be meeting the next day, he would not be able to meet him, needs to travel the next day.
(d) where they could meet the following day, he would not be able to meet him, would be traveling the next day.

3. Read the conversation given below and complete the paragraph that follows.

Julie When is the fancy - dress competition in your school?
Mona It is after two weeks.
Julie Are you taking part in it?

Mona Yes, I am taking part as an engine driver.

Julie Why have you chosen that?

Mona So that I can reach late.

Julie asked Mona when the fancy dress competition in her school was. To that Mona replied that .... Julie enquired whether .... Mona said that she was taking part as an engine driver. Julie asked why .... She answered ....

(a) it was after two weeks, if she was taking part in it, she had chosen that, so that she could reach late
(b) It was two week later, whether she planned on taking part in it, she had decided that, so that she could come late
(c) It is two weeks after, if she was participating in it, she will be choosing that, so she can reach late
(d) it was after two weeks, if she was taking part in it, she had decided that, so that she could come late

4. Change the following into indirect speech.

(i) I said to Prerna, "How do you travel to office everyday?"
(ii) Shivam said to his mother, "Where does the rain come from?"
(iii) "Do you know the way to the paradise?" A crazy man said to me.
(iv) Maria said to her daughter, "At what time will you come back?"
(v) The man said to the mechanic, "By what time will you have fixed the tyre of my bike?"
(vi) Varun says to Tarun, "Where did you go yesterday?"
(vii) "Is there anything special in it?" She asked.
(viii) "Hark! I can smell something here" said Mr. Naik to his colleagues.
(ix) "Alas! we have lost the game." said Shishir to his friend.
(x) "How intelligent you are!" Manjiri said to her grandfather.

5. Rewrite the sentences into direct speech from indirect speech.

(i) Miara said that she wrote a letter.
(ii) Kiran said that she was going to the temple.
(iii) The teacher said that the Sun rises in the East.
(iv) He said that he had been reading a novel.
(v) Nelson said that he had been playing badminton.
(vi) He ordered her to be careful.
(vii) Raman exclaimed joyfully that she was very beautiful.
(viii) He asked where she was going.
(ix) He said that he didn't know the way and asked her if she did.
(x) The Science teacher told the class that ice floats on water.

ANSWERS

1. (i) (a) Nancy said that she might leave the next day.
(ii) (a) I reiterated that I did not care about the job.
(iii) (c) She told me that she had taken breakfast in the morning.
(iv) (a) Bala's mother asked Bala if he would lock the door.
(v) (c) He said that the Sun rises in the East.
(vi) (d) He said to me, "Why didn't you come on time yesterday?"
(vii) (c) The kids yelled in a loud voice that they loved their family.
(viii) (d) He said, "I have been waiting here for a long time."
(ix) (a) Rahul said that he would do it then or never.
(x) (d) The teacher exclaimed that I was suspended.
(xi) (b) Manisha said that she was going out that night.
(xii) (c) Kiara said, "I have been planning for this for a while."
(xiii) (c) The head said to the staff, "We have thought of a solution."
(xiv) (a) The coach said to us, "Do you have any doubts?"
(xv) (d) Anne said that it was time to leave for the meeting.
(xvi) (c) George said, "Hurrah! I am happy with my result."
(xvii) (b) The kids yelled in a loud voice that they were going out.
(xviii) (a) The King said, "We should celebrate our victory."
(xix) (a) I asked the boy if he would step with me into the garden.
(xx) (d) Mr. Steven said, "This explanation is easier."

2. (b) where they could meet the following day, he might not be able to meet him, would be traveling the next day.

3. (a) it was after two weeks, if she was taking part in it, she had chosen that, so that she could reach late.

4. (i) I asked Prerna how she travels to office everyday.
(ii) Shivam asked his mother where the rain comes from.
(iii) A crazy man asked me whether I knew the way to Paradise.

(iv) Maria asked her daughter at what time she would come back.
(v) The man asked the mechanic by what time he would have fixed the tyre of his bike.
(vi) Varun asks Tarun where he went yesterday.
(vii) She asked whether there was anything special in it.
(viii) Mr. Naik exclaimed with fear and said to his colleagues that he could smell something there.
(ix) Shishir exclaimed with sorrow and told his friend that they had lost the game.
(x) Manjiri told her grandfather that he was very intelligent.

5. (i) Miara said, "I write a letter."
(ii) Kiran said, "I am going to the temple."
(iii) The teacher said, "The Sun rises in the East."
(iv) He said, "I have been reading a novel."
(v) Nelson said, "I have been playing badminton."
(vi) "Be careful", he said to her.
(vii) "How beautiful she is!" said Raman.
(viii) He said, "Where is she going?"
(ix) "I don't know the way. Do you?" he said to her.
(x) The science teacher said to the class, "Ice floats on water."

Word Power

15.1 Antonyms

Antonyms are the words that have opposite meaning.

Word	Antonym
Abundant	scarce
Accept	decline, refuse
Accomplishment	failure
Accurate	inaccurate
Adjacent	distant
Admire	detest
Admit	deny, reject
Adore	hate
Advance	retreat
Affirm	deny
Afraid	confident
Aid	hinder
Allow	forbid
Amateur	professional
Ally	enemy

Word	Antonym
Amuse	bore
Ancient	modern
Appear	disappear, vanish
Arrive	depart
Arrogant	humble
Artificial	natural
Ascend	descend
Attack	defend
Awkward	graceful
Bent	straight
Bitter	sweet
Blame	praise
Bless	curse
Blunt	sharp
Bold	timid, meek
Borrow	lend

Word	Antonym
Boundless	limited
Brief	long
Broad	narrow
Busy	idle
Calm	windy, troubled
Captive	free
Capture	release
Careful	careless
Cause	effect
Center	edge
Clear	vague, cloudy, opaque
Clever	stupid
Common	rare
Complex	simple
Compliment	insult
Conceal	reveal
Constant	variable
Continue	interrupt
Crazy	sane
Crooked	straight
Cunning	simple
Dainty	clumsy
Deep	shallow
Demand	supply
Despair	hope
Dismal	cheerful
Dusk	dawn
Expand	contract, shrink
Export	import
Exterior	interior
Fade	brighten
Feeble	sturdy, strong, powerful
Fiction	fact
Float	sink
Frequent	seldom
Gather	distribute
Generous	stingy, mean
Gentle	rough, violent
Gloomy	cheerful
Grant	refuse
Harsh	mild
Heaven	hell

Word	Antonym
Humble	proud
Ignore	notice
Imitation	genuine
Immense	minute, tiny, small
Immigrate	emigrate
Important	trivial
Imprison	free
Jeopardise	secure
Keen	uninterested
Kind	cruel, nasty
Knowledge	ignorance
Lack	abundance, plenty
Lenient	strict
Messy	neat
Miser	spendthrift
Mend	break
Narrow	wide, broad
Native	foreigner, stranger
Obedient	disobedient
Occasionally	frequently
Often	seldom, sometimes
Optimist	pessimist
Outskirts	center
Permanent	temporary
Permit	forbid
Please	displease
Plentiful	scarce
Polite	rude, impolite
Plant	harvest
Rough	smooth, soft, gentle
Rude	courteous
Safe	unsafe, dangerous
Scatter	collect
Serious	trivial, funny
Simple	complex, hard, complicated
Sink	float
Slim	fat, thick, stout
Sow	reap
Straight	crooked
Synonym	antonym
Tame	wild
Transparent	opaque

Word	Antonym
Urban	rural
Urgent	leisurely
Vacant	occupied
Victory	defeat
Virtue	vice
Voluntary	compulsory
Wax	wane
Wisdom	folly, stupidity
Zenith	nadir

15.2 Synonyms

Synonyms are the words that have similar meaning.

Word	Synonyms
Amazing	astonishing, startling
Awesome	impressive, fabulous
Awful	dreadful, alarming
Bad	wicked, defective
Beautiful	attractive, appealing
Begin	commence, initiate
Boring	tedious, tiresome
Change	alter, transform
Definitely	unquestionably, precisely
Easy	effortless, natural
Excellent	superior, unsurpassed
Exciting	thrilling, stirring
Fast	swift, quick
Finish	complete, conclude
Fun	pleasure, Frolic
Funny	comical, amusing
Get	obtain, receive
Give	donate, supply
Good	satisfactory, fine
Got	received, obtained
Great	tremendous, remarkable
Happy	pleased, joyous
Hard	complex, complicated
Help	serve, sustain
Hurt	injure, impair
Important	significant, substantial
Interesting	absorbing, fascinating

Word	Synonyms
Keep	retain, control, possess
Kind	type, variety
Know	comprehend, understand
Mad	angry, frustrated
Make	build, construct
New	recent, modern
Next	subsequently, thereafter
Nice	pleasant, satisfying
Old	archaic, ancient
Part	section, portion
Perfect	flawless, faultless
Pleasant	agreeable, gratifying
Prove	demonstrate, confirm
Quick	brisk, prompt
Really	truly, genuinely
Regular	usual
Scared	afraid, fearful
Small	minor, tiny

15.3 One Word Substitutions

One word substitutions are defined as single words that are used in place of a group of words to denote a person, an object, a place etc.

Word	Meaning
One who believes in total abolition of war	Pacifist
Study of fossils	Paleontology
A shortened form of a word or phrase	Abbreviation
Which can be approached	Accessible
A person who attacks first	Aggressor
A person who loves everybody	Altruist
A person representing a state in a foreign country.	Ambassador
A study of man	Anthropology
State of being unmarried	Bachelorhood
One who can't pay the debts	Bankrupt
A life history written by somebody else	Biography
A government by the officials	Bureaucracy
A person who is above hundred years	Centenarian
Belonging to the same period of time	Contemporary
One who cannot speak	Dumb

Word	Meaning
One who has strange habits	Eccentric
Study of environment	Ecology
A person who believes in fate	Fatalist
One who advocates for equal rights of women	Feminist
One who eats too much	Glutton
A position for which no salary is paid	Honorary
Study of Earth	Geology
The point where the Earth and sky seem to meet	Horizon
That which is against law	Illegal
A person who cannot read or write	Illiterate
A sound that cannot be heard	Inaudible
That which cannot be avoided	Inevitable
A man who is easily irritated	Irritable
A planned route or journey	Itinerary
A hundred years	Century
New word coined by an author	Neologism
One who is new to a trade or profession	Novice
One who is present everywhere	Omnipresent
One who looks at the brighter side of things	Optimist
Belonging to the middle ages	Medieval
Subject to death	Mortal
One who loves own country	Patriot
One who has no money	Pauper
Study of art of teaching	Pedagogy
One who looks at the dark side of things	Pessimist
Study of stamp collection	Philately
One who knows many languages	Polyglot
Stanza of four lines	Quatrain
One who speaks less	Reticent
Violating the sanctity of a church	Sacrilege
One who helps others	Samaritan
The art of making dolls	Sculpture
One who believes in God	Theist
Belonging to all parts of the world	Universal
A woman whose husband is dead	Widow
A man whose wife had died	Widower

15.4 Idioms and Phrases

The expression that have a different meaning from its literal meaning.

Idiom	Sentence
To beat about the bush	He is always beating about the bush and never comes to the main point.
To blow one's own trumpet	One who blows one's own trumpet is not a good fellow.
To break the ice	The two friends broke the ice when they met in a party.
To build castles in the air	Daydreamers often build castle in the air.
A big cheese	The general manager of a company is always a big cheese in the scene.
Between the devil and the deep sea	Leaving the job and a failure in the new venture has lead him between the devil and the deep sea.
Bite your tongue	A leader will never bite his tongue anywhere.
Birds of same feather flock together	One can often see rogue students sitting together as birds of same feather flock together always.
Back to square one	Broken hearts go back to square one when it comes to reunion.
In black and white	To avoid conflict, I need everything in black and white.
Pick someone to pieces	The boss picked the lazy employee to pieces when he was caught sitting idle.
To fight like cat and dog	The bargain lead the two to a fight like cat and dog.
To let the cat out of the bag	I wanted to give my mother a surprise but my brother let the cat out of the bag.
To mind one's own business	Good and worthy people always mind their own business.
Action speaks louder than words	Sachin has always replied his critics by a splendid performance once and it is what we call action speaks louder than words.
Every cloud has a silver lining	Don't lose your heart man! There must be a silver living in the cloud.
An empty vessel sounds much	When a duffer speaks, I always recall that an empty vessel sounds much.
A drop in the ocean	The bail-out package to the company which is having a great loss looks like a drop in the ocean.
As you sow, so you reap	The robber has been put in jail and this proves as you sow, so you reap.

Idiom	Sentence
Crying over spilt	It's no use crying over spilt milk.
A nine days wonder	If you pass an exam by cheating, you must not be happy because it is a nine days wonder.
Finding one's feet	Getting some runs in the last match, the batsman is finding his feet now.
To hold one's horse	Hold your horse if you want to gain from your shares.
Kick up a row	His abuse in the public place kicked up a row with other people.
Avarice is the root of all evils	You should control your greed of gaining so much of physical wealth as avarice is the root of all evils.

15.5 Homophones

The words that pronounce the same, but have different meanings are called Homophones.

Homophones	Sentence
Aloud Allowed	Speak aloud, I can't hear it. You are allowed to go there.
Blew Blue	The bomb blew all the houses. She loves wearing blue dress.
Brake Break	The driver has applied the brakes. Don't break the rules.
Born Borne	She was born in March. You have to borne all the costs.
Earn Urn	She used to earn a lot. An urn was kept before the God.
Eight Ate	Eight people were killed. She ate the apples.
Flair Flare	I have a flair for writing. The flare of the bulb keeps me awake and amazed.
Hair Hare	She has curly hair. They have a hare as a pet.
Higher Hire	She went for higher studies. We hired a taxi to go to the railway station.
Morning Mourning	We go to exercise in the morning. The family were mourning the deceased.
Peace Piece	Countries should maintain peace. She collected the broken piece of the glass.
Plane Plain	She travels by plane. Plain dress is liked by us.
Principle Principal	Honesty is his principle. He is a school principal.
Road Rode	Follow the road manuals. I rode an elephant for the first time.
Sell Cell	They sell fresh flowers. Amoeba has a single cell.
Wait Weight	Don't wait for me. Weight of the packet is ten kilogram.
Waist Waste	People in England wear waist coat. Lots of food go as waste.
Weather Whether	Goa has a pleasant weather. I want to know whether you were involved in it or not.
Yoke Yolk	The yoke is a ploughing supplement. Yolk is the most nutritional part of an egg.

Integrated Exercise

Type I : Gap Filling

I. Directions (Q. Nos. 1-20) Fill in the blanks with suitable words.

1. She has bought some ....

(a) furniture (b) furnitures
(c) good furnitures (d) cheap furnitures

2. She ..... not go park yesterday.

(a) was (b) did
(c) does (d) had

3. I ..... have done this tough task.

(a) myself (b) me
(c) ourselves (d) mine

4. It has been raining ..... 3 o' clock.

(a) from (b) for
(c) upto (d) since

5. ..... Ganga is a holy river.

(a) The (b) A
(c) An (d) No article

6. She was crying, ... she?

(a) isn't (b) wasn't
(c) hasn't (d) hadn'

7. I love chicken ..... my brother loves fish.

(a) and (b) where
(c) but (d) though

8. She ..... come inside now.

(a) might (b) could
(c) may (d) would

9. Delhi is ..... crowded city.

(a) the (b) an
(c) a (d) No article

10. She jumped ..... the river.

(a) in (b) inside
(c) to (d) into

11. Why are you ..... there like a statue?

(a) stand
(b) stood
(c) standing
(d) been standing

12. She can do all .... work by herself.

(a) his (b) him
(c) their (d) her

13. Mahi can run as .... as Juhi these days.

(a) quickly (b) quick
(c) quicker (d) quickest

14. Taj Mahal is one of the .... wonder in the world.

(a) great (b) greater
(c) greatly (d) greatest

15. One must adhere .... the disciplines of life.

(a) to (b) for
(c) into (d) at

16. This good book is written .... me recently.

(a) to (b) at
(c) by (d) from

17. One .... breathe in order to survive.

(a) can (b) must
(c) may (d) could

18. Japanese .... making great advancement is technology.

(a) has been (b) are
(c) were (d) had been

19. I refused to do this at the call .... my conscience.

(a) to (b) from
(c) of (d) in

20. Countrymen should love .... another.

(a) each (b) ones
(c) all (d) one

II. Direction (Q.Nos. A-D) : Choose the correct options to fill in the blanks to complete the passages.

A. Fill in the following blanks by choosing the most appropriate option from the ones given below.

(1) .... the first prize in the debate competition, Raghu decided to put in his maximum effort in all the (2) .... inter-school competitions. His teacher advised him not (3) .... overconfident. (4) .... is not always necessary. (5) .... a good student, he knew the meaning of what his teacher advised him.

1. (a) Win (b) Won (c) To win (d) Winning
2. (a) comes (b) come (c) came (d) coming
3. (a) feeling (b) to feel (c) felt (d) feel
4. (a) Winning (b) Will win (c) Win (d) Won
5. (a) Be (b) Is (c) Being (d) Be

B. Fill in the following blanks by choosing the most appropriate option from the ones given below.

All life on Earth can ultimately be (1) .... back in the sea. Creatures (2) .... limbs with fingers rather than fins evolved from fishes about 335 millions years (3) .... The new fossil (4) .... in the rock formation near Scotland provides one of the few (5) .... to what has been happening in these 30 million years.

1. (a) traced (b) trace (c) will trace (d) traceds
2. (a) is (b) has (c) had (d) having
3. (a) ago (b) past (c) away (d) before
4. (a) find (b) found (c) finds (d) was found
5. (a) cluing (b) clued (c) clue (d) clues

C. Read the passage given below. Fill in the blanks by choosing the most appropriate words/phrases from the given options.

My deadline for the day's incredible, awe inspiring column (1) .... the Tribune was three hours away and I was in a jam. I (2) .... already tossed three ideas into the recycle bin and was staring at a blank screen again. The really tricky thing about (3) .... a 'witty' column is that between Mark Twain, Oscar Wilde and Dorothy Parker, everything worth saying (4) .... already been said.

1. (a) at (b) on (c) in (d) for
2. (a) had (b) have (c) will have (d) am
3. (a) drawing (b) creating (c) making (d) writing
4. (a) had (b) has (c) have (d) did

D. Fill in the blanks in the following sentences by choosing the most appropriate options from the ones given below. (Any four)

It was an old tree. A seed had been carried (1)...... the island by (2)...... strong wind some fifty years back. It (3)...... found shelter (4)...... two rocks and had (5)...... up to give shelter to a small family.

1. (a) over (b) on (c) at (d) to
2. (a) the (b) a (c) an (d) some
3. (a) have (b) has (c) had (d) having
4. (a) between (b) in (c) on (d) over
5. (a) spring (b) sprang (c) sprung (d) springing

III. Directions (Q. Nos. A-D)

A. Fill in the blanks in the passage given below with the correct option from those given in brackets.

In 1911, the British *(i)* .... (shift/shifted) their capital from Calcutta to Delhi. After *(ii)* .... (a, the) First World War, *(iii)* .... (a/the) government *(iv)* .... (get/got) down to the task of building a new capital.

B. Fill in the blanks in the following passage with one word only in each blank.

The people in the restaurant seemed *(i)* .... lonely as the place itself. Two men in untidy work shirts *(ii)* .... at the counter, *(iii)* .... weirdly the at the cups of coffee. I thought that they *(iv)* .... shift workers *(v)* ...., for some reason, didn't want to go home. A little away from them sat *(vi)* .... couple. The man was staring into space, idly tapping his spoon on the table *(vii)* .... the woman drew aimless parallel lines on her paper napkin with *(viii)* .... fork.

C. Fill in the blanks in the following passage with one word only in each blank.

The ancient Egyptians believed that a person's soul lived after *(i)* .... body died. To make *(ii)* .... soul live they developed ways to prevent the body from *(iii)* .... At first, they used to bury their bodies under *(iv)* .... hot desert sand.

D. Fill in the blanks in the following passage with one word only in each blank.

From a very young age I had *(i)* .... aversion to water when I was *(ii)* .... it. This started when I was three *(iii)* .... four years old and my father took me *(iv)* .... a beach in California.

Type II : Jumbled Sentences/ Sentence Reordering

I. Directions (Q.Nos. 1-20) The questions given below consists of certain phrases. Rearrange these phrases to form a meaningful sentence.

1. **the only creature (1) / laughter (2)/ blessed with the power of (3)/ man is (4)**

(a) 2134 (b) 4132
(c) 1324 (d) 4321

2. **by keeping (1) /oblige me (2) /your (3) / to yourself (4)/ suspicion (5)**

(a) 32154 (b) 35421
(c) 21354 (d) 21345

3. **the managing director (1)/ in listening to her (2)/ was not interested (3) /explanation about why profits were lessening (4)**

(a) 1234 (b) 1243
(c) 1324 (d) 2341

4. **supported by soft term loans (1) / to supply the raw material worth Rs. 5 lakh (2) / the dealer has agreed (3) / with a very low rate of interest. (4)**

(a) 3214 (b) 4213
(c) 1432 (d) 2134

5. **when meat (1) / the food poisoning occurred (2)/ added in the food preparations (3)/ of low quality was (4)**

(a) 3214 (b) 2341
(c) 1423 (d) 2143

6. **I wanted to tell her (1)/not to talk to him (2)/not listen to me (3)/but she would (4)**

(a) 1234 (b) 1243
(c) 1423 (d) 2314

7. **for thousands of years (1)/ famous symbols of ancient civilisations (2)/ Monuments have been created (3)/ and they are often the most durable and (4)**

(a) 3142 (b) 1234
(c) 2143 (d) 4321

8. **is one of the most widely used indicators (1)/ of ecosystems and their biodiversity (2)/ for assessing the condition (3)/ The conservation status of plants and animals (4)**

(a) 4132 (b) 4321
(c) 2314 (d) 1234

9. **photos which were submitted (1)/ in the fire last night (2)/ for the exhibition (3)/ have been totally burnt (4)**

(a) 1432 (b) 2134
(c) 1342 (d) 3142

10. **In the wintertime (1)/ the 2022 World Cup in Qatar (2) / would best be staged (3) / will not be held in June and July but (4)**

(a) 2314 (b) 3412
(c) 1432 (d) 2431

11. **She saw her opportunity (1)/to make amends (2)/ when he came to her home (3)/ to borrow some sugar(4)**

(a) 2341 (b) 1234
(c) 2314 (d) 1423

12. **the mutterings of (1)/ As lightning accompanies thunder (2)/ so was mingled with in my character (3)/ my wrath a flash of humour (4)**

(a) 2314 (b) 2413
(c) 1342 (d) 2134

13. **coal as a fuel (1)/ in place of wood (2)/ during this period (3)/ people were beginning to use (4)**

(a) 2413 (b) 1342
(c) 3412 (d) 4312

14. **The CEO (1)/ of making the right decision (2)/ was not scared (3) /despite a loss in profits (4)**

(a) 1234 (b) 1243
(c) 1324 (d) 2341

15. **Half its beauty and usefulness (1)/ knowledge would lose (2)/ without hard toil (3)/ if we could acquire it (4)**

(a) 3241 (b) 2143
(c) 3421 (d) 4312

16. containing memorable letters of Churchill (1)/ Recently a book (2)/ has been published (3)/ by a reputed publisher (4)

(a) 2134 (b) 1234
(c) 2314 (d) 2314

17. We can give him (1)/ and let him do nothing (2)/ to lock up a man (3)/ is one of the cruelest punishments (4)

(a) 1432 (b) 3241
(c) 2431 (d) 4312

II. Directions (Q. Nos. 1-20) Rearrange the words to form meaningful sentences.

1. so / to / itchy / is / that / I / wait / my / off / uniform / can't / take / it
2. is / good / both / for / and / early / rising / old / adults
3. the / weekend / I / can / love / down / be / I / myself / because / and / dress
4. finish / work / early / one / can / go / and / a / for walk / one's
5. place / our lives / music / important / has / in / an
6. its / urbanisation / in India / everywhere / has / tentacles / spread
7. light up / in every home / good / the lamp / books / magazines / and / of / knowledge
8. 'The year of Books' / are / we / this / celebrating / year
9. I'd / thought / nervous! / the / get / interview; / I / I / through / was / never / so
10. Reshma / year / to / to / the / come / back / hopes / Disneyworld / for / next / a /holiday
11. want / do / me / see / you / you / at / to / the / airport? / off
12. you/ betrays / once / it's / his / fault / someone / fault / betrays / it's / if he / twice/ If /your / you
13. baby / gave / apple / her / the / mother / a / red
14. that / lived in / hills / I dreamt / I / Malabar
15. Mohit / and / skating / Saturday / went / on / Preeti
16. way / good / eating / cream / ice / to / off / is / a / cool
17. spoil / broth / the / too / many / cooks
18. money / me? / how / give / can / much / you
19. the / was / that / authority / curbed / King / annoyed / his / was
20. strike / opportunity / the / wait / I/ to / right / for / will

Type III : Editing

Directions (Q. Nos. 1-4) The following passages have not been edited. There an error in each line. Spot the error and rectify them. One has been done as an example in each.

1. My class was filling with excitement — **filling** — **filled**
because someone have discovered that — (a) ....
the next day is our teacher's birthday. — (b) ....
Our teacher was the kindest persons — (c) ....
I have ever met. Thus, it was not the — (d) ....
surprise that he was his favourite teacher. — (e) ....

2. When I return from the school I saw that — **return** — **returned**
my mother were in the kitchen and my — (a) ....
younger brother was played with his — (b) ....
friends. I entered my room where books was lying scattered. So, I called — (c) ....
my mother to helping me — (d) ....
arrange all these book is no time. — (e) ....

3. People all over in world are now health-conscious. They did not want to fall ill and so they usually exposes themselves to exercise who is the best way to staying fit. We must exercise on a regularly basis.

	in	the
(a)	....	....
(b)	....	....
(c)	....	....
(d)	....	....
(e)	....	....

4. No matter how good a team be on paper, what matter the most is how they performs in the field. South Africa was a very good team but even they lose to ordinary teams recently. It meant that they are 'chokers'.

	be	is
(a)	....	....
(b)	....	....
(c)	....	....
(d)	....	....
(e)	....	....

Type IV : Omitting

Directions (Q. Nos. 1-4) In the following paragraph one word has been omitted in each line. Write the missing words in any four lines of the given paragraph, along with the words that come before and the words that come after it in the space provided.

1.

		Before	Missing	After
Most the people	e.g.	Most	of	the
are annoyed passwords.	(a)	....	....	....
They have many remember.	(b)	....	....	....
On any given day are	(c)	....	....	....
bound forget them	(d)	....	....	....
This creates difficulties the people.	(e)	....	....	....

2.

		Before	Missing	After
Do you remember last time you laughed	e.g.	remember	the	last
loudly? For most us laughing out loud is an	(a)	....	....	....
uphill task. More often not people think	(b)	....	....	....
that they no time to laugh. There are more	(c)	....	....	....
important things do. Says Sudha Chandra,	(d)	....	....	....
"Hiring laughter coach is my aim here."	(e)	....	....	....

3.

		Before	Missing	After
In 2018, Indian Women's cricket team a	e.g.	team	played	a
T - 20 Match Pakistani team.	(a)	....	....	....
India won toss and	(b)	....	....	....
chose field first. The Pakistani team	(c)	....	....	....
lost three wickets no time.	(d)	....	....	....
The fourth wicket they tried level best to save the match.	(e)	....	....	....

4.

Police have launched special teams catch the snatchers. Each the teams will move into the crime affected areas. The teams directly report the district unit.

police teams residents will work together to catch snatchers.

	Before	Missing	After
e.g.	teams	to	catch
(a)	....	....	....
(b)	....	....	....
(c)	....	....	....
(d)	....	....	....
(e)	....	....	....

ANSWERS

Type I : Gap Filling

I.
1. (a) furniture
2. (b) did
3. (a) myself
4. (d) since
5. (a) The
6. (b) wasn't
7. (c) but
8. (c) may
9. (c) a
10. (d) into
11. (c) standing
12. (d) her
13. (b) quick
14. (d) greatest
15. (a) to
16. (c) by
17. (b) must
18. (b) are
19. (c) of
20. (d) one

II.A.
1. (c) To win
2. (d) coming
3. (b) to feel
4. (a) Winning
5. (c) Being

B.
1. (a) traced
2. (d) having
3. (a) ago
4. (b) found
5. (d) clues

C.
1. (d) for
2. (a) had
3. (d) writing
4. (b) has

D.
1. (d) to
2. (b) a
3. (c) had
4. (a) between
5. (c) sprung

III. A. (i) shifted (ii) the (iii) the (iv) got

B. (i) as (ii) sat (iii) staring (iv) were (v) who (vi) a (vii) while (viii) a

C. (i) the (ii) the (iii) decaying (iv) the

D. (i) an (ii) in (iii)or (iv) to

Type II : Jumbled Sentences

I.
1. (b) 4132
2. (c) 21354
3. (c) 1324
4. (a) 3214
5. (d) 2143
6. (b) 1243
7. (a) 3142
8. (a) 4132
9. (c) 1342
10. (d) 2431
11. (b) 1234
12. (a) 2314
13. (c) 3412
14. (c) 1324
15. (b) 2143
16. (a) 2134
17. (b) 3241

II.
1. My uniform is so itchy that I can't wait to take it off.
2. Early rising is good for both old and adults.
3. I love the weekend because I can be myself and dress down.
4. One can finish one's work early and go for a walk.
5. Music has an important place in our lives.
6. Urbanisation has spread its tentacles everywhere in India.
7. Good books and magazines light up the lamp of knowledge in every home.
8. This year, we are celebrating 'The Year of Books'.
9. I never thought I'd get through the interview; I was so nervous!
10. Reshma hopes to come back to the Disneyworld for a holiday next year.

11. Do you want me to see you off at the airport?
12. If someone betrays you once, it's his fault. If he betrays you twice, it's your fault.
13. The mother gave her baby a red apple.
14. I dreamt that I lived in Malabar hills.
15. Mohit and Preeti went skating on Saturday.
16. Eating ice cream is a good way to cool off.
17. Too many cooks spoil the broth.
18. How much money can you give me?
19. The king was annoyed that his authority was curbed.
20. I will wait for the right opportunity to strike.

Type III : Editing

1. (a) have - has
   (b) is - was
   (c) persons - person
   (d) the - a
   (e) his - our
2. (a) were - was
   (b) played - playing
   (c) was - were
   (d) helping - help
   (e) book - books
3. (a) did - do
   (b) exposes - expose
   (c) who - which
   (d) staying - stay
   (e) regularly - regular
4. (a) matter - matters
   (b) performs - perform
   (c) was - is
   (d) lose - lost
   (e) meant - means

Type IV : Omitting

1.	(a) annoyed	at	passwords
	(b) many	to	remember
	(c) day	we	are
	(d) bound	to	forget
	(e) difficulties	for	the
2.	(a) most	of	us
	(b) often	than	not
	(c) they	have	no
	(d) things	to	do
	(e) Hiring	a	laughter
3.	(a) match	against	Pakistani
	(b) won	the	loss
	(c) chose	to	field
	(d) wickets	in	no
	(e) -	in	the
4.	(a) Each	of	the
	(b) teams	will	directly
	(c) report	to	the
	(d) teams	and	residents
	(e) catch	the	snatchers

1 Sentences

- **Assertive/Declarative Sentences** Make general statements, end with full stop (.)
- **Interrogative Sentences** Ask questions, end with question mark (?)
- **Imperative Sentences** Give commands, request, advice etc., generally end with full stop (.)
- **Exclamatory Sentences** Present extreme emotions, end with exclamation mark (!)

2 Nouns

1 Types

1. **Proper Noun** Unique name, begin with capital letters e.g. Parth, XYZ cafe, London, etc.
2. **Common Noun** General name of people place or thing e.g. boy, cafe, bird etc.
3. **Collective Noun** Name given to a group e.g. herd, choir, etc.
4. **Abstract Noun** Name given to a feeling, state, idea, quality e.g. anger, childhood, freedom, beauty etc.
5. **Material Noun** From which, things, are made e.g. gold, silk, wood etc.
6. **Compound Noun** Noun made from two words e.g. black board, X-ray, etc.

2 Number Noun

- **Countable Noun** can be counted e.g. pens, cap.
  - **Singular** Refer one noun e.g. pen, boy, ant. etc.
  - **Plural** Refer more than one noun e.g. pens, boys, ants, etc.
- **Uncountable Noun** cannot be counted e.g. milk, hair, etc.

3 Gender Noun

1. **Masculine Gender** Refer to a male noun e.g. boy, king, lion etc.
2. **Feminine Gender** Refer to a female noun e.g. girl, queen, lioness, etc.
3. **Common Gender** Refer to a both male and female noun e.g. child, doctor, etc.
4. **Neuter Gender** Refer to a non-living things e.g. chair, ring, etc.

3 Pronouns

- **Personal Pronouns** Used in place of person or thing (He, she, I, you, we, him, her, they, then, it and us)
- **Possessive Pronouns** Shows ownership (Mine, his, hers, ours, yours and theirs)
- **Demonstrative Pronouns** Points to a particular noun (This, that, these and those)
- **Distributive Pronouns** Refers to each noun (Each, either, and neither)
- **Indefinite Pronouns** Does not refer to specific nouns e.g. any body, something, etc.
- **Relative Pronouns** Refers to noun mentioned before it (Who, whom, that, which and where)
- **Interrogative Pronouns** Ask questions (Who, whom, what, which and whose)
- **Reciprocal Pronoun** Expresses mutual action between two or more people (Each-other and one-another)
- **Reflexive Pronoun** Use to refer back to the noun (Himself, herself, yourself, myself, ourselves, themselves)
- **Emphatic Pronoun** Emphasise the noun (Same as reflexive pronoun)

4 Adverbs

- **Adverbs of Time** Indicates when action performed e.g. now, yesterday, still, yet, later etc.
- **Adverbs of Frequency** Indicates how often an action takes place e.g. regularly, rarely etc.
- **Adverb of Place** Indicates where an action is performed e.g. here, outside, near, away etc.
- **Adverb of Manner** Indicates how an action performed e.g. gracefully, angrily, fast, happily etc.
- **Adverb of Degree** Indicates intensity of an action e.g. completely, entirely, perfectly etc.
- **Interrogative Adverbs** Used to ask questions e.g. why, when, where, why, how

10 Determiners

- **Articles** Placed before noun to indicate whether is specific or general (A, an, the)
- **Possessive** Use to indicate ownership (My, your, his, her, our, their)
- **Demonstrative** Use to point to a specific noun (This, that, these, those)
- **Quantifiers** Denote the amount or quantity of a countable noun. (Enough, much, many, some, few, a few, the few, etc.)

Grammar at a Glance

9 Modals

- **Can** Expresses ability, request, possibility, suggestion
- **Could** Expresses polite request, past ability, future possibility
- **Will** Expresses request, future action, assumption, prediction
- **Would** Expresses future possibility, future action
- **Shall** Expresses future action, advice, request
- **Should** Expresses duty, obligation, possibility
- **May** Expresses polite request, wish, formal permission, present possibility
- **Might** Expresses less possibility, guess, ask permission
- **Must** Expresses necessity, prohibition, strong probability
- **Ought to** Expresses obligation, duty
- **Dare** Expresses warning, used in negative and in interrogative sense
- **Need to** Expresses absence of necessity in negative and interrogative sense

8 Conjunctions

- **Coordinating Conjunctions** Join two or more clause of equal importance. e.g. for, and, nor, but, or, yet and so.
- **Subordinating Conjunctions** Join dependent clause to main clause e.g. as, because since, while, until etc.
- **Correlative Conjunctions** Used in pairs to join two independent clause. e.g. either....or, neither ....nor, not only....but also.

7 Prepositions

- **Prepositions of Time** Denote when person or thing performs action e.g. by, on, at, in, from, to, for, since, ago, before, till.
- **Preposition of Place** Denote the location e.g. on, at, in, between, among, behind, above, under, below.
- **Preposition of Movement** Denote movement or direction e.g. to, towards, into, from, up, down, over, across, through.

6 Adjectives

- **Adjectives of Quality** Describes the quality of noun or pronoun e.g. beautiful, tall etc.
- **Adjective of Quantity** Describes the quantity of noun or pronoun e.g. lot of, much, enough
- **Adjective of Number** Shows how many or how much quantity of nouns or pronouns e.g. one, two, first, second, etc.
- **Demonstrative Adjectives** point out the specific nouns/pronouns being refer to e.g. this, that, these and those.
- **Possessive Adjectives** shows ownership e.g. my, our, his, her, their and your.
- **Interrogative Adjectives** asks question about noun e.g. which, whose and what.
- **Proper Adjectives** formed by proper noun e.g. Indian, Spanish etc.
- **Degree of Comparison Used to Compare Noun**

  Positive Degree of Adjective No comparison made e.g. good, clever, etc.

  Comparative Degree of Adjective Comparison between two nouns e.g. Better, cleverer, etc.

  Superlative Degree of Adjective Comparison between more than two nouns e.g. best, cleverest, etc.

5 Verbs

- **Main Verbs or Action Words** Denote an action

  Transitive Verbs Requires an object

  Intransitive Verbs Does not require object
- **Linking Verbs** Serves as a connectors e.g. is, am, are, has, have, had, do, does and did
- **Helping Verbs** Used with main verbs

  Primary (Same as linking verbs)

  Modals
- **Finite Verbs** Changes forms with numbers and tenses
- **Non-finite Verbs** Do not change forms

  Gerunds (Used as nouns)

  Infinitives (Used as nouns, adjectives or adverb)

  Participles (Used as adjectives)

SECTION D : LITERATURE

Prose	- Honeydew
Poetry	- Honeydew
Supplementary	- It so happened...

The Best Christmas Present in the World

by Micheal Morpungo

CHAPTER 1

CHAPTER SUMMARY 'The Best Christmas Present in the World' is a heart touching story written by Micheal Morpungo. The story revolves around a letter found by the narrator in an old desk. The letter was written by Jim Macpherson, a captain of the English army, to his wife-Connie. It narrates the incident that took place during the war between the British and Germans in 1914 on Christmas.
The letter is important as it presents how wars are useless. They only bring destruction and sadness to the world. The story, then, points out that only the path of peace will lead to happiness and welfare of mankind.

Part – I

The Narrator Finds a Roll-Top Desk

The story starts at the point when the narrator found a roll top desk made of oak in a junk shop in Bridport. The desk was made in the 19th century. The narrator had always wanted a roll-top desk but found them to be very expensive. However, this roll-top desk was cheap as it was damaged. It was broken at a number of places, was not properly mended and had burn marks on it.

The narrator thought that he could fix the desk even though he knew that it was difficult. So, he bought the desk and kept it in a workroom at the back of his garage.

The Secret Drawer

The narrator started to repair the desk on 24th December, Christmas Eve. He removed the roll top and took out the drawers. While doing so, he found that besides fire, water had also damaged the desk.

As the narrator was removing the drawers, he found that the last drawer was stuck. He tried to take it out gently. But when it did not work, he used force to open the drawer. He struck the drawer with his fist and the drawer opened. The narrator found that this drawer had another secret drawer inside it. This secret drawer had a black tin box with a note taped on it. The note said "Jim's last letter, received 25th January, 1915. To be buried with me when the time comes."

The Narrator Reads the Letter

The narrator knew that he should not open the box. However, he was curious; so, he opened the box. Inside the box, the narrator found an envelope with the address to Mrs. Jim Macpherson. The narrator opened the letter and found that it was written with pencil on 26th December, 1914.

Part – II

In this part the narrator is reading the letter.

The Letter

The letter that the narrator had found in the tin box was written for Connie (Mrs. Jim Macpherson). The writer (Jim Macpherson) states that he was happier because of something that had happened to him. He wanted Connie to know about the incident. He tells her that on a cold and beautiful Christmas morning, he and his team were standing in their hiding places. He tells Connie that he is embarrassed to tell her that the incident was started by the German Soldiers (Fritz).

The Incident

The writer tells Connie that he and his team saw a German soldier wave a white flag from their hiding places. The German soldiers wished them a 'Happy Christmas' and they replied back. Then, the German soldiers wearing a grey coat started coming out one by one. They told the English soldiers not to shoot them. This surprised the writer and his team. They thought that the German Soldiers were trying to trick them. However, it was not the case.

Christmas Celebration Invitation

The German soldiers waved a bottle above their heads and invited them to celebrate Christmas. They told the writer and his team that they had schnapps and sausage. Then, many German soldiers were seen walking towards the writer and his team. From the English soldiers, Little Private Morris was the first to stand up. He told his team that the German soldiers were trying to celebrate and they should join them.

The writer felt that he should have stopped his team. However, he and his team joined the German soldiers in the middle of the land which belonged to no government or state. They were making peace in the middle of the war between them.

Hans Wolf and Jim Macpherson

The writer tells Connie that he cannot describe the feeling he felt when a German soldier came to him and shook his hand. The German soldier introduced himself as Hans Wolf who belonged to Dusseldorf. He told the writer that he played cello in orchestra and wished him a Happy Christmas. The writer also introduced himself as Jim Macpherson who was a school teacher from Dorset located in the west of England.

The writer adds that the German soldier started a conversation with him. He told the writer about how he knew about Dorset. Then, the writer offered him his drink while the German soldier shared his sausage. The writer tells his wife that the German soldier had never been to Dorset but had read about it in his school and from reading books in English. He loved books written by Thomas Hardy and his favourite book was 'Far from the Maddening Crowd'.

The writer and the German soldier talked about Bathsheba, Gabriel Oak, Sergeant Troy and Dorset. The German soldier told him that he was married and had a 6 month old son. They looked at the others enjoying the celebration and ate the Christmas cake. The writer, then, tells his wife that the German soldier, Hans, and he were very similar even though Hans was his enemy.

The Football Match

The writer tells his wife that this was a unique and special Christmas for him. Then, he tells her about the football match they had played after the Christmas celebration. The writer states that after the celebration, someone took out a football. The soldiers took off their coats into piles which acted as goalposts. He adds that Hans, the German soldier, and him were clapping and cheering the players.

While the other soldiers were playing football. Hans looked at the writer with a smile and told him that they should solve the war with a football match. This is so because then no one will be killed, no wife will lose their husband and no child will lose a parent. The writer agreed and told Hans that he believes that instead of football, they should play cricket as then the English team would have more chances of winning.

After the Match

The writer further tells Connie that the German soldiers won the football match with two goals. However, Hans told him that the German team won because their goal post was wider.

After the game ended and the food was finished, the English and German soldiers bid each other goodbyes. The writer told Hans that he wished for the war to end soon so that Hans got to see his family and they could all go home. Hans told the writer that all the soldiers from both the English and the German teams wanted the same thing- to go back home. Then, they both left with their teams.

The writer adds that late at night, they heard the German soldiers singing a Christmas carol- Silent Night (Stille Nacht). The English soldiers also joined them by singing another carol- While Shepherds Watched. Then, everything was silent. The writer feels that he would treasure the day as long as he would live.

Ending of the Letter

The writer, then, address Connie and tell her that by next Christmas, the war would be over. But he knows that all the soldiers wanted peace. He, ends the letter telling her that he would meet her soon.

Part – III

Looking for Connie Macpherson

After reading the letter, the narrator decided to return it to Connie Macpherson. So, he drove into Bridport and asked a boy where Cooper Beeches was. However, when he reached house number 12, he found that the house was completely destroyed. The narrator, then, went to the neighbouring house and asked if they knew where Mrs. Macpherson was.

Mrs. Macpherson

An old man in his slipper came and told the narrator that Mrs. Macpherson was a lovely 101 years old lady. She has been in the house when her house caught fire. No one knew about how the fire started but some people believe it to be candles as Mrs. Macpherson used candles. She did not use electricity because she thought that it was expensive. She was saved by a fireman. Now, she was in a nursing home named Burlington House on Dorchester road located in the other side of the town.

The Nursing Home

The narrator found the Burlington House Nursing home easily. As he entered the Nursing Home. he found that the place was decorated with paper chains and Christmas tree. He saw the dining room where people were celebrating Christmas. To meet Mrs. Macpherson, he told the matron that he was a friend of the lady and had come with a gift for her.

The matron was happy to see the narrator and offered him mince pie. When the narrator told her about the reason for the visit, she told her that Mrs. Macpherson was not feeling well and so was resting. She also told the narrator that Mrs. Macpherson had no family to visit her and that she would be happy to see the narrator. Then, the matron took the narrator to a conservatory.

Meeting Mrs. Macpherson

In the conservatory, the narrator found an old woman sitting in a wheelchair. Her hand were on her lap, her hair was pinned in a bun and she was looking out in the garden. The narrator greeted the lady and wished her Christmas. He, then, gave her the letter.

Mrs. Macpherson was looking at the narrator with a blank expression when the narrator was telling her about how he found the letter. But as soon as she saw the letter, Mrs. Macpherson became happy. She recognised the letter and took it from the narrator.

Mrs. Macpherson's Mistake

Suddenly, she took the narrator's hand and remembered the promise that Jim had made to her. She thought that the narrator was Jim and called meeting him again 'the best Christmas present in the world'. Then, the narrator sat with Mrs. Macpherson and she kissed his cheek. Mrs. Macpherson addressed the narrator as Jim and told the narrator that she has been waiting for him and had read the letter many times. Now, she wanted him to read the letter because she wanted to hear his voice. She added that after he had read the letter, she would make a nice Christmas cake with marzipan all around because she knows that her husband loves marzipan.

Word Meaning

Word	Meaning
Clumsily	lacking grace in movement or posture.
Mended	restored by replacing a part or putting together what is torn or broken.
Scorch marks	to become dried or colourless due to slight burning
Veneer	a thin decorative covering of plastic or fine wood to cover a coarse wood
Taken their toll on	damaged
Stuck fast	shut tight
Brute	strong and blunt
Shallow	having little depth
Scruples	the feeling of doubt or hesitation with regards to the morality of an action
Trenches	long deep ditcher in the ground where soldier hide, from the enemy
Frosty	cold, chilly
Fritz	a name for a German soldier (common German name)
No man's land	an unused land which is not under the rule of any government
Tommy	an English soldier (common English name)

Word	Meaning
That would be that	that was all; that was the end of the matter
Schnapps	a kind of strong alcohol, resembling gin
Cello	a four stringed musical instrument, resembling a large violin
Parapet	a low protective wall
Outstretched	extended or stretched out
Marzipan	a sweet yellow or white paste made of sugar and almonds
Dumped	to discard
Dugout	trench
Burned out	destroyed by fire
Gaping	wide and open
Boarded-up	covered with wooden boards
Whereabouts	the location
Muddle-headed	confused
Conservatory	greenhouse
Wispy	fluffy
Lit up	became bright with happiness and excitement
Suffused with	glow of happiness spread all over the face
Tenderly	caringly

NCERT FOLDER

NCERT Intext and Exercise Questions

BEFORE YOU READ (NCERT PAGE 9)

Q.1 Do you know which events the dates below refer to?

(i) 4th July, 1776

Ans. American Declaration of Independence

(ii) 17th December, 1903

Ans. Wilbur and Orville Wright made the first flight, remaining in the air for 12 seconds and covering 120 feet.

(iii) 6th August, 1945

Ans. Hiroshima Day or the day when an atomic bomb was dropped on Hiroshima in Japan on this day.

(iv) 30th January, 1948

Ans. Assassination of Mahatma Gandhi

(v) 12th April, 1961

Ans. Yuri A. Gagarin became the first human to orbit the Earth.

(vi) 20th July, 1969

Ans. Neil Armstrong became the first human to set foot on the moon.

COMPREHENSION CHECK❶ (NCERT PAGE 10)

Q.1 What did the author find in a junk shop?

Ans. The author found an old roll- top desk in a junk shop in Bridport. It was made of oak wood in the early 19th century.

Q.2 What did he find in a secret drawer? Who do you think had put it in there?

Ans. In the secret drawer, the narrator found a small tin box that contained a letter. In the tin box, there was a note which said that it was Jim's last letter which was received on 25th January, 1915.

I think the letter was put by the receiver Mrs. Connie Macpherson there for safety.

CHECK❷ (NCERT PAGE 14)

Q.1 Who had written the letter, to whom and when?

Ans. Jim had written the letter to his wife, Connie, when he was away on the war front fighting the war against the Germans. The letter was written a day after Christmas i.e. on 26th December, 1914. It reached Mrs. Macpherson on 25th January, 1915.

Q.2 Why was the letter written–what was the wonderful thing that had happened?

Ans. Jim wrote this letter to his wife, Connie to describe certain unusual events that took place on the previous day. The wonderful thing that happened was that in the midst of the war, the British and the German soldiers had come together to celebrate Christmas.

They shared their food, drinks and cake. It was unbelievable for Jim and perhaps for others too to think of enemies setting aside their weapons and making peace. Jim shared with Connie all the details of the way that they celebrated Christmas Day together on no man's land.

Q.3 What jobs did Hans Wolf and Jim Macpherson have when they were not soldiers?

Ans. The jobs that Hans Wolf and Jim Macpherson had in their daily lives were very different from that of a soldier. Hans Wolf played the cello in an orchestra in Dusseldorf. Jim Macpherson, on the other hand, was a school teacher in Dorset.

Q.4 Had Hans Wolf ever been to Dorset? Why did he say he knew it?

Ans. Hans Wolf had never been to Dorset. Despite that, he knew fairly well about the place. He had read a lot about Dorset in school and had read about it in English books.

Q.5 Do you think Jim Macpherson came back from the war? How do you know this?

Ans. No. Jim Macpherson never came back from the war. This can be concluded from the fact that even at the end of the chapter when Jim's wife Connie is a hundred and one years old. She is still waiting for Jim to come back from the war. This shows that Jim probably died in the war soon after writing that letter to Connie.

CHECK❸ (NCERT PAGE 15)

Q.1 Why did the author go to Bridport?

Ans. The author went to Bridport to meet Connie and return Jim's last letter to her. The tin box that contained the letter had Connie's message pasted upon it, "To be buried with me when the time comes." This showed that the letter was very important to her.

So, the narrator could not restrain himself from taking the letter to its rightful owner.

Q.2 How old was Mrs. Macpherson now? Where was she?

Ans. Mrs. Macpherson was now a hundred and one years old. She was admitted to Burlington House Nursing Home after her house had caught fire.

CHECK❹ (NCERT PAGE 16)

Q.1 Who did Connie Macpherson think her visitor was?

Ans. Connie Macpherson thought that the visitor was her husband Jim who had promised to come back home from the war by next Christmas.

Q.2 Which sentence in the text shows that the visitor did not try to hide his identity?

Ans. The following sentence shows that the visitor did not try to hide his identity from Connie Macpherson :
"I found this. I think it's yours."

WORKING WITH THE TEXT (NCERT PAGE 16)

Q.1 For how long do you think Connie had kept Jim's letter? Give reasons for your answer.

Ans. Connie must have kept her husband, Jim's letter for a very long time as she used to read it very often. Jim was a British officer fighting in the war against the Germans. The soldiers in armies are usually young men. This tells us that Connie must also have been a young lady when she received her husband's letter on 25th January, 1915.

When we meet Mrs. Macpherson in the Burlington House Nursing Home, she is an old lady, aged hundred and one. The time lapse clearly indicates that Connie must have preserved Jim's letter for more than 70 years in the hopes that he would come back and read the letter to her.

Q.2 Why do you think the desk had been sold and when?

Ans. Judging by the damaged physical condition of the desk, it is probable that the desk must have been sold after Connie's home caught fire and she was taken to the nursing home.

Q.3 Why do Jim and Hans think that games or sports are good way of resolving conflicts? Do you agree?

Ans. Jim and Hans thought that games or sports are better ways of resolving conflicts than going to war because war only leads to death and destruction. No matter which side wins the war, loss of life and sorrow are common to both the armies. Families are ruined, children are orphaned and wives are widowed.
I completely agree with this line of thought as no one dies during sport matches. Peace constructs the society whereas war destroys it.

Q.4 Do you think the soldiers of the two armies are like each other or different from each other? Find evidence from the story to support your answer.

Ans. There is enough evidence in the story to prove that the soldiers of both the armies are no different from each other. The soldiers from both the sides love the idea of peace and harmony. They lose no time in coming together to celebrate Christmas with each other, forgetting that they are supposed to be each other's enemies. They bring their drinks, sausages and cakes and unite in perfect brotherhood.

Also, the soldiers on both the sides became sad again when they had to return to their trenches and continue with the war. Jim Macpherson also regretted that he was not the first one to initiate the celebration.

Q.5 Mention the various ways in which the British and the German soldiers become friends and find things in common at Christmas.

Ans. The British and German soldiers became friends on Christmas because of the festive spirit which they all had in common. The way that they eagerly come together to celebrate shows that the soldiers on both sides wished for the war to end so that they could go home to their families. This is further proved when Hans Wolf says that this is what every soldier wants.

During the Christmas celebration, all the soldiers enjoy drinks, sausages (meat) and cakes. They play a friendly match of football and sing Christmas carols with each other as well.

Q.6 What is Connie's Christmas present? Why is it 'the best Christmas present in the world'?

Ans. Connie's Christmas present was the last letter that Jim had written to her and her belief that Jim had come back to her.

It is called the best Christmas present because Connie thought that she had most probably lost the letter in the house fire. Now, not only did she get the letter but Jim (actually the narrator) had fulfilled his promise of coming back to her.

Q.7 Do you think the title of this story is suitable for it? Can you think of any other title(s)?

Ans. According to me, the title of the story 'The Best Christmas Present in the World' is very suitable, as all the events in the story revolve around Christmas. Each of the primary characters receives a present on the day of Christmas.

Jim Macpherson and Hans Wolf rejoice in the merriment of Christmas along with their armies. Away from home in a war, they get to be happy, even though temporarily.

The narrator manages to buy the desk he had been longing to buy. Connie Macpherson gets her special letter back and believes that on Christmas her husband has finally returned to her, as he had promised years ago in the letter.

WORKING WITH LANGUAGE

(NCERT PAGE 17-19)

Q.1 Look at these sentences from the story.

I *spotted* it in a junk shop in Bridport... The man *said* it was made in the early 19th century... This one *was* in a bad condition...

The italicised verbs are in the past tense. They tell us what happened in the past, before now.

(i) Read the passage below and underline the verbs in the past tense.

A man got on the train and sat down.
The compartment was empty except for one lady.
She took her gloves off. A few hours later the police arrested the man. They held him for 24 hours and then freed him.

Ans. A man got on the train and sat down. The compartment was empty except for one lady. She took her gloves off. A few hours later the police arrested the man. They held him for 24 hours and then, freed him.

Now, look at these sentences.

The veneer *had lifted* almost everywhere. Both fire and water *had taken* their toll on this desk.

Notice the verb forms *had lifted*, *had taken* (their toll). The author found and bought the desk in the past. The desk was damaged before the author found it and bought it.

Fire and water had damaged the desk *before* the author found it and bought it.

- We use verb forms like *had damaged* for an event in the 'earlier past'. If there are two events in the past, we use the 'had...' form for the event that occurred first in the past.
- We also use the past perfect tense to show that something was wished for or expected before a particular time in the past. e.g. I *had always wanted one...*
- Discuss with your partner the difference in meaning in the sentences below.
  When I reached the station, the train left.
  When I reached the station, the train had left.

(ii) Fill in the blanks using the correct form of the verbs in brackets.

My little sister is very naughty. When she ....(come) back from school yesterday, she had ....(tear) her dress. We .... (ask) her how it had .... (happen). She .... (say) she .... (have) .... (quarrel) with a boy. She .... (have) .... (beat) him in a race and he .... (have) ....(try) to push her. She ..... (have) .... (tell) the teacher and so he ....(have) .... (chase) her and she ....(have)................(fall) down and.............. (have) .... (tear) her dress.

Ans. My little sister is very naughty. When she came back from school yesterday, she had torn her dress. We asked her how it had happened. She said she had quarreled with a boy. She had beaten him in a race and he had tried to push her. She had told the teacher and so, he had chased her and she had fallen down and had torn her dress.

(iii) Underline the verbs and arrange them in two columns, Past and Earlier past.

(a) My friends set out to see the caves in the next town, but I stayed at home, because I had seen them already.

(b) When they arrived at the station, their train had left. They came back home, but by that time I had gone out to see a movie.

(c) So they sat outside and ate the lunch I had packed for them.

(d) By the time I returned, they had fallen asleep.

Past	Earlier Past

Ans. (a) My friends set out to see the caves in the next town, but I stayed at home, because I had seen them already.

(b) When they arrived at the station, their train had left. They came back home, but by that time I had gone out to see a movie!

(c) So they sat outside and ate the lunch I had packed for them.

(d) By the time I returned, they had fallen asleep!

Past	Earlier Past
stayed	had seen
arrived	had left
came	had gone
sat, ate	had packed
returned	had fallen

Q.2 Dictionary Work

By the end of the journey, we had run out of drinking water.

Look at the verb *run out* of in this sentence. It is a phrasal verb: it has two parts, a verb and a preposition or an adverb.

Phrasal verbs often have meanings that are different from the meanings of their parts.

Find these phrasal verbs in the story.

burn out, lit up, looked on, run out, keep out

Write down the sentences in which they occur. Consult a dictionary and write down the meaning that you think matches the meaning of the phrasal verb in the sentences.

Ans. (i) **Burn out** completely burnt

House number 12 turned out to be nothing but a **burned-out** shell.

(ii) **Lit up** glow

That was the moment her eyes **lit up** with recognition and her face became suffused with a sudden glow of happiness.

(iii) **Looked on** watched

Hans Wolf and **I looked on** and cheered, clapping our hands and stamping our feet.

(iv) **Run out** finished

The time came and all too soon, when the game was finished, the schnapps and the rum and the sausage had long since **run out** and we knew it was all over.

(v) **Keep out** Prevent from entering

Hans, Wolf and I looked on and cheered clapping our hands and stamping our feet, to **keep out** the cold as much as anything.

Q.3 Noun phrase

Read the following sentence.

I took out a small *black tin box*.

- The phrase in italics is a noun phrase.
  - It has the noun—box—as the head word and three adjectives preceding it.
  - Notice the order in which the adjectives occur—*size* (small), *colour* (black) and *material* (tin) of which it is made.

We rarely use more than four adjectives before a noun and there is no rigid order in which they are used, though there is a preferred order of modifiers/adjectives in a noun phrase, as given below.

Determiner	Modifier 1 (opinion, feeling)	Modifier 2 (size, shape, age)	Modifier 3 (colour)	Modifier 4 (material)	Head word
A/ an/ the	nice/lazy/ beautiful	tall/round/ old/young	red/ white/ light/dark	silk/ cotton/ woollen	woman/man / table/chair

Q.4 The table below contains a list of nouns and some adjectives. Use as many adjectives as you can to describe each noun. You might come up with some funny descriptions!

Nouns	Adjectives
elephant	circular, stripped, enormous,
face	multicoloured, round, cheerful, wild, blue,
building	red, chubby, large, medium-sized, cold
water	

Ans.

Nouns	Adjectives
elephant	enormous, multicoloured
face	stripped, round, cheerful, red, chubby sized
building	large, medium-sized, multicoloured
water	blue, cold

SPEAKING (NCERT PAGE 19)

Q.1 In groups discuss whether wars are a good way to end conflicts between countries. Then present your arguments to the whole class.

Ans. War is definitely not a good way of resolving conflicts between countries. They only lead to destruction and devastation with loss of both human life and property.

Human loss War is responsible for the death of trained, skilled, zealous and patriotic soldiers. Many a times when a soldier returns, he has injuries that bring life long sufferings. This suffering is also extended to his family members who constantly mourn separation, death and sufferings.Children are orphaned, wives are widowed and parents lose their sons. War also affects civilians who fall prey to the war.

Economic loss A lot of money is spent by the government in maintaining armies. Also, during war there is an increased expenditure on maintaining weapons and ammunition that are essential in combating the enemy. This money could be spent on welfare programmes, infrastructural developments and so on.

In a civilised society, discussions, negotiations and peace treaties could be good alternatives to avoid war and live in a peaceful and harmonious atmosphere.

Q.2 What kind of presents do you like and why? What are the things you keep in mind when you buy presents for others? Discuss with your partner.

Ans. Presents are usually tokens of love and blessings. It is good to receive them. One feels loved and pampered. I like receiving painting materials and books as presents. I use them to create paintings to decorate my home. While buying presents for others, there are two points to be kept in mind which are as follow

(i) The preferences of the person for whom we are buying the present. It is good to keep aside our personal likes and think of what would be suitable had that person been buying something for himself/ herself.

(ii) The efficacy or the worth of the present. Presents are also good ways of inculcating and encouraging good habits in others. For instance, gifting a book that could be read by people over a period of time and also be shared with others. It is also a good source of knowledge. Gifting a potted plant is another good method of improving our surroundings and environment and aiming at creating cleaner and greener spaces around us. It is also good to buy and give presents to children at orphanages as they have no one who could give them this happiness.

WRITING (NCERT PAGE 20)

Q.1 Imagine that you are Jim. You have returned to your town after the war. In your diary, record how you feel about the changes you see and the events that occur in your town. You could begin like this,
25th December, 1919, it's Christmas today, but the town looks......

Ans. 25th December, 1919 9:00 PM

The war is over. I have returned home and today is Christmas, but Christmas doesn't have its usual cheer and gaiety. Hardly any people can be seen on the streets dancing, singing, and making merry. It's been more than a month since the war has been over. However, people are still terrorised and are hesitant to step out.

The empty streets are not the same either. The parks, fountains and almost every other building have been reduced to debris. The purity of air has been replaced by the smell of blood and fire.

I just cannot connect with this town. I get lost while wandering, because all those familiar landmarks have been reduced to heaps of garbage. I feel so sad and helpless.

Connie is sad too. She is traumatised and gets lost in the web of her thoughts. I wish this war had never happened. How I wish that last Christmas celebrations should not have been further followed by war. Things would have been different today. Things would have been normal today.

Jim

Or

Suppose you are the visitor. You are in a dilemma. You don't know whether to disclose your identity and disappoint the old lady or let her believe that her dear Jim has come back. Write a letter to a friend highlighting your anxiety, fears and feelings.

Ans. House No. 10,

XYZ Street,

Burlington

25th December, 19XX

Dear Peter

How have you been, my friend? I have been fine physically. It's been a long time since we last met. I had come to Burlington for some work and have encountered a string of strange events. My thoughts are all muddled up. I am sharing my feelings with you hoping you could help. The string of strange events started with my buying a roll-top desk. It was in a bad condition, so I started working on its repair and while doing so, I saw a secret drawer which contained a letter. The letter was written by Jim, an army officer, to his wife Connie while he was away at the war with Germans. It was quite an old letter dated 1914.

Having read the letter, I immediately knew how special and treasured this letter was. So, the next morning I thought of meeting Mrs. Macpherson.

With the help of the address indicated on the envelope, I reached there and got to know that their house had caught fire and Mrs. Macpherson was now in a nursing home. I went to see her in the hospital. She had turned so old and was sitting on a wheelchair. I tried explaining her how I had found it. However, she had become lost in her thoughts and somehow she thought that I was Jim, her dead husband. She kissed my cheek, held my hands, asked me to talk to her and I animatedly did it all.

I came back home after a little while and my thoughts were entirely stuck as to what to do next. Should I tell her the truth and disappoint her? Or should I allow her to die peacefully thinking that finally her husband had returned to her?

Dear friend, please help me understand what should be the right course of action.

Yours truly

Tom

Q.2 Given below is the outline of a story. Construct the story using the outline.

A young, newly married doctor .... freedom fighter .... exiled to the Andaman and Nicobar Islands by the British .... infamous Cellular Jail .... prisoners tortured ....revolt by inmates ....doctor hanged .... wife waits for his return .... becomes old .... continues to wait with hope and faith.

Ans. A young newly married doctor, who was also a freedom fighter, was detained a day after his marriage and exiled to the Andaman and Nicobar Islands by the British to the infamous Cellular Jail. All this happened so suddenly and discreetly that nobody got to know what had happened.

In the jail, the prisoners were tortured and beaten up. They were not allowed to write letters to their relatives. They were expected to silently endure all this, but one fine day there was a revolt by the inmates. They decided to get together and protest.

The authorities did not know how to handle it and to suppress the revolt, many inmates were hanged to death. The doctor too was hanged. His wife didn't get the news of his death. She kept waiting for him to return. Endlessly waiting, she became old, but her husband never returned. Despite that, she continues to wait with hope and faith.

REVIEW EXERCISE
Including Competency Based Questions

Multiple Choice Questions

1. Where did the narrator buy the old desk from?

(a) Junk shop (b) Charity
(c) Mall (d) Pawn shop

Ans. (a) Junk shop

2. When did the narrator start working on the restoration of the old desk?

(a) New Year's Eve (b) Christmas Eve
(c) Black Friday (d) Easter

Ans. (b) Christmas Eve

3. Where did the narrator buy the old desk from?

(a) Bridport (b) Dusseldorf
(c) Dorset (d) Dorchester

Ans. (a) Bridport

4. When did Connie receive Jim's letter? Diksha

(a) 25th January, 1915 (b) 20th January, 1920
(c) 25th December, 1947 (d) 15th January, 1950

Ans. (a) 25th January, 1915

5. Who was the letter addressed to?

(a) Connie MacGonagall (b) Jim McGonagall
(c) Connie Macpherson (d) Jim Macpherson

Ans. (c) Connie Macpherson

6. British soldiers are called ...., while the German soldiers are called .... Diksha

(a) Tommy, Fritz (b) Fritz, Tommy
(c) Timmy, Schapps (d) Schnapps, Timmy

Ans. (a) Tommy, Fritz

7. Schnapps is a kind of .... , and sausage means .... Diksha

(a) meat, sauce (b) German wine, meat
(c) snack, soup (d) British dish, vegetable

Ans. (b) German wine, meat

8. The favourite book of Hans Wolf is .... It has been written by ....

(a) Gone with the wind, Margaret Mitchell
(b) Far from the Madding Crowd, Thomas Hardy
(c) The Return of the Native, Thomas Hardy
(d) Fathers and Sons, Ivan Turgenev

Ans. (b) Far from the Madding Crowd, Thomas Hardy

9. Which of these most clearly conveys the importance of the letter? Competency Based

(a) It was locked in a tin box.
(b) It was written on Christmas Eve.
(c) Jim stopped writing further letters.
(d) Connie was able to save it from the fire.

Ans. (b) It was written on Christmas Eve.

10. Who are Bathsheba, Gabriel Oak and Sergeant Troy? Competency Based

(a) Hans' family
(b) Officers in the army
(c) Jims neighbours in Dorset
(d) Characters from Hans's favourite book.

Ans. (d) Characters from Hans's favourite book.

11. Based on the events of the text, which statement is true? Competency Based

(a) Jim's optimism about returning home was misplaced.
(b) Jim's army was being tricked by the Germans.
(c) Jim' did not believe he would survive the war.
(d) Jim was proud of his achievements.

Ans. (a) Jim's optimism about returning home was misplaced.

12. Which of these does the author do? Competency Based

(a) Starts the story with an exciting event.
(b) Ends with a revelation that changes the plot.
(c) Teaches a life lesson through the characters.
(d) Narrates events from the past to set the context.

Ans. (c) Teaches a life lesson through the characters.

13. Read the statements given below and choose the correct answer.

Statement 1 The narrator was happy for the old Mrs. Machpherson.

Statement 2 Old Mrs. Macpherson had lost her memory.

(a) Statement 1 is true but Statement 2 is false.
(b) Statement 1 is false but Statement 2 is true.
(c) Both the statements are true.
(d) Both the statements are false.

Ans. (a) Statement 1 is true but Statement 2 is false.

14. Which of the following best describes the ending of the story?

(a) Sad (b) Open-ended
(c) Full of dilemma (d) Joyous

Ans. (c) Full of dilemma

Extract Based Questions

1. Read the extract given below and answer the following questions.

"I spotted it in .... on Christmas Eve" I spotted it in a junk shop in Bridport, a roll-top desk. The man said it was early nineteenth century, and oak. I had wanted one, but they were far too expensive. This one was in a bad condition, the roll-top in several pieces, one leg clumsily mended, scorch marks all down one side. It was going for very little money. I thought I could restore it. It would be a risk, a challenge, but I had to have it. I paid the man and brought it back to my workroom at the back of the garage. I began work on it on Christmas Eve.

(i) Why hadn't the narrator bought an oak desk before?

Ans. The narrator hadn't bought an oak desk before because oak desks were very expensive.

(ii) Why was the oak desk in the junk shop being sold at a cheap rate?

Ans. The oak desk in the junk shop being sold at a cheap rate because it was quite damaged.

(iii) When and where did the narrator begin restoring the desk?

Ans. The narrator began restoring the oak desk in his garage on Christmas Eve, 24th December.

(iv) What kind of damage do 'scorch marks' suggest?

Ans. 'Scorch marks' suggest damage by fire.

(v) What is the meaning of the phrase 'clumsily mended'?

Ans. 'Clumsily mended' means badly repaired.

2. Read the extract given below and answer the following questions.

I should like to be able to tell you that we began it. But the truth, I'm ashamed to say, is that Fritz began it. First someone saw a white flag waving from the trenches opposite. Then they were calling out to us from across no man's land, "Happy Christmas, Tommy! Happy Christmas!" When we had got over the surprise, some of us shouted back, "Same to you, Fritz! Same to you!" I thought that would be that. We all did. But then suddenly one of them was up there in his grey greatcoat and waving a white flag. "Don't shoot, lads!" someone shouted. And no one did. Then there was another Fritz up on the parapet, and another. "Keep your heads down," I told the men, "it's a trick." But it wasn't.

(i) Why did Jim call the German soldiers 'Fritz'?

Ans. Jim called the German soldiers 'Fritz' because it was a common German name.

(ii) Whom does 'Tommy' refer to in the extract?

Ans. In the extract, Tommy refers to the British soldiers.

(iii) In your opinion, why is Jim ashamed?

Ans. Jim is ashamed because instead of him, it was the German side that initiated the truce and the Christmas party.

(iv) What is the meaning of the word 'parapet'?

Ans. The word 'parapet' means a protective wall along the top of a trench.

(v) What does the phrase 'keep your head down'?

Ans. The phrase 'keep your head down' means to try to avoid trouble.

3. Read the extract given below and answer the following questions.

"Then they were calling out to us from across no man's land, "Happy Christmas, Tommy ! Happy Christmas!" When we had got over the surprise, some of us shouted back, 'Same to you, Fritz! Same to you' thought that would be that. We all did. But then suddenly one of them was up there in his grey greatcoat and waving a white flag.

"Don't shoot lads!" someone shouted. And no one did. Then there was another Fritz up on the parapet, and another. "Keep your heads down," I told the men, "it's a trick." But it wasn't.

(i) Who is the speaker of these lines?

(a) Jim (b) Tommy
(c) Hans Wolf (d) The narrator

Ans. (a) Jim

(ii) What is the 'trick' that the speaker is talking about?

(a) The waving of flag by the Germans.
(b) Germans wishing Christmas.
(c) Germans offering their food and drinks.
(d) Germans' playing football.

Ans. (a) The waving of flag by the Germans.

(iii) What was the speaker's reaction when he realises that it wasn't a trick?

(a) He was ashamed (b) He gets very angry
(c) He was embarrassed (d) He began to cry

Ans. (a) He was ashamed

(iv) **In the context of war, what does 'waving a white flag' mean?**

(a) The waving party is offering a truce.
(b) The waving party is surrendering.
(c) The waving party is pulling back.
(d) The waving party is activating landmines.

Ans. (a) The waving party is offering a truce.

(v) **Which of the following words is an antonym of 'shout'?**

(a) Scream (b) Whisper (c) Roar (d) Bellow

Ans. (b) Whisper

4. Read the extract given below and answer the following questions.

"That was the moment her eyes lit up with recognition and her face became suffused with a sudden glow of happiness. I explained about the desk, about how I had found it, but I don't think she was listening. For a while she said nothing, but stroked the letter tenderly with her fingertips."

(i) **Who is the 'her' in these lines?**

(a) The matron
(b) Old Mrs. Macpherson
(c) Young Mrs. Macpherson
(d) The neighbour

Ans. (b) Old Mrs. Macpherson

(ii) **Why did she become happy?**

(a) Because it was Christmas
(b) At the sight of the visitor
(c) Because the matron had served apple pie
(d) On seeing the decorations and the Christmas tree

Ans. (b) At the sight of the visitor

(iii) **Who did she think had come?**

(a) Jim (b) Hans Wolf
(c) Her father (d) Her brother

Ans. (a) Jim

(iv) **What is the meaning of the word 'suffuse'?**

(a) Lacking clarity or conciseness.
(b) Gradually spread through or over.
(c) Produced or given in large amounts.
(d) Succeed in persuading someone to do something.

Ans. (b) Gradually spread through or over.

(v) **Which of the following words is not a synonyms of 'tender'?**

(a) Caring (b) Kind (c) Callous (d) Gentle

Ans. (c) Callous

Very Short Answer Type Questions

1. Which war does the story talk about?

Ans. The story talks about the First World War, 1914-1918.

2. How did the table most likely get scorch marks? **Competency Based**

Ans. The most likely way that the table had gotten scorch marks was during the fire in Connie's house.

3. What was the colour of the box that contained Jim's letter?

Ans. The box that contained Jim's letter was a small black coloured tin box.

4. Who all were there in Hans Wolf's family?

Ans. Hans Wolf had a wife and a 6 month old son.

5. Which game did Jim prefer to play, as a solution to war?

Ans. Jim thought it was better to resolve the war by playing cricket.

6. What did the old man, Mrs. Macpherson's neighbour tell the narrator about her?

Ans. The old man told the narrator that Mrs. Macpherson was a lovely lady, but also muddle-headed because of her age.

7. Why did Mrs. Macpherson continue using candles for light?

Ans. Mrs. Macpherson used to burn candles for light because she thought that electricity was expensive.

8. What was the atmosphere of the Burlington House Nursing home when the author reached there? **Diksha**

Ans. The atmosphere of the Burlington House was festive and cheerful when the author reached there.

9. What did the matron offer to the narrator?

Ans. The matron offered a mince pie to the narrator.

10. What did the Matron inform the narrator? **Diksha**

Ans. The Matron informed the narrator that Mrs. Macpherson will be pleased to meet the narrator because she doesn't have any family, and so no one visits her.

Short Answer Type Questions

1. What was Jim ashamed of?

Ans. Jim was ashamed of the fact that he was not the first one to initiate peace between the soldiers of the two armies. This initiative was taken by the Germans. He was also ashamed because he had been suspicious of the Germans when they waved a white flag to indicate peace. He thought it to be one of their dirty tricks.

2. On the 'No man's land' what does the mingling of the breaths of Hans and Jim signify? **Diksha**

Ans. When Hans and Jim were watching the football match, their breaths mingled and they both smiled. It was significant because a human's breath is the symbol of life. Even though Jim and Hans were enemies by nationalities with a disputed border between them, they are essentially the same. This shows how stupid human conflicts are.

3. According to Hans Wolf, how is football a better way to resolve war? Diksha

Ans. According to Hans Wolf, a football match was the better way to resolve war because no one dies in a football match. No children are orphaned and no wives become widows. The thinking of Hans Wolf is right since war means bloodshed, loss and pain.

4. Why was the narrator unable to sleep, having read Jim's letter to Connie?

Ans. The narrator could not sleep the whole night after having read Jim's letter addressed to Connie because of the special status that the letter held in Connie's life. The note on the tin box that contained the letter had Mrs. Macpherson's message, "To be buried with me when the time comes." This forced him to think of Connie and the letter and also of a way to return it to her.

5. How did Mrs. Macpherson's house catch fire?

Ans. Mrs. Macpherson's house caught fire because she used to light up a lot of candles. Mrs. Macpherson used candles for light as she believed that electricity was very expensive. She was very old and therefore, she could have left a candle burning in a dangerous place.

6. Why was the matron happy to take the narrator to meet Mrs. Macpherson.

Ans. The matron very happily and willingly took the narrator to a conservatory, which had cane chairs and lots of plants. In the room, old Mrs. Macpherson was seated all by herself for she had no relatives and therefore no one came to meet her. The matron was happy that finally somebody had come to meet Mrs. Macpherson.

7. Briefly note down the initial reaction of Mrs. Macpherson after seeing the tin box? Diksha

Ans. The moment Mrs. Macpherson saw the tin box, her eyes lit up with recognition and her face became suffused with a sudden glow of happiness. She did not listen to anything the narrator said. Instead, she kept stroking the letter gently.

8. Why did old Mrs. Macpherson become happy when she met the narrator?

Ans. Old Mrs. Macpherson's face suffused with a sudden glow of happiness as she met the narrator. First, she saw the tin box that contained Jim's last letter and was happy to get it back. She, then, also mistakenly assumed the narrator to be her husband, Jim and was happy to see him return.

Long Answer Type Questions

1. Discuss the significance of the letter.

Ans. The letter is significant as it is a symbol of hope. It's the only thread of communication between Connie and her husband, Jim. Jim promises in the letter that he will return home before Christmas, a promise that Connie hopes will be fulfilled, hoping her husband would return soon.

For Connie, the letter becomes a substitute for her absent husband. She could feel her husband's presence whenever she read the letter. This made her read the letter over and over again.Years later, the letter also becomes Connie's "best Christmas present" for she mistakenly assumes that her husband has finally returned, bringing the letter with him.

2. What is the author conveying through this story?

Ans. The story 'The Best Christmas Present in the World' conveys many things. First, it presents the futility (uselessness) of war. Wars bring death and destruction for all. It leads to death of men leaving women widowed and children orphaned.

Hence, no one wants it. Even the soldiers want the war to end without any bloodshed. They want to return to their homes. The story further states that wars bring people who are similar, in conflict.

At the same time, the story also conveys the importance of hope. It celebrates unions over loneliness, joy over sadness, celebration over destruction and peace over war. The author shares with his readers, the true spirit of Christmas, love and hope and not destruction and death.

3. Elucidate the peculiar features of Jim's Christmas party.

Ans. Jim had the most peculiar Christmas party while he was at war. After the Germans initiated the peace truce, Jim saw the 'khaki clad men' and men in 'grey coats' mingling with each other. They were eating, drinking, laughing, smoking and having lots of fun. No one remembered that they were each other's enemies. They celebrated Christmas like friends. During this Christmas party, the two sides even played a friendly match of football while their in charge officers watched with happiness as their breaths mingled. Perhaps, the most peculiar thing about Jim's Christmas party is that it took place over no man's land.

4. Should the narrator reveal his identity to old Mrs. Macpherson or should he allow her to believe that he was her husband?

Ans. The narrator should not reveal his identity to old Mrs. Macpherson. Mrs. Macpherson was fairly young when her husband went to war. She spent her entire life waiting for her husband to return to her. When the narrator meets Mrs. Macpherson in the hospital, she was hundred and one years old. Since Mrs. Macpherson had no relatives in the last days of her life, she also had no visitors.

This mistaken identity of her visitor could give her some happiness. It is true that the narrator would be telling a lie and cheating her by hiding his identity knowingly. However, it would be worth Mrs. Macpherson's endless wait and a peaceful death.

ASSESSMENT EXERCISE

Multiple Choice Questions

1. Read the given statements and choose the correct option.

Statement 1 The German soldiers were very angry and aggressive.

Statement 2 The German and British soldiers played a friendly football match.

(a) Statement 1 is true but Statement 2 is false.
(b) Statement 1 is false but Statement 2 is true.
(c) Both the Statements are true.
(d) Both the Statements are false.

2. Which instrument did Hans play?

(a) Flute (b) Cello
(c) Guitar (d) Drums

3. What was the best Christmas present, according to Connie?

(a) The letters safe return.
(b) Jim's presence during Christmas.
(c) The visitor reading the letter for her.
(d) Sharing the marzipan cake with the visitor.

4. 'But the truth, I'm ashamed to say, is that Fritz began it.' What does the statement show?

(a) Jim was wary of the Germans.
(b) Jim felt guilty about the whole incident.
(c) Jim admired the German's bold gesture.
(d) Jim regretted interacting with the Fritz officer.

5. "We have Schnapps. We have sausage. We meet you? Yes?" Who said this to whom?

(a) Fritz to Mrs. Macpherson (b) Tommy to Fritz
(c) Fritz to Tommy (d) Jim to Mrs. Macpherson

Extract Based Question

Read the extract given below and answer the following questions.

Suddenly she reached out and took my hand. Her eyes were filled with tears. "You told me you'd come home by Christmas, dearest," she said. And here you are, the best Christmas present in the world. Come closer, Jim dear, sit down.'

(i) Who are the lines addressed to?

(a) Jim (b) Connie
(c) Hans Wolf (d) Narrator

(ii) What is the "best Christmas present in the world"?

(a) Jim's letter (b) Jim's return
(c) Jim's present (d) Jim's picture

(iii) By which Christmas did Jim promise to be back home?

(a) 1913 (b) 1914 (c) 1915 (d) 1916

(iv) Comment on the ending of the story.

(v) Comment on the nature of conflict faced by the narrator as the story ends.

Very Short Answer Type Questions

1. On which date does Connie receive Jim's letter?

2. What was the colour of the uniforms of the German and British soldiers?

3. Why couldn't the narrator sleep after reading the letter?

4. What is the importance of the day on which the narrator returns the letter to Mrs. Macpherson?

5. How is the Christmas party of the soldiers connected to hope?

6. Jim had been feeling upset before the Chritsmas Eve of 1914. Give evidence to support the statement.

Short Answer Type Questions

1. Why did Connie hide away the letter in a secret drawer of her desk?

2. Why was Jim amused when he first met Hans Wolf?

3. Explain the emotional state of Hans Wolf when he said — "No children are orphaned. No wives become widows".

4. Why was the matron happy to take the narrator to Mrs. Macpherson?

5. Describe Mrs. Macpherson's appearance when the narrator met her.

Long Answer Type Questions

1. Why did Mrs. Macpherson mistake the narrator to be her husband?

2. What were the 'wider goals' that Jim and Hans Wolf were most concerned of during the war?

3. Is war the only way of resolving conflicts between nations?

4. Both Jim and Hans favoured games or sports as peaceful solution to settle disputes. How can settlement of disputes by games or sports be different from that of war?

The Tsunami

Tsunami is a large and powerful wave caused by earthquakes under the sea. On 26th December, 2004, a tsunami hit Thailand and parts of India such as Andaman and Nicobar Islands and the Tamil Nadu coast. This chapter recounts some stories of courage and survival from that tsunami.

Part – I

Stories from Andaman and Nicobar Islands

The Story of Ignesious

Ignesious was the manager of a cooperative society in Katchall of Nicobar Islands. He was woken up by his wife at 6 a.m. because she felt an earthquake. So, he carefully placed the TV set on the ground to make sure it would not fall and break. Then, he rushed out of the house with his family. When the tremors stopped, he along with his family noticed the sea rising. In the confusion, his family got separated. Two of his children ran in the opposite direction with their maternal grandfather and uncle. Ignesious never saw any of them again. His wife got swept away by the waves. The only people to survive were the three children that went with him.

The Stories of Sanjeev and Meghna

Sanjeev was a policeman in Katchall island of the Nicobar groups of islands. He had managed to save himself, his wife and baby girl when he heard the cries of help from his cook John's wife. When he jumped into the water to save her, they were both taken away by the waves.

Meghna was a thirteen-year-old girl who was swept away with her parents and seventy-seven other people. She survived by holding onto a wooden door and floating on the sea for two days. During this time, she saw relief helicopters eleven times but she wasn't rescued because they couldn't see her. She was washed ashore by a wave two days later and was found walking along the shore blankly.

The Story of Almas Javed

Almas Javed was a 10 year old student at Carmel Convent in Port Blair where her father had a petrol pump. Her family was visiting Nancowry Island to celebrate Christmas at her mother Rahila's home. When the tremors came early in the morning, her family was sleeping. When her father saw the sea water recede (to go back), he immediately understood that the water would come rushing back with great force.

He woke everyone up and began rushing them to a safer place. While running away, her grandfather was hit on the head and he fell down. When her father went to rescue him, they both got swept away by the first giant wave. Her mother and aunts were clinging to the leaves of a coconut tree and calling out to her. A wave swept the tree away and they were both lost. Almas climbed onto a log of wood and fainted. When she woke up she was in a hospital in Kamorta. From there, she was taken to Port Blair. She was traumatised and doesn't talk about the incident due to which she lost all of her family.

Part – II

Stories from Thailand

The Story of Tilly Smith

Tilly Smith, a ten years old British school girl saved many people when the tsunami struck the Phuket beach in Southern Thailand. She won many awards because of her heroic acts. The Smith family was from South-East England and were celebrating Christmas at a beach resort in Southern Thailand. Tilly had a seven-years-old sister and her parents were Penny and Colin Smith. A massive earthquake in Northern Sumatra had triggered the tsunami on the morning of 26th December, 2004. Penny recalls that the water kept swelling and the beach was getting smaller. She couldn't understand what was happening. However, her daughter Tilly remembered the geography lesson where she had learned about Tsunamis two weeks before she took the trip.

Tilly Saves Many Lives

When she saw the foaming and whirlpools in the sea, she was reminded of the video of the tsunami that had hit the Hawaiian Islands in 1946. Tilly began screaming at her family to get off the beach. She kept talking about earthquake under the sea. While Penny didn't know what a tsunami was, she realised the danger they were in because her daughter was frightened and crying badly. So, Tilly's parents took the girls to the hotel along with some other tourists. Just then, the tsunami struck the beach looking like the entire sea had come out.

Her family took refuge in the third floor of the hotel and survived the tsunami. Tilly's education saved the lives of many tourists and their entire families. Later, Tilly went back to England and shared her terrifying tale with her classmates.

Part – III

Animals and their Sixth Sense

Before the tsunami hit the coasts of India and Sri Lanka, it was observed that the wild and domestic animals began panicking and fled to safety. Elephants screamed while running for higher ground, dogs refused to go outside, Flamingoes flew away, and zoo animals rushed into their shelters and refused to come out. It is commonly believed that animals possess a sixth sense and they are aware of when the earth is going to shake. Some people believe that the animal's strong sense of hearing allows them to hear or feel the Earth's vibrations.

Animals Survive the Tsunami

While the tsunami killed more than 150,000 people in a dozen countries, hardly any animals were reported dead. Thousands of people died along India's Cuddalore coast but buffaloes, dogs, and goats were found unharmed. In the Yala National Park in Sri Lanka, which is home to elephants, leopards and more than 130 species of birds, sixty people were washed away from the Patanangala beach. However, no animal bodies except that of two water buffaloes were found. People had also observed three elephants running away from the beach an hour before the tsunami hit.

A Sri Lankan gentleman, who lives on the coast near Galle, remarked that although his dogs love to go for their daily run on the beach, they refused to go that day and thus, saved his life.

Word Meaning

Word	Meaning
Archipelago	a group of many islands and the surrounding sea
Tremor	a shake, quiver or vibration
Chaos	complete disorder or confusion
Relief helicopters	helicopters bringing help to people
Recede	to move back
Daze	blank look
Clinging	to grip tightly
Traumatised	disturbed, due to shock
Triggered	to start something
Swelling	to extend or expand
Massive	heavy, bulky
Swept away	to be washed away
Terrifying	scary

Word	Meaning
Hysterical	uncontrolled emotions
Withstood	survive, endured
Refuge	shelter or protection from danger
Surge	a sudden rush or flood, force.
Whirlpool	a swirling body of water
Forewarned	to warn someone before something happens.
Slammed	to shut with a sudden force, to strike forcefully
Entice	to attract or lure
Acute	sensitive, quick
Species	a type or a kind of organisms
Perish	to die
Carcass	dead body

NCERT FOLDER

NCERT Intext and Exercise Questions

BEFORE YOU READ (NCERT PAGE 24)

Q.1 Now read the sentences below. Rewrite the incorrect ones after correcting the mistakes.

(i) Katchall is an island.

(ii) It is part of the Andaman group of islands.

(iii) Nancowry is an island in the Nicobar group.

(iv) Katchall and Nancowry are more than a hundred miles apart. (Hint: the scale of the map is given)

(v) The Andaman and Nicobar islands are to the West of India.

(vi) The Nicobar islands are to the North of the Andaman islands.

Ans. (i) Correct

(ii) Incorrect
Katchall is part of the Nicobar group of Islands.

(iii) Correct

(iv) Incorrect
Katchall and Noncowry are not more than hundred miles apart.

(v) Incorrect
The Andaman and Nicobar Islands are to the South-East of India.

(vi) Incorrect
The Nicobar Islands are to the South of the Andaman Islands.

NCERT COMPREHENSION CHECK

CHECK ❶ (NCERT PAGE 27)

Say whether the following are True or False.

Q.1 Ignesious lost his wife, two children, his father -in-law and his brother-in-law in the tsunami.

Q.2 Sanjeev made it to safety after the tsunami.

Q.3 Meghna was saved by a relief helicopter.

Q.4 Alma's father realised that a tsunami was going to hit the island.

Q.5 Her mother and aunts were washed away with the tree that they were holding on to.

Ans. 1. True 2. False 3. False 4. True 5. True

CHECK❷ (NCERT PAGE 28-29)

Answer the following in a phrase or sentence.

Q.1 Why did Tilly's family come to Thailand?

Ans. Tilly's family came from England to Thailand to celebrate Christmas.

Q.2 What were the warning signs that both Tilly and her mother saw?

Ans. Both Tilly and her mother saw the sea water swelling and coming towards them, while the beach was getting smaller and smaller.

Q.3 Do you think Tilly's mother was alarmed by them?

Ans. No. Tilly's mother was not alarmed by them. She was alarmed by her daughter's reactions and when Tilly screamed and asked the family to get off the beach, she was sure that something serious was happening.

Q.4 Where had Tilly seen the sea behaving in the same strange fashion?

Ans. Tilly had seen the sea behaving in a similar fashion in one of the videos shown by her geography teacher to her class.

The video was of the tsunami that had struck the Hawaiian islands in 1946.

Q.5 Where did the Smith family and the others on the beach go to escape from the tsunami?

Ans. The Smith family and the other tourists who were forewarned by Tilly took refuge in the third floor of the hotel to-escape the tsunami.

Q.6 How do you think her Geography teacher felt when she heard about what Tilly had done in Phuket?

Ans. Tilly's geography teacher must have been very proud of Tilly's presence of mind and the way Tilly had applied the teachings during that Geography lesson. The teacher must also have been overwhelmed because indirectly she was also responsible in the safeguarding of so many lives.

CHECK❸ (NCERT PAGE 30)

Q.1 In the tsunami 150,000 people died. How many animals died?

Ans. 'Although' the death count of human beings was very high, hardly any animals were reported dead in the tsunami.

Q.2 How many people and animals died in Yala National Park?

Ans. Sixty visitors died in the Yala National Park and only two water buffaloes were found dead.

Q.3 What do people say about the elephants of Yala National Park?

Ans. People at Yala National Park had observed three elephants running away from the Patanangala beach at Yala National Park.

Q.4 What did the dogs in Galle do?

Ans. Dogs in Galle refused to go for their daily run, something that they were usually excited about.

WORKING WITH THE TEXT (NCERT PAGE 30-31)

Discuss the following questions in class. Then write your own answers.

Q.1 When he felt the earthquake, do you think Ignesious immediately worried about a tsunami? Give reasons for your answer.
Which sentence in the text tells you that the Ignesious family did not have any time to discuss and plan their course of action after the tsunami struck?

Ans. No, Ignesious only feared the earthquake. He did not know it was a tsunami. He only thought about protecting the television set and his family from the earthquake. No other measures were taken by him.

The Ignesious family indeed did not have any time to discuss or plan their course of action. This is proved by the fact that half of the family members ran in one direction, while the others ran in the opposite direction in utter chaos and confusion.

Q.2 Which words in the list below describe Sanjeev, in your opinion?
(Look up the dictionary for words that you are not sure of.)

cheerful	ambitious	brash	brave	careless
heroic	selfless	heartless	humorous	

Use words from the list to complete the three sentences below.

(i) I don't know if Sanjeev was cheerful, ... or ....

(ii) I think that he was very brave, ... and ....

(iii) Sanjeev was not heartless, ... or ....

Ans. (i) humorous, ambitious
(ii) heroic, selfless
(iii) brash, careless

Q.3 How are Meghna and Almas's stories similar?

Ans. Meghna and Almas's stories are similar because both lost their families at a very young age.

Both Meghna and Almas managed to survive by holding on to wooden planks. Meghna held on to a wooden door and Almas held on to a log of wood.

Q.4 What are the different ways in which Tilly's parents could have reacted to her behaviour? What would you have done if you were in their place?

Ans. Tilly's parents could have scolded her for her extreme reactions, not knowing that their daughter could be knowledgeable about the graveness of the matter. Also, they could have simply ignored her.

Had I been in their place, I would have heard her and would have done what she said as a precautionary measure, as the sea was surely behaving strangely.

Q.5 If Tilly's award was to be shared, who do you think she should share it with—her parents or her Geography teacher?

Ans. If Tilly's award was to be shared, it must be shared with her Geography teacher. This is so because it was the lesson that she was taught and the video that she was showed that enabled Tilly to understand what was happening.

Q.6 What are the two different ideas about why so few animals were killed in the tsunami? Which idea do you find more believable?

Ans. Very few animals died in the tsunami because it is believed that the animals have a sixth sense. They had an intuition about the upcoming danger and therefore, managed to survive the tsunami.

Experts also believe that the animals have acute hearing powers. They could, therefore, feel the vibrations of the Earth much in advance. Both the theories are equally believable.

WORKING WITH LANGUAGE (NCERT PAGE 31)

Q.1 Go through Part - I carefully and make a list of as many words as you can find that indicate movement of different kinds. (There is one word that occurs repeatedly—count how many times!) Put them into three categories.

fast movement, slow movement and neither slow nor fast

Can you explain why there are many words in one column and not in the others?

Fast Movement	Slow Movement	Neither Slow nor Fast
• Rushed out • Rushed in • Jumped into • Rushing back • Rush them • Ran • Rushed to • Entire sea had come out after • Surge Slammed • Fled to safety	• Floating • Brought to the shore • Walking	• Swept away (thrice) • Recede • Washed away (twice) • Kept coming in

Ans. The word 'rushed' occurred repeatedly, at least 6 times. This was so because during tsunami, people were rushing away from the sea or rushing to the aid of their dear ones and family members. The number of words are more under the category of 'Fast Movement' because the suddenness and the force of the waves compelled the people to move faster than usual.

Q.2 Fill in the blanks in the sentences below (the verbs given in brackets will give you a clue).

(i) The Earth trembled, but not many people felt the .... (tremble)

(ii) When the zoo was flooded, there was a lot of .... and many animals escaped into the countryside. (confuse)

(iii) We heard with .... that the lion had been recaptured. (relieve)

(iv) The zookeeper was struck in a tree and his .... was filmed by the TV crew. (rescue)

(v) There was much .... in the village when the snake charmer came visiting. (excite)

Ans. (i) tremors (ii) confusion (iii) relief (iv) rescue (v) excitement

Q.3 Study the sentences in the columns A and B.

Column A	Column B
Meghna was swept away.	The waves swept Meghna away.
Alma's grandfather was hit on the head.	Something hit Alma's grandfather on the head.
Sixty visitors were washed away.	The waves washed away sixty visitors.
No animal carcasses were found.	People did not find any animal carcasses.

Compare the sentences in A to the ones in B. Who is the 'doer' of the action in every case? Is the 'doer' mentioned in A or in B?

Notice the verbs in A: 'was swept away', 'was hit', 'were washed away', 'were found'. They are in the passive form.

The sentences are in the Passive voice. In these sentences, the focus is not on the person who does the action.

In B, the 'doer' of the action is named. The verbs are in the Active form.

The sentences are in the Active voice. Say whether the following sentences are in the Active or the Passive Voice. Write A or P after each sentence as shown in the first sentence.

(i) Someone stole my bicycle. ....

(ii) The tyres were deflated by the traffic police. ....

(iii) I found it last night in a ditch near my house. ....

(iv) It had been thrown there. ....

(v) My father gave it to the mechanic. ....

(vi) The mechanic repaired it for me. ....

Ans. (i) A (ii) P (iii) A (iv) P (v) A (vi) A

SPEAKING AND WRITING (NCERT PAGE 32-33)

Q.1 Suppose you are one of the volunteers who went to the Andaman and Nicobar islands for relief work after the tsunami. You work in the relief camps, distributing food, water and medicine among the victims. You listen to the various stories of bravery of ordinary people even as they fight against odds to bring about some semblance of normalcy in their lives. You admire their grit and determination. Write a diary entry.

You may start in this way.

31st December, 2004

The killer tsunami struck these islands five days ago. But the victims are being brought in even now. Each one has a story to tell...

Ans. 31st December, 2004 10:00 P.M.

Dear Diary,

The killer Tsunami struck these islands five days ago. But the victims are being brought in even now. Each one has a story to tell, a story of the sheer destruction and devastation. The sight of the islands told the story of how nature had wrecked havoc in these areas. This story became more vivid and painful as the number of victims continued to increase in the relief camps bringing in images of loss, pain and suffering.

There was not one person who had not lost a dear one or had not been injured by the giant waves or had not been rendered homeless because of the tsunami. All stories were different yet so similar. Loss became a common theme for all.

As a volunteer working in the relief camp, I thought of restoring some sense of normalcy to the victims and therefore, brought with me packets of food, bottles of water, some clothes and medicines. However, these are bare essentials. The victims have not just suffered physically but also mentally.

They have been traumatised to the worst degree. The suddenness of the tsunami has rendered some mute. However, there are many others who have exhibited courage and saved the lives of many. There are some who rescued others, not caring about their own lives. I salute such masters of humanity.

However, even stories of courage could stop my tears as I saw these people's sufferings. I developed cold feet as I saw small children orphaned but still searching for their parents.

It was impossible to bear the sight, but I have decided to stay here and do my bit of service towards humanity. May God give all of us strength to cope with this face of nature.

Q.2 The story shows how a little girl saved the lives of many tourists when a tsunami struck the beach, thanks to the geography lesson that she had learnt at school. She remembered the visuals of a tsunami and warned her parents.

Do you remember any incident when something that you learnt in the classroom helped you in some way outside the classroom? Write your experiences in a paragraph of about 90-100 words or narrate it to the whole class like an anecdote.

Ans. My mother while working in the kitchen, absent mindedly left the burner on, while there was very little oil in the pan that was placed above the stove. The pan soon caught fire as the little oil in the pan was heated to an extreme level. On seeing the situation, everybody in my house, that is my mother, my elder sister and my younger brother, began to panic. Not knowing what to do, they began to scream.

I immediately took a towel, placed it under the tap of running water and then, used the wet towel to extinguish the fire. I had learnt at school that water acts as an insulator of heat, but pouring water directly may be harmful, as the splash might momentarily increase the expanse of fire. I also immediately turned off the burner for further contact between fire and the gas supply. I had also learnt that the next good insulator of heat is sand.

I remembered my teacher telling us that on the beaches, sand acts as an insulator to Sun's heat. Therefore, I immediately went downstairs where some construction work was going on, got some sand in a packet and emptied the contents of the packet on the pan as the final remedial measure.

REVIEW EXERCISE

Including Competency Based Questions

Multiple Choice Questions

1. A tsunami is a very large and powerful wave caused by ....

(a) high tide
(b) sea storm
(c) earthquakes on the land
(d) earthquakes under the sea

Ans. (d) earthquakes under the sea

2. On 26th December, 2004, a tsunami hit the coasts of ....

(a) Thailand
(b) Andaman and Nicobar islands
(c) Tamil Nadu
(d) All of the above

Ans. (d) All of the above

3. How are the three sections of the text related to each other? Competency Based

(a) They analyse the cause of related incidents
(b) They compare different but similar incidents
(c) They place a series of incidents in proper sequence
(d) They relate the same incident from different perspectives

Ans. (d) They relate the same incident from different perspectives

4. Why did Ignesious take the television set off the table and put it down on the ground?

(a) Because of the earthquake
(b) To make sure it would not fall and break
(c) Both (a) and (b)
(d) None of the above

Ans. (c) Both (a) and (b)

5. Choose the correct option.

(a) Meghna was rescued by a relief helicopter.
(b) Meghna was rescued after four days.
(c) Meghna was rescued by a rescue boat.
(d) Meghna was not rescued by a relief helicopter.

Ans. (d) Meghna was not rescued by a relief helicopter.

6. How did the father of Almas Javed know about the tsunami?

(a) He heard the emergency alert on the radio.
(b) He felt the tremors and saw the water recede.
(c) He heard the panicked shouting of the neighbours.
(d) He saw the emergency alert on his phone.

Ans. (b) He felt the tremors and saw the water recede.

7. Penny Smith's initial reaction to the tsunami was Competency Based

(a) terror
(b) anxiety
(c) confusion
(d) indifference

Ans. (c) confusion

8. What convinced Penny Smith to leave the beach? Competency Based

(a) Seeing how upset her daughter was.
(b) The severity of the earthquake.
(c) Seeing other people leave.
(d) The size of the waves.

Ans. (a) Seeing how upset her daughter was.

9. What triggered the deadly tsunami waves of 26th December, 2004?

(a) Massive earthquake off the coast of Hawaii.
(b) Massive earthquake off Northern Sumatra.
(c) Massive earthquake off the Southern Nicobar Islands.
(d) Massive earthquake off the coast of Thailand.

Ans. (b) Massive earthquake off Northern Sumatra.

10. Tilly had seen the video of a tsunami that had hit the Hawaiian islands in ....

(a) 1932
(b) 1946
(c) 1954
(d) 1963

Ans. (b) 1946

11. What is the main idea of the third section? Competency Based

(a) Animals were not affected much by the tsunami.
(b) Animals helped many humans from the tsunami.
(c) Animals seem to be able to sense natural calamities early.
(d) Animals in different places react differently to natural calamities.

Ans. (c) Animals seem to be able to sense natural calamities early.

12. In the third section, the writer mainly .... Competency Based

(a) makes an argument
(b) provides information
(c) describes new findings
(d) recounts some incidents

Ans. (b) provides information

13. The second paragraph of the third section begins with .... **Competency Based**

(a) a new discovery
(b) a well-known fact
(c) a commonly held opinion
(d) an unsupported argument

Ans. (c) a commonly held opinion

14. Read the given statements and choose the correct answer.

Statement 1 The Tsunami had destroyed many families in different parts of Asia.

Statement 2 Animals saved themselves due to their sixth sense.

(a) Statement 1 is true but Statement 2 is false.
(b) Statement 2 is true but Statement 2 is false.
(c) Both the Statements are true.
(d) Both the Statements are false.

Ans. (c) Both the Statements are true.

Extract Based Questions

1. Read the extract given below and answer the following questions.

Sanjeev was a policeman, serving in the Katchall island of the Nicobar group of islands. He somehow managed to save himself, his wife and his baby daughter from the waves. But then he heard cries for help from the wife of John, the guesthouse cook. Sanjeev jumped into the water to rescue her, but they were both swept away.

Thirteen year-old Meghna was swept away along with her parents and seventy-seven other people. She spent two days floating in the sea, holding on to a wooden door. Eleven times she saw relief helicopters overhead, but they did not see her. She was brought to the shore by a wave, and was found walking on the seashore in a daze.

(i) What does the story reveal about the incident?

Ans. The story reveals the suddenness of the incident and the chaos and panic created by it. People did not have the time to think before acting; they just did whatever they could do to save themselves and their loved ones.

(ii) Can Sanjeev be called a failure?

Ans. Sanjeev cannot be called a failure. Even though he couldn't survive, he bravely jumped into the water to save the life of his cook's wife.

(iii) Why couldn't the relief helicopters rescue Meghna?

Ans. The rescue helicopters couldn't rescue Meghna because she was holding onto a wooden door to stay afloat, so she must not have been visible to the helicopters.

(iv) State True or False.

Sanjeev was unable to save the wife of the cook; therefore, he was ashamed for many years.

Ans. The given statement is false. Since Sanjeev died in the attempt to save the cook's wife, he couldn't have been shamed for years after that.

Ans. Choose the word in the passage which means 'to save someone from danger'.

Ans. The word 'rescue' means 'to save someone from danger'.

2. Read the extract given below and answer the following questions.

Tilly's parents took her and her sister away from the beach, to the swimming pool at the hotel. A number of other tourists also left the beach with them. "Then itwas as if the entire sea had come out after them. I was screaming, 'Run!'"

The family took refuge in the third floor of the hotel. The building withs tood the surge of three tsunami waves. If they had stayed on the beach, they would not have been alive. The Smiths later met other tourists who had lost entire families. Thanks to Tilly and her Geography lesson, they had been forewarned. Tilly went back to her school in England and told her classmates her terrifying tale.

(i) How did Tilly forewarn her family and the tourists on the beach?

Ans. Tilly forewarned her family and the tourists on the beach by screaming about the earthquake under the water.

(ii) What does Penny Smith describe the tsunami as?

Ans. Penny Smith describes the tsunami like this – 'as if the whole sea had come out after them'.

(iii) Where did the Smith family take refuge during the tsunami?

Ans. The Smith family took refuge in the third floor of the hotel during the waves of tsunami.

(iv) Select the word from the extract which means 'a place providing safety or shelter'.

Ans. The word 'refuge' means 'a place providing safety or shelter'.

(v) Select the word from the extract which means 'a sudden powerful forward or upward movement'.

Ans. The word 'surge' means 'a sudden powerful forward or upward movement'.

3. Read the extract given below and answer the following questions.

Before the giant waves slammed into the coast in India and Sri Lanka, wild and domestic animals seemed to know what was about to happen. They fled to safety. According to eye witness accounts, elephants screamed and ran for higher ground; dogs refused to go outdoors; flamingoes abandoned their low-lying breeding areas; and zoo animals rushed into their shelters and couldnot be enticed to come back out.

Many people believe that animals possess a sixth sense and know when the earth is going to shake. Some experts believe that animals' more acute hearing helps them to hear or feel the earth's vibration. They can sense an approaching disaster long before humans realise what's going on.

(i) Which of the following knew about the tsunami in advance?

(a) Wild animals
(b) Domestic animals
(c) Both (a) and (b)
(d) None of the above

Ans. (c) Both (a) and (b)

(ii) Why did the elephants run for higher ground?

(a) Because the water from the tsunami waves would not reach higher ground.
(b) Because the higher ground contained a safety shelter for elephants.
(c) Because the elephants prefer to live on higher grounds.
(d) Because higher ground had the advantage of a better point of view.

Ans. (a) Because the water from the tsunami waves would not reach higher ground.

(iii) What do people believe about animals and their sixth sense?

(a) That their sixth sense allows help them to see ghosts.
(b) That their sixth sense allows them know about life after death.
(c) That their sixth sense allows them to know about shaking of the Earth.
(d) That their sixth sense allows them to escape from predators.

Ans. (c) That their sixth sense allows them to know about shaking of the Earth.

(iv) Select the phrase from the extract that means 'a place where animals breed and produce their animals'.

(a) low lying (b) breeding areas
(c) slammed (d) coast

Ans. (b) breeding areas

(v) Which word from the extract is a synonym of 'sharp' and 'sensitive'?

(a) domestic (b) rushed
(c) acute (d) disaster

Ans. (c) acute

4. Read the extract given below and answer the following questions.

Along India's Cuddalore coast, where thousands of people perished, buffaloes, goats and dogs were found unharmed. The Yala National Park in Sri Lanka is hometo a variety of animals including elephants, leopards, and 130 species of birds. Sixty visitors were washed away from the Patanangala beach inside the park; butno animal carcasses were found, except for two water buffaloes. About an hour before the tsunami hit, people at Yala National Park had observed three elephants running away from the Patanangala beach.

A Sri Lankan gentleman who lives on the coast near Galle said his two dogs would not go for their daily runon the beach. "They are usually excited to go on thisouting," he said. But on that day they refused to go and most probably saved his life.

(i) List the animals that lived in the Yala National Park.

(a) Kangaroos, buffaloes, leopards, and goats
(b) Buffaloes, goats, dogs, and elephants
(c) Tiger, lion, chimpanzee and dogs
(d) Buffaloes, goats, sheep, and horse

Ans. (b) Buffaloes, goats, dogs, and elephants

(ii) How many people died in the Patanangala beach?

(a) Eighty
(b) Sixty
(c) One hundred and thirty
(d) Two hundred

Ans. (b) Sixty

(iii) Why were no animal carcasses found?

(a) Because they were all eaten by vultures.
(b) Because they all got swept away by the waves.
(c) Because their sixth sense allowed them to escape.
(d) Because there were no animals at the Patanangala beach.

Ans. (c) Because their sixth sense allowed them to escape.

(iv) **Which of the following word is not an antonym of 'perished'?**

(a) Appear (b) Arrive (c) Build (d) Cease

Ans. (d) Cease

(v) **What does the phrase 'washed away' mean?**

(a) To bathe for a long time

(b) To be taken away by the sea waves

(c) To play among the sea waves at the beach

(d) To scrub away the dirt and dust

Ans. (b) To be taken away by the sea waves

Very Short Answer Type Questions

1. Where was Ignesious working?

Ans. Ignesious worked in a co-operative society in Katchall group of Nicobar islands.

2. Why is the television mentioned in the second paragraph? Competency Based

Ans. The television is mentioned in the second paragraph because the tremors from the earthquake could have caused it to misbalance and fall on the floor. Ignesious takes the time to make sure it doesn't break due to the earthquake.

3. List the survivors of the Ignesious family.

Ans. Ignesious and his three children who accompanied him survived the tsunami. His other two children and his wife and wife's father and brother were probably dead.

4. For whom did Sanjeev risk his life?

Ans. Sanjeev risked his life for the sake of humanity. He jumped to save the guesthouse cook's wife.

5. In which school did Almas Javed study?

Ans. Almas Javed was a student of Carmel Convent School in Port Blair.

6. How did Tilly become aware of the upcoming calamity?

Ans. Tilly had become aware of the upcoming calamity because of a video that she had seen in her Geography class.

7. What according to the experts helps the animals sense dangers accurately? Diksha

Ans. Experts believe that animals have an acute hearing ability, which enables them to sense the vibrations of the earthquake, forewarning them of the danger.

8. During the tsunami, what was common between the Indian and the other stories from other parts of the globe?

Ans. Death, destruction and devastation were the common features between the stories from India and elsewhere during the tsunami.

Short Answer Type Questions

1. Sanjeev's actions were more heroic than the actions of Almas's father. Do you agree? Justify your answer. Competency Based

Ans. Almas's father tried to save his own father from the waves, whereas Sanjeev was already safe but still risked his life for someone who wasn't even related to him i.e. the wife of his cook, John. Hence, the actions of Sanjeev were more heroic than those of Almas's father.

2. How could Meghna save herself from the tsunami of 2004? Diksha

Ans. Meghna floated in the sea for two days during which she clung on to a wooden door. She saw relief helicopters eleven times, but they didn't rescue her because they couldn't see her. Finally, she was brought to the shore by a wave.

3. Who was responsible for the deaths of Almas Javed's father and grandfather? Competency Based

Ans. In their attempt to rush out of the house and save themselves from the waves, Almas's grandfather hit his head against something and fell on the ground.

Almas's father came to his father's rescue, but it was too late to do something to save their lives. They were not initially swept by the waves, but the chaos and panic created by the giant waves was responsible for their deaths.

4. Why does Almas Javed refuse to talk about the incident?

Ans. Almas Javed lost her grandfather, father, mother and aunts in the tsunami. Hence, she refused to talk about the incident because she was in a state of shock and traumatised because of the intensity of loss.

5. What helped Tilly understand that a tsunami was coming? Competency Based

Ans. Tilly's Geography lesson in which she had learned the features of a tsunami, as well as the video of the Hawaiian island tsunami of 1946 that was shown in the class helped her understand that a tsunami was coming.

6. How was the fate of other tourists different from the tourists who were present on the Phuket beach?

Ans. The fate of the other tourists was very different from that of the tourists present at the Phuket beach. The tourists on the beach had been forewarned by Tilly's screaming and shouting.

Alongwith Tilly's family, they too left the beach. The other tourists, however, had lost their entire families. They were swept away by enormous waves.

7. Who all lived in the Yala National Park?

Ans. The Yala National Park in Sri Lanka was home to a variety of animals including elephant, leopards and more than 130 species of birds.

Elephants, dogs, goats, water buffaloes, flamingoes and various other animals and birds lived in the National Park which also had a good number of visitors.

8. How did the animals react prior to the tsunami? **Diksha**

Ans. When the animals sensed the tsunami, the wild and domestic animals fled to safety, elephants screamed and ran for higher ground, dogs refused to go outdoors, flamingoes abandoned their low-lying breeding areas and zoo animals rushed into their shelters.

Long Answer Type Questions

1. How did Tilly's knowledge about the Tsunami save many lives during the tsunami in Thailand? **Diksha**

Ans. Tilly had learnt of the tsunami and its indicators in her Geography lessons a few days ago in her hometown in England. She had also seen the video of the sea during a 1946 tsunami that had struck the Hawaiian Islands. Therefore, she was aware of the strangeness of the sea on that morning.

As she and her family members were in the beach, she realised that something was wrong with the waves and that a disaster was approaching. She used that knowledge to warn her family and the tourists who were present on the Phuket beach when the tsunami struck that area. Thus, she along with her parents and other tourists evacuated well before time and saved themselves.

2. Discuss the stories of the tsunami victims as narratives of pain and suffering.

Ans. Tsunami is a Japanese word which means 'harbor wave'. But the word itself symbolises endless suffering and death. The stories shared in the chapter all stand evidence to this reality. None of the people involved in the natural disaster were aware of their impending doom. This unpreparedness is a common thread in all of these stories.

Another thing to note is that any natural disaster doesn't care for the gender or age of its victims. Old people like Almas's grandfather and Ignesious's father-in-law were some of the first people killed by the waves. Young children like Almas and Meghna lost their entire families in one sweep and suffered through trauma that cannot be described. Brave people like Sanjeev paid for their morals, while their families were left destroyed in the aftermath. This amount of pain and loss is indescribable in its magnitude.

3. Tilly's story had some important messages attached to it. What were they?

Ans. Tilly's story had many important messages attached to it.

(i) It is important that students are taught such lessons which give them knowledge about their immediate environment.

(ii) Tilly not just learned about tsunami in the Geography lesson, but also applied her knowledge and with her presence of mind saved many lives.

(iii) Tilly could have shared this Geography lesson with her parents and sister, thereby increasing the number of people who were of the coming tsunami and therefore, quicken the rescue works.

ASSESSMENT EXERCISE

Multiple Choice Questions

1. Ignesious and his family rushed out of the house because

(a) they feared the coming of a tsunami.
(b) they felt the tremors of an earthquake.
(c) they heard loud noises from outside.
(d) there was a snake in their house.

2. The little girl who saved many live during the 2004 tsunami was

(a) Meghna (b) Tilly Smith
(c) Almas Javed (d) Penny Smith

3. Read the given statements and choose the correct answer.

Statement 1 Tsunami is a very large and powerful wave caused by earthquakes under the sea.

Statement 2 Ignesious lost all of his children in the tsunami of 2004.

(a) Statement 1 is true, but Statement 2 is false.
(b) Statement 1 is false, but Statement 2 is true.
(c) Both the Statements are true.
(d) Both the Statements are false.

4. Fill in the blank with the correct options.

He woke everyone up and tried to .... them to a safer place. Her father .... to help him but got swept away.

(a) rush, rushed (b) rushed, rush
(c) rushing, rushed (d) rushed, rushes

5. The Yala National Park is located in

(a) USA (b) Phuket
(c) India (d) Sri Lanka

Extract Based Question

Read the given extract and answer the following questions.

These stories are all from the Andaman and Nicobar archipelago.

Ignesious was the manager of a cooperative society in Katchall. His wife woke him up at 6 a.m. because she felt an earthquake. Ignesious carefully took his television set off its table and put it down on the ground so that it would not fall and break. Then the family rushed out of the house.

When the tremors stopped, they saw the sea rising. In the chaos and confusion, two of his children caught hold of the hands of their mother's father and mother'sbrother, and rushed in the opposite direction. He never saw them again. His wife was also swept away. Only the three other children who came with him were saved.

(i) Ignesious's wife woke him up at 6 a.m. because
   (a) she felt very ill.
   (b) he was the manager of a cooperative society.
   (c) she felt an earthquake.
   (d) she felt like watching television.

(ii) The first thing Ignesious did upon being alerted about the earthquake was
   (a) run out of the house with his wife and kids.
   (b) run to his children's room to wake them up.
   (c) placing the television on the ground.
   (d) hide under the dining table with his wife and children.

(iii) What did Ignesious see when he ran out of the house and the tremors stopped?
   (a) He saw the relief helicopters.
   (b) He saw the impact of the earthquake
   (c) He saw the sea waves rising.
   (d) He saw the beautiful sunrise with his family.

(iv) Which words from the passage describe a state of disorder and uncertainty?

(v) Which word from the given passage means 'a group of islands'?

Very Short Answer Type Questions

1. Why were the water buffaloes unable to escape the tsunami?
2. Tilly remembered seeing a video of the sea about a tsunami in her Geography class. Where did the tsunami in the video take place?
3. Did Meghna have the will to live?
4. Why did Almas refuse to talk about the tsunami?
5. How does the trauma of Almas and Meghna compare?

Short Answer Type Questions

1. Is there a difference between the nature of suffering of Ignesious's family and Sanjeev's family?
2. What are the theories that explain why hardly any animal deaths were reported?
3. What happened after the tremors from the earthquakes stopped?
4. How was the expectations of the Smith family different from their experiences in the Thailand?
5. What happened long before the tsunami waves crashed into the coasts of India and Sri Lanka?

Long Answer Type Questions

1. How did the tsunami affect the areas along India's Cuddalore coast?
2. What did people see in the Yala National Park an hour before the tsunami hit? Explain the reason and the significance behind it.
3. Write a diary entry from the perspective of Meghna recounting her experience in the two days she was adrift in the sea. Mention how she must have felt upon seeing various relief helicopters pass her by.
4. Tilly shared the terrifying tale of her experiences in Thailand with her friends. Write a diary entry from the perspective of one of Tilly's friends. Include the measures you would take to be prepared for a tsunami.

Glimpses of the Past

by S.D. Sawant

The following chapter has been taken from 'Our Freedom Movement' written by S.D. Sawant. It presents some pictures of the history of our country from 1757 to 1857 when the First War of Independence was fought.

1. The Martyrs

The picture recounts the brave martyrs who fought for their country in the First War of Independence of 1857. The famous song of Lata Mangeshkar 'Oh my countrymen!' perfectly remembers the sacrifices made by the brave men and women of India.

2. The Company's Conquests (1757-1849)

The British East India Company had superior weapons and were extending their power in 18th century India. The Indian Princes were not wise and could not see how their actions were going to affect Indian freedom. Their insignificant rivalries allowed the English merchants to gain power. The Britishers used these rivalries to their advantage and defeated many Indian Princes. In contrast, wise rulers like Tipu Sultan of Mysore could see the realities of the situation. He gave up his life while fighting the British.

Meanwhile, Indians of different stages of life had varying reactions. The Indian Princes thanked the British as they stopped the looting by thugs (thieves) and wars. They felt that the Britishers were sent by God to help them. However, the common people believed that the Britishers had killed Indian rulers and taken their positions. They realised that they were beginning to become the slaves of Britishers.

3. British Rule (1765-1836)

India was being held back by some religious leaders who taught immoral things like untouchability, child marriages, and hatred towards women. They believed that anyone who leaves their land and crosses the sea loses their religion or that the world is full of sorrow because of women.

The Britishers disliked the Indian people for such practices and dishonesty, causing Indians to lose self-respect. They destroyed the Indian industries for quick profits. They not only took away the crops produced by farmers but also imposed heavy taxes on them. They also decided to import English goods without any import duty. As a result, there was shortage of food and 15 lakh farmers died of starvation between 1822 and 1836. Further, the British policies also ruined the artisans and their businesses.

4. Ram Mohan Roy (1772-1833)

Ram Mohan Roy was a learned man from Bengal who valued the Indian tradition while also recognising the need of reform. He knew that superstitions were ruining us and told his wife Uma that just like cows of all colours give milk, all religions are the same. He used scientific and modern knowledge to reform Indian societies through his newspaper. The Britishers grew suspicious and stopped the newspaper in 1823. So, he went to England to see what made the Britishers so powerful. There, he accepted British rule on the condition that they are willing to fulfill their responsibilities towards their Indian subjects.

5. Oppression (1765-1835)

The Britishers ignored the ideas of Ram Mohan Roy and continued to oppress the Indian people. In 1818, they passed the Regulation III under which any Indian could be jailed without trial in the court. At the same time, Britishers profited from their large salaries and private businesses. By 1829, they were exporting British goods worth seven crore rupees to India. The British prospered from the loot while the Indian industries began to die. Looking at the condition of Indian farmers who had their lands as well as the crops they produce, the Governor-General Bentick said 'The bones of cotton weavers are bleaching the plains of India'.

6. Dissatisfaction (1835-1856)

A Britisher named Thomas Macaulay was dissatisfied with the Indian education that took place in Persian and Sanskrit. He suggested a change wherein English education can produce Indian clerks who could do the small jobs of the British. However, this created a set of individuals who wanted betterment of their society. They wanted to educate other Indians to help them reduce their poverty. For the same, they decided to convey their thoughts to the British Parliament. But in reality, as the Britishers conquered the whole of India by 1856, the Indians lost their existing jobs and lands. People were angry and wanted to drive the Britishers out of their nation.

7. The Sparks (1855-1857)

The discontent among Indians began taking the form of rebellion. Taxes had destroyed peasants and the Santhals in Bengal had lost their lands under the new land rule. Hence, they rose in rebellion in 1855 and killed Europeans and their supporters. Meanwhile, the Indian soldiers in the East India Company's army were also dissatisfied. They understood that their English counterparts were getting much better salaries, servants, and bungalows to live in while they got least salaries and slow promotions. Furthermore, they also felt that they were losing their age-old customs and religion by crossing the seas to distant lands. As a result, Sepoy Mangal Pande attacked the adjutant of his regiment and was executed. Other soldiers revolted but they were insulted and prisoned.

Some soldiers were angered that the bullet grease was made from cow and pig fat, which was against the Indian religion. The message for support in fighting the Britishers spread through villages via chapaties. Indian soldiers used the symbol of a lotus flower and began getting ready for revolt.

8. Revolt and the Fight for Freedom (1857)

The revolt began through a violent outbreak in Meerut and continued to spread through the country. Sepoys marched to Delhi with the support of the landlords who had lost their land to British policies. Emperor Bahadur Shah was praised while slogans such as 'Death to the Foriegners' were chanted.

This war of Independence was supported by former rulers such as Begum Hazrat Mahal of Lucknow. Popular leaders like Maulvi Ahmedulla of Faizabad called the people to fight. Azimulla Khan told Tatya Tope that Peshwa Nana Saheb should lead the war of Independence against the British. Eighty year old Kunwar Singh of Bihar was one of many patriots who fought in the First War of Independence.

Word Meaning

Word	Meaning
Pictorial	expressed in pictures
Glimpses	a momentary or partial view
Conquest	invasion and assumption of control
Martyrs	one who willingly accepts death
Short-sighted	not wise or thinking about the future
Subdue	control
Dethroned	overthrow
Preach	sermonise
Scorned	disrespect, contempt
Unworthy	undeserving
Arrears	debts
Artisans	craftsperson
Cripple	physically disabled
Inevitably	impossible to avoid
Famines	extreme scarcity of food
Starvation	suffering or death caused by lack of food
Despise	hate
Superstitions	false notion, blind faith
Essence	core
Prosper	become successful
Achievement	accomplishment/success
Oppress	dominate, subdued

Word	Meaning
Trial	examination
Bleaching	lighten, to become white or pale with chemical process
Petty	of little importance
Grievances	a cause of complaint
Regulations	to guide, prescribe
Conquered	occupied
Coverting	change
Massacred	slaughter
Brewing	prepare a drink
Discontent	dissatisfaction
Pittance	meagre amount
Abolish	eliminate
Adjutant	a military officer who acts as an administrative assistant to a senior officer
Executed	perform
Regiment	brigade
Sepoy	soldiers of Indian origin
Stripped of	exposed
Sore	painful
Upsurge	rise
Pitched	inclined

NCERT FOLDER

NCERT Intext and Exercise Questions

COMPREHENSION CHECK (NCERT PAGE 45)

Q.1 Look at picture 1 and recall the opening lines of the original song in Hindi. Who is the singer? Who else do you see in this picture (Refer Picture of NCERT Page no 36)?

Ans. "Ae mere watan ke logon, zara aankh mein bhar lo paani, jo shaheed hue hain unki zara yaad karo kurbaani" are the opening lines of the song sung by Lata Mangeshkar. Pandit Jawaharlal Nehru, the first Prime Minister of the Independent India, Lal Bahadur Shastri and Indira Gandhi can also be seen in the picture, sitting in the audience.

Q.2 In picture 2 what do you understand by the Company's "superior weapons" (Refer Picture 2 of NCERT page no 37)?

Ans. The Company's 'superior weapons' could mean the mind-games that the British played to establish and spread their rule in India. Also, their superior guns and artillery are referred to as the Company's 'superior weapons'.

Q.3 Who is an artisan? Why do you think the artisans suffered? (Refer to Picture 3 of NCERT Page no 38)

Ans. The artisans are skilled craftsmen who created goods manually. They suffered because the British imported their goods to India at a bulk scale. The artisans could not keep pace with the quantity and cheap price of machine manufactured goods that flooded the Indian markets even when the artisan's skill was of a much higher quality. As a result, artisans lost their businesses and had to look at other ways to earn a living.

Q.4 Which picture, according to you, reveals the first sparks of the fire of revolt?

Ans. Picture 4 reveals the first spark of revolt when the Europeans were massacred by the 'Santhals' of Bengal in 1855.

WORKING WITH THE TEXT (NCERT PAGE 45)

Answer the following questions.

Q.1 Do you think the Indian princes were short-sighted in their approach to the events of 1757?

Ans. The Indian princes were surely short-sighted in their approach to the events of 1757 because they failed to understand the consequences of the foreign help that they sought in order to resolve their internal matters.

Q.2 How did the East Indian Company subdue the Indian princes?

Ans. The East Indian Company subdued the Indian prince by the trick of divide and rule. They assisted and encouraged wars among the Indian princes while continually gaining power.

Q.3 Quote the words used by Ram Mohan Roy to say that every religion teaches the same principles.

Ans. According to Ram Mohan Roy, "Cows are of different colours. But the colour of their milk is the same. Different teachers have different opinions, but the essence of different religions is the same."

Q.4 In what ways did the British officers exploit Indians?

Ans. The British officers exploited Indians in following ways

(a) They scorned the Indians for dishonesty and made them lose self-respect.

(b) They imposed heavy taxes on the farmers, forcing them to abandon their fields.

(c) They imposed British goods to India without any import duty.

(d) Their policies ruined the expert articans and Indian industries.

(e) They imposed Regulation III under which, any Indian could be jailed without trial.

(f) They changed the language of education from Persian and Sanskrit to English.

(g) They recruited Indian men to fight their wars.

Q.5 Name these people.

(i) The ruler who fought pitched battles against the British and died fighting.

(ii) The person who wanted to reform the society.

(iii) The person who recommended the introduction of English education in India.

(iv) Two popular leaders who led the revolt (choices may vary).

Ans. (i) Tipu Sultan (ii) Ram Mohan Roy

(iii) Lord Macaulay

(iv) Tatya Tope and Peshwa Nana Saheb

Q.6 Mention the following.

(i) Two examples of social practices prevailing then.

(II) Two oppressive policies of the British.

(iii) Two ways in which common people suffered.

(iv) Four reasons for the discontent that led to the 1857 War of Independence.

Ans. (i) Untouchability and child marriage.

(ii) Regulation III and import of British goods without import duty.

(iii) The farmers were heavily taxed and Indian artisans lost their businesses.

(iv) (a) Taxes that ruined the farmers.

(b) Loss of land due to new land rules.

(c) Disparity in the perks, privileges and wages of British soldiers and the Indian soldiers.

(d) The grease used on the bullets was made from the fat of cows and pigs.

WORKING WITH LANGUAGE

(NCERT PAGE 45–46)

In comics, what the characters speak is put in bubbles. This is direct narration. When we report what the characters speak, we use the method of indirect narration.

Study these Examples

First farmer Why are your men taking away the entire crop?

Second farmer Your men have taken away everything.

Officer You are still in arrears. If you don't pay tax next week, I"ll send you to jail.

- **The first farmer asked the officer why his men were taking away the entire crop.**
- **The second farmer said that their men had taken away everything.**
- **The officer replied that they were still in arrears and the warned them that if they did not pay tax the following week, he (the officer) would send them (the farmers) to jail.**

Q.1 Change the following sentences into indirect speech.

(i) First man : We must educate our brothers.
Second man And try to improve their material condition.

Third man : For that we must convey our grievances to the British Parliament.

The first man said that................................

The second mand added that ....

The third man suggested that ....

Ans. The first man said that they must educate their brothers. The second man added that they had to try to improve their material condition. The third man suggested that they must convey their grievances to the British Parliament.

(ii) First soldier : The white soldier gets huge pay, mansions and servants.

Second soldier : We get a pittance and slow promotions.

Third soldier : Who are the British to abolish our customs?

The first soldier said that ....

The second soldier remarked that ....

The third soldier asked ....

Ans. The first soldier said that the white soldier got huge pay, mansions and servants. The second soldier remarked that they only got a pittance and slow promotions. The third soldier asked who the British were to abolish their customs.

SPEAKING AND WRITING (NCERT PAGE 46–49)

Q.1 Playact the role of farmers who have grievances against the policies of the government. Rewrite their 'speech bubbles' in dialogue form first.

Ans. First Farmer These foreigners are worse than our Indian princes.

Second Farmer Yes, you are absolutely right. They have taken away our entire crop.

Third Farmer As if this wasn't enough, they have levied heavy taxes on us and arrears too.

First Farmer The rain gods don't seem to be very happy either. The famine would ruin our entire family.

Second Farmer Despite so much suffering, we are further being threatened that we would be put into jail.

Third Farmer Someone was talking about some Regulation III which says that Indians could be jailed without any trial.

Second Farmer We are damned forever. Death be to the foreigner!

Q.2 Look at the pictures.

Fox accidentally falls into a well

"How do I get out of here?"

"Hello ! Is this water sweet?"

"Too sweet! I've had so much, I might faint."

"Let me taste it."

"Thanks for the help. Come out when you can."

"My mother used to say: Be careful how you take the advice of people you don't know."

(i) Ask one another questions about the pictures.

- Where is the fox?
- How did it happen?
- What is the fox thinking?
- Who is the visitor?
- What does she want to know?
- What is the fox's reply?
- What happens next ?
- Where is the goat?
- Where is the fox now?
- What is the goat thinking?

Ans. Do it yourself.

(ii) Write the story in your own words. Give it a title.

Ans. The Clever Fox

Once, a fox accidentally fell into the water. It did not know what to do or how to get out of the water. At that very instance, a goat arrived there.

It asked the fox a silly question, "Is the water sweet?" The fox pretended that it was inside the well only to drink plenty of the sweet water. Hearing this, the goat gots tempted and unthinkingly jumped into the well.

The fox had been waiting for this opportunity. It immediately climbed the back of the goat and jumped out of the well. He, then, sarcastically told the goat to come out whenever it can.

The goat understood that it had been fooled by the clever fox and remembered its mother's saying: "Be careful how you take the advice of people you don't know."

Q.3 Read the following news item.

History Becomes Fun at this School

Mumbai Students in the sixth grade of a certain school in Navi Mumbai love their history lessons thanks to a novel teaching aid. It is not surprising given the fact that their study material includes comic books and they use their textbooks for reference to put things into perspective. Besides, students are encouraged to tap other sources of information as well. During history classes, students pore over comic strips of historical periods, enact characters of emperors and tyrants and have animated discussions on the subject. History has become fun.

In the class, students are asked to read the comic strip aloud after which they break up into groups of four, discuss what they have heard and write a summary. Each group leader reads his group's summary aloud and the whole class jumps into discussion and debate, adding points, disagreeing and qualifying points of view. A sixth grade student says, "It's a lot of fun because everyone gets a chance to express themselves and the summary takes everyone's ideas into account."

According to the school principal, the comic strip format and visuals appeal to students. A historian feels that using comics in school is a great idea. Comics and acting help students understanding what characters in the story are actually thinking.

(adapted from The Times of India, New Delhi, October, 2007)

Based on this news item, write a paragraph on what you think about this new method of teaching history.

Ans. This new method of teaching sounds very promising because students understand better through visuals and popular culture such as comic reading. This method is a good alternative to the boring text book reading sessions. Since these are activity based sessions, students participate with a lot of energy and enthusiasm.

This method blurs the line between playing and learning and therefore, it is the most suitable method. Acting the roles of various characters, the students are made to apply their knowledge and think as the characters would have thought which forces them to be imaginative and creative.

Q.4 Find the chapters in your history book that correspond to the episodes and events described in this comic. Note how the information contained in a few chapters of history has been condensed to a few pages with the help of pictures and 'speech bubbles'.

Ans. Do it yourself.

Q.5 Create a comic of your own using this story.

Once, the Sun and the Wind began to quarrel, each one saying that he was stronger than the other. At last they decided to test each other's strength. A man with a cloak around his shoulders was passing by.

The wind boasted, "Using my strength I can make that man take off the cloak". The Sun agreed. The wind blew hard. The man felt so cold that he clasped his cloak round his body as tightly as possible. Now, it was turn of the Sun which shone very hot indeed. The man felt so hot that he at once removed the cloak from his body. Seeing the man taking off the cloak, the wind conceded defeat.

Ans. Do it yourself.

REVIEW EXERCISE
Including Competency Based Questions

Multiple Choice Questions

1. How were the Indian princes shortsighted? Competency Based

(a) They were inefficient rulers
(b) They did not respect far-sighted rulers like Tipu
(c) They gave the British opportunities to gain power
(d) They overlooked the superiority of British weapons

Ans. (c) They gave the British opportunities to gain power

2. What does the panel "How did Indians react to these conquests?" convey? Competency Based

(a) It reveals the hypocrisy of Indians
(b) It highlights the patriotism of Indians
(c) It shows that the Indians were unhappy with the British rulers
(d) It contrasts the attitudes of the princes and the common man

Ans. (d) It contrasts the attitudes of the princes and the common man

3. The Britishers' policy of no import duty brought into India from Britain Diksha

(a) increased untouchability
(b) stopped the education of Indians
(c) led to the downfall of Indian industries
(d) increased the income of artisans

Ans. (c) led to the downfall of Indian industries

4. 'Abandon their fields'. What does the word abandon mean?

(a) The land becomes barren (b) To give up completely
(c) Sold their fields (d) Give land on loan

Ans. (b) To give up completely

5. The farmers during British rule abandoned their fields because: Diksha

(a) The Britishers took heavy taxes from them
(b) They were not allowed to work on the fields
(c) They had no equipment to work on the fields
(d) There was no rain

Ans. (a) The Britishers took heavy taxes from them

6. "Cows are of different colours but colour of their milk is the same". Ram Mohan Roy said this to mean that Diksha

(a) All people are equal
(b) Milk is healthy for us
(c) We should treat cows with respect
(d) Different teachers have different opinions but essence of every religion is the same

Ans. (d) Different teachers have different opinions but essence of every religion is the same

7. "Let us not despise ourselves. Our ancient culture is great". What is the meaning of 'despise'?

(a) Feel worthless (b) Feel unhappy
(c) Feel confident (d) Feel insignificant

Ans. (a) Feel worthless

8. According to Ram Mohan Roy, what was the solution to India's problems? Competency Based

(a) Absolute faith in religion
(b) Pride in one's own heritage
(c) Putting an end to internal fights
(d) Respecting religious differences

Ans. (b) Pride in one's own heritage

9. Governer-General Bentick's words show that the British were Competency Based

(a) sly
(b) wrathful
(c) indifferent
(d) condescending

Ans. (a) sly

10. The main causes of violent revolt by the Indians were

(a) Britishers took heavy taxes from the farmers. Diksha
(b) Indian industries began to die
(c) Indians could be jailed without trials
(d) All of the above

Ans. (d) All of the above

11. 'While we get a pittance and slow promotions.' This statement of Indian soldiers in British army shows that Diksha

(a) They were working for money
(b) They wanted their own army
(c) They were discontented and wanted to revolt
(d) They were not loyal soldiers

Ans. (c) They were discontented and wanted to revolt

12. **What do the sections 'Revolt' and 'The Fight for Freedom' together mainly convey?** Competency Based

(a) Show the impact of the revolt on British rule in India
(b) Demonstrate the damage caused by the revolt
(c) Highlight the extent of the revolt
(d) Identify the leaders of the revolt

Ans. (d) Identify the leaders of the revolt

13. **The speech bubbles in the lesson help us to understand** Diksha

(a) the bravery of Indian rulers
(b) how Britishers earned money
(c) the condition which led to first war of Independence
(d) the growth of child marriage and untouchability

Ans. (c) the condition which led to first war of Independence

Extract Based Questions

1. **Read the comic clip given below and answer the following questions.**

(i) What did the East India Company focus on during the 18th century?

Ans. The East India Company focused on extending its power throughout India during the 18th century.

(ii) How did the Indian princes prefer to deal with the kings and princes who opposed them?

Ans. The Indian princes preferred to call the English merchants to defeat the kings and princes who opposed them.

(iii) How was the plan of Indian princes a drawback for the freedom of the country?

Ans. The plan of the Indian princes was a drawback for the freedom of the country because it allowed the Britishers to gain power and subjugate the Indian population.

(iv) Which word from the given comic strip is a synonym of 'higher ranking'?

Ans. The word 'superior' from the comic strip means 'higher ranking'.

(v) State True or False. "The Indian princes were very wise and far-sighted."

Ans. The given statement is false.

2. **Read the comic clip given below and answer the following questions**

(i) What kind of wrong ideas did the religious leaders preach?

Ans. Religious leaders preached ideas such as untouchability and child marriage.

(ii) What did the religious leaders say about crossing the seas?

Ans. The religious leaders said that crossing the seas causes any person to lose their religion.

(iii) What kind of attitude did the religious leaders have about women?

Ans. The religious leaders believed that all the misery in the world was due to women.

(iv) Which word from the given comic strip is connected to discrimination on the basis of caste?

Ans. Untouchability means discrimination on the basis of caste.

(v) Which word from the given passage is a synonym of 'suffering'?

Ans. The word 'misery' from the given passage is a synonym of 'suffering'.

3. Read the comic clip given below and answer the following questions.

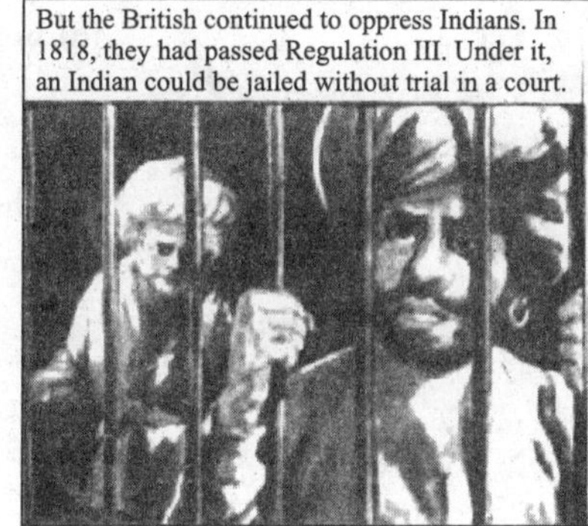

(i) When was Regulation III introduced?

(a) 1816 (b) 1817
(c) 1818 (d) 1819

Ans. (c) 1818

(ii) Whom was the Regulation III disastrous for?

(a) British officers (b) Indians
(c) Landowners (d) Rulers without male child

Ans. (b) Indians

(iii) All the time British officers in India drew ....

(a) beautiful paintings (b) caricatures of Indian kings
(c) big salaries and huge profits (d) sketches of Indian temples

Ans. (c) big salaries and huge profits

(iv) Which of the given words is not a synonym of 'oppress'?

(a) Abuse (b) Tyranny
(c) Delight (d) Injustice

Ans. (c) Delight

(v) Which of the given words means 'belonging to one person'?

(a) Private (b) Community
(c) Autocrate (d) Public

Ans. (a) Private

4. Read the extract given below and answer the following questions.

(i) Which language was traditionally the mode of education in India?

(a) Sanskrit (b) English (c) Persian (d) Both (a) and (c)

Ans. (d) Both (a) and (c)

(ii) Who suggested the change in the mode of education in India?

(a) G. M. Trevelyan (b) Thomas Macaulay (c) Edward Gibbon (d) Thomas Carlyle

Ans. (b) Thomas Macaulay

(iii) What was the purpose behind changing the language of education to English?

(a) To distance the Indians from their culture
(b) To make the Indians lose self-esteem
(c) To produce English speaking Indians that could do the petty jobs of the British
(d) All of the above

Ans. (d) All of the above

(iv) The word .... means 'a person associated with a place by birth'?

(a) native (b) persian (c) indian (d) british

Ans. (a) native

(v) Which of the following words is not an antonym of 'grievance'?

(a) Comfort (b) Happiness (c) Injustice (d) Blessing

Ans. (c) Injustice

Very Short Answer Type Questions

1. What were the two conflicting views with which the Indians welcomed the British during the years 1757 and 1849?

Ans. The Indian princes looked at the British as help sent by the Gods. The native people, however, regretted that they had become slaves to the foreigners.

2. Identify two ways in which the British earned profits from India. Competency Based

Ans. British earned profits from India through the following ways:

(i) They levied heavy taxes on the Indian farmers.
(ii) They imported British goods to India without any import duty.

3. Ram Mohan Roy's concept of knowledge was very different from that of the traditional idea of knowledge in the Indian scheme of things. Why?

Ans. Ram Mohan Roy put a lot of emphasis on knowledge being scientific and practical. This modern form of knowledge was very different from the traditional ways of looking at life.

4. Why did Ram Mohan Roy go to England?

Ans. Ram Mohan Roy went to England to see what made the British powerful. On his return, he accepted the British as their ruler, but only if the British were willing to take responsibility of its citizens.

5. What is Regulation III and why was it oppressive? Diksha

Ans. The Regulation III, passed in the year 1818, was oppressive because it refused to acknowledge the existence of Indians before law. It entailed that the Indians could be jailed without any trial.

6. Who suggested that English education should be introduced in India?

Ans. An Englishman, named Thomas Macaulay in the year 1835, suggested that English education should be introduced in India.

7. What were the grievances of the native people during 1835-56?

Ans. The native men could see that their kings had become puppets in the hands of the British. The British cared little about the Indians and were also making attempts at converting Indians into their faith/religion.

8. During 1855-57, what way was adopted by the rebels to send their message to the villagers?

Ans. The rebels sent their message that the emperor would soon need the services of the villagers by sending chapattis from village to village.

9. Name the people who participated in the First War of Independence, 1857.

Ans. Begum Hazrat Mahal of Lucknow, Maulvi Ahmedulla of Faizabad, Azimulla Khan, Tatya Tope and Kunwar Singh from Bihar were few among many who participated in the First War of Independence, 1857.

10. In which languages was the Indian education conducted initiallly?

Ans. Initially, Indian education was conducted in Persian and Sanskrit.

Short Answer Type Questions

1. How did the Indians react to the Company's conquest? Diksha

Ans. Indians of different ranks of life had varying reactions to the company's conquest. While the Indian Princes thanked the intervention of the British that stopped the looting, common people were beginning to see that they were becoming slaves to the British.

2. Why did Tipu fight with the British till his last breath?

Ans. Tipu Sultan of Mysore was a far-sighted and wise ruler. He understood that the British were taking an advantage of the fights between the Indian princes and would later fulfill their ulterior motives. Therefore, Tipu Sultan fought against the establishment of the British rule in India.

3. Was Ram Mohan Roy against his culture?

Ans. No. Ram Mohan Roy was not against his culture. Rather, he was a great admirer of his ancient culture and invested a lot of faith in its capacities to attain great merits. However, he believed that his society was in need of reform because superstitions had ruined it.

4. Why was Mangal Pandey executed?

Ans. The discontent in the East India Company's army was increasing day-by-day as the Indian soldiers had understood that they were being discriminated against.

Mangal Pandey, one of the sepoys, led a rebellion against his regiment and attacked one of the adjutants. He was executed for daring to rebel.

5. Why did Indian industries begin to die? Competency Based

Ans. Indian industries began to die because the Britishers imposed heavy taxes on the Indian farmers and artisans while importing cheap, machine made products from England. This caused the Indian artisans to go out of business. Thus, the Indian industries were destroyed by the policies of the British.

6. Why did the Indian soldiers feel that they had lost their religion on account of the British?

Ans. The Indian soldiers felt that they lost their religion because they had to travel to different lands across the sea, for the British. Also, the grease used on the bullet was made from the fat of pigs and cows. Both these things were considered wrong in their religion.

7. Mention two reasons for the discontent that led to the 1857 War of Independence. Diksha

Ans. The following two reasons of discontent led to the 1857 war of independence

(i) The Santhals had lost their lands due to the oppressive policies of the British. They became desperate and started killing the Europeans as well as their supporters.

(ii) The salaries and living condition of the British soldiers were much better and higher than those of the Indian soldiers. This caused a lot of discontentment among the Indian soldiers.

8. How did the masses help the rebels?

Ans. Through chapattis and lotus flowers, a message was sent to the masses by the rebels that their services would be needed. The masses stood in full support and gave shelter to patriots, safeguarding them from the British police imprisoning them.

Long Answer Type Questions

1. Which spheres of the Indian society were targeted by the British in gaining control over the Indians?

Ans. The British, being merchants first and foremost, targeted the economic base of the Indians. They ruined the cottage and small-scale industries, thereby hitting the backbone of the country.

They also targeted the social and religious practices of the Indians leading to the destruction of the moral fabric of the Indian existence. Politically, they had already turned the Indian kings and princes into puppets to play with. Also, the changes in existing laws were introduced with an aim to reduce Indians into nothingness before the legal bodies.

2. What happened with the introduction of English education?

Ans. The English education not only replaced the traditional forms of education, especially the modes/languages in which education was imparted, but also created a new class of intellectuals. These intellectuals served as middle men between the native Indians and the British. Since English education was not introduced uniformly, this new class invested a lot of faith in English mannerisms.

3. On the basis of your reading of the text, write a character sketch of Ram Mohan Roy.

Ans. Ram Mohan Roy was a very learned man from Bengal. He was unbiased and objective in his perspectives about his society. He realised both merits and demerits of his society. He could foresee that various social evils and superstitions were ruining Indian society. He, therefore, tried to bring about a reform in his society. He started his newspaper for such causes. He was also a great appreciator of the Western thinking for it laid emphasis on practical and scientific forms of knowledge.

4. What were the superstitions that were being spread by the religious leaders of the time?

Ans. The religious leaders of the time talked about ideas like untouchability and child marriage, ideas that were orthodox and regressive in nature. They also preached against women: "All the misery in the world is due to women." This led to women suffering because of a lower social status.

The religious leaders of the time also encouraged people to believe that travelling to distant lands over the seas would make them lose their religion.

5. Do you think that a society should always resist change or reform in order to preserve its traditional values?

Ans. No. Society should not always resist the changes or reforms that occur because with the changing times certain traditional ideas and values may become meaningless. Also, certain rituals suppress the existence of certain sections of the society. If there is no reform, these sections would always remain oppressed and subjugated, for instance, the women, lower caste and lower class people.

ASSESSMENT EXERCISE

Multiple Choice Questions

1. How many Indians died during the years 1822 and 1836?
   (a) Ten thousand (b) Fifteen lakh
   (c) Fifty thousand (d) Forty lakh
2. What did the British impose on the Indian farmers?
   (a) Heavy taxes (b) Service taxes
   (c) Regulation II (d) Regulation III
3. What was the value of British goods exported to India in 1829?
   (a) Five crores (b) Six crores
   (c) Seven crores (d) Eight crores
4. When was the First War of Independence fought?
   (a) 1829 (b) 1818 (c) 1857 (d) 1847
5. Read the given statements and choose the correct answer.

   Statement 1 Indian princes were short-sighted and fought petty wars amongst themselves.

   Statement 2 Tipu Sultan of Mysore was a brave king who died fighting against the British.

   (a) Statement 1 is true but Statement 2 is false.
   (b) Statement 1 is false but Statement 2 is true.
   (c) Both the Statements are true.
   (d) Both the Statements are false.

Extract Based Question

Read the extract given below and answer the following questions.

Sepoy Mangal Pande attacked the adjutant of his regiment and was executed

humiliated and put in irons.

(i) How were the Indian soldiers discriminated against in the army?
   (a) They got slower promotions.
   (b) They got lower wages.
   (c) They didn't get mansions to live in.
   (d) All of the above

(ii) What could cause the Indian soldiers to lose their religion?
   (a) Eating beef
   (b) Biting bullets
   (c) Crossing the seas
   (d) Killing people

(iii) What was the name given by the Indian soldiers to the Britishers?
   (a) Jootewala   (b) Topiwala
   (c) Lathiwala   (d) Daftarwala

(iv) Which word from the comic strip means 'dissatisfaction with one's circumstances'?

(v) What does the phrase 'put in irons' mean?

Very Short Answer Type Questions

1. Name the Englishman who reported the ruin of Indian industries to England.
2. What was the medium used by Ram Mohan Roy to spread knowledge so as to bring reforms in Indian societies?
3. By which year had the British conquered the whole of India?
4. What were the views of religious leaders about excluded sections of the society?
5. Why were the farmers unable to pay arrears?

Short Answer Type Questions

1. What weapons did the British have that were superior to Indian weapons?
2. What did Governer General Bentnick say about the suffering of Indian farmers?
3. What was the role of Mangal Pandey in the rebellion?
4. What were the views of Raja Ram Mohan Roy about religion?
5. On what condition did Raja Ram Mohan Roy accept the rule of the British?

Long Answer Type Questions

1. Look at the years between 1757 and 1857 and analyse the changing reactions of the Indians towards the British rule.
2. Comment on the faults committed by the Indian leaders and masses which led to the strengthening of the British rule.
3. How did the hatred towards the foreigners grow into armed revolt?
4. Explain the events of the First War of Independence in 1857. Mention the names of the people involved in the revolt.

Bepin Choudhury's Lapse of Memory

by Satyajit Ray

CHAPTER SUMMARY Bepin Choudhury's Lapse of Memory is a suspense story written by Satyajit Ray. The story is divided into 4 parts and revolves on Bepin Babu who is made to believe that he had been to Ranchi while he himself believes that he had never been to the place before. In reality, he is tricked by his old friend named Chunilal, who Bepin does not help in time of need.

The humorous story has conspiracy and a surprise ending which aims to teach us to be generous and kind to others in their time of need.

Part – I

Stranger in the Bookshop

Bepin Choudhury came to Kalicharan's shop in New Market to buy books like every Monday. He had a habit of buying at least five books of crime stories, ghost stories, and thrillers that he would read through the week. He was not a social person and had only a few friends. As he was buying the books, he noticed someone observing him. It was a round-faced and humble looking man who smiled at Bepin Babu and asked if he recognised him. When Bepin babu failed to identify him, the man was surprised.

Bepin Babu's Strange Encounter

The stranger introduced himself as Parimal Ghose and claimed to have met him every day for a whole week. He also said that he arranged a car for Bepin Babu to take him to Hudroo Falls in Ranchi in 1958. However, Bepin Babu insisted that the stranger was making a mistake because he had never been to Ranchi, though he had greatly wished to visit the place. However, the stranger correctly identified him as Bepin Babu and proceeded to share some personal details about Bepin Babu on his sight-seeing trips.

The Stranger Shares Details

To make Bepin Babu believe him, Ghose told Bepin Babu that the injury on Bepin's right knee was from a fall at Hudroo falls. He added that he was the one who bought him medicine and also arranged a car for him to go to Netarhat but he did not go due to pain. Further, Ghose claimed that Dinesh Mukerji (a friend of Bepin) was also in Ranchi at that time. He recounted that Bepin stayed in a bungalow because he didn't like hotel food and preferred to have his meals cooked by a bawarchi. Mr. Ghose shared that Mr. Mukerji stayed with his sister and they had a big argument about the moon landing. He also stated that Bepin always carried a big bag of books with him.

Bepin Babu gets Confused

The details shared by Ghose made Bepin Babu anxious. So, he asked Ghose to tell him the month of his visit. Mr. Ghose replied that it was October of 1958. Bepin Babu was sure that he had spent Puja with a friend in Kanpur that year. However, Ghose kept insisting that he knew Bepin and recalled drinking tea and chatting about his family. He recalled that Bepin Babu told him that he had no children and that he lost his wife ten years ago. His only brother had died in a mental asylum and that's why he didn't visit the mental hospital in Ranchi. Confused and anxious, Bepin Babu bought his books and left the shop leaving Ghose completely surprised.

Part – II

Bepin Babu Questions Everything

After the encounter with the stranger, Bepin Babu sat in his car that was parked in Bertram Street by the Lighthouse Cinema and told his driver Sitaram to drive by the Ganga. While in his car, Bepin began regretting paying attention to the strange man because he was quite sure that he hadn't ever been to Ranchi.

He could not have forgotten an incident that took place only six or seven years ago because he had an excellent memory. But then, he considered that he could be losing his mind. Even though he worked in a big firm and nothing ever went wrong with his job, he still began doubting his own mind because the man had known many personal details about him.

Bepin Babu Examines his Memories

Bepin Babu could clearly remember that he had spent the Puja of 1958 in Kanpur with his friend Haridas Bagchi. He could write to Haridas to clarify the matter but Haridas had left for Japan with his wife, and Bepin didn't have his address anymore. However, Bepin kept doubting himself and insisted that he hadn't ever gone to Ranchi. When they reached near Hastings, Bepin checked his right knee and found an inch-long old cut, but he couldn't remember where he had gotten it from.

Then he remembered the stranger had claimed that Dinesh Mukerji had also been in Ranchi at the same time. He lived in Beninandan street which was very close. Bepin Babu could visit Dinesh and ask him, but he decided against it because Dinesh would surely make fun of him.

Bepin Babu is Restless

Bepin only began to feel comfortable when he had dinner and went to bed with a thriller book. By now, he had completely forgotten about the strange man. Next day, Bepin Babu couldn't concentrate on his work and thus, decided to call Dinesh. He felt that a call would be better because his embarrassment wouldn't be seen by Dinesh. However, when Dinesh confirmed that they had been to Ranchi in the October of 1958, Bepin Babu cut the call. He was left completely shocked and did not want to eat his food.

Part – III

Bepin Babu Calls Dinesh

Bepin babu was known to be a tireless and careful worker. However, for the first time in 25 years he couldn't focus on his work after the shocking call with Dinesh. He reached home at two-thirty in the afternoon and laid down in his bed to figure things out. He knew that people could lose their memory due to injuries in the head but he hadn't ever heard of someone remembering everything except just one incident. Later that evening, his friend Chuni visited him at seven thirty.

Bepin Babu Talks to Chunilal

Chunilal was Bepin's School friend and had been visiting him in hopes of getting a job. However, Bepin Babu couldn't do anything about that. So, he told his servant to send him away. Yet, Chunilal kept on visiting Bepin. This time also, Bepin told his servant to send him away. But then, he thought that Chuni might remember something about the trip to Ranchi and so he rushed to talk to him. Chuni looked at Bepin Babu in amazement and asked if he had taken drugs. Then, he replied that not only had Bepin gone to Ranchi but that Chuni himself had booked his ticket via his last job at a travel agency. He had even gone to the station with Bepin and had gotten a fan fixed in his compartment.

Bepin Babu Visits the Doctor

After talking to Chunilal, Bepin Babu concluded that he had been working too hard and that he would go see a specialist doctor. So, Bepin visited Paresh Chanda, a young physician with bright eyes and a sharp nose. When Bepin asked the doctor to cure him of his illness, Dr. Chanda replied that he had never dealt with a case such as Bepin's before and that it was outside his experience. He suggested that Bepin Babu should visit Ranchi again, because the familiar sights might bring his memory back. He prescribed a nerve tonic and a tranquiliser to Bepin Babu and told him to get proper sleep. Next morning, Bepin Babu called his office to give some instructions and booked a first class ticket to Ranchi for the same evening.

Part – IV

Bepin Babu Visits Ranchi

When Bepin Babu reached the Ranchi station the next morning, he realized that he had never been there before. He took a taxi and drove around the town in search of anything familiar. He visited the buildings, hotels, bazaars, and even the Moradabadi hill but couldn't find anything familiar. Then, he arranged for a car to take him to Hudroo Falls. He was found unconscious around five o'clock by two Gujrati men from a group of picnickers. When he woke up, he cried that there was no hope of him remembering the trip.

Bepin Babu Gets Back

Next morning, Bepin Babu went back to Calcutta and began worrying about the fact that he was going to lose everything. He wondered if he might end up at the asylum. He asked Dr. Chanda to come over while he showered and went to bed with an ice bag clamped on his head. Then, his servant brought a green envelope with his name as well as 'Urgent and Confidential' written in red ink.

The Truth of the Matter

Bepin Babu opened the envelope and found that it was written by Chunilal who had taken revenge on Bepin Babu by arranging for the entire Ranchi incident. Chunilal had been hurt that Bepin Babu hadn't helped him because of his pride in money. Then, he informed Bepin that he would be alright since a publisher was taking a look at his novel.

When Dr. Chanda arrived, Bepin lied to him that he had remembered everything as soon as he got off the train at Ranchi. Dr. Chanda remarked that it was a unique case and decided to write about it in a medical journal. Meanwhile, Bepin Babu replied that he had hip pain due to the fall he had in Ranchi and asked if he could get a painkiller.

Word Meaning

Word	Meaning
Idle chat	a necessary routine conversation
Meek	humble, modest, meager
Contrary	housing, barracks or living space
Bawarchi	cook in hindi
Inconceivable	unable to be conceived, unbelievable
Utter disbelief	complete surprise
Head reeled	was shocked and confused
Intimate	closely acquainted or familiar
Bracing	stimulating
Linger	to stay or remain in a place or situation especially as if unwilling to depart
Losing his mind	becoming mad
Ridiculous	deserving of ridicule; foolish; absurd
Ruthless	without pity or compassion; cruel
Sarcasm	a form of humor that is marked by mocking with irony
Nuisance	an annoying person or situation
Snuggling	lying
Embarrassment	a state of discomfort arising from bashfulness or consciousness of having violated a social rule
Going nuts	going mad or crazy
Getting into people's hair	interfering with and annoying people
Thriller encounter	a suspenseful story
Sleuthing	careful investigation into a crime or mystery
Slammed	to shut with sudden force so as to produce a shock and noise

Word	Meaning
Appetite	a strong desire for something specially food
Reputation	what somebody is known for
Sweating	to think hard
Conscientious	thorough, careful; implies a desire to do a task well
Head was in a whirl	confused and unable to think clearly
Gather his wits together	make an effort to become calm and think clearly
Having a rough time	having a lot of problems
Turning up like a bad penny	appearing at a place where one is not welcomed
Didn't beat around the bush	came straight to the point
Throw your mind back	think back and recall a past event
Must see about consulting	may have to consult
Incredulous	skeptical or unable to believe
Tranquilliser	a drug used to reduce anxiety or tension; a sedative
Procured	to acquire or to obtain
Slightest	smallest amount
Boulder	a large piece of stone
Clamped	a band to hold things
Confidential	secret
Affluence	an abundant flow or supply
In retribution of	as a punishment for

NCERT FOLDER

NCERT Intext and Exercise Questions

COMPREHENSION CHECK❶ (NCERT PAGE 58)

Q.1 Why did the man stare at Bepin Babu in disbelief?

Ans. The man stared at Bepin Babu in disbelief because Bepin Babu refused to recognise him.

Q.2 Where did Bepin Babu say he went in October, 1958?

Ans. Bepin Babu said that in October, 1958 he had gone to Kanpur to celebrate 'Puja' with his friend, Haridas Bagchi.

Q.3 Mention any three (or more) things that Parimal Ghose knew about Bepin Babu.

Ans. Parimal Ghose knew quite a few things about Bepin Choudhury and his life. These include

(i) Bepin Choudhury's wife had died about ten years ago.

(ii) Bepin Babu had no children.

(iii) Bepin Babu's brother had died of insanity and for this reason Bepin Babu did not like visiting mental hospitals.

(iv) Bepin Babu was not fond of hotel food.

(v) Bepin Babu carried a bag with his books in it.

CHECK❷ (NCERT PAGE 61)

Q.1 Why did Bepin Babu worry about what Parimal Ghose had said?

Ans. Bepin Babu was worried about the things Parimal Ghose had shared with him because these were all intimate details of his life, not known to strangers. Parimal Ghose was correct about everything, except for Bepin being to Ranchi in 1958. Bepin Babu began to worry if there was something wrong with his mental health.

Q.2 How did he try to decide who was right — his memory or Parimal Ghose?

Ans. Bepin Choudhury decided to call his friend, Haridas Bagchi, with whom he had spent the 'Puja' of 1958. Since Bagchi was away to Japan, he rolled up his trousers to see for himself the cut on his knee. He, later, decided to call up Dinesh Mukerji and Chunilal, to get a confirmation.

Q.3 Why did Bepin Babu hesitate to visit Mr. Mukerji? Why did he finally decide to phone him?

Ans. Bepin Babu was a little hesitant to visit Mr. Mukerji because he thought that it would be quite embarrassing for him to ask details of his life from his friend.

Also, if Dinesh Mukerji would confirm their Ranchi visit, Mukerji would get to know about his state of mind and humiliate him. Therefore, Bepin Babu decided to phone him.

Q.4 What did Mr. Mukerji say? Did it comfort Bepin Babu or add to his worries?

Ans. Mr. Mukerji confirmed that both of them had been to Ranchi in the year 1958. This quite obviously added on to Bepin Babu's worries.

CHECK❸ (NCERT PAGE 64)

Q.1 Who was Chunilal? What did he want from Bepin Babu?

Ans. Chunilal was a very old friend of Bepin Babu. They had been together at school. Chunilal was going through a very rough time as he didn't have a job at present. He had been coming to meet Bepin Babu over and over again for job prospects.

Q.2 Why was Dr. Chanda puzzled? What was unusual about Bepin Babu's loss of memory?

Ans. Dr. Chanda was puzzled because Bepin Babu seemed to remember everything about his life, except this one episode.

The peculiarity of Bepin Babu's case was that unlike patients who seem to forget parts of their memory, Bepin Babu had forgotten just this one episode of his life.

CHECK❹ (NCERT PAGE 66)

Q.1 Had Bepin Babu really lost his memory and forgotten all about a trip to Ranchi?

Ans. No, Bepin Babu had not lost his memory or forgotten anything. He had been fooled by Chunilal to believe that he had made a trip to Ranchi and then, he was unable to remember it.

Q.2 Why do you think Chunilal did what he did? Chunilal says he has no money; what is it that he does have?

Ans. Chunilal had been a very old friend of Bepin Choudhury. He was asking for help from Bepin Babu on account of this age old friendship. According to Chunilal, the privileged circumstances of Bepin Babu seemed to make him overlook the ill condition of his friend. This deeply hurt Chunilal. As his revenge, he played this trick upon Bepin Babu. Chunilal wrote in his letter that he had no money, but what he did have was his imagination. He was using his imagination to take revenge from his friend.

WORKING WITH THE TEXT (NCERT PAGE 66)

Q.1 The author describes Bepin Babu as a serious and hardworking man. What evidence can you find in the story to support this?

Ans. The author describes Bepin Babu as a serious and hard working man. He took his job quite seriously and did all his work with great dedication. The proof for this is the fact that even while Bepin Choudhury was quite unwell because of the Ranchi episode and when Dr. Chanda recommended him to go to Ranchi once again, he called up at his office, gave a set of instructions before setting on this journey. This clearly proves that even in condition of ill health, he placed his office work at priority.

Q.2 Why did Bepin Babu change his mind about meeting Chunilal? What was the result of this meeting?

Ans. Chunilal had been coming over and over again to meet Bepin Babu to appeal for a job. Bepin Babu, therefore, asked him to leave. Immediately, however, Bepin Babu changed his mind because he thought Chunilal might have a fair idea about his Ranchi visit in 1958.

After this meeting, Bepin Babu was left further troubled, since Chunilal confirmed Bepin Babu's Ranchi visit.

Q.3 Bepin Babu lost consciousness at Hudroo Falls. What do you think was the reason for this?

Ans. Bepin Babu lost consciousness at Hudroo Falls perhaps because that was his lost hope at regaining the lost parts of his memory.

He was already in bad health, worrying too much about his lapse of memory. So, when he failed to recollect that episode, at Hudroo Falls, he probably got over burdened by his thoughts and lost consciousness.

Q.4 How do you think Bepin Babu reacted when he found out that Chunilal had tricked him?

Ans. Bepin Babu must have been shocked, dumbfounded and embarrassed when he found out that Chunilal had tricked him. That is why he didn't wish to share his embarrassment with anyone and therefore, in keeping with Chunilal's lie, he told Dr. Chanda that on visiting Ranchi he had recollected everything.

WORKING WITH LANGUAGE (NCERT PAGE 67-69)

Q.1 Look at these two sentences.

He had to buy at least five books to last him through the week.

Bepin had to ask Chuni to leave.

Had *to* is used to show that it was very important or necessary for Bepin Babu to do something. He had no choice. We can also use 'have to'/ 'has to' in the same way.

Fill in the blanks below using 'had to' / 'have to'/ 'has to'.

(i) I .... cut my hair every month.

(ii) We .... go for swimming lessons last year.

(iii) She .... tell the principal the truth.

(iv) They .... take the baby to the doctor.

(v) We .... complain to the police about the noise.

(vi) Romit .... finish his homework before he could come out to play.

(vii) I .... repair my cycle yesterday.

Ans. (i) have to (ii) had to
(iii) had to (iv) had to
(v) had to (vi) has to
(vii) had to

Q.2 Here are a few idioms that you will find in the story. Look for them in the dictionary in the following way.

First, arrange them in the order in which you would find them in a dictionary.

(Clue: An idiom is usually listed under the first noun, verb, adjective or adverb in it. Ignore articles or prepositions in the idiom). To help you, we have put in bold the words under which you must look for the idioms in the dictionary.

(i) at/from **close** quarters (**close** :adjective)

(ii) **break** into a smile (**break** :verb; look under 'break into something')

(iii) **carry** on (**carry** : verb)

(iv) have a clean **record** (you may find related meanings under both these words)

(v) **beat** about the bush (verb)

Now, refer to your dictionary and find out what they mean.

Ans. The dictionary order

(i) beat about the bush (ii) break into a smile
(iii) carry on (iv) from close quarters
(v) have a clean record of

Meaning

(i) Not to talk in a straight forward manner

(ii) Smile abruptly or suddenly

(iii) To continue

(iv) Nearby or close by

(v) Without any blemish

Q.3 Study the sentences in the columns A and B below.

Column A	Column B
I saw this movie yesterday.	I have seen this movie already.
Bepin Babu worked here for a week last year.	Bepin Babu has worked here since 2003.
Chunilal wrote to a publisher last week.	Chunilal has written to a publisher.
I visited Ranchi once, long ago.	I have visited Ranchi once before.

Compare the sentences in two columns, especially the verb forms. Answer the following questions about each pair of sentences.

(i) Which column tells us that Bepin Babu is still working at the same place?

(ii) Which column suggests that Chunilal is now waiting for a reply from the publisher?

(iii) Which column suggests that the person still remembers the movie he saw?

(iv) Which column suggests that the experience of visiting Ranchi is still fresh in the speaker's mind?

Ans. (i) Column B–Bepin Babu has worked here since 2003.

(ii) Column A–Chunilal wrote to a publisher last week.

(iii) Column B–I have seen this movie already.

(iv) Column B–I have visited Ranchi once before.

Q.4 Given below are jumbled sentences. Working in groups, rearrange the words in each sentence to form correct sentences.

You will find that each sentence contains an idiomatic expression that you have come across in the lesson. Underline the idiom and write down its meaning. Then use your dictionary to check the meaning.

One sentence has been worked out for you as an example.

***Jumbled sentence:* vanished/ The car/ seemed to/into thin/have/air.**

Ans. The car seemed to have vanished into thin air.
Idiom: **vanished into thin air** : disappeared or vanished in a mysterious way.

(i) Stop/ and tell me/ beating about/what you want/ the bush

(ii) don't pay/If you/attention/you might/the wrong train/ to the announcement/ board

(iii) The villagers/tried/the crime/on the young woman/to pin

(iv) Bepin Babu/orders to/telling people/under/ loved/doctor's/eat early/that he was

(v) the students/The teacher/ his eyebrows/ when/said that/all their lessons/raised/they had revised

Ans. (i) Stop beating about the bush and tell me what you want.
Idiom: **beating about the bush** which means to not talk about something directly.

(ii) If you don't pay attention to the announcement you might board the wrong train.
Idiom: **Pay attention** which means to be attentive

(iii) The villagers tried to pin the crime on the young woman.
Idiom: **To pin the crime** which means to accuse someone for any crime.

(iv) Bepin Babu loved telling people that he was under doctor's orders to eat early.
Idiom : **Under orders** which means to follow the instructions.

(v) The teacher raised his eyebrows when the students said that they had revised all their lessons.
Idiom: **raised his eyebrows** which means to be shocked or surprise mildly.

SPEAKING AND WRITING (NCERT PAGE 69)

Q.1 What do you think happened after Bepin Babu came to know the truth? Was he angry with this friend for playing such a trick on him? Or do you think he decided to help a friend in need?

Ans. When Bepin Babu discovered the truth, he was completely shocked. He could never imagine in his wildest dreams that he would be fooled in this manner. Initially, he became quite upset with Chunilal and could not understand how Chunilal could play such a serious prank on a friend. He was also disturbed by Dinesh Mukerji's lie as it had made him believe in the gravity of the situation.

However, he soon realised that what disturbed him most was that his friends were responsible for his present condition, his mental misbalance and ill health.

Bepin Choudhury, then, understood how he was responsible for Chunilal's poor economic condition. As a friend, how he had failed to be a pillar of strength and help his friend, in the hour of need.

He, therefore, decided to help his friend in whatever ways possible and do so without any delay. He also wrote an apology letter to his friend and went to see his friend in person and sought forgiveness from him.

Q.2 Imagine you are Bepin Choudhury. You have received Chunilal's letter and feel ashamed that you did not bother to help an old friend down on his luck.

Now, you want to do something for him. Write a letter to Chunilal promising to help him soon.

Ans. XYZ Street

Calcutta

25th January, 19XX

Dear Chunilal

How are you doing? I am fine here and hoping well for you. I have written this letter regarding your last letter which I received yesterday.

I had just been back from Ranchi and was in poor health when I was shocked by the revelation your letter made. I was dumbfounded and went numb for a considerable amount of time. I did not know how to react. The way I had suffered in the past week, I should have been very angry with you. However, realising how you might have been suffering for the past two months on my account left me speechless. I am really ashamed of how I handled your case. I could have put in a little effort and helped you gain a position. But, my unfeeling attitude has hurt you, and left me in pain today. My friend, I beg you, for the sake of our old friendship, to forgive me and I promise to help you out in the best possible way. I wish to meet you soon but I am too embarrassed to come and face you. Do let me know that you have forgiven me and I will make all things better.

Looking forward to your reply.

Yours truly

Bepin Choudhury

Or

A prank is a childish trick. Do you remember any incident when someone played a prank on you or your friends? Describe the prank in a paragraph.

Ans. When I was young, I was very scared of lizards. One day, one of my cousins threw a plastic lizard on me. I was scared to death, thinking it to be a real one. I was so scared that I wanted to have revenge on my cousin. So, I called him from another phone and pretended to be his teacher and asked him to pass the phone to his father so that I could complain about his mischievous behaviour in class. Thinking of me as his teacher, my cousin was so apologetic for all his wild acts that it gave me a lot of pleasure.

REVIEW EXERCISE

Including Competency Based Questions

Multiple Choice Questions

1. What can be said about Bepin Choudhury from the first paragraph? Competency Based

(a) He was a hard worker
(b) He was a man of routine
(c) He had an active lifestyle
(d) He was a keen judge of character

Ans. (b) He was a man of routine

2. Where would Bepin Babu drop every monday while returning home from work? Diksha

(a) Kalicharan's shop (b) Mr. Mukerji's house
(c) Ganag riverbank (d) Chunilal's place

Ans. (a) Kalicharan's shop

3. How many books did Bepin Babu require for a week? Diksha

(a) Minimum five
(b) Two to three
(c) Three to five
(d) More than five

Ans. (a) Minimum five

4. How can you tell that Bepin was a regular reader? Competency Based

(a) He visited bookstores
(b) He read a variety of books
(c) He bought new books every week
(d) He visited the market only to buy books

Ans. (c) He bought new books every week

5. What could be the reason behind Bepin not being a good mixer? Competency Based

(a) Bepin's preference of keeping less friends
(b) Bepin's preference of spending more time with books
(c) Bepin's living condition
(d) Bepin's preference of not engaging in idle talk

Ans. (b) Bepin's preference of spending more time with books.

6. Who was staring at Bepin Babu at the book stall? Diksha

(a) Chunilal (b) Parimal Ghose
(c) Mr. Mukerji (d) Kalicharan

Ans. (b) Parimal Ghose

7. Where did Bepin Babu say he went in October '58? Diksha

(a) Kanpur (b) Ranchi
(c) Kolkata (d) Jaipur

Ans. (a) Kanpur

8. Why did Bepin Choudhury start doubting himself? Competency Based

(a) The man narrated his story with conviction
(b) The man was familiar with the places in Ranchi
(c) The man remembered who Bepin lived with in Ranchi
(d) The man had information about Bepin that few people knew

Ans. (d) The man had information about Bepin that few people knew

9. What did Bepin most likely feel after the conversation with Dinesh? Competency Based

(a) Panic (b) Disgust
(c) Exhaustion (d) Resentment

Ans. (a) Panic

10. Which of the following best describes Bepin's attitude towards Chuni? Competency Based

(a) Insincere (b) Malicious
(c) Dismissive (d) Patronising

Ans. (c) Dismissive

11. "I know that old friendships don't mean much to you, but at least you had a good memory." What would most likely have been Chuni's attitude when he said the above lines? Competency Based

(a) Bitter (b) Amused
(c) Defensive (d) Accusatory

Ans. (a) Bitter

12. What is the tone of Chuni's letter? Competency Based

(a) Formal (b) Nostalgic
(c) Vindictive (d) Miserable

Ans. (c) Vindictive

13. What did Chuni's letter to Bepin prove? Competency Based

(a) Bepin was losing his memory
(b) Bepin was not good at his job
(c) Bepin had never been to Ranchi
(d) Bepin's visit to Ranchi had upset Chunilal

Ans. (c) Bepin had never been to Ranchi

14. Fill in the blank with the correct option.

The best thing surely would be to ask him. He lived quite near-in ....Street. What about going right now?

(a) Hargobindan (b) Ramanujan
(c) Beninandan (d) Parmanandan

Ans. (c) Beninandan

15. What reason did Bepin Babu give for calling Dr. Chanda to his home?

(a) Bepin had a terrible headache
(b) Bepin had forgotten even more things
(c) Bepin had remembered his trip to Ranchi
(d) Bepin had hip pain due to falling down

Ans. (d) Bepin had hip pain due to falling down

Extract Based Questions

1. Read the extract given below and answer the following questions.

"No, sir," said Bepin Babu. "I spent Puja in '58 with a friend in Kanpur. You're making a mistake. Good day." But the man didn't go, nor did he stop talking. "Very strange. One evening I had tea with you in a veranda of your bungalow. You spoke about your family. You said you had no children, and that you had lost your wife ten years ago. Your only brother had died insane, which is why you didn't want to visit the mental hospital in Ranchi..."

(i) Where did Bepin Babu visit during the Durga Puja of 1958?

Ans. Bepin Babu visited his friend in Kanpur.

(ii) How had the brother of Bepin Babu died?

Ans. The brother of Bepin Babu had died insane.

(iii) Why did Bepin Babu not have any children?

Ans. Bepin Babu didn't have any children because his wife had died ten years ago.

(iv) State True or False. "Bepin Babu and Parimal Ghose drank coffee on the verandah of the bungalow in Ranchi".

Ans. False. Bepin Babu and Parimal Ghose drank tea on the verandah of the bungalow in Ranchi'.

(v) **What is the meaning of the word 'insane'?**

Ans. The word 'insane' means 'a person who is mentally ill'.

2. Read the extract given below and answer the following questions.

And yet the man knew a great deal about him. How? He even seemed to know some intimate details. The bag of books, wife's death, brother's insanity... The only mistake was about his having gone to Ranchi. Not a mistake; a deliberate lie. In '58, during the Pujas, he was in Kanpur at his friend Haridas Bagchi's place. All Bepin Babu had to do was write to – no, there was no way of writing to Haridas. Bepin Babu suddenly remembered that Haridas had left with his wife for Japan some weeks ago, and he didn't have his address. But where was the need for proof? He himself was fully aware that he hadn't been to Ranchi – and that was that.

(i) What intimate details did the stranger know about Bepin Babu?

Ans. The stranger knew that Bepin Babu carried a bag of books with him. He also knew about the death of his wife and his brother's insanity.

(ii) According to Bepin Babu, where had he been during October of 1958?

Ans. According to Bepin Babu, he had been visiting the place of his friend Haridas Bagchi in Kanpur.

(iii) Why couldn't Bepin write to his friend Haridas Bagchi to confirm the details of his travels in 1958?

Ans. Bepin couldn't write to his friend Haridas Bagchi to get confirmation about his travels because Haridas and his wife had shifted to Japan and he didn't know their address anymore.

(iv) From the passage, choose a word that is synonymous of 'personal'.

Ans. From the passage, the word 'intimate' means 'personal'.

(v) What is the meaning of the word 'deliberate'?

Ans. The word 'deliberate' means 'doing something with intention'.

3. Read the extract given below and answer the following questions.

Every Monday, on his way back from work, Bepin Choudhury would drop in at Kalicharan's in New Market to buy books. Crime stories, ghost stories and thrillers. He had to buy at least five at a time to last him through the week. He lived alone, was not a good mixer, had few friends, and didn't like spending time in idle chat. Today, at Kalicharan's, Bepin Babu had the feeling that someone was observing him from close quarters. He turned round and found himself looking at a round faced, meek looking man who now broke into a smile.

(i) Where was the book shop of Kalicharan situated?

(a) Old market (b) Sunday book market
(c) New market (d) Monday book market

Ans. (c) New Market

(ii) What kind of books did Bepin Choudhury prefer to read?

(a) Crime stories (b) Ghost stories
(c) Thrillers (d) All of these

Ans. (d) All of these

(iii) Which of the following are known habits of Mr. Bepin Choudhury?

(a) Cooking tasty dishes
(b) Reading thrillers and crime stories
(c) Going on solo travel trips
(d) Writing Novels

Ans. (b) Reading thrillers and crime stories

(iv) Which of the following is not a synonym for 'meek'?

(a) Docile (b) Gentle
(c) Bold (d) Timid

Ans. (c) Bold

(v) What does the phrase 'not a good mixer' mean?

(a) Extrovert (b) Sociable
(c) Ambivert (d) Introvert

Ans. (d) Introvert

4. Read the extract given below and answer the following questions.

"What are you saying, Mr. Choudhury? You had a fall in Hudroo and cut your right knee. I brought you iodine. I had fixed up a car for you to go to Netarhat the next day, but you couldn't because of the pain in the knee. Can't you recall anything? Someone else you know was also in Ranchi at that time. Mr. Dinesh Mukerji. You stayed in a bungalow."

(i) Who is the speaker of the above lines?

(a) Mr. Parimal Ghose
(b) Mr. Dinesh Mukerji
(c) Kalicharan
(d) Mr. Bepin Choudhury

Ans. (a) Mr. Parimal Ghose

(ii) Why did he bring iodine for Bepin Babu?

(a) Because he needed to eat salt
(b) Because he had to purify his water
(c) Because he had cut up his right knee
(d) Because he had cut up his left knee

Ans. (c) Because he had cut up his right knee

(iii) Where couldn't Bepin Babu visit because of his injury?

(a) Ranchi (b) Hudroo
(c) Kanpur (d) Netarhat

Ans. (d) Netarhat

(iv) Fill in the blank wih\th the appropriate option.

Someone else you know was also in Ranchi at that time. ....

(a) Mr. Parimal Ghose (b) Mr. Dinesh Mukerji
(c) Kalicharan (d) Mr. Bepin Choudhury

Ans. (b) Mr. Dinesh Mukerji

(v) What does the phrase 'had a fall' mean?

(a) Autumn has arrived
(b) He fell down
(c) He bought a sweater
(d) He had a fall-themed party

Ans. (b) He fell down

Very Short Answer Type Questions

1. Discuss a regular feature of Bepin Choudhury's Monday evenings.

Ans. Every Monday, after work, Bepin Choudhury used to go to Kalicharan's book shop in new market to buy at least five books that would last him the entire week.

2. According to Parimal Ghose he had arranged a car for Bepin Babu to travel to which place?

Ans. Parimal Ghose had arranged a car for Bepin Babu to travel to Hudroo Falls and Netarhat.

3. Do you think Bepin was well known? Support your answer with evidence from the story. **Competency Based**

Ans. From the chapter, we can assume that Bepin Babu was well known because Parimal Ghose said 'who doesn't know Bepin Choudhury!'

4. Why was Bepin Choudhury unable to consult his friend, Haridas Bagchi?

Ans. Bepin Choudhury was unable to call Haridas Bagchi because Haridas Bagchi and his wife had gone to Japan.

5. Why did Bepin hesitate to contact Dinesh? **Competency Based**

Ans. Bepin hesitated to contact Dinesh because Dinesh was known for his ruthless sarcasm.

6. What was the nature of Chunilal's last job?

Ans. In his previous job, Chunilal had worked at a travel agency.

7. Is Dr. Chanda successful in diagnosing Bepin Babu's problem?

Ans. No, Dr. Chanda was unable to diagnose Bepin Choudhury's problem. He thinks that it was quite a peculiar case.

8. Where did Bepin Choudhury spend the October of 1958?

Ans. During October 1958, Puja, Bepin Choudhury was in Kanpur with his friend, Haridas Bagchi and his family.

9. Did Parimal Ghose know Bepin Choudhury?

Ans. No, Parimal Ghose was not familiar with Bepin Choudhury. He was merely acting in accordance with Chunilal's instructions.

Short Answer Type Questions

1. Why does Dr. Chanda call Bepin Babu's case a peculiar case?

Ans. Dr. Chanda called Bepin Babu's case peculiar because he had never heard of any case of partial lapse of memory. He had heard of people losing their partial memory. But he had never known someone forgetting only a particular incident of his life and remembering everything else without any difficulty.

2. What role does Dinesh Mukerji play in the story?

Ans. Dinesh Mukerji's confirmation of Bepin Choudhury's Ranchi visit is a turning point in the story. Only after receiving this piece of information, he gets convinced that something was the matter with him and he begins to consider Parimal Ghose's claims seriously.

3. What were Bepin Choudhury's biggest fears concerning his present condition?

Ans. Bepin Choudhury begins to believe that he was losing his sanity and was going mad. His biggest fear was that he might end up in a lunatic asylum.

His brother had died of insanity and he hated going to a mental hospital, but he feared that his fate might be the same. He also feared losing his job and reputation.

4. What did Bepin Choudhury want to confirm after visiting Hudroo Falls?

Ans. Bepin Choudhury wanted to confirm whether he had visited Ranchi or not by visiting Hudroo falls. He was hoping that visiting a familiar place might jog his memory.

5. With what intention does Chunilal reveal the truth in the end?

Ans. Chunilal reveals the truth in the end and showcases himself as the mastermind of the entire game to teach Bepin Choudhury a lesson.

He lets Bepin Babu know that he had played this prank on him to seek revenge and reduce Bepin Choudhury to as pitiable a situation as he himself was in.

Long Answer Type Questions

1. Discuss the theme of revenge as it emerges in this story.

Ans. The treatment of the revenge theme in this story is fairly unusual. The revenge in this case is neither murdering the opponent nor robbing his valuables or in any way physically abusing him. It is trapping one in a way such that escape becomes difficult. The revenge is executed in a very subtle way. Chunilal manages to take his revenge all the while teaching a lesson to Bepin Choudhury for not having tried enough to help his age old friend.

2. Discuss the significance of the phrase, 'Lapse of Memory', in the title of the story.

Ans. The chapter looks at memory and its power to integrate the past, present and future as a crucial part of human existence. The phrase, 'Lapse of Memory' becomes crucial in two ways.

The 'Lapse of Memory', on one hand, could refer to Chunilal's central plot in tricking Bepin Babu. On the other hand, 'Bepin Babu's Lapse of Memory' was actually a reality as he was unconfident about the events of his life and believes that there was a 'Lapse of Memory' in reality.

3. The story makes certain comments about the changing faces of friends. Discuss.

Ans. The story makes serious comments about the changing faces of friends and their friendships. Chunilal approaches Bepin Choudhury for seeking help to find a job on the strength of their age old friendship.

Bepin Choudhury, however, proves to be unhelpful and inconsiderate, something that greatly disturbs Chunilal.

Bepin Choudhury is aware of Dinesh Mukerji's sarcasm, yet Dinesh Mukerji comes across as a good acquaintance of Bepin Choudhury.

However, by the end of the story, it is amply clear that Dinesh Mukerji functioned more as an ally of Chunilal, than as a friend of Bepin Babu. Chunilal also mirrors Bepin Choudhury's coldness by playing a prank on Bepin Babu that unnerves him completely.

Unlike a friend, Chunilal too becomes inconsiderate of the affect that his prank was having on Bepin Babu's health.

4. Chuni took a lot of effort to convince Bepin that he had been to Ranchi. Justify. **Competency Based**

Ans. Chuni made the entire plan to convince Bepin that not only had he been to Ranchi, he couldn't remember a single detail from that trip. This was a difficult task because Bepin Choudhury was a detail oriented person who had a very good memory. Therefore, Chunilal planned his scheme in such a way that it would produce doubt within Bepin's mind.

He planted Parimal Ghose at the bookstore which Bepin would visit and also told Parimal all the secrets about Bepin. Chuni even let Dinesh in on the plan and asked him to confirm that he and Bepin had gone to Ranchi in October of 1958.

Finally, to make sure that he could eliminate all doubt as well as witness the bad state of Bepin Choudhury, he visited him and further confirmed Bepin's suspicions. Chunilal took so much effort in making sure that Bepin would fall for his trap because he wanted to get revenge for the way Bepin had behaved when Chunilal was in need of help.

ASSESSMENT EXERCISE

Multiple Choice Questions

1. What does the word 'acquaintance' mean?

(a) Distant (b) Familiar
(c) Opponent (d) Stranger

2. Bepin Babu did not like spending time in ....

(a) idle chat (b) home
(c) Kalicharan's shop (d) office

3. Read the statements given below and choose the correct answer.

Statement 1 Bepin Babu had an excellent memory.

Statement 2 Dinesh was ruthless in his sarcasm.

(a) Statement 1 is true but Statement 2 is false.
(b) Statement 1 is false but Statement 2 is true.
(c) Both the Statements are true.
(d) Both the Statements are false.

4. Read the statements given below and choose the correct answer.

Statement 1 Bepin Babu visited Ranchi in 1958.

Statement 2 Bepin Babu visited Kanpur in 1958.

(a) Statement 1 is true but Statement 2 is false
(b) Statement 1 is false but Statement 2 is true
(c) Both the Statements are true
(d) Both the Statements are false

5. According to Dr. Chanda, the trip to Ranchi would

(a) worsen his condition
(b) help him recover
(c) soothe him
(d) not affect him at all

Extract Based Question

Read the given extract and answer the following questions.

"Dear Bepin, I had no idea that affluence would bring about the kind of change in you that it has done. Was it so difficult for you to help out an old friend down on his luck? I have no money, so my resources are limited. What I have is imagination, a part of which I used in retribution of your unfeeling behavior. Well, you'll be alright again now. A novel I've written is being considered by a publisher. If he likes it enough, it'll see me through the next few months.

Yours, Chunilal

When Dr. Chanda came, Bepin Babu said, "I'm fine. It all came back as soon as I got off the train at Ranchi." "A unique case," said Dr. Chanda. "I shall certainly write about it in a medical journal." "The reason why I sent for you," said Bepin Babu, "is that I have a pain in the hip from a fall I had in Ranchi. If you could prescribe a painkiller..."

(i) What did the letter reveal about the motivations of Chunilal?

(a) He had made this plan because Bepin had insulted him.
(b) He had made this plan because Bepin had asked for money.
(c) He had made this plan because Bepin had refused to help him.
(d) He had made this plan because he was writing a novel.

(ii) What reason did Chunilal attribute to the unfeeling behaviour of Bepin Babu?

(a) His memory (b) His money
(c) His freedom (d) His job

(iii) What did Bepin tell Dr. Chanda?

(iv) What does the word 'affluence' mean?

(v) What did Dr. Chanda describe Bepin's lapse of memory as?

Very Short Answer Type Questions

1. What was the name of Bepin Babu's driver?

2. In the year 1958, how many times had Dinesh Mukerji been out of Calcutta?

3. What was the suggestion of Dr. Chanda to cure Bepin of his condition?

4. How did Bepin try to figure out whether he was right about Parimal?

5. Why did Bepin Babu need a painkiller?

Short Answer Type Questions

1. Write a short note on the sarcasm of Dinesh Mukerjee.

2. Evaluate the acting talent of Parimal Ghose.

3. What does Chuni make Bepin realise through his letter?

4. Describe the theme of friendship as it emerges in the story.

5. What was the intention behind Chunilal's plan?

Long Answer Type Questions

1. Was Chunilal's plan justified? Explain through instances from the story.

2. Discuss the title of the story in the context of the events of the chapter.

3. On the basis of the chapter, write a character sketch of Bepin Babu.

4. On the basis of the chapter, write a character sketch of Chunilal.

The Summit Within

by Major H.P.S. Ahluwalia

CHAPTER 5

The following chapter is written by Major H.P.S. Ahluwalia. He was a member of the first successful Indian expedition to Mount Everest in 1965. He remembers the challenging journey to the highest point in the world and explains how being an Everester has changed his life for the better.

The First Successful Indian Expedition

When Major Ahluwalia stood at the summit of Everest, the strongest emotion he felt was humility. Although his body was thankful that the challenging climb was over, he wasn't completely happy. He felt a little sad. This is so because he had done the ultimate and biggest thing in climbing and now every future achievement would be below it.

Major Ahluwalia says that the joy and gratitude one feels upon climbing the Everest stays forever. The experience changes one completely because the man who has been to the mountains undergoes a change. Looking back on his life after Everest, Major Alhuwalia insists that the summit of the mind is as frightening and difficult.

Why do People Climb Mountains?

The Major remembers that while he was getting down from summit, he asked himself why he had climbed the Summit. He questioned why the act of reaching the summit had been on his mind now that he had already climbed the Everest. He knows that as time passes, the event would become a past event. He asks himself whether his memories would fade away. His thoughts lead him to think about why people climb mountains. He thinks that it is not an easy question to answer. The simplest response would be that people climb the mountain simply because it is there.

The Three Physical Qualities

Major Ahluwalia reasons that mankind finds pleasure in overcoming obstacles and mountains present great difficulty. A climb to a summit requires a demonstration of three physical qualities – endurance, persistence, will power. Major Ahluwalia has a personal answer to the question. He had been attracted to mountains since childhood and believes that they are nature at its best. The beauty and majesty of mountains poses a great challenge and he believes that they are a means of communication with God.

The Greatest Challenge

Now, Major Ahluwalia thinks why people choose Mount Everest. He finds that people choose Everest as it is the highest and mightiest of all mountains. Many previous attempts to climb it had failed. Climbing Everest is a struggle with rock and ice and requires all of one's energy. It is not something that one can abandon halfway even if one has to risk one's life because the passage back is just as dangerous as the passage forward. However, when the summit is climbed, one feels the joy of doing something like going into a battle and gaining victory.

Climbing Everest is a Spiritual Experience

Major Ahluwalia talks about how he experienced a change within himself. He states that looking at the peak from a distance, he gets transported to another world. The beauty, aloofness, and ruggedness (the property of being big and strong) of the mountain peaks attracted him and presented a challenge that was difficult to resist.

He, then, goes back to his question of why he climbed Everest. He explains that he hasn't been able to give an answer because there is no final answer to the question. According to him, climbing Everest is not merely physical. A person who has been to the peak of Everest becomes aware of his smallness against the large universe. There is a sense of fulfillment and a satisfaction of having risen above one's surroundings. Humankind's eternal love for adventure makes the climb an emotional as well as a spiritual experience.

Companions on the Climb

Major Ahluwalia asks the reader to consider the climb when the climber has almost reached the top. The climber is sharing a rope with another climber. They move together through the ice, going one after the other. He talks about how famous climbers have left records of how they had needed and received help due to which they could keep going. When breathing gets difficult and a climber feels like giving up and going back down, there is something that doesn't let him give up. This is the companionship of the other climber. The climbers draw strength and inspiration from each other and make sure they keep going forward feet by feet. This is the way climbers reach the summit without even being aware of it.

The View from the Highest Point in the World

From the top of Everest, one can see other silvery peaks appear through the clouds. When the sun shines, it looks like a jeweled necklace around the neck of Everest. Looking down from the top is an experience that makes a person nobler and enriches their life. It inspires people to submit to their God and show their respect. Thus, all the climbers leave a religious symbol on the top of Everest. Major Ahluwalia left a picture of Guru Nanak, Rawat left a picture of Goddess Durga, Phu Dorji left a relic of Buddha, and Edmund Hillary buried a cross.

The Summit Within

Just like the summit of Everest, there is a summit inside the mind of every human. People must climb this summit to gain better knowledge of themselves. This summit is fearful and unscalable. No other person can climb this mountain for you. You yourself have to do it. The process and the effects of climbing both these summits outside and inside are the same. It will change you and teach you about the world and yourself.

Major Ahluwalia considers that his experience as an Everester has given him inspiration and strength to fight the problems of life with determination. He considers that the summits within one's mind are perhaps, even higher than Everest.

Word Meaning

Word	Meaning
Expedition	a journey or voyage made for a specific purpose
Surged	arose suddenly and intensely
Panorama	view of a wide area
Humility	the quality of being humble
Jubilant	very happy because of success
Tinge	trace/shade
Overwhelmed	become filled with uncontrollable emotion
Formidable	arousing fear
Remote	located for away, far away in time
Endurance	power of bearing pain
Persistance	determination
Exhilarating	very exciting
Exhaustion	tiredness/ fatigue
Brutal	punishing harsh
Communion	a communication between people who share a close relationship
Defied	frustrated/resisted
Ounce	tiny bit
Glimpsing	a brief view or look
Mystical	spiritual
Aloof	distant in manner
Ruggedness	having a rough surface

Word	Meaning
Fulfillment	a feeling of satisfaction at having achieved your desires
Eternal	something timeless
Belays	fixes a rope
Strain	test the limits of
Ascent	an upward slope, climb
Grim	rigid or harsh
Sheer	real
Snap out	to get out
Jewelled	treasured or esteemed
Ennobling	to make noble or dignifying
Enriching	improve in quality
Make your obeisance	show your obedience or submission
Relic	something that has survived passage of time
Cairn	a mound erected as a marker
Reverence	an act of showing respect
Unscalable	unclimbable
Akin	essentially similar or related
Venture	to expose to danger or risk
Worthwhile	important to be worth one's time
Ordeals	painful experiences
Resolutely	with determination or firmness

NCERT FOLDER

NCERT Intext and Exercise Questions

COMPREHENSION CHECK[1] (NCERT PAGE 76)

Q.1 Standing on Everest, the writer was

(i) overjoyed (ii) very sad

(iii) jubilant and sad

Choose the right item.

Ans. (iii) jubilant and sad

Q.2 The emotion that gripped him was one of

(i) victory over hurdles.

(ii) humility and a sense of smallness.

(iii) greatness and self importance.

(iv) joy of discovery.

Choose the right item.

Ans. (ii) humility and a sense of smallness.

Q.3 'The summit of the mind' refers to

(i) great intellectual achievements.

(ii) the process of maturing mentally and spiritually.

(iii) overcoming personal ambition for common welfare.

(iv) living in the world of thought and imagination.

(v) the triumph of mind over worldly pleasures for a noble cause.

(vi) a fuller knowledge of oneself.

Mark the items(s) not relevant.

Ans. The summit of the mind does not refer to (iv) living in the world of thought and imagination.

WORKING WITH THE TEXT (NCERT PAGE 77)

Q.1 Answer the following questions.

(i) What are the three qualities that played a major role in the author's climb?

Ans. The three qualities that played a major role in the author's climb were endurance, persistence and will power.

(ii) Why is adventure, which is risky, also pleasurable?

Ans. The adventure, though risky, gives pleasure because man takes delight in overcoming obstacles and doing what is difficult.

(iii) What was it about Mount Everest that the author found irresistible?

Ans. The author finds it difficult to answer this question in its entirety. One reason quite obviously was because the Everest is the highest and the mightiest and the earlier attempts to reach its top had failed.

Also, the author found in climbing mountains a way to have a communion with God and nothing could be better than the Everest.

(iv) One does not do it (climb a high peak) for fame alone. What does one do it for, really?

Ans. According to the author, one does not just climb the highest peak for fame or because of the undying love that man has for adventure. He does so to lift himself above his immediate surroundings. Climbing the mountains is a life changing experience and it teaches you lessons that last a life time.

(v) "He becomes conscious in a special manner of his own smallness in this large universe." This awareness defines an emotion mentioned in the first paragraph. Which is the emotion?

Ans. Humility is the emotion defined in the first paragraph. According to the author, climbing the mountain peak makes you really humble.

Looking from the mountain peak, one finds his surroundings really small and one's position in that surrounding further smaller. This makes you aware of your nothingness.

(vi) What were the 'symbols of reverence' left by members of the team on Everest?

Ans. Every climber left a symbol of reverence or what they associated with God. These 'symbols of reverence' were a picture, an idol, a relic or an emblem of the God they worshipped.

Therefore, Ahluwalia left a picture of Guru Nanak, whereas Rawat left a picture of Goddess Durga. Phu Dorji left a relic of Buddha and Edmund Hillary buried a cross.

(vii) What, according to the writer, did his experience as an Everester teach him?

Ans. The author learnt various lessons as an Everester. The first lesson he learnt was of endurance, persistence and will power. To be able to reach the top and not leave the venture half way, one needs all three.

The second lesson learnt was of team spirit and helping your fellow climbers. Each climber's life was deeply entangled with the actions of the other climbers. You could not risk the life of others due to your errors and also team work could help others emerge out of their difficulties too. The third lesson was of humility and gratitude. You thank God for every breath that you breathe.

Q.2 Write a sentence against each of the following statements. Your sentence should explain the statement. You can pick out sentences from the text and rewrite them. The first one has been done for you.

(i) The experience changes you completely. (i) <u>One who has been to the mountains is never the same again.</u>

(ii) Man takes delight in overcoming obstacles.

....

(iii) Mountains are nature at its best.

....

(iv) The going was difficult but the after-effects were satisfying.

....

(v) The physical conquest of a mountain is really a spiritual experience ....

Ans. (ii) It is the eternal love for adventure in man.

(iii) The beauty of nature is found best in the mountains.

(iv) When the summit is climbed, there is the exhilaration, the joy of having done something, the sense of a battle fought and won.

(v) Mountains are a means of communion with God.

WORKING WITH LANGUAGE

(NCERT PAGE 78-79)

Q.1 Look at the italicised phrases and their meanings given in brackets.

Mountains are *nature at its best.*	(nature's best form and appearance)
Your life is *at risk.*	(in danger; you run the risk of losing your life).
He was *at his best worst* in the last meeting.	(it was his best/worst performance).

Fill in the blanks in the following dialogues choosing suitable phrases from those given in the box.

at hand at once at all at a low ebb at first sight

(i) Teacher. You were away from school without permission. Go to the principal .... and submit your explanation.

Pupil: Yes, Madam. But would you help me write it first?

(ii) Arun: Are you unwell?

Ila: No, not .... Why do you ask?

Arun: If you were unwell, I would send you to my uncle. He is a doctor.

(iii) Mary: Almost every Indian film has an episode of love ....

David: Is that what makes them so popular in foreign countries?

(iv) Asif: You look depressed. Why are your spirits .... today? (Use such in the phrase)

Ashok: I have to write ten sentences using words that I never heard before.

(v) Shieba: Your big moment is close .... Jyoti: How should I welcome it?

Shieba: Get up and receive the trophy.

Ans. (i) at once (ii) at all
(iii) at first sight (iv) at a low ebb
(v) at hand

Q.2 Write the noun form of the following words adding -ance or -ence to each.

(i) Endure......... . (ii) Persist......... .
(iii) Signify......... . (iv) Confide......... .
(v) Maintain......... . (vi) Abhor......... .

Ans. (i) Endurance (ii) Persistence
(iii) Significance (iv) Confidence
(v) Maintenance (vi) Abhorrence

Q.3 (i) Match words under A with their meanings under B.

A	B
Remote	difficult to overcome
Means	most prominent
Dominant	be overcome/overpowered
Formidable	method(s)
Overwhelmed	far away from

Ans.

A	B
Remote	far away from
Means	method(s)
Dominant	most prominent
Formidable	difficult to overcome
Overwhelmed	be overcome/overpowered

(ii) Fill in the blanks in the sentences given below with appropriate words from under A.

(a) There were .... obstacles on the way, but we reached our destination safely.

(b) We have no ...... of finding out what happened there.

(c) Why he lives in a house .... from any town or village is more than I can tell.

(d) .... by gratitude, we bowed to the speaker for his valuable advice.

(e) The old castle stands in a .... position above the sleepy town.

Ans. (a) formidable (b) means
(c) remote (d) Overwhelmed
(e) dominant

SPEAKING AND WRITING (NCERT PAGE 79)

Q.1 Write a composition describing a visit to the hills, or any place which you found beautiful and inspiring.

Before writing, work in small groups. Discuss the points given below and decide if you want to use some of these points in your composition.

- Consider this sentence
  Mountains are a means of communion with God.
- Think of the act of worship or prayer. You believe yourself to be in the presence of the divine power. In a way, you are in communion with that power.
- Imagine the climber on top of the summit - the height attained; limitless sky above; the climber's last ounce of energy spent; feelings of gratitude, humility and peace.
- The majesty of mountains does bring you close to nature and the spirit and joy that lives there, if you have the ability to feel it.

Some composition may be read aloud to the entire class afterwards.

Ans. During the last vacation, I went to Mussoorie with my family and friends. The cottage, where we stayed, was very close to the river and the mountains. Everyone was enjoying the place, when I proposed climbing the mountains.

The purity of the air, the delight of seeing the early morning rays of the Sun are just available at the mountains.

However, everyone was resistant and too lazy for a trek. I, however, could not resist the temptation of going up the mountains and enjoying the purity of air, the sight of the early morning rays of the sun; these feelings are just indescribable.

The peace that one attains in the mountains cannot be matched elsewhere. I automatically began to chant the name of God as I was climbing up.

With every foot forward you come closer to God, for you begin to value life, something that we take for granted in the rush of city life. The beauty around makes you admire the craft of the master creator, God, who has invested so much in creating life on Earth.

The vibrant colours, the fragrance of flour, the sound of birds chirping, all overpower your senses and your own achievements begin to diminish in front of these. You really begin to attain God in his grace.

REVIEW EXERCISE

Including Competency Based Questions

Multiple Choice Questions

1. What is the purpose of the first paragraph of the text? Competency Based

(a) To express the writer's fear of returning home after the journey

(b) To highlight the conflicting reactions of the writer's mind and body

(c) To explain the reasons behind the writer's decision to climb Everest

(d) To describe how the writer's emotional nature affected his Everest experience

Ans. (d) To describe how the writer's emotional nature affected his Everest experience

2. What is the writer worried about at the beginning of the text? Competency Based

(a) Whether his efforts to climb Everest would be recognised

(b) Whether the success in scaling Everest was worth celebrating

(c) Whether future events would be as inspiring as climbing Everest

(d) Whether he would be able to go on other adventurous journeys in the future

Ans. (c) Whether future events would be as inspiring as climbing Everest

3. Which of these words best describes the writer's attitude towards mountains? Competency Based

(a) Nostalgic (b) Inquisitive

(c) Intimidated (d) Passionate

Ans. (a) Nostalgic

4. According to the writer, the appeal of climbing Everest is mainly related to what? Competency Based

(a) Its size

(b) Its location

(c) Its lack of inhabitants

(d) The difficulty of the return journey

Ans. (a) Its size

5. "The man who has been to the mountain-top becomes conscious in a special manner of his own smallness in this large universe".

In which line does the writer express a similar sentiment? Competency Based

(a) Of all the emotions which surged through me as I stood on the summit of Everest, looking over miles of panorama below us, the dominant one I think was humility.

(b) By climbing the summit of Everest you are overwhelmed by a deep sese of joy and thankfulness.

(c) Their beauty and majesty pose a challenge, and like many, I believe that mountains are a means of communion with God.

(d) And then, when the summit is climbed, there is the exhilaration, the joy of having done something, the sense of a battle fought and won.

Ans. (a) Of all the emotions which surged through me as I stood on the summit of Everest, looking over miles of panorama below us, the dominant one I think was humility.

6. According to the writer, what is the summit within? Competency Based

(a) The ability to face challenges fearlessly

(b) The ability to conquer the temptations of the mind

(c) The ability to develop an understanding about oneself

(d) The ability to build physical strength to finish tiring tasks

Ans. (a) The ability to face challenges fearlessly

7. Which of these words best describes the writer's tone?

(a) Factual (b) Reflective (c) Detached (d) Optimistic

Ans. (b) Reflective

8. What does the writer mainly do through the text? Competency Based

(a) Narrated the ways in which an external event changed his personality

(b) Gives a detailed description of the various stages of a difficult journey

(c) Providing instructions to aspiring climbers of Everest
(d) Describes a significant personal experience

Ans. (d) Describes a significant personal experience

9. Imagine you are Major HPS Alhuwalia answering a telephonic interview. Complete the dialogue as Major Alhuwalia. Diksha

(a) I'm eager to tell you. The journey was good and you must all scale the mountain to know the answers.
(b) Perseverance, persistence, and hard work are the key to success. The journey was no doubt tiring but it had its own pleasures.
(c) I really enjoyed talking to you. Hope to meet you again
(d) He would keep mum.

Ans. (b) Perseverance, persistence, and hard work are the key to success. The journey was no doubt tiring but it had its own pleasures.

10. According to the text, the word 'obstruction' has many meanings except one of the given options. Choose the dissimilar option. Diksha

(a) Stumbling block (b) Clogged
(c) Blocked (d) Pathway

Ans. (d) Pathway

11. "However, instead of being jubilant, there was a tinge of sadness". What is the synonym of jubilant? Diksha

(a) Sad (b) Blissful (c) Haughty (d) Healthy

Ans. (b) Blissful

12. Statement 1 Major Ahluwalia was a part of the first successful Indian expedition to Mount Everest.

Statement 2 He was worried that any other adventure would not feel as daring as this expedition.

(a) Statement 1 is true, but Statement 2 is false.
(b) Statement 1 is false, but Statement 2 is true.
(c) Both the Statements are true.
(d) Both the Statements are false.

Ans. (c) Both the Statements are true.

13. The noun form of the verb 'dominate' is Diksha

(a) dominative (b) dominating
(c) conquer (d) dominance

Ans. (d) dominance

14. Imagine you are Major HPS Ahluwalia. You faced many troubles while scaling Mount Everest. One of them was pollution. You need to write a letter to the editor regarding the issue of pollution. The correct format of the letter would be Diksha

(a) Day, date, time
(b) Sender's address, receiver's address
(c) Sender's address and date
(d) Receiver's address, date, and sender's address

Ans. (d) Receiver's address, date, and sender's address

Extract Based Questions

1. Read the extract given below and answer the following questions.

Of all the emotions which surged through me as I stood on the summit of Everest, looking over miles of panorama below us, the dominant one I think was humility. The physical in me seemed to say, 'Thank God, it's all over!" However, instead of being jubilant, there was a tinge of sadness. Was it because I had already done the 'ultimate' in climbing and there would be nothing higher to climb and all roads hereafter would lead down? By climbing the summit of Everest you are overwhelmed by a deep sense of joy and thankfulness. It is a joy which lasts a lifetime. The experience changes you completely. The man who has been to the mountains is never the same again.

(i) What was the dominant emotion felt by the speaker upon reaching the summit and why?

Ans. The speaker felt humility upon reaching the summit of Mount Everest because he could see the entire world below him. This instilled in him a sense of smallness in relation to the huge summit he had conquered.

(ii) Why did the speaker say 'thank god, it's all over'?

Ans. The speaker was thankful that it was over because the climb to the top of Everest was extremely challenging (physically) for a human body.

(iii) Why do you think the experience of climbing Everest completely changes a person?

Ans. Climbing Everest completely changes people because it is the tallest mountain in the world. The experience of defeating such a great challenge, and then, looking at the entire world below you must be overwhelmingly profound.

(iv) What is the meaning of the word 'panorama'?

Ans. The word panorama means an unbroken view of the whole region surrounding an observer.

(v) Which word from the given extract is the antonym of 'pride'?

Ans. The word 'humility' is the antonym of 'pride'.

2. Read the extract given below and answer the following questions.

As I look back at life after climbing Everest I cannot help remarking about the other summit — the summit of the mind — no less formidable and no easier to climb. Even when getting down from the summit, once the physical exhaustion had gone, I began asking myself the question why I had climbed Everest. Why did the act of reaching the summit have such a hold on my imagination? It was already a thing of the past, something done yesterday. With every passing day, it would become more remote. And then what would remain? Would my memories fade slowly away?

(i) According to the writer, which summit is as difficult to climb as the summit of Everest?

Ans. According to the writer, the summit of the mind is as difficult to climb as the summit of Everest.

(ii) What question did the speaker ask himself after getting down from the summit?

Ans. After getting down from the summit, the speaker asked himself why he had climbed Everest and why the achievement of reaching the summit had such a hold on his imagination.

(iii) What did the speaker fear would happen as time passed by?

Ans. The speaker feared that his memories of the summit of Everest would fade away as time passed.

(iv) State True or False. "The summit of the mind is much easier to climb than the summit of Everest."

Ans. False

(v) What does the phrase 'memory fades away' mean?

Ans. The phrase 'memory fades away' means that the finer details of the experience would be lost and soon only a blurred picture would stand in the place where the memory was once vibrant.

3. Read the extract given below and answer the following questions.

All these thoughts led me to question myself as to why people climb mountains. It is not easy to answer the question. The simplest answer would be, as others have said, "Because it is there." It presents great difficulties. Man takes delight in overcoming obstacles. The obstacles in climbing a mountain are physical. A climb to a summit means endurance, persistence and will power. The demonstration of these physical qualities is no doubt exhilarating, as it was for me also.

(i) What question did the speaker ask himself?

(a) Why do people like to swim across the oceans?
(b) Why do people like to climb the mountains?
(c) Why do people like to challenge nature?
(d) Why do people like to surf the waves?

Ans. (b) Why do people like to climb the mountains?

(ii) What does man take delight in?

(a) Overcoming difficult obstacles
(b) Surfing the highest waves
(c) Climbing the highest mountains
(d) Diving the deepest seas

Ans. (a) Overcoming difficult obstacles

(iii) Which qualities are required to climb the summit of a mountain?

(a) Endurance (b) Sincerity
(c) Determination (d) All of these

Ans. (d) All of these

(iv) Which of the following words is a synonym of 'endurance'?

(a) Apathy (b) Cowardice
(c) Tolerance (d) Idleness

Ans. (c) Tolerance

(v) Which of the following words is not a synonym of 'persistence'?

(a) Endurance (b) Stamina
(c) Lethargy (d) Perseverance

Ans. (c) Lethargy

4. Read the extract given below and answer the following questions.

Looking round from the summit you tell yourself that it was worthwhile. Other silvery peaks appear through the clouds. If you are lucky the Sun may be on them. The surrounding peaks look like a jewelled necklace around the neck of your summit. Below, you see vast valleys sloping into the distance. It is an ennobling, enriching experience to just look down from the summit of a mountain. You bow down and make your obeisance to whichever God you worship. I left on Everest a picture of Guru Nanak. Rawat left a picture of Goddess Durga. Phu Dorji left a relic of the Buddha. Edmund Hillary had buried a cross under a cairn (a heap of rocks and stones) in the snow. These are not symbols of conquest but of reverence.

(i) What did the surrounding peaks look like around the summit of Everest?

(a) A necklace of pearls
(b) A necklace of jewels
(c) A necklace of beads
(d) A necklace of diamonds

Ans. (b) A necklace of jewels

(ii) **What is Major Ahluwalia feeling in the given extract?**

(a) A sense of accomplishment
(b) A sense of relief
(c) A sense of pride
(d) A sense of humility

Ans. (a) A sense of accomplishment

(iii) **Why did the Everesters leave relics of their faith on the summit of Everest?**

(a) They were relics of faith
(b) They were relics of religion
(c) They were symbols of respect
(d) They were symbols of conquest

Ans. (c) They were symbols of respect

(iv) **What is the meaning of the word 'obeisance'?**

(a) A symbol of obesity (b) A symbol of love
(c) A symbol of hatred (d) A symbol of respect

Ans. (d) A symbol of respect

(v) **Edmund Hillary had buried a cross under a ....**

(a) rock (b) cavern
(c) cairn (d) cliff

Ans. (c) cairn

Very Short Answer Type Questions

1. **In which year did H.P.S. Ahluwalia undertake the expedition to Everest?**

Ans. HPS Ahluwalia undertook the expedition to Everest in 1965.

2. **Which was the most dominant emotion that he experiences on reaching the top?**

Ans. The most dominant emotion experienced by Major Ahluwalia when he reached the peak of Everest was humility.

3. **According to the writer, why do people usually climb mountains?** **Competency Based**

Ans. According to H.P.S. Ahluwalia, people climb mountains because they wish to face challenges and overcome difficult obstacles.

4. **What personal answer does the author give to the question of why people climb mountains?** **Competency Based**

Ans. The author's personal answer is that he had always been attracted to mountains since childhood, and believed them to be nature at its best.

5. **What does Ahluwalia have to say about the relationship between mountain climbing and life?**

Ans. According to H.P.S. Ahluwalia, there is a very close connection between climbing and the journey of life. His experience as an Everester gave him the inspiration to face life's ordeals with great confidence.

6. **How does the author view himself in the light of his surroundings, as he reaches the summit?**

Ans. As the author reaches the summit, he becomes more and more conscious of his smallness as he sees the universe from the mountain peak.

Short Answer Type Questions

1. **Why does the author become sad on reaching the top of the mountain?**

Ans. On reaching the top of the mountain, the author becomes sad because their ultimate goal had been attained and now, they lack another aim. In addition, the highest peak had been reached and the author realises that from here on the journey would only lead downwards.

2. **Discuss the significance of leaving religious or spiritual symbols on mountain tops.**

Ans. Leaving the pictures or symbols of God on the mountain top is a way of expressing gratitude for having attained that point and being safe and hearty. The author also discusses how reaching the mountain top is symbolic of attaining God. The act of leaving symbols of God, then, makes attaining God on reaching the top both literally and metaphorically true.

3. **Why does the author not abandon the climb halfway?**

Ans. Even in moments of sheer exhaustion, the author refuses to abandon the climb because climbing the mountain is all about team work. Further, companions are always a source of inspiration for each other. They keep pushing the limits till they reach the peak.

4. **Was reaching the top of the Everest the last challenge that the author wished to face?**

Ans. No, reaching the top of the Everest was not the last challenge the author wished to face. Infact after sucessfully completing task of climbing Everest, the author feels a little sad as there would be no other task for him.

5. **The success of the climber is also dependent on their companions. Justify the statement using evidence from the text.** **Competency Based**

Ans. The success of the climber is certainly dependent on their companions. Major Ahluwalia recalls that when a climber loses confidence and will power to keep climbing, a look shared with their companion climber can boost the confidence of the climbers. The presence of another person upon the frigid heights of Everest reassures the human mind.

Long Answer Type Questions

1. The success of the climber is dependent not only on their companion but also their will power. Justify the statement using evidence from the story.

Ans. The success of a climber doesn't depend only on their physical capabilities. It also depends on their companion climber as well as their own will power. Climbing a mountain peak is a task that demands every last drop of energy from a person's body. As such, a climber cannot succeed solely on their physical strength.

The main battle in climbing a mountain that is as challenging as Mount Everest means a battle of will. Only people with extremely strong will power can climb the highest peak in the world. But even their will power many weaken upon the difficult, icy slopes. In such a scenario, a shared glance with your fellow climber can bring a new boost of confidence and encourage the climber to keep going forwards because it assures the climber that they are not alone.

2. Describe the scene that offers delight to the author as he reached the top of the Everest.

Ans. From the summit, the author could see other silvery peaks, which gave him a lot of pleasure. He could also see other peaks through the clouds giving the glimpses of great picturesque beauty. The Sun rays created an illusion of a jewelled necklace around the neck of the summit. A little below the mountains were various sloping valleys that added to the beauty of the place. Also, as one looked down, it appeared as if the ultimate worship to God was being offered.

3. Discuss the importance of the records left by famous climbers.

Ans. The records left by famous climbers primarily discuss and share their experiences and difficulties at having made it to the top. These records equip the future climbers with knowledge to deal with similar difficulties and overcome those obstacles.

These records are also stories of inspiration. They inspire the future climbers to not abandon their climb midway, nor get depressed because of the difficulties.

They, on the other hand, are enthused with optimism on remembering these stories.

4. Why does H.P.S. Ahluwalia compare climbing the mountain to a battle?

Ans. While climbing the mountain, one faces many obstacles and hindrances which consume every bit of the climber's energy. The passage back is as difficult as the passage forward and it exhausts you entirely.

Just like in a battle, it is a matter of life and death; similarly in mountain climbing, the climbers are always putting their life at sake with every single movement that they make. All these facts make climbing the mountain similar to a battle.

ASSESSMENT EXERCISE

Multiple Choice Questions

1. Seeing a mountain peak from a distance Ahluwalia feels that
   (a) It looks very beautiful.
   (b) Its beauty is great.
   (c) It offers a challenge which is difficult to resist.
   (d) It brings fear to the mind.
2. How does the experience of the other summit change one completely?
   (a) It makes the writer more conscious and aware.
   (b) It makes the writer proud.
   (c) It makes the writer jubilant.
   (d) It makes the writer compassionate.
3. The author talks about two summits in the text. What are they?
   (a) Kanchanjunga and the internal summit
   (b) Mount Everest and the internal summit
   (c) Mount Everest and physical well-being
   (d) Mount Everest and K2
4. Read the statements given below and choose the correct answer.

   Statement 1 The first successful Indian expedition to the summit of Mount Everest was in 1965.

   Statement 2 Major Ahluwalia left a picture of Guru Nanak at the summit.

   (a) Statement 1 is true, but Statement 2 is false.
   (b) Statement 1 is false, but Statement 2 is true.
   (c) Both the Statements are true.
   (d) Both the Statements are false.
5. The obstacles in climbing a mountain are ....
   (a) physical (b) psychological
   (c) Both of these (d) None of these

Extract Based Question

Read the extract given below and answer the following questions.

"However, instead of being jubilant, there was a tinge of sadness. Was it because I had already done the ultimate in climbing and there would be nothing higher to climb and all roads hereafter would lead down? By climbing the summit of Everest you are overwhelmed by a deep sense of joy and thankfulness. It is a joy which lasts a lifetime.

The experience changes you completely. The man who has been to the mountains is never the same again."

(i) Why is the person who has been to the mountains never the same again?
   (a) The experience changes him completely
   (b) He gets hurt
   (c) The experience makes him proud
   (d) He goes mad

(ii) Why is the climber filled with gratitude?
   (a) For having reached the summit safely
   (b) For having reached the summit first
   (c) For having become victorious
   (d) For having left everyone behind

(iii) What is the 'ultimate' in these lines?
   (a) Climbing the mountain
   (b) Climbing the highest mountain
   (c) Climbing the other summit
   (d) The journey back

(iv) What does the author mean when he says that " the man who has been to the mountains is never the same again?

(v) Write four synonyms of the word 'jubilant'.

Very Short Answer Type Questions

1. "Major Ahluwalia's jubilance was not unmixed." Justify the statement.
2. "A climb on the mountains is a demonstration of some great human qualities." Explain the given statement.
3. What is the author's personal answer to the question of why people climb mountains?
4. What do the pictures of God left on Everest symbolise?
5. What has the experience as an Everester taught the narrator?

Short Answer Type Questions

1. How does the author describe the scene including the other peaks from the top of the summit?
2. How do companion climbers support each other mentally throughout the climb?
3. What problems do the climbers encounter during their journey to the top of the mountain?
4. Justify the appropriateness of the title of the chapter.
5. What life lessons can be learned from this chapter?

Long Answer Type Questions

1. Explain in detail the relevance of the summit within.
2. The success of the climbers is also dependent on their companions. Justify the statement using evidence from the text.
3. Write a character sketch of Major Ahluwalia based on his views about the summit of Everest.
4. How does his experience as an Everester prepare him for graver and more serious challenges in life?

This is Jody's Fawn

by Marjorie Kinnan Rawlings

CHAPTER 6

The following chapter written by Marjorie Kinnan Rawlings is an emotional story about a child's feeling regarding a baby animal. The story is divided in three parts and revolves around the moral conflict of a child whose father had killed a mother deer to save his own life after being bit by a rattlesnake. The child worries about the fawn left all alone.

Part – I

Jody Talks to His Father

Jody kept thinking about the fawn (baby deer) and even saw it in his dreams. He went to his father's bedside and looked at him. Penny, Jody's father was resting but his eyes were open and indicated that he was ill. He asked his father about his health. Penny replied that he was feeling fine. He praised how Jody had kept calm in the serious situation. Then, Jody asked him about the doe and the fawn. Penny replied that he could never forget them since the poor doe saved him.

Jody gets Permission to Raise the Fawn

Jody told his father that the fawn might be scared and hungry in the forest. Then, he asked his father if he could go and look for the fawn so that he could raise it. To convince Penny, he added that it wouldn't take much to raise it since the fawn would soon start eating leaves and acorns. Further, he stated that they killed the doe and separated the fawn from its mother. Penny was surprised. He told Jody that he was smarter than other boys. He added that he couldn't say no as it would seem ungrateful to leave the fawn to starve. Penny agreed with Jody who told his father that he would come back with the Mill-wheel if he found him.

Jody Talks to Ma Baxter

Jody's mother was pouring coffee for everyone when he told her that Penny had allowed him to bring the fawn back. He told his mother about how they had used the heart and liver of the doe to draw the poison of the rattlesnake out and save his father, Penny. Ma Baxter was hesitant but Doc Wilson told her that nothing in the world comes free and that both Jody and Penny were right in their decision. To convince Ma Baxter, the Mill-wheel stated that he would take Jody to the forest to help find the fawn. Ma Baxter agrueed on the condition that Jody would give his own milk to the fawn since they had nothing else to feed it.

Jody and Mill-wheel Ride to the Forest

Jody readily agreed to Ma Baxter's condition and set out with Mill-wheel on his horse. When Jody questioned if they would be able to find the fawn, Mill-wheel asked him how Jody could know that the fawn was male. Jody replied that the spots on the doe-fawn were in a line, whereas his Pa had told him that on a female-fawn, the spots are in different directions.

Part – II

Jody and Mill-Wheel in the Forest

Jody gave directions to the Mill-wheel to reach the place where Penny was bitten by the snake. As they were about to reach the place, Jody found himself unwilling to take Mill-wheel to the fawn. If the fawn was dead then he didn't want the Mill-wheel to see his disappointment. If the fawn was alive then, he didn't want to share their lovely and secret meeting. So, he asked the Mill-wheel to leave him saying that they were not far from the spot and he would be able to search on foot, while the horse would have trouble with the bushes.

Mill-Wheel Quizzes Jody about Directions

The Mill-wheel was afraid to leave Jody alone in the forest because he could get lost or get bitten by a snake too. Jody assured that he would be careful. The Mill-wheel asked him to point the directions North and East. Jody did so correctly and informed that the tall pine tree helped him find the directions. When the Mill-wheel was assured, he left Jody in the forest.

Jody Searches for the Fawn

As soon as the Mill-wheel left, Jody changed his direction and moved to the right. He looked around in the still and silent forest and wondered if he was lost. Then, he saw a buzzard (a scavenger bird) flying away. Following it, Jody reached a clearing under oak trees where many buzzards were sitting around the dead body of the doe in a circle. Jody threw his stick (a branch of a tree) at them and began to study the footprints in the sand. The footprints looked like that of big cat. However, there were no big cats (tigers and leopards) around because they ate fresh prey. Then, he went to the place where he had seen the fawn the last time. He found that the fawn was not there. He dropped on hands and knees to spot small hoof prints in the sand. However, the night's rain had washed all prints of the fawn away.

Part – III

Jody Finds the Fawn

As Jody was looking for the fawn, a movement surprised him. The fawn was staring at Jody and examining him while making no move to run away. Jody stayed still and placed a careful hand on his neck as the fawn smelled him. Jody carefully picked up the fawn and gently stroked him. The fawn's skin was clean, smooth and soft, and it smelled of grass. Jody slowly got up and lifted the fawn. To save the fawn from seeing his dead mother, he went around the clearing. He struggled to carry the fawn through the bushes while trying to shield their faces from the thorns.

Jody Takes the Fawn Home

Jody was surprised to notice that the fawn had accepted him. Without wasting any time, he reached the road that would take him home. There, he stopped to rest and put the fawn down. When the fawn bleated at him, Jody was enchanted and told it that he would carry him after catching his breath. Then, Jody remembered that his father had told him that a fawn that has been carried will follow him. So, he started to walk away slowly. Initially, the fawn stared at Jody but after Jody returned and patted it, the fawn took a few shaky steps and cried. Jody was filled with joy to know that the fawn would follow him. He was so happy to own the fawn that he wanted to play with it but he did not want to scare it.

The Long Road Home

Jody picked up the fawn again and carried it without effort. Whenever his arms began to ache, he would put the fawn down and it would follow him. Then, he would pick it up again. Jody was so happy with the fawn that he could have walked and watched him follow through the entire day and into the night. When they reached the house, the fawn followed him but couldn't get up the steps. So, Jody picked it up and went to his father to show him the fawn. Penny observed that Jody's eyes were as bright as the fawn's.

Jody Feeds the Fawn

After showing the fawn to his father, Jody went into the kitchen with the fawn following him. He took the morning's milk, separated the cream and poured the milk into a gourd (a bowl). The fawn was unable to drink the milk from the gourd. So, Jody dipped his fingers in the milk and allowed the fawn to suck the milk off them. Then, he lowered his fingers into the milk as the fawn keeps sucking the milk greedily. Jody felt great joy at the feel of the fawn's tongue against his fingers. Soon, the fawn had finished the milk.

Word Meaning

Word	Meaning
Drift back to	to move back to someone or something slowly
Dilated	having been widened; expanded
A close shave	a narrow escape
Kept your head	to remain calm and sensible in an awkward situation
Thieving	stealing quietly
Hemmed in	to trap or enclose someone
Acorns	nut with base shaped like cup
Doe	female deer
Fawn	a young deer
Sidled back	to avoid something or someone by moving back
Anxious	nervous
Every which way	in different directions
Gasped	quick intake of breath
Endure	suffer something unpleasant over long period
Scrub	shrubs
Makes a bearing	acts as a compass and helps finding directions
Hooves	hard part of horse's foot
Crackling	sound something makes when it cracks
Twigs	very small thin branch of tree or bush
Buzzard	a large bird that eats other birds or dead animals
Carcass	body of dead animal
Scrawny	very thin
Bough	a big branch on a tree
Hoof prints	foot prints of an animal
Startled	suddenly frightened or surprised by something
Quivering	shake with short quick movements
Delirious	extremely excited and happy

Word	Meaning
Convulsion	extreme change that causes problems or harm
Parted	pushed aside
A China deer	a clay deer that is easily broken
Hoist	pull up higher
Limply	walk with difficulty because of injured leg
Bleat	complain in weak voice or annoying way
Prickling	feel something sharp and uncomfortable on skin
Vines	plant on which grapes grow
Bobbed	moved up and down
Stride	long confident step
Thumped	attack or punish someone by hitting them
Dangling	hang or swing somewhere
Piteous	deserving pity
Fondle	touch lightly
Romp	to run and bounce around playfully
Latch	bar for keeping door, gate etc shut
Gourd	type of container for liquids
Precariously	likely to change or become dangerous suddenly
Frantic	marked by uncontrolled emotion
Balked	a sudden and obstinate stop
Skimmed	to pass lightly
Sleek	smooth and shiny
Light-headed	unable to think clearly
Snorted	sudden loud noise made through nose
Ecstasy	a feeling of great happiness and pleasure
Gurgling	make a low sound that water makes

NCERT FOLDER

NCERT Intext and Exercise Questions

COMPREHENSION CHECK❶ (NCERT PAGE 86)

Q.1 What had happened to Jody's father?

Ans. Jody's father was bitten by a rattlesnake.

Q.2 How did the doe save Penny's life?

Ans. The doe was killed and its heart and liver were used to draw the poison out of Jody's father, Penny.

Q.3 Why does Jody want to bring the fawn home?

Ans. Jody wished to bring the fawn home and look after it as he held himself and his family responsible for its pitiable situation. Its mother was killed to save the life of his father and neither the fawn nor the doe was to be blamed for this.

Q.4 How does Jody know that the fawn is a male?

Ans. Jody knew that the fawn was a male because its spots were in a line.

CHECK❷ (NCERT PAGE 87)

Q.1 Jody didn't want Mill-wheel with him for two reasons. What were they?

Ans. Jody didn't want Mill-wheel with him for the following two reasons

(i) If he was unable to find the fawn then, he didn't want Mill-wheel to see his disappointment.

(ii) If he was able to find the fawn then, he didn't want to share his happiness at that secret meeting with anyone.

Q.2 Why was Mill-wheel afraid to leave Jody alone?

Ans. The Mill-wheel was afraid that Jody might get bitten by a snake or lose his direction and get lost.

CHECK❸ (NCERT PAGE 90)

Q.1 How did Jody bring the fawn back home?

Ans. Jody had to carry the fawn in his arms to bring him back home.

Q.2 Jody was filled with emotion after he found the fawn. Can you find at least three words or phrases which show how he felt?

Ans. Jody was filled with happiness and relief after he found the fawn.

The following lines from the lesson indicates this

(i) Jody put his arms around its body.

(ii) He stroked its sides as gently as though the fawn were a China deer and he might break it.

(iii) He rose slowly and lifted the fawn from the ground.

Q.3 How did the deer drink milk from the gourd?

Ans. Jody had to dip his fingers in the milk and keep them immersed in the gourd in order to feed the fawn. Gradually, the fawn began to drink milk from the gourd.

Q.4 Why didn't the fawn follow Jody up the steps as he had thought it would?

Ans. The fawn did not follow Jody up the steps because it was too young and did not know how to climb the staps.

WORKING WITH THE TEXT (NCERT PAGE 90-92)

Q.1 Why did Penny Baxter allow Jody to go find the fawn and raise it?

Ans. Penny Baxter allowed Jody to find the fawn and raise it because he was obliged to the doe that was killed to save his own life. Also, he could not deny Jody's wish, for he loved him dearly.

Q.2 What did Doc Wilson mean when he said, "Nothing in the world ever comes quite free"?

Ans. Doc Wilson's statement that "Nothing in the world comes quite free" meant that they had to pay a price for everything. Raising the dead doe's fawn could be their price for the doe's sacrifice.

Q.3 How did Jody look after the fawn, after he accepted the responsibility for doing this?

Ans. Jody sacrificed his portion of milk in order to feed the fawn. He also took care of the needs of the fawn such as teaching him how to sip milk from the gourd, climbing stairs and so on.

Q.4 How does Jody's mother react when she hears that he is going to bring the fawn home? Why does she react in this way?

Ans. Jody's mother became anxious when she heard that Jody was bringing the fawn home. She also became worried because the family could not afford sufficient food for the fawn. There was no extra milk or food to be given to the fawn.

WORKING WITH LANGUAGE (NCERT PAGE 90-92)

Q.1 **Look at these pairs of sentences.**

Penny said to Jody, "Will you be back before dinner?"

Penny asked Jody if he would be back before dinner.

"How are you feeling, Pa?" asked Jody.

Jody asked his father how he was feeling.

Here are some questions in direct speech. Put them into reported speech.

(i) Penny said, "Do you really want it son?"

(ii) Mill-wheel said, "Will he ride back with me?"

(iii) He said to Mill-wheel, "Do you think the fawn is still there?"

(iv) He asked Mill-wheel, "Will you help me find him?"

(v) He said, "Was it up here that Pa got bitten by the snake?"

Ans. (i) Penny asked his son if he really wanted it.

(ii) Mill-wheel asked if he'll ride back with him.

(iii) He asked Mill-wheel if he thought the fawn was still there.

(iv) He asked Mill-wheel if he would help to find him.

(v) He asked if it was up there that his Pa had got bitten by the snake.

Q.2 **Look at these two sentences.**

He tumbled backward.

It turned its head.

The first sentence has an intransitive verb, a verb without an object.

The second sentence has a transitive verb. It has a direct object. We can ask: "What did it turn?" You can answer: "Its head. It turned its head."

Say whether the verb in each sentence below transitive or intransitive. Ask yourself a 'what' question about the verb, as in the example above. (For some verbs, the object is a person, so ask the question 'who' instead of 'what').

(i) Jody then went to the kitchen.

(ii) The fawn wobbled after him.

(iii) You found him.

(iv) He picked it up.

(v) He dipped his fingers in the milk.

(vi) It bleated frantically and butted him.

(vii) The fawn sucked his fingers.

(viii) He lowered his fingers slowly into the milk.

(ix) It stamped its small hoofs impatiently.

(x) He held his fingers below the level of milk.

(xi) The fawn followed him.

(xii) He walked all day.

(xiii) He stroked its sides.

(xiv) The fawn lifted its nose.

(xv) Its legs hung limply.

Ans. (i) Transitive (ii) Intransitive

(iii) Transitive (iv) Transitive

(v) Transitive (vi) Intransitive, transitive

(vii) Transitive (viii) Transitive

(ix) Transitive (x) Transitive

(xi) Transitive (xii) Intransitive

(xiii) Transitive (xiv) Transitive

(xv) Intransitive

Q.3 **Here are some words from the lesson. Working in groups, arrange them in the order in which they would appear in the dictionary. Write down some idioms and phrasal verbs connected to these words. Use the dictionary for more idioms and phrasal verbs.**

close	draw	make
wonder	scrawny	parted
clearing	sweet	light
pick		

Ans. Order in dictionary: Clearing, close, draw, light, make, parted, pick, scrawny, sweet, wonder

Clearing	–	Clearing out
Close	–	Close up, Close quarters, Close in, Close down
Draw	–	Draw back, Draw the line
Light	–	Light up, In the light of, Lighten
Make	–	Make merry, Make up, Make much of, Make after
Parted	–	Parted with
Pick	–	Pick on, Pick up, Pick out, Pick and Choose
Scrawny	–	Scrawny neck
Sweet	–	Sweet tooth, Short and Sweet
Wonder	–	Works wonders

SPEAKING (NCERT PAGE 92)

Q.1 **Do you think it is right to kill an animal to save a human life? Give reasons for your answer.**

Ans. It is morally incorrect to kill animals. However, in order to save a life in the absence of any other alternative, it sometimes becomes imperative to kill animals. Animals have been killed for ages in order to satisfy the superfluous needs of human beings.

For instance, animals are killed for consumption. Their skin and hair are used for making fur, leather purses and so on. Such unwanted and pointless needs, however, could be controlled and killing of animals could be avoided.

Q.2 Imagine you wake up one morning and find a tiny animal on your doorstep. You want to keep it as a pet but your parents are not too happy about it. How would you persuade them to let you keep it? Discuss it in groups and present your arguments to the class.

Ans. Last Sunday, I woke up early to go to the park to play cricket with my friends. When I stepped out of the house, I saw a small puppy hiding in the gap between the staircase and the main gate. I immediately brought it with me and wanted to keep it as a pet.

My mother, however, strongly reacted against this idea. She did not want me to touch such filthy animals or play with them.

She also put forward her discomfort in maintaining pets in the household and how it would affect her routine. My father had his concerns too.

However, I explained to them how animals are also worthy of love and in return for that love they would give their unconditional devotion. A dog in the house would also take care of our safety. Finally, my parents were convinced.

WRITING (NCERT PAGE 92)

Q.1 Imagine you have a new pet that keeps you busy. Write a paragraph describing your pet, the things it does and the way it makes you feel. Here are some words and phrases that you could use.

Frisky, smart, disobedient, loyal, happy, enthusiastic, companion, sharing, friend, rolls in mud, dirties the bed, naughty, lively, playful, eats up food, hides the newspaper, drinks up milk, runs away when called, floats on the water as if dead.

Ans. I just received a new pet as my birthday gift. It is a dog. I was overwhelmed to receive such a gift. It is wonderful to have pets around. They keep us happy and are a constant source of joy. Its friskiness is a guaranteed remedy for my lethargy. When I am tired or sad, it would revive lost energy in me with its playfulness. It would run away with my things and make me run after it. It would force me to be happy and smile.

Every morning, I take it for a morning walk. It's such a delight to see it roll in the mud, running away when called and being as naughty as it could. It is a perfect start to my day.

Q.2 Human life is dependent on nature (that's why we call her Mother Nature).

We take everything from nature to live our lives. Do we give back anything to nature?

(i) Write down some examples of the natural resources that we use.

(ii) Write a paragraph expressing your point of view regarding our relationship with nature.

Ans. (i) It is true that human life is entirely dependent upon nature.

We can't survive without it. From the air we breathe to the food we eat and the water we drink, we constantly draw on innumerable natural resources.

Yet, we take all these resources for granted and neither do we thank Mother Nature for them, nor do we give anything to Mother Nature in return.

(ii) Mankind is dependent on nature for everything but this relationship is one-sided. We only take from Mother Nature without thinking about her needs. We ruthlessly and greedily destroy nature to satisfy our needs. Hence, it is essential that we become aware of our dependence on nature and take necessary steps to keep it clean and protected.

Q.3 In *This is Jody's Fawn*, Jody's father uses a 'home remedy' for a snake bite. What should a person now do if he or she is bitten by a snake? Are all snakes poisonous? With the help of your teacher and others, find out answers to such questions. Then write a short paragraph on - What to do if a snake chooses to bite you.

Ans. No, not every snake is poisonous, but most are. Due care should be taken in case of a snake bite.

If a snake bites me, I would first wash the bite with soap and water. I would then cover the bite with a clean, dry dressing. Immediately after this, I would head to see a doctor who could provide me with necessary first aid.

REVIEW EXERCISE
Including Competency Based Questions

Multiple Choice Questions

1. What does the first paragraph suggest? **Competency Based**
   (a) Jody has been thinking about the fawn for a while.
   (b) Jody was afraid to discuss the fawn with his father.
   (c) Jody felt relieved that his father was out of danger.
   (d) Jody wondered whether he had done the right thing.

Ans. (a) Jody has been thinking about the fawn for a while.

2. Which word best describes Pa's attitude towards the doe? **Competency Based**
   (a) Sympathetic (b) Remorseful
   (c) Indifferent (d) Thankful

Ans. (d) Thankful

3. Why did Jody want to bring the fawn home? **Competency Based**
   (a) He wanted to own a pet.
   (b) He felt responsible for its loss.
   (c) He felt that the fawn was its friend.
   (d) He wanted to show that he could be responsible.

Ans. (b) He felt responsible for its loss.

4. Which word best describes Ma's reaction to the idea of bringing the fawn home?
   (a) Angry (b) Hesitant
   (c) Desperate (d) Suspicious

Ans. (b) Hesitant

5. Why did Jody want to search for the fawn on its own? **Competency Based**
   (a) He feared that Mill-wheel would be bitten by a snake.
   (b) He wanted to prove to Mill-wheel that he was fearless.
   (c) He feared that Mill-wheel might try to befriend the fawn.
   (d) He wanted to keep his emotions for the fawn from Mill-wheel.

Ans. (d) He wanted to keep his emotions for the fawn from Mill-wheel.

6. Why were the big cats not feeding on the doe? **Competency Based**
   (a) The doe was already dead.
   (b) The buzzards found the doe first.
   (c) Jody's presence scared the big cats away.
   (d) They had eaten the doe and left the remains for the buzzards.

Ans. (a) The doe was already dead.

7. 'The touch made him delirious'. What does the given line suggest? **Competency Based**
   (a) Jody was relieved that the fawn was alive.
   (b) Jody was scared that the fawn would run away.
   (c) Jody was delighted to make contact with the fawn.
   (d) Jody was thinking about how to take the fawn home safely.

Ans. (c) Jody was delighted to make contact with the fawn.

8. Which of these words best describes Jody?
   (a) Patient (b) Modest
   (c) Optimistic (d) Compassionate

Ans. (d) Compassionate

9. Who is the speaker of the line "Nothing in the world comes quite free"?
   (a) Jody (b) Jody's father
   (c) Mill-wheel (d) Doctor Wilson

Ans. (d) Doctor Wilson

10. Who was supposed to drink the milk that Jody gave to the fawn?
    (a) Jody's Father (b) Jody's Mother
    (c) Mill-Wheel (d) Jody

Ans. (d) Jody

11. Read the given statements and choose the correct answer.
    Statement 1 Jody wanted the fawn to drink milk.
    Statement 2 Mill-wheel didn't want Jody to find the fawn.
    (a) Statement 1 is true, but Statement 2 is false.
    (b) Statement 1 is false, but Statement 2 is true.
    (c) Both the Statements are true.
    (d) Both the Statements are false.

Ans. (a) Statement 1 is true, but Statement 2 is false.

Extract Based Questions

1. Read the extract given below and answer the following questions.

"What fawn? The fawn belonging to the doe we killed. We used the doe's liver to draw out the poison and save Pa." She gasped. 'Well for pity's sake- "Pa said it would be ungrateful to leave it to starve." Doc Wilson said, "That's right, Ma'am. Nothing in the world comes quite free. The boy's right and his daddy's right."

(i) Who is the main speaker?

Ans. Jody is the main speaker.

(ii) How many opinions do we get to read in the above passage?

Ans. We get to read four opinions from the reading of the above passage.

(iii) What was the argument of the main speaker?

Ans. The argument of the main speaker was to bring home the fawn of the dead doe and raise it.

(iv) What does Doc Wilson mean by "Nothing in the world comes quite free"?

Ans. Through the given phrase Doc Wilson seems to suggest the price that must be paid for the sacrifice of the doe. He seems to suggest a sense of responsibility that they owe towards the life of the sacrificed doe and its fawn.

(v) Why would it be ungrateful to leave the fawn unattended?

Ans. It would be ungrateful to leave the fawn unattended because its mother was killed on purpose to save the life of Penny Baxter. As an expression of gratitude, the fawn must be looked after.

2. Read the extract given below and answer the following questions.

"He was afraid that it might kick and bleat at sight and smell of its mother. He skirted the clearing and pushed its way into the thicket. It was difficult to fight through with his burden. The fawn's legs caught in the bushes and he could not lift his own with freedom. He tried to shield its face from prickling vines. Its head bobbed with its stride. His heart thumped with the marvel of its acceptance of him."

(i) Who is the 'it' in the first line of the passage?

Ans. 'It' refers to the fawn in the first line of the passage.

(ii) Pick two sensory terms from the passage.

Ans. Sight and smell are two sensory terms present in the passage.

(iii) What all did Jody do to make the journey home easier for the fawn?

Ans. Jody carried the fawn in his arms, despite its weight and long legs. He avoided the direct route because the carcass of the doe lay in the middle and Jody didn't wish the fawn to see it. He also tried to shield the fawn's face from getting scratched by prickly vines.

(iv) State the meaning of the expression, "marvel of its acceptance of him."

Ans. Jody was overwhelmed by the fact that the fawn had surrendered itself to Jody. It had accepted Jody and the decisions Jody took to protect it.

This is what Jody meant by the expression, "the marvel of its acceptance of him."

(v) Make sentences with

(a) Shield **(b) Freedom**

Ans. (a) **Shield** The warrior carried a gleaming shield to the battlefield.

(b) **Freedom** The freedom fighters sacrificed their lives for the sake of their country.

3. Read the extract given below and answer the following questions.

Movement directly in front of him startled him so that he tumbled backward. The fawn lifted its face to his. It turned its head with a wide, wondering motion and shook him through with the stare of its liquid eyes. It was quivering. It made no effort to rise or run. Jody could not trust himself to move. He whispered, "It's me." The fawn lifted its nose, scenting him. He reached out one hand and laid it on the soft neck. The touch made him delirious. He moved forward on all fours until he was close beside it. He put his arms around its body.

(i) What happened when there was movement in front of Jody?

(a) He got startled (b) He stumbled backwards
(c) Both of these (d) None of these

Ans. (c) Both of these.

(ii) How does the author describe the eyes of the doe?

(a) Piercing eyes (b) Brown eyes
(c) Doe eyes (d) Liquid eyes

Ans. (d) Liquid eyes

(iii) Why was Jody hesitant to move?

(a) To defend himself from the wild animals in the area
(b) To not draw the attention of the buzzards in the area to himself
(c) To make sure that the doe would not get startled and run
(d) To move safely upon his injured leg

Ans. (c) To make sure that the doe would not get startled and run

(iv) What of the following words is a synonym of 'trembling'?

(a) Firm (b) Steady
(c) Quivering (d) Controlled

Ans. (c) Quivering

(v) **Which word from the given extract means 'in a state of wild excitement'?**

(a) Quivering (b) Delirious

(c) Startled (d) Scenting

Ans. (b) Delirious

4. Read the extract given below and answer the following questions.

He reached the trail and walked as fast as he could until he came to the intersection with the road home. He stopped to rest and set the fawn down on its dangling legs. It wavered on them. It looked at him and bleated. He said, enchanted, "I'll carry you after I get my breath." He remembered his father saying that a fawn would follow if it had first been carried. He started away slowly. The fawn stared after him. He came back to it and stroked it and walked away again. It took a few wobbling steps toward him and cried piteously. It was willing to follow him. It belonged to him. It was his own. He was light-headed with his joy. He wanted to fondle it, to run and romp with it, to call for it to come to him. He dared not alarm it.

(i) **How does Jody describe the legs of the fawn?**

(a) Lanky (b) Dangling

(c) Elegant (d) Scrawny

Ans. (b) Dangling

(ii) **Why was Jody enchanted?**

(a) Because the fawn was magical

(b) Because the fawn snuggled up to Jody

(c) Because the fawn tried to talk to Jody

(d) Because the fawn began leaping and dancing

Ans. (c) Because the fawn tried to talk to Jody

(iii) **What did Jody conclude from his experiment?**

(a) That the fawn was intelligent

(b) That the fawn was injured

(c) That the fawn wanted to follow him

(d) That the fawn wanted to find his mother

Ans. (c) That the fawn wanted to follow him

(iv) **What is the meaning of 'piteous'?**

(a) Deserving jealousy (b) Deserving anger

(c) Deserving pity (d) Deserving love

Ans. (c) Deserving pity

(v) **Which word from the extract suggests that the fawn was weak?**

(a) Wobbling (b) Piteous

(c) Bleat (d) Fondle

Ans. (a) Wobbling

Very Short Answer Type Questions

1. Why was Penny proud of his son?

Ans. Penny was proud of his son for keeping calm in a difficult situation.

2. Penny Baxter was worried about how they would feed the fawn. What does Jody suggest?

Ans. Jody suggests that since he was now a grown up boy, his share of milk could be given to the fawn.

Also, the fawn would soon start eating leaves and acorns. So, nothing much would be required to raise him.

3. Were Doc Wilson and Mill-wheel supportive of Jody's decision?

Ans. Yes, both Doc Wilson and Mill-wheel were supportive of Jody's decision to bring the fawn back home.

Mill-wheel even offered help in giving Jody a ride to the location.

4. How does Jody manage to find his direction in the forest?

Ans. Jody manages to find his direction by looking at the tall pine trees. They acted like a compass and helped him in finding direction.

5. What were the buzzards doing in the scrub?

Ans. Buzzards are scavenging birds. They were eating the flesh of the dead doe's carcass.

6. In which way does Jody manage to get rid of the buzzards?

Ans. As the buzzards came towards Jody, Jody threw a bough at them and they flew into adjacent trees.

7. Why was Jody afraid of carrying the fawn through the clearing?

Ans. Jody was afraid that the fawn might see or smell the carcass of the doe and begin to bleat and get out of control.

8. What was the observation of Penny when Jody brought the fawn into Penny's room?

Ans. Penny felt that Jody's eyes were as bright as that of the fawn. Jody was brimming with happiness at having brought the fawn home.

Short Answer Type Questions

1. What excuse does Jody give to Mill-wheel for not accompanying him?

Ans. Jody didn't want Mill-wheel to accompany him so he gave him the excuse that the horse would have trouble going through the bushes. So, Jody insisted that he would go find the fawn alone.

2. **Describe the meeting between Jody and the fawn.**

Ans. The meeting of Jody and the fawn was lovely. While the fawn must have been feeling an immense feeling of safety, Jody was enchanted by the tiny fawn. Soon, the fawn began trusting Jody and even followed him home on his weak legs.

3. **Why was it difficult for Jody to carry the fawn back home?**

Ans. It was difficult for Jody to carry back the fawn because the fawn was a little heavy. Further, the legs of the fawn were fairly long and they hung limply, making it difficult for Jody to carry it. Jody was also afraid that the fawn might get out of control at the sight of its mother's carcass and then it would get even more difficult to carry the burden.

4. **Why did Penny feel trapped on hearing Jody's request?**

Ans. Penny felt trapped on hearing Jody's request because he was left with no option other than saying yes. The doe had saved Penny's life and leaving its fawn unattended would have been morally incorrect. Therefore, Penny was forced to comply with Jody's demand of bringing the fawn home.

5. **Jody knew his way around the forest. Justify the statement using evidence from the story.**

Competency Based

Ans. It is true that Jody knew his way around the forest. This is proved by the fact that he could guide the Mill-wheel to the exact spot that his father had been bitten. He even knew the answers to all the questions Mill-wheel asked to make sure that he wouldn't get lost. Later, he was able to take the fawn home by himself without getting lost.

Long Answer Type Questions

1. **Why did the fawn have difficulty in drinking the milk?**

Ans. The fawn was perhaps used to drinking the milk by suckling its mother. It did not know how to drink milk any other way. Therefore, when Jody dipped his fingers in the milk and offered them to the fawn, the fawn felt as if it was drinking milk in the same old fashion and began to suck Jody's finger.

When Jody withdrew his fingers, it again became difficult for the fawn to take milk. Therefore, Jody had to keep his fingers immersed in the gourd to make it easier for the fawn to drink milk.

2. **Discuss an important lesson imparted by the story.**

Ans. The story 'This is Jody's Fawn' puts a lot of emphasis on questions of morality behind killing of animals. Therefore, both the prime characters as well as the minor characters in the story are seen dealing with questions concerning the fawn from a moral perspective.

Jody's thoughts constantly revolve around the abandoned fawn of the doe that they had to kill in order to save Penny. Penny, too, is forced to agree to Jody's demand because it would be immoral to leave the fawn starving, knowing that its mother saved his life. Ma Baxter, though treating the question practically, also gives in when Doc Wilson reminds her of the 'moral price' they must pay, since the doe saved her husband's life.

Both Doc Wilson and Mill-wheel were supportive of Jody's decision of raising the fawn. The story does not justify the unnecessary killing of animals nor does it seem to suggest that the killing of animals is not a serious issue. Thus, looking at animals with love, care and sensitivity is highlighted by the story.

3. **Why was it so important for Jody to bring the fawn home?**

Ans. Jody was stirred by feelings of love and guilt and this was his reason in bringing home the fawn. The doe was killed so that its heart and liver could be used to neutralise the effect of poison in Penny's body.

Jody held himself responsible for the fate of the doe and its fawn; they had to suffer for no fault of theirs. This forced Jody to think about the fawn. Also, Jody had met the fawn earlier. When Jody goes to look for the fawn in the scrub, the fawn is able to recognise Jody from his smell, which is indicative of some prior meeting or relation between the two.

4. **Describe the relationship between Jody and the fawn.**

Ans. Jody and the fawn shared a unique relationship of love and compassion. Jody feels a certain degree of compassion for the fawn, whose mother was killed in order to save Penny's life. Jody realises that neither the doe nor the fawn was to blame.

He, therefore, wanted to take the responsibility of raising the fawn. The fawn, on the other hand, was bonded to Jody through a strong chain of love. It felt safe and protected in Jody's company. When it meets Jody after its mother's death, it became delirious with joy at finding that familiar touch and smell.

ASSESSMENT EXERCISE

Multiple Choice Questions

1. Jody feared that his parents might not allow him to bring the fawn home because ....
   (a) they had a small house
   (b) of the expenses of feeding an animal
   (c) the fawn was a dangerous animal
   (d) it was illegal to keep a fawn
2. Jody's mother held the coffee-pot in the air. This shows that
   (a) she was stunned at what Jody said
   (b) she had heard a sound
   (c) she saw doctor Wilson which upset her
   (d) she didn't want to give coffee to Jody
3. What is the meaning of 'buzzard'?
   (a) A big animal that hunts and kills
   (b) A bird that flies high up in the sky
   (c) A bird that makes a lot of noise
   (d) A large bird like the vulture
4. Read the given statements and choose the correct answer.
   Statement 1 Jody's father was bitten by a poisonous snake.
   Statement 2 The fawn was very excited and energetic when Jody found her.
   (a) Statement 1 is true, but Statement 2 is false.
   (b) Statement 1 is false, but Statement 2 is true.
   (c) Both the Statements are true.
   (d) Both the Statements are false.
5. Why was Mill-wheel afraid to leave Jody alone in the woods?
   (a) He was afraid that Jody would get lost
   (b) He was afraid that Jody would get bitten by a snake
   (c) Both (a) and (b)
   (d) None of the above

Extract Based Question

Read the extract given below and answer the following questions.

"Pa, I'm a big boy now and don't need to drink milk.
Why don't I go and see if I could find the fawn?
"And bring it here?"
"And raise it."
Penny lay quiet, staring at the ceiling.
"Boy, you've got me hemmed in."

(i) Who is the speaker of these lines?
   (a) Jody (b) Penny
   (c) Doc Wilson (d) Mill-wheel

(ii) Was the speaker guilty?
   (a) For not drinking milk
   (b) For having killed the doe
   (c) For leaving the fawn to starve
   (d) For being rude to his father

(iii) Why was the doe killed?
   (a) To save Penny's life
   (b) To be consumed for meat
   (c) To be separated from its fawn
   (d) To save Jody's life

(iv) What ways did Jody suggest to make the raising of the fawn affordable for the family?

(v) What do you think was the first reaction of Penny on listening to Jody's demand?

Very Short Answer Type Questions

1. What did Penny Baxter mean by, "You've got me hemmed in"?
2. Who all were supportive of Jody's decision?
3. What were buzzards doing in the scrub?
4. Who took Jody to the forest to rescue the fawn?
5. Why did the fawn suck milk greedily?

Short Answer Type Questions

1. Why was Ma Baxter against the idea of bringing the fawn home?
2. Jody asks the Mill- wheel to go back. Why?
3. What did Jody do that made Penny feel proud?
4. How did Penny explain to his son that he was feeling fine?
5. Why was Jody afraid of carrying the fawn through the clearing?

Long Answer Type Questions

1. Imagine yourself to be the fawn. Write a paragraph on how you felt on meeting Jody after your mother's death.
2. "You are smarter than boys of your age." How far is this true?
3. Jody could not leave the fawn all alone in the forest. What does this say about his nature?
4. Is the killing of innocent animals justified? How did the characters of the story react to the killing of the doe? Explain with evidence from the chapter.

A Visit to Cambridge

by Firdaus Kanga

This chapter is an excerpt from Firdaus Kanga's book 'Heaven on Wheels'. It recounts the extraordinary meeting of Firdaus Kanga with Stephen Hawking, the renowned astrophysicist. It's important to note that both of these men are differently-abled and wheelchair users. Stephen Hawking is confined to his wheelchair because of a form of paralysis that allows him to speak only by punching buttons on a machine. Firdaus Kanga is an Indian writer and journalist from Mumbai who was born with weak bones that broke easily as a child.

This chapter discusses the views of these two great men on topics like life in a wheelchair, and society's opinions.

Kanga in Cambridge

Writer and journalist Firdaus Kanga was travelling through Cambridge on his travels in England. For him, when he talked of Cambridge, he talked of England. However, it all changed when he met Stephen Hawking. When the guide mentioned Stephen Hawking, the disabled but worthy successor to Isaac Newton at the university, Kanga was surprised. He had forgotten that the brilliant astrophysicist, who had written the bestselling book *A Brief History of Time,* lived at Cambridge.

After the tour, Kanga immediately called Stephen Hawking's house from a phone booth to request a meeting with him. He told the assistant that he had come in a wheelchair from India and would love to meet him even for ten minutes. The assistant gave him half an hour to talk to Professor Hawkins and told him to come at 3:30 pm.

Kanga's Experience of Growing up Disabled

Upon getting the meeting fixed, Kanga felt weak. He remarked that disabled people get fed up with others asking them to be brave. He stated that seeing other disabled people achieve something big was the only thing that made him feel stronger. This is so because it allowed other disabled people to see the possibilities of what they could achieve.

Firdaus Kanga Meets Stephen Hawking

When Firdaus Kanga met Stephen Hawking, he asked Hawking if he has been told to be brave. Hawking replied that he hadn't been brave and that he did not have a choice. Kanga wanted to say that living creatively even with the paralysis must have been a choice, but he stopped himself. This was so because he felt guilty every time he forced Hawking to respond.

Hawking would communicate by tapping on a switch in his hand. When he struggled to find the right words, he would close his eyes in frustration. Kanga felt his irritation because Hawking's mind was filled with thoughts. However, he could only express his thoughts in emotionless and mechanical phrases and sentences.

On Happiness

Kanga remarked that although society believes that disabled people are always sad, he knew that wasn't true. Then, he asked if Hawking was often laughing on the inside. Hawking took three minutes to reply and answered that he found it amusing when people treated him as if he was inferior to them. Kanga further asked if he found people like him who disturbed his work annoying. To this, Hawking replied 'yes' and smiled. Kanga remarked that he found Stephen Hawking to be the most beautiful man in the world.

The Appearance of Stephen Hawking

Kanga found the first glimpse of Hawking very shocking because he looked exactly like he did in the photographs found in magazines and newspapers. His head was twisted sideways, the torso inside his pale blue shirt was shrunk, and his legs were unused. But his eyes could speak and they were saying something huge and urgent that Kanga couldn't understand. Through the almost useless body of Stephen Hawking, he could see the inner glow/soul of the man. He realised that the physical body was not important. He found that even though he didn't believe in eternal souls, this inner glow/soul was the essence of what humans were.

Conversations on Disability

Kanga asked Hawkins what he thought was the best thing about being disabled. Hawking replied that there was nothing good about being disabled. Kanga told that he had found how much kindness there was in the world through being disabled. Although Hawking said yes, there was no emotion behind the mechanical voice. Therefore, Kanga could not know how enthusiastically Hawking had agreed with him.

Shifting Viewpoints

Kanga remarked that while sitting in front of Stephen Hawking he became very aware of the things that his disabled body could do. Every little movement such as shifting in his chair or turning his wrist to watch the time made him very happy. It almost didn't matter to Kanga that he would never walk or stand.

Hawking had been a great source of inspiration to Kanga and others. So, he asked Hawking whether the thought helped him. When Hawking replied no, Kanga realised that it had been a stupid thing to ask because when you are trapped within a body that is like being locked in a room, it doesn't matter if people on the outside are admiring you for being alive.

Hawking's Advice to Disabled People

When Kanga asked if Hawking had any advice to give to other disabled people, Hawking said that disabled people should focus on what they are good at. He also believed that things like disabled Olympics were a waste of time. Kanga replied that he had spent years trying to play a Spanish guitar that was much larger than him and fondly remembered how he had unstringed it one night.

When the half hour was finished, Kanga began to leave after thanking Stephen Hawking. However, Hawking asked him to stay for tea and to see the garden with him.

Kanga and Hawking in the Garden

The garden was as big as a park, but they covered every inch of it in their wheelchairs. The sunlight made it impossible for Stephen Hawking to look at the letters on his machine, so they didn't talk much. One hour later when Kanga was ready to leave, he didn't know what to do. He didn't kiss Stephen or cry but touched his shoulder and wheeled out. As he was leaving, he felt as if Hawking was waving him goodbye. Stephen Hawking was the embodiment of the bravest self of Kanga, and looking at him Kanga realised that for now his journey was over.

Word Meaning

Word	Meaning
Paralysis	inability to act or function properly
Brittle	easily breakable
Metaphor	figurative meaning
Astrophysicist	a scholar of astrophysics - branch of physics dealing with stars and planets
Propelled	to drive or cause to move, forward or onward: to propel a boat by rowing
Fed up	very tired of something
Draw a cheque	to take some courage
Disembodied	lacking a body or freed from the body
Disintegrating	to lose strength and gradually fail
Anguish	pain and sadness
Buoyant	intensely active and vibrant
Corpse	dead body
Chronically	serious and lasting for a long time
Patronise	taking sponsorship of
Slump	be suddenly reduced to much lower level

Word	Meaning
Torso	upper part of body
Incandescence	inner glow or light
Accessory	objects added to make something better
Eternal	something that lives forever.
Synthesiser	an electrical equipment that produces sounds
Inflection	rise and fall of the voice in speaking
Enthusiastically	with excitement
Exhilaration	make someone feel extremely happy or excited
Cliche	phrase or idea used so often that it loses its meaning
Claustrophobic	fear of a very small and suffocating enclosed space
Gleefully	very happily
Unstringed	to remove the string
Rumbling	a noise (of thunder)
Embodiment	representation of something in a visible form

NCERT FOLDER

NCERT Intext and Exercise Questions

COMPREHENSION CHECK (NCERT PAGE 97)

Which is the right sentence?

Q.1 "Cambridge was my metaphor for England." To the writer,

(i) Cambridge was a reputed university in England.

(ii) England was famous for Cambridge.

(iii) Cambridge was the real England.

Ans. (iii) Cambridge was the real England.

Q.2 The writer phoned Stephen Hawking's house

(i) from the nearest phone booth.

(ii) from outside a phone booth.

(iii) from inside a phone booth.

Ans. (ii) from outside a phone booth.

Q.3 Every time he spoke to the scientist, the writer felt guilty because

(i) he wasn't sure what he wanted to ask.

(ii) he forced the scientist to use his voice synthesiser.

(iii) he was face to face with a legend

Ans. (ii) he forced the scientist to use his voice synthesiser.

Q.4 "I felt a huge relief... in the *'possibility of my body'*. 'In the given context, the highlighted words refer to

(i) shifting in the wheelchair, turning the wrist.

(ii) standing up, walking.

(iii) speaking, writing.

Ans. (i) shifting in the wheelchair, turning the wrist.

WORKING WITH THE TEXT (NCERT PAGE 97-98)

Q.1 (i) Did the prospect of meeting Stephen Hawking make the writer nervous? If so, why?

Ans. Yes, the prospect of meeting Stephen Hawking made the writer nervous. This was because Stephen Hawking was a brilliant man and a big source of inspiration for Firdaus Kanga, not only for his reputation as a genius but also because of the fact that just like Kanga, Hawking was also a differently-abled man.

(ii) Did he at the same time feel very excited? If so, why?

Ans. The author got extremely excited when Hawking's assistant gave him an appointment to meet Hawking for half an hour. This was so because Kanga idolised Stephen Hawking for being differently-abled and yet achieving something huge.

Q.2 Guess the first question put to the scientist by the writer.

Ans. The first question that the writer asked Stephen Hawking was how he had managed to be so brave.

Q.3 Stephen Hawking said, "I've had no choice." Does the writer think there was a choice? What was it?

Ans. Yes, the writer believed that Stephen Hawking did have a choice. According to him, the brilliant astrophysicist had chosen to live creatively despite his complete paralysis.

Q.4 "I could feel his anguish." What could be the anguish?

Ans. Hawking felt anguished, frustrated and tired due to his inability to express his thoughts. This was so because he was unable to find the letters on his machine through which he used to express himself.

Q.5 What endeared the scientist to the writer so that he said he was looking at one of the most beautiful men in the world?

Ans. The one-way smile of Stephen Hawking and the fact that he was not getting emotional or silly endeared the scientist to the writer. Kanga felt that he was looking at one of the most beautiful men in the world.

Q.6 Read aloud the description of the beautiful man. Which is the most beautiful sentence in the description?

Ans. The following sentence is the most beautiful one in the author's description of Stephen Hawking:- "Before you, like a lantern whose walls are worn so thin you glimpse only the light inside, is the incandescence of a man."

Q.7 (i) If 'the lantern' is the man, what would its walls' be?

(ii) What is housed within the thin walls?

(iii) What general conclusion does the writer draw from this comparison?

Ans. (i) The walls would be the body of the scientist which had been reduced to nothingness.

(ii) The inner glow of the man which refers to the eternal soul is housed within the thin walls or the thin body.

(iii) The author draws the conclusion that ultimately it is not the body but the soul that is significant.

Q.8 What is the scientist's message for the disabled?

Ans. The scientist's message for the disabled people is that they should do what they are good at and not what people want to extract out of them to view disabilities in a glorious light.

Q.9 Why does the writer refer to the guitar incident? Which idea does it support?

Ans. The writer refers to the time when he gleefully unstringed his Spanish guitar to illustrate that differently-abled people shouldn't waste their energies on doing things they aren't good at. It supports Stephen Hawking's idea that things like the disabled Olympics are a waste of time.

Q.10 The writer expresses his great gratitude to Stephen Hawking. What is the gratitude for?

Ans. The writer expresses his gratitude to Stephen Hawking for living bravely and creatively and giving differently abled people like the author the courage and inspiration to live better lives.

Q.11 Complete the following sentences taking their appropriate parts from both the boxes below.

(i) There was his assistant on the line...

(ii) You get fed up with people asking you to be brave, ...

(iii) There he was, ...

(iv) You look at his eyes which can speak, ...

(v) It doesn't do much good to know ....

A

- tapping at a little switch in his hand
- and I told him
- that there are people
- as if you have a courage account
- and they are saying something huge and urgent

B

- trying to find the words on his computer.
- I had come in a wheelchair from India.
- on which you are too lazy to draw a cheque.
- smiling with admiration to see you breathing still.
- it is hard to tell what.

Ans. (i) There was his assistant on the line and I told him I had come in a wheelchair from India.

(ii) You get fed up with people asking you to be brave, as if you have a courage account on which you are too lazy to draw a cheque.

(iii) There he was, tapping at a little switch in his hand trying to find the words on his computer.

(iv) You look at his eyes which can speak, and they are saying something huge and urgent it is hard to tell what.

(v) It doesn't do much good to know that there are people smiling with admiration to see you breathing still.

WORKING WITH LANGUAGE

(NCERT PAGE 99-100)

Q.1 Fill in the blanks in the sentences below using the appropriate forms of the words given in the following box.

guide	succeed	chair	travel
pale	draw	true	

(i) I met a .... from an antique land.

(ii) I need special .... in mathematics. I can't count the number of times I have failed in the subject.

(iii) The guide called Stephen Hawking a worthy .... to Issac Newton.

(iv) His other problems .... into insignificance beside this unforeseen mishap.

(v) The meeting was .... by the youngest member of the board.

(vi) Some people say 'yours .... when they informally refer to themselves.

(vii) I wish it had been a .... match. We would have been spared the noise of celebrations, at least.

Ans. (i) traveller (ii) guidance
(iii) successor (iv) paled
(v) chaired (vi) truly
(vii) drawn

Q.2 Look at the following words.

walk	stick

Can you create a meaningful phrase using both these words?

(It is simple. Add ing to the verb and use it before the noun. Put an article at the beginning.)

.........a walking stick

Now, make six such phrases using the words given in the box.

read/session	smile/face	revolve/chair
walk/tour	dance/doll	win/chance

Ans. (i) A reading session (ii) A smiling face
(iii) A revolving chair (iv) A walking tour
(v) A dancing doll (vi) A winning chance

Q.3 Use all or both in the blanks. Tell your partner why you choose one or the other.

(i) He has two brothers. .... are lawyers.

(ii) More than ten persons called. .... of them wanted to see you.

(iii) They.......... cheered the team.

(iv) ....her parents are teachers.

(v) How much have you got? Give me .... of it.

Ans. (i) both (ii) all (iii) all
(iv) both (v) all

Q.4 Complete each sentence using the right form of the adjective given in the brackets.

(i) My friend has one of the ....cars on the road. (fast)

(ii) This is the ..... story I have ever read. (interesting)

(iii) What you are doing now is .... than what you did yesterday. (easy)

(iv) Ramesh and his wife are both......... (short)

(v) He arrived .... as usual. Even the chief guest came .... than he did (late, early)

Ans. (i) fastest (fast)
(ii) most interesting (interesting)
(iii) easier (easy)
(iv) short (short)
(v) late, earlier (late, early)

SPEAKING AND WRITING

(NCERT PAGE 100-101)

Q.1 Say the following words with correct stress. Pronounce the parts given in colour loudly and clearly.

camel	balloon	decent	opinion
fearless	enormous	careful	fulfill
father	together	govern	degree
bottle	before		

- In a word having more than one syllable, the stressed syllable is the one that is more prominent than the other syllable(s)
- A word has as many syllables as it has vowels.
  – man (one syllable)
  – manner (two syllables)
- The mark (') indicates that the first syllable in 'manner' is more prominent than the other.

Ans. Do it yourself.

Q.2 Underline stressed syllables in the following words. Consult the dictionary or ask the teacher if necessary.

artist	mistake	accident	moment
compare	satisfy	relation	table
illegal	agree	backward	mountain

Ans.

artist	mis**take**	**accident**	**mo**ment
compare	sa**ti**sfy	rela**tion**	**ta**ble
ille**gal**	ag**ree**	**back**ward	**moun**tain

Q.3 Write a notice for the School Notice Board.

Step 1

Discuss why notices are put up on the notice board.

What kinds of 'notices' have you lately seen on the board?

How is a notice different from a letter or a descriptive paragraph?

Step 2

Suppose you have lost or found something on the campus.

What have you lost or found?

You want to write a notice about it. If you have lost something, you want it restored to you in case someone has found it. If you have found something, you want to return it to its owner.

Step 3

Write a few lines describing the object you have lost or found. Mention the purpose of the notice in clear terms. Also write your name, class, section and date.

Step 4

Let one member of each group read aloud the notice to the entire class.

Compare your notice with the other notices and make changes, if necessary, with the help of the teacher.

or

- **Imagine that you are a journalist.**
- **You have been asked to interview the President of the village Panchayat.**
- **Write eight to ten questions you wish to ask.**
- **The questions should elicit comments as well as plans regarding water and electricity, cleanliness and school education in the village.**

Ans. Notices are put on the notice board to give important and relevant information to all the students or whosoever is the reader. A notice answers all important questions related to the central topic for which it has been put up. For instance, date, time, venue etc of an upcoming event; or the colour, size, contents of something lost or found. Lately, I have come across a number of notices on the notice board. For instance, lost and found notices, notice giving details about activities or events or the school cultural and academic calendar.

ABC Public School

NOTICE

5th September, 20XX

Lost! Lost! Lost!

I have lost a wallet, a purple coloured rectangular wallet. The wallet contained my school Identity card and a few more personal belongings. I lost it during my PT session in the playground. Anyone who finds it is requested to kindly return it.

XYZ,

Student of VIII A

Q.2 Imagine that you are a journalist.

You have been asked to interview the President of the Village Panchayat.

Write eight to ten questions you wish to ask.

The questions should elicit comments as well as plans regarding water and electricity, cleanliness and school education in the village.

Ans. Interview with the Village Panchayat

Self, Journalist: J

Village Panchayat: VP

J : Hello Sir, I have come to take your interview. Can you please tell me the population or head count of your village?

VP : Yes. There are approximately 500 people living in our village.

J : Do you provide the villagers with basic facilities like hospitals, schools etc?

VP : Yes. Our village has one hospital and a school.

J : Sir, don't you think considering the number of people that live in your village, one hospital and one school is insufficient?

VP : We are planning to get at least one more of both the hospital and the school constructed.

J : Good to hear. Is there regular electricity in your village.

VP : No, not yet.

J : What are your plans regarding getting the village access to electricity?

VP : We are in constant negotiation with the district officials to introduce electricity and replace kerosene lit lamps.

J : I am glad that you are doing a lot for this village.

REVIEW EXERCISE

Including Competency Based Questions

Multiple Choice Questions

1. What was the writer's first reaction when he realised that Hawking lived in Cambridge? Competency Based

(a) Shock (b) Surprise
(c) Excitement (d) Nervousness

Ans. (a) Shock

2. What was the request made by Firdaus Kanga to the assistant of Stephen Hawking? Diksha

(a) He would be obliged if he got to meet Stephen Hawking even for ten minutes.
(b) He would be obliged if he got to meet Stephen Hawking even for thirty minutes.
(c) He would be obliged if he got a copy of books written by Stephen Hawking.
(d) He would be obliged if he got a chance to write his biography.

Ans. (a) He would be obliged if he got to meet Stephen Hawking even for ten minutes.

3. Which of the following sentences does not have the correct use of the word 'successor'? Diksha

(a) A person or thing that succeeds another person or thing is called a successor.
(b) The antonym of the word successor is predecessor.
(c) Ramesh was the successor of the company after his father Mohanlal.
(d) Tanya was the successor in the 500m race.

Ans. (d) Tanya was the successor in the 500m race.

4. According to the writer, what gives courage to a disabled person? Competency Based

(a) The success of people with disabilities
(b) Spending time with inspirational people
(c) Ignoring people who ask them to be brave
(d) Doing things that others suggest they could not

Ans. (a) The success of people with disabilities

5. Kanga felt guilty everytime he spoke to Hawking because

(a) Hawking had to work hard to respond
(b) he was wasting his own time
(c) he was wasting Hawking's time
(d) Hawking had asked him to keep quiet

Ans. (a) Hawking had to work hard to respond

6. When did Hawking feel amused?

(a) When people spoke to him
(b) When people disturbed him
(c) When people sympathised with him
(d) When people patronised him

Ans. (d) When people patronised him

7. "And sitting opposite him I could feel his anguish, the mind buoyant with thoughts that came out in frozen phrases and sentences stiff as corpses."

In the line above, the writer is trying to highlight how Competency Based

(a) he communicated with Hawking
(b) Hawking's intelligence intimidated him
(c) Hawking struggled to use the machine
(d) the disability limited Hawking's expression

Ans. (d) the disability limited Hawking's expression

8. What was actually shocking about the first glimpse of Hawking? Competency Based

(a) The lack of movement
(b) The expression of his eyes
(c) The resemblance to photographs
(d) The uniqueness of his appearance

Ans. (c) The resemblance to photographs

9. What did meeting Hawking help the writer realise? Competency Based

(a) The irrelevance of the accessories that aid disabled people
(b) The ways in which he judged himself for his disability
(c) The similarities between Hawking and himself
(d) The importance of spirit over body

Ans. (d) The importance of spirit over body

10. Based on the interaction, what best describes Hawking?

(a) Optimistic
(b) Generous
(c) Considerate
(d) Straightforward

Ans. (d) Straightforward

11. Read the given statements and choose the correct answer.

Statement 1 Stephen Hawking believed that disabled people should focus on what they are good at.

Statement 2 Stephen Hawking believed that things like the disabled Olympics were a waste of time.

(a) Statement 1 is true but Statement 2 is false.
(b) Statement 1 is false but Statement 2 is true.
(c) Both the Statements are true.
(d) Both the Statements are false .

Ans. (c) Both the Statements are true.

12. How did the author describe the fingers of Stephen Hawking?

(a) Long and pale (b) Stubby
(c) Crooked (d) Elegant

Ans. (a) Long and pale

Extract Based Questions

1. Read the extract given below and answer the following questions.

Cambridge was my metaphor for England and it was strange that when I left it had become altogether something else, because I had met Stephen Hawking there. It was on a walking tour through Cambridge that the guide mentioned Stephen Hawking, "poor man, who is quite disabled now, though he is a worthy successor to Issac Newton, whose Chair he has at the university". And I started, because I had quite forgotten that this most brilliant and completely paralysed astrophysicist, the author of A Brief History of Time, one of the biggest best-sellers ever, lived here.

(i) What was the author doing in Cambridge?

Ans. The author was taking a walking tour through Cambridge.

(ii) Who was the predecessor of Stephen Hawking?

Ans. Isaac Newton was the predecessor of Stephen Hawking.

(iii) What is the name of the best-selling book written by Stephen Hawking?

Ans. The name of the bestselling book written by Stephen Hawking is 'A Brief History of Time'.

(iv) How does the idea of Stephen Hawking affect him?

Ans. The idea of Stephen Hawking shocks Kanga as he had completely forgotten that the great scientist lived in Cambridge.

(v) Write a synonym and antonym for the word 'worthy'?

Ans. The synonym for the word 'worthy' is 'deserving'. Its antonym is 'unworthy'.

2. Read the extract given below and answer the following questions.

"I haven't been brave," said his disembodied computer-voice, the next afternoon. "I've had no choice." Surely, I wanted to say, living creatively with the reality of his disintegrating body was a choice? But I kept quiet, because I felt guilty every time I spoke to him, forcing him to respond. There he was, tapping at the little switch in his hand, trying to find the words on his computer with the only bit of movement left to him, his long, pale fingers. Every so often, his eyes would shut in frustrated exhaustion. And sitting opposite him I could feel his anguish, the mind buoyant with thoughts that came out in frozen phrases and sentences stiff as corpses.

(i) Why was the voice of Stephen Hawking 'disembodied'?

Ans. The voice of Stephen Hawking was 'disembodied' because he couldn't speak and used a machine to speak for him.

(ii) Why didn't the author agree with Stephen Hawking's belief that he had no choice?

Ans. The author didn't agree with Stephen Hawking's belief that he had no choice because he could see that Hawking had chosen to live creatively.

(iii) How did Stephen Hawking show his frustration at being unable to find the appropriate words?

Ans. Stephen Hawking would show his frustration at being unable to find the appropriate words by closing his eyes.

(iv) What is the meaning of the word 'disembodied'?

Ans. The word 'disembodied' means 'separated from or existing without the body'.

(v) Write an antonym for the word 'buoyant'.

Ans. The antonym of the word 'buoyant' is 'depressed'.

3. Read the extract given below and answer the following questions.

About three minutes later, he responded, "I find it amusing when people patronise me." "And do you find it annoying when someone like me comes and disturbs you in your work?" The answer flashed. "Yes." Then he smiled his oneway smile and I knew, without being sentimental or silly, that I was looking at one of the most beautiful men in the world. A first glimpse of him is shocking, because he is like a still photograph — as if all those pictures of him in magazines and newspapers have turned three-dimensional.

(i) **Which word best describes the emotional state of Hawking, whenever people pitied him?**

(a) Amusement (b) Anger
(c) Jealousy (d) Frustration

Ans. (a) Amusement

(ii) **Why did Stephen Hawking reply three minutes later?**

(a) Because the author had asked an insulting question
(b) Because he was thinking about his answer very carefully
(c) Because he had to find the words on his machine
(d) Because he did not understand the question

Ans. (c) Because he had to find the words on his machine

(iii) **What did the author think when Stephen Hawking smiled at him?**

(a) That he was being sarcastic
(b) That he was the most beautiful man
(c) That he was insulting the author
(d) That his smile was very strange

Ans. (b) That he was the most beautiful man

(iv) **Which of the following words means "treat someone in a way that is apparently kind but betrays a feeling of superiority"?**

(a) Amusing (b) Patronising
(c) Sentimental (d) Shocking

Ans. (b) Patronising

(v) **Which of the following words is not a synonym of 'shocked'?**

(a) Astonished (b) Stunned
(c) Amazed (d) Nonchalant

Ans. (d) Nonchalant

4. Read the extract given below and answer the following questions.

"Yes," he said; it was a disadvantage of his voice synthesiser that it could convey no inflection, no shades or tone. And I could not tell how enthusiastically he agreed with me. Every time I shifted in my chair or turned my wrist to watch the time — I wanted to make every one of our thirty minutes count — I felt a huge relief and exhilaration in the possibilities of my body. How little it mattered then that I would never walk, or even stand. I told him how he had been an inspiration beyond cliche´ for me and, surely, for others — did that thought help him?

(i) **Why was the voice synthesiser a disadvantage?**

(a) Because Stephen Hawking couldn't speak
(b) Because the voice synthesiser produced confusing speech
(c) Because there was no voice modulation
(d) Because it took a long time to operate

Ans. (c) Because there was no voice modulation

(ii) **Why did the author check his watch repeatedly?**

(a) To make sure that he could still move
(b) To make sure that he wouldn't be late for his next appointment
(c) To make sure that he would use every bit of the thirty minutes provided to him
(d) To make sure that he celebrated the possibilities of his body

Ans. (c) To make sure that he would use every bit of the thirty minutes provided to him

(iii) **What did the author think upon seeing Stephen Hawking?**

(a) That his own body was capable of many things
(b) That Stephen Hawking lived a sad life without any possibilities
(c) That he was much more fortunate than Stephen Hawking
(d) That he was more good looking than Stephen Hawking

Ans. (a) That his own body was capable of many things

(iv) **Which of the following is not a synonym of 'enthusiastic'?**

(a) Passionate (b) Keen
(c) Apathetic (d) Vigourous

Ans. (c) Apathetic

(v) **Which of the following words means "a phrase that is overused and betrays a lack of original thought"?**

(a) Enthusiastic (b) Synthesiser
(c) Inflection (d) Cliche

Ans. (d) Cliche

Very Short Answer Type Questions

1. Who reminds Kanga of Hawking's presence in Cambridge?

Ans. The guide of the walking tour to Cambridge reminds Kanga of Stephen Hawking.

2. Why had the writer come to England?

Ans. The writer had come to England as he was writing a book about his travels in Britain.

3. What makes the writer feel stronger in weak times?

Ans. Looking at physically disabled people like him doing well in life, makes the writer feel stronger in weak times.

4. List a couple of emotions that the writer saw in the scientist when he first saw him talking.

Ans. The emotions that writer saw in the scientist when he first saw him talking were exhaustion, frustration and anguish.

5. **"Before you like a lantern whose walls are worn thin you glimpse only the light inside, is the incandescence of a man." What does the lantern represent?**

Ans. In this simile, the lantern represents the disintegrating body of Stephen Hawking.

6. **What does Stephen Hawking find most annoying?**

Ans. People pitying his disability and patronising him annoyed Stephen Hawking.

7. **State one disadvantage of Hawking's voice synthesiser.**

Ans. The synthesiser was unable to convey the inflection or the rise and fall of the speaker's voice. According to Kanga, this was one disadvantage of the synthesiser.

8. **Hawking didn't talk much to the writer while they were in the garden. Why?**

Ans. In the garden, the rays of the Sun shone over the letters on the machine. This made it difficult for Stephen to look for the appropriate letters to be able to express himself.

Short Answer Type Questions

1. **How does the writer overcome his depression over his disintegrated body?**

Ans. On seeing the state of Stephen Hawking and how creatively he lived, the writer overcomes his depression and becomes glad at observing the possibilities of his own body. Unlike Hawking, the writer had been blessed with greater movement. He could move his upper body, finger, his hands, his neck and so on. Meanwhile Hawking could only use his fingers.

2. **Why does the writer's association with England change altogether by the time his journey comes to an end?**

Ans. For the writer, England was synonymous with Cambridge. However, by the time his journey ends, England had taken an entirely new meaning.
This meaning came through his meeting with Stephen Hawking. Now, England stood for much more than Cambridge. It now stood for creativity, positivity, optimism and endless possibilities.

3. **While describing the scientist, what does the writer compare him to?**

Ans. The writer compares the sight or appearance of Hawking to a picture that one sees in a newspaper or a magazine. It was as stiff and lifeless as those pictures, except it was three-dimensional.

4. **What were the six questions that the writer asked the scientist?**

Ans. The writer asked the following six questions from the scientist

(i) Had the scientist been brave?
(ii) Did he laugh often?
(iii) Did the scientist find it annoying when he is disturbed by people?
(iv) What is the best thing about being a disabled person?
(v) If he was relieved or felt better on knowing that people admired him.
(vi) Hawking's message for other disabled people.

5. **What did the writer have to say about the body-soul nexus?**

Ans. According to the writer, he had never been a believer in the idea of transcendence (supremacy) of the soul. Yet, after seeing Stephen Hawking, he became sure that the body was merely the irrelevant outward covering. The only thing worthwhile was the soul or the spirit of the human being.

6. **How has Firdaus Kanga described Professor Hawking achievements that he had accomplished in spite of his physical disailty?** Diksha

Ans. Firdaus Kanga mentions the following achievements of Stephen Hawkings

(i) He is the most brilliant astrophysicist.
(ii) He is the author of the Best-selling book 'A Brief History of Time'.

7. **How is Professor Hawking an inspiration beyond cliché for people?** Diksha

Ans. Professor Stephen Hawking is an inspiration beyond cliché for people because he not only challenged the stereotypical notion of people towards differently-abled people, he is also a recognised and celebrated genius.

8. **The limited time he spent with Hawking was precious to the writer. Support using evidence from the text.**

Ans. The writer kept checking his wrist watch while talking with Stephen Hawking because he wanted to make the most of every minute. This proves that the limited time he spent with the scientist was precious to the writer.

Long Answer Type Questions

1. **Give detailed account of the appearance of Stephen Hawking.**

Ans. The writer was shocked at the first glimpse of the scientist because he looked exactly like his photographs. He was wearing a pale blue shirt over his shrunken torso.
His legs were wasted from disuse. But his eyes were alive in a way that the rest of his body wasn't. They were speaking

something urgent and huge, but the writer could not understand the message.

The writer states that Stephen's body was so thin that he could see his soul.

It was as if one is looking at a lantern whose walls are worn so thin that one can glimpse the light inside. Since he was completely paralysed and thus couldn't speak, he used a computerised synthesiser that produced automated sounds.

2. "I knew that my journey was over." Elaborate with reference to the lesson.

Ans. The writer was doing research and writing about his travels to Britain in a book. His meeting with Stephen Hawking, the living genius and a great source of inspiration, was the ultimate part of his journey. For the writer, the journey had ended right there because he was fully content with his visit to England and couldn't have asked for anything better. It was also a metaphorical way of calling it the end of journey as he had attained a merger with his inspiration and had become aware that this is exactly how he would like to view himself in the future.

3. Is it right to judge a person on the basis of his physical ability? Elaborate with reference to the lesson.

Ans. No, it is not right to judge a person on the basis of his physical ability. People should be judged on the basis of their mental strength. It is possible that people without any disability are weak and pitiable.

At the same time, disabled people need not necessarily be weak. It is possible for such people to have a strong will power and determination to overcome challenges, as in the case of Stephen Hawking.

ASSESSMENT EXERCISE

Multiple Choice Questions

1. Cambridge was my .... for England.

(a) alliteration (b) personification (c) simile (d) metaphor

2. How long did the meeting between Firdaus Kanga and Stephen Hawking last?

(a) Less than an hour (b) More than an hour (c) Two hours (d) Four hours

3. What was the reason behind the disability of Firdaus Kanga?

(a) He had been born with a physical disability.
(b) He had been born with brittle bones.
(c) He had been in a car accident.
(d) He had fallen off a roof.

4. Read the given statements and choose the correct answer.

Statement 1 Both Stephen Hawking and Firdaus Kanga were wheel-chair users.

Statement 2 Firdaus Kanga had come to Cambridge to meet Stephen Hawking.

(a) Statement 1 is true but Statement 2 is false.
(b) Statement 1 is false but Statement 2 is true.
(c) Both the Statements are true.
(d) Both the Statements are false.

5. The ending of the text shows that for the writer, the meeting with Hawking was.

(a) emotional (b) nostalgic (c) humbling (d) thrilling

Extract Based Question

Read the extract given below and answer the following questions.

"When the walking tour was done, I rushed to a phone booth and almost tearing the cord so it could reach me outside, phoned Stephen Hawking's house. There was his assistant on the line and I told him I had come in a wheelchair from India (perhaps he thought I had propelled myself all the way) to write about my travels in Britain. I had to see Professor Hawking-even ten minutes would do. "Half an hour", he said, "From three-thirty to four." And suddenly I felt weak all over. Growing up disabled, you get fed up with people asking you to be brave..."

(i) Where had the writer come from?

(a) India (b) China (c) Japan (d) Sri Lanka

(ii) Why did he wish to meet Hawking?

(a) Hawking was a living genius
(b) Hawking was too depressed
(c) Hawking had called him
(d) Hawking was on his death bed

(iii) How long did the writer expect to be allowed to meet the scientist?

(a) Ten minutes (b) Half an hour (c) One hour (d) Two hours

(iv) Why was the writer fed up with certain people?

(v) Write a synonym and a homonym for the word 'weak'.

Very Short Answer Type Questions

1. How long did Kanga think would be the maximum time granted to him to meet Stephen Hawking?
2. Firdaus Kanga had indulged himself in learning which activity?
3. How did Kanga feel when he went to meet Hawking?
4. With what intention were events like the disabled Olympics introduced?
5. What does the writer mean by "an embodiment of my bravest self"?

Short Answer Type Questions

1. Would you say that Stephen Hawking and Firdaus Kanga were brave people?
2. Elaborate upon Hawking's dismissal of the disabled Olympics.
3. What does the writer mean when he says that meeting Hawking meant the end of his journey?
4. How did the writer and Stephen Hawking bid each other goodbye?
5. What are the thoughts of the writer on the advice given by Stephen Hawking to disabled people?

Long Answer Type Questions

1. Why do people think that disabled people are chronically unhappy?
2. Was it relieving for Hawking to hear that he had many admirers?
3. Firdaus Kanga called Stephen Hawking "one of the most beautiful men in the world". What is his idea of beauty and how does it connect to society's ideas about beauty?
4. How does Firdaus Kanga relate to the advice given by Stephen Hawking?

A Short Monsoon Diary

by Ruskin Bond

'A Short Monsoon Diary' is an excerpt taken from the diary of a renowned Indian author, Ruskin Bond. The chapter is divided into two parts and does not have a story as such. It portrays the beauty of nature in the author's hometown, Mussoorie and the emotions it produces within the author.

Part - I

24th June

The writer described the first day of monsoon mist (thin fog). He remarked how the birds had fallen silent when the mist covered the hills and believed that it makes the monsoon mist lonely and sad. The birdsong, that could be heard an hour ago, had become silent and it felt as if it were midnight. The writer could hear Bijju calling to his sister while running on the hillside through the mist but he couldn't see him.

25th June

The writer celebrated the warm monsoon rain that was falling during this time and expressed his dislike for the cold weather that had continued throughout the year. He added that on the day when he walked up to the bank and the post office, he noticed the first cobra-lily beginning to bloom. Thus, he believed that the plants also knew that monsoon had arrived.

The writer also remarked that since it made it difficult to see, the mist offered some privacy.
Further, when a school boy asked the writer to describe the hill-station and the valley in one sentence, the author could only say that it was 'A paradise that might have been'.

27th June

As soon as the rainy season arrived, one could see a leopard and many leeches. The writer mentioned that just a day before in the noon time, the leopard had taken a dog from near the servant's quarter below the school. It had even tried to attack Bijju's cows in the evening but his mother had scared the leopard with her shouts. The writer accepted that he'll get used to losing blood to the leeches soon.

The writer celebrated the arrival of birds like scarlet minivets who look like bright jewels among the green trees. The female minivets are yellow in colour. The birds are so brightly coloured that they are unable to hide themselves among the trees. However, sometimes they would stay silent and remain hidden. Along with the minivets, another species of birds, the aggressive drongo, was seen in the season. These birds would chase the minivets away.

In this season, creeper trees grew the trunk of the oak tree. Further, there was no lack of food for insect eating birds due to rainy season.

Part – II

2nd August

The writer mentioned that it had been raining continuously all night without any storm or thunder. The sound of the raindrops against the tin roof helped him stay awake, but at the same time also helped him sleep. He admitted that it is a good sound. He remarked that the rain outside was contrasted by the quiet inside his room. He felt untouched by the rain leaking from the roof, but still in connection with it.

3rd August

The writer mentioned that the rain had stopped. When the clouds cleared up and Sun could be seen near the hill on his left side, he could hear the sound of a woman cutting sticks. He could also hear the sound of cowbells. He heared a crow cawing in an oak tree and the water leaking from a drain pipe. Suddenly, he could hear the clear and pure song of a whistling thrush (a bird) coming from a valley.

12th August

The writer was gloomy because of the continuous rain and mentioned that the sun had not been seen for eight or nine days. He could not go anywhere because of the rain and moved in his room watching people with umbrellas pass by through his window. He was relieved that the rain wasn't cold. He also remarked that he could see the late monsoon flowers like wild balsam, dahlias, begonias and ground orchids covering the hillsides.

31st August

Monsoon season had reached its peak as August ended. The seeds of cobra lily flowers were turning red signaling that the rains would end soon. The writer predicted that the ferns would begin turning yellow soon but at the time they were green and firm. Plants like ground orchids, mauve lady's slipper and the white butterfly orchids covered the hillside of Mussoorie. Red, yellow and magenta wild dahlias had begun blooming from rocky cracks. Snakes and little animals had been flooded out of their holes and had taken shelter in roofs attics and godowns.

The writer mentioned that a weak-sighted shrew (chuchundar) had been wandering in the rooms of his house amusing the children. But the grandmother had forbidden them from killing it because shrews are considered lucky as they bring money. The writer believed the grandmother as he soon received a check for a small amount of money in the mail.

3rd October

Monsoon had turned into winter rain and it had been snowing higher up the hill. An evening hailstorm had filled the valley and the hills with a beautiful, golden light.

26th January

Winter Rains in the Hills

The writer had written an original poetry in this diary entry. He has described the silence and loneliness after his friend had left. The rain was falling in a pattern on the leaves and the roof, and the mist had covered his house. He would move to the window and observe that the rain would stop and start again. The gray trees had filled him with loneliness.

23rd March

Winter was ending and the blackest cloud had covered the sky of Mussoorie. But the hailstorm that lasted half an hour had cleared the sky. The writer mentioned that he could see a rainbow forming.

Word Meaning

Word	Meaning
Miracles	an extraordinary and welcome event
Mist	haze
Melancholy	very sad
Blankets	covers
Genuine	true
Humid	relatively high level of water vapour in the atmosphere
Rears	lifts
Ferns	a flowerless plant with feathery green leaves
Heralded	announced or brought the news of
Leech	a bloodsucking parasite that is found during the rainy season
Imprecations	curses
Scarlet minivets	bright red bird like a cuckoo
Bloodletting	losing blood
Flitting	moving swiftly and lightly
Drongo	a song-bird with a stout bill
Conceal	hide
Contrive	manufacture
Aggressive	likely to attack
Creeper	climbing plant
Insectivorous	feeding on insects
Dearth	shortage
Corrugated	ridged
Tropical downpour	a sudden and unexpected heavy fall of rain
Steady	stable
Swish	move with or make a swishing sound
Leaks	seeps out

Word	Meaning
Drumming	falling noisily
Cowbell	a bell hung around a cow's neck
Disconsolately	unhappily
Ravine	valley
Soggy	wet and soft
Tinkle	chime
Mauve	a pale purple colour
Landour	another name for Mussoorie
Thrush	a small songbird
Damp	moist
Bobbing	up and down movement
Lush	abundant
Crevices	narrow openings or cracks in rock or wall
Rodent	a small mammal
Shrew	chuchundar
Blunder	mistake
Balsam, dahlias and begonias	are a variety of flowers
Burrows	hole
Altitude	height of an object or point in relation to sea level
Hailstorm	a storm that produces hail
Suffused	covered
Hushed	quiet
Drenched	thoroughly wet
Squatted	sit on your heels
Caress	touching or holding lovingly
Menace	threaten

NCERT FOLDER

NCERT Intext and Exercise Questions

COMPREHENSION CHECK[1] (NCERT PAGE 106)

Q.1 Why is the author not able to see Bijju?

Ans. The author was unable to see Bijju because of the monsoon mist.

Q.2 What are the two ways in which the hills appear to change when the mist comes up?

Ans. The hills appear to change in the following two ways when the mist comes up

(a) When the mist covers the hills, the forests become silent.

(b) When the mist covers the hills, it makes it difficult to see anyone and thus offers privacy.

CHECK[2] (NCERT PAGE 108)

Q.1 When does the monsoon season begin and when does it end? How do you prepare to face the monsoon?

Ans. The monsoon season begins in the month of June and ends by the time August ends. One prepares for the rainy season by arranging umbrellas and raincoats.

Q.2 Which hill-station does the author describe in this diary entry?

Ans. The author is describing the monsoon rains of Mussoorie in these diary entries.

Q.3 For how many days does it rain without stopping? What does the author do on these days?

Ans. It rained continuously for almost eight to nine days.

The author could not do anything much or go anywhere because of the rains. He would only pace up and down the room and gaze out of the windows, at the people with umbrellas passing by.

Q.4 Where do the snakes and rodents take shelter? Why?

Ans. The snakes and rodents take shelter in the roofs, attics and godowns. They did so because they had been flooded out of their holes and burrows.

Q.5 What did the author receive in the mail?

Ans. The author received a cheque of small amount in his mail.

WORKING WITH THE TEXT (NCERT PAGE 109)

Q.1 Look carefully at the diary entries for 24-25th June, 2nd August and 23rd March. Now write down the changes that happen as the rains progress from June to March.

Ans. On 24th June, mist covered the hillside and announced the arrival of monsoon. By the next day, i.e. June 25th, warm monsoon rain had begun pouring and the flowers began to bloom.

On 2nd August, the writer notes that the non-stop rain had been creating beautiful sounds against the tin roof of his house. He considered it a good sound. By 23rd March, the winter had finally ended. As the skies cleared after a hailstorm, the writer could see rainbows forming in the sky.

Q.2 Why did the grandmother ask the children not to kill the *Chuchundar*?

Ans. The grandmother asked the children not to kill the chuchundar because she believed that the 'chuchundars' brought good luck and money.

Q.3 What signs do we find in nature which show that the monsoons are about to end?

Ans. The seeds of the cobra lily flower were turning red. This was nature's way of showing that the monsoon rains were coming to an end.

Q.4 Complete the following sentences.

(i) Bijju is not seen but his voice is heard because ....

(ii) The writer describes the hill station and valley as ....

(iii) The leopard was successful in .... but had to flee when ....

(iv) The minivets are easily noticed because ....

(v) It looks like a fashion display on the slopes when ....

(vi) During the monsoon season, snakes and rodents are found in roofs and attics because ....

Ans. (i) of the mist that concealed everything.

(ii) a paradise that might have been.

(iii) attacking Bijju's cow, Bijju's mother screamed at it.

(iv) of their attractive and bright colours

(v) ground orchids, mauve lady's slipper and white butterfly orchids appear.

(vi) the rain water floods their holes and burrows.

Q.5 'Although tin roofs are given to springing unaccountable leaks, there is a feeling of being untouched by and yet in touch with, the rain.'

(i) Why has the writer used the word, 'springing'?

Ans. The writer uses the word 'springing' to suggest that the roof tins begin to leak without giving any warning.

(ii) How is the writer untouched by the rain?

Ans. The writer is literally untouched by the rain because he is inside the room and that protects him from it.

(iii) How is the writer in touch with the rain at the same time?

Ans. The writer is in touch with the rain by listening to the rhythmic sounds it makes against the tin roof.

Q.6 Mention a few things that can happen when there is endless rain for days together.

Ans. Endless rains create a number of problems. Work gets obstructed as it makes difficult for people to step outside their homes, while the holes of snakes and rodents get flooded.

If there is no proper drainage system, it leads to problems of water logging and traffic jams on roads. During rains, there is an increase in the insect population, which could also cause diseases. Sometimes, due to excessive rains, the crop gets destroyed.

Q.7 What is the significance of cobra lily in relation to the monsoon season, its beginning and end?

Ans. The blooming of cobra lily is an indication that the monsoons have arrived. As the seeds of cobra lily turn red, it signifies the end of the season.

WORKING WITH LANGUAGE

(NCERT PAGE 109-111)

Q.1 Here are some words that are associated with the monsoon. Add as many words as you can to this list. Can you find words for these in your languages?

downpour, floods, mist, cloudy, powercuts, cold, umbrella

Ans.

Rainwater	-	वर्षा का पानी
Water logging	-	जल जमाव
Traffic jam	-	यातायात जाम
Damp	-	नम
Soggy	-	गीला
Leaks	-	रिसाव
Thunder	-	गरज
Floods	-	बाढ़
Mist	-	धुंध
Powercuts	-	बिजली कटौती
Cold	-	शीत
Umbrella	-	छाता

Q.2 Look at the sentences below.

(i) Bijju wandered into the garden in the evening.

(ii) The trees were ringing with birdsong.

Notice the highlighted verbs.

The verb wandered tells us what Bijju did that evening. But the verb was ringing tells us what was happening continually at same time in the past (the birds were chirping in the trees).

Now look at the sentences below. They tell us about something that happened in the past. They also tell us about other things that happened continually, at the same time in the past.

Put the verbs in the brackets into their proper forms. The first one is done for you.

(i) We (get out) of the school bus. The bell (ring) and everyone (rush) to class.

(ii) The traffic (stop). Some people (sit) on the road and they (shout) slogans.

(iii) I (wear) my raincoat. It (rain) and people (get) wet.

(iv) She (see) a film. She (narrate) it to her friends who (listen) carefully.

(v) We (go) to the exhibition. Some people (buy) clothes while others (play) games.

(vi) The class (is) quiet. Some children (read) books and the rest (draw).

Ans. (i) We got out of the school bus. The bell was ringing and everyone was rushing to class.

(ii) The traffic stopped. Some people were sitting on the road and they were shouting slogans.

(iii) I was wearing my raincoat. It was raining and people were getting wet.

(iv) She had seen a film. She was narrating it to her friends who were listening carefully.

(v) We went to the exhibition. Some people were buying clothes while others were playing games.

(vi) The class was quiet. Some children were reading books and the rest were drawing.

Q.3 Here are some words from the lesson which describe different kinds of sounds.

drum, swish, tinkle, caw, drip

(i) Match these words with their correct meanings.

(a) to fall in small drops

(b) to make a sound by hitting a surface repeatedly.

(c) to move quickly through the air, making a soft sound

(d) harsh sound made by birds

(e) ringing sound (of a bell or breaking glass, etc.)

(ii) Now fill in the blanks using the correct form of the words given below.

(a) Ramesh .... on his desk in impatience.

(b) Rain water .... from the umbrella all over the carpet.

(c) The pony .... its tail.

(d) The .... of breaking glass woke me up.

(e) The .... of the raven disturbed the child's sleep.

Ans. (i) (a) drip (b) drum (c) swish (d) caw (e) tinkle

(ii) (a) drummed (b) dripped (c) swished (d) tinkle (e) caw

Q.4 And sure enough, I received a cheque in the mail.

Complete each sentence below by using appropriate phrase from the ones given below.

sure enough	colourful enough	serious enough
kind enough	big enough	fair enough
brave enough	foolish enough	anxious enough

(i) I saw thick black clouds in the sky. And .... it soon started raining heavily.

(ii) The blue umbrella was .... for the brother and sister.

(iii) The butterflies are .... to get noticed.

(iv) The lady was .... to chase the leopard.

(v) The boy was .... to call out to his sister.

(vi) The man was .... to offer help.

(vii) The victim's injury was .... for him to get admitted in hospital.

(viii) That person was .... to repeat the same mistake again.

(ix) He told me he was sorry and he would compensate for the loss. I said, ' ....'.

Ans. (i) sure enough (ii) big enough
(iii) colourful enough (iv) brave enough
(v) anxious enough (vi) kind enough
(vii) serious enough (viii) foolish enough
(ix) fair enough

SPEAKING (NCERT PAGE 111)

Q.1 Do you believe in superstitions? Why or why not? Working with your partner, write down three superstitious beliefs that you are familiar with.

Ans. No, I don't believe in superstitions. Superstitions are nothing but obsolete truths of a previous age.

There is no logic behind these truths. They are generally believed by ignorant and conservative people.

Three familiar superstitions are

(i) not to broom any surface in evening.
(ii) not to cut nails at night.
(iii) not to sneeze while stepping out of the house.

Q.2 How many different kinds of birds do you come across in the lesson? How many varieties do you see in your neighbourhood? Are there any birds that you used to see earlier in your neighbourhood but not now? In groups discuss why you think this is happening.

Ans. There are a number of birds that we come across in the lesson. These include minivets, drongos, thrush, crow and so on.
Birds that could be seen very often in the neighbourhood, but have now disappeared are eagles, peacocks and white parrots.

These birds can no longer be seen because of high-rise buildings and increase in the levels of pollution.

WRITING (NCERT PAGE 112)

Q.1 The monsoons are a time of great fun and even a few adventures: playing in the rain and getting wet, wading through knee-deep water on your way to school, water flooding the house or the classrooms, powercuts and so on. Write a paragraph describing an incident that occurred during the rains which you can never forget.

Ans. The monsoons indeed are a time of great fun. It is easy to use rains as an excuse for not attending school. One day, I did not go to school on the account of rain.
My mother agreed to this only on the condition that I would not drench myself in the rains.

However, my father made paper boats for me and encouraged me to make them swim in the rainwater that had collected in the roads outside our house. It was such a fun-filled moment seeing my father enjoying the boat game like a young child.

Or

Write a poem of your own about the season of spring when trees are in full bloom.

Ans. When spring comes, flowers begin to bloom.
It puts an end to the last autumn's gloom.
Anywhere we see, there is a lot of colour.
The birds, the flowers, the Earth; nothing is duller.
It is the season of joy.
Everyone seems to sing.
Be it a girl or a boy. Such a joyful seasons is spring.

REVIEW EXERCISE

Including Competency Based Questions

Multiple Choice Questions

1. Choose the flowers that you came across in the lesson. DIKSHA

(a) Jasmine (b) Lotus (c) Dahlia (d) Rose

Ans. (c) Dahlia

2. What is the author's tone when he describes the minivets?

(a) Appreciation (b) Pride
(c) Envy (d) Joy

Ans. (a) Appreciation

3. Why does the writer associate mist with sadness? Competency Based

(a) Mist brings darkness (b) The birds stop singing
(c) Mist envelopes the hills (d) The weather becomes cold

Ans. (b) The birds stop singing

4. Based on the text, the writer finds early monsoon rain to be Competency Based

(a) inconvenient (b) unexpected
(c) energising (d) pleasing

Ans. (d) pleasing

5. What effect do the monsoon rains not have on the writer's surroundings?

(a) The flowers start blooming
(b) A variety of wildlife emerges
(c) The animals become docile
(d) Disease causing insects become common

Ans. (c) The animals become docile

6. What makes the minivets different? Competency Based

(a) They hide amongst colorful plants
(b) They are very common
(c) They are easy to spot
(d) They do not sing

Ans. (c) They are easy to spot

7. What best describes the writer's feelings during pouring rain?

(a) Uneasy (b) Hopeful
(c) Indifferent (d) Comfortable

Ans. (a) Uneasy

8. What is true about the writer's style? Competency Based

(a) He describes images vividly
(b) He recounts personal events to add context
(c) He reveals several endearing details about himself
(d) He maintains a pessimistic attitude towards the world

Ans. (a) He describes images vividly

9. Look at the given statements and choose the correct answer.

Statement 1 The author feels lonely during monsoons.

Statement 2 The author loves looking at the blooming flowers at the hillside.

(a) Statement 1 is true but Statement 2 is false.
(b) Statement 1 is false but Statement 2 is true.
(c) Both the Statements are true.
(d) Both the Statements are false.

Ans. (b) Statement 1 is false but Statement 2 is true.

10. "I can hear him running about on the hillside but I cannot see him." Why couldn't the writer see 'him'?

(a) Because of the hailstorm (b) Because of the rain
(c) Because of the mist (d) Because of the thunderstorm

Ans. (c) Because of the mist

11. Read the given statements and choose the correct answer.

Statement 1 Ruskin Bond is fond of the natural environment and this reflects in his writing.

Statement 2 Ruskin Bond can recreate the scenic beauty of nature very vividly through words.

(a) Statement 1 is true but Statement 2 is false.
(b) Statement 1 is false but Statement 2 is true.
(c) Both the Statements are true.
(d) Both the Statements are false.

Ans. (c) Both the Statements are true.

12. "In the evening it attacked one of Bijju's cows but fled at the approach of Bijju's mother, who came screaming imprecations". From the given statement, it can be concluded that

(a) Bijju's mother liked to hunt leopards
(b) Bijju's mother was not afraid of the leopard
(c) The leopard liked to eat cows
(d) The leopard was a coward

Ans. (b) Bijju's mother was not afraid of the leopard

13. **"..not only does it conceal the hills, it blankets them in silence too". What is the writer speaking about in the given line?**

(a) The writer is speaking about the rain
(b) The writer is speaking about the mist
(c) The writer is speaking about the fog
(d) The writer is speaking about the snow

Ans. (b) The writer is speaking about the mist

Extract Based Questions

1. **Read the extract given below and answer the following questions.**

24th June The first day of monsoon mist. And it's strange how all the birds fall silent as the mist comes climbing up the hill. Perhaps that's what makes the mist so melancholy; not only does it conceal the hills, it blankets them in silence too. Only an hour ago the trees were ringing with birdsong. And now the forest is deathly still as though it were midnight. Through the mist Bijju is calling to his sister. I can hear him running about on the hillside but I cannot see him.

(i) What strange thing does the writer notice about the approaching mists?

Ans. The writer notices that when the mist begins to cover the hills, strangely all the birds fall silent.

(ii) Why does the writer associate mist with the feeling of melancholy?

Ans. The writer associates mist with the feeling of melancholy because it silences the birds and cuts people off from each other by making it difficult to see.

(iii) What could the writer hear on the hillside even after the birds had stopped singing?

Ans. The writer could hear Bijju calling for his sister in the mist.

(iv) The way the writer portrays the mist gives it a human attribute. Which sentence matches this description?

Ans. The following sentence shows how the writer gives mist a human attribute - 'as the mist comes climbing up the hill'.

(v) Which word from the given passage is a homonym of the word 'wringing'?

Ans. The word 'ringing' is the homonym of the given word 'wringing'.

2. **Read the extract given below and answer the following questions.**

27th June The rains have heralded the arrival of some seasonal visitors—a leopard and several thousand leeches. Yesterday afternoon the leopard lifted a dog from near the servants' quarter below the school. In the evening it attacked one of Bijju's cows but fled at the approach of Bijju's mother, who came screaming imprecations. As for the leeches, I shall soon get used to a little bloodletting every day.

(i) Name the seasonal visitors of Mussoorie during the rainy season.

Ans. The seasonal visitors are a leopard and a thousand leeches.

(ii) Where did the leopard attack the dog?

Ans. The leopard attacked the dog near the servant's quarters below the school.

(iii) Why does the writer say that he will get used to a little bloodletting?

Ans. The writer states that he will get used to a little bloodletting every day because the beginning of monsoon meant the arrival of thousands of blood-sucking leeches.

(iv) What is the meaning of the word 'herald'?

Ans. The word 'herald' means 'a sign that something is about to happen'.

(v) What is the meaning of the word 'imprecations'?

Ans. The word 'imprecations' means 'spoken curses'.

3. **Read the extract given below and answer the following questions.**

All night the rain has been drumming on the corrugated tin roof. There has been no storm, no thunder, just the steady swish of a tropical downpour. It helps me to lie awake; at the same time, it doesn't keep me from sleeping. It is a good sound to read by – the rain outside, the quiet within – and, although tin roofs are given to springing unaccountable leaks, there is a feeling of being untouched by and yet in touch with, the rain.

(i) Which word describes the sound quality of the rain falling?

(a) Thunder
(b) Drumming
(c) Swish
(d) Spring

Ans. (b) Drumming

(ii) The rain came along with a feeling of .... for the writer.

(a) thunder (b) hail
(c) storm (d) peace

Ans. (d) peace

(iii) What were the tin roofs expected to do during the rainy season?

(a) Crack (b) Rust
(c) Leak (d) Bend

Ans. (c) Leak

(iv) Why does the writer emphasise the feeling of "being untouched by and yet in touch with the rain"?

(a) Because the writer did not like getting wet by the rain.
(b) Because the writer was troubled by the frequent leaks in his roof during the rainy season.
(c) Because the writer wanted to be connected to the rain without getting wet.
(d) Because the writer didn't like to go out in the rain with an umbrella.

Ans. (c) Because the writer wanted to be connected to the rain without getting wet

(v) What dual quality of the sound of the rain does the author admire?

(a) The way it can help him sleep or help him stay awake
(b) The way it can make him feel cool in the warm summer
(c) The way it can create noise but still sound pleasant
(d) The way it can make a boring book interesting

Ans. (a) The way it can help him sleep or help him stay awake

4. Read the extract given below and answer the following questions.

It is the last day of August and the lush monsoon growth has reached its peak. The seeds of the cobra lily are turning red, signifying that the rains are coming to an end. In a few days the ferns will start turning yellow, but right now they are still firm, green and upright. Ground orchids, mauve lady's slipper and the white butterfly orchids put on a fashion display on the grassy slopes of Landour. Wild dahlias, red, yellow and magenta, rear their heads from the rocky crevices where they have taken hold.

(i) What signified the end of monsoon?

(a) The seeds of the cobra lily turned red
(b) The blooming of the cobra lily flower
(c) The seeds of the cobra lily turned yellow
(d) The blossoming of wild dahlias

Ans. (a) The seeds of the cobra lily turned red

(ii) The ferns were firm, green and upright but they would soon start turning ....

(a) brown (b) red (c) yellow (d) gray

Ans. (c) yellow

(iii) Who put on a fashion display on the grassy slopes of Landour?

(a) Ground Orchids
(b) Mauve Lady's Slipper
(c) White Butterfly Orchids
(d) All of the above

Ans. (d) All of the above

(iv) Which of the following words is not a synonym of the word 'lush'?

(a) Lavish
(b) Abundant
(c) Barren
(d) Plush

Ans. (c) Barren

(v) "In a few days the ferns will start turning yellow, but right now they are still firm, green and upright." The specified mention of the terms 'yellow' and 'upright' serves to explain that .... was coming.

(a) winter (b) autumn
(c) spring (d) summer

Ans. (b) autumn

Very Short Answer Type Questions

1. What reference does the writer use to show both the beginning and the ending of monsoons? **Competency Based**

Ans. The writer uses the reference of the cobra lily flowers blooming to show the beginning of monsoon. When the seeds of the cobra lily turn red it signifies the end of monsoon.

2. Write two adjectives used to describe the early monsoon rain.

Ans. Warm and humid are the two adjectives used to describe the early monsoon rain.

3. What is the colour of the minivets that arrive with the rains? How does the writer describe them?

Ans. The minivets are brightly coloured with the female ones being yellow. The writer describes them as 'brilliant jewels'.

4. "There is no dearth of food for the insectivorous birds". Explain, why?

Ans. With monsoon comes a lot of insects. The birds that survive on insects therefore, have food in abundance during this season.

5. What happens when the rain stops on 3rd August?

Ans. As the rains stop, people resume with their day-to-day activities. A woman begins chopping the wood and the sound of cowbells could now be heard. The birds shake off rainwater from their feathers and crows start cowing.

6. Why does Bijju's mother shout imprecations at the leopard?

Ans. Bijju's mother shouted a series of curses at the leopard because it attacked the cows belonging to her son Bijju.

7. Why does the writer feel lonely?

Ans. The writer feels lonely as his friend had gone and everything was quiet except for the rhythm of the rain.

8. What changes in the trees does the writer describe in his diary entry on 26th August?

Ans. The writer notes that the rain had put a dark blanket on everything around the house. The trees didn't appear green anymore. They had gone grey; threatening the arrival of writer with their darker shades.

Short Answer Type Questions

1. Why was the writer unable to sleep on the night of 2nd August?

Ans. The writer was unable to sleep on the night of 2nd August as he was kept awake by the sound of the rain water falling on the tin roofs. It provided him some kind of peace and he spent the night observing the pattern of the rain.

2. How does the writer get to know that the monsoon was coming to an end?

Ans. The writer noticed the leaves of the cobra lily turning red and realised that soon the ferns would turn yellow too, though as of now they were firm and green.
The writer knew that these changes signify the end of the monsoon season.

3. Give description of the atmosphere when the winter came to an end.

Ans. As the winter was coming to an end, the writer saw the blackest cloud cast in the sky hailing marbles.

The hailstorm cleared the sky. No sooner had this happened that the writer saw the appearance of rainbow in the sky.

4. Describe the general atmosphere of the hill-station. How does it get changed with the coming of the monsoons?

Ans. The general atmosphere of the hill station, Mussoorie, is cold. With the coming of the monsoons, it turns warm and humid.

The writer celebrates this change, as the mist offers some warmth and privacy and turns the entire place into a paradise.

5. Which incident supported grandmother's belief? Competency Based

Ans. The writer's grandmother believed that the chuchundars bring good luck and money with them. This belief was supported by the incident where the writer received a check in the mail soon after the arrival of a chuchundar to their house.

6. What makes the entry on 26th January different?

Ans. The entry on 26th January is different from the rest of the diary entries because it contains an original poem written by Ruskin Bond. He had gotten inspired by the winter rains in the hills and thus, created a poem describing the quiet and lonely atmosphere.

7. The writer feels unsettled during winter rain. Which lines from the entry of 26th January most clearly show this?

Ans. The following line from the diary entry of 26th January shows that the writer was feeling unsettled: "And the trees no longer green but grey, menace me with their loneliness."

Long Answer Type Questions

1. Assume yourself to be a tourist who has gone to Mussoorie during the monsoon. Write a note describing your experiences.

Ans. As I reached Mussoorie, the weather was extremely cold and unbearable. Within two days, however, with the onset of the monsoons it changed to become warm and pleasant. Not only did the weather change, but the entire place also got transformed. A variety of birds and flowers that were not to be seen in the first two days of my stay came from somewhere and added a lot of colour to the surroundings.

Along with the sound of the rain, the songs of the birds reverberated in the air turning the hill-station into a paradise.

2. Describe the writers day on 31st August.

Ans. The last day of August marks the last few days of the monsoon. The writer notices that the monsoons have already reached the peak and now the rains would come to an end as indicated by different elements of nature.

He sees the seeds of cobra lily turning red and the ferns beginning to get yellowish in colour. At the same time, he also sees a variety of colourful flowers and butterflies. It gives delight to the writer. The writer also gets a pay cheque on this day.

3. "The winter rains unsettled the writer and made him feel lonely and sad." Justify the given statement with evidence from the story.

Ans. The diary entry of 26th January contains a description of the writer's feelings in the winter rain. Through a poem, he describes how the house was completely silenced after the departure of his friend. He states that the atmosphere was 'very lonely, very quiet', as the rain drummed on the window panes in a rhythmic pattern. It can also be understood that the writer was pacing his room due to a feeling of unease, because he would 'pause near a window' and observe the gray trees menacing him with their loneliness. All of these instances portray that the writer was in a sad and uneasy mood and the winter rains had made him feel lonely in his quiet house.

4. What message does 'A Short Monsoon Diary' convey to the readers of Ruskin Bond?

Ans. The given chapter is a compilation of a few diary entries written by the world renowned author, Ruskin Bond. In these entries, he describes the way monsoon rain affects his beautiful hometown of Mussoorie. The author has a talent for describing the images he sees in all their beauty. The way he gives the most importance to the little changes in the nature around him shows that he believes nature to be healer of the soul. It is clear that he takes out specific time from his day to watch the nature around him, especially from his last entry that states the appearance of a rainbow while he was writing. This is the message that Ruskin Bond wishes to convey to his readers.

ASSESSMENT EXERCISE

Multiple Choice Questions

1. What best describes the writer's feelings during the formation of the rainbow?

(a) Hopeful (b) Indifferent (c) Sullen (d) Gloomy

2. What is true about the writer's style of writing?

(a) He focuses exclusively on the wild animals of Mussoorie.
(b) He writes extensively about the little changes in nature.
(c) He notes down the minutest change in his feelings.
(d) He marked down the different hues of the sky.

3. Read the given statements and choose the correct answer.

Statement 1 The writer feels angry at the leeches for sucking his blood.

Statement 2 The writer admits that he will get used to the bloodletting.

(a) Statement 1 is true but Statement 2 is false.
(b) Statement 1 is false but Statement 2 is true.
(c) Both the Statements are true.
(d) Both the Statements are false.

4. The writer describes Mussoorie as "A .... that might have been".

(a) paradise (b) dream (c) heaven (d) wonderland

5. "There is a feeling of being untouched by, yet in touch with ...."

(a) sadness (b) daydream (c) rain (d) snow

Extract Based Question

Read the extract given below and answer the following questions.

"The rain stops. The clouds begin to break up, the sun strikes the hill on my left. A woman is chopping up sticks. I hear the tinkle of cowbells. In the oak tree, a crow shakes the raindrops from his feathers and caws disconsolately. Water drips from a leaking drainpipe. And suddenly, clean and pure, the song of the whistling thrush emerges like a dark sweet secret from the depths of the ravine."

(i) What does the scene describe?

(a) Scene before the rains
(b) Scene during the rains
(c) Scene after the rains
(d) Scene after the season came to an end

(ii) Give the adjectives that describe the bird's song.

(a) Clean and pure
(b) Chopping and tinkle
(c) Nice and sweet
(d) Sweet and secretive

(iii) The word 'ravine' means ....

(a) Earth (b) valley (c) hillside (d) plains

(iv) What does the writer compare the thrush's song with?

(v) What does the crow do after the rain stops?

Very Short Answer Type Questions

1. How does the writer describe the hill station during monsoon?
2. Name the various unpleasant visitors that come to the hill station during the rains.
3. What does the writer mean by 'bloodletting'?
4. Why do the leopards and the leeches come to the hills in the monsoon?
5. How does Bijju's cow escape death?

Short Answer Type Questions

1. Why did the valley look as if it was hosting a fashion show?
2. Describe the writer's emotions during the rainy season.
3. What does the writer's grandmother instruct to the children?
4. Why did the snakes and rodents seek shelter in the roofs, attics and godowns?
5. What happened to the author that unwittingly proved a superstition of his grandmother?

Long Answer Type Questions

1. Write a letter to your friend describing the beauty of nature.
2. Write a diary entry comparing the weather during the summer with that during the monsoon.
3. When did the leopard enter the hills of the writer's hometown? What made him escape back to the forest?
4. Sum up the main ideas of the author's monsoon diaries in about a hundred words.

The Ant and the Cricket

by Adapted from Aesop's Fables

CHAPTER 1

Introduction The poem 'The Ant and the Cricket' is taken from the infamous Aesop's Fables. The poem describes the story of an ant and a cricket and how their actions had different results. The poem emphasises the importance of planning ahead to lead a better life.

Stanzawise Explanation

Stanza 1

A silly young cricket, accustomed to sing
Through the warm, sunny months of
gay summer and spring,
Began to complain when he found that, at home,
His cupboard was empty, and winter was come.

Explanation The poem begins with the introduction of a young and silly cricket (an insect). During the warm weather of the summer and spring, he used to spend all his time singing. However, as winter came, he started to complain that his cupboards were empty and he had no food at home.

It is important to note here that the poet describes the seasons of summer and spring as 'gay' (happy) because during these seasons, the surroundings are warm and vibrant, everything is flourishing and food is available in abundance.

Stanza 2

Not a crumb to be found
On the snow-covered ground;
Not a flower could he see,
Not a leaf on a tree.
"Oh! what will become,"
says the cricket, "of me?

Explanation The cricket realised that the ground was covered with snow and he could not find any crumb (pieces of food) on it. The tree didn't bear any flowers or leaves. Seeing it, he started to think about how he would be able to survive.

Stanza 3

At last by starvation and famine made bold,
All dripping with wet, and all trembling with cold,
Away he set off to a miserly ant,
To see if, to keep him alive, he would grant

Explanation Now, because of lack of food both inside and outside, the cricket became hungry and bold. Hence, completely wet and shaking terribly due to the cold, he went to meet the ant. He wanted to plead the ant to provide him certain things to survive.

The use of the word 'famine' here suggests that due to the harsh winter conditions, no food could be found anywhere.

Stanza 4

Him shelter from rain,
And a mouthful of grain.
He wished only to borrow;
He' d repay it tomorrow;
If not, he must die of starvation and sorrow.

Explanation The cricket approached the ant. He, then, asked the ant to help him take shelter from the rain and to provide him some food. He told the ant that he was only borrowing and would pay back whatever he took from the ant soon. He emphasised that if the ant didn't provide him with anything, he would surely die as a result of extreme hunger and sadness.

Stanza 5

Says the ant to the cricket,
"I'm your servant and friend,
But we ants never borrow;
we ants never lend.
But tell me, dear cricket did you lay nothing by
When the weather was warm?"
Quoth the cricket "Not I!

Explanation After listening to the cricket's request, the ant told the cricket that he was his servant and friend. However, ants follow a rule of never borrowing or lending things. He, then, asked the cricket whether he had saved anything during the warm weather. To this question, the cricket answered that he did not do so.

Stanza 6

My heart was so light
That I sang day and night,
For all nature looked gay."
"You sang, Sir, you say?
Go then," says the ant,
"and dance the winter away"

Explanation The cricket told the ant that he was so happy during the warm weather that he only sang day and night as the nature looked so pleasant. The ant got annoyed and told the cricket that since he had spent the entire warm weather singing, he should go and spend the winter dancing.

This stanza is important as it presents the moral of the poem. The cricket had been so busy in merry-making that he forgot to think about the future. This resulted in him facing hardships during the winter season.

Stanza 7

Thus ending, he hastily lifted the wicket,
And out of the door turned the poor little cricket.
Folks call this a fable.
I'II warrant it true:
Some crickets have four legs,
and some have two.

Explanation After refusing the cricket's request, the ant ended the conversation. It asked the cricket to leave and closed his door. Then, the poet tells us that although many would call this story a fable (a story with a moral lesson), he would like to believe that it is not. He thinks that just as there are four-legged crickets, two-legged crickets also exist.

The last line of the stanza may seem meaningless at first. However, the lines indicate that the habit of not planning for the future can be found among human too.

Word Meaning

Word	Meaning
Stanza 1	
Accustomed	used to
Gay	happy
Stanza 3	
Dripping	to leak slowly
Trembling	shaky
Warrant	guarantee
Hastily	urgently
Fable	story that teaches a moral lesson (usually with animal characters)
Stanza 4 and 5	
Mouthful of grain	a little amount of food
Quoth	said
Lay nothing by	keep or save anything

NCERT FOLDER | NCERT Exercise Questions

WORKING WITH THE POEM (NCERT PAGE 23)

Q.1 The cricket says, "Oh! What will become of me?" When does he say it, and why?

Ans. The cricket says, "Oh! What will become of me?" when he realises that winter had arrived. He says this because he realises that there was no food to be found either in the house or outside.

Q.2 (i) Find in the poem the lines that mean the same as "Neither a borrower nor a lender be" (Shakespeare)

Ans. "We ants never borrow; we ants never lend."

(ii) What is your opinion of the ant's principles?

Ans. In my opinion, the ant's principles seem quite fair. Ants are self sufficient and have managed to do so because of sheer hard work. They consume what is required and store the remaining. Therefore, they never need to borrow. For the same reasons, they do not wish to lend because that might lead to depletion of their resources.

Q.3 The ant tells the cricket to "dance the winter away". Do you think the word 'dance' is appropriate here? If so, why?

Ans. Yes, the word 'dance' seems quite appropriate as it is used in a sarcastic manner in this line. The cricket had fun during the happy and pleasant months of summer. The ant tells him that he might as well have fun in the winter, without any food or shelter.

Q.4 (i) Which lines in the poem express the poet's comment? Read them aloud.

Ans. "Folks call this a fable. I'll warrant it true Some crickets have four legs and some have two."

(ii) Write the comment in your own words.

Ans. These lines state that for many, the tale of the ant and the cricket is just a fictional tale with animal characters. However, the problem faced by the cricket is something that makes it true especially for humans. Like the cricket, humans too forget to save for the difficult times.

REVIEW EXERCISE | Including Competency Based Questions

Part – I

Multiple Choice Questions

1. Why did the cricket complain? Competency Based

(a) He could not sing.
(b) The ant refused to help him.
(c) He did not have anything to eat.
(d) His house was covered in snow.

Ans. (c) He did not have anything to eat.

2. What was the reaction of the cricket when he realised that his cupboard was empty in the winter season? Diksha

(a) He began to sing louder.
(b) He approached the ant for help.
(c) He was worried about himself.
(d) He began to tremble.

Ans. (c) He was worried about himself.

3. '...Go then,' says the ant, 'and dance the winter away.' Which of these best describes the ant's tone when it says this? Competency Based

(a) Encouraging (b) Sarcastic
(c) Amused (d) Furious

Ans. (b) Sarcastic

4. Which of these best describes the ant? Competency Based

(a) Wicked (b) Modest (c) Righteous (d) Annoying

Ans. (c) Righteous

5. Which of these is true about the cricket? Competency Based

(a) He was not brave enough to face his struggles.
(b) He did not take responsibility for his actions.
(c) He learned from his life experiences.
(d) He trusted other creatures blindly.

Ans. (a) He was not brave enough to face his struggles.

6. **Read the following statements and choose the correct answer.**

Statement 1 The ant was a miser because he worked hard to collect his food.

Statement 2 The cricket was sure that the ant would not help him at all.

(a) Statement 1 is true but Statement 2 is false.
(b) Statement 1 is false but Statement 2 is true.
(c) Both the Statements are true.
(d) Both the Statements are false.

Ans. (a) Statement 1 is true but Statement 2 is false.

7. **Which of these ideas does the poem mainly convey?** **Competency Based**

(a) Never borrow food or money.
(b) A friend in need is a friend indeed.
(c) Think ahead and save for the future.
(d) Always live in the present and enjoy life.

Ans. (c) Think ahead and save for the future.

8. **According to the poet, the incident in the poem** **Competency Based**

(a) mirrors real-life experiences of some people.
(b) shows how nature teaches us important lessons.
(c) illustrates the struggles faced by animals during winter.
(d) explains why some creatures survive longer than others.

Ans. (a) mirrors real-life experiences of some people.

9. **What does the poem do?** **Competency Based**

(a) Describe (b) Instruct (c) Explain (d) Narrate

Ans. (b) Instruct

10. **Read the given stanza from the poem and answer the following question** **Competency Based**

At last by starvation and famine made bold,
All dripping with wet, and all trembling with cold,
Away he set off to a miserly ant,
To see if, to keep him alive, he would grant
Him shelter from rain,
And a mouthful of grain.
He wished only to borrow;
He'd repay it tomorrow;
If not, he must die of starvation and sorrow.

What made the cricket ask the ant for food?

(a) His food had gone bad.
(b) He was friends with the ant.
(c) He was facing an extreme shortage of food.
(d) The ant had borrowed food from him earlier.

Ans. (c) He was facing an extreme shortage of food.

Extract Based Questions

1. **Read the extract given below and answer the following questions.**

A silly young cricket, accustomed to sing
Through the warm, sunny months of
gay summer and spring,
Began to complain when he found that, at home,
His cupboard was empty, and winter was come.
Not a crumb to be found
On the snow covered ground;
Not a flower he could see,
Not a leaf on a tree.
Oh! What will become, says the cricket, of me?

(i) Why does the poet call the cricket silly?

Ans. The poet called the cricket silly because he hadn't saved anything for the winter.

(ii) Where did the cricket look for food?

Ans. The cricket looked for food in his cupboards. He also tried find any food on the trees or the ground outside.

(iii) What is the weather described in the extract?

Ans. The given extract described the winter season. The ground was covered with snow. Also, there was rain.

(iv) Find a word from the extract which means 'habituated'.

Ans. 'Accustomed'

(v) What emotion is the poet trying to show in this extract?

Ans. In the given extract, the poet is trying to show the cricket's worry.

2. **Read the extract given below and answer the following questions.**

But tell me, dear cricket,
Did you lay nothing by
When the weather was warm?
Quoth the cricket, Not I!
My heart was so light/
That I sang day and night,
For all nature looked gay.
You sang, Sir, you say?
Go then, 'says the ant and dance the
winter away.

(i) Who sang day and night?

Ans. The cricket sang day and night.

(ii) Why did the ant ask the cricket to 'dance the winter away'?

Ans. The ant asked the cricket to dance the winter away because all through the summer he had done nothing but had fun. He might as well have fun in the winter too.

(iii) What were the consequences of the cricket's actions during the warm weathers?

Ans. The consequences of the cricket's actions during the warm weather were that during winter he had no food, no shelter and he was cold and starving.

(iv) Explain the meaning of the phrase, 'lay nothing by.'

Ans. 'Lay nothing by' means saving nothing.

(v) What is the poetic device used in the following line?

"When the weather was warm"

Ans. Alliteration

3. Read the extract given below and answer the following questions.

At last by starvation and famine made bold,
All dripping with wet, and all trembling with cold,
Away he set off to a miserly ant,
To see if, to keep him alive, he would grant
Him shelter from rain,
And a mouthful of grain.
He wished only to borrow;
He'd repay it tomorrow;
If not, he must die of starvation and sorrow.

(i) Why was he dripping with wet and trembling with cold?

(a) Because of the winter weather
(b) Because he had taken a bath
(c) Because he had fever
(d) Because he was in shock

Ans. (a) Because of the winter weather

(ii) What is the poetic device used in the following lines?

Away he set off to a miserly ant,
To see if, to keep him alive, he would grant

(a) Anaphora (b) Repetition
(c) Alliteration (d) Rhythm

Ans. (d) Rhythm

(iii) What is the rhyme scheme of the following lines from the extract?

Him shelter from rain,
And a mouthful of grain.
He wished only to borrow;
He'd repay it tomorrow;
If not, he must die of starvation and sorrow.

(a) ababa (b) abbcc (c) aabbc (d) aabbb

Ans. (d) aabbb

(iv) What did he ask from the ant?

(a) Raincoat
(b) Sweater
(c) Shelter and grain
(d) Umbrella

Ans. (c) Shelter and grain

(v) What would happen if he didn't get what he wanted?

(a) He would not sing
(b) He would break the friendship with the ant
(c) He would die of starvation and sorrow
(d) He would find it somewhere else

Ans. (c) He would die of starvation and sorrow

4. Read the extract given below and answer the following questions.

Thus ending, he hastily lifted the wicket,
And out of the door turned the poor little cricket.
Folks call this a fable. I'll warrant it true:
Some crickets have four legs, and some have two.

(i) 'Lifted the wicket' in the lines implies

(a) lifted the cricket
(b) lifted a heavy object
(c) ended the conversation
(d) lifted the cricket's hopes

Ans. (c) ended the conversation

(ii) A fable is

(a) a fictional novel
(b) a biography
(c) a real life story
(d) a story that has a moral or teaches a lesson

Ans. (d) a story that has a moral or teaches a lesson

(iii) Which of the following is an antonym of the word 'hastily'.

(a) Deliberately (b) Quickly
(c) Suddenly (d) Briefly

Ans. (a) Deliberately

(iv) The cricket ....

(a) went out of the window
(b) wanted to go and dance
(c) got the help he needed
(d) was refused help and went out the door

Ans. (d) was refused help and went out the door

(v) What is the poetic device used in the line?

"Some crickets have four legs, and some have two"

(a) Anaphora (b) Metaphor
(c) Simile (d) Personification

Ans. (b) Metaphor

Part – II

Very Short Answer Type Questions

1. When did the cricket realise a change in his circumstances?

Ans. The cricket realised a change in his circumstances when he saw that his cupboards were empty and the winter had come.

2. Why is the adjective 'gay' used to describe summer and spring?

Ans. The adjective 'gay' is used to describe summer and spring because these were the warm and sunny months and there was no shortage of any kind.

3. What did the cricket seek from the ant?

Ans. The cricket asked for shelter and a handful of grain from the ant in order to survive.

4. What belief did ants live by? Competency Based

Ans. The ants lived by the belief to never lend or borrow.

5. 'Some crickets have four legs, and some have two.'
According to the poet, who are the crickets with two legs? Competency Based

Ans. According to the poet, humans are the crickets with two legs.

6. How did the ant react to cricket's confession that he had spent his precious time in singing during summer and spring? Diksha

Ans. The ant reacted to the cricket's confession by saying that since he had spent the summer singing, he should go and dance the winter away too as it was too late to save himself from the cold and hunger.

Short Answer Type Questions

1. What are some of the signs of approaching winter as mentioned by the poet in the poem? Diksha

Ans. The poet mentions that not even a piece of food could be found on the ground which was covered with snow when the winter approached. The trees became lifeless as there was neither flowers nor leaves on them. The surroundings were wet and cold.

2. Which line from the poem most clearly shows that the cricket approached the ant only because he was forced to? Competency Based

Ans. The line 'At last by starvation and famine made bold, all dripping with wet, and trembling with cold' most clearly shows that the cricket approached the ant only because he was forced to.

3. Describe the sufferings of the cricket.

Ans. The cricket suffered a great deal as the winter set in. He realised that he had no food and his cupboards were empty. Even the nature had nothing to offer. There were no flowers or leaves on the trees as they were covered with snow. The cricket was cold and starving under these circumstances.

4. Discuss the moral lesson imparted by the poem.

Ans. The poem showcases how the cricket is left with nothing to sustain itself as it spent all the time in merry making without worrying about the future.

In order to sustain itself, he is dependent on begging and asking for mercy of fellow creatures like the ant.

Long Answer Type Questions

1. Describe the differences between the ant and the cricket.

Ans. The ant called himself a friend of the cricket. However, both the friends were very different from each other. The cricket was silly and foolish. He did not work during the summer or the spring and didn't store anything for the winter. The ant, on the other hand, worked according to his principles. He planned ahead and worked hard when the weather was warm and saved enough food to last the whole winter without depending on anybody else.

2. Does the poet criticise the ant for his unhelpful behaviour?

Ans. The poet doesn't criticise the ant for his unhelpful behaviour, except saying that the ant was miserly in nature. However, he surely doesn't glorify the cricket's behaviour. Through the cricket's example, he extends the moral of the tale that human beings should work hard and save for the bad times rather than depending on others.

The critique of cricket's ways doesn't justify ant's unhelpful behaviour, but it surely details that ant's way of living was better than that of the cricket.

ASSESSMENT EXERCISE

Multiple Choice Questions

1. The cricket asked the ant for a .... of grain.
   (a) crumb (b) mouthful
   (c) little (d) lot
2. When was the cricket going to pay the ant back if he lent him anything?
   (a) Never (b) Soon
   (c) When the winter was over (d) When it stopped raining
3. How did the cricket address the ant as?
   (a) Friend (b) Servant
   (c) Miserly (d) Poor little
4. Read the statements carefully and choose the correct answer from the following options.

   Statement 1 The cricket sang, dance and slept during the summer and spring.

   Statement 2 The cricket only asked the ant for food.
   (a) Statement 1 is true but Statement 2 is false.
   (b) Statement 1 is false but Statement 2 is true.
   (c) Both the Statements are true.
   (d) Both the Statements are false.
5. "You sang, Sir, you say?

   Go then," says the ant, "and dance the winter away"

   What is the tone of the ant when he said this?
   (a) Annoyance (b) Tiredness
   (c) Teasing (d) Playful

Extract Based Question

Read the extract given below and answer the following questions.

Thus ending, he hastily lifted the wicket,
And out of the door turned the poor little cricket.
Folks call this a fable. I'll warrant it true:
Some crickets have four legs, and some have two.

(i) Find a word from the extract which is an antonym of the word 'deliberately'.
(ii) What was the result of the conversation? Was the cricket able to convince the ant?
(iii) What is the poetic device used in the line?
"Some crickets have four legs, and some have two"
(iv) 'Lifted the wicket' in the lines implies
(a) lifted the cricket (b) lifted a heavy object
(c) ended the conversation (d) lifted the cricket's hopes
(v) A fable is
(a) a fictional novel
(b) a biography
(c) a real life story
(d) a story that has a moral or teaches a lesson

Very Short Answer Type Questions

1. Pick out the phrases in which we directly hear the poet's voice.
2. List as many adjectives that describe the cricket and the ant.
3. What were the main pre-occupations of the cricket?
4. When was the happiest time for the cricket?
5. Give one reason why the life of the ant was better than that of the cricket.

Short Answer Type Questions

1. Explain the meaning of the line, "Some crickets have four legs and some have two."
2. Why does the poet say that this fable is true?
3. Why is the ant called miserly?

Long Answer Type Questions

1. How far was the cricket responsible for his fate?
2. Discuss the moral lesson imparted by the poet.

Geography Lesson

by Zulfikar Ghose

Introduction The poem 'Geography Lesson' by Zulfikar Ghose talks about the Earth and its physical features when seen from different heights. He represents the relationships between the locations of civilisations to different geographical features of the planet. While doing so, the poet also finds that there is no logic in the hatred and the borders that man has created on the planet.

Stanzawise Explanation

Stanza 1

When the jet sprang into the sky,
it was clear why the city
had developed the way it had,
seeing it scaled six inches to the mile.
There seemed an inevitability
about what on ground had looked haphazard,
unplanned and without style
When the jet sprang into the sky.

Explanation The poem begins with the poet's description of the city when it is viewed from the sky. When the jet took off from the ground into the sky, the poet could see the city in its smaller version. The poet observed that an area which was spread over a mile was reduced to six inches, when it is seen from above. On seeing it, the poet understood why the city had developed in such a manner. The city looked unplanned and seemed to have been made without style from the ground. However, when it is seen from a higher place, he could not help but see the reason why there was no order or symmetry in it.

Stanza 2

When the jet reached ten thousand feet,
it was clear why the country
had cities where the rivers ran
and why the valleys were populated.
The logic of geography -
that land and water attracted man -
was clearly delineated
When the jet reached ten thousand feet.

Explanation When the jet reached ten thousand feet in the sky, the poet could understand why the cities were developed along the rivers in the country. The poet had also realised the reasons behind the inhabitation of people in the valleys. He could understand the significance of geography and clearly pointed out that land and water attracted man.

In this line, the poet notes that land and water allowed man to sustain life. Man used land and water for agricultural practices and to make shelters for themselves. Hence, cities were found near rivers and on valleys.

Stanza 3

When the jet rose six miles high,
it was clear the earth was round
and that it had more sea than land
But it was difficult to understand
that the men on the earth found
causes to hate each other, to build
walls across cities and to kill.
From that height, it was not clear why.

Explanation When the jet had risen to six miles from the ground, the poet could see that Earth is indeed round and its maximum portion is covered by sea. While the poet was observing all these details from above, he still couldn't figure out some things. He found it hard to understand why there is so much hatred among men. He could not find any reason to justify why men find ways to hate and kill each other and stay divided by building walls across cities.

Word Meaning

Word	Meaning
Stanza 1	
Sprang	leap
Scaled	to climb up a steep surface
Inevitability	that cannot be avoided
Haphazard	without plan or order
Stanza 2	
Delineated	shown

NCERT FOLDER

NCERT Exercise Questions

WORKING WITH THE POEM (NCERT PAGE 35)

Q.1 Find three or four phrases in stanzas one and two which are likely to occur in a geography lesson.

Ans. The following phrases usually occur in a geography lesson.

Stanza 1

(a) Scaled six inches to a mile

Stanza 2

(a) It was clear why the country had cities where the river ran and why the valleys were populated.

(b) Land and water attracted man

(c) Clearly delineated

Q.2 Seen from the window of an aeroplane, the city appears

(i) as haphazard as on ground.

(ii) as neat as a map.

(iii) as developed as necessary.

Mark the right answer.

Ans. (iii) as developed as necessary.

Q.3 Which of the following statements are examples of 'the logic of geography'?

(i) There are cities where there are rivers.

(ii) Cities appear as they are not from six miles above the ground.

(iii) It is easy to understand why valleys are populated.

(iv) It is difficult to understand why humans hate and kill one another.

(v) The earth is round, and it has more sea than land.

Ans. The following statements are examples of 'the logic of geography'

(i) There are cities where there are rivers.

(iii) It is easy to understand why valleys are populated.

(v) The earth is round and it has more sea than land.

Q.4 Mention two things that are

(i) clear from the height.

(ii) not clear from the height.

Ans. (i) It becomes clearer from the height that the earth is round and that land and water attract man.

(ii) Even from the height, it was not clear why men hate and kill each other and build walls around their cities.

REVIEW EXERCISE

Including Competency Based Questions

Part - I

Multiple Choice Questions

1. The poet was on a

(a) ship (b) jet (c) mountain (d) bike

Ans. (b) jet

2. What became clear to the poet when he was in the sky?

(a) That he was still on the ground
(b) That there was more land than water
(c) That the city was unorganised
(d) Why the city developed the way it had

Ans. (d) Why the city developed the way it had

3. What was the poet's opinion about the city before he saw it from above? Competency Based

(a) He thought it was too crowded.
(b) He thought it was disorganised.
(c) He thought it developed naturally.
(d) He thought it was too far from the river.

Ans. (b) He thought it was disorganised.

4. At what height did the poet understand the logic of geography?

(a) Six inches (b) Twenty thousand feet
(c) Six miles (d) Ten thousand feet

Ans. (d) Ten thousand feet

5. What phrase best describes the poet? Competency Based

(a) Unpredictable (b) Meticulous
(c) Observant (d) Ignorant

Ans. (c) Observant

6. The poem ends on a note of Competency Based

(a) Grief (b) Despair
(c) Uncertainty (d) Contemplation

Ans. (d) Contemplation (thought provoking ideas)

7. What is the main point the poet is making in the poem? Competency Based

(a) Geography limits the potential of human development.
(b) Geography highlights human ingenuity and achievement.
(c) Geography is a significant factor in harmful human behaviour.
(d) Geography is a primary factor in the course of human development.

Ans. (d) Geography is a primary factor in the course of human development

8. In the poem, the poet mainly Competency Based

(a) argues a position (b) narrates an incident
(c) describes new insights (d) expresses his frustration

Ans. (c) describes new insights

Read the given stanza from the poem and answer the following questions. Competency Based

When the jet rose six miles high,
it was clear the earth was round
and that it had more sea than land.
But it was difficult to understand
that the men on the earth found
causes to hate each other, to build
walls across cities and to kill.
From that height, it was not clear why.

9. What was clear to the poet when the jet reached six miles high?

(a) Jet planes could fly higher than he imagined
(b) The earth was round and had more sea than land
(c) Cities of the world stood out compared to other regions
(d) The buildings on earth were not visible from that height

Ans. (b) The earth was round and had more sea than land

10. During his flight, the poet felt that the hatred between men on earth was .... Competency Based

(a) normal (b) harmful
(c) reasonable (d) meaningless

Ans. (d) meaningless

Extract Based Questions

1. Read the extract given below and answer the following questions.

When the jet reached ten thousand feet,
it was clear why the country
had cities where the rivers ran
and why the valleys were populated.
The logic of geography-
that land and water attracted man -
was clearly delineated
when the jet reached ten thousand feet.

(i) **How much height did the jet attain?**

Ans. The jet attained a height of ten thousand feet.

(ii) **What became clear as the jet attained that height?**

Ans. As the jet attained that height it became clear why cities had developed near the flowing rivers.

(iii) **What became obvious on seeing the city from that height?**

Ans. Seeing the city from that height, it became obvious that land and water were essential for habitation.

(iv) **What is the logic of geography?**

Ans. The logic of geography mentioned in the extract is why cities and civilisation exist near rivers.

(v) **Find a word from the poem which means 'clearly shown'.**

Ans. 'Delineated'

2. Read the extract given below and answer the following questions.

When the jet rose six miles high,
It was clear the earth was round
and that it had more sea than land.
But it was difficult to understand
that the men on the earth found
causes to hate each other.

(i) **What was the height that the jet attained?**

(a) Ten thousand feet
(b) Six miles
(c) A few hundred feet
(d) Ten thousand miles

Ans. (b) Six miles

(ii) **What does the poet learn about the earth?**

(a) That the earth was round
(b) That the earth had boundaries
(c) That the earth had no land
(d) That the earth was entirely made of water

Ans. (a) That the earth was round

(iii) **Who posed a threat to the poet's understanding of the logic of geography?**

(a) Men (b) Animals
(c) Water (d) Land

Ans. (a) Men

(iv) **Which of the following statements remains unclear to the poet.**

(a) Men are filled with negative emotions and actions.
(b) Earth consists of more water than land.
(c) Earth is round when it is viewed from above.
(d) Men live on Earth.

Ans. (a) Men are filled with negative emotions and actions.

Part – II

Very Short Answer Type Questions

1. "scaled six inches to the mile" What does the phrase mean? Competency Based

Ans. The phrase means that the city appeared very small as a mile seemed to be equal to six inches when it is viewed from above.

2. Why did the city look haphazard on the ground?

Ans. The city looked haphazard on the ground because it was impossible to get a wider view of the city.

3. The poet failed to find answers to certain questions. What were these questions?

Ans. The poet failed to understand why men hated men and were ready to kill each other. He also could not comprehend why men built walls around cities.

Short Answer Type Questions

1. What were the thoughts of the poet when he sees the city from the sky?

Ans. On seeing the city from a certain height in the sky, the poet was able to understand why the city had developed in a certain way. The city was developed in accordance to the needs of man and therefore, though it looked haphazard on the ground, it followed a logical plan.

2. What is the central theme as conveyed by the poet?

Ans. The poet wishes to convey the irrational and illogical grudges and grievances that people nurture for each other. The poet fails to understand why people discriminate and judge on the basis of regional and territorial lives when geography and nature does not establish these differences.

Long Answer Type Questions

1. Why is the poem titled Geography Lesson? **Competency Based**

Ans. The poem is titled 'Geography Lesson' as the poet learns a lesson from geography. Due to his jet flight, he was able to understand why the city was built in the manner that it was. Earlier, he had found it to be haphazard but now, he was clear that it had developed according to the needs of man.

He was also able to understand the logic of geography- man being attracted by water and land. It became clear to him that Earth had more sea than land and that it was round in shape. However, he was unable to understand the reason behind the hatred of men for each other and the reasons for building walls across the cities and killing each other.

2. Discuss the tone of the poem.

Ans. In the opening stanzas of the poem, the poet adopts a fairly descriptive tone. He describes the landscape the way he views it from a certain height. He accurately records the height that the plane attains and the way that alters his view of the city.

However, as the poem progresses, especially in the final stanza, the tone of the poet becomes contemplative and philosophical. He ponders upon the reasons as to why man has become an enemy of man, why is he willing to kill people of his own species and why they are trying to separate from each other by building walls.

ASSESSMENT EXERCISE

Multiple Choice Questions

1. What did the men on Earth build across the cities?
   (a) Walls
   (b) Health centres
   (c) Airports
   (d) Water bodies
2. At what height did the poet realise that the Earth was round?
   (a) Ten thousand feet
   (b) Six miles
   (c) Sixty miles
   (d) Five thousand feet
3. When the jet sprang into the sky
   What is the poetic device used in the above line?
   (a) Personification
   (b) Alliteration
   (c) Anaphora
   (d) Metaphor
4. Read the statements carefully and choose the correct answer from the following options.
   Statement 1 The poet was clear that Earth was round when the jet rose ten thousand feet from the ground.
   Statement 2 It was clearly shown that what attracted man were the land and water.
   (a) Statement 1 is true but Statement 2 is false.
   (b) Statement 1 is false but Statement 2 is true.
   (c) Both the Statements are true.
   (d) Both the Statements are false.
5. How did the development of the city not look like when viewed from the ground?
   (a) Haphazard
   (b) Unplanned
   (c) Unstylish
   (d) Unprincipled

Extract Based Question

Read the extract given below and answer the following questions.

When the jet sprang into the sky,
it was clear why the city
had developed the way it had,
seeing it scaled six inches to the mile.
There seemed an inevitability
about what on ground had looked haphazard.

(i) What became clear when the jet sprang into the sky?
(ii) Explain the meaning of the phrase 'scaled into'.
(iii) What looked haphazard on the ground?
(iv) Into how many inches did a mile get reduced to?
(a) Three (b) Four
(c) Five (d) Six
(v) The word haphazard means ....
(a) lacking order (b) confused
(c) complex (d) perspective

Very Short Answer Type Questions

1. Where were the cities built?
2. What looked haphazard and unplanned to the poet?
3. What did the poet fail to understand?

Short Answer Type Questions

1. What lesson did the poet acquire?
2. What did the poet observe about the country?

Long Answer Type Question

1. Borders and wars seem vain to the poet. Do you agree? Justify your answer.

The Last Bargain

by Rabindranath Tagore

The poem 'The Last Bargain' is written by Rabindranath Tagore. It conveys the strong message that freedom is more important than all worldly comforts that the world may offer.

Stanzawise Explanation

Stanza 1

"Come and hire me," I cried, while in the morning
I was walking on the stone-paved road.
Sword in hand the King came in his chariot.
He held my hand and said, "I will hire you with my power,
But his power counted for naught, and he went away in
his chariot.

Explanation The poem starts with the speaker walking along a stone-paved road in the morning. He is requesting the passersby to hire him for some work. The first person who heard his request was a King who carried a sword in his hand. He came in his chariot and while holding the narrator's hand told him that he would like to hire him by using his power. However, the speaker found the King's power to be insignificant. So, the King left the place in his chariot.

Stanza 2

In the heat of the mid-day the houses stood with
shut doors.
I wandered along the crooked lane.
An old man came out with his bag of gold.
He pondered and said, "I will hire you with my money.
He weighed his coins one by one, but I turned away.

Explanation It was noon and the speaker was wandering along a deformed path. The houses along this path were closed. An old man who had a lot of money came to the speaker to hire him. He carried a bag of gold and after a moment of thought, he started weighing the coins one by one. However, the speaker refused to work for him.

In the last line, the poet seems to imply that the speaker wasn't interested in money or wealth.

Stanza 3

It was evening. The garden hedge was all a flower.
The fair maid came out and said, "I will hire you
with a smile.
"Her smile paled and melted into tears, and she went
back alone into the dark.

Explanation When evening came, the speaker came across a garden in which flowers were blossoming. A young lady came out of this garden and told the speaker that she would hire him. She further told him that she would offer the speaker her smile as payment. However, her smile faded and changed into tears. She decided to go back alone into the dark.

Stanza 4

The sun glistened on the sand, and the sea
waves broke waywardly.
A child sat playing with shells.
He raised his head and seemed to know me and said,
"I hire you with nothing.
"From henceforward that bargain struck in child's play
made me a free man.

Explanation In this stanza, the speaker meets a child near the sea. The Sun was shining and its rays were reflected on the sand while the waves coming to the shore were difficult to be controlled. The child was sitting there and playing with shells. When he lifted his head, it appeared that he knew the speaker. He, then, told the speaker that he would hire him with nothing. From that moment onwards, the speaker accepted the deal as it seemed to be fair and made him a free man.

The last deal made by the speaker is important as it indicates that more than money, power or beauty, one's work or passion is needed to make one free and happy.

Word Meaning

Word	Meaning
Stanza 1	
Stone paved	(road or path) covered with stone on the surface
Chariot	carriage which is usually drawn by horses
Naught	nothing
Stanza 2	
Crooked	curved or bent
Pondered	thinking carefully
Stanza 3	
Hedge	fence
A flower	filled with blooming flowers
Paled	reduced or less end
Stanza 4	
Glistened	gleamed
Waywardly	uncontrollable
Bargain	agreement in which both parties promise to do something for each other.

NCERT FOLDER

NCERT Exercise Questions

WORKING WITH THE POEM (NCERT PAGE 71)

Q.1 Who is the speaker in the poem?

Ans. The speaker in the poem is an ordinary man who is looking for work.

Q.2 'The king, sword in hand' suggests

(i) wealth

(ii) power

(iii) more power than wealth

Mark the appropriate item in the context of stanza 1.

Ans. (ii) power

Q.3 The old man offered the speaker a lot of money. Why did he turn down the offer?

Ans. The speaker turned down the offer for a lot of money because his freedom was more important than any materialistic wealth.

Q.4 Find in the poem, lines that match the following. Read both one after another.

(i) I have nothing to give you except goodwill and cheer.

(ii) Her happiness was no more than sorrow in disguise.

(iii) The king's might was not worth much.

Ans. (i) I hire you with nothing.

(ii) Her smile paled and melted into tears.

(iii) But his power counted for naught.

Q.5 How did the speaker feel after talking to the child on the beach?

Ans. The speaker felt like a 'free man' after talking to the child on the beach. He felt happy and relieved. Now, he did not need to compromise his freedom and in return, he was to get goodwill and cheer. To him, it was a fair deal.

REVIEW EXERCISE

Including Competency Based Questions

Part – I

Multiple Choice Questions

1. What does the poet want at the beginning of the poem? Competency Based

(a) He wants to be offered work.
(b) He wants to impress the king.
(c) He wants someone to listen to his sorrows.
(d) He wants someone to join him on his journey.

Ans. (a) He wants to be offered work.

2. Who comes in a chariot?

(a) The old man (b) The fair maiden
(c) The King (d) The child

Ans. (c) The King

3. Which word best describes the poet's attitude towards the king's power? Competency Based

(a) Fearful (b) Wishful
(c) Dismissive (d) Overwhelmed

Ans. (c) Dismissive

4. The old man came out with his.

(a) chariot (b) seashells
(c) bag of gold (d) smile

Ans. (c) bag of gold

5. Her smile paled and melted into tears What does the poet try to indicate in the line above? Competency Based

(a) The loneliness of the maid.
(b) The insincerity of her smile.
(c) The transient nature of beauty.
(d) The maid's sadness at the poet's rejection.

Ans. (c) The transient nature of beauty.

6. How does the tone in the third stanza change? Competency Based

(a) Sympathetic to angry (b) Excited to indifferent
(c) Curious to confused (d) Hopeful to dismal

Ans. (d) Hopeful to dismal

7. What made the poet accept the child's offer? Competency Based

(a) He already knew the child.
(b) He felt that it would give him liberty.
(c) He did not want to hurt the child.
(d) He felt the child's innocence was trustworthy.

Ans. (b) He felt that it would give him liberty.

8. Why did the poet say that the bargain had made him a free man? Competency Based

(a) He could go where he wanted to.
(b) It ensured that he was not in anyone's debt.
(c) He had already fulfilled his obligations.
(d) It allowed him to look after the child as he wanted.

Ans. (b) It ensured that he was not in anyone's debt.

9. What main idea is conveyed in the poem? Competency Based

(a) Children possess the inner wisdom that adults lack.
(b) Pride in wealth, money and beauty will lead to downfall.
(c) It is important to balance material needs with spirituality.
(d) Freedom of the spirit is more important than worldly comforts.

Ans. (d) Freedom of the spirit is more important than worldly comforts.

10. Which word best describes the style of the poet? Competency Based

(a) Simple
(b) Formal
(c) Flowery
(d) Emphatic

Ans. (a) Simple

Extract Based Questions

1. Read the extract given below and answer the following questions.

"In the heat of the mid-day
the houses stood with shut doors.
I wandered along the crooked lane.
An old man came out with his bag of gold
He pondered and said,
'I will hire you with my money'
He weighed his coins one by one,
but I turned away."

(i) What was the weather on that day?

Ans. The weather on that day was hot.

(ii) Does the speaker accept the offer made by the old man?

Ans. No, the speaker does not accept the offer. He was not lured by money.

(iii) **Complete the sentence appropriately. When the old man came out with a lot of money, he ....**

Ans. thought for a moment. Then, he told the speaker that he would hire him with his money.

(iv) **Find a word from the extract which means the opposite of 'linear'.**

Ans. Crooked

(v) **What is the meaning of the phrase 'turned away' according to the extract?**

Ans. The meaning of the phrase 'turned away' means to reject or dismiss something or someone.

2. Read the extract given below and answer the following questions.

"The sun glistened on the sand, and the sea
waves broke waywardly.
A child sat playing with shells.
He raised his head and seemed to
know me and said,
'I hire you with nothing.'
From henceforward that bargain
struck in child's play
Made me a free man."

(i) **Who is the speaker of these lines?**

(a) The king (b) The poet
(c) The child (d) The man

Ans. (d) The man

(ii) **Where did the speaker meet the child?**

(a) At the seashore (b) At the stone-paved road
(c) In the garden (d) Near the crooked lane

Ans. (a) At the seashore

(iii) **What was the child doing when the speaker met him?**

(a) Playing with a sword
(b) Playing with the sea shells
(c) Plucking flowers
(d) Counting coins

Ans. (b) Playing with the sea shells

(iv) **What is the antonym of the word 'glistening'?**

(a) Fading (b) Flickering
(c) Draining out (d) Gliding

Ans. (a) Fading

(v) **Which of the following is a homonym of the word 'made'?**

(a) mad (b) made (c) maid (d) mate

Ans. (c) maid

Part II

Very Short Answer Type Questions

1. What does the king and his sword represent in the poem?

Ans. The king and his sword represent power in the poem.

2. What did the old man offer the poet? Competency Based

Ans. The old man offered the poet money from his bag of gold.

3. He weighed his coins one by one, but I turned away. Why did the poet turn away? Competency Based

Ans. The poet turned away from the old man because his freedom was more important to him than the gold coins offered to him.

4. What was the child doing when the speaker met him?

Ans. The child was playing with shells when the speaker met him on the seashore.

5. Who had the man encountered till the evening?

Ans. The man encountered the king in the morning, the old man towards mid-day and the fair maid in the evening.

6. Did the man compromise?

Ans. No, the man did not compromise. He didn't accept the offers made by the king, the old man and the fair maid because none provided him freedom.

Short Answer Type Questions

1. Why did the man turn down the offers made by the king, the old man and the fair lady?

Ans. The man turned down the offers made by the king, the old man and the fair lady because no wealth, power and beauty attracted him. The man was looking for a job, but not at the cost of his freedom. He desired goodwill and happiness.

2. What do the sword, the gold and the smile of the fair lady signify? What do they not offer to the speaker?

Ans. The sword signified power, the gold signified wealth, and the smile of the fair lady signified beauty. None of these were capable enough to give the man everlasting happiness or freedom.

Long Answer Type Question

1. The poem invests a lot of faith in the idea of freedom. Comment on it.

Ans. It is true to say that the poem invests a lot of faith in the idea of human freedom. In the poem, the speaker was offered power by the king, money by the old man and beauty by the lady. But, he showcases a wilful rejection of power, wealth and beauty as none of these are as necessary for human growth and development as freedom. He only struck the deal with the child because the child promised him 'nothing' in return which can be taken as free of any commitment.

ASSESSMENT EXERCISE

Multiple Choice Questions

1. What did the king carry?
   (a) Sword (b) Bag of gold
   (c) A beautiful smile (d) Seashell
2. The man cried 'Come and hire me' at/in the ....
   (a) evening (b) night
   (c) morning (d) afternoon

Extract Based Questions

Read the extract given below and answer the following questions.

"It was evening. The garden hedge was all a flower.
The fair maid came out and said, "I will hire you with a smile."
Her smile paled and melted into tears,
And she went back alone in the dark.

(i) What was the offer made by the fair maid?
(ii) Why did her smile melt into tears?
(iii) Find two words from the passage which are antonyms of each other.
(iv) Where did the speaker meet the fair maid?
   (a) At the seashore (b) At the stone-paved road
   (c) In the garden (d) Near the crooked lane
(v) "The garden was all a flower" means ....
   (a) there was an abundance of flowers in the garden
   (b) there were no flowers in the garden
   (c) the garden had only flowers
   (d) the garden is artificial

Very Short Answer Type Questions

1. Where did the speaker meet the old man?
2. What was the king carrying in his hand?
3. What did the king ride on?
4. When did the speaker meet the fair maid?
5. What was breaking waywardly?

Short Answer Type Questions

1. What was the offer made by the king?
2. With what did the fair maid thought of hiring the speaker's services?
3. How did the conversation between the fair maid and the speaker end?

Long Answer Type Question

1. Discuss the title of the poem 'The Last Bargain'.

The School Boy

by William Blake

Introduction The poem 'The School Boy' written by William Blake is about an unhappy school boy. The boy feels that by forcing him to go to school, his happiness and freedom are being taken away by his parents and teachers. He enjoys nature and explains that a young child in his prime of growth should be given the right amount of freedom to be able to grow up well.

Stanzawise Explanation

Stanza 1

I love to rise in a summer morn,
When the birds sing on every tree;
The distant huntsman winds his horn,
And the skylark sings with me.
O! what sweet company.

Explanation The poem begins with the speaker (a young school-going boy) explaining the things that he likes to do. He describes how he loves to wake up early in the morning during the summer season. During this time, birds sing on trees and he could hear the huntsman (hunter) blowing the horn from a far place. The speaker feels that when he sings, the skylark (a bird) sings along with him. He enjoys the sweet company of the skylark and the nature around him.

Stanza 2

But to go to school in a summer morn,
O! it drives all joy away;
Under a cruel eye outworn,
The little ones spend the day,
In sighing and dismay.

Explanation The speaker of the poem now says that he has to go to school in the summer mornings. He doesn't enjoy going to school and states that it takes away all the happiness he feels. In school, the young students spend their whole day under the strict control of the teachers. As a result, they feel bored and sad throughout the whole time.

This stanza makes it clear that the speaker loves to spend his time in nature. He wants to enjoy the joys and pleasure of the summer time in nature. However, he has to go to school and remain there for the whole day under the strict rules and regulations of the teacher. The phrase 'cruel eye outworn' is an important reference that depicts how the teachers at school keep their eyes on the students all day and restrict their freedom.

Stanza 3

Ah! then at times I drooping sit,
And spend many an anxious hour.
Nor in my book can I take delight,
Nor sit in learning's bower,
Worn thro' with the dreary shower.

Explanation This stanza presents how the speaker spends his day at school. The speaker conveys that he feels tired when he is at school. He has to unwillingly sit at one place in his class. While sitting in his seat, he hangs down his head as he is uninterested, bored and impatient. He cannot find any joy or interest in learning from his books. He finds learning while sitting in a shady place (classroom) to be unpleasant and continuous lectures given by the teachers to be dull.

In this stanza, the classroom is called a 'learning's bower' indicating that the school is a shady place that should bring pleasant experiences. However, for the boy it is a place of "dreary shower". The phrase 'dreary shower' refers to the lectures and education that are dull.

The lines reveal the speaker's impatience to free himself from the repetitive school life, get out of the walls of his classroom and experience the true beauty the summer has to offer. The stanza also reveals the schoolboy's dissatisfaction with the way schoolwork or education is done.

Stanza 4

How can the bird that is born for joy,
Sit in a cage and sing.
How can a child when fears annoy,
But droop his tender wing,
And forget his youthful speing.

Explanation In this stanza, the boy compares himself with a caged bird. According to him, a bird is a creature that is meant to be free to sing and fly as it wishes. It should not be confined in a cage. When birds are caged, their very nature to fly and be free is taken away from them.

Similarly, a young boy like him should be left free to explore and create. However, he is scared of his teachers and parents who have taken away his freedom (wings). As a result, he seems to be forgetting the youthful days of his growing stage.

It is to be noted here that the poet compares the boy to a caged bird as both are confined and have lost all the freedom that they should have. Further, these lines also point out that schools are often associated with punishments and fear. They stop the kids from being creative and imaginative. As a result, the boy lacks motivation and feels like his wings of freedom have been locked.

Stanza 5

O! Father and Mother, if buds are nip'd,
And blossoms blown away,
And if the tender plants are strip'd
Of their joy in the springing day,
By sorrow and cares dismay,

Explanation In this stanza, the speaker can be seen trying to make his parents see why it is pointless to go to school. He explains his unhappiness and disappointment by comparing himself to young plants and flowers. He tells his parents that if buds and young plants are destroyed at an early stage or if the flowers are blown away before it grows in the spring season, then there would be no joy in it. Similarly, just as he had begun to grow up, he is left in sadness and disappointment because of the meaningless education system which takes away his individuality and independence.

Stanza 6

How shall the summer arise in joy,
Or the summer fruits appear?

Explanation This stanza is a continuation of the previous stanza. The speaker continues telling his parents about his sorrow and disappointment. He asks his parents how could summer be enjoyable and how would the trees bear summer fruits, if the flowers are destroyed in the spring season. Likewise, how can a child grow into a talented, caring, creative and successful person if the very childhood is stolen away from them.

The poet seems to be implying that just like how natural elements need the right time and atmosphere to grow and flourish, a child requires the right amount of love, care, environment and freedom to become joyful and pleasant. However, it is not possible in the present education system and the intolerable pressure as well as expectations forced upon the kids by their parents.

Word Meaning

Word	Meaning
Stanza 1	
Morn	morning
Skylark	a small bird that sings while flying
Winds	to produce a sound by blowing into an instrument
Stanza 2	
Outworn	outdated
Sighing	a deep audible breathing sound indicating sadness
Dismay	disappointment
Stanza 3	
Drooping	to bend
Anxious	feeling worried or nervous

Word	Meaning
Delight	happiness or joy
Bower	pleasant shady area generally covered by trees
Dreary	boring, uninteresting
thro'	through
Stanza 4	
Tender	soft, sensitive
Stanza 5	
Nip'd	nipped, to stop or destroy it at an early stage of its development
Strip'd	taken away
Blossoms	flowers
Springing day	growing days

NCERT FOLDER | NCERT Exercise Questions

WORKING WITH THE POEM (NCERT PAGE 81-82)

Q.1 Find three or four words/phrases in stanza 1 that reflect the child's happiness and joy.

Ans. The words/phrases that reflect the child's happiness and joy are
- 'love to rise'
- 'birds sing'
- 'skylark sings'
- 'sweet company'

Q.2 In stanza 2, the mood changes. Which words/phrases reflect the changed mood?

Ans. The words/phrases that reflect the changed mood are
- "O! It drives all joy away."
- "Under a cruel eye outworn."
- "Sighing and dismay."

Q.3 'A cruel eye outworn' (stanza 2) refers to

(i) the classroom which is shabby/noisy.

(ii) the lessons which are difficult/uninteresting.

(iii) the dull/uninspiring life at school with lots of work and no play.

Mark the answer that you consider right.

Ans. (iii) the dull/uninspiring life at school with lots of work and no play.

Q.4 'Nor sit in learning's bower worn thro' with the dreary shower'

Which of the following is a close paraphrase of the lines above?

(i) Nor can I sit in a roofless classroom when it is raining.

(ii) Nor can I learn anything at school though teachers go on lecturing and explaining.

(iii) Nor can I sit in the school garden for fear of getting wet in the rain.

Ans. (ii) Nor can I learn anything at school though teachers go on lecturing and explaining.

Q.5 Read the following poem and compare it with 'The School Boy'.

The One Furrow
When I was young,
I went to school
With pencil and footrule
Sponge and slate,
And sat on a tall stool
At learning's gate.
When I was older, the gate sung wide;
Clever and keen-eyed
In I pressed,
But found in the mind's pride
No peace, no rest.
Then who was it taught me back to go
To cattle and barrow,
Field and plough:
To keep to the one furrow, As I do now?

RS Thomas

Ans. The two poems, 'The School Boy' by William Blake and 'The One Furrow' by RS Thomas are quite similar to each other in terms of invoking the nature to derive pleasure and joy. However, 'The School Boy' restricts itself entirely to the boy's school going phase. 'The One Furrow,' on the other hand, discusses the speaker's utter disillusionment with life at large. The boy in 'The School Boy' is bored of the dull and boring teaching methodology at school. The speaker of 'The One Furrow' finds peace missing from his life, perhaps because of the over-activity associated with city life.

REVIEW EXERCISE | Including Competency Based Questions

Multiple Choice Questions

1. Who is 'sweet company' for the boy?

(a) Skylark (b) Father (c) Teacher (d) Mother

Ans. (a) Skylark

2. What does the poet mainly talk about in the first stanza? Competency Based

(a) The sights on his way to school
(b) The things that he loves about morning
(c) The desire to befriend the birds in his garden
(d) The things that makes staying at home enjoyable

Ans. (b) The things that he loves about morning

3. How does the poet's tone change from the first stanza to the second stanza? Competency Based

(a) Happy to miserable (b) Peaceful to anxious
(c) Excited to frightened (d) Respectful to irreverent

Ans. (a) Happy to miserable

4. Under a cruel eye outworn
What does the line above indicate? Competency Based

(a) The poet is tired after studying hard.
(b) The poet spends all day in school crying.
(c) The poet tries hard to stay awake during lessons.
(d) The poet feels that teachers don't allow students freedom.

Ans. (d) The poet feels that teachers don't allow students freedom.

5. What is the main idea of the third stanza? Competency Based

(a) The poet's inability to read
(b) The poet's fear of teachers
(c) The poet's restlessness in school
(d) The poet's dislike for rainy weather

Ans. (c) The poet's restlessness in school

6. What does the poet do in the fourth stanza? Competency Based

(a) Compares two dissimilar things
(b) Says one thing but means another
(c) Uses an interesting sound to convey pain
(d) Uses sarcasm to add drama to the situation

Ans. (a) Compares two dissimilar things

7. What is the main idea of the fourth stanza? Competency Based

(a) The beauty of a caged bird's song
(b) The gentleness of a new-born bird
(c) The loss of children's freedom in schools
(d) How fear suppresses the talent of students

Ans. (c) The loss of children's freedom in schools

8. Which word best describes the poet's tone in the fifth stanza? Competency Based

(a) Fierce (b) Pleading
(c) Defeated (d) Complaining

Ans. (b) Pleading

9. What does the poet mainly do in the 6th stanza?

(a) Complaining
(b) Questioning
(c) Getting angry
(d) Giving up

Ans. (b) Questioning

10. What is the main purpose of the poem? Competency Based

(a) To inspire readers to cherish their school days
(b) To reflect on the poet's fondest childhood memories
(c) To highlight how schooling deprives the joy of childhood
(d) To describe the ways in which children try to escape school

Ans. (c) To highlight how schooling deprives the joy of childhood

11. Read the statements carefully and choose the correct answer from the following options.

Statement 1 The boy only fears being scolded by his teachers.

Statement 2 The boy sits throughout the class in sorrow and annoyance.

(a) Statement 1 is true but Statement 2 is false.
(b) Statement 1 is false but Statement 2 is true.
(c) Both Statements are true.
(d) Both Statements are false.

Ans. (b) Statement 1 is false but Statement 2 is true.

Extract Based Questions

1. Read the extract given below and answer the following questions.

But to go to school in a summer morn,
O! it drives all joy away;
Under a cruel eye outworn,
The little ones spend the day,
In sighing and dismay.

(i) Whose plight is the boy describing?

Ans. The boy is describing the plight of the school boys.

(ii) Choose a phrase from the extract that indicates the 'plight' of the child.

Ans. The little ones spend the day in sighing and dismay.

(iii) What is the meaning of the phrase 'in sighing and dismay'?

Ans. The phrase 'in sighing and dismay' expresses sadness and discomfort.

(iv) What kills the joy for the boy?

Ans. Going to school kills all joy for the boy.

(v) Find the word from the extract which has the opposite meaning of 'satisfy'.

Ans. Dismay

2. Read the extract given below and answer the following questions.

O! Father and Mother, if buds are nip'd,
And blossoms blown away,
And if the tender plants are strip'd
Of their joy in the springing day,
By sorrow and cares dismay,
How shall the summer arise in joy,
Or the summer fruits appear?

(i) Who are these lines addresse to?

(a) Parents
(b) School boys
(c) School teachers
(d) School principal

Ans. (a) Parents

(ii) Which of the following is the antonym of the word 'Tender'?

(a) Soft (b) Slender
(c) Tough (d) Fast

Ans. (c) Tough

(iii) What are the two seasons that the boy refers to?

(a) Spring and summer
(b) Summer and winter
(c) Spring and autumn
(d) Autumn and summer

Ans. (a) Spring and summer

(iv) What is the rhyme scheme of the first four lines of the extract?

(a) abab (b) aabb (c) abba (d) abac

Ans. (a) abab

(v) 'And blossoms blown away'
What is the poetic device used in this line?

(a) Repetition (b) Simile
(c) Metaphor (d) Alliteration

Ans. (d) Alliteration

Very Short Answer Type Questions

1. Why is the speaker of the poem unhappy?

Ans. The speaker of the poem, a little boy, is unhappy because he doesn't like going to school.

2. What is the boy fond of doing?

Ans. The boy is fond of waking up in a summer morning and hearing the birds sing. He also likes singing with the skylark.

3. How does the boy spend his day at school?

Ans. The boy spends his day drooping. He does nothing but sighs in distress and disappointment.

4. Whom does the boy try to explain his situation to?

Ans. The boy tries to explain his situation to his mother and father.

5. What are children compared to in the fifth stanza? Competency Based

Ans. In the fifth stanza, children are compared to birds.

Short Answer Type Questions

1. What does the poet intend to convey through this poem?

Ans. The poet intends to convey the message of how a child should not be burdened with heavy school responsibilities and should be allowed to enjoy nature and his freedom.

The poet expresses that young children spend their days 'sighing in dismay' when they are at school.

2. Do, you think the boy is imaginative?

Ans. Yes, the boy is imaginative. He compares himself with caged birds, buds and plants. He relates the mentioned things with himself to present how their freedom and innocence is lost when their natural capabilities are destroyed in their early stages.

3. Which lines clearly show the poet's lack of interest in classroom activities? Competency Based

Ans. The lines 'Nor in my book can I take delight, Nor sit in learning's bower, Worn thro' with the dreary shower' clearly show the poet's lack of interest in classroom activities.

Long Answer Type Questions

1. A child's growth is restricted and the joy of childhood is taken away by formal schooling. Justify the statement in context with the poem 'The School Boy'.

Ans. It is true to say that a child's growth is restricted and the joy of childhood is taken away by formal schooling. According to the poet, childhood is the time when a child should enjoy his best days in life. However, the child is forced to sit in a confined classroom. The school boy's joy is driven away the moment he thinks of school. He fears the annoyance of his teachers and so, he spends his whole time at school in disappointment and sorrow. He does not derive any delight from his books nor does he get any happiness out of school.

The poet compares the school going boy to a caged bird. He wonders how can a bird that is born to fly live in a cage. Similarly, how will a child grow and develop properly when their innocence and independence is taken away. Thus, a child's growth to perfection depends largely on the joyful environment the child grows in and not under the restrictions of formal schooling.

ASSESSMENT EXERCISE

Multiple Choice Questions

1. The boy loves to rise in a summer morn when
   (a) he has to sit in the classroom and listen
   (b) he has to do his homework
   (c) he has to go to school
   (d) the birds sing on every tree
2. The boy can't take delight in
   (a) watching birds sing on every tree
   (b) his book at school
   (c) the skylark singing with him
   (d) being absent from school
3. Read the statements and choose the correct answer from the following options.

   Statement 1 The boy compares himself with a bird because it can fly anywhere without any restriction.

   Statement 2 The boy was very angry at his parents.
   (a) Statement 1 is true but Statement 2 is false.
   (b) Statement 1 is false but Statement 2 is true.
   (c) Both the Statements are true.
   (d) Both the Statements are false.
4. The boy feels afraid when his teachers are
   (a) angry (b) annoyed (c) screaming (d) teaching
5. What drives the boy's joy away?
   (a) The singing of birds (b) Skylark singing with him
   (c) Going to school (d) Rising in a summer morning

Extract Based Question

Read the extract given below and answer the following questions.

How can the bird that is born for joy,
Sit in a cage and sing.
How can a child when fears annoy,
But droop his tender wing,
And forget his youthful spring.

(i) Whom does the child fear?
(ii) Why might the child forget the youthful spring?
(iii) Who does the boy compare himself with?
(iv) Who is the speaker of these lines?
   (a) The school boy
   (b) The poet
   (c) The mother
   (d) The school teacher
(v) The meaning of droop is ....
   (a) tired
   (b) shocked
   (c) annoyed
   (d) disgusted

Very Short Answer Type Questions

1. What makes the boy unhappy?
2. Why does the boy compare himself to a bird?
3. Why does the boy think that skylarks were singing with him?
4. What does the phrase 'droop his tender wing' mean?
5. Where doesn't the boy take delight in?

Short Answer Type Questions

1. Why does the boy compare himself to objects that wither?
2. Was the boy unhappy with the school teachers?
3. What does the boy compare himself with?

Long Answer Type Questions

1. Discuss the title of the poem 'The School Boy'.
2. The poet criticises the present system of education in the poem. Do you agree? Justify.

On the Grasshopper and Cricket

by John Keats

Introduction 'On the Grasshopper and Cricket' is a fourteen-line poem (also called a sonnet), written by John Keats. The poem emphasises on how nature keeps itself alive season after season with the help of the grasshopper and cricket. The poetry (sound) of Earth never stops to exist even during the extremely hot summer and the chilling cold winter.

Stanzawise Explanation

Stanza 1

The poetry of earth is never dead:
When all the birds are faint with the hot sun,
and hide in cooling trees, a voice will run
From hedge to hedge about the new-mown mead,
That is the grasshopper's–he takes the lead
In summer luxury–he has never done
With his delights, for when tired out with fun
He rests at ease beneath some pleasant weed.

Explanation The poem begins with the poet saying that the poetry of earth is always alive. The sound of earth exists all round the year making it wonderful and graceful forever. During summer, when the birds feel drained and take cover under the shady parts of trees, a voice could be heard from the ground. This voice that runs from hedge to hedge (corner to corner) and around the newly cut grasslands (meadows) belongs to the Grasshopper. The Grasshopper takes the lead in the nature's song and keeps its beauty alive. Summer season is a luxury for the grasshopper as he becomes joyous and cheerful during this time. When he gets tired of singing, he takes rest under some pleasant weed (grass).

In this stanza, the poet tries to convey the importance of how the voice of the grasshopper travels far and wide to keep the spirit of nature alive. He sings tirelessly so that he could provide ease and comfort to anyone that is burdened by the hot Sun. In the environment, various elements are available to tackle heat during summer, such as 'cooling trees' and 'pleasant weed' which refer to the shades provided by trees and the beautiful grass.

Stanza 2

The poetry of earth is ceasing never:
On a lone winter evening when the frost
Has wrought a silence, from the stone there shrills
The cricket's song, in warmth increasing ever,
And seems to one in drowsiness half lost;
The grasshopper's among some grassy hills.

Explanation In this stanza, the poet repeats that the poetry of earth doesn't come to an end even during the winter season. In winter evenings, the cold weather brings complete silence. It is a time of inactivity: trees look barren, birds have migrated, and people stay inside their homes. In such silence, a loud and sharp voice of a cricket singing could be heard from the stone. The songs sung by the cricket makes one feel warm throughout the winter. Sometimes, a person who is half- asleep would assume that a grasshopper is singing somewhere in the grassy hills. However, it is the cricket's song.

The last line of the poem seems to imply that when people hear the songs sung by the cricket in winter, they are reminded of the grasshopper's songs during summer. This gives them the feeling of warmth of the summer in winter.

From this stanza, it can be concluded that the poetry of earth never comes to an end whatever season it may be. Just as the grasshopper provides easiness and comfort during the summer, the cricket provides warmth during winter. Hence, nature is kept alive by the merry-making and singing every season.

Word Meaning

Word	Meaning
Stanza 1	
Faint	weak or dizzy
Hedge	border
New mown mead	newly cut grassland
Weed	wild plant/grass
Stanza 2	
Lone	alone/single
Frost	thin layer of ice/snow
Ceasing	stopping
Wrought	brought about
Shrills	comes through loud and clear
Drowsiness	sleepiness

NCERT FOLDER

NCERT Exercise Questions

Part – I

WORKING WITH THE POEM

(NCERT PAGE 114)

1. Discuss with your partner the following definition of a poem. A poem is made of words arranged in a beautiful order. These words, when read aloud with feeling, have a music and meaning of their own.

Ans. It is true that a poem is made of words arranged in a beautiful order. The words create music and produce a certain rhythm because of various poetic elements such as rhythm, rhyme and meter.

2. 'The poetry of earth' is not made of words. What is it made of, as suggested in the poem?

Ans. The poetry of the earth is made of various sounds that change with each season.

3. Find in the poem lines that match the following.

(i) The grasshopper's happiness never comes to an end.

Ans. "He has never done with his delights."

(ii) The cricket's song has a warmth that never decreases.

Ans. "The cricket's song, in warmth increasing ever."

4. Which word in stanza 2 is opposite in meaning to 'the frost'?

Ans. 'Warmth'

5. The poetry of earth continues round the year through a cycle of two seasons.
Mention each with its representative voice.

Ans. The two seasons that seem to create a continuous natural cycle are summer and winter. The grasshopper's song is a representative voice of the summer and the cricket's song is a representative voice of the winter.

REVIEW EXERCISE

Including Competency Based Questions

Part – I

Multiple Choice Questions

1. The poetry of earth is never dead
What is the poet trying to convey in the line above? Competency Based

(a) There is always something to do on earth.
(b) There is always movement on earth.
(c) There is always sound on earth.
(d) The earth is always beautiful.

Anrs. (d) The earth is always beautiful.

2. Why do the birds hide? Competency Based

(a) It's too hot. (b) It's too quiet.
(c) They are sick. (d) They are scared.

Anrs. (a) It's too hot.

3. According to the poet, the grasshopper finds the summer . Competency Based

(a) Tiring (b) Peaceful (c) Beautiful (d) Enjoyable

Ans. (d) Enjoyable

4. The grasshopper rests .... some pleasant weed when he is ....

(a) beneath, tired out with fun
(b) under, tired
(c) at, singing happily
(d) at, tired

Ans. (a) beneath, tired out with fun

5. "The frost has wrought a silence"
Which poetic device is used in the above line?

(a) Personification (b) Simile
(c) Rhythm (d) Anaphora

Ans. (a) Personification

6. Read the statements carefully and choose the right answer from the following options.

Statement 1 The grasshopper always feels joyous and cheerful.
Statement 2 People sometimes mix up the cricket's song with that of the grasshopper.

(a) Statement 1 is true but Statement 2 is false.
(b) Statement 1 is false but Statement 2 is true.
(c) Both the Statements are true.
(d) Both the Statements are false.

Anrs. (c) Both the Statements are true.

7. From where does the cricket sing? Diksha

(a) Under the stones (b) From the trees
(c) From grassy hills (d) From mountains

Ans. (a) Under the stones

8. Why does the poet compare the cricket and the grasshopper? Competency Based

(a) Their noise disturbs people.
(b) They make noises that sound similar.
(c) They make noise in the same season.
(d) They make noise when other animals are quiet.

Ans. (d) They make noise when other animals are quiet.

9. What is the poet mainly trying to do in the poem? Competency Based

(a) Highlight how nature is symmetrical
(b) Convey his appreciation of the earth
(c) Suggest that the earth is never silent
(d) Convince people to listen to the sounds of nature

Ans. (c) Suggest that the earth is never silent

10. What is the tone of the poem? Competency Based

(a) Admiring (b) Nostalgic
(c) Passionate (d) Appreciative

Ans. (d) Appreciative

Extract Based Questions

1. Read the extract given below and answer the following questions.

The poetry of earth is never dead
When all the birds are faint with the hot sun,
And hide in cooling trees, a voice will run
From hedge to hedge about the new-mown mead,

(i) What does the word 'cooling' mean in this extract?

Ans. Comforting

(ii) What does the poet mean by 'the poetry of earth'?

Ans. By the phrase, 'the poetry of earth', the poet means the sounds that are abundantly found in nature.

(iii) Where will the voice run?

Ans. The voice will run from hedge-to-hedge about the newly cut grasslands.

(iv) What is the rhyme scheme of the given lines of the extract?

Ans. The rhyme scheme of the given lines of the extract is abbc.

(v) The grasshopper's song is representative of which season?

Ans. The grasshopper's song is representative of the summer.

2. Read the extract given below and answer the following questions.

On a lone winter evening when the frost
Has wrought a silence, from the
stone there shrills
The cricket's song, in warmth increasing ever,
And seems to one in drowsiness half lost;
The grasshopper's among some grassy hills.

(i) Whose voice is heard from the stones?

(a) The grasshopper (b) The cricket
(c) The poet (d) The nature

Ans. (b) The cricket

(ii) Which element of nature has been personified in these lines?

(a) Winter (b) Frost
(c) Silence (d) Wrought

Ans. (b) Frost

(iii) Why do some people confuse the singing of the cricket with that of the grasshopper's song?

(a) The people are in half-asleep state.
(b) They don't know the difference between the two sounds.
(c) Both sounds are coming from the same direction.
(d) The cricket is imitating the grasshopper.

Ans. (a) The people are in half-asleep state.

(iv) 'from the stone there shrills'
What is the poetic device used in the above line?

(a) Alliteration (b) Anaphora
(c) Personification (d) Simile

Ans. (a) Alliteration

(v) Which of the following is a homonym of the word 'wrought'?

(a) Worth (b) Rot (c) Rode (d) What

Ans. (b) Rot

Part – II

Very Short Answer Type Questions

1. What happens to birds during summer?

Ans. The birds become faint and quiet under the hot Sun during summer.

2. Where do the birds hide to avoid the heat of the Sun?

Ans. The birds hide themselves under the shade of the trees in order to protect themselves from the heat of the sun.

3. Which words or phrases suggest a sense of relief from the heat of summer in stanza 1?

Ans. 'Cooling trees' and 'pleasant weeds' offer a sense of relief from the heat of summer in stanza 1.

4. And hide in cooling trees, a voice will run
Whose voice is the poet talking about? **Competency Based**

Ans. In the given line, the poet is talking about the voice of the grasshopper.

5. What does the grasshopper do when he has finished his fun? **Competency Based**

Ans. When the grasshopper has finished his fun and he is tired, he rests at ease beneath some pleasant weed.

6. Who are half lost in drowsiness and why?

Ans. During winter, people get half lost in drowsiness because the weather is extremely cold.

7. What happens during winter?

Ans. The frost casts complete silence over all aspects of nature during winter.

8. Who thinks the cricket sounds like the grasshopper? **Competency Based**

Ans. The people who are half lost in drowsiness think that the cricket sounds like the grasshopper.

9. How many creatures have been discussed in the poem 'On the Grasshopper and Cricket'? Who are they? **Diksha**

Ans. Three creatures have been discussed in the poem 'On the Grasshopper and Cricket'. They are the birds, grasshopper and cricket.

Short Answer Type Questions

1. Discuss the common features between the grasshopper and the cricket?

Ans. Both the grasshopper and the cricket are the representative voices of nature's sound or poetry. They offer a soothing effect from the unpleasant feeling caused by the extreme weather.

The grasshopper's song balances the extreme heat during the summer by providing music that is comforting and pleasing. The cricket does the same during winter by providing warmth.

2. Why does the poet believe that the poetry of earth is never dead?

Ans. The poet believes that poetry of nature is never ending or never ceasing because it continues to offer its service all year round, irrespective of change in seasons, change in day and night and so on. There are so many pleasant sounds in nature that provide relief to people from the harsh climate conditions.

3. Why does the poet repeat a similar line at the beginning of both stanzas? Competency Based

Ans. The poet repeats a similar line at the beginning of both stanzas to show that nature always remains beautiful and thriving regardless of whether it is summer or winter. The grasshopper sings in the summer and the cricket in the winter when all other animals are silent. Hence, the sound of nature never comes to an end.

Long Answer Type Questions

1. Describe the summer season in context with the poem 'On the Grasshopper and Cricket'.

Ans. According to the poem, the poetry or the sounds of earth is alive in the summer season. As the weather is hot during the summer days, the birds that usually produce the sounds in nature are all hidden in the shades of the tree to seek comfort. They feel faint and remain quiet.

The grasshopper takes delight in summer and he takes the lead to keep the sounds of nature alive throughout the summer. He sings with such a voice that the song can be heard from one corner to another. The grasshopper is always cheerful and also spreads the happiness all around. When he gets tired, he rests under beautiful grass. Then, he starts singing again and enjoying the various pleasures that the nature offers.

ASSESSMENT EXERCISE

Multiple Choice Questions

1. The birds were drained out due to the ....
(a) grasshopper (b) new-mown mead
(c) heat (d) continuous singing

2. The cricket's song brings
(a) warmth (b) noise
(c) rain (d) frustration

3. Read the statements carefully and choose the correct answer from the following options.
Statement 1 The cricket feels that summer is a luxury for it.
Statement 2 The cricket broke the silence and provides sound to nature.
(a) Statement 1 is true but Statement 2 is false.
(b) Statement 1 is false but Statement 2 is true.
(c) Both the Statements are true.
(d) Both the Statements are false.

4. "The cricket's song, in warmth increasing ever"
What is the poetic device used in the above line?
(a) Alliteration (b) Metaphor
(c) Simile (d) Personification

5. "A voice will run from hedge to hedge"
What does this line indicate about the grasshopper?
(a) Grasshopper has a powerful voice.
(b) Grasshopper runs from one corner to the other.
(c) Grasshopper has such a voice that it reaches far and wide.
(d) Grasshopper likes to run around while singing his songs.

Extract Based Question

Read the extract given below and answer the following questions.

...He takes the lead In summer luxury—he has never done
With his delights, for when tired out with fun
He rests at ease beneath some pleasant weed."

(i) Explain the meaning of the phrase, 'summer luxury.'
(ii) Indicate a line which means that 'he' is very happy.
(iii) Who takes the lead?
(a) The poet
(b) The grasshopper
(c) The cricket
(d) The frost
(iv) Where does the one who takes the lead rest?
(a) Behind the stones
(b) Beneath some pleasant weeds
(c) In summer luxury
(d) Under the cooling trees
(v) Which of the following is an antonym of the word 'luxury'?
(a) Necessity (b) Plenty
(c) Required (d) Unnecessary

Very Short Answer Type Questions

1. When does the grasshopper sing?
2. How does the cricket's song sound?
3. How are the people spending their time when the cricket sings?

Short Answer Type Questions

1. What is the theme of the poem?
2. Are the grasshopper and the cricket characters in the poem?
3. Discuss the significance of poetry or music as discussed in this poem.

Long Answer Type Question

1. The poetry of Earth is never dead.
Justify the statement with reference to the poem 'On the Grasshopper and Cricket?

How the Camel got his Hump

by Rudyard Kipling

The story 'How the Camel got his Hump' by Rudyard Kipling is an imaginative tale describing the reason behind the Camel's Hump. Through the tale, the author presents the importance of doing one's own work to not burden others with extra work.

Part – I

The Lazy Camel and the other Animals

In the beginning when the world was new, Animals had just started working for Man. There was a Camel that lived in the middle of the Howling Desert because he didn't want to work. He only ate sticks, thorns, and prickles. When anyone tried to talk to him, he would only say 'Humph!'.

On the Monday morning, the horse with a saddle on his back came to the Camel and asked him to work like all other animals. The Camel only said 'Humph!'. So, the Horse went away and told the Man. The Dog came to him with a stick in his mouth and asked the Camel to play fetch and carry like them. Again, the Camel only said 'Humph!'. So, the Dog went away and told the Man. Then, the Ox asked the Camel to plough like them. The same procedure was repeated. The Camel only replied with 'Humph!' and the Ox went back and told the Man.

The Man Makes them Work Double-time

At the end of the day, the Man called the Horse, Dog and Ox together. He told them that since the Camel can't work, they would have to work harder to compensate for it. This made the three animals angry and they called a panchayat at the edge of the Desert. The Camel came chewing food, laughed at them, said 'Humph!', and went away again. Then, the Djinn who was in charge of all Desert came there rolling in a cloud of dust.

The Djinn Meets the Animals

The Horse asked the Djinn if it was right for anyone to be lazy. He replied that it wasn't right. Then, the Horse told him about the animal with long neck and legs, who lived in the desert and hadn't done any work since Monday morning. The Djinn said that it was his Camel. The Ox told the Djinn that the Camel only replies with 'Humph!' and wouldn't plough. The Djinn assured them that he will solve the problem.

Part – II

The Djinn talks to the Camel

The Djinn rolled himself in his dust cloak and went to meet the Camel. When he found the Camel, it was looking at his own reflection in the water. He asked the Camel why he wouldn't work, but the Camel didn't answer. The Djinn told him that the other three animals had to do extra work because of his laziness. The Camel said 'Humph!'. The Djinn, then, warned him to not say that word again and told him to get to work. But the Camel once again said 'Humph!'.

The Camel Grows a Hump

As soon as the Camel said 'Humph!', his back puffed into a big hump. The beautiful back that he was proud of had swollen to form a humph. The Djinn told him that it was the result of his own laziness since he hadn't worked since Monday and it was already Thursday. The Camel asked how he could work with the big Humph on his back. The Djinn told him that the Humph served a purpose. Since he missed three days of work, he will now be able to work for three days without eating. Then, the Djinn told him to go out of the desert and get to work.

So the Camel joined the other animals in work but he hasn't been able to catch up for the three days of work that he missed. He still has the Humph on his back, which is now called a 'hump' to spare the Camel's feelings. But he still hasn't learned how to behave.

Word Meaning

Word	Meaning
Djinn	a spirit that has strange powers and can assume any form, human or animal
Prickle	thorn
Saddle	leather seat
Trot	work
Fetch	to get something
Yoke	piece of wood attached to the neck of animals
Plough	turn up the soil of an area

Word	Meaning
Edge	the outside boundary of an area
Chewing cud	food for chewing
Idle	lazy
Stroke of work	any work
Whew	an expressive sound of relief
I'll humph him	I'll set him right/deal with him
Puffing up	out of breath

NCERT FOLDER

NCERT Intext and Exercise Questions

COMPREHENSION CHECK❶ (NCERT PAGE 3)

Q.1 What tasks, do you think, were assigned to the dog and the ox?

Ans. The dog was assigned the task to fetch and carry things. The ox, on the other hand, was asked to carry the yoke on his back and plough the fields.

Q.2 Why did the camel live in the middle of the desert?

Ans. The camel lived in the middle of the desert because he did not wish to do any work. He merely ate sticks, thorns and prickles to survive.

Q.3 What made the dog, the horse and the ox very angry?

Ans. The dog, the horse and the ox were very angry with the camel because the man had asked the three animals to do the camel's share of work alongwith their own. This meant double work for the three of them.

Q.4 How did the Djinn know the horse was complaining against the camel?

Ans. The Djinn knew that the horse was talking about the camel because of the following description given by the horse–'long neck and long legs'. The Djinn was also in charge of all deserts and was therefore, familiar with all animals.

CHECK❷ (NCERT PAGE 5)

Q.1 The camel was looking at his own reflection in the pool. What does it suggest to you about the camel?

Ans. The camel was looking at his image in the pool because he loved how he looked. It suggests that the camel only cared about himself.

Q.2 The camel said, 'Humph' repeatedly. How did it affect him?

Ans. The camel said 'humph!' repeatedly whenever someone talked to him. Even the Djinn warned him not to say the word again, but the camel didn't listen. When he said 'Humph!' again, his beautiful back puffed up into a big hump.

Q.3 What, according to the Djinn, was the use of the 'humph'?

Ans. According to the Djinn, because of his hump, the camel could work continuously for 2-3 days. The hump on the camel's back was a storehouse of food and water.

Q.4 **"...he has never yet learnt to behave". In the light of this, what is the writer's opinion about the camel?**

Ans. According to the writer, the camel has never learnt to behave because he is still an arrogant and non-cooperative animal.

EXERCISE (NCERT PAGE 5)

Discuss the following topics in groups.

Q.1 **Can this story be factually true?**

Ans. No. This story cannot be factually true. This story is a fable. It has animal characters to convey a moral lesson.

Q.2 **What, according to you, is the story about? Consider the following**

(i) How the world began?

(ii) Why everyone should do his/her share of work seriously?

(iii) How animals are important to humans?

(iv) How the camel got his hump?

Ans. As the title of the story suggests, the story is about how the camel got his hump.

In doing so, it does not tell us how the world began. However, it does tell us that everyone of us should do our share of work to not burden others with extra work. It also tells us that animals are important to humans as they share the humans' workload. Through the story of how the camel was given a hump, we also learn not to be lazy and arrogant like the camel. Otherwise, we will all suffer in one way or another just like the camel who got his hump as a punishment for his laziness.

Q.3 **What did you do over the weekend? Were you generally active or idle? Please check your back before starting to discuss or answer the question.**

Ans. Do it yourself.

Q.4 **There are broadly two categories of workers- those who prefer to do today what they can do tomorrow and those who prefer to do tomorrow what they can do today. Where do you belong?**

Ans. It is better to do today what you can do tomorrow because time flies away quickly. I belong to the first category of workers who prefer to do today what they can do tomorrow.

REVIEW EXERCISE

Including Competency Based Questions

Part – I

Multiple Choice Questions

1. **Fable is a fictional story that features animals, legendary creatures, plants or inanimate objects to lead a particular moral lesson.**

   Parable is a short story that teaches a lesson, specially one told by Jesus in the bible.

   The story 'How the camel got his hump' is a .... Diksha

   (a) rhyme (b) fable
   (c) parable (d) None

Ans. (b) fable

2. **What did the camel eat?**

   (a) Sticks
   (b) Thorns
   (c) Prickels
   (d) All of the above

Ans. (d) All of the above

3. **What problem does the camel create for others?** Diksha

   (a) They were scolded by the Djinn.
   (b) They had to do work double time.
   (c) They could not get anything to eat.
   (d) They had to leave the forest.

Ans. (b) They had to do work double time.

4. **What was the purpose of the panchayat?**

   (a) To plan an attack against the man
   (b) To plan an attack against the Djinn
   (c) To plan a mass bunk from work
   (d) To decide how to make the camel work

Ans. (d) To decide how to make the camel work

5. **What did the camel do in the panchayat meeting?**

   (a) Apologised to everyone
   (b) Began working double-time
   (c) Began insulting the three animals
   (d) Laughed at the three animals and went away

Ans. (d) Laughed at the three animals and went away

6. **How did the horse complain against the camel without naming him?**
   (a) He drew a picture of the camel
   (b) The Djinn could know this through his magic
   (c) He described his features such as long legs and long neck
   (d) He made a video of the camel

Ans. (c) He described his features such as long legs and long neck

7. **Why was the camel punished?**
   (a) Because he was rude
   (b) Because he was lazy and grew fat
   (c) He says 'Humph!' too many times to the Djinn, so he makes a hump magically appear
   (d) Because he insulted the Djinn

Ans. (c) He says 'Humph!' too many times to the Djinn, so he makes a hump magically appear

8. **"But that Humph-thing in the Desert can't work, or he would have been here by now, so I am going to leave him alone". What is the 'humph thing' here?** DIKSHA
   (a) A Pile of Corn (b) The camel
   (c) The Djinn (d) The ox

Ans. (b) The camel

9. **"But no sooner he had said it, than he saw his back that he was so proud of, puffing up and puffing up into a great big hump."**

   What is the meaning of the word 'puffing up' in this sentence based on the context clues? DIKSHA
   (a) Growing bigger (b) Getting harder
   (c) Ripening (d) Blooming

Ans. (a) Growing bigger

10. **"How can I," said the camel, "with this humph on my back?" "That has a purpose," said the Djinn, "all because you missed those three days." What was the purpose according to the Djinn?** DIKSHA
    (a) The hump is the mark of laziness that all can see.
    (b) The camel can live off the hump for three days.
    (c) The hump allows people to sit safely upon the camel's back.
    (d) The camel carries the hump to show that he belongs to the Djinn.

Ans. (b) The camel can live off the hump for three days.

11. **What characteristic can be given to the camel based on the story?**
    (a) Energetic (b) Productive
    (c) Laziness (d) Efficient

Ans. (c) Laziness

12. **Read the given statements and choose the correct answer.**

    Statement 1 The Djinn was angry at the camel.

    Statement 2 Camel is now known for its laziness.
    (a) Statement 1 is true but Statement 2 is false
    (b) Statement 2 is true but Statement 1 is false
    (c) Both the Statements are true
    (d) Both the Statements are false

Ans. (c) Both the statements are true

Extract Based Questions

1. **Read the given extract carefully and answer the questions.**

   In the beginning, when the world was new and the Animals were just beginning to work for Man, there was a camel, and he lived in the middle of a Howling Desert because he did not want to work. He ate sticks and thorns and prickles, and when anybody spoke to him he said 'Humph!'

   Just 'Humph!' and no more. Presently the Horse came to him on Monday morning, with a saddle on his back and said, "camel, O camel, come out and trot like the rest of us."

   'Humph!' said the camel, and the Horse went away and told the Man.

   (i) **When did the animals start working for man?**

   Ans. The animals started working for man in the beginning when the world was new.

   (ii) **Did the camel live in the desert because he loved being in the Sun?**

   Ans. No, the camel didn't live in the desert because he loved being in the Sun. He lived in the desert because he didn't want to work.

   (iii) **What did the horse say when he went to meet the camel on the Monday morning?**

   Ans. The horse went to meet the camel on Monday morning and asked him to come out and trot like him.

   (iv) **Which word from the given passage means 'a loud, painful sound'?**

   Ans. Howling

   (v) **Which word from the given passage is the antonym of 'crawl'?**

   Ans. Trot

2. Read the given extract carefully and answer the questions.

At the end of the day the Man called the Horse and the dog and the ox together, and said, "Three, O Three, I'm very sorry for you; but that Humph-thing in the Desert can't work, or he would have been here by now, so I am going to leave him alone, and you must work double-time to make up for it."

That made the Three very angry, and they held a panchayat on the edge of the Desert; and the camel came chewing cud and laughed at them. Then he said 'Humph!'and went away again.

(i) Why was the man sorry for the three animals?

Ans. The man was sorry for the three animals because they would have to work double-time in order to make up for the laziness of the camel.

(ii) What did the man call the camel?

Ans. The man called the camel 'that humph thing in the desert'.

(iii) What did the three animals do when they became angry?

Ans. The three animals called a panchayat when they became angry.

(iv) Which phrase from the passage means 'working your fingers to the bone'?

Ans. The phrase 'work double-time' means 'working your fingers to the bone'.

(v) Which word from the given passage means 'a large dry area, with very little rain and plants'?

Ans. The word 'desert' means 'a large dry area, with very little rain and plants'.

3. Read the given extract carefully and answer the questions.

Presently there came along the Djinn who was in charge of All Deserts, rolling in a cloud of dust. Djinn of All Deserts," said the Horse, "is it right for anyone to be idle?"

"Certainly not," said the Djinn.

"Well," said the Horse, "there's a thing in the middle of your Desert with a long neck and long legs, and he hasn't done a stroke of work since Monday morning. He won't trot."

"Whew!" said the Djinn whistling, "that's my camel. What does he say about it?"

"He says 'Humph!', and he won't plough," said the ox.

"Very good," said the Djinn. "I'll humph him if you will kindly wait a minute."

(i) What was the Djinn in charge of?

(a) All lakes (b) All deserts
(c) All jungles (d) All camels

Ans. (b) All deserts

(ii) What did the horse say about the legs of the camel?

(a) They were weird (b) They were long
(c) They were short (d) They were stumpy

Ans. (b) They were long

(iii) According to the horse, since when had the camel been idling?

(a) Since last night
(b) Since the beginning of time
(c) Since he got a promotion
(d) Since Monday morning

Ans. (d) Since Monday morning

(iv) Which word is the synonym of 'idle'?

(a) Active (b) Useless
(c) Employed (d) Diligent

Ans. (b) Useless

(v) Which word from the given passage means 'to turn up soil from an area of land before sowing'?

(a) Idle (b) Desert
(c) Whistle (d) Plough

Ans. (d) Plough

4. Read the given extract carefully and answer the questions.

And the camel said 'Humph!' again; but no sooner had he said it than he saw his back, that he was so proud of, puffing up and puffing up into a great big hump.

"Do you see that?" said the Djinn. "That's your very own humph that you've brought upon your very own self by not working. Today is Thursday, and you've done no work since Monday, when the work began. Now you are going to work."

"How can I," said the camel, "with this humph on my back?"

"That has a purpose," said the Djinn, "all because you missed those three days. You will be able to work now for three days without eating, because you can live on your humph; and don't you ever say I never did anything for you. Come out of the Desert and go to the Three, and behave."

(i) **What was the camel proud of?**

(a) His back (b) His eyes (c) His hump (d) His hair

Ans. (a) His back

(ii) **What did the hump carry?**

(a) Seven days of water (b) Three days of food
(c) Three days of snacks (d) Seven days of oxygen

Ans. (b) Three days of food

(iii) **What did the Djinn do to the camel?**

(a) The Djinn exciled the camel from desert.
(b) The Djinn gave the camel a reward.
(c) The Djinn gave the camel a hump.
(d) The Djinn punished the camel.

Ans. (c) The Djinn gave the camel a hump.

(iv) **Which word is the antonym of 'proud'?**

(a) Glad
(b) Dignified
(c) The camel gave the Djinn a hump
(d) Undignified

Ans. (d) Undignified

(v) **The hump of the camel was the ...... of his own actions.**

(a) consequence
(b) inconsequence
(c) subsequence
(d) sequence

Ans. (a) consequence

Part – II

Very Short Answer Type Questions

1. What was the task assigned to the horse?

Ans. The task assigned to the horse was to carry goods or the man from one place to another. That is why he had a saddle on his back.

2. What work did man assign to the horse, the dog and the ox at the end of the day?

Ans. At the end of the day, the man told the three animals to do double-work to compensate for the work loss on account of the camel.

3. What question did the horse ask the Djinn?

Ans. The horse asked the Djinn if it was 'right for anyone to be idle.'

4. Since how many days had the camel done no work?

Ans. The camel had done no work since three days. It was Monday when the horse came to call the camel. Till Thursday, when the Djinn met the camel, the camel had been idle.

5. Does the camel realise his mistake by the end of the story?

Ans. No, the camel does not realise his mistake because he had not learned to behave well till the end of the story.

Short Answer Type Questions

1. What were the different tasks assigned to the three animals?

Ans. The horse was assigned the task to carry goods and even the man from one place to another. The dog was assigned the task of fetching things. The task of ploughing the fields was assigned to the ox.

2. Why didn't the man go to call the camel for work?

Ans. The man does not go to call the camel for work because he believed that if the camel would have been capable of work, it would have come for work on its own. It had been three days and the camel had not shown up even once for work.

3. Did the Djinn look at the camel's hump as a punishment for not working?

Ans. Yes, the Djinn looks at the camel's hump as a punishment for not working. During his conversation with the camel, the Djinn tries to explain that he had brought the hump on himself by choosing not to do his share of work.

4. What did the Djinn mean by "I'll humph him"?

Ans. When the Djinn said that he'll 'humph' the camel, he meant that he will set the camel straight by scolding him. Since the Djinn was in charge of the entire desert, it was his duty to punish the camel.

5. Do you think it is good to impose our share of work on the others?

Ans. No. It is not good to impose our share of work on others. Everyone should do his/her share of work. We should not exploit others by making them do the work that we are meant to do.

Working collectively and with sincerity also increases the efficiency of doing work.

6. Compare and contrast the character of the camel vis-a-vis the other animals? Diksha

Ans. The actions of the camel show that he is a solitary creature who is extremely lazy, even to the point of eating sticks and prickles just so he wouldn't have to work. He is also a vain creature because he spends his time looking at his own reflection in the water. On the other hand, the other animals are hardworking and united. They have team spirit and even call the panchayat to discuss situations.

Long Answer Type Questions

1. Imagine you are the camel. Write a diary entry describing his feelings on being reprimanded by the Djinn.

Ans. 5th November, 20XX 9:00 pm

Dear diary,

I am very disturbed by what has happened in the desert today. As if those three were not enough, namely the horse, the dog and the ox; today the Djinn too came to scold me.

I do not feel like doing any work, then why should I be compelled to work. These daily reminders make me feel worse. I am fond of lazing around and admiring my beauty that I can see in the pool water.

The Djinn has punished me with a hump on my beautiful back. Now, I cannot bear to look at myself in the water. The Djinn said that it'll help me work continuously for three days but I don't want to work!

The Camel

2. How do we get to know which task was assigned to which animal?

Ans. We can figure out which task was provided to which animal based on the clues provided in the chapter. When the horse came to meet the camel, he had a saddle on his back and he asked the camel to trot like the other animals. This means that the horse was being used for travelling from one place to another.

The dog came to meet the camel with a stick in his mouth. The dog asked the camel to fetch things like all other animals. This indicates that the dog was assigned the task of fetching and carrying things.

The ox, likewise, came with a yoke on his neck, asking the camel to plough like the other animals; indicating that the task assigned to him was ploughing the fields.

3. 'Hard work is very important in life'. Justify this statement based on the chapter.

Ans. It is true that hard work is very important in life. It makes our character and personality pleasant. Without hard work, no one can ever succeed in life. The importance of hard work and doing one's own task is especially pointed out in the story 'How the Camel got his Hump'.

All animals, the horse, the dog and the ox, respectively had been doing their work sincerely, except for the camel. As a result, the camel is disliked by all the other animals.

The Djinn also feels the need to scold the camel. Towards the end of the story, we learn that the camel had got his hump because he had refused to do his share of work. The Djinn sees the camel's hump as a punishment for him. Hence, hard work is very important.

4. "I am who I am today because of the choices I made yesterday". Justify this statement based on the camel from the story.

Ans. The given statement fits the camel perfectly. This statement depicts why the camel received a punishment as well as came to be known as lazy and bad mannered. While all the other three animals worked diligently every day, the camel preferred to laze about and look at himself in the water. Even though the other animals came to persuade him to work, he didn't listen to them. He didn't even listen to the words of the Djinn who was in charge of all the deserts. Because of this attitude, he made all the other animals his enemy. He also got punished with a hump on his back.

Nowadays, the camel is known as the animal with a hump on his back. The way it is recognised today is directly related to his actions in the past. Therefore, it is true that the camel is who he is today because of the choices he made yesterday.

ASSESSMENT EXERCISE

Multiple Choice Questions

1. The three animals wanted the camel to ....

(a) dance (b) sleep
(c) work (d) sing

2. It is right for anyone to be idle?

(a) Yes (b) No
(c) Sometimes (d) On special occasions

3. The Djinn .... the camel by giving him a hump.

(a) mocks (b) punishes
(c) degrades (d) angers

4. Read the given statements and choose the correct answer.

Statement 1 The camel didn't want to work.

Statement 2 The Djinn gave the camel silky hair.

(a) Statement 1 is true, but Statement 2 is false.
(b) Statement 1 is false, but Statement 2 is true.
(c) Both the Statements are true.
(d) Both the Statements are false.

5. Select the odd one out.

(a) Dog (b) Djinn
(c) Camel (d) Horse

Extract Based Question

Read the given extract and answer the following questions.

The Djinn rolled himself up in his dust-cloak, and took a walk across the Desert, and found the camel looking at his own reflection in a pool of water.

"My friend," said the Djinn, "what's this I hear of your doing no work?"

The Djinn sat down, with his chin in his hand, while the camel looked at his own reflection in the pool of water.

"You've given the Three extra work ever since Monday morning, all on account of your idleness," said the Djinn. And he went on thinking with his chin in his hand.

(i) What was the Djinn's cloak made of?

(ii) What was the camel doing when the Djinn found him?

(iii) How did the Djinn address the camel?

(iv) What is the meaning of the word 'cloak'?

(a) Headband (b) Bracelet
(c) Skirt (d) Coat

(iv) "You've given the Three extra work ever since Monday morning, all on account of your....."

(a) haste (b) perfection
(c) idleness (d) efficiency

Very Short Answer Type Questions

1. Choose from the list below the objects that belong to the dog, Saddle, hump, yoke, stick.

2. What was the camel's reply to all the animals that came to call him?

3. Why did the man apologise to the other three animals?

4. Why do you think the other animals went to the Djinn to complain about the house?

5. Why did the Djinn warn the camel before punishing him?

Short Answer Type Questions

1. Why was the camel conscious of his image?

2. Why were the horse, the ox and the dog angry with the camel?

3. What was the purpose of the panchayat?

4. Why did the man give double work to the three animals?

5. Why did the animals believe that the Djinn would solve their problem?

Long Answer Type Questions

1. Explain the moral of the story.

2. Write a paragraph describing how did the camel get a humph.

3. How did the camel's punishment turn out to be a reward?

4. "He who struggles is better than he who never attempts." Justify this statement with the context of the chapter.

Children at Work

by Gita Wolf, Anushka Ravishankar, Orijit Sen

CHAPTER 2

CHAPTER SUMMARY The story 'Children at Work' is an excerpt from 'Trash – On Ragpicker Children and Recycling' written by Gita Wolf, Anushka Ravishankar and Orijit Sen. The story is divided into three parts and revolves around a 11 year old boy named Velu who had run away from his village. He hopes to live a better life in the city but is turned into a ragpicker. By showing Velu's emotions and thoughts through his experiences, the story presents a realistic depiction of the underprivileged and poor children.

Part – I

Velu at Chennai Central Station

Velu got off the Kanyakumari Express at Chennai Central station. He was standing on the platform as a porter screamed at him to get out of the way. Feeling scared of so many people around him, Velu sat down on a bench. He had only seen so many people at a village fair before. People bumped into him with their suitcases and an announcement was made on a loudspeaker. Some people were sitting on the platform and looking at the TV. Hence, Velu found the station to be very noisy.

Journey to Chennai

Velu put his head on his knees as he was feeling very tired and sad. He had run away from his village two days ago and hadn't eaten anything except jaggery and some peanuts. He only had a shirt, a towel, and a comb which he kept in a bundle. The first day after running from home, he had walked the entire day to Kanur. From there, he got on a train to Chennai without a ticket because he had no money. He was lucky that the ticket collector hadn't come to check the unreserved compartment. He had tried to sleep near the door, but a group of men playing cards had kept shouting.

Velu Meets a Strange Girl

Velu was sitting on the platform when a rough voice asked if he was new to town. Velu looked around to find a girl his age wearing a long banian. She had stiff, brownish hair and carried a huge sack on her shoulder. She was picking up dirty plastic cups and putting them in her sack. Velu was surprised and did not answer the girl. So, she asked his name, to which Velu replied. Then, she asked if he ran away from home.

Velu didn't want to tell a stranger that he ran away from home because his father would take away all the money that he and his sisters earned to drink and beat him. When Velu did not reply, the girl told him that there were many children like him who came to the city to get rich. Then, she sat with him while Velu held his stomach which was aching due to hunger. She noticed that he was hungry and told him that he wouldn't find food by sitting there and looking sad. Then, she offered to find some food for him and walked away. After a little hesitation, Velu followed her.

Part – II

Velu Followed the Strange Girl

Velu followed the girl out of the station and across the busy road where the vehicles never stopped for anyone. The dust and smoke from the vehicles confused Velu and he was slow to walk. So, the girl made him cross the road. When they had crossed the road safely, Velu was scolded by the girl who asked why he was moving slowly. She told him to move quickly to avoid being killed. Velu was shocked as he couldn't understand how they had crossed the road.

Talking to the Strange Girl

Velu and the strange girl were walking along the side of the road under many signboards. Velu couldn't read the signboards because they were written in English.

Velu followed the girl across a bridge and she showed him the Central Jail. She cautioned him to not get caught otherwise he'll be put into the jail. Velu was confused because he did not know why he would be jailed when he hadn't done anything wrong. Then, he asked her what she carried in the sack and she told him that it was things like bottles or papers. He wanted to ask some more questions but felt shy. So, they kept walking barefoot for over an hour in hot Sun over a tar road that burned his feet.

The Girl Helped Velu Find Food

Velu and the strange girl walked for more than an hour. They arrived at a wedding function in a huge building which had a sign saying 'Sri Rajarajeshwari Prasanna Kalyana Mandapam'. The girl pulled away one rose from a decorated car and put it in her hair. Velu thought that they would eat in the wedding but the girl took him behind the hall where the garbage bin was. She found a crushed banana and a vada for him to eat.

When Velu refused to eat, she scolded him by saying that neither of them had any money to buy food. So, he must eat what she had found for them. Velu ate the banana and a vada but he was still very hungry. The girl could find only one more banana which she ate. She, then, told him to wait for lunch if he wanted to eat some more and walked away again.

The Strange Girl's Name

The strange girl told Velu that she had work and had to leave. Velu panicked and followed her as he did not know where he was and what he should do. He called her and asked her name. The girl laughed and told him that her name was Jaya. Velu then asked if he could go with her. The girl told him she was going home to get another bag because this one was full.

Jaya's Home

Velu followed Jaya for half an hour before they came across a bridge. There, she told him that they were at Triplicane and pointed to the Buckingham Canal. As Velu looked around, he spotted rows of the strangest huts he had ever seen. They were made of metal sheets, plastic, bricks, tyres, etc. and they looked as if they could fall at any moment. Velu told Jaya that the houses in his village were made of mud and palm leaves. Jaya kept on moving to one hut where she put down her full sack and picked up an empty one.

Jaya and Velu Go to Work

After taking an empty sack, Jaya asked Velu to help her. She gave Velu a pair of old shoes without laces along with a stick and a sack which confused Velu. He had only worked at farms, weeding and grazing cows. So, he asked Jaya if there were any farms in the city. Jaya laughed and told him that there were no farms or farmers in the city. She added that they were ragpickers. She explained that they collected things like paper, plastic, and glass from the garbage bins and sold it to Jaggu of Jam Bazaar who sold it to a factory.

Velu felt even more confused as he thought that rubbish was to be thrown and not bought. Velu thought that he hadn't run from his home to dig through garbage bins when Jaya screamed at him to hurry otherwise they wouldn't get anything. Velu decided to become a ragpicker until he could find a better job.

Word Meaning

Word	Meaning
Livelihood	a means of securing the necessities of life
Pulled in	direct oneself towards something
Get off	to leave a place, here
Wobbly	moving unsteadily from side to side
Porter	a person who carries luggage
Bumping	colliding
Miserable	very unhappy
Exhausted	very tired
Unreserved	general (used about seats in train etc.)
Stiff	not easily bent or changed in shape
Sack	a bag
Snatch	quickly seizing something in a rude way
Pinching	squeeze someone's skin
Grimace	an expression indicating pain
Glumly	gloomily
Make his head spin	make him confused
Hesitating	be uncertain
Dragged	to forcefully take someone
Grazing	eat grass growing in a field
Chutney	crushed (as per context)
Peeped	peek
Rubbish	waste material

Word	Meaning
Squinted	look sideways
Grinned	smiled
Blasted down	to be in full intensity
Buzzed	murmuring sound
Squashy	not having stiffness
Distaste	mild dislike
Stomach squeezed him	indication of hunger
Gulped	ate
Stick to her	stay with her
Trickle	drip
Puddles	small pool of water
Crookedly	not straight
Dumped	kept
Shove	push
Weeding	working in a field, removing grass
Thumped	punch
Ragpickers	a person who collects or sells rags
Blockhead	fool
Poked	thrust abruptly
Posing	looking important
Sighed	exhale noisily

NCERT FOLDER

NCERT Intext and Exercise Questions

COMPREHENSION CHECK❶ (NCERT PAGE 9)

Q.1 Velu stood on the platform but he felt 'as if he was still on a moving train'. Why?

Ans. Velu felt that he was 'still on a moving train' because his legs were shaking. He was tired and exhausted because of the journey. This was so because Velu had not eaten anything except some peanuts and jaggery. Further, he had walked the entire day.

Q.2 What made him feel miserable?

Ans. Velu felt miserable because he had run away from his home. He was hungry, tired and scared to be all alone in the noisy big city that had so many people bumping into him and shouting at him.

Q.3 (i) Velu travelled without a ticket. Why?

Ans. Velu travelled without a ticket because he had no money to buy one.

(ii) How did he escape the ticket collector's attention?

Ans. He escaped the ticket collector's attention because the ticket collector didn't come to the unreserved coach.

Q.4 Why had Velu run away from home?

Ans. Velu ran away from home because his father was a drunkard and Velu was tired of the beating that he received from his father. He could also not keep any money that he earned, because it was snatched away by his father.

Q.5 Why did he decide to follow the 'strange' girl?

Ans. Velu decided to follow the strange girl because he neither knew where to go nor did he know what to do in the city. He thought it was better to follow the girl who seemed friendly and knew about the city.

CHECK❷ (NCERT PAGE 13)

Q.1 Can Velu read Tamil and English? How do you know?

Ans. Velu could read Tamil, but not English. We know this because he manages to read the banner, Central Jail, which was written in Tamil. However, he could not read what was written on the signboards as the writing was all in English.

Q.2 "If you are not careful, you will soon be counting bars there." the girl said.

(i) What is she referring to?

Ans. She was referring to the Central Jail.

(ii) What does she mean when she says "If you are not careful..." (She says something a little later which means the same. Find that sentence.)

Ans. The girl tries to tell Velu that the police can catch or arrest him even if he hasn't done anything wrong.

The sentence, "You don't have to do anything. Just don't get caught" means the same thing.

Q.3 (i) Where did the girl lead Velu to?

Ans. The girl leads Velu to a wedding hall, which had a sign that read - Sri Rajrajeshwari Prasanna Kalyan Mandapam.

(ii) What did they get to eat?

Ans. They got to eat leftover food like bananas and vadas from the garbage bin placed behind the marriage hall.

Q.4 What work did she do? Think of a one word answer.

Ans. Ragpicking

CHECK❸ (NCERT PAGE 15)

Q.1 (i) What material are the 'strange' huts made out of?

Ans. The strange hunts were made out of metal sheets, tyres, bricks, wood and plastic.

(ii) Why does Velu find them strange?

Ans. Velu finds them strange because they were very different from the houses in his village. In Velu's village, the houses were made of mud and palm leaves.

Q.2 What sort of things did Jaya and children like her collect and what did they do with those things?

Ans. Jaya and children like her collect paper, empty bottles, plastic and glass. They sold all such stuff to Jam Bazaar Jaggu, who later sold these to a factory.

Q.3 Is Velu happy or unhappy to find work? Give a reason for your answer.

Ans. Velu was not happy to work as a ragpicker, but he had no choice till he could find a better job.

EXERCISE (NCERT PAGE 16)

Discuss the following questions in small groups. Write their answers afterwards.

Q.1 Is Velu a smart boy? Which instances in the text show that he is or isn't?

Ans. No, Velu was not a smart boy. There are several instances in the text that depict this

(i) He had run away from home without any money. He knew nothing about the place he had travelled to.

(ii) Further, he expected to find work in a farm, not knowing that there were no farms in the city. He also chooses to follow Jaya without knowing anything about her.

Q.2 Do you think Jaya is a brave and sensitive child with a sense of humour? Find instances of her courage, kind nature and humour in the text.

Ans. Yes, Jaya is a brave and sensitive child with a good sense of humour. She is a brave girl as she supports herself in this big and cruel world. She was sensitive towards the plight of Velu and tries to help him.

She guides Velu, helps him find food and also assists him in finding work. Her sense of humour emerges at various points.

The way she shows Velu the Central Jail, gives tips on not being caught, gets Velu to eat food and calls the trickling water Buckingham Canal, displays her brilliant sense of humour.

Q.3 What one throws away as waste may be valuable to others. Do you find this sentence meaningful in the context of this story? How?

Ans. Yes. For people who cannot afford proper food, leftover and thrown away food is important for survival. The rich people waste a lot of food, but this food supports Velu, Jaya and the other children like them.

Jaya is a ragpicker and as a ragpicker she collects trash which is of no use to many people. Velu, himself, fails to understand the worth of collecting rubbish, something that is very important to Jaya, Jam Bazaar Jaggu and other ragpickers.

REVIEW EXERCISE

Including Competency Based Questions

Part – I

Multiple Choice Questions

1. Velu's legs felt wobbly because .... Diksha

(a) Velu was tired
(b) he felt he was still on a moving train
(c) he carried heavy luggage
(d) he travelled without ticket

Ans. (b) he felt he was still on a moving train

2. What was the group of people doing?

(a) Sitting on the platform
(b) Shouting at other
(c) Watching TV
(d) Both (a) and (c)

Ans. (d) Both (a) and (c)

3. Velu had walked most of the first day to ....

(a) Chennai (b) Thiruvananthapuram
(c) Kanur (d) Mysore

Ans. (c) Kanur

4. Read the given statements and choose the correct answer.

Statement 1 Velu saw many people when he was sitting on the bench on the platform.

Statement 2 A man was announcing something on the loudspeaker.

(a) Statement 1 is true but Statement 2 is false
(b) Statement 2 is true but Statement 1 is false
(c) Both the Statements are true
(d) Both the Statements are false

Ans. (a) Statement 1 is true but Statement 2 is false

5. Velu had slept near .... in the train to chennai.

(a) the seats (b) the door (c) the toilets (d) can't say

Ans. (b) the door

6. The girl asked Velu if he had run away from home because .... Diksha

(a) he looked exhausted
(b) he was watching the people around
(c) he was alone and confused
(d) he travelled in an unreserved compartment

Ans. (c) he was alone and confused

7. Velu decided to follow the girl as .... Diksha

(a) he had no money
(b) he was new to Chennai
(c) he did not know anyone there
(d) All of the above

Ans. (d) All of the above

8. Jaya told Velu if 'he was grazing cows' because .... Diksha

(a) he was standing in the middle of the road
(b) he had not seen a city before
(c) he was busy watching vehicles on the road
(d) he was missing his fields in the village

Ans. (a) he was standing in the middle of the road

9. Jaya says to Velu, "You'll be counting bars there if ....". Diksha

(a) Velu does not help her
(b) Velu goes back home
(c) Velu can't read Tamil
(d) Velu isn't careful

Ans. (d) Velu isn't careful

10. Jam Bazaar Jaggu .... Diksha

(a) sold old bottles
(b) employed children
(c) sold and bought rubbish
(d) collected and burnt rubbish

Ans. (c) sold and bought rubbish

11. Jaya gave Velu .... to wear.

(a) a cap (b) a shirt
(c) a pair of shoes (d) a trouser

Ans. (c) a pair of shoes

12. Arrange the following events in ascending order as given in the story.

(i) Jaya took a rose from a decorated car.
(ii) Velu sat on the bench at the station.
(iii) Jaya gave Velu a vada to eat.
(iv) Jaya took Velu to her home.

(a) (i) (ii) (iii) (iv) (b) (ii) (i) (iii) (iv)
(c) (iv) (i) (iii) (ii) (d) (iii) (ii) (iv) (i)

Ans. (b) (ii) (i) (iii) (iv)

Extract Based Questions

1. Read the given extract and answer the questions carefully.

WHEN the Kanyakumari Express pulled in at Chennai Central, it took Velu some time to get off. When he finally stood on the platform, his legs felt wobbly, as if he was still on a moving train. "Oy, out of the way!" A porter went by with a loaded trolley. Velu jumped aside.

He sat on a bench on the platform, putting his small bundle down. In all his eleven years, he had never seen so many people, except once a year at the fair in his village. People walked by, bumping into him with their suitcases. A voice announced something on a loudspeaker.

Near him a group of people sat on their luggage, looking at a TV hanging from the roof. The noise was terrible.

Velu put his head down on his knees, feeling miserable and exhausted. He had run away from his village two days ago. For two days he had eaten nothing but some peanuts and a piece of jaggery. In his bundle he carried a shirt, a towel and a comb.

(i) Why did Velu take time in getting off the Kanyakumari Express?

Ans. Velu took time in getting off the Kanyakumari Express because he was weak and tired.

(ii) When could Velu see so many people as he saw on the platform?

Ans. Velu could see so many people as he saw on the platform at a fair in his village.

(iii) How old was Velu?

Ans. Velu was eleven years old.

(iv) Complete the sentence appropriately.

For two days he had eaten ....

Ans. some peanuts and a piece of jaggery

(v) Which word from the given passage is the antonym of 'energetic'?

Ans. The word 'exhausted' is the antonym of 'energetic'.

2. Read the given extract and answer the questions carefully.

He had walked for most of the first day to Kanur and then got on the train to Chennai. Velu had no money for a ticket but luckily the ticket collector didn't come to the unreserved compartment. He had tried to sleep on the floor near the door. A group of men next to him had played cards and shouted all night.

"Aiy! What, new to town eh?" called out a rough voice.

Velu opened his eyes. There were a lot of people standing around, but nobody was looking at him.

"Here! Aiy!" He turned around. Behind him was a girl around his own age, wearing a long banian that came down to her knees. Her hair was stiff and brownish and she had a huge sack on one shoulder.

She was picking up dirty plastic cups from the floor and stuffing them into her sack. Why is she calling me, thought Velu. And why is a girl wearing a banian?

"No need to stare stupidly. What's your name?"

"Velu," muttered Velu, looking away.

"So Mr Velu," said the girl, looking at his bundle. "Run away from home?"

(i) What is the name of the place from which Velu caught the train for Chennai? How did he reach there?

Ans. Velu caught the train to Chennai from Kanur. He reached Kanur by walking for almost a day.

(ii) Why did Velu resort to sleeping on the floor near the door of the train?

Ans. Velu had to sleep on the floor near the door of the train because he did not have a ticket and therefore, he did not have a seat.

(iii) What did the strange girl ask Velu when she saw him?

Ans. When the strange girl saw Velu, she asked him if he was new to the town.

(iv) State true or false.

"Velu got a good night's sleep on the train to Chennai".

Ans. False. Velu did not get a good sleep on the train to Chennai because of the shouting of the men playing cards.

(v) From the given passage, find a homonym for the word 'stair'.

Ans. The homonym of 'stair' is 'stare'.

3. Read the given extract and answer the questions carefully.

He caught up with the girl as she was leaving the station. When they got to the road, Velu found that the vehicles kept coming and never stopped for anyone. Smoke and dust flew at him from all sides, making his head spin. They had to wait for a long time before they could find a gap to run through. Velu kept hesitating and the girl finally dragged him to the other side.

"What do you think you're doing? Grazing cows? If you stand around in the middle of the road like that, you'll be chutney."

Velu's heart was still beating fast. He looked back at Central Station and the traffic speeding by. How had they managed to come through that? They walked along the side of the road under some huge signboards. Velu looked up at the pictures: banians, car tyres, pens, a woman holding a box. The writing was all in English, so he didn't know what it meant.

(i) Why did Velu have trouble crossing the road?

(a) Because the vehicles never stopped coming.
(b) Because his legs were wobbly.
(c) Because his head was spinning.
(d) Because there was dust in his eyes.

Ans. (a) Because the vehicles never stopped coming.

(ii) "What do you think you're doing? Grazing cows?" What does 'grazing cows' mean in this context?

(a) Taking cows out to graze.
(b) Shaving the cows growing hair.
(c) Moving at a very slow pace.
(d) Moving at a very fast pace.

Ans. (c) Moving at a very slow pace.

(iii) Why does Jaya tell Velu that he will become chutney?

(a) Because the vehicles will flatten him.
(b) Because Jaya wanted to eat chutney.
(c) Because Velu loved eating chutney.
(d) Because Velu had brought chutney from home.

Ans. (a) Because the vehicles will flatten him.

(iv) What language could Velu not read?

(a) Tamil
(b) Malyali
(c) Telegu
(d) English

Ans. (d) English

(v) Which of the following words is not a synonym of 'dragged'?

(a) Pulled (b) Hauled
(c) Tugged (d) Pushed

Ans. (d) Pushed

4. Read the given extract and answer the questions carefully.

Velu stared. This was a canal? Near some puddles of water was a row of the strangest huts he had ever seen. They were built out of all sorts of things – metal sheets, tyres, bricks, wood and plastic. They stood crookedly and looked as if they would fall any moment.

"Is this where you live? These houses are strange!" said Velu. "In our village, the houses are made of mud and palm leaves."

Jaya went around to one of the huts and dumped her sack outside. Then she picked up an empty one.

"Let's go."

She turned to Velu and gave him a shove. "At least help me now. Here, wear these and come with me."

She threw him a pair of old shoes without laces and pushed a sack and a stick into his hands. Velu was confused. What work did she want him to do with these things? The only work he had ever done was on the landowner's farm, weeding and taking cows out to graze.

"Are there any farms in the city?" he asked Jaya.

(i) What were the strange huts made of?

(a) Metal sheets (b) Tyres
(c) Plastic (d) All of these

Ans. (d) All of these

(ii) What did Jaya do at the hut?

(a) Dumped her full sack (b) Picked up an empty sack
(c) Both of these (d) None of these

Ans. (c) Both of these

(iii) What did Jaya give to Velu?

(a) Old shoes without laces
(b) Stick
(c) Sack
(d) All of the above

Ans. (d) All of the above

(iv) Which of the following words means 'distorted'?

(a) Puddle (b) Strange (c) Crooked (d) Lace

Ans. (c) Crooked

(v) Which of the following words is an antonym of 'clear'?

(a) Structured (b) Confused
(c) Neat (d) Methodical

Ans. (b) Confused

Part – II

Very Short Answer Type Questions

1. Which station did the Kanyakumari Express stop at? Diksha

Ans. The Kanyakumari Express stopped at Chennai Central Station.

2. What were the contents of the bundle that Velu carried with him?

Ans. In his bundle, Velu had brought with him a shirt, a towel and a comb.

3. Why does Velu get surprised on seeing Jaya?

Ans. Velu gets surprised on seeing Jaya because she was a complete stranger. Velu could not understand why she could be calling him.

4. What was Jaya's first act of help for Velu?

Ans. After offering to find food for Velu, Jaya helps Velu in crossing the road.

5. What does Velu make out of the signboards?

Ans. Velu didn't know how to read English. Therefore, he could not understand anything that was written on the signboards. He only saw the pictures of banians, car tyres, pens and a woman holding a box.

6. What catches Velu's attention as he reaches the wedding hall?

Ans. Velu's attention got caught by the big cars parked outside the wedding hall. The car that was decorated with roses and garlands of flowers attracted Velu's attention the most.

7. Who was Jam Bazaar Jaggu?

Ans. Jam Bazaar Jaggu was the person to whom Jaya and the children like her used to sell the rubbish they used to collect. Jaggu used to sell it further to factories.

8. Why was Velu shocked upon seeing the food given to him by Jaya?

Ans. Velu was shocked upon seeing the food given to him by Jaya because it was taken from the garbage bins behind the marriage hall.

9. What is the theme of the story 'Children at Work'? Diksha

Ans. The theme of the story is the plight of poor children.

10. What are the reasons due to which children have to work? Diksha

Ans. Children have to work because they don't have parents or other adults to take care of them. Another reason is that their parents are irresponsible adults who waste time and money in drinking and beat their kids.

Short Answer Type Questions

1. Describe the difficulties faced by Velu while crossing the road.

Ans. Velu found that vehicles kept coming on the road and never stopped; making it impossible to cross. Smoke and dust confused him and there was hardly any gap to go to the other side of the road. So, he did not know how to cross the road.

2. What was similar between Velu and Jaya?

Ans. Both Jaya and Velu had nobody to depend on. They were all alone and had to look after themselves in the big city. Both Jaya and Velu had to work hard to survive in this world. Jaya is also able to understand that Velu had run away from home because perhaps she had done the same.

3. What warning does Jaya give to Velu?

Ans. Jaya warns Velu against getting caught by the police and being put into the jail. Jaya specially points out to the building of the Central Jail to advice Velu to be cautious as one need not have done anything wrong to be jailed.

4. Why do you think Velu chooses to do the work of ragpicking? Is it in any way linked to food?

Ans. Yes, Velu chooses to work as a ragpicker in order to support and sustain himself. The main need of the poor people is to somehow ensure food for themselves in order to survive.

Velu understood that getting food without doing any work was difficult. He, therefore, decides to temporarily work as a ragpicker till he finds a new job.

5. Was Velu content and satisfied after he got work? Elaborate on the basis of the chapter.

Ans. Velu was not content or satisfied after he got work because the work was that of a ragpicker. Velu felt disgusted at the thought of looking through garbage bins for things that are usually not useful but he knew that the job provided him a method of feeding himself. So, he accepted the work of a ragpicker temporarily.

6. What qualities can we learn from Jaya? Diksha

Ans. We can learn many qualities from Jaya. Even though she lives in a heartless world where she can depend on nobody, she herself helps Velu who is clueless about his new situation. Jaya is kind, strong, brave and active. She doesn't sit and cry over her fate, she gets up and does whatever it takes to make it through to the next day.

7. Why did Velu run away from home? Diksha

Ans. Velu ran away from home because of the horrible behaviour of his father. Velu's father was a drunkard who would regularly beat Velu and his sisters.

He would also snatch away all the money that Velu and his sisters earned.

Long Answer Type Questions

1. "Velu realised that if the girl left him, he had no idea where he was and what to do." Justify the statement in the context of the chapter.

Ans. It is true to say that Velu realised that if the girl left him, he had no idea where he was and what to do. Velu was new to Chennai. He had no idea about the life in the city as he belonged to a village. He was sad and dejected as he did not know what to do at the place. So, when the strange girl talked to him and helped him get the food. He realised that the girl knew about the place.

Although, Velu was hesitant in doing what the strange girl asked him to do, he knew that if the girl left him or if he leaves the girl, he would be left helpless. He realised that the girl could help him get a job so that he can survive in the strange city.

2. Describe the events of Velu's day when he left his home.

Ans. On the first day, Velu had to walk for most of the day from his village to Kanur before he got on the train for Chennai. Since, Velu had no money, he could not buy a ticket and had to travel without one. Fortunately for him, the ticket collector didn't come to his compartment. He had to sleep on the floor near the door, amidst the noise produced by a group of men who played cards.

The next day he was tired and weak from hunger. He was completely lost in the crowd and noise of the Chennai Central Station.

3. What does the food overflowing from the garbage bin indicate? Should one be more conscious of food wastage?

Ans. The food overflowing from garbage bin indicates wastage of food. It is not an uncommon sight to find that in rich people's weddings and social gatherings, a lot of food gets wasted. The untouched excess food and the leftover food are indiscriminately thrown into the garbage bin.

Yes, people could become more conscious and take only the amount of food that they can actually consume and avoid wastage. We should be very conscious of the wastage of food because it is a pity to see that poor children like Velu, Jaya and many others like them often have nothing to eat.

ASSESSMENT EXERCISE

Multiple Choice Questions

1. Jaya was a .... by profession.
(a) student (b) beggar
(c) cleaner (d) ragpicker

2. What did Velu's bundle have?
(a) Towel
(b) Shirt
(c) Comb
(d) All of the above

3. What was Velu's profession before reaching Chennai?
(a) Field worker (b) Student
(c) Ragpicker (d) Dancer

4. Which characteristic can be attached to Jaya?
(a) Independent (b) Timid
(c) Shy (d) Angry

5. Read the given statements and choose the correct answer.

Statement 1 Velu had run away from home.

Statement 2 Velu had a loving and caring father.

(a) Statement 1 is true, but Statement 2 is false.
(b) Statement 1 is false, but Statement 2 is true.
(c) Both the Statements are true.
(d) Both the Statements are false.

Extract Based Question

Read the given extract and answer the following questions.

She laughed and thumped her stick on the ground. "Farms! There are no farmers here. We are ragpickers."

"Ragpickers?"

"See my sack? Full of things I collected."

"Collected? From where?" asked Velu.

"From rubbish bins, where else?"

"You collect rubbish?" Velu had never heard of such a thing

"*Ayye*, blockhead. It's not any rubbish. Only paper, plastic, glass, such things. We sell it to Jam Bazaar Jaggu."

Velu was puzzled. He had heard of people throwing away rubbish. But why would anyone want to buy rubbish? "Who's Jam Bazaar Jaggu? Why's he buying all this?"

"You think he buys it for show? He sells it to a factory. Come on, I don't have time to waste, like you."

Velu did not move. He hadn't run away and come to this new place to dig through garbage bins. Jaya poked at him with her stick.

"Look here!" she shouted. "If someone gets there before us we don't get anything. Don't just stand there, posing. Big hero. I'm trying to help you. Who filled your stomach today?"

Velu scratched his head and sighed. I'll do it for now, he thought, until I find a better job.

(i) What did Jaya reply about her job when Velu asked about farmers?
(ii) What did Jaya collect? Where did she collect it from?
(iii) Who is Jam Bazaar Jaggu? What does he do?
(iv) Which of the following is not a synonym of 'rubbish'?
(a) Garbage (b) Trash
(c) Pearl (d) Junk
(v) What does Jaya address Velu as?
(a) Big hero (b) Blockhead
(c) Both of these (d) None of these

Very Short Answer Type Questions

1. Why does Jaya laugh at Velu when he asks her about the farms?

2. Why does Velu accept the job as a ragpicker?

3. What was the Buckingham Canal?

4. Why do Velu's feet get burnt?

5. Whom does Velu compare himself with on seeing Jaya offering him leftover food?

Short Answer Type Questions

1. Why does Velu panic when Jaya was leaving him, while going to find food for him?

2. Velu's difficulty with the English language would have proved an obstacle for living in the city. Why?

3. Describe the appearance of Jaya.

4. Before coming to Chennai, when had Velu seen so many people?

5. What was the significance of the big building to Jaya and Velu?

Long Answer Type Questions

1. How different is Velu from Jaya?

2. Make a list of differences between city and village life that we gather from our reading of the story.

3. Comment on the title of the story, 'Children at Work'.

4. Under which circumstances did Velu become a ragpicker?

The Selfish Giant

by Oscar Wilde

The story 'The Selfish Giant' written by Oscar Wilde is a simple tale which teaches us not to be selfish through the character of the giant.

Part – I

The Beautiful Garden

Every afternoon, the children used to go play in the Giant's garden. It was a very lovely and large garden with soft green grass and flowers that looked like stars. There were twelve peach trees that bore pink and pearl coloured flowers in the Spring and gave rich fruits in the Autumn. The birds would sing so beautifully that even the kids would stop playing to listen. They would often say how happy they were in the Giant's beautiful garden.

The Giant Comes Back Home

The Giant had gone away for seven years to meet his friend, the Cornish Ogre. When he came back home, he saw the children playing in the garden and rudely told them to go away. He said that he won't allow anyone to play in his garden as he was a selfish person. Then, he built a high wall around the garden and put up a notice board that said "Trespassers will be prosecuted". The children became sad because now they had nowhere to play. They did not like to play on the road as it was dusty and full of stones. So, they would move around at the high wall and talk about the beautiful garden and how happy they had been there.

The Giant's Garden doesn't Get Spring

In the Spring time, the entire country was filled with flowers and little birds. However, the Giant's garden was still in winter. The birds didn't sing because there were no children, and the trees forgot to blossom. One beautiful flower rose up. But when it saw the notice board, it was so sorry for the children that it went back into the ground. The only happy people in the garden were Snow and Frost. When they realised that spring had forgotten the garden, they decided to stay there for the entire year. Snow covered the grass in a white layer, and Frost painted the trees silver. They even invited the North Wind and the Hail to visit the garden. The North Wind blew down the chimneys and the Hail would knock against the roof and break all the slates. Dressed in grey with a breath like ice, the Hail would run round and round in the garden.

The Selfish Giant is Confused

The Giant would sit at his window and wonder why the Spring was so late. He would look at his garden and hope for a change in the weather. But Spring and Summer never came. Even Autumn refused to give his garden any flowers because she thought that the Giant was too selfish. So, the North Wind, Hail, Snow, and Frost covered the trees. One morning, the Giant heard a lovely music. It was so sweet that he believed the music must be played by the King's musicians passing by. A little linnet (bird) was singing outside his window. The Hail and North Wind had also stopped and as he smelled sweet perfume he believed that the Spring had finally arrived. Happily, he came out of his bed and looked outside.

Part – II

Spring in the Giant's Garden

When the Giant got out of bed to see the garden, he saw that children had crept into the garden through a small hole in the wall and were playing in the garden. A child was sitting in every tree of the garden. The trees had finally blossomed and were waving their arms gently, above the children's head. The birds were dancing and singing with delight and the flowers were laughing.

It was a beautiful scene, but one corner of the garden still had winter. A little boy was trying to climb up a tree but he could not reach up to the branches, so he cried bitterly. The scene melted the Giant's heart who realised how selfish he had been. He decided to help the little boy, then knock down the high wall and convert the garden into a playground for children forever.

The Giant Helps the Little Boy

The Giant went out in the garden to help the little boy but the children got scared and ran away. Winter came to the Giant's garden again. However, since the little boy was crying, he couldn't see the Giant coming. The Giant gently took the boy in his hands and put him up into the tree. Immediately, the tree blossomed and birds came to sing on it.

The little boy was so happy that he threw his arms around the Giant's neck and kissed him on the cheek. The other children saw that the Giant was no longer evil and ran back into the garden to play. The Giant took his axe and knocked down the high wall. When the people were going to the market, they saw that the Giant was playing with the children in the most beautiful garden.

In the evening when all the children said their goodbyes to the Giant, he asked about the little boy. The children told him that the boy had gone away.

The Giant Misses the Little Boy

Every afternoon, the children would play in the garden, but the little boy never came back. The other children didn't know where he lived so they couldn't tell him to come play either. The Giant missed him very much and wanted to meet him again. As time passed, the Giant grew old and too weak to play with the children. So, he would sit in his huge armchair and watch the kids as they played in his garden. He would say that the children are the most beautiful flowers. When winter arrived in his garden he didn't hate it anymore because he understood that the Spring was just sleeping.

The Giant Meets the Little Boy Again

One winter morning, the Giant woke to see that in the farthest corner of his garden, there was a beautiful tree covered in white flowers. Its branches were gold and the fruits were silver in colour. Under the tree, the little boy that the Giant loved was sitting. He ran out to meet him. When he reached the boy he became angry because the palms and feets of the little boy had prints of nails. He asked the boy who injured him so the Giant could take up his huge sword and kill them.

The Giant Goes to Paradise

To the Giant's query, the boy replied that the wounds were of love. The Giant sat in front of the boy and gently asked him who he was. The child smiled at him and told him that since the Giant had let him play in his garden, now he shall play in the garden of the little boy, which is paradise. That afternoon, the children discovered the Giant lying dead under the tree, covered in white flowers.

Word Meaning

Word	Meaning
Blossoms	flower
Bore	gave
Ogre	a cruel giant who eats people, a very frightening person
Gruff	rough, surly
Trespassers	those who enter somebody's land without his/her permission
Prosecuted	tried in a court of law; punished
Wander	travel without purpose
Cloak	cover
Frost	ice
Hail	frozen rain
Rattled	make short sharp knocking sounds
Linnet	a brownish songbird

Word	Meaning
Ceased	finish
Casement	window that opens on hinges like a door
Waving	movement of hand
Twittering	chirping
Crept	sneak
Wicked	evil
Knocked down	removed
Feeble	weak
Hastened	hurry
Dared	had the courage
Wound	injury
Nay	no
Who art thou?	who are you?

NCERT FOLDER

NCERT Intext and Exercise Questions

COMPREHENSION CHECK❶ (NCERT PAGE 20)

1. Why is the Giant called selfish?

Ans. The Giant is called selfish because he doesn't allow the children to play in his garden. He even built a huge wall around the garden to keep the children out.

2. On one occasion the children said "How happy we are here!" Later they said: "How happy we were there!"
What are they referring to in both the cases?

Ans. In both the cases, the children are referring to the Giant's beautiful garden, which was a perfect play ground for them. The first statement is made in happiness, when the children played in the garden freely.

The second statement is a sad longing of the children after they are prohibited from entering the garden by the Giant.

3. (i) When spring came, it was still winter in the garden. What does winter stand for or indicate here?

Ans. The winter, in the story, stands for lack of joy and activity. It stands for lack of music, colours and everything positive in contrast to the blossoms of the spring, the sound of birds singing and the perfumed fragrance of the flowers.

(ii) Winter has been presented like a story with its own characters and their activities. Describe the story in your own words.

Ans. Oscar Wilde presents winter as a separate story. It has various characters such as snow, frost, hail and North wind. These characters have their separate identities, motives and desires. They are clothed in different costumes and do different things such as snow covering the grass or frost painting the trees silver. All of them have a common goal-an eternal winter.

4. Was the Giant happy or sad over the state of the garden?

Ans. The Gaint was very sad over the state of his beautiful garden. He could not understand why the spring wasn't visiting his garden and why the garden was stuck in an eternal winter.

5. What effect did the linnet's song have over hail and the North wind?

Ans. The linnet's song made the rattling hail and the roaring wind stop. The song was so sweet that the Giant believed it to be played by the king's musicians passing by.

CHECK❷ (NCERT PAGE 24)

1. (i) The Giant saw a most wonderful sight. What did he see?

Ans. The Giant saw his lifeless garden regain its beauty. He saw children sitting on the branches of every tree and the trees were laid with fruit and blossoms. He could smell the perfumed fragrance of the flowers and hear the birds singing.

(ii) What did he realise on seeing it?

Ans. He realised his mistake of being selfish. He realised that the real beauty was to be found in the laughter of children.

2. Why was it still winter in one corner of the garden?

Ans. There was still winter in one corner of the garden because a little boy was unable to climb the tree.

3. Describe the first meeting of the little boy and the Giant.

Ans. The first meeting between the little boy and the Giant takes place when the Giant had realised his mistake. The Giant picked up the little boy in his arms and helped him to climb the tree. The boy was surprised at the Giant's act of kindness and hugged and kissed him, in return.

4. Describe their second meeting after a long interval.

Ans. The second meeting between the Giant and the boy takes place many years later when the Giant had grown old. The Giant ran with joy to meet the little boy, when he saw him. The little boy smiled at the Giant.

Despite it being winter, the Giant saw white flower blossoms at the place where the boy stood.

The boy informed the Giant that he had come to take the Giant with him, to his garden, the Paradise.

5. The Giant lay dead, all covered with white blossoms. What does this sentence indicate about the once selfish Giant?

Ans. This sentence indicates that the Giant had been blessed with Christ's love and mercy. White flowers are indicative of peace and compassion, something that the Giant had learnt from the children in his garden.

EXERCISE (NCERT PAGE 24)

Discuss the following topics in groups.

1. The little child's hands and feet had marks of nails. Who does the child remind you of ? Give a reason for your answer.

Ans. The little child reminds us of Jesus Christ who was crucified on a cross, nailed on his hands and feet, the impressions of which the child had on his hands and feet.

2. Is there something like this garden near where you live? Would you like one (without the Giant perhaps) and why? What would you do to keep it in good shape?

Ans. Yes, I have a beautiful garden in front of my house. It has many colourful flowers and swings to play on. The garden is loved by all the people who stay there. The elders use it for exercise and the children use it to play. To maintain it properly, we should make sure that more and more plants are planted and that nobody litters the place.

REVIEW EXERCISE

Including Competency Based Questions

Part – I

Multiple Choice Questions

1. The Giant built a .... all around his garden.

(a) low wall
(b) high wall
(c) narrow lane
(d) spiked wall

Ans. (b) high wall

2. What did the Giant write on the notice board to dissuade the children from coming to his garden? Diksha

(a) Trespassers will be persecuted
(b) Trespassers will be prosecuted
(c) My garden is my own garden
(d) I do not like children

Ans. (b) Trespassers will be prosecuted

3. Which of the following set of values are upheld in the story? **Diksha**

(a) Truth, charity, honesty
(b) Affection, co-operation, selflessness
(c) Bravery, courtesy, dignity
(d) Empathy, generosity, peace

Ans. (b) Affection, co-operation, selflessness

4. "The only people pleased were the Snow and the Frost. 'spring has forgotten this garden', they cried." What figure of speech is used in these lines? **Diksha**

(a) Hyperbole (b) Personification
(c) Oxymoron (d) Simile

Ans. (b) Personification

5. "This is a delightful spot", said the North Wind to the Snow and the Frost. Pick up the antonym of the word 'delightful' from the following words. **Diksha**

(a) Blissful (b) Pleasurable
(c) Distressing (d) Pleasing

Ans. (c) Distressing

6. "The giant longed to see that child specially who had kissed and changed him". What does the word 'longed' mean here? **Diksha**

(a) Keenly desire (b) Eagerly waited
(c) Strong wish (d) Desires and wishes

Ans. (a) Keenly desire

7. When the Giant woke up one morning he was mesmerised by the melody of the bird song. Which bird was singing outside his window?

(a) Koyal (b) Mynah
(c) Linnet (d) Thrush

Ans. (c) Linnet

8. When the little boy came to the garden the second time the tree ....

(a) was covered with white blossoms
(b) had golden branches
(c) had silver fruits
(d) All of the above

Ans. (d) All of the above

9. What did the Giant intend to use to slay the people who had hurt the little boy?

(a) A Giant club
(b) A Giant axe
(c) A Giant bow
(d) A Giant sword

Ans. (d) A Giant sword

10. Which statement covers the moral of this story most appropriately? **Diksha**

(a) Children are the most beautiful flowers of all.
(b) Selflessness leads to salvation.
(c) Distributing happiness lead to receiving happiness.
(d) We should always help others.

Ans. (c) Distributing happiness lead to receiving happiness.

11. Read the given statements and choose the correct answer.

Statement 1 The Spring loves the children.
Statement 2 The Giant did not know that the children were playing in the garden.

(a) Statement 1 is true but Statement 2 is false.
(b) Statement 2 is true but Statement 1 is false.
(c) Both the Statements are true.
(d) Both the Statements are false.

Ans. (c) Both the Statements are true.

Extract Based Questions

1. Read the following extract carefully and answer the questions.

Every afternoon, as they were coming from school, the children used to go and play in the Giant's garden. It was a large lovely garden, with soft green grass. Here and there over the grass stood beautiful flowers like stars, and there were twelve peach-trees that in the springtime broke out into delicate blossoms of pink and pearl, and in the autumn bore rich fruit. The birds sat on the trees and sang so sweetly that the children used to stop their games in order to listen to them. "How happy we are here!" they cried to each other.

One day the Giant came back. He had been to visit his friend, the Cornish ogre, and had stayed with him for seven years. When he arrived he saw the children playing in the garden.

"What are you doing here?" he cried in a very gruff voice, and the children ran away.

(i) When would the children go to the Giant's garden to play?

Ans. The children would go to the Giant's garden in the afternoon after coming back from school.

(ii) What sort of trees were there in the garden?

Ans. Peach trees were found in the garden.

(iii) What made the children stop playing in the garden?

Ans. The children would stop playing in the garden to listen to the singing of the birds.

(iv) **State True or False. "The Giant was very happy to see the children playing in his garden".**

Ans. False

(v) **Which word from the given passage means 'rough'?**

Ans. Gruff

2. Read the following extract carefully and answer the questions.

"My own garden is my own garden," said the Giant; "anyone can understand that, and I will allow nobody to play in it but myself." So he built a high wall all round it, and put up a notice-board:

Trespassers Will Be Prosecuted

He was a very selfish Giant. The poor children had now nowhere to play. They tried to play on the road, but the road was very dusty and full of hard stones, and they did not like it. They used to wander round the high walls when their lessons were over, and talk about the beautiful garden inside. "How happy we were there!" they said to each other.

Then the Spring came, and all over the country there were little blossoms and little birds. Only in the garden of the Selfish Giant it was still winter. The birds did not care to sing in it as there were no children, and the trees forgot to blossom. Once a beautiful flower put its head out from the grass, but when it saw the notice-board it was so sorry for the children that it slipped back into the ground again, and went off to sleep.

(i) **What did the Giant do to keep the children out of his garden?**

Ans. The Giant built a high wall around his garden to keep the children out.

(ii) **Why was the Giant called selfish?**

Ans. The Giant was called selfish because he did not want to share his garden with the children and let them play in it.

(iii) **What did the beautiful flower do upon waking up and looking around?**

Ans. The beautiful flower read the notice board. It felt sorry for the children and went back to sleep.

(iv) **State true or false. "The children preferred playing on the road".**

Ans. False

(v) **Which word from the given passage means 'greedy'?**

Ans. Selfish

3. Read the following extract carefully and answer the questions.

The only people who were pleased were the Snow and the Frost. "Spring has forgotten this garden," they cried, "so we will live here all the year round." The Snow covered up the grass with her great white cloak, and the Frost painted all the trees silver. Then they invited the North Wind to stay with them, and he came. He was wrapped in furs, and he roared all day about the garden, and blew the chimney-pots down. "This is a delightful spot," he said, "we must ask Hail on a visit." So the Hail came.

Every day for three hours he rattled on the roof of the castle till he broke most of the slates, and then he ran round and round the garden as fast as he could go. He was dressed in grey, and his breath was like ice.

"I cannot understand why the Spring is so late in coming," said the Selfish Giant, as he sat at the window and looked out at his cold, white garden; "I hope there will be a change in the weather." But the Spring never came, nor the Summer. The Autumn gave golden fruit to every garden, but to the Giant's garden she gave none. "He is too selfish," she said. So, it was always Winter there, and the North Wind and the Hail, and the Frost, and the Snow danced about through the trees.

(i) **Who was pleased that the spring had forgotten the Giant's garden?**

(a) Snow
(b) Frost
(c) Both (a) and (b)
(d) None of the above

Ans. (c) Both (a) and (b)

(ii) **The .... covered up the grass with her great ...... cloak.**

(a) snow, white
(b) Frost, pink
(c) hail, grey
(d) summer, yellow

Ans. (a) snow, white

(iii) **Who was wrapped in furs and roared all day about the garden?**

(a) Snow
(b) Frost
(c) North Wind
(d) Fur

Ans. (c) North Wind

(iv) **Which of the following words is the antonym of 'rattled'?**

(a) Bewildered
(b) Crushed
(c) Clear
(d) Confounded

Ans. (c) Clear

(v) Which of the following words is a synonym of 'wrapped'?

(a) Benevolent (b) Trespass
(c) Enclosed (d) Kind

Ans. (c) Enclosed

4. Read the following extract carefully and answer the questions.

One Winter morning he looked out of his window as he was dressing. He did not hate the Winter now, for he knew that it was merely the Spring asleep, and that the flowers were resting.

Suddenly he rubbed his eyes in wonder and looked and looked.

It certainly was a marvellous sight. In the farthest corner of the garden was a tree quite covered with lovely white blossoms. Its branches were golden, and silver fruit hung down from them, and underneath it stood the little boy he had loved.

Downstairs ran the Giant in great joy, and out into the garden. He hastened across the grass, and came near to the child. And when he came quite close his face grew red with anger, and he said, "Who hath dared to wound thee?" For on the palms of the child's hands were the prints of two nails, and the prints of two nails were on the little feet.

(i) Why didn't the Giant hate the winter anymore?

(a) Because he knew that winter is important too.
(b) Because he knew that spring was just sleeping.
(c) Because he had grown fond of winter.
(d) Because he hated being hot and sweaty.

Ans. (b) Because he knew that spring was just sleeping.

(ii) What did the flowers do during the winter?

(a) They tended to the Sun.
(b) They rested in the ground.
(c) They waited for the children.
(d) They played in the snow.

Ans. (b) They rested in the ground.

(iii) Its branches were ...., and .... fruit hung down from them.

(a) brown, yellow (b) green, red
(c) silver, gold (d) gold, silver

Ans. (d) gold, silver

(iv) Which of the following words means 'causing great wonder'?

(a) Credulous (b) Marvellous
(c) Superfluous (d) Biased

Ans. (b) Marvellous

(v) Which of the following words means 'moving really fast'?

(a) Crawl (b) Hasten (c) Slide (d) Drag

Ans. (b) Hasten

Part – II

Very Short Answer Type Questions

1. Where had the Giant gone?

Ans. The Giant had gone to visit his friend the Cornish Ogre for seven years.

2. What effect did the songs of the birds have on the children?

Ans. The children used to get spellbound by the songs that the birds sang. They would stop playing to listen to the birds singing.

3. Where did the children play after the Giant pushed them out of his garden?

Ans. On being pushed out of the garden, the children tried to play on the road. However, it was difficult to play on the road because the road was dusty and had hard stones.

4. Why was it still winter in corner of the garden? **Diksha**

Ans. It was still winter in the corner of the garden because the little boy couldn't reach the branches and climb up the tree.

5. Who did the Giant credit to the source of the sweet music?

Ans. The Giant credited the source of the sweet music to the king's musicians that must have been passing by.

6. Where did the music come from?

Ans. The music was not produced by the king's musicians but it was a linnet singing. The spring had finally come to the Giant's garden and with it came the birds who sang sweet music.

7. What did the children say when the Giant questioned them about the little boy?

Ans. On being questioned about the little boy, the children told the Giant that they didn't know where the little boy lived, nor had they seen him before.

8. Why did the Giant get red with anger on seeing the little boy?

Ans. The Giant got red on seeing the little boy because he saw that the child had horrible injuries. Both palms of his hand and both feet had the imprints of nails. This angered the Giant and he asked the boy who hurt him so that he could slay them.

Short Answer Type Questions

1. Why did the Giant not allow the children to his garden?

Ans. The Giant was selfish. He believed that his garden belonged only to him and should be used only by him. For this reason, he banned the entry of children from his garden and put up a notice board stating, 'Trespassers will be prosecuted'.

2. What were the differences between the Giant's garden and the other gardens during the spring season?

Ans. During spring, the trees in all other gardens were filled with golden fruits except for the Giant's garden. All other gardens had little blossoms and little birds. The Giant's garden had none and was white and cold. Winter and snow became the permanent residents in his garden.

3. Why did the Giant knock down the wall that he himself had built?

Ans. The Giant knocked down the wall when he realised that he was being selfish. He realised that the change in seasons skipped his garden because of his attitude.

He understood that he was deprived of the joy of spring because the real source of joy was to be found in the children.

4. Why was the Giant sad, despite spring having had come to his garden? **Diksha**

Ans. The Giant was sad because he missed his dear little friend, the little boy whom he had helped climb the tree.

He asked the other children to tell the little boy to come and play in his garden. The children, however, informed him that they didn't know the boy nor did they know where he lived.

5. Describe the Giant during his old age.

Ans. During his old age, the Gaint grew old and weak. He could not play with the children any longer. So, he would sit in his huge armchair and watch the children play their games. He would admire his beautiful garden and say that the children were the most beautiful of all flowers.

6. Why was the Giant filled with a 'strange awe' on meeting the little boy?

Ans. When the Giant meets the little boy for the second time, he was filled with a strange sense of awe because it is hinted that the little boy was Jesus Christ.

On seeing Christ stand before him and having come to take him to Paradise, the Giant was overwhelmed with strange emotions.

7. Which value does the chapter strongly condemn?

Ans. The chapter strongly condemns the idea of being 'selfish'. Till the point the Giant was selfish he failed to enjoy the gifts of nature and God. Despite having a big garden, it remained barren. The moment he realised his mistakes and worked to correct them, the Giant's garden began to bloom. The chapter critiques every man considering himself as the supreme ruler of the benefits of nature.

Long Answer Type Questions

1. The line, "My own garden is my own garden" gets transformed in the course of the story. Explain why?

Ans. The line, "My own garden is my own garden" gets transformed into "It is your garden now, dear children." The Giant kept waiting for the spring to come. The spring, however, comes only when the children come back.

The Giant is quick to realise that the real flowers to be found in the trees are the children. Therefore, through these lines the Giant welcomes back the children into his garden.

2. How did the Giant express his repentance over his rude behaviour towards the children? **Diksha**

Ans. After a long winter season full of snow and hail, one day the Giant found the garden full of sweet smell, bird song, and flowers.

The change in weather was because the children had sneaked into the garden through a small hole in the wall bringing spring with them.

When the Gaint realised that he had been selfish, he helped the little boy climb the tree. He knocked down the high wall and told the children that garden would be their playground forever. He also used to play with the children daily.

3. "But these are the wounds of love." Justify the statement in the context of the chapter.

Ans. The little boy utters these lines, "but these are the wounds of love", when the Giant sees him wounded with the prints of nails on his hands and feet. Through these lines, the little boy reveals himself to be the Christ himself. He calls these wounds the 'wounds of love' because he chose to die and sacrifice his life for the sake of his love for man and mankind. These wounds were Christ's love and ultimate sacrifice for humanity.

ASSESSMENT EXERCISE

Multiple Choice Questions

1. Which cold-weather related attributes has been personified in the chapter?

(a) Snow (b) Hail
(c) Frost (d) All of these

2. The little boy whom the Giant loved was an allegory of ....

(a) God (b) Santa Claws
(c) Christ (d) Vishnu

3. Arrange the following events in the correct order.

(i) The Giant went to meet the Cornish Ogre.
(ii) The Giant knocked down the wall.
(iii) The Giant put up a sign saying "Trespassers will be prosecuted".
(iv) The Giant saw the injuries of the little boy.

(a) (iv) (iii) (ii) (i) (b) (i) (ii) (iii) (iv)
(c) (i) (iii) (ii) (iv) (d) (iv) (ii) (i) (iii)

4. The Giant became .... with time.

(a) old (b) weak
(c) wise (d) All of these

5. Read the given statements and choose the correct answer.

Statement 1 The Giant built a high wall around his garden.

Statement 2 The Giant knocked down the high wall around his garden.

(a) Statement 1 is true, but Statement 2 is false.
(b) Statement 1 is false, but Statement 2 is true.
(c) Both the Statements are true.
(d) Both the Statements are false.

Extract Based Question

Read the following extract and answer the following questions.

One morning the Giant was lying awake in bed when he heard some lovely music. It sounded so sweet to his ears that he thought it must be the King's musicians passing by. It was really only a little linnet singing outside his window, but it was so long since he had heard a bird singing in his garden that it seemed to him to be the most beautiful music in the world. Then the Hail stopped dancing over his head and the North Wind ceased roaring and a delicious perfume came to him through the open casement. "I believe the Spring has come at last," said the Giant and he jumped out of bed and looked out.

He saw a most wonderful sight. Through a little hole in the wall the children had crept in and they were sitting in the branches of the trees. In every tree that he could see there was a little child and the trees were so glad to have the children back again that they had covered themselves with blossoms and were waving their arms gently.

(i) What did the Giant hear when he woke up?
(ii) Who did the Giant think was playing that music?
(iii) What was happening in the garden?
(iv) Then the Hail stopped dancing over his head and the .... Wind ceased roaring.

(a) North (b) South
(c) East (d) West

(v) What does the word 'cease' mean?

(a) Snatching something
(b) Stopping something
(c) Sewing something
(d) Sailing something

Very Short Answer Type Questions

1. How long had the Giant lived with his friend?
2. From the story choose the synonym for the word 'Giant'.
3. How do the trees welcome the children?
4. Why does the little boy disappear in the middle of the story?
5. Who had wounded the little boy?

Short Answer Type Questions

1. What was the notice that the Giant had put up for the children?
2. Describe the activities of the North wind and the Hail.
3. Why didn't the Giant hate the winter in his old age?
4. Describe the scene of the Giant's death.

Long Answer Type Questions

1. Discuss an important moral imparted by the story.
2. Assume yourself to be the Giant. Write a letter to your friend discussing the changes that have lately occurred in you.
3. Do we find traces of the Giant in ourselves? Answer in the context of the given story.
4. What do winter and spring symbolise in the story?

The Treasure Within

CHAPTER 4

The chapter describes a conversation between Hafeez Contractor, a leading architect and Ms. Bela Raja, Editor of the newsletter Sparsh. It discusses the importance of knowing the potential of each and every child and their style and area of interest to lead them to the right path.

Part – I

Hafeez Contractor's Biggest Nightmare

Hafeez Contractor(HC) shares with Bela(RJ) that till 4- 5 years ago, he used to get nightmares that he was appearing for a mathematics exam and he was not prepared for it. It is only now that he settled in his professional life that he has got over these bad dreams.

When Bela asks Hafeez about his earliest memories of school, he tells her that he was a good student but only till the second standard. He informs her that after the third standard, he suddenly lost interest in studies and would spend all his time playing pranks on others. He also used to cheat in exams by copying and getting hold of the prepared examination paper to be able to pass the examination. He added that he could not remember what had been taught to him in class.

Advice that Changed His Life

Hafeez recollects how a sentence spoken by his school Principal had a life changing impact on him. When Hafeez reached the eleventh standard, the Principal told him that he was a good student but he never studied. He also told Hafeez that he would no longer be able to take care of him. The Principal added that after the death of Hafeez's father, his mother had worked very hard to raise him. However, he had only played games. It was now his turn to repay and take care of his mother.

Hafeez tells Bela that he was a good sportsman and a champion along with being the cricket captain. But after that incident, he stopped playing and concentrated entirely on his studies. All he did during that first year was to eat, pray and study. He knew that he could not pass SSC by copying. At the end of that year, he scored very well in his SSC exams and secured 50% marks which the Principal said was like a distinction.

Hafeez – His Memory and Pranks

On being asked other questions, Hafeez tells Bela that he couldn't remember things and would often forget very easily. He could only remember it when it was presented to him as a photograph.

When Bela enquired about how his teachers helped him when he did badly in school, Hafeez replied that since he was too interested in playing, he never felt anything and instead got punished every week.

Upon being asked about his state of mind when punished, Hafeez tells Bela that he understood that he had made his teachers angry but his state of mind was to go and play so he would forget the pain. He did not feel insecure or threatened. He adds that he had the most interest in funny pranks. He even created a distraction to the class by playing 'chor police' for a full hour just because he didn't want to study.

He also tells Bela that once in a week, they were allowed to go watch a movie. So, he would not eat his lunch. He would collect money from 40-50 students and go to buy the movie ticket. He would eat only when they were returning from the hall. Further, he states that he was the leader of his gang and what interested him were gang fights and planning strategies for the same and not academics. Therefore, his juniors would ask for his textbooks as he probably only opened them one day before exams.

Part – II

Hafeez's Days at Jaihind College

Bela was curious about Hafeez's journey to the field of architecture. So, Hafeez tells her that the cut-off mark in any architecture college was 80-85 percent and he only had 50 percent. He actually wanted to join the Army and even got the admission letter but his aunt tore up that letter. He, then, wanted to join the Police force. His mother asked him to do graduation instead. So, he went to Jaihind College in Bombay. There, he had to choose between German and French. He had studied French for seven years but he was bad at it so he opted for German. He studied German till his teacher died. After the death of his teacher, the college told him to take French or take admission in other college. He knew that it was not possible because he got admission in Jaihind College due to influence. So, he took French and started learning it from his cousin whose husband was an architect.

Journey to the Field of Architecture

Hafeez started going to an architect's office to learn French. One day, he saw somebody drawing a window in detail. He was able to pin-point the mistakes in the drawing correctly. His brother-in-law was surprised and to test his skills, asked Hafeez to draw a couple of things. When Hafeez was able to do so, his brother-in-law asked him to join architecture.

Hafeez also tells Bela that his Principal of the college allowed him to give the entrance exam and had told him that if he failed, Hafeez could not join architecture. In the entrance exam for architecture, Hafeez got an 'A+' and got admitted in the architecture course. He managed to get a first class first throughout. He explains that all this understanding came from what he used to play and do during school.

Hafeez adds that in his architecture college, he had a friend named Behram Divecha with whom he used to compete for designing forts, guns and ammunition in their own different ways.

Hafeez Goes Back to Meet Mrs. Gupta

Hafeez remembers that when he was in second or third standard, one of his teachers Mrs. Gupta had told him on seeing his sketches that he could become a good architect. For everything else, he was quite useless. When he finally did become an architect, he went to meet her and let her know that she was quite right in her evaluation of him.

Reasons for Hafeez's Disinterest in Studies

Bela asks for his reasons for not being interested in studies and if the curriculum was what made him disinterested. Hafeez explains that he was very bad at languages and Maths but he could deal with Science and Geography. Also, he used to forget everything that was taught. There was no application of mind. Bela, then, continues to ask if the lessons were boring or if it was because once he understood the concept, he just lost interest. He tells Bela that life in boarding school was very difficult. There were many tests and they used to copy and made the teacher assume they did their work.

Giftedness and Learning Disabilities

Bela questions him about the general belief about giftedness and disabilities going hand-in-hand. Hafeez remarks that he has observed toppers of his class doing ordinarily in life. He observes that his street-smartness is helping him today. Many lessons were learnt independently, outside the academics. Bela adds that Hafeez was able to do so because of his personality and skills which helped him in doing everything he wanted to do.

Hafeez shares with Bela that his mind worked differently. If he saw that it was raining outside, he used to start thinking of ways to stop the water, of ways to construct a dam for the same and so on. He also shares how he used to cut a perfect button from a chalk for students whose buttons got lost.

Hafeez Works Instinctively

On being asked how he decided what he was to offer to his clients, Hafeez informed that observation was the key to it. He would observe how they talked, what they wore, what they ate and he was able to assess their taste. He would try to relate to his clients and draw the design spontaneously. He adds that now, design is like mathematics to him. This mathematics includes putting design, construction, psychology and sociology together.

Word Meaning

Word	Meaning
Potential	possible
Detested	disliked
Psyche	mind or mentality
As far as my things are concerned	perhaps he is referring to matters other than course materials and their details
Caning	punishment/ beating
Incurred the wrath of your teacher	made your teacher furious
Distraction	something that doesn't allow one to concentrate
Eat to my heart's content	eat as much as I wanted

Word	Meaning
Stumbled on	got into (architecture) by chance
Offbeat	unusual or unconventional
Calling	work or vocation of his choice
Cakewalk	smooth ride, something easy to achieve
Ammunition	weapons
Cope	manage, handle, deal with
Curriculum	prescribed courses of study
Giftedness	having special abilities
Defied	broke
Instinctively	naturally

NCERT FOLDER

NCERT Intext and Exercise Questions

COMPREHENSION CHECK❶ (NCERT PAGE 28)

Q.1 What did Hafeez Contractor have nightmares about?

Ans. Hafeez Contractor had nightmares that he was appearing for a maths examination and he did not remember anything.

Q.2 What did the Principal say to him, which influenced him deeply?

Ans. The Principal explained to Hafeez that he was a good student but didn't study. Now, he should start taking care of himself instead of playing around. He reminded Hafeez about how hard his mother had worked after the death of his father in order to raise him. It was now Hafeez's turn to repay the debt. These words had a deep influence on Hafeez Contractor.

Q.3 "... that year I did not step out onto the field." What was he busy doing that year?

Ans. That particular year Hafeez Contractor dedicated his entire time to his studies for the SSC exam. He would only pray, eat and study the whole time.

Q.4 (i) What 'distraction' did Hafeez Contractor create one day?

Ans. One day, Hafeez Contractor created a distraction. He made everyone play 'chor police' for one whole hour.

(ii) Would you have liked to participate in the 'distraction' had you been with him?

Ans. It is tempting to play the games that everyone else is playing. I, too, might have participated in the 'distraction' if I had been with him.

CHECK❷ (NCERT PAGE 32)

Q.1 Hafeez Contractor wanted to join the police force. Why didn't he?

Ans. Hafeez Contractor wanted to join the police force, but he didn't because his mother was not in its favour. His mother asked him to finish his graduation instead.

Q.2 In the architect's office. Hafeez Contractor was advised to drop everything and join architecture. Why?

Ans. In the architect's office, he was advised to drop everything and join architecture because his drawing and sketching was excellent. On being asked to make a few sketches, he was able to draw in detail. His brother-in-law, then, urged him to go to the architecture field as he had talent there.

Q.3 (i) What was Mrs. Gupta's advice to Hafeez Contractor?

Ans. Mrs. Gupta advised Hafeez to join architecture as she felt that he would excel in nothing, but architecture.

(ii) What made her advise him so?

Ans. Mrs. Gupta was impressed by his sketches and therefore, she gave him this piece of advice.

Q.4 How did he help fellow students who had lost a button?

Ans. Hafeez Contractor helped fellow students who had lost a button by cutting a perfect button from chalk, a button that would stay fixed till the school ended.

Q.5 Which rules did he break as a school boy?

Ans. As a school boy, Hafeez Contractor broke all rules. He used to cheat in exams and use unfair means to attain a copy of the question paper. He was also good at distracting the class and insisted the fellow students to play 'chor police'. He also indulged in gang fights.

Q.6 (i) What is Hafeez Contractor's definition of mathematics?

Ans. According to Hafeez Contractor, putting together designs, constructions, psychology and sociology and making a sketch from it is 'mathematics.'

(ii) How would you want to define mathematics? Do you like the subject?

Ans. I would define mathematics as that branch of science that makes use of numericals to derive and prove concepts.

I truly love this subject for it is very interesting.

EXERCISES (NCERT PAGES 32)

Answer the following questions.

Q.1 Is it likely that someone who is original and intelligent does not do very well at school? Should such a learner be called a failure? If not, why not?

Ans. It is quite possible that people who are intelligent do not do well at school. Such people think differently and imaginatively, something that doesn't match with the standard expectations of the school as schools follow a particular curriculum.

Such a learner is not necessarily a failure, but a learner with different capacities.

Q.2 Who, in your view, is an 'unusual' learner?

Ans. An 'unusual' learner is someone who may not be good in all subjects, but can do exceptionally well in another field. Usually, he is a person who proves himself to be a genius at some later point.

Q.3 What can schools do to draw out the best in unusual learners? Suggest whatever seems reasonable to you.

Ans. These schools should enable the students to increase their potential in whatever they are good at. Also, extracurricular activities such as music, painting, dance and sports should be kept at par with academic subjects such as maths, sciences and languages.

REVIEW EXERCISE

Including Competency Based Questions

Part – I

Multiple Choice Questions

1. Hafeez was interested in Diksha

(a) games, running, playing jokes and pranks on others
(b) doing science experiments
(c) earning a livelihood as he had lost his father
(d) taking part in singing and dancing competitions

Ans. (a) games, running, playing jokes and pranks on others

2. Read the given statements and choose the correct answer.

Statement 1 Hafeez's school fees were paid by his mother all those years.

Statement 2 They were not well-off as Hafeez's father had passed away.

(a) Statement 1 is true but Statement 2 is false.
(b) Statement 2 is true but Statement 1 is false.
(c) Both the Statements are true.
(d) Both the Statements are false.

Ans. (c) Both the Statements are true.

3. 'That year I did not step out onto the field.' What was Hafeez busy doing that year? Diksha

(a) He was busy teaching his younger brother.
(b) He was busy practising drawing.
(c) He was busy in taking care of his mother.
(d) He was focusing on his studies for SSC.

Ans. (d) He was focusing on his studies for SSC.

4. Students used to book Hafeez's textbooks because

(a) they were almost brand new
(b) they had important information related to the course
(c) he would offer them for free
(d) they wanted to see his designs

Ans. (a) they were almost brand new

5. Choose the correct option to complete the sentence appropriately.

During exam times, Hafeez would ....

(a) copy and try to get hold of the prepared examination paper
(b) copy and try to get hold of the study papers
(c) try to cheat
(d) run around and play pranks on others

Ans. (a) copy and try to get hold of the prepared examination paper.

6. Hafeez went to Jaihind College in Bombay to study ....

(a) English (b) German (c) Spanish (d) Architecture

Ans. (b) German

7. Hafeez learnt French from ....

(a) his cousin (b) his friend
(c) his cousin's husband (d) his mother

Ans. (a) his cousin

8. Every child is a potential achiever and is different from other children in her/his style of learning and are of interest. What was the role of Mrs. Gupta in the career of Hafeez Contractor? Diksha

(a) She was the one who told him that he would become an architect.
(b) She was the one who helped him financially.
(c) She was the one who fixed his job in police force.
(d) She encouraged him to take more and more part in sports.

Ans. (a) She was the one who told him that he would become an architect.

9. Those who do not concentrate on studies are known as unusual learners. They admit that there are lots of things to learn and they always criticise the study materials according to their own interpretation. Choose the right statement in context with the lesson.

(a) Hafeez Contractor was a bright child who always scored good marks in studies.
(b) He could not study as he was very weak in mathematics.
(c) He was an unusual learner learning from other activities and pranks.
(d) None of the above

Ans. (c) He was an unusual learner learning from other activities and pranks.

Extract Based Questions

1. Read the extract given below and answer the following questions.

In the college for architecture, nobody who had got below 80-85 per cent was allowed to enter. I had only 50 per cent. I wanted to join the Army. I got my admission letter but my aunt tore it up. Then I decided that I wanted to join the police force. My mother said, "Don't join the police force, just do your graduation!" So I went to Jaihind College in Bombay. There, I was to either take French or German. Though I had studied French for seven years, I did not know seven words of French. So I took German.

(i) Who is the speaker of these lines?

(a) Bela Raja (b) Hafeez Contractor
(c) Mrs. Gupta (d) Behram Divecha

Ans. (b) Hafeez Contractor

(ii) The speaker didn't join the army because

(a) his mother was against it
(b) his father was against it
(c) his aunt was against it
(d) he was not interested

Ans. (c) his aunt was against it

(iii) The speaker's mother wanted him to

(a) join the police (b) join the army
(c) do his graduation (d) join the navy

Ans. (c) do his graduation

(iv) The speaker

(a) knew French decently well
(b) was as fluent in French as a native
(c) didn't know French well
(d) was a French professor

Ans. (c) didn't know French well

(v) According to the extract, which subject did the speaker pick at Jaihind College in Bombay?

(a) French (b) German (c) Spanish (d) English

Ans. (b) German

2. Read the extract given below and answer the following questions.

Actually, it all happened quite by chance. In the architect's office, I saw somebody drawing a window detail. A window detail is a very advanced drawing. I told him that his drawing was wrong — that the window he had drawn would not open. He then had a bet with me and later he found that indeed, his drawing was wrong! My cousin's husband was surprised. He asked me to draw a few specific things, which I immediately did. He asked me to design a house and I designed a house. After that, he told me to drop everything and join architecture. We went to meet the Principal of the college. The Principal warned me, "I will allow you to take part in the entrance exams, but if you do not do well I will not allow you to join. I got an 'A+' in the entrance exam and from that day it was a cakewalk."

(i) What does Hafeez mean by 'it all happened quite by chance'?

Ans. In the given line, Hafeez is trying to say that he pursued architecture quite by chance.

(ii) Why did Hafeez go to the architect's office?

Ans. Hafeez went to the architect's office to learn French from his cousin, whose husband was an architect.

(iii) Why was Hafeez's cousin's husband surprised?

Ans. Hafeez's cousin's husband was surprised because Hafeez had told one person in the architect's office that the window he had drawn would not open. To his surprise, Hafeez was right.

(iv) State true or false.

The Principal of the architecture college didn't let Hafeez join.

Ans. False

(v) What was the result of Hafeez's entrance exam?

Ans. Hafeez got an A+ in the entrance exam and joined the architecture college. It was like a cakewalk for him after that.

Part – II

Very Short Answer Type Questions

1. What was the designation of Bela Raja?

Ans. Bela Raja was an editor of Sparsh, a newsletter from the Resource Centre, The Valley School, Bangalore.

2. What made Hafeez Contractor feel that the phase of getting nightmares was now over?

Ans. Hafeez Contractor thought that since he doesn't need to think about examinations anymore, he had gotten over the phase of getting nightmares.

3. What did Hafeez Contractor wish to do?

Ans. Hafeez Contractor wished to join the Army at first. Later, he thought of joining the Police force.

4. What did Hafeez Contractor plan strategies for?

Ans. Hafeez Contractor planned strategies for fighting against the other gangs.

5. For how many years had Hafeez Contractor learnt French?

Ans. Hafeez Contractor had spent 7 years learning French.

6. Who was Behram Divecha?

Ans. Behram Divecha was a friend of Hafeez Contractor with whom Hafeez used to have competitions for designing forts, guns and ammunition.

7. Which were the subjects that Hafeez was able to deal with?

Ans. Hafeez could deal with Science and Geography. However, he was extremely bad at Maths and languages.

8. When and with whom did Hafeez Contractor commence his career?

Ans. Hafeez Contractor began his career in 1977 under the apprenticeship of T Khareghat.

9. Whom does Hafeez Contractor give credit for the lessons he had learnt about life?

Ans. Hafeez Contractor gave credit to his boarding school life for the lessons he had learnt about life. According to him, the life there made him street smart and what he learnt when doing things on his own.

10. What does Hafeez Contractor have to say about the class toppers?

Ans. Hafeez Contractor says that the class toppers and other good students are doing ordinarily in life from his observations.

Short Answer Type Questions

1. Why did the students use to book Hafeez Contractor's books in advance?

Ans. The students used to book Hafeez Contractor's books in advance as he hardly opened his books to study, except a little before the exams. His books were almost brand new.

The students knew this. His juniors, therefore, could buy second hand books which were almost new.

2. What does Hafeez Contractor say about his memory?

Ans. Hafeez Contractor says that he used to forget things very easily. He could remember only those things that he saw as a photograph. If he read a book, he could remember the matter like a photograph, but not so through his mind.

3. What used to be Hafeez Contractor's state of mind after incurring the wrath of his teachers?

Ans. Hafeez Contractor used to incur the wrath of his teachers quite often. However, he informed Bela Raja that he hardly had any time to reflect on the beating or scolding that he would have received from his teachers. He would be so busy wanting to go and play.

4. Why did Contractor opt for German in College?

Ans. Hafeez Contractor had to choose either French or German at Jaihind College. He choose to opt for German because he had spent 7 years learning French and he could hardly utter any words in French. So, he thought of trying his hand at German.

5. Describe Hafeez Contractor's activities during his eleventh grade.

Ans. During his eleventh grade, Hafeez Contractor was deeply stirred by the advise given to him by his school Principal.

That entire year, Hafeez withdrew from the field and the various games he used to play and devoted his entire time to his studies. He used to merely eat, pray and study.

Long Answer Type Questions

1. What did Hafeez Contractor do in the architect's office that led to his becoming an architect himself?

Ans. In the architect's office, Hafeez Contractor saw someone making a drawing of a window. He pointed out the mistakes in the drawing and said that according to the sketch, the window would never open.

Later, he made some specific drawings when asked by his brother-in-law and he was found to possess impressive qualities in that particular field. This led to the future course of actions which in turn facilitated his becoming an architect.

2. Give examples from the book to indicate that Hafeez Contractor looked at things differently.

Ans. There are many instances in the chapter that prove that Hafeez Contractor looked at things differently. For instance, when it began to rain outside while he was in class, his mind would drift to think about ways to build a dam in order to block the flowing water.

He would also probe questions like how much water would the dam be able to hold and so on. To save his friends, he would apply his skill to cut buttons from a chalk with the help of a blade. The buttons fit so perfectly that they stayed fixed for a whole day.

3. Why are students who are original in their thinking labelled as failures at school?

Ans. A school usually adheres to fixed and standard teaching and learning practices in accordance with a given curriculum. It, therefore, fails to acknowledge originality in children as it is constantly forcing them to be good in everything. However, in the process of becoming good in every subject, original thinkers at times forget what they are brilliant in. They end up being branded as failures.

4. What important lesson do we learn by looking closely at Hafeez Contractor's life?

Ans. Hafeez Contractor's life teaches us two important lessons. It, first, teaches us that it is never too late to decide to work hard. In his eleventh grade, when Contractor decides to work hard, he fairs quite well in his exams. His life also teaches us that we should not underestimate anyone's capabilities. Just because someone is a different learner doesn't mean that they are a failure.

ASSESSMENT EXERCISE

Multiple Choice Questions

1. According to Hafeez, students from his class who stood first or second
   (a) had all become scientists
   (b) were all writers
   (c) were doing very ordinary jobs
   (d) had become doctors
2. When students lost a button, Hafeez would
   (a) lend them another uniform
   (b) lend his own buttons
   (c) carve a button for them from chalk
   (d) tell the teacher
3. Read the given statements and choose the correct answer.

   Statement 1 Hafeez Contractor's aunt didn't like him to join the Army.

   Statement 2 Hafeez made an advanced drawing at the architect's office.

   (a) Statement 1 is true but Statement 2 is false
   (b) Statement 1 is false but Statement 2 is true
   (c) Both Statements are true
   (d) Both Statement are false
4. Complete the following sentence in context with the lesson.

   Hafeez was too interested in playing and he did badly in school so he would receive ....

   (a) a caning every week (b) lecture on discipline every week
   (c) an earful of scolding (d) praise from his fellow classmates
5. Which subject did the speaker pick at Jaihind College in Bombay?
   (a) French (b) German
   (c) Architecture (d) Both (a) and (c)

Extract Based Question

Read the given extract and answer the following questions.

I was just interested in playing and nothing else. I was most interested in funny pranks. One day, I did not want to study, so I created a distraction, for one whole hour we played 'chor police'.

Every Saturday, we were allowed to go into town to see a movie. So what I would do was have no lunch and collect money from 40–50 students and run and buy the tickets. On my way back, I would eat to my heart's content.

I used to be the leader of a gang. We would have fights and plan strategies. These things used to interest me more than any academics. Students used to book my textbooks for the following year because they were almost brand new. I probably opened them one day before exams.

(i) What did Hafeez do when he lost interest in studies?
(ii) Why did Hafeez skip lunch on Saturdays?
(iii) When did Hafeez open his school textbooks?
(iv) When were the students allow to go see a movie?
   (a) One Saturday (b) Saturdays of every week
   (c) Anytime (d) None of the above
(v) How long did the students play 'chor police'?
   (a) Full one hour (b) Almost one hour
   (c) More than one hour (d) Less than one hour

Very Short Answer Type Questions

1. Did Hafeez Contractor ever feel insecure or threatened by his teachers?
2. Which all games did Hafeez Contractor play at school?
3. How did his competition with Behram Divecha help him later?
4. How did Hafeez Contractor manage to get admission to Jaihind College?
5. How did he fair in the entrance exam for architecture?

Short Answer Type Questions

1. What did Hafeez Contractor have to say about boarding schools?
2. In the present, what comes handy when Contractor tries to comprehend what his clients desire?
3. Why did Mathematics give shivers to Hafeez Contractor?
4. Explain the meaning of 'street smart.'

Long Answer Type Questions

1. Write about your experiences of having met a potential achiever.
2. What was Hafeez Contractor's understanding of an ideal learning?
3. Describe the series of chance events that led to Hafeez Contractor's becoming an architect.

Princess September

by Somerset Maugham

CHAPTER SUMMARY 'Princess September' by Somerset Maugham is a story that presents the importance of freedom for all living birds. In the story, the Princess cages a bird which sings beautifully. However, when she realises that the bird would die, she frees him.

The King and his Nine Daughters

The King of Siam had nine daughters. Since the Queen used to have difficulty remembering so many names, the King named his daughters after the names of the months of the year. Therefore, the eldest was called January and the youngest was named September. The King had a unique habit of giving gifts rather than receiving them on his birthday. One year, he gifted a green parrot in a golden cage to each of his daughters. The daughters loved their gifts and were proud of their parrots. They taught their parrots to say 'God save the King' and 'Pretty Polly in seven Oriental languages.

Princess September's Parrot Dies

One morning, Princess September saw her parrot lying dead at the bottom of its golden cage. The Princess cried so much that not even her Maids of Honour able to comfort her. The Queen found all this stupid and ordered the Maids of Honour to put the Princess in her bed without serving her any dinner.

The Little Bird

The Maids of Honour wanted to go to a party. So, they quickly put Princess September to bed. While the Princess lay in her bed, crying in sadness for her dead parrot, a little bird came into her room. As the Princess saw him, he began to sing a beautiful song, about the lakes, the trees, the willow and the goldfish. When he had finished singing, the Princess was not crying anymore and she had forgotten that she was hungry. When she praised the bird, he asked her if he could take her parrot's place. He told her that even though he was ugly, he can sing well. So, the Princess agreed happily.

The Princess is Proud and Happy

The next morning when Princess September woke up, the little bird wished her Good morning. Later, when the Maids of Honour brought in her breakfast, the bird ate rice out of the Princess' hands and had his bath in her cup. After this, the bird began to sing again so beautifully that the Maids of Honour were quite surprised. The Maids of Honour had never heard anything like it and Princess September was very proud and happy.

Little Bird's Introduction

With great delight, the Princess showed the little bird to all her sisters. For each of the sisters, the bird sang a new and beautiful song. Then, the Princess showed her new friend to the King and the Queen. They were delighted to see the bird, as the bird sang beautifully and was unlike the parrots who just knew how to say, 'God save the King' and 'Pretty Polly.'

The Sisters Grew Jealous of September

Seeing the King speaking favourably of the little bird and hearing him sing beautifully, the eight sisters grew jealous of September. Even their parrots looked sad. The sisters, then, decided to plan a strategy to get rid of the little bird. They made an offer to September. They told her that they would give their pocket money in helping September to buy a new parrot. When September refused they questioned the freedom of the bird by pointing out his absence every now and then, making September insecure. They also advised her not to take any risks and put the bird in the cage.

September Begins to Worry

On realising that the bird had been away too long, September began to worry about the safety of her bird. She feared that hawks and snares might have harmed it. She also began to think that the bird might have forgotten her and become a pet to someone else. All these ideas greatly disturb her.

When the bird returned, the Princess asked the bird the reasons behind his delay. The bird unaware of the circumstances, honestly tells her that his father-in-law was giving a party and he initially intended not to come back that night. Hearing this, September makes up her mind and puts the bird in the cage. Initially, the bird thought that September was putting him in the cage until morning. However, when he realised that he was being caged forever, he became very unhappy.

The Bird's Condition

As soon as the bird realised that he had been caged permanently, he tried to get out. He tried to get out from between the bars of the cage and even tried to open the door. However, nothing happened and he could not escape. Then, the other Princesses came to Princess September and told her that she did the right thing. When the bird cried to be freed, Princess September scolded him. She told him that she had kept him in a cage because she loved him and wanted to protect him from her mother's cats.

The Bird's Freedom

Now in a cage, the bird stopped singing. This worried Princess September and she asked the bird to sing. The bird told her that he could not sing any further as he was unable to feel the beauty of lakes, trees and green rice growing in the fields. When the Princess told him that she would take him out everyday, the bird told her that it was different. He could no longer see nature as he could when he was free. Hence, the bird wouldn't sing and also refused to have food. Princess September was worried but her sisters told her that she was doing the right thing. They told her that she should remain firm. The Princess agreed thinking that bird would get used to it. However, the next morning, the bird laid lifeless at the bottom of the cage. As a result, Princess September thought that the bird had died and started to cry.

However, the bird was alive and upon waking up, he told the Princess that he could not sing if he couldn't fly and if he didn't sing he would die. Princess September felt very sorry for what she had done and therefore, freed the bird. The bird promised that he loved her and would keep coming to meet the Princess.

Princess September is Lonely

As the bird got free, he was happy. However, Princess September became sad and lonely. Her sisters made fun of her and told her that the bird would never return. But the bird kept on returning. He ate food from September's hands and sang her the beautiful songs he had learned while he was flying. September kept her window open day and night so that the little bird might come into her room.

Princess September's Future

Princess September grew up to be very beautiful. She got married to the King of Combodia and was sent to the king on a white elephant. Meanwhile her other sisters grew up ugly and had to be married off to the King's councillors by offering a pound of tea and a Siamese cat.

Word Meaning

Word	Meaning
Siam	former name of Thailand
Peculiar	strange
Handy	useful (here)
Oriental	of the East
Maids of Honour	women attending the Princess
Hop	jump
Willow	tree with narrow leaves
Glided	move smoothly
Perch	a place where a bird sits or rests
Vexed	distressed; worried
Lark	a songbird
Put their heads together	discussed amongst themselves to take a decision
Pop	put; push
Ominously	threateningly
Hawks	bird that kills other animals for food
Snares	traps for catching birds or animals
Alighted	sat
Thump	beat
Suspected	doubted
Ivory	a precious metal
dawn	morning
Perch	moving about quietly
Sulking	bad temper
Obstinate	stubborn
Startled	shocked
Sob	cry
Sill	ridge
Mocked	teased
Inclined	interested

NCERT FOLDER

NCERT Intext and Exercise Questions

COMPREHENSION CHECK[1] (NCERT PAGE 38)

Q.1 How many daughters did the royal couple have?

Ans. The royal couple had nine daughters.

Q.2 Why were they named after the months of the year?

Ans. They were named after the months of the year because their Queen Mother found it difficult to remember so many names.

Q.3 The King had a peculiar habit. What was it? Why is it called peculiar?

Ans. The peculiar habit that the King had was that instead of receiving gifts, he gave gifts to his daughters on his birthday. It was called peculiar because usually people receive gifts on their birthdays.

Q.4 (i) What was Princess September's reaction to the loss of her parrot?

Ans. Princess September burst into tears when she saw her parrot lying dead in its cage.

(ii) What was her mother's reaction to it?

Ans. Her mother found it stupid to be crying over a dead bird and hardly paid any heed to the Princess's loss.

(iii) What do the reactions indicate about the nature and temperament of each?

Ans. The Princess was attached to her parrot and therefore, got sentimental over its death.

The Queen, on the other hand, looked at it in a mature manner. She doesn't attach any importance to the incident of the parrot's death.

Q.5 What pulled the Princess out of her gloom?

Ans. A little bird that came hopping into her room and the beautiful song that it was singing pulled the Princess out of gloom.

Q.6 How did the Maids of Honour come to know that the Princess and the bird had become intimate friends?

Ans. When the Maids of Honour brought the Princess breakfast, the little bird was still there.

He ate rice from the hands of the Princess, had bath in her saucer and then, sang a beautiful song for the Princess. The Maids of Honour, thus, came to know that they had become intimate friends.

Q.7 The new bird was full of new songs, but the old parrots always repeated themselves. What did they say?

Ans. The old parrots only said, 'God save the King' and 'Pretty Polly'.

Q.8 What is the King's opinion about his Councillors? Why did he form that opinion?

Ans. The King felt that his councillors only sang empty praises of him. Like the parrots, they could say the same thing in seven different languages but they never meant anything that they said.

Q.9 (i) The eight Princesses made an offer to Princess September. What was it?

Ans. The other eight Princesses made an offer to put together their pocket money to buy a green and yellow parrot for their sister.

(ii) Why, in your view, did they do it?

Ans. The eight sisters made the offer because were jealous of the little bird that their sister had, who sang beautifully. They were also unhappy with how the king was looking favourably at her bird.

Q.10 What did the sisters advise the Princess to do about her bird?

Ans. The sisters advised the Princess to put her little bird in a cage so that it does not fly away from her.

CHECK❷ (NCERT PAGE 43)

Q.1 In the following sentence elaborate the underlined part in sentence. <u>Under the circumstances</u> it was <u>a very unfortunate remark</u> for the bird to make.

Ans. When the Princess was giving in to the advise given by her sisters, suspecting that the bird may never come back, the little bird made unfortunate remarks such as "The fact is I very nearly didn't come back tonight at all. My father-in-law was giving a party...."

Q.2 (i) What did Princess September do to ensure the safety of her pet?

Ans. To ensure the safety of the little bird, the Princess put the bird into the cage.

(ii) How did the bird react to it?

Ans. The bird refused to be caged and put behind the bars. He grew very unhappy and told the Princess that he could no longer sing and would die.

Q.3 Why did the bird refuse to be taken out in her cage?

Ans. The bird refused to be taken out in the cage because he could not see the trees, the lake and the rice fields in the same way as he would be able to see as a free bird. He told the Princess that everything looked different when viewed from behind the bars.

Q.4 (i) What persuaded Princess September to give the bird his freedom again?.

Ans. The bird had become so unhappy in the cage that it almost looked lifeless. The Princess gave him his freedom back because she loved him and didn't want him to die.

(ii) How did the bird react to it?

Ans. He thanked the Princess and told her that he loved the Princess so he would come back and sing a song. Then, spreading his wings he flew into the open sky.

Q.5 Princess September kept her window open day and night.

(i) How did it help the bird?

Ans. Princess September kept the window open day and night so that the bird could easily come and go whenever it liked.

(ii) How did it help the Princess herself?

Ans. The open breeze that came in from the window helped in making the Princess extremely beautiful. Later, she was married to the King of Cambodia.

Q.6 The eight sisters kept their windows shut. How did it affect them?

Ans. The eight sisters that kept their windows closed became ugly and disagreeable. Only the king's councellors were left to marry them, with gifts such as a Siamese cat and a pound of tea.

EXERCISE (NCERT PAGES 44)

Discuss the following questions in small groups. Write their answers later.

Q.1 Are the sisters unkind and cruel? Find evidence in the text to support your idea.

Ans. Yes, the sisters were unkind and cruel to Princess September. They were jealous of her little bird because it sang sweet songs for her. Also, every time he was asked to sing, he sang a new song.

The parrots of the sisters only knew how to say 'God save the King' or 'Pretty Polly.' They, therefore, instigated Princess September to put her little bird in the cage and aroused unnecessary fear in her.

Q.2 Which to you, is the most important idea in this story and why?

(i) Importance of music **(ii) Value of freedom**
(iii) Beauty of nature

Ans. (ii) The most important idea in the chapter is the value of freedom. When the little bird's freedom is taken away, he almost becomes lifeless.
On being given his freedom, he is able to live life happily, sing beautiful songs and also remains grateful and loyal to the Princess. Thus, freedom is the birth right of every living being as they should be able to live freely without any bondages.

REVIEW EXERCISE

Including Competency Based Questions

Part – I

Multiple Choice Questions

1. The King decided to name his daughters after the names of the month because

(a) they were born in those months
(b) the Queen felt confused having to remember so many names
(c) the King was fond of astrology
(d) the King didn't know any other good names

Ans. (b) the Queen felt confused having to remember so many names

2. On his birthday, the King gave each of his daughters a

(a) yellow parrot (b) grey parrot
(c) lark (d) green parrot

Ans. (d) green parrot

3. How did the Maids of Honour react to the death of Princess September's Parrot?

(a) Sadness (b) Indifference
(c) Regret (d) Nostalgia

Ans. (b) Indifference

4. Read the statements given below and choose the correct answer.

Statement 1 Princess September forgot her sorrow because of the little bird.
Statement 2 Her parents liked the little bird.

(a) Statement 1 is true but Statement 2 is false
(b) Statement 2 is true but Statement 1 is false
(c) Both the Statements are true
(d) Both the Statements are false

Ans. (c) Both the Statements are true

5. The Princesses taught their parrots to say 'Pretty Polly' in .... different languages.

(a) seven (b) five (c) eight (d) ten

Ans. (a) seven

6. What did the Princesses want to buy for September with their pocket-money?

(a) Her favourite food for supper
(b) A new book
(c) A green and yellow parrot
(d) A golden cage

Ans. (c) A green and yellow parrot

7. The Princesses asked September to

(a) take the bird to the garden
(b) lock the bird in a cage
(c) not feed the bird
(d) get rid of the bird

Ans. (b) lock the bird in a cage

8. Why was the little bird late in coming back to September?

(a) He didn't like September
(b) His father was sick
(c) His father-in-law was giving a party
(d) His mother had died

Ans. (c) His father-in-law was giving a party

9. The little bird couldn't sing because

(a) his freedom was restricted
(b) he was tired of singing songs and wanted a change
(c) his throat wasn't well after the party he attended
(d) he didn't like Princess September

Ans. (a) his freedom was restricted

10. Which of the following statements is not true in context with the story?

(a) The fourth daughter of the king was named Princess June.
(b) The Queen thought the Princess crying over a death bird was nonsensical.
(c) The King knew that his councillors never meant what they say to him in seven different ways.
(d) The little bird sang of the lake, willow trees and goldfish.

Ans. (a) The fourth daughter of the king was named Princess June.

Extract Based Questions

1. Read the extract given below and answer the following questions.

She gave a sob of relief, for she felt that his little heart was beating still. "Wake up, wake up, little bird," she said. She began to cry and her tears fell on the little bird. He opened his eyes and saw that the bars of the cage were no longer around him. "I cannot sing unless I'm free, and if I cannot sing I die," he said. The Princess gave a great sob. "Then take your freedom," she said. "I shut you in a golden cage because I loved you and wanted to have you all to myself. But I never knew it would kill you. I love you enough to let you be happy in your own way." She threw open the window and gently placed the little bird on the sill. He shook himself a little. "Come and go as you will, little bird," she said. "I will never put you in a cage anymore." "I will come because I love you, little Princess," said the bird.

(i) Why was 'she' relieved?

Ans. Princess September was relieved because her little bird was still alive as its heart was beating. She had thought he had died.

(ii) Why could the bird not sing?

Ans. The bird could not sing as he was locked inside a cage and he was not free anymore.

(iii) State whether the following statement is True or False.

The Princess caged the little bird as she wanted him all by herself and didn't love the bird much.

Ans. False

(iv) Find a word from the extract which means 'trembled'.

Ans. Shook

(v) Did the bird come back after being set free? Why/Why not?

Ans. Yes, the bird did come back to the Princess and sang many songs for her after being set free. He returned to her because he loved her and had made a promise that he would come back.

2. Read the extract given below and answer the following questions.

September kept her window open day and night so that the little bird might come into her room whenever he felt inclined and this was very good for her; so she grew extremely beautiful and when she was old enough she married the King of Cambodia and was carried on a white elephant all the way to the city in which the King lived but her sisters never slept with their windows open, so they grew extremely ugly as well as disagreeable and when the time came to marry them off they were given away to the King's Councillors with a pound of tea and a Siamese cat.

(i) September kept her window open every day because

(a) she wanted to allow the bird to come to her room whenever he wanted
(b) she wanted to see what was happening in the garden
(c) there was no light in her room
(d) she was short of breath and wanted fresh air

Ans. (a) she wanted to allow the bird to come to her room whenever he wanted

(ii) How did Princess September go to the city of her husband?

(a) On foot with her little bird
(b) In a motor car
(c) On a horse chariot
(d) On a white elephant

Ans. (d) On a white elephant

(iii) Choose the word from the following options which means 'disagreeable'.

(a) Ugly (b) Unpleasant
(c) Absent-minded (d) Always disagree

Ans. (b) Unpleasant

(iv) September's sisters grew ugly and disagreeable because

(a) they always lied
(b) they were cursed
(c) they never kept their windows open
(d) they didn't have a good bathroom

Ans. (c) they never kept their windows open

(v) What does the phrase 'given away' mean in context with the extract?

(a) To give up or abandon
(b) To bestow as a gift
(c) To expose a secret
(d) To present a bride to her spouse formally

Ans. (d) To present a bride to her spouse formally

Part – II

Very Short Answer Type Questions

1. What were the king's nine daughters named after?

Ans. The King's daughters were named after the names of the months in an year, but in the Siamese language.

2. What was the gift that the King gave to his daughters on his birthday?

Ans. The King gifted a green parrot in a golden cage to each of his daughters on his birthday.

3. **Why did the Maids of Honour put the crying Princess in the bed and went away?**

Ans. The Maids of Honour had wanted to go to a party. They, therefore, quickly put the Princess in the bed and went away.

4. **What was the little bird's song based upon?**

Ans. The little bird's song was based upon the lake in the king's garden, the willow trees that reflected its image in the water and the goldfish that glided in and out of the branches in that image.

5. **What did the little bird tell the Princess to convince her to be friends?**

Ans. The little bird asked the Princess to take him in place of her parrot. He told her that he was not as beautiful as the parrot, but had a lovely voice.

6. **Whom does the king compare the parrots with?**

Ans. The King compares his councellors with the parrots. Both of them said the same thing, 'God save the King' or 'Pretty Polly' in different languages, without meaning it.

7. **Why were the other sisters vexed?**

Ans. The eight sisters were vexed because Princess September's bird sang beautifully whereas their parrots only knew to say two phrases.

8. **Where had the little bird gone when the sisters came to meet Princess September?**

Ans. The bird had gone to pay a visit to his father-in-law when the sisters came to meet Princess September.

9. **What does the little bird do when the Princess puts him into the cage?**

Ans. The little bird gets shocked and couldn't say anything when the Princess puts him into the cage. He didn't expect the Princess to have thought of putting him there.

10. **What reason does the Princess give the bird for putting him into the cage?**

Ans. The Princess tells the bird that her mother's cats had been prowling around and to ensure the bird's safety she was putting him in the cage.

Short Answer Type Questions

1. **Why does the Princess get worried about her bird?**

Ans. The Princess gets worried because the bird had been away for a very long time. She fears that the hawks and the snares might have harmed the bird. She also thinks that the bird might have forgotten her or taken fancy to someone else.

2. **What does the Princess fear the next morning?**

Ans. When the Princess woke up next morning and called out to the bird, the bird gave no reply. He laid at the bottom of the cage with its eyes closed. The Princess feared that the bird might have died.

3. **What according to the author was very difficult to do?**

Ans. According to the author, it is very difficult to put the happiness of someone you love before your own. The Princess, however, finally places the happiness of the bird before her own happiness and lets him go, knowing that without him she would become lonely.

4. **What did the little bird say when the Princess released him from the cage?**

Ans. The little bird promised the Princess that he would never forget her and would come back as he loved the Princess. He also told the Princess that no matter how far he went he would always come back to meet and spend time with the Princess.

Long Answer Type Questions

1. **Why do the sisters end up marrying the people they do?**

Ans. When Princess September grew up, she became extremely beautiful. The reason was that she had kept window open throughout day and night so as to allow the bird to come in whenever he liked. The cool open breeze was good for her physical health. Her sensitivity to the bird and his freedom made her amicable. She was, therefore, married to the King of Cambodia and was carried on a white elephant all the way to the city in which the King lived.

The other sisters grew up to be ugly and disagreeable as they slept with their windows closed and didn't get fresh air. They were given away to the King's Councillors by offering them a pound of tea and a Siamese cat.

2. **Why did the sisters mock Princess September?**

Ans. The eight sisters mocked Princess September because they were jealous of Princess September. When they get to know that Princess September had let her little bird fly freely and didn't put him in a cage, they made fun of her for her stupidity. They envied Princess September inwardly as she had a bird that sang beautifully while their parrots only knew how to say 'God save the King' and 'Pretty Polly'.

They told her that her little bird would never come back and that she had made a blunder. But, the bird did come back and sang a beautiful song for the Princess. He also ate from her hand and used to love the Princess dearly.

3. Does the story recommend the idea of birds being made pets?

Ans. No, the idea of birds as pets may sound cute and loveable but birds should never be turned into pets and thereby put in cages. The inherent nature of birds is to fly.

By putting them behind bars of cages, we curb what they are meant for. Unlike human beings and animals that do not have wings, birds are blessed with wings so that they could fly.

By controlling their flight, we are going against the laws of nature. The little bird in the story almost becomes lifeless when he realises that he could be caged forever. The parrot could have also died for similar reasons.

ASSESSMENT EXERCISE

Multiple Choice Questions

1. Princess September had .... sisters.
   (a) twelve (b) eleven (c) eight (d) seven
2. Read the given statements and choose the correct answer.
   Statement 1 The King of Siam didn't love the princesses equally.
   Statement 2 The Queen didn't regret making Princess September starve when her parrot died.
   (a) Statement 1 is true but Statement 2 is false.
   (b) Statement 1 is false but Statement 2 is true.
   (c) Both Statements are true.
   (d) Both Statements are false.
3. Who said 'God save the King' and 'Pretty Polly' often?
   (a) The parrots (b) The princesses
   (c) The councillors (d) Both (a) and (c)
4. What was the reaction of the King and Queen when they first heard the little bird sing?
   (a) The King and Queen were delighted but not surprised.
   (b) The King and Queen were surprised but not delighted.
   (c) The King and Queen were tired of hearing it sing.
   (d) The King and Queen were both delighted and surprised.
5. How did the princesses sit down around Princess September when they came to meet her?
   (a) In a circle (b) In a semi-circle
   (c) In a triangle shaped (d) Scattered

Extract Based Question

Read the given extract and answer the following questions.

The bird wouldn't sing a song and he wouldn't eat a thing. The Princess was a little anxious at this, and asked her sisters what they thought about it.

"You must be firm," they said.

"But if he won't eat, he'll die," she answered.

"That would be very ungrateful of him," they said. "He must know that you're only thinking of his own good. If he's obstinate and dies it'll serve him right and you'll be well rid of him."

September didn't see how that was going to do her very much good, they were eight to one and all older than she, so she said nothing.

"Perhaps he'll have got used to his cage by tomorrow," she said.

(i) Complete the following sentence appropriately.
Princess September was worried that as her little bird was refusing to eat and ....

(ii) What was her sisters' response to her worry?

(iii) Why did Princess September do when her sisters explained their thoughts on her worries?

(iv) Which one of the following words means the opposite of 'obstinate'?
(a) Stubborn
(b) Complaint
(c) Stiff
(d) Contrary

(v) What did Princess September expect to happen the next day?
(a) For the bird to get used to the cage
(b) For the bird to start eating again
(c) For the bird to start singing again
(d) For the bird to get his freedom

Very Short Answer Type Questions

1. What was the name of the third oldest daughter of the King of Siam?
2. Why were the eight Princesses jealous of Princess September?
3. Explain the meaning of the phrase, 'put their heads together'.
4. Describe the qualities of the Princess's little bird.
5. Whom does Princess September get married to?

Short Answer Type Questions

1. Why does Princess September become uneasy when her bird is late in coming back?
2. Why did the Princess let lose the bird?
3. Why does Princess September fear that the bird might die?

Long Answer Type Questions

1. Write a character sketch of the eight sisters.
2. What lesson does the story impart?

The Fight

by Ruskin Bond

Part – I

CHAPTER SUMMARY

'The Fight' by Ruskin Bond is a story about two boys who fight with each other over something that does not belong to anyone. The boys don't know each other and so participate in a useless fight. However, in the end, they become friends and decide to help each other in gaining some skills.

Discovery of the Pool

It had been less than a month living in Rajpur when Ranji discovered a pool. The summer was at its extreme and Ranji's school hadn't opened yet. He didn't have any friends in this semi-hill station. While wandering all by himself in a hot and tired day, he discovered a pool in the forest. On the day when Ranji discovered the pool, it was extremely hot and Ranji's brown feet had turned chalky with dust.

The water had a gentle transparency on that day. In monsoon, however, the water would come rushing down the hills. But, during the summer the water was merely a trickle. Unlike in the plains, here the rocks held the water and therefore, the pool did not dry up.

Ranji Goes into the Pool

Ranji had never seen a pool like this. Pools in Rajputana were sticky and muddy. Only buffaloes wallowed in those pools and women washed their clothes in it. This pool was clean and cold and therefore, inviting. Ranji had often gone for swimming with his friends and even alone. Therefore, he didn't hesitate to jump into the pool. His dark body shined as patches of sun-lit water touched it.

The Fighter Meets the Warrior

The next day when Ranji came to the pool, he was there for almost an hour when he noticed another boy, who was a little older than him, staring at him. Ranji was taken aback by the hatred displayed this stranger. The boy told Ranji that the pool belonged to him and he liked to swim alone. He added that he didn't appreciate uninvited visitors. The boy also informed Ranji that he was a warrior and didn't like speaking to villagers. Hearing this, Ranji told him that he was not a villager but a fighter. Hence, both of them reached a situation which could not be solved.

A Fight Broke Out

When none of them said anything and Ranji didn't make any move to leave, the stranger made a strange sound and slapped Ranji across the face with all his force. There were red finger marks on Ranji's cheek. Ranji almost fell down and felt quite dizzy but then, he mustered courage and punched the stranger. Soon, they were rolling over in dust, mud, and even in the water while fighting with each other.

The Fight Exhausted the Boys

The boys fought with each other for five minutes but nobody emerged victorious. Their bodies were exhausted and they needed to put effort to be able to speak. Each, after reiterating their status as a warrior and a fighter, decided that they were not going to lose. The warrior asked Ranji if he would leave the pool. Ranji continued to answer that he would not. They resolved the matter for the time being by deciding to continue with the fight the next day.

Part II

After the First Fight

As Ranji got back home, he found it difficult to explain to his mother the cause of his injuries. Although his mother instructed him to stay at home, he thought of going to the market and finding peace in a bottle of lemonade and hot and sweet jalebis wrapped in a banana leaf. In the market he saw the stranger, who was his enemy. He wanted to throw the bottle of lemonade on him or to look in another direction. But, Ranji choose to angrily stare at him. The warrior also glared back at Ranji.

The Next Day

The next day, Ranji felt weak and lazy. He was not at all eager for a fight. However, he did not wish to accept his defeat by not showing up at the pool and refusing a challenge. He also believed that he needed to fight to gain his respect. He went to the pool thinking that he had the right to the pool as long as he fought. He also hoped that the warrior might have forgotten the challenge by now. On reaching the pool, however, he saw his opponent on the other side of the rock.

Challenging Each Other

Ranji's opponent saw him and called out the challenge. So, Ranji asked him to come to his side for the fight.

The warrior challenged Ranji to swim to his side if he knew how to swim. Ranji was pretty good at swimming so he dived into the pool and came swimming to the other side. Seeing this, the warrior was shocked.

Becoming Friends

The warrior told Ranji that he was very good at diving. However, the warrior found diving a difficult task. At this, Ranji told the warrior that diving was fairly easy. Ranji demonstrated to the warrior how to dive. The warrior tried doing it, but fell into the water. Seeing this, Ranji began to laugh. Ranji tried to teach the warrior one more time. Ranji also showed him how to breathe underwater and swim at the bottom of the pool. The warrior asked Ranji to teach him both the skills. Soon, both boys had forgotten the fight and the challenge. They exchanged names with each other. The warrior Suraj promised Ranji that he would teach him how to become a pahelwan if Ranji taught him how to dive. On this note, both became friends. Suraj told Ranji that now it was their pool and not his alone. Ranji smiled that he had actually won that day.

Word Meaning

Word	Meaning
Plunges	dive
Ensues	follow
Interminably	endlessly
Chalky	feeling or tasting like chalk
Parched	hot and dry
Translucency	clarity
Cluster	group

Word	Meaning
Feed	fill
Gushing	talkative
Torrent	rushing stream of water
Cascading	coming down like a waterfall
Supple	agile
Quench	satisfy
Glistened	sparkle

Word	Meaning
Thickset	stout/solidly built
Limpid	clear
Taken aback	surprised
Strode	progress
Impasse	deadlock
Penetrated	gone through/into
Muster	gather
Staggered	stumbled
Assailant	the person who attacks
Swung	moved to and fro
Bony	skinny
Gasping	out of breath
Groped	touch someone in a rough way
Spluttering	speaking quickly/confusedly
Clawing	scrape
Muster	collect or gather
Swaying	moving from side to side

Word	Meaning
Frenzied	violent
Heaving	breathing heavily
Solace	comfort
Impulse	reaction
Adversary	opponent
Scowled	looked angrily
Ferocity	fierceness
Acquiesce	accept quietly
Dashed	in trouble
Vigour	strength
Superiority	authority
Treading water	keeping oneself upright in deep water by moving the feet
Seer	ser; a unit of weight
Spouting	executed
Unflinching	looking straight at each other

NCERT FOLDER

NCERT Intext and Exercise Questions

COMPREHENSION CHECK[1] (NCERT PAGE 49)

Q.1 In what way is the forest pool different from the one which Ranji knew in the Rajputana desert?

Ans. The forest pool was cleaner than the pool in the Rajputana desert. It was also so clear that the smooth round pebbles could be seen at the bottom of the pool. A small stream provided the water to the pool. It also had cold water. The water in the Rajputana desert pool was muddy and sticky.

Q.2 The other boy asked Ranji to 'explain' himself.

(i) What did he expect Ranji to say?

Ans. The other boy expected Ranji to apologise for swimming in the pool without asking his permission to use it.

(ii) Was he in your opinion, right or wrong to ask this question?

Ans. He was wrong in putting those questions to Ranji. The pool was not his personal property.

Q.3 Between Ranji and the other boy, who is trying to start a quarrel? Give a reason for your answer.

Ans. The other boy was trying to start a quarrel. He stared at Ranji in a hostile manner and threw questions at him in a threatening way. Ranji, on the other hand, welcomed him to join him and give company.

Q.4 "Then we will have to continue the fight," said the other.

(i) What made him say that?

Ans. After having fought for five minutes, the boys felt exhausted. However, none of them had emerged victorious. Also, Ranji refused to leave the pool. Therefore, the other boy said that they will have to continue the fight tomorrow.

(ii) Did the fight continue? If not, why not?

Ans. No, the fight did not continue. Although the next day, they met with an intention to continue the fight, the warrior was so impressed with the way Ranji dived that he wanted Ranji to teach him the same. This brought an end to the fight.

CHECK❷ (NCERT PAGE 53-54)

Q.1 What is it that Ranji finds difficult to explain at home?

Ans. Ranji finds it difficult to give an explanation for the wounds and bruises on his face, legs and arms that he incurred during the fight.

Q.2 Ranji sees his adversary in the bazaar.

(i) What does he wish to do?

Ans. Ranji wished to look in the other direction or throw the bottle of lemonade on his adversary, when he sees him in the bazaar.

(ii) What does he actually do and why?

Ans. Ranji actually stood still and angrily stared at his adversary.

Q.3 'Ranji is not at all eager for a second fight. Why does he go back to the pool', then?

Ans. Ranji felt weak for the second fight. He goes back to the pool because he fears that his absence might be understood as his defeat.

Q.4 Who was the better swimmer? How do you know it?

Ans. Ranji was the better swimmer. He knew how to dive and could also swim under water. The other boy neither knew how to dive nor did he know how to swim under the water.

Q.5 What surprises the warrior?

Ans. The warrior was surprised to see Ranji diving into the water.

Q.6 Now that they are at the pool, why don't they continue the fight?

Ans. The warrior and the fighter do not continue the fight as they had become friends. Suraj asked Ranji to teach him to swim. In return, he told Ranji that he would help him become a 'pahelwan'.

Q.7 Ranji's superiority over the other boy is obvious in the following:
physical strength, good diving, sense of humour, swimming under water, making a good point, willingness to help Underline the relevant phrases.

Ans. Physical strength, <u>good diving</u>, <u>sense of humour</u>, <u>swimming under water</u>, making a good point, <u>willingness to help</u>.

Q.8 What, according to you, makes the two adversaries turn into good friends in a matter of minutes? Explain it as you have understood it.

Ans. The two adversaries turn into good friends because they wished to learn something from each other. Also, Ranji had come to fight merely for the sake of self respect. He, otherwise, had no intention to fight.

EXERCISE (NCERT PAGE 54)

Discuss the following topics in small groups.

Q.1 Is fighting the only way of resolving differences of opinion? What else can be done to reach a mutually acceptable settlement?

Ans. No. Fighting is not the only way of resolving differences of opinion. Rather, differences of opinions could be resolved in much better ways. For instance, having a dialogue is a much better way to reach a mutually acceptable settlement.

Q.2 Have you ever been in a serious fight only to realise later that it was unnecessary and futile? Share your experience/views with others frankly and honestly.

Ans. Yes. I have been in a serious fight. Later, I realised that it was unnecessary and futile.

I could have easily controlled the situation had I been a little more calm and patient.

Instead of pointing out the mistakes in others, had I concentrated on my own faults, the fight could have been avoided.

Q.3 Why do some of us find it necessary to prove that we are better than others? Will you be amused or annoyed to read the following sign at the back of the car in front of you?
I may be going slow but I am ahead of you.

Ans. Do it yourself.

REVIEW EXERCISE

Including Competency Based Questions

Part – I

Multiple Choice Questions

1. Where did Ranji discover the pool?

(a) Beach (b) Grassland (c) Forest (d) Desert

Ans. (c) Forest

2. The water in the pool didn't dry up because

(a) it was monsoon period (b) people took care of it
(c) the weather was cold (d) the rocks held the water

Ans. (d) the rocks held the water

3. What was the expression of the boy looking at Ranji while he was lying in the shade near the pool?

(a) Hostile (b) Amused
(c) Curious (d) Sad

Ans. (a) Hostile

4. Complete the sentence appropriately by using the correct answer from the given options.

The other boy asked Ranji if he didn't know he was a warrior and that he did not ....

(a) give permission to Ranji to use the pool
(b) like Ranji using the pool as his own
(c) take replies from villagers like Ranji
(d) like Ranji's physical appearence

Ans. (c) take replies from villagers like Ranji

5. Ranji called himself a

(a) villager (b) fighter
(c) warrior (d) newcomer

Ans. (b) fighter

6. Read the statements properly and choose the correct answer from the following options.

Statement 1 Ranji found it difficult to conceal the cuts and bruises on his body.

Statement 2 Ranji was not able to explain the fact that he had been in a violent fight.

(a) Statement 1 is true but Statement 2 is false.
(b) Statement 1 is false but Statement 2 is true.
(c) Both Statements are true.
(d) Both Statements are false.

Ans. (c) Both Statements are true.

7. How does the warrior react on seeing Ranji dive?

(a) Anger (b) Envy (c) Regret (d) Shock

Ans. (d) Shock

8. Ranji went to the pool the next day even though he was stiff and sore because

(a) he was confident of victory
(b) not going would be an acknowledgement of defeat
(c) he was tired of staying home
(d) he wanted to show off his power

Ans. (b) not going would be an acknowledgement of defeat

9. Ranji was half hoping that the warrior

(a) would not turn up at the pool
(b) would have forgotten about the challenge
(c) would be well prepared to fight
(d) was going to drown in the water of the pool

Ans. (b) would have forgotten about the challenge

10. The warrior wanted to be .... one day.

(a) a policeman
(b) professional swimmer
(c) the world's champion wrestler
(d) villager

Ans. (c) the world's champion wrestler

Extract Based Questions

1. Read the extract given below and answer the following questions.

When Ranji got home, he found it difficult to explain the cuts and bruises that showed on his face, leg and arms. It was difficult to conceal the fact that he had been in an unusually violent fight, and his mother insisted on his staying at home for the rest of the day. That evening, though, he slipped out of the house and went to the bazaar, where he found comfort and solace in a bottle of vividly coloured lemonade and a banana leaf full of hot, sweet jalebis. He had just finished the lemonade when he saw his adversary coming down the road. His first impulse was to turn away and look elsewhere, his second to throw the lemonade bottle at his enemy.

(i) **How did Ranji get cuts and bruises on his body?**

Ans. Ranji got cuts and bruises on his body because he had been in an unusually violent fight with the warrior at the pool in the forest.

(ii) **What did Ranji's mother ask him to do?**

Ans. Ranji's mother asked him to stay home for the rest of the day.

(iii) **Find a word from the extract which means 'distinctly'.**

Ans. Vividly

(iv) **What is the meaning of the phrase 'slipped out' in the extract?**

Ans. In the given extract, the phrase 'slipped out' means to leave a place without being noticed.

(v) **What did Ranji want to do when he saw his enemy?**

Ans. When Ranji saw his enemy coming down the road, his first impulse was to turn away and look elsewhere, his second was to throw the lemonade bottle at him.

2. Read the extract given below and answer the following questions.

"You are strong," said Ranji. "You are a real pahelwan." "One day I will be the world's champion wrestler," said Suraj, slapping his thighs, which shook with the impact of his hand. He looked critically at Ranji's hard, thin body. "You are quite strong yourself," he conceded. "But you are too bony. I know, you people do not eat enough. You must come and have your food with me. I drink one seer of milk every day. We have got our own cow! Be my friend, and I will make you a pahelwan like me! I know – if you teach me to dive and swim underwater, I will make you a pahelwan! That is fair, isn't it?"

(i) **Ranji calls the warrior a**

(a) real pahelwan (b) villager
(c) skinny boy (d) weak warrior

Ans. (a) real pahelwan

(ii) **Why did Suraj's thighs shake?**

(a) He was exhausted from the fight
(b) As a result of him slapping his thighs
(c) Ranji slapped his thighs
(d) As a result of him jumping from one side to the other

Ans. (b) As a result of him slapping his thighs

(iii) **Suraj asks Ranji to**

(a) leave the pool
(b) take his cow
(c) settle the fight with him
(d) have food with him

Ans. (d) have food with him

(iv) **Suraj drank one seer of .... everyday.**

(a) lemonade (b) milk
(c) apple juice (d) orange juice

Ans. (b) milk

(v) **Which word in the following options means 'concede'?**

(a) acknowledge (b) praise
(c) gives in to (d) allow

Ans. (a) acknowledge

Part – II

Very Short Answer Type Questions

1. In which city did Ranji discover the pool?

Ans. Ranji discovered the pool in Rajpur.

2. Describe Ranji's appearance when he was introduced.

Ans. Ranji was wearing vest and shorts and his brown feet had become chalky with dust because of walking in extreme heat.

3. How would the stream that Ranji came across look during monsoon?

Ans. During monsoon, the stream that Ranji came across would be a gushing torrent coming down like a waterfall from the hills.

4. How did Ranji and the stranger introduce themselves to each other?

Ans. The stranger introduced himself as a Warrior. Ranji, on the other hand, introduced himself as a Fighter.

5. What instructions were given by Ranji to the stranger to make a good dive?

Ans. Ranji asked the stranger to stand on the rock, stretch out his arms and allow his head to displace his feet.

Short Answer Type Questions

1. What was the atmosphere of Rajpur when Ranji visits the place?

Ans. It was extremely hot in Rajpur when Ranji visits the place. The earth was parched and the grass was brown.

The trees had become listless and were hardly stirring, as if waiting for a cool wind or a refreshing shower of rain.

2. What happened when Ranji went to the bazaar?

Ans. Ranji went to the bazaar to find solace in a bottle of lemonade and hot and sweet jalebis. When he had just finished his lemonade, he saw Suraj coming down to the bazaar. Ranji wanted to ignore him or through his bottle of lemonade on him. He merely stared at his opponent, though.

3. Why did Ranji go to the pool the next day, despite feeling weak for the fight?

Ans. Despite feeling weak for the fight, Ranji went to the pool the next day because he didn't wish to accept defeat quietly. Refusing the challenge would mean cowardice. Ranji didn't wish to accept defeat or let go off the pool without fighting for it because as long as he fought he reserved a right to the pool.

4. Describe the physical appearances of Suraj and Ranji.

Ans. Suraj was tall and solidly built. He had a broad nose and thick red lips. He was older than Ranji, and stronger too. Ranji, on the other hand, was thin and bony. Though Ranji was strong, too, his limbs were supple and free from any fat.

Long Answer Type Questions

1. Give details of the fight that took place between Ranji and Suraj.

Ans. When Ranji refused to leave the pool, Suraj took on a violent expression. He made hissing sounds and both Ranji and Suraj kept staring at each other. Then, Suraj slapped Ranji with great force. Gathering himself, Ranji swung his arm up and pushed a hard bony fist into Suraj's face. Soon, both were at each other's throats and were rolling over and over in the dust.

Their fight continued for sometime in which both were groping for each other's head and throat.

2. "Ranji smiled with the knowledge that he had won the day." Justify the statement in context of the story.

Ans. Towards the end of the story, Ranji understood that even without fighting, he had won the match and he had a claim over the pool. Suraj was now willing to address the pool as 'our pool'. This was what Ranji had wanted when he met the stranger, Suraj.

Ranji displays a calm and composed self by not imposing his triumph or victory on Suraj and thereby maintaining a peaceful truce that had happened between the two of them.

Ranji doesn't display the hostility that Suraj had showed towards him and thus, avoids causing any more fights between the two.

ASSESSMENT EXERCISE

Multiple Choice Questions

1. When Ranji saw his adversary at the bazaar, he

(a) turned away and looked elsewhere
(b) threw the bottle of lemonade at him
(c) smiled and shook his hand
(d) scowled at his passing enemy

2. According to Suraj, if Ranji didn't teach him to swim, he would

(a) never let him enter the forest
(b) never let him swim in the pool
(c) beat him
(d) never talk to him again

3. Read the given statements and choose the correct answer.

Statement 1 The warrior made thick red finger marks on Ranji's cheek.

Statement 2 Ranji tried to swing his fist but he failed to land a blow to the warrior's face.

(a) Statement 1 is true but Statement 2 is false.
(b) Statement 1 is false but Statement 2 is true.
(c) Both Statements are true.
(d) Both Statements are false.

4. How was the weather of the next day of fight between Ranji and the warrior?

(a) Cold (b) Hot (c) Windy (d) Sweaty

5. Why did Suraj think the reason for Ranji being bony was?

(a) Ranji did not eat enough food.
(b) Ranji didn't drink enough milk.
(c) Ranji did not exercise like he did.
(d) Ranji was naturally skinny.

Extract Based Question

Read the given extract and answer the following questions.

And then they were at each other's throats, swaying on the rock, tumbling on to the sand, rolling over and over, their legs and arms locked in a desperate, violent struggle. Gasping and cursing, clawing and slapping, they rolled into the shallows of the pool.

Even in the water, the fight continued as, spluttering and covered with mud, they groped for each other's head and throat. But after five minutes of frenzied, unscientific struggle, neither boy has emerged victorious. Their bodies heaving with exhaustion, they stood back from each other, making tremendous efforts to speak.

(i) Complete the sentence appropriately.
They were at each other's throat and head, as the fight ....

(ii) Why was the fight considered as an unscientific struggle?

(iii) Find a word from the extract which has the same meaning as 'heave'.

(iv) What were locked in a desperate attempt in the fight?
(a) Throats
(b) Legs and arms
(c) Throats and heads
(d) Bodies

(v) Which one of the given options is an antonym of 'tremendous'.
(a) Ample (b) Excellent
(c) Slight (d) Fixed scale

Very Short Answer Type Questions

1. For how long did the fight continue between Ranji and his opponent?

2. Why did the two boys reach an impasse?

3. What does Ranji's mother suggest him to do after he returns from the fight?

4. "I will have to beat you," said the stranger.
What did the stranger do next to show his violent attitude?

5. "Then we shall have to continue the fight," said the other. "All right," said Ranji.
Which incident followed this conversation between the two boys?

Short Answer Type Questions

1. Do you affirm Suraj's sole claim to the pool?

2. Explain the meaning of, "Ranji, smiling with the knowledge that he had won the day."

3. How does Ranji save his honour?

4. How different was the pool in Rajpur from the one in Rajputana?

Long Answer Type Question

1. Justify the title of the story 'The Fight'.

Jalebis

by Ahmed Nadeem Qasmi

Part – I

CHAPTER SUMMARY

The story 'Jalebis' by Ahmed Nadeem Qasmi is a value based moral story teaching children about not using money for something other than its actual use. In the story, a boy uses the money he gets to pay his fee to buy jalebis. In the end, he has no money to pay his fees and is punished.

The Narrator has Money

The narrator was in the fifth standard at the government school of Kambelpur, now called Atak. One day, he had gone to school with four rupees in his pocket. The money was given to him to pay the school fees and the fund. When the narrator reached the school, the teacher who collected the fees, Master Ghulam Mohammed, was on leave. So, the fees would be collected the next day. The coins he had were quiet in school but as soon as the school got over the coins started talking.

The Talking Coins

The narrator says that he knows that coins don't talk. They make a noise. However, that day they talked. One coin told him that he should go and buy hot jalebis with it. The coin urged the boy to spend it as money was meant to be spent. The boy answered the coins that he was a good boy and the coins should not be misguiding him. He told the coins that he was well fed at home and buying anything from the shops would be bad. He also told the coins that the money was meant for his fees.

He asked the coins how would he be able to face Master Ghulam Mohammed and Allah Miyan at Qayamat if he spent his money. On top of it, when Master Ghulam Mohammed got mad, he might even make him stand on the bench till the last bell rang.

Silencing the Coins

The coins didn't appreciate the argument given by the young boy. They, therefore, all began to talk at the same time and made a lot of sound. They made such noise that passersby began to stare at the boy. The boy closed them tight in his fist. They were silent for some time. A little later, the boy loosened his fist and the coins again began to lure him. The oldest coin tempted him by saying that he could pay his fees with scholarship money.

The Boy Thinks about the Situation

The boy knew that what the coins were telling him was not right, but he thought that they were not wrong either. The boy began to think about the hot, fresh jalebis full of sweet sugar. He was tempted but he was also thinking about the entire situation. He came from a well-to-do family and had enjoyed a considerable prestige and status in his class. Masterji had often asked him to beat the other boys in the class. Eating jalebis in the middle of the bazaar was not easy for him. So, he clenched his fist again and came back home.

The Boy Finally Gave In

The coins, however, wouldn't stop making noises. The boy could not bear the noise created by the coins. He finally gave in to their wish. Without wearing his shoes, he rushed to the bazaar and asked the halwai to weigh him jalebis worth a rupee. The halwai opened a whole newspaper and heaped a pile of jalebis on it.

Eating and Giving Away the Jalebis

He had hardly gathered the heap of jalebis when he saw his chachajaan (uncle) returning from court. So, the boy immediately held the jalebis and ran into a gali (street). Reaching a safe corner, he began eating the jalebis and he ate so many that he felt that jalebis would pop out from his ears and nostrils. Soon, he saw that the boys from the neighbourhood had assembled in the gali. He was so full that he started handing out jalebis to the children around. Soon, more and more children came. He stood on the chabutara and distributed the jalebis to the children like the Governor Saheb. He kept distributing the jalebis and one by one, spent all the four coins to buy jalebis. He even felt that he would be elected to the assembly if children were allowed.

The Boy's Stomach is Full

After having washed his hands and mouth, he got back home pretending innocence. He feared that he might burp and jalebis would pop out. At night he had to eat his dinner, though his stomach was full with the jalebis he had eaten. Not eating the dinner would demand an explanation. And if doctor was called, then he would be exposed. So, he simply had his dinner, and spent rest of the night suffering a stomach ache. The next morning, he was absolutely fine.

The Bad News

Getting ready for school, he headed towards it feeling secure that he would receive four rupees as scholarship money. He would use that money to pay his fees. However on reaching the school, he found out that the scholarship money would be paid next month. Master Ghulam Mohammed announced that the money for the fees would be collected during the recess.

Not knowing what to do, the boy ran away from the school after the recess. He started praying to Allah Miyan (God) to send a farishta (angel) who would drop four rupees into his pocket, promising that he would not eat jalebis this time. He kept walking and walking till he reached the point where the Kambelpur railway station began.

The Boy is Sad

The boy sat down under a shade-giving tree besides the railway track. There, he realised that the things that seemed too simple had unnecessarily become complex. He thought that if he had known that they would get the money next month, he would not have spent his money. Now, he was missing school, for the first time and sitting under a tree. As a result, the boy wanted to cry. He began to pray to Allah Miyan that somehow he should give four rupees to him.

The Boy Keeps Praying

The boy kept praying the rest of the day, making promises to offer namaaz, recite the ten surats and Ayat-al-Kursi and so on. But, nothing happened. The next day, too, he walked directly to the spot and offered endless prayers. Then, he decided to play a game with Allah Miyan. He decided to run from the tree to the signal and asked Allah Miyan to place four rupees under the rock. All he could find under the rock, however, was a hairy worm. He kept playing this game in the hope that Allah Miyan would give in to his wishes.

The Boy Gets Caught

On the second day, the boy decided to think of strategies to strike a deal with Allah Miyan. However, that very day the report of him being absent from school had reached his home. He thought it needless to share what the consequences were, but till his eighth standard he kept wondering what harm would have occurred had Allah Miyan granted him four rupees. Only later, he realised that if Allah Miyan was to grant everything merely by listening to man's prayers and demands, man would not have learnt to do anything. As a result, man would still be living in nests like vultures and crows. They wouldn't even have known the art of making jalebis.

Word Meaning

Word	Meaning	Word	Meaning
Kadhao	large open pot for cooking	Gobbled	eaten quickly/greedily
Clamour	loud noise	Summoned	sent for/called
Wretched	evil	Burp	make noise when air from stomach leaves mouth
Blabbering	talking confusedly	Tucked	inserted
Clenched	compress	Crouching	sitting
Kissa khatam paisa hazam	end of story	Racket	uproar/ loud noise
Persuasion	coaxing	Surats	verses from the holy Quran
Hand cart	cart pushed by hand	Ayat-al-Kursi	title of a verse in the holy Quran
Devour	eat greedily	Treasury	wealth
Popped	come out	Decreed	command
Jalebi-wielding hand	the hand that held jalebis	Curling	bending
		Wriggled	move about

NCERT FOLDER

NCERT Intext and Exercise Questions

COMPREHENSION CHECK (NCERT PAGE 58)

Q.1 Why didn't he pay the school fees on the day he brought money to school?

Ans. He didn't pay the school fees on the day he brought the money because the teacher who was supposed to collect the fees money was on leave.

Q.2 (i) What were the coins 'saying' to him?

Ans. The coins were asking him to spend them by buying fresh and sweet syrupy jalebis.

(ii) Do you think they were misguiding him?

Ans. Yes, they were misguiding him by tempting the boy.

Q.3 Why didn't he take the coins' advice? Give two or three reasons.

Ans. He didn't take the coins's advice because he thought that he came from a good house and was well fed at home. Spending money to buy things from the bazaar would be a sin. He was also conscious of the fact that the money he had was meant for his fees, which he had to pay the next day.

Q.4 (i) What did the oldest coin tell him?

Ans. The oldest coin told him that they were trying to tell him something for his own good. The coin told him that if he spends the fees money on jalebis, he can still pay the fees with the scholarship money he was going to get the next day.

After all, the oldest coin questioned him, didn't he wish to have hot jalebis.

(ii) Did he follow his advice? If not, why not.

Ans. No, he didn't follow his advice. He knew that what he was saying was not wrong. Further, he was afraid that by doing something of that sort, his prestige must be put on stake.

Q.5 He reached home with the coins in his pocket. What happened then?

Ans. As he reached his home with the coins in his pocket, the coins began to talk again. When he went to take his lunch, the coins were shrieking.

He got frustrated with the sound that the coins made and finally gave in. He rushed to the bazaar to buy jalebis for a whole rupee from the halwai.

CHECK❷ (NCERT PAGE 61)

Q.1 (i) Why didn't he eat all the jalebis he had bought?

Ans. He didn't eat all the jalebis he bought because there were too many jalebis and his stomach was already full.

(ii) What did he do with the remaining jalebis?

Ans. He distributed the remaining jalebis to the boys from the neighbourhood who had assembled in the gali.

Q.2 "The fear was killing me." What was the fear?

Ans. The fear was that with every burp, a jalebi or two might pop out since he had eaten too many jalebis. Furthermore, at night he was also to have his dinner.

Q.3 "Children's stomachs are like digestion machines." What do you understand by that? Do you agree?

Ans. The phrase means that children can digest greater amount of food without much problem. Whatever the boy ate, he was able to digest by next morning.

I do not agree with this because overeating may cause digestive problems and upset the metabolism of the child leading to various other problems.

Q.4 How did he plan to pay the fees the next day?

Ans. The next day, he planned to pay the fees with the four rupees he was supposed to get as scholarship money.

Q.5 When it is time to pay the fees, what does he do? How is he disobeying the elders by doing so?

Ans. As he didn't get the scholarship money that day, when the time came to pay the fees, he simply carried his bag and left the school. He disobeyed his elders by spending the fees money on sweet jalebis and by crossing the railway track, something he was warned against.

CHECK❸ (NCERT PAGE 65)

Q.1 What was the consequence of buying jalebis with the fees money?

Ans. The consequences of buying jalebis with the fees money was that he was not left with any money to pay his fees. In order to escape the punishment of not being able to pay the fees, he would dress up for school but go to the railway station, thus missing his classes.

Q.2 His prayer to God is like a lawyer's defence of a bad case. Does he argue his case well? What are the points he makes?

Ans. He argues his case well by giving good logic for having spent the fees money on buying jalebis.
He tells God that the problem would not have occurred had he got the scholarship money on time. He further say that had he known this before then he would have postponed buying jalebis till the next month.

He also tries to strike a deal with God by promising to recite the ten Surats, Ayat-al-Kursi and Namaaz.

Q.3 He offers to play a game with Allah Miyan. What is the game?

Ans. The game was that he would run up till the signal and before he returned from the signal, Allah Miyan should place four rupees under the rock. He would touch the signal, come back to the place and look underneath said rock.

Q.4 Did he get four rupees by playing the game? What did he get to see under the rock?

Ans. No, he didn't get the four rupees. All that he got to see under the rock was a hairy worm.

Q.5 If God has granted his wish that day, what harm would it have caused him in later life.

Ans. If God would have granted his wish that day he wouldn't have learnt a very important lesson.

He would not have understood that if God fulfilled all the wishes of man then he wouldn't have understood that hard work was important.

And if man doesn't learn anything, then he would have been like birds and wouldn't have known how to make jalebis.

EXERCISE (NCERT PAGE 65)

Work in small groups

Q.1 Select and read sentences that show

- **that the boy is tempted to eat jalebis.**

Ans. The following statements from the chapter show that the boy is tempted to eatjalebis.

(i) Jalebis are meant to be eaten and only those with money in their pocket can eat them.

(ii) But then, these jalebis are no common sort of jalebis either. They're crisp, fresh and full of syrup.
My mouth watered.

- **that he is feeling guilty.**

Ans. The following statements from the chapter show that the boy was feeling guilty.

(i) My head started to spin. I felt as if I was standing on my head and could not get on to my feet again if I tried.

(ii) When the recess bell rang, I tucked my bag under my arm and left the school.

(iii) Now for the crime of eating the jalebis, for the first time in my life I was absent from the school.

(iv) Sitting under a tree, at first I felt like crying.

- **that he is justifying a wrong deed.**

Ans. The following statements from the chapter show that the boy was justifying a wrong deed.

(i) I didn't eat them all by myself and I fed them to a whole lot of children.

(ii) Allah Miyan, I am a very good boy. I have memorised the whole Namaaz.

Discuss the following points.

- **Is the boy intelligent? If so, what is the evidence of it.**

Ans. The narrator is an intelligent boy. He has won a scholarship and is one of the most promising students.

- **Does his outlook on the jalebis episode change after class VIII? Does he see that episode in a new light?**

Ans. Yes. His outlook on the jalebis episode changes after Class VIII. He is able to look at the episode with a new light. He is able to understand that he tried to tempt and lure God without understanding the ways of God and man. If God was to grant man everything that man asked for, man wouldn't have understood the need to work and would be no better than words.

- **Why are 'coins' made to talk in the story? What purpose does it serve?**

Ans. The coins are made to talk in the story because the voice of the coins is the boy's own confused mind, trying to resolve the conflict between eating or not eating the jalebis. He was tempted to eat the jalebis, at the same time he was hesitant because of his prestige.

REVIEW EXERCISE

Including Competency Based Questions

Part – I

Multiple Choice Questions

1. The writer was in .... standard at the .... school, Kambelpur.

(a) fifth, government (b) fifth, public

(c) eight, government (d) eighth, public

Ans. (a) fifth, government

2. What was the four rupees for?

(i) School fees **(ii) Fund**

(iii) Tuition fees **(iv) Jalebis**

(a) Both (i) and (ii) (b) Both (ii) and (iv)

(c) Both (i) and (iv) (d) (i), (ii) and (iv)

Ans. (a) Both (i) and (ii)

3. The coins began talking when

(a) the boy was in school

(b) the boy spoke to his friends

(c) the boy left home for school that day

(d) the school was over and he was outside

Ans. (d) the school was over and he was outside

4. The boy considered even looking at something in the bazaar a sin because

(a) he was poor

(b) the bazaar didn't have anything good to eat

(c) the sellers at the bazaar used to cheat him

(d) he got so much at home

Ans. (d) he got so much at home

5. According to the boy, when Master Ghulam Mohammed gets angry and makes someone stand on the bench,

(a) he lets them sit soon afterwards

(b) he simply forgets to let them sit till the last bell rings

(c) he slaps them on the face

(d) he sends word to their parents

Ans. (b) he simply forgets to let them sit till the last bell rings

6. Why did the boy consider himself to be of a high status?

(a) He was among the most promising students and had a scholarship.

(b) He came from a well-to-do family and enjoyed considerable prestige.

(c) Masterji got him to beat the other boys at school.

(d) All of the above

Ans. (d) All of the above

7. Read the statements properly and choose the correct answer from the following options.

Statement 1 During those years, one rupee of jalebis would fetch the same amount of jalebis as twenty rupees these days.

Statement 2 Jalebis were not expensive items.

(a) Statement 1 is true but Statement 2 is false.

(b) Statement 1 is false but Statement 2 is true.

(c) Both Statements are true.
(d) Both Statements are false.

Ans. (c) Both Statements are true.

8. What did the boy do with the leftover jalebis?

(a) Threw them in the dustbin
(b) Took them home with him
(c) Returned them to the halwai
(d) Distributed it to the boys assembled in the gali

Ans. (d) Distributed it to the boys assembled in the gali

9. The boy had to eat dinner after eating a lot of jalebis because

(a) if he hadn't eaten he would have to explain the reason
(b) he wanted to get sick and miss school the next day
(c) he wanted a change of taste
(d) he was still hungry

Ans. (a) if he hadn't eaten he would have to explain the reason

10. Who sent the boy one Id card last Id?

(a) Master Ghulam Mohammed (b) Mamu
(c) Chachajaan (d) Chaprasi

Ans. (b) Mamu

Extract Based Questions

1. Read the extract given below and answer the following questions.

Just as I was gathering up the heap, in the distance I spotted our tonga. Chachajaan was returning from Court. I clutched the jalebis to my chest and ran into a gali. When I reached a safe corner, I began to devour the jalebis. I ate so many... so many jalebis that if anyone pressed my stomach a little, jalebis would have popped out of my ears and nostrils. Very quickly, boys from the entire neighbourhood assembled in the gali. By that time I was so pleased with my stomach full of jalebis that I got into the mood for some fun. I started handing out jalebis to the children around.

(i) Which heap was the boy gathering up?

Ans. The boy was gathering up the heap of jalebis that he had bought from the halwai in an entire newspaper.

(ii) Why does the boy say that jalebis would have popped out of his ears and nostrils?

Ans. According to the boy, he had eaten so many jalebis that if anyone pressed his stomach a little, jalebis would have popped out of his ears and nostrils.

(iii) State whether the statement is True or False.

The boy devoured jalebis at a safe place because he was afraid someone else would take them from him and eat them.

Ans. False

(iv) Find a word from the extract which means 'gobble up'.

Ans. 'Devour'

(v) Complete the sentence appropriately.

The boy was pleased with his stomach which was full of jalebis that by the time ....

Ans. boys from the entire neighbourhood gathered in the gali, he felt like having some fun.

2. Read the extract given below and answer the following questions.

"Look here, you four rupees, I said to them. I am a good boy. Don't misguide me or it won't be good for you. I get so much at home that I consider even looking at something in the bazaar a sin. Besides, you are my fees and fund money. If I spend you today, then how shall I show my face to Master Ghulam Mohammed in school tomorrow and after that to Allah miyan at Qayamat? You probably don't know it but when Master Ghulam Mohammed gets angry and makes you stand on the bench, he simply forgets to let you sit till the last bell rings. So it's best you stop chewing at my ears like this and let me go home straight."

(i) Who is the boy talking to in the given extract?

(a) Chachajaan (b) Halwai
(c) The coins (d) Master Ghulam Mohammed

Ans. (c) The coins

(ii) How did the boy warn 'them' for misguiding him?

(a) By telling them off
(b) By telling them to keep their mouths shut
(c) By pleading them to not do that
(d) By ignoring them

Ans. (a) By telling them off

(iii) What did Master Ghulam do when he got angry?

(a) Canned the students
(b) Make the students stand on the bench
(c) Makes the students stand till the last bell
(d) Both (b) and (c)

Ans. (d) Both (b) and (c)

(iv) Whom should the boy meet the next day?

(a) Allah Miyan (b) Master Ghulam Mohammed
(c) His Chachajaan (d) School Principal

Ans. (b) Master Ghulam Mohammed

(v) What does the phrase 'chewing at one's ears' mean?

(a) To bite someone's ear
(b) To talk or nag at someone
(c) To twist someone's ears
(d) To listen to someone's worries

Ans. (b) To talk or nag at someone

Part – II

Very Short Answer Type Questions

1. What happened to the boy during his fifth standard?

Ans. The jalebi episode happened when the boy was in the fifth standard at the government school in Kambelpur.

2. The boy fears that if he spent the money, he would not be able to show his face. Who were these people whom he would not be able to show his face to?

Ans. The boy fears that if he would spend the money he would not be able to show his face to Master Ghulam Mohammed at school and to Allah Miyan at Qayamat.

3. Who would have caught the boy when he purchased the jalebis?

Ans. Chachajaan would have caught the boy had he seen him while returning from the court on his tongo.

4. Whom does the boy compare himself to while distributing the jalebis to the children?

Ans. While distributing the jalebis, the boy compares himself to the Governor Saheb who used to distribute rice to the poor and needy on Independence Day.

5. While distributing jalebis, the boy assumes a certain importance. Which lines from the text indicate that?

Ans. "If children could be elected to the Assembly, my success would have been assured that day. Because one little signal from my jalebi wielding hand and the mob would have been willing to kill and get killed for me." These lines from the text indicate the statement given.

6. What were the contents of the boy's bag, when he was expecting God to have put four rupees in it?

Ans. The contents of the boy's bag were a few textbooks and notebooks, one pencil, one sharpener and an Id card his mamu had sent him last Id.

Short Answer Type Questions

1. What prayers did the boy promise to offer God?

Ans. The boy promised to offer Namaaz, recite ten surats, Ayat-al-Kursi, Kalma-e-Tayyab and in fact everything he remembered in order to attain four rupees from God. When his various attempts failed, he even decided to do wazu, wear clean clothes and read namaaz from morning to noon.

2. How does the boy escape from the punishment for not having paid the fees?

Ans. On not being able to pay the fees, the boy feared the punishment which was given by Master Ghulam Mohammed. So, he left the school after recess, the time decided for collection of fees. The next day, he left home for school but never went. On third day, too, he decides to do the same. Thus, he escapes from the punishment for not having paid the fees.

3. What did the oldest coin mean by, 'kissa khatam, paisa hazam'?

Ans. The oldest coin was trying to persuade the boy to spend the coins on buying jalebis. It was trying to argue that he could buy jalebis with the fees money and pay fees with the scholarship money and that would be the end of the story, 'kissa khatam, paisa hazam'.

4 "The coins were so eager to be spent that day." Do you agree?

Ans. No, the truth is that the coins don't speak. It is the boy's greed and temptation to devour the hot, fresh and sugar syrupy jalebis that was becoming uncontrollable. All the arguments presented by the coins, in fact, was the debate going on in the mind of the boy.

Long Answer Type Questions

1. Describe the tone of the second encounter between the boy and the halwai.

Ans. Not having been able to pay the fees, the boy left the school after the recess and came back when the school was going to get over to walk down home with the other children. On being asked by the halwai if he wanted to buy jalebis even that day, the boy felt like telling him that he wanted to roast his liver and eat, that instead. Although, he ended up saying nothing and moved away from there, the boy was full of regret and anger which got reflected in their second meeting.

2. Describe the various metaphors employed in the story.

Ans. The story employs quite a few metaphors.
The jalebis, hot and syrupy, stand as a metaphor for various temptations that young children could come across. The boy in the story is lured by the prospect of buying jalebis with his fees money. The four coins, similarly, are metaphors in the story. The noises produced by the coins, their jingle and clamour, is representative of the mental conflict going on in the boy's mind. He was unable to control his temptation. Therefore, the 'talking coins', are metaphors that represents the conflict going on in the boy's mind in regard to the temptation.

3. "No one can erase what fate has decreed". Justify the statement in context with the story.

Ans. The boy had been warned by his elders never to misuse the fees money. Despite that, he spends the fees money on jalebis. The lesson he learns is that he should never misuse the funds and money which his parents have worked hard to earn. Also, he learns that one can never be too sure of one's circumstances. Most importantly, he learned the importance of making efforts.

If Allah Miyan provided everything that men ask for, then, there will be no progress in life and man would still be living in nests like birds.

Fate has its own role to play. Therefore, the scholarship money that he used to get every month was so late in coming on that particular day when he had already spent his fees money. This resulted in the boy having to miss his classes to avoid punishment and to stray around the railway station for a few days.

ASSESSMENT EXERCISE

Multiple Choice Questions

1. Who did the boy see when he was gathering up his heap of jalebis?

(a) His father (b) His mother
(c) Chachajaan (d) Master Ghulam Mohammed

2. The boy compares children's stomach to

(a) digestion machines (b) newborn babies
(c) jalebis (d) halwai

3. How do coins usually present themselves?

(i) By jingling (ii) By clamouring
(iii) By talking
(a) Both (i) and (ii) (b) Both (i) and (iii)
(c) Only (i) (d) Only (iii)

4. Read the statements carefully and choose the correct answer.

Statement 1 In the shade of a tree in a deserted corner of the railway station, the boy sat down and shed tears.

Statement 2 His thoughts went from God to the fees to Master Ghulam's cane.

(a) Statement 1 is true but Statement 2 is false.
(b) Statement 1 is false but Statement 2 is true.
(c) Both Statements are true.
(d) Both Statements are false.

5. What did the worm do when the boy lifted the rock for the second time?

(a) It started moving towards the boy.
(b) It stared at the boy.
(c) It got smashed by the rock.
(d) It coiled towards the opposite direction.

Extract Based Question

Read the given extract and answer the following questions.

I didn't even realise that I was standing near the jalebiwala's shop. Suddenly, the halwai called out, "Kyon bhai, shall I weigh a rupee's worth? Don't want jalebis today?"

I felt like saying I won't eat your jalebis today but, I'd sure like to roast your liver and eat that instead. But I wasn't feeling too well that day, so I simply moved away.

The next day, I did the same thing. I got dressed and left home, went up to the school gate and then turned off to the railway station. Under the same tree I sat and began to say the same prayers. I repeatedly pleaded, Allah Miyan! At least give it to me today. Today is the second day.

(i) "I felt like saying I won't eat your jalebis today but, I'd sure like to roast your liver and eat that instead."
What was the attitude of the boy towards the halwai when he thought this?

(ii) Complete the sentence appropriately.
The halwai asked the boy if ....

(iii) The next day, I did the same thing.
What was the 'same thing' that he did?

(iv) Why did the boy move away without saying anything to the halwai?
(a) He wasn't feeling well
(b) He would get angrier if he talked to him
(c) Because the halwai tricked him into buying jalebis
(d) He had indigestion from overeating

Very Short Answer Type Questions

1. Whom did the boy ask Allah Miyan to send in order to save him that day?

2. What was the worth of one rupee in those times?

3. What kind of status did the boy enjoy in his class?

4. What happened when the boy lifted the big rock while playing a game with Allah Miyan?

Short Answer Type Questions

1. What were the consequences that the boy was forced to bear pretending he hadn't eaten anything during the day?

2. How did the boy silence the coins?

3. How did the boy have fun, after he had pleased his stomach with jalebis?

Long Answer Type Questions

1. State the arguments presented by the coins and the boy during the debate they had on jalebis.

2. What was the divide between the fanciful and the factual, that the boy experienced that day?

Ancient Education System of India

Part – I

This chapter factually explains the existence of the ancient education system in India. It is known that India has been the centre of learning since ancient times. The source of its information and evidence are found in the form of inscriptions on stones, metals and palm leaf records. During ancient period, various travellers from around the world visited India. They discussed the rich cultural heritage, traditions and education system of India in detail. The ancient education system acted as a source of all knowledge, traditions and practices that led to the upliftment of humanity.

Salient Features of Ancient Education System

Since the Rigveda, the ancient education system focused on an overall development of the inner and outer self of an individual. It also focused on moral, physical, spiritual and intellectual development. It emphasised on the values such as humbleness, truthfulness, discipline, self-reliance and respect for all creations etc. It also taught to appreciate the harmony between humans and nature. It followed the principles of the Vedas and Upanishads that focused on the duties towards self, family and society. It emphasised on a healthy mind and a healthy body. In other words, education was practical, achievable and interrelated to life.

Sources of Education

Vedas, Brahmanas, Upanishads and Dharmasutras comprised the ancient education system. Writings of Aryabhatta, Panini, Katyayana and Patanjali alongwith medical treatises of Charaka and Sushruta were also sources of learning.

The branches of various disciplines display a rich and wide range of subjects taught in the ancient system. Shastras (learned disciplines), Kavyas (imaginative and creative literature), Itihas (history), Anviksiki (logic), Mimamsa (interpretation), Shilpashastra (architecture), Arthashastra (polity), Varta (agriculture, trade, commerce, animal husbandry), Dhanurvidya (archery), etc. were some of few disciplines. As physical education was also an important area, there were many disciplines like Krida (games, recreational activities), Vyayamprakara (exercises), Archery and Yogasadhana (training the mind and body). In addition, debates (Shastrartha), peer learning and group teachings were an integral part of education.

Ancient Education System in India : A Way of Life

There existed both formal and informal ways of education during that time. Temples, schools, pathshalas, tols, chatuspadis and gurukuls were places where people guided children. They were centres of learning and also promoted knowledge of our ancient system. Viharas and Universities were attended by students to earn higher knowledge.

Gurukuls

Gurukuls were residential places of learning situated in serene and peaceful forests. Within these gurukuls, students (shishyas) lived together with their gurus. They participated together in their day to day activities. The emphasis was on developing the outer as well as the inner dimensions of personality.

Women too had access to education. Some women Vedic scholars are Maitreyi, Viswambhara, Apala, Gargi, Lopamudra etc.

Part – II

Monasteries

Various monasteries/viharas were set up for monks and nuns. Here, they meditated and discussed their thoughts for their quest of knowledge. In addition, many educational centres of higher education developed around those viharas. These centres attracted students from China, Korea, Tibet, Burma, Ceylon, Java, Nepal, etc.

Viharas and Universities

The educational centres around viharas were a result of the interest of the kings and societies in promoting education as per the accounts given by Xuan Zang (Hiuen Tsang), I-Qing (I-tsing), and Jataka Tales. Some of the most prominent universities were situated in Takshashila, Nalanda, Valabhi, Vikramshila, Odantapuri and Jagaddala. Some education centres at Benaras, Navadeep and Kanchi were developed by connecting with temples.

These students joined these centres of learning and advanced their knowledge through discussions and debates among scholars. Apart from getting knowledge from institutions, a king would sometimes organise a gathering with various scholars of the country to meet, debate and exchange views.

Since Takshashila or Taxila and Nalanda Universities were considered among the best centres of learning in the world, they have been declared heritage sites by the United Nations Educational, Scientific and Cultural Organisation (UNESCO).

Takshashila or Taxila

Takshashila is one of the universities which is named after the ancient Indian city called Takshashila now Pakistan. It was a noted centre of learning including Buddhism till its destruction in 5th century CE. It attracted students from around the world for many centuries. Its curriculum included study of ancient scriptures, laws, medicines, astronomy, military science and arts or the eighteen silpas.

Among its noted pupils were Panini (grammarian) who authored 'Ashtadhyayi', Jivaka (physician) and Chanakya (skilled exponent of statecraft). Students had to commute to Takshashila from Kashi, Kosala, Magadha, etc. after a long and hard journey.

The ruins of Takshashila were discovered in the mid 19th century. Today, Takshashila is a World Heritage site as declared by UNESCO in 1980.

Role of the Teacher

Teachers had complete freedom to select their students as well as to design the course. When a teacher was satisfied with students, the course concluded. They used debates and discussions as methods of teaching. The advanced level students would help the teachers in the teaching process.

Nalanda University

Another prestigious university in higher learning was Nalanda University. During the visit of Xuan Zang, it was called Nala. He along with I-Qing gave clear and concise accounts of the university. They noted that around hundred discourses happened on a daily basis on a variety of disciplines.

Xuan Zang himself became a student of Nalanda. He studied Yogashastra and mentioned that the chancellor Shilabhadra was the highest living authority in yoga. The university had a wide range of syllabus including vedic fine arts, medicine, mathematics, astronomy, politics and warfare.

Role of Community

In ancient India as knowledge was sacred no fee was paid by students. Contribution in education was considered highest form of donation. Financial support, gifts of buildings and lands was given by rich merchants, wealthy parents and society.

In Southern India, Agraharas, Ghatika and Brahmapuri were centres of learning and teaching. A Ghatika included a small religious centre of learning. An Agrahara was a whole settlement of Brahmins that was maintained by generous donations from society. Some other sources of learning were at Temples, Mathas, Jain Basadis and Buddhist Viharas.

Continuation of Indian Education System

The education of India continued in the form of ashrams, in temples and in schools. During medieval period, Maktabas and Madrassas became a part of the education system. In addition, the informal system of education flourished as an extension of the formal system. They were mostly religious and spiritual forms of education which were taught in tols in Bengal, Pathshalas in Western India, Chatuspadis in Bihar and so on.

With the focus on an overall development, the modern education system has a lot to learn from ancient education system. Today, educationists understand the role of multilingual and multicultural education, thereby connecting the ancient and traditional knowledge with modern learning.

Word Meaning

Word	Meaning
Evolved	to develop gradually
Holistic	dealing with the whole of something
Intellectual	ability to think and understand things
Humility	lack of pride
Tenets	a principle of belief
Encompassing	surround and have within
Pragmatic	practical
Complementary	to combine in such a way as to enhance or emphasise the qualities of each other
Treatises	a written work dealing formally with a subject
Conscientiously	in a through and responsible way
Proficient	skilled in doing something
Indigenous	originating in a particular place
Imparted	to make known
Imbibing	to absorb
Pious	strongly religious

Word	Meaning
Prominent	important
Dimensions	a feature of a situation
Enriching	improving or enhancing the quality or value
Quest	the act of seeking/searching
Catered	provide people with
Expertise	a high level of knowledge
Legendary	very famous or admired
Arduous	difficult or tiring
Autonomy	self-governing freedom
Vivid	intensely clear image
Discourses	discussions
Warfare	the activities involved in war
Sacred	connected to god
Memoirs	a historical account
Centralised	bring together in one place
Foundations	an underlying basis or principle

NCERT FOLDER

NCERT Intext and Exercise Questions

COMPREHENSION CHECK❶ (NCERT PAGE 69)

Q.1 Why were travellers attracted towards India?

Ans. Travellers were attracted towards India because for them India was a land of wonder. Its culture, wealth, religions, philosophies, art, architecture and its educational practices encouraged them to visit the land of wonder.

Q.2 What were the sources of the ancient education system?

Ans. The sources of the ancient education system included education of the Vedas, Brahmanas, Upanishads and Dharmasutra. It also included the study of writings of Aryabhatta, Panini, Katyayana, Patanjali, medical treatises of Charaka and Sushruta.

Q.3 What were the features of education system in ancient India?

Ans. Following are the features of education system in ancient India.

- The education system of ancient India focused on the overall development of an individual.
- It emphasised on moral, physical, spiritual and intellectual development.
- It taught to appreciate the balance between human beings and nature.
- It instilled values like respect, self-reliance, discipline and humility.
- It encourages people to fulfill their obligations to family, friends society and oneself.
- It focuses on healthy mind as well as body.

Thus, the education in India was practical, achievable and complementary to life.

Q.4 What was the role of guru in pupils' lives?

Ans. In ancient education system, the guru played a very important role in a pupil's life. The guru and the pupil lived together and helped each other in their day-to-day activities. The guru while living with his pupil taught the student (pupil) how to live a disciplined life and realise one's true potential. They honed their skills to become efficient in all areas of learning.

CHECK❷ (NCERT PAGE 74)

Q.1 Where did nuns and monks receive their education?

Ans. Nuns and monks received their education in monasteries or viharas where they meditated, debated and discussed with the learned.

Q.2 What is Panini known for?

Ans. Panini is known for his expertise in language and grammar. He was a legendary Indian grammarian who had authored one of the greatest works on grammar called Ashtadyayi.

Q.3 Which University did Xuan Zang and I-Qing study at?

Ans. Xuan Zang and I-Qing studied at Nalanda University.

Q.4 Which subject did Xuan Zang study in India?

Ans. Xuan Zang studied Yogashastra in the Nalanda University in India.

Q.5 How did society help in the education of the students?

Ans. To help the education of the students, the society donated contributions in the field of education in some form or another. Financial support came from rich merchants, wealthy parents and society. Besides gifts of buildings, the universities also received gifts of land. Thus, the society played an important role in promoting education.

EXERCISE (NCERT PAGE 74)

Discuss the following questions in small groups and write your answers.

Q.1 Which salient features of the ancient education system of India made it globally renowned?

Ans. The salient features of the ancient Indian education that made it globally renowned are

(i) It focused on the complete development of the inner and outer selves, moral, physical, spiritual and intellectual of an individual.

(ii) It placed immense weight on the importance of values such as humility, truthfulness, discipline, self-reliance and respect for all creations.

(iii) The principles of the Vedas and Upanishads which focused on the duties towards self, family and society were a part of the curriculum.

(iv) It taught the significance of maintaining a healthy body and a healthy mind.

Q.2 Why do you think students from other countries came to India to study at that time?

Ans. During the ancient times, students from other countries like China, Korea, Tibet, Burma, etc. came to India to study because of the development of educational centres of higher learning around the monasteries and viharas.

Q.3 Why is education considered a way of life?

Ans. Education is considered a way of life because it was imparted in day-to-day lives, homes, in temples, pathshalas, tols, chatuspadis and gurukuls. The elders and teachers guided the children-or-students to live a pious and disciplined life.

Q.4 What do you understand by holistic education?

Ans. Holistic education includes on overall development of the inner and outer self of an individual. It includes moral, physical, spiritual and intellectual growth. It emphasised on values of discipline, respect, etc. and also focused on all aspects of life.

Q.5 Why do you think Takshashila and Nalanda have been declared heritage sites?

Ans. Takshashila and Nalanda Universities were considered as the best centres of learning in ancient India. Hence, they have been declared as world heritage sites by UNESCO.

REVIEW EXERCISE

Including Competency Based Questions

Part – I

Multiple Choice Questions

1. In the view of travellers from various regions, ancient India was

(a) unorthodox (b) uneducated
(c) poor (d) a land of wonder

Ans. (d) a land of wonder

2. Ancient Indian education system focused on

(i) physical and mental development
(ii) enforcing spiritual values
(iii) appreciating the harmony among humans beings

(a) Only (i) (b) Both (i) and (ii)
(c) Both (i) and (iii) (d) Both (ii) and (iii)

Ans. (b) Both (i) and (ii)

3. What were Kavyas?

(a) Imaginative and creative literature
(b) Learned disciplines
(c) History
(d) Architecture

Ans. (a) Imaginative and creative literature

4. The younger pupils received .... from the pupils at advanced stage of learning and there was a system of .... learning.

(a) lessons, peer (b) strict discipline, group
(c) guidance, peer (d) contempt, group

Ans. (c) guidance, peer

5. Students went to .... for higher knowledge.

(a) viharas and universities (b) temples
(c) village homes (d) mountains

Ans. (a) viharas and universities

6. Which type of learning place was a Gurukul?

(a) Pathshalas (b) Temples
(c) Commercial (d) Residential

Ans. (d) Residential

7. Which of the following was a prominent Vedic scholar?

(a) Viswambhara (b) Panini
(c) Katyayana (d) Patanjali

Ans. (a) Viswambhara

8. Choose the correct answer by matching the following words.

A. Gargi	1. Gurukul
B. Chanakya	2. Taxila
C. Xuan Zang	3. Nalanda

Codes

(a) A-3, B-2, C–1 (b) A-3, B-1, C–2
(c) A-1, B-2, C–3 (d) A-1, B-3, C–2

Ans. (c) A-1, B-2, C–3

9. Which of the following was not a student in Takshashila?

(a) Jivaka (b) Kautilya (c) Panini (d) Apala

Ans. (d) Apala

10. The ruins of Takshashila were discovered by

(a) Howard Carter (b) Kathleen Kenyon
(c) Alexander Cunningham (d) Mortimer Wheeler

Ans. (c) Alexander Cunningham

Extract Based Questions

1. Read the extract given below and answer the following questions.

Nalanda, when Xuan Zang visited it, was called Nala and was a centre of higher learning in various subjects. The University attracted scholars from the different parts of the country as well as world. The Chinese scholars I-Qing and Xuan Zang visited Nalanda in the 7th century CE. They have given vivid accounts of Nalanda. They have noted that as many as one hundred discourses happened on a daily basis, in a variety of disciplines through the methods of debate and discussions. Xuan Zang himself became a student of Nalanda to study yogashastra. He has mentioned that the Chancellor of Nalanda, Shilabhadra, was the highest living authority in yoga. The courses of study offered by Nalanda University covered a wide range, almost the entire circle of knowledge then available.

(i) When did Nala University change its name?

Ans. During the time when Xuan Zang visited Nala, it changed its name to Nalanda University.

(ii) Which region did I-Qing and Xuan Zang belong to and when did they visit Nalanda?

Ans. The scholars I-Qing and Xuan Zang belonged to China and visited Nalanda in the 7th century CE.

(iii) What did Xuan Zang study at Nalanda?

Ans. Xuan Zang studied yogashastra as a student in Nalanda.

(iv) Find a word from the extract which means 'discussions'.

Ans. Discourses

(v) State whether the given statement is true or false.
Nalanda University attracted students from different parts of the country only.

Ans. False

2. Read the extract given below and answer the following questions.

The Indian education system continued in the form of ashrams, in temples and as indigenous schools. During the medieval period, maktabas and madrassas became part of the education system. During the pre-colonial period, indigenous education flourished in India. This was an extension of the formal system that had taken roots earlier. This system was mostly religious and spiritual form of education. Tols in Bengal, pathshalas in western India, chatuspadis in Bihar, and similar schools existed in other parts of India. Local resources via donations supported education. References in texts and memoirs inform that villagers also supported education in southern India.

(i) Which of the following were institutes of Indian Education System?

(a) Temples (b) Ashrams
(c) Indigenous schools (d) All of the above

Ans. (d) All of the above

(ii) The form of education in indigenous schools comprised of .... and .... learning.

(a) pre-colonial, system (b) maktabas, madrassas
(c) spiritual, religious (d) pathshalas, chatuspadis

Ans. (c) spiritual, religious

(iii) How did education get its support during the ancient times?

(a) Through knowledge sharing
(b) Through donations
(c) Through establishments of library
(d) Through the people

Ans. (b) Through donations

(iv) Find the word which means 'memoirs'.

(a) Remembrance (b) Encounter
(c) Historical account (d) Connection

Ans. (c) Historical account

(v) Find the one word substitute for 'occurring naturally in a particular place'.

(a) Indigenous (b) Pre-colonial
(c) Flourish (d) Extension

Ans. (a) Indigenous

Part – II

Very Short Answer Type Questions

1. How were the learning of pupil evaluated?

Ans. The learning of the pupils were evaluated or assessed through debates or discussions (Shastrartha).

2. Which sources tell us that kings and society promoted education?

Ans. The Jataka Tales written by Xuan Zang and I-Qing alongwith other sources tell us that kings and society took interest in promoting education.

3. **What was Takshashila known for?**

Ans. Takshashila was known for being a noted centre of learning of Buddhism and for its higher education facility.

4. **What did Xuan Zang think about Shilabhadra?**

Ans. Xuan Zang thought that Shilabhadra, the chancellor, of Nalanda was the highest living authority in yoga.

5. **What were the courses offered in Nalanda?**

Ans. The courses of study offered by Nalanda covered the Vedas. The students were trained in fine arts, medicine, mathematics, astronomy, politics and warfare. It was almost the entire circle of knowledge which was available at that time.

6. **What were the centres of learning in the South of India?**

Ans. In the South of India, Agraharas, Ghatika and Brahmapuri served as the centres of learning and teaching.

Short Answer Type Questions

1. **How were Gurukuls a centre of learning?**

Ans. Gurukuls/Ashrams were the residential places of learning situated in peaceful forests. Hundred of students came together in gurukuls wherein they lived together with their gurus. They helped each other in their day-to-day lives and learned to live a disciplined life. The students within the gurukuls pursued their education in history, art of debate, law, medicine, etc.

2. **What was a teacher's role in education?**

Ans. In ancient education, a teacher had complete authority over the selection process of the students. They designed their syllabi and when they were satisfied with students, they concluded the course. They taught the courses that their students were keen to learn and were assisted by their advanced level students in teaching.

3. **How did the Indian education system continue?**

Ans. The ancient Indian education system continued in the form of ashrams, in temples and in indigenous schools. Different types of education system were introduced during the middle/medieval and pre-colonial period.

Maktabas and madrassas were part of the education system in the middle period and indigenous education during the pre-colonial period.

Indigenous education evolved as an extension of the formal religious and spiritual forms of education.

Long Answer Type Questions

1. **What were the sources of education? Where did the ancient education take place?**

Ans. The ancient education system of India had sources from the Vedas, Brahmanas, Upanishads and Dharmasutras. Various prominent scholars such as Aryabhata, Panini, Katyayana, Patanjali, Charaka, Sushruta, etc and their works were also some sources of learning.

These sources were divided into various academic as well as physical subjects and were taught through formal and informal means.

Education was imparted at homes, in temples, pathshalas, tols, chatuspadis and gurukuls. Along with them monasteries, viharas and universities were build for higher knowledge. Such institutions were set up on donations of kings and society in various places including Takshashila, Nalanda, etc.

2. **What kinds of subjects were taught in ancient education system? How were the students evaluated?**

Ans. The various subjects that were taught in the ancient education system were drawn from the ancient Indian scriptures. The studies derived from the scriptures were divided into various different subjects including Shastras (learned disciplines), Kavyas (imaginative and creative literature), Itihas (history), Anviksiki (logic), Mimamsa (interpretation), Shilpashashtra (architecture), Arthashastra (polity), Varta (agriculture, trade, commerce, animal husbandry), Krida (games), Vyayamaprakara (exercises) and Yogasadhana (training the mind and body).

The gurus worked with the pupils to achieve a level of learning. The teacher would assess the pupils, learning through debate and discussions.

3. **The education system today is way different from the education system of ancient India. Justify the above statement with reference to the text.**

Ans. The education system today is way different from the education system of ancient India. The education system of earlier times focused on the holistic development of a child. It focused on an all-round growth of an individual within one's social life. This made the education system practical, achievable and complementary to life.

However, the education system of the present world ceases to be practical. There is an inherent focus on the theoretical academic knowledge.

So, there is a need to reduce this difference. It is to ensure that the stress is being laid on connecting learning to the real world outside the school.

ASSESSMENT EXERCISE

Multiple Choice Questions

1. Read the statements carefully and choose the correct answer.

   Statement 1 Gurukuls were named after the Vedic scholars and sages.

   Statement 2 Gurukuls encouraged the enrichment of inner dimensions of personality.

   (a) Statement 1 is true but Statement 2 is false.
   (b) Statement 1 is false but Statement 2 is true.
   (c) Both the Statements are true.
   (d) Both the Statements are false.

2. Which of the following is a UNESCO world heritage site?

   (a) Odantapuri (b) Jagaddala
   (c) Valabhi (d) Taxila

3. The students of higher learning centres developed their knowledge by .... and .... with renowned scholars.

   (a) discussions, debates (b) discussions, writings
   (c) writings, debates (d) writings, discussion

4. Which of the following universities were developed in connection with temples?

   (i) Benaras (ii) Kanchi (iii) Valabhi

   (a) Only (i)
   (b) Both (i) and (ii)
   (c) Both (ii) and (iii)
   (d) Only (iii)

5. When was Takshashila destroyed?

   (a) 5th century CE
   (b) Mid-19th century
   (c) 7th century CE
   (d) 12th century CE

Extract Based Question

Read the given extract and answer the following questions.

At that time, knowledge was considered sacred and no fee was charged. Contributions towards education were considered the highest form of donation. All members of the society contributed in some form or the other. Financial support came from rich merchants, wealthy parents and society. Besides gifts of buildings, the universities received gifts of land. This form of free education was also prevalent in other ancient universities like Valabhi, Vikramshila and Jagaddala. At the same time in the south of India, agraharas served as centres of learning and teaching. South Indian kingdoms also had other cultural institutions known as Ghatika and Brahmapuri.

(i) Since there were no charges of fees, how did education survive?

(ii) Complete the sentence appropriately.
All members of the society including ....

(iii) Find the two words from the extract which are synonyms of each other.

(iv) Which university existed at the same time as Ghatika in another part of India?

   (a) Agraharas (b) Brahmapuri
   (c) Valabhi (d) Ancient University

(v) Choose the ways in which the society had made their donations to education.

   (a) Financial support, buildings and land
   (b) Financial support
   (c) Buildings and land
   (d) Gifts

Very Short Answer Type Questions

1. How had Xuan Zang and I-Qing contributed to our knowledge of ancient education system of India?
2. Where were the gurukuls located?
3. What methods were used by teachers of the ancient Indian education system to promote learning?
4. What could be concluded from the references in texts and memoirs from Southern India?
5. How did Aryabhata, Panini and Charaka contribute to the ancient Indian education system?

Short Answer Type Questions

1. How did the kings and the society contribute to education?
2. What are the salient features of the ancient education system?
3. State the difference between Ghatika and Agrahara.

Long Answer Type Questions

1. Justify the ancient education system as a way of life.
2. Describe the relation between the viharas and universities.

SAMPLE QUESTION PAPERS

Sample Question Paper 1 (Solved)
English

Time : 3 hrs M.M. : 80

General Instructions

1 The Question Paper contains four sections- Reading, Grammar, Writing and Literature.

2 Attempt questions based on specific instructions for each part.

Section A : Reading Skills

1. Read the passage carefully and answer the questions that follow.

1. Food is an important part of our identity and culture. We are known by what we eat. It reflects the geography to which we belong and the locally available resources used in our cuisine. Adivasi food systems are deeply embedded in local culture and traditions, given that the way of life of these indigenous people is so closely linked to nature and its resources.
2. Jharkhand is a natural abode and home to numerous Adivasi communities constituting a little over 25% of the total population. These communities, in addition to their rich social and cultural traditions, practice immensely diverse food practices which are based on locally available resources and techniques. Such Adivasi food systems have been instrumental in maintaining the sovereignty and self-reliance of these communities. They have taken many varieties of vegetables and tubers, wild or grown, to enrich their diet and also to meet their requirements of calcium, iron, minerals and vitamins.
3. The realm of medicinal plants and herbal products is even vaster. According to the All India Coordinated Research Project on Ethnobiology, tribal communities are acquainted with the use of over 9,000 species of plants including food plants, while specifically for the purpose of healing they know the use of around 7,500 species of plants.
4. The Adivasi food of Jharkhand may be defined in terms of a few characteristic features: food is influenced by physiological needs and geographical conditions and the habit is closely associated with habitat. This means food habits are guided by locally available resources. Adivasis consume boiled food like rice, pulses, herbs or 'saag' and on some occasions, animal or bird meat is roasted on a fire. Because of these consistent food habits that are based on locally available resources, instances of serious diseases are considerably lower among Adivasis.
5. Nutrition Value: Ingredients used in Adivasi food are a great source of nutrition in addition to taste. Studies have revealed that Adivasi food provides high immunity to diseases and protection from deformities. Food like tubers, shoots, berries, nuts, etc. are a good source of protein and fat. The consumption of meat, fish, egg, shellfish, etc. provides good quality protein apart from important vitamins and minerals. Widely consumed wild or grown tubers enrich their dietary requirement of calcium, iron, mineral elements and vitamins.

Questions

On the basis of your reading of the passage, answer the following questions. (10)

(i) The sentence "We are known by what we eat" means that

(a) it's important to eat good food in order to be healthy and fit.

(b) we become famous by the kind of food we eat.

(c) healthful and nutritious food is the reason behind our fame.

(d) people remember us because of our eating habits.

(ii) Select the option that states the reason behind the statement "Adivasi food provides high immunity to diseases and protection from deformities".

(a) The food of Adivasis has more protein and fibre.

(b) The food of Adivasis has a rich balance of protein, vitamins and minerals.

(c) Adivasis grow their own food themselves.

(d) Adivasis know the use of around 7,500 species of plants.

(iii) When the writer says "food is an important part of our identity and culture", he means that

(a) culture is what makes everyone different from who we are to where we originate.

(b) food is family treasure in a way that the recipes are passed on from one generation to another.

(c) as the world becomes more globalised, it is easier to access cuisines from different cultures.

(d) how we eat and talk about food is a different key part of our identities.

(iv) How have Adivasi food systems been instrumental?

(a) They maintain the sovereignty of these communities.

(b) They maintain the self-dependency of these communities.

(c) They encourage inter-dependence in a community.

(d) Both (a) and (b)

(v) From which of the following is the Adivasi food of Jharkhand influenced?

(a) Physiological needs

(b) Geographical conditions

(c) Locally available resources

(d) All of the above

(vi) The word .... in the passage means the same as 'included'.

(a) revealed (b) dietary

(c) embedded (d) linked

(vii) Why are the instances of serious diseases considerably lower among Adivasis?

(viii) List the locally available food of Adivasi's.

(ix) How are the Adivasi's food systems linked to nature and its resources?

(x) Do you agree with the statement that 'Adivasi systems are more medically advanced'?

2. Read the following poem and answer the questions that follow.

Rhyme of the River Aven
By : Bhavna Ramakrishnan

1. The river flows, where it goes, nobody knows
The trees are like towers touching the stars

Down they blow their heads in a row
To the river as it flows
Down the town the river flow as, swirling it goes
Meandering the playground and houses in rows

2. The rocks on the bank look still and stern
The waves, from eddies that twirl and turn
Water bubbles drench the flowers and ferns Lovers gaze with a far away look and yearn Children enter into boats that cruise
and return

3. Slipping and sliding through the hills and forest green
The blue waters roaring, and then placid and serene
The bard's town sliced by enigmatic stream

The waves dancing on the rainbow coloured sun beams
Through the labyrinth of branches, filtered sunlight gleams

4. The river flows, silent and deep
Life's lesson learnt as it bound and leaps
Spread the message of peace, friendship you reap
Forget all sorrows, wonderful memories you keep
Life is a playground and sometimes mountains steep

5. The river never stops till it merges with the ocean
Success and failure in life unfold in slow motion
Cut your own path and stay steadfast in this notion
Let ambition and determination be interspersed with emotion
Like the river, never stop until you reach your destination

On the basis of your reading of the poem answer the given questions. (10)

(i) Trees are compared to
  (a) towers so tall that they are reaching heads
  (b) towers so tall that they are reaching houses
  (c) towers so tall that they are reaching the sky
  (d) towers so tall that they are reaching the clouds

(ii) The poet calls life a
  (a) playground and enigmatic stream
  (b) playground and steep mountains
  (c) playground and coloured rainbow
  (d) playground and grasslands

(iii) The blue waters are
  (a) like the ocean
  (b) like raging waterfall
  (c) sometimes placid and quiet
  (d) absolutely quiet

(iv) Rocks on the shore appear to be
  (a) still and stern (b) moving with the river
  (c) filled with fungus (d) still and moving

(v) The waves of the river appear to be dancing due to the
  (a) eddies (b) meandering path
  (c) sunlight falling on them (d) coloured rainbow

(vi) The flowing river flashes the message that
  (a) life is deep and silent
  (b) forget all sorrows of life and live life king size
  (c) hustle till you reach your destination
  (d) give in to troubles

(vii) At which point does the river stop?

(viii) How does the sunlight come to the river?

(ix) Find a word from the poem that means course following a winding path.

(x) Find a word from the poem that means irregular network of passages or paths/a maze.

Section B : Writing

3. A. You are Reshma/Rajan Head Girl/Head Boy of Moonrise Public School, Chandigarh. A cooking competition is going to take place in your school. Write a notice to be displayed on the school notice board informing the members of the Culinary Club to attend a meeting with the Principal for the organisation of the competition. Draft the notice in about 50 words giving all necessary details. **(5)**

Or

B. **Read the following conversation carefully.**

Anoki : Hello ! is it 90350225XX?

Radhya : Yes, please. Who am I speaking to?

Anoki : I'm Anoki, a friend of Vidya. Where is she?

Radhya : Oh! Sorry. Actually she has forgotten her mobile here. She has gone to the market. How can I help you?

Anoki : Oh, sure. In fact, I wanted to convey to her that today's music class is suspended because the teacher is not well. Instead it will be held on Sunday.
Could you please pass this message to her?

Radhya : Oh! Sure. Thank you.

Anoki : Thank you too.

As Radhya is going to her dance classes, she needs to write the message for Vidya. Write the message on her behalf with every detail.

4. A. When children watch TV, adults generally scold them without realising that some programmes on TV can be educative too. Write an article in 150-200 words on 'Do Television spoil Children?' Your are Navtej/Navita. **(5)**

Or

B. Write an original short story that begins with the words "I was returning to India after having completed my studies from abroad. The yearning to meet my parents and friends grew ...."

5. A. You are pained to see that in your city, there is no proper arrangement for cleaning of drains. There are heaps of accumulated garbage and stagnant water. Write a letter to the Municipal Commissioner of your city complaining about the same as there is a fear of outbreak of disease. You are Alka/Ashish. (Word limit 100-120) **(5)**

Or

B. You are Ishant of Meerut. Your friend Manik of Agra has recently got a place in Under 16 Cricket Team of India. Write a letter of congratulations to him.

Section C : Grammar

6. Choose the correct options to fill in the blanks to complete the passages. **(3)**

Modern ....(i) of communication such as emails and telephones have reduced the ......(ii) of time people spend seeing their friends. This has had a negative effect .... (iii) their social lives.

(i) (a) forms (b) method (c) medium (d) types

(ii) (a) amount (b) portion (c) quality (d) quantity

(iii) (a) on (b) in (c) for (d) of

7. Select the option that identifies the error and supplies the correction for the following line
The children cheers loudly when their captain scored the winning goal. **(1)**

Option	Error	Correction
(a)	cheers	cheered
(b)	when	by
(c)	scored	scoring
(d)	winning	winner

8. Select the options that identify the errors and supply the corrections for the following line **(1)**
You don't run here. It is not allowed.

Option	Error	Correction
(a)	you	your
(b)	don't	shouldn't
(c)	run	ran
(d)	allowed	allow

9. The following paragraph has not been edited. There is one error in each line. Identify the error and write it along with the corrections. **(3)**

		Error	Correction
Gold prices have now touched an all time			
high. Some says it could be a bubble	(a)	....	....
that may grown but will at last	(b)	....	....
burst after recession in a	(c)	....	....
West was over. So, investing			
in gold may not be a good idea now.			

10. Rearrange the following words to make meaningful sentences. **(2)**

(i) the garbage / dispose of / properly / Please

(ii) clapped happily / entered / as Santa Claus / The children

Section D : Literature

11. Read the following extracts to answer the given questions. (5)

A. I should like to be able to tell you that we began it. But the truth, I'm ashamed to say, is that Fritz began it. First someone saw a white flag waving from the trenches opposite. Then they were calling out to us from across no man's land. "Happy Christmas, Tommy! Happy Christmas!" When we had got over the surprise, some of us shouted back, "Same to you, Fritz! Same to you!" I thought that would be that. We all did. But then suddenly one of them was up there in his grey greatcoat and waving a white flag. "Don't shoot, lads!" Someone shouted. And no one did. Then there was another Fritz up on the parapet, and another. "Keep your heads down", I told the men, "it's a trick." But it wasn't.

(i) Why is the writer ashamed?

(ii) Who was waving the white flag?

(a) Children (b) Germans
(c) Britishers (d) Common people

(iii) Why does the speaker think that the act presented in the extract is a trick?

(iv) What do you think is the speaker's occupation?

(a) Athlete (b) Soldier
(c) Manager (d) Police officer

(v) What is the weather as per the given extract?

(a) Summer (b) Autumn
(c) Monsoon (d) Winter

Or

B. "If I spend you today, then how shall I show my face to Master Ghulam Mohammed in school tomorrow and after that to Allah Miyan at Qayamat? You probably don't know it but when Master Ghulam Mohammed gets angry and makes you stand on the bench, he simply forgets to let you sit till the last bell rings. So it's best you stop chewing at my ears like this and let me go home straight." The coins disliked what I'd said so much.

(i) Who is the speaker of the given lines and to whom is he speaking?

(ii) How much money does the speaker has to spend?

(a) Two rupees (b) Three rupees
(c) Four rupees (d) Six rupees

(iii) Why does the speaker say these lines?

(iv) Who is Master Ghulam Mohammed?

(a) Teacher (b) Father
(c) Principal (d) Uncle

(v) The tone with which the speaker is speaking is

(a) happy (b) regret
(c) angry (d) scolding

12. Read the following extracts to answer the given questions. (5)

A. A silly young cricket, accustomed to sing
Through the warm, sunny months of gay summer and spring,
Began to complain when he found that, at home,
His cupboard was empty, and winter was come.
Not a crumb to be found
On the snow-covered ground;
Not a flower could he see,
Not a leaf on a tree

(i) Why is the cricket called silly?

(ii) What is the reason behind the cricket's complaint?

(iii) Which qualities are attached to summer and spring?

(a) Festive (b) Colourful
(c) Mourning (d) Dry

(iv) The word 'crumb' refers to

(a) leaves (b) flowers (c) food (d) shelter

(v) Who will the cricket ask for help?

(a) Grasshopper (b) Ant
(c) Butterfly (d) No one

Or

A. O! Father and Mother, if buds are nip'd,
And blossoms blown away,
And if the tender plants are strip'd
Of their joy in the springing day,
By sorrow and cares dismay,
How shall the summer arise in joy,
Or the summer fruits appear?

(i) Name the poem and the poet.

(ii) Who is the speaker of the lines?

(a) A school going boy (b) An orphan
(c) A poor boy (d) Children in general

(iii) What does the speaker compare himself with?

(a) Flowers (b) Birds

(c) Saplings (d) All of these

(iv) The word 'dismay' means

(a) anger (b) disappointment

(c) regret (d) nostalgia

(v) Why does the speaker make the comparison?

13. Answer the following questions in about 15-20 words. (4)

(i) "Don't shoot lads!" – Explain the statement with reference to 'The Best Christmas Present in the world'.

(ii) How did Tilly sense that something was wrong?

(iii) Why does the school boy sit dully in the school?

(iv) Which skill of Ranji impress Suraj?

14. Answer any three of the following in 30-40 words. (9)

(i) "And yet the man knew a great deal about it."- What did he know about Bepin Babu's personal life?

(ii) What were the six questions that the writer asked Stephen Hawking?

(iii) How does the attitude and understanding of self- worth help a person succeed in life? (With reference to 'The treasure within)

(iv) What is Panini known for?

(v) What is the speaker's last bargain? Why does he call it the best?

15. Answer any one of the following in 100-150 words. (6)

A. Write in your words how Chunilal planned and executed the punishment he wanted to give to Bepin Babu.

Or

B. Describe the summer season in context with the poem 'On the Grasshopper and Cricket'.

16. Answer any one of the following in 100-150 words. (6)

A. "I am who I am today because of the choices I made yesterday." Justify this statement based on the camel from the story.

Or

B. "Service for welfare of other should be the aim of human deeds". Elaborate. with reference to the story 'The Selfish Giant'.

Answers

1. (i) (a) it's important to eat good food in order to be healthy and fit.

(ii) (b) The food of Adivasis has a rich balance of protein, vitamins and minerals.

(iii) (b) food is family treasure in a way that the recipes are passed on from one generation to another.

(iv) (d) Both (a) and (b)

(v) (d) All of the above

(vi) (c) embedded

(vii) The Adivasi food of Jharkhand is influenced by physiological needs and geographical conditions. This means food habits are guided by locally available resources. Because of this, instances of serious diseases are considerably lower among Adivasis.

(viii) Some locally available food of Adivasi's include rice, pulses, herbs, saag and in some occasions, animal or bird meat is roasted on fire.

(ix) It is mentioned in the passage that the Adivasi food system are embedded in the manner they live their life which is closely linked to their surrounding nature and its resources.

(x) Yes, I agree with the statement that Adivasi systems are more medically advanced as they are acquainted with over 9000 species of plants which can be used to heal.

2. (i) (c) towers so tall that they are reaching the sky

(ii) (b) playground and steep mountains

(iii) (c) sometimes placid and quiet

(iv) (a) still and stern

(v) (b) meandering path

(vi) (c) hustle till you reach your destination

(vii) The river stops only at the point where it meets the ocean.

(viii) The sunlight reaches the river after being filtered by the labyrinth of tree branches.

(ix) Meandering (x) Labyrinth

3. A.

Moonrise Public School, Chandigarh

NOTICE

12th September, 20XX

Meeting Regarding Cooking Competition

All members of the Culinary Club are hereby informed to attend a meeting with the Principal on 15th September, 20XX at 4 pm in the Principal's Cabin. The meeting will be held to decide the process and organisation of the cooking competition. Members are expected to come up with ideas for the competition, decoration, awards, Chief Guest among other things.

Reshma/Rajan
(Head Girl/Head Boy)

B.

MESSAGE

1st March, 20XX 11:11 AM

Dear Vidya

Your friend Anoki called to inform you that today's music class is suspended because the teacher is not well. Instead, it will be held on Sunday.

Radhya

4. A.

Do Television Spoil Children?

by Navtej

The question of whether television is useful or not has been a topic of great debate ever since it was invented. On one hand, it is credited of keeping the masses informed; on the other hand, it is wrongly accused of causing distraction. Children watching television is also a supposed sign of being spoilt. But is this argument still valid? No, it is not.

With the advancement in technology and communication industry, the amount of content telecast on the television is also increasing. This provides a variety of age appropriate television programmes for children. Seeing the love of kids for television, multiple educational channels have been launched. These channels aim at making learning a fun process for the kids. However, most parents fail to realise this. They ban children from watching television. Hence, the argument that television spoils children is completely invalid in today's era. So, instead of scolding your children for watching television, parents have to let them watch educational programmes so that they learn and have fun at the same time.

B. I was returning to India after having completed my studies from abroad. The yearning to meet my parents and friends grew with every passing minute as I boarded the plane. Seated next to me was a boy who was about five years old. No sooner had the plane taken off from London Airport than the boy jumped out of his seat and started roaming about in the plane. Soon, the air-hostess brought some snacks and tea. After having my refreshment, I settled down to complete a novel that I had brought with me.

I had almost completed my novel when the captain told us that we were about to land at the Palam Airport. Just then, a young man got up and caught hold of the boy, placing a knife on his neck. He warned us to sit and entered the cockpit where he ordered the pilot not to land the plane. Suddenly, one of the old ladies collapsed on the floor. Seeing this, the other lady shouted at the hijacker for having caused a heart attack.

The hijacker's attention was momentarily diverted. Sensing this, a well built man sitting in the front just near the hijacker, knocked the knife out of his hand. Soon, everyone jumped on the unarmed hijacker, freeing the boy in the process. He was overpowered and everybody heaved a sigh of relief. The plane finally landed at the airport and the hijacker was arrested.

We were all given a warm welcome from the crowd which had gathered at the airport as news of the hijacking had spread. The child jumped into the open arms of his grandma who hugged him lovingly. It was indeed a very eventful homecoming for all of us.

5. A. 3/4, Anand Nagar
New Delhi

21st April, 20XX

The Municipal Commissioner
Municipal Corporation
Delhi – 110 006

Subject Complaint about lack of cleanliness and hygiene in Anand Nagar

Sir/Ma'am

This is to inform you that I, Alka/Ashish, am a resident of Anand Nagar, Delhi. On behalf of the residents of Anand Nagar, I have written this letter to draw your kind attention towards the prevailing unsanitary and unhygienic conditions of our locality.

Of late, Anand Nagar has become a place identified because of its dirt and drain. The sewage are not cleaned and are always overflowing. Garbage is littered at almost all corners and stagnant water can be found accumulated at various places. This is not to say that no sweepers come to the place. The sweepers come but they do not perform their duties properly. They keep on piling the garbage at corners day-by-day without removing it. Moreover, the rubbish collection van does not come regularly. It has created a terrible smell and has made the life of residents miserable. Besides, mosquitoes, flies and other disease carriers breed in these garbage dumps and pose a serious health hazard.

I, therefore, request you to look into the matter. Garbage should be collected daily or atleast on alternate days so as to prevent the accumulation of waste.

Kindly do the needful at the earliest.

Thanking you

Yours sincerely
Alka/Ashish
(Resident, Anand Nagar)

B. XYZ Street
Meerut
25th October, 20XX

Dear Manik

How are you? I am hale and hearty here and hope the same for you. I received your letter today and was thrilled to know about you being accepted in the under 16 Indian Cricket Team. Accept my heartiest congratulations on your wonderful achievement on being selected.

With the way you played, I knew someday you would make a place for yourself in the world of cricket. You have really done it and made all of your near and dear ones proud. Your parents must be really happy. When are you going to play your first match and against whom? Do let me know so that I can also witness the game. Put in your best and please do keep in touch.

Once again, I congratulate you and pray to God for your successful future.

Yours lovingly
Ishant

6. (i) (c) medium (ii) (a) amount
(iii) (a) on

7.

Options	Error	Correction
(a)	cheers	cheered

8.

Options	Error	Correction
(b)	don't	shouldn't

9.

Options	Error	Correction
(a)	says	say
(b)	grown	grow
(c)	a	the

10. (i) Please dispose of the garbage properly.
(ii) The children clapped happily as Santa Claus entered.

11. A. (i) The writer is ashamed because he wasn't the person who started the act of peace and celebration among the warring teams.
(ii) (b) Germans
(iii) The speaker thinks that the act presented in the extract is a trick because his team (English soldiers) is at war with the other, German soldiers.
(iv) (b) Soldier (v) (d) Winter

B. (i) The speaker of the given lines is a school going boy. He is speaking to the coins.
(ii) (c) Four rupees
(iii) The speaker says these lines because the coins have been luring him to buy jalebis.
(iv) (a) Teacher 4(v) (d) scolding

12. A. (i) The cricket is called silly because he wastes his time instead of thinking about the future.
(ii) The reason behind the cricket's complaint is the lack of food and shelter in winters.
(iii) (a) Festive (iv) (c) food (v) (b) Ant

B. (i) The given lines have been taken from 'The School Boy' written by William Blake.
(ii) (a) A school going boy
(iii) (d) All of these
(iv) (b) disappointment
(v) The speaker makes the comparison to make the parents realise the importance of freedom for a child like him.

13. (i) This statement was made by one of the soldiers. It was made so because after wishing Christmas, one of the German soldiers got up on the parapet in grey great coat and started waving a white flag.

(ii) Tilly saw the sea slowly rise and start to form bubble and whirlpools. She remembered that she had seen this in class in a video of Tsunami.

(iii) The school boy sits dully in the school because he is bored, impatient and anxious to go out and enjoy nature.

(iv) When Ranji was called upon to the other side of the pool, he dived into the pool and reached the other side by swimming. The way Ranji dived unpressed Suraj. Ranji's swimming skills impressed Suraj as he was really good at it.

14. (i) The person named Parimal Ghose knew much about Bepin Babu's personal life. He knew about his wife who died ten years ago and had no children. His brother died insane as a result of which he was not willing to visit the mental hospital of Ranchi.

(ii) The six questions that the writer asked Stephen Hawking are

- Had the scientist been brave?
- Did he laugh often?
- Did the scientist find it annoying when he is disturbed by people?
- What is the best thing of being a disabled person?
- If he was relieved or felt better on knowing that people admired him.
- Hawking's message for other disabled people.

(iii) Hafeez is a trendsetter who had a normal childhood yet became a renowned Indian architect. His interest was more in sports rather than academics. He dreamt of making dams, drew sketches, planned strategies.
His mind can be seen in more observant and creative. His success can be seen in his curiosity and understanding of his clientele.

(iv) Panini was a Sanskrit grammarian who gave a comprehensive and scientific theory of phonetics, phonology, and morphology. He was an expert in language and grammar and authored one of the greatest works on grammar called Ashtadhyayi.

(v) The speaker's final bargain is with a child playing with shells on the sea beach. The child has nothing to pay in return. Still the man strikes the deal. Playing with the child will make him a free man, not a slave or servant.

15. A. Chunilal had planned and executed the punishment he wanted to give Bepin Babu precisely to the last detail. He fitted a man named Parimal Ghose, whom Bepin Babu didn't know about. He was made to tell that he had met Bepin Babu in Ranchi in the year of 1958 during the puja. He even told intimate details about Bepin Babu. Chunilal had got the information that Haridas along with his wife had left for Japan a few weeks ago. He even involved Bepin' friends and got them to lie to him. As a result, it became easier for him to execute the plan. After his mission was accomplished, he went to him and again told that he knew about Bepin Babu's Ranchi trip. He even suggested him to consult with a specialist doctor.

B. According to the poem, the poetry or the sounds of Earth is alive in the summer season. As the weather is hot during the summer days, the birds that usually produce the sounds in nature are all hidden in the shades of the tree to seek comfort. They feel faint and remain quiet.

The grasshopper takes delight in summer and he takes the lead to keep the sounds of nature alive throughout the summer. He sings with such a voice that their sounds can be heard from one corner to another. The grasshopper is always cheerful and also spreads the happiness all around. When he gets tired, he rests under beautiful grass. Then, he starts singing again and enjoying the various pleasures that the nature offers.

16. A. The given statement fits the camel perfectly. This statement depicts why the camel received a punishment as well as came to be known as lazy and bad mannered. While all the animals worked diligently every day, the camel preferred to laze about and look at himself in the water. Even though the other animals came to persuade him to work, he didn't listen to them. He didn't even listen to the words of the Djinn who is in charge of all the deserts. Because of this attitude, he made all the other animals his enemy. He also got punished with a hump on his back.

B. 'Humanity is the service of others.' Owing things is the basic human instinct. Accumulation of wealth and resources make one greedy. The Giant was selfish and blocked the entry of the children. But nature punished him. No spring refreshed his garden. When he realised his mistake, he showed generosity towards children and earned their love. Owning things is humane but sharing is divine. When the Giant learnt coexistence, he became contented and lead exemplary life for others.

Sample Question Paper 2 (Unsolved)
English

Time : 3 hrs | M.M. : 80

General Instructions

1 The Question Paper contains four sections- Reading, Grammar, Writing and Literature.
2 Attempt questions based on specific instructions for each part.

Section A : Reading Skills

1. Read the following passage and answer the questions that follow.

In the last week of September 2019, Keerthi Jeyaraj, Director of EduRight Foundation, flew from Texas, the US, to Pallichandai Thidal, a nondescript mound at the far end of Keeladi, a tiny hamlet located 12 km South-East of the historic city of Madurai in Tamil Nadu. The next week, three Sri Lankan Tamils arrived at the same spot. It was their second visit to the excavation site. Also on his way by rail was Chennai-based documentary filmmaker Amshan Kumar. To accommodate these visitors and thousands more, a temporary parking lot was created in Keeladi. A stall selling snacks and coffee sprung up at what looked like a new picnic spot.

An astonishing 1.16 lakh people visited the site between 20th September and 10th Octobar. The visitors flocked to the hamlet in curiosity and fascination following the publication of a report by the Tamil Nadu State Department of Archaeology (SDA) on 18th September. Earlier, carbon samples from Keeladi had been sent to the Beta Analytic Lab in Miami, Florida, for carbon dating, a widely accepted tool to ascertain the age of archaeological and historical remains. The Lab had found that the cultural deposits unearthed during the fourth excavation at Keeladi in Sivaganga district could be safely dated to a period between 6th century BCE and 1st century CE. These place Keeladi artefacts about 300 years earlier than previously believed.

Questions

On the basis of your reading of the passage, answer the following questions. **(10)**

(i) What can you infer about what happened in Keeladi by the usage of the word 'flocked' in the second paragraph?
(a) The population of Keeladi suddenly exploded as there was a massive number of people moved into the town.
(b) There was a brief surge in the number of people who went to Keeladi to see the archaeological site.
(c) Every person who rushed to Keeladi had read the study published by the SDA.
(d) Keeladi became a major centre for tourist holidays.

(ii) What can you say about how long ago Indian people had lived in the Keeladi excavation site?
(a) Between 300 and 600 years ago
(b) Between 600 and 1000 years ago
(c) Between 1000 and 2000 years ago
(d) Between 2000 and 2500 years ago

(iii) Which other word in the passage is closest in meaning to the word 'artefacts' in the last sentence?
(a) hamlet
(b) remains
(c) site
(d) samples

(iv) Based on the information in the passage, why do you think that carbon dating is a "widely accepted tool to ascertain the age of archaeological and historical remains"?
(a) It is a highly accurate dating method.
(b) It is not available in all countries, only some developed countries have it.
(c) It is perhaps the best tool that is available at present.
(d) It is a very safe method of dating historical remains.

(v) Which of the following phrases used in the excerpt supports the idea that Pallicandai Thidal was a 'nondescript mound'?
   (a) '...what looked like a new picnic spot'
   (b) '...a temporary parking lot was created'
   (c) 'An astonishing 1.16 lakh people visited the site'
   (d) 'excavation site'

(vi) What is the use of carbon dating?
   (a) To scan the archeological data
   (b) To ascertain the age of archeological history and remains
   (c) To make a report on the historical site
   (d) To further the excavation for more findings

(vii) Where did Keerthi Jayaraj Travel and why?

(viii) A new picnic spot was created to accomodate people. Give reasons for your answer.

(ix) Which word from the passage means 'found/ discovered'?

(x) What does the word 'hamlet' mean in the passage?

2. Read the given passage and answer the questions that follow.

The Mastermind quiz is billed as a 'battle of minds'. This battle is fought in two halves. In the first, each of four participants faces a barrage of questions, for two minutes, on any topic of his or her choice. In the second round, the questions are on general knowledge. There are two points for each correct answer and zero for wrong answers and passes. In the event of a tie, the person who has passed fewer questions wins.

Questions can be bizarre, but they are answered nonetheless. "It absolutely amazes you that these guys know so much. In KBC, it used to be that this guy knows so little," says Basu after the show. Siddhartha Basu was the director of Kaun Banega Crorepati (KBC).

This year's Mastermind final was won by Ramanand Janardhana, a 22 year-old software engineer from Pune. Janardhana had Agatha Christie's 'Tommy and Tupence' novels as his specialist topic. He even knew that Tommy used asofoetida to create a stink in his room.

There are, of course, all sorts of quizzers. The diary-toting, Manorama yearbook, wielding variety will typically prepare for a contest by 'studying'. He knows that the best questions, the ones that get the 'wah-wahs', are always repeated. He is a solid quizzer, because he knows the obvious.

There is the other kind, like Janardhana, who claim they do nothing extra to prepare for quizzes. They read the papers and magazines, watch TV, and become quizzers because they enjoy the test of recall.

It was a test the nation took when KBC fever was at its height. But long before KBC, there were quiz societies across the country, in places from Guwahati to Gandhinagar. Kolkata was the hub of the game; quizzing in India began here in 1967. Even now, the majority of quizzers are from Kolkata. Of the four 2002 Mastermind finalists, two were from that city.

Quizzing is big in school and college festivals. It's the 'literary' highlight of all fests. There are even professional quizzers, who, like mercenaries, play for money and the thrill of the game. They represent various organisations at different times.

Most quizzers grow out of active quizzing after college. Some, the really hardcore devotees of the game, keep at it. "I don't get tired of quizzing," says Pinaki Prasad Roy, a Mastermind finalist. "I get excited." Roy is a 46-year old finance professional from Kolkata, and has been a quizzer for three decades.

Curiosity is the most essential quality for a quizzer. A fantastic memory and instant recall help. And for Mastermind at least, the choice of specialist subject is critical. In this year's event, Janardhana took an unassailable lead in the specialist round itself.

Answer the following questions by choosing the most appropriate option. **(10)**

(i) The Mastermind quiz is called a 'battle of minds' because ....
   (a) it is a duel of wits
   (b) the participants are the most intelligent persons
   (c) the participants face a shower of questions
   (d) the mind is on the anvil

(ii) The participants in the quiz seem 'Masterminds' because ....
   (a) they seem to know so little
   (b) they have very polished manner
   (c) they show lot of self confidence
   (d) they seem to know so much

(iii) Ramanand Janardhana won as ....
(a) he had mastery over the specialist topic
(b) he had gone through the quiz columns in magazines
(c) he had chinks in his memory/recall
(d) he knew all the often repeated questions asked by quizmasters

(iv) The studious quizzers are called 'solid' quizzers because ....
(a) they prepare expected questions
(b) they know the obvious
(c) they bank on general awareness
(d) they enjoy the test of recall

(v) The quality most essential for a quizzer is ....
(a) love of learning
(b) mathematical accuracy
(c) curiosity to know
(d) comprehensive learning

(vi) The word 'mercenaries' in para 7 means ....
(a) those who seek mercy
(b) those who work on machines
(c) those who are lively and quick
(d) those who fight for money

(vii) Why did Ramanand Janardhana win Mastermind final?

(viii) Who are called solid quizzers?

(ix) Which is the most essential quality of a quizzer?

(x) How is Kolkata associated with quizzing game?

Section B : Writing

3. A. Your friend, Kunal is fond of reading good books. Write a letter to him inviting him to visit the Food Festival which is going to be held in your city in December. You are Rajiv Mittal.

Or

B. Recently you went to attend a lecture about the increasing pollution on our planet. The focus of the lecture was e-waste. Write a Diary Entry talking about the lecture and what you learnt from it.

4. A. Write a short story in 100-120 words beginning with the following lines. Give a suitable title to the story. **(5)**

Mr. Gupta was returning from work at around 11 : 30 pm that night. On his way home, he heard a rustling sound from the bushes ... .

Or

B. Write a speech to be delivered in the morning assembly on the topic, "Water, a valuable asset, conservation at home and at school". You are Karuna/Karan. You can use the following image to frame your answer.

5. A. You are Mudit, a student of J. P. Public School, Karnal. You have just returned from a trekking expedition. Write a letter to your friend Lakshya of Jhansi sharing the experience of the same.

Or

B. As a regular commuter by bus from Noida to Delhi, you have been witnessing rash driving by the busdrivers daily without an exception. Write a letter to the Editor, 'The Times of India' in 120-150 words drawing the attention of the General Manager, Delhi Transport Corporation to this problem. You are Priti/Prakash, 15 Udyog Vihar, Noida. (120-150 words)

Clues

- Creates a sense of panic among the pedestrians and commuters
- Leads to accidents
- Drivers should be fined heavily
- Strict enforcement of traffic rules.
- Time to time training must be encouraged

Section C : Grammar

6. Choose the correct options to fill in the blanks to complete the passages. **(3)**

Once upon a time, a hyena and a hare were ...... (i) friends. However, both of them liked the monkey daughter. ....(ii) of them wished to marry her. Both went to father monkey and told him so. Father monkey asked them to come well-dressed so that he could .... (iii) one of them for his daughter.

(i) (a) great (b) greet (c) grate (d) grete

(ii) (a) Two (b) Both (c) None (d) Neither

(iii) (a) choose (b) chose (c) chosen (d) have chosen

7. Select the option that identifies the error and supplies the correction for the following line
Breaking and entering are against the law. **(1)**

Options	Error	Correction
(a)	breaking	broken
(b)	and	or
(c)	are	is
(d)	law	laws

8. Select the options that identify the errors and supply the corrections for the following line
I remember in my youth that I was used to go with my father to the book fair and buy storybooks. **(1)**

Options	Error	Correction
(a)	Remember	Remembered
(b)	in	at
(c)	was used	used
(d)	buy	bought

9. Following paragraph has not been edited. There is an error in each numbered write the correction against the correct blank number. **(3)**

When it comes to nutrients, almonds really know how to shine! This all in one nut is snacked with multiple benefits who help in weight management, maintain blood glucose levels and providing essential nutrients. Almonds is an excellence source of vitamin-E, magnesium, and manganese.

	Error	Correction
(a)	....	....
(b)	....	....
(c)	....	....

10. Rearrange the following words to make meaningful sentences. **(2)**

(i) the desert / A camel / carries / trough / travellers

(ii) prince / The young / far and wide / travelled

Section D : Literature

11. Read the following extracts to answer the given questions. (5)

A. Tilly started to scream at her family to get off the beach. "She talked about an earthquake under the sea. She got more and more hysterical," said her mother Penny. "I didn't know what a tsunami was. But seeing my daughter so frightened, I thought something serious must be going on." Tilly's parents took her and her sister away from the beach, to the swimming pool at the hotel. A number of other tourists also left the beach with them. "Then it was as if the entire sea had come out after them. I was screaming, 'Run!'"

(i) Why did Tilly scream?

(ii) Why did Penny listen to Tilly?
(a) Because Tilly was too frightened.
(b) Because Tilly reacted unnaturally.
(c) Because Tilly was angry.
(d) Because Tilly was getting ill.

(iii) Where did Tilly and her family take refuge?
(a) On a hill
(b) On the third floor
(c) On the terrace
(d) On a wooden plank

(iv) The word 'hysterical' means
(a) crazy (b) uncontrollable
(c) ill (d) angry

(v) On the basis of the extract, how would you define Tsunami?

Or

B. The poor children had now nowhere to play. They tried to play on the road, but the road was very dusty and full of hard stones, and they did not like it. They used to wander round the high walls when their lessons were over, and talk about the beautiful garden inside. "How happy we were there!" they said to each other. Then the Spring came, and all over the country there were little blossoms and little birds. Only in the garden of the Selfish Giant it was still winter.

(i) Why did the poor children have no place to play?

(ii) The children did not play on the road because of
(a) its dirtiness (b) stones
(c) probability of injuries (d) Both (a) and (b)

(iii) Why did spring skip the Giant's garden?

(iv) On the basis of the extract, which characteristic would you attach to the Giant?
(a) Crafty (b) Cruel
(c) Kind (d) Evil

(v) What was the children's tone when they said 'How happy we were there!'?
(a) Regret (b) Disappointment
(c) Nostalgia (d) Angry

12. Read the following extracts to answer the given questions. (5)

A. There seemed an inevitability
about what on ground had looked
haphazard,
unplanned and without style
When the jet sprang into the sky.
When the jet reached ten thousand feet,
it was clear why the country
had cities where the rivers ran and
why the valleys were populated.

(i) What was the inevitability?

(ii) How did the view from the ground differ from that in the air?

(iii) What did these thing teach the poet?
(a) About different perspectives
(b) Lack of logic behind man's action
(c) Logic of geography
(d) All of the above

(iv) Where were the cities located?
(a) On hills (b) Near rivers
(c) In forest (d) Both (a) and (b)

(v) What is the rhyme scheme of the first four lines of the poem?
(a) abcb
(b) abbc
(c) abab
(d) No rhyme scheme

Or

B. The poetry of Earth is ceasing never:
On a lone winter evening when the frost
Has wrought a silence, from the stone there shrills
The cricket's song, in warmth increasing ever,
And seems to one in drowsiness half lost;
The grasshopper's among some grassy hills.

(i) Whose voice is heard from the stones?
(a) The grasshopper
(b) The cricket
(c) The poet
(d) The nature

(ii) The frost has wrought a silence
Which poetic device is used in the above line?
(a) Personification (b) Simile
(c) Rhythm (d) Anaphora

(iii) What is the tone of the extract?
(a) Admiring (b) Nostalgic
(c) Passionate (d) Appreciative

(iv) How does the cricket's song spread warmth?

(v) Who does the cricket's song resemble to people lost in drowsiness?

13. Answer the following questions in about 15-20 words. **(4)**

(i) How did Tipu Sultan react to the Britishers?

(ii) What does the poet find difficult to understand in the poem 'The Geography Lesson'?

(iv) What does the song of cricket remind people of?

(v) Why do Ranji and Suraj engage in a fight?

14. Answer any three of the following in 30-40 words. **(9)**

(i) Write a short note on Nalanda University.

(ii) Why does the ant refuse to help the grasshopper?

(iii) What frustrated Stephen Hawking while giving the interview?

(iv) What does the school boy tell his parents in the poem 'The School Boy'?

(v) How did the Giant react when he saw the children playing in his garden when he returned after seven years?

15. Answer any one of the following in 100-150 words. **(6)**

A. How did both the British and Germans spend the Christmas night?

Or

B. What does the poet in 'The Last Bargain' prefer? What is the reason for his preference?

16. Answer any one of the following in 100-150 words. **(6)**

A. Justify the title of the story 'The Treasure Within'.

Or

B. How does Velu feel in the city? Elaborate in detail.

Sample Question Paper 3 (Unsolved)
English

Time : 3 hrs	M.M. : 80

General Instructions

1 The Question Paper contains four sections- Reading, Grammar, Writing and Literature.

2 Attempt questions based on specific instructions for each part.

Section A : Reading Skills

1. Read the following passage and answer the questions that follow.

It is an indisputable fact that the world has gone too far with the innovation of new technologies such as mobile phones, the internet and so on, due to which people are able to tour the cosmos virtually sitting at one place using their smart devices or other technological gadgets. Though mobile internet access is ten times hurried and short, it can still provide common internet features like alerts, weather data, emails, search engines, instant messages, and game and music downloading.

Due to the easy access of smartphones, communication has been very effective and instant. People are able to convey their message all around the globe to their loved ones without spending hefty sums of money. Adults are always fond of such gadgets and they always welcome and adopt such new technology readily. Further, young people have been able to broaden their minds and improve their skills by doing research on the Internet. For instance, they use smartphones to look up any new word they come across. As we know that most of the universities have online teaching provisions and smartphones assist the students to complete their assignments on time. The mobile phone has been a life saver for a lot of people in case of an emergency. Likewise, the use of smartphones can be of vital importance in preventing crimes in society by providing information to the security forces in time.

Nonetheless, for the young, the use of mobile phones can be like an addiction and they can misuse it. Young people are also prone to getting involved in undesirable activities on the Internet. This might have an adverse effect on their academic performance. Therefore, young people should always be monitored and made aware of its bad outcomes.

Also, a major contributor to its popularity is the availability of prepaid or pay as you go services from a phone shop or an online store. This allows subscribers to load text or airtime credits to their handsets by the use of their credit cards, debit cards or by buying a prepaid card from the network they subscribe to. This plan also doesn't commit a particular customer to a contract. If the prepaid card is not that appealing to you, then you can opt to subscribe using the pay by month plan.

Questions

Based on your understanding of the above passage, answer the questions given below. **(10)**

(i) How has the world advanced?

(a) Introduction of new technologies
(b) Strengthening the political ties
(c) Helping each other
(d) Maintaining world peace

(ii) What are the benefits of mobile phones for the young generation?

(a) Help in online learning
(b) Help look up new word they come across
(c) Help complete assignments on time
(d) All of these

(iii) How can mobile phones be considered 'lifesavers'?

(a) They automatically connect you to a doctor.
(b) They warn you of an impending crime.
(c) They prevent crimes by providing information to security forces.
(d) They give life saving tips.

(iv) Mention any one demerit of mobile phones.

(a) Very expensive
(b) Take a lot of time to charge
(c) Affect academic performance
(d) Difficult to avail services

(v) Through mobile, internet access is .... times hurried and short.

(a) ten (b) fifty
(c) hundred (d) more than ten

(vi) Pick out the words/phrases from the passage which mean the same as 'availablity'.

(a) indisputable (b) access
(c) effective (d) provisions

(vii) How is a prepaid card useful to mobile phone users?

(viii) How can mobile phones be considered 'lifesavers'?

(ix) Mention any two demerits of mobile phones.

(x) How is a prepaid card useful to mobile phone users?

2. Read the given poem and answer the following questions.

My child is still a star
Treading a path so far
Let me not mock him for his marks,
Making him a fish amongst sharks.

God give me the patience to see him bloom.
He's still growing and needs lot of room.
It's a big bad world which puts him down.
No, I don't want to see him ever frown.

My child is still a star
Treading a path so far.
He may not be the best
He may not top the test
God give me the sense not to treat him like a scale
His worth being measured by pass or fail.
He's a fine piece of art!
My lovely child because
God created him with
Strokes so mild.
Someday, he'll unfold his mind and soul.
until then let not the false world take a toll.
God give me the strength to teach him to rise.
for every fall will surely make him wise.
For now, I shall just let him be
And live his life with mirth and glee.
However, I hope he may someday shine.
Or even if he doesn't he's still just fine.
Because a star is always a star.

(Dr. Arundhati Patil)

Based on your understanding of the above poem, answer the questions given below. (10)

(i) Generally people make fun of the children who ....

(a) are like fish
(b) are shining stars
(c) get poor marks
(d) are young children

(ii) The poet compares the little one with a fish because they ....

(a) look like fish
(b) live in water
(c) are helpless and weak
(d) cannot walk

(iii) In the poem, the poet is trying to ....

(a) assess and appreciate a weak child
(b) appreciate and encourage a weak child
(c) encourage and evaluate a weak child
(d) humiliate a weak child

(iv) A 'fall' helps a child as ....

(a) he gets up again
(b) he gets an experience
(c) he gets good marks
(d) he gets free treatment

(v) The poet wants her son to ....

(a) be a star
(b) be a great achiever
(c) go by his natural instincts
(d) get good marks

(vi) Which word in the poem means the same as walking?

(a) Treading (b) Growing
(c) Unfold (d) Strokes

(vii) On what occasion is this poem composed?

(viii) The poet prays God for patience. Why?

(ix) How has the poet criticised the world?

(x) Find a word from the poem that means 'amusement'.

Section B : Writing

3. A. You have met your school friend after five years. Write a dialogue about your conversation discussing your life, career choices, etc. **(5)**

Or

B. Describe a handcrafted item which you made yourself.

4. A. Hard work and punctuality are essential for a happy and successful life. They help in meeting the desired targets of our life. You are Kavya/Kanha. Write an article highlighting the importance of hard work punctuality in a student's life. **(5)**

Use the following clues

foundations for future life of students-important character-importance of time–source of discipline and confidence–meeting deadlines–wards off the stress–life is full of challenges–no shortcuts. It trains a student's mind and body for future.

Or

B. Look at the given image and write a story titled 'The Missing Fortune'.

5. A. As a regular commuter by bus from Noida to Delhi, you have been witnessing rash driving by the bus drivers daily without an exception. Write a letter to the Editor, 'The Times of India' in 120-150 words drawing the attention of the General Manager, Delhi Transport Corporation to this problem. You are Priti/ Prakash, 15 Udyog Vihar, Noida. **(5)**

Or

B. The tourism industry can bring valuable income to the country. Write a letter to the Editor of a popular daily on how the government and the public can boost the development of this industry in 100-120 words. You are Rama/Ram, 4 Rani Road, Ranchi.

Section C : Grammar

6. Choose the correct options to fill in the blanks to complete the passages. **(3)**

Ernest Hemingway was .... (i) of America's most beloved authors. He was born in 1898. ...... (ii) World War I, he served as a volunteer ambulance driver in Italy, ... (iii) later served in the Italian infantry.

(i) (a) best (b) one (c) alone (d) only

(ii) (a) During (b) At (c) In (d) On

(iii) (a) but (b) and (c) further (d) also

7. Select the option that identifies the error and supplies the correction for the following line. **(1)**

The sounds of laughter was echoing in the corridor.

Options	Error	Correction
(a)	sounds	sound
(b)	laughter	laughing
(c)	was	were
(d)	in	of

8. Select the options that identify the errors and supply the corrections for the following line. **(1)**

I must to call him at once.

Options	Error	Correction
(a)	must	should
(b)	to call	call
(c)	him	his
(d)	at	by

9. In the following passage, one word has been omitted in each line. Write the omitted word with the word before and after indicated in it. (3)

(i) The human eye is often called

(ii) king of senses. It gathers 80% of all the knowledge

(iii) but only a few people are blessed appreciate eyes.

10. Rearrange the following words to make meaningful sentences. (2)

(i) wear/these/people/a majority/of/days/a watch

(ii) time/it/in/measures/seconds/and/hours /minutes

Section D : Literature

11. Read the given extracts and answer the questions that follow. (5)

A. Of all the emotions which surged through me as I stood on the summit of Everest, looking over miles of panorama below us, the dominant one I think was humility. The physical in me seemed to say, 'Thank God, it's all over!" However, instead of being jubilant, there was a tinge of sadness. Was it because I had already done the 'ultimate' in climbing and there would be nothing higher to climb and all roads hereafter would lead down?

(i) Who is I?

(a) A soldier without a name
(b) Major Ahluwalia
(c) Bachendri Pal
(d) A randon climber

(ii) List the emotions felt by the writer in the extract.

(iii) Why do you think that the writer felt 'humility'?

(iv) Which of the following words can replace 'dominant' in the extract?

(a) Superior (b) Strongest
(c) Overwhelming (d) Extreme

(v) The word .... in the extract means the same as 'landscape'.

(a) summit (b) panorama
(c) ultimate (d) humility

Or

B. She picked up her sack and started to walk away. Velu stayed on the bench. What should he do? Should he follow this girl? Where was she going to take him? She was disappearing into the crowd, so he had to make up his mind quickly. Alright, he decided. Anyway I have no idea where to go. He jumped up and ran after her. She wasn't even looking back to see where he was.

(i) Who is 'she'?

(a) A beggar
(b) A ragpicker
(c) An orphan
(d) A school going girl

(ii) Where is Velu?

(a) At a bus stop
(b) At a fair
(c) At a railway platform
(d) At a park

(iii) Where was 'she' taking him?

(a) To a wedding
(b) To the police station
(c) To get food
(d) To the bus stop

(iv) Why did Velu hesitate to follow the girl?

(v) For what reason did Velu follow the girl?

12. Read the following extracts to answer the given questions that follow. (5)

A. In the heat of the mid-day the houses stood with shut doors.
I wandered along the crooked lane.
An old man came out with his bag of gold.
He pondered and said, "I will hire you with my money."
He weighed his coins one by one, but I turned away.

(i) Why was the speaker moving in lanes?

(ii) What does the old man offer to the speaker?

(a) Power (b) Wealth
(c) Beauty (d) Freedom

(iii) Why does the speaker refuse to work for the old man?

(iv) The word 'pondered' in the extract indicates ....

(a) will (b) debate

(c) thought (d) confusion

(v) What time of the day is it in the extract?

(a) Morning (b) Evening

(c) Night (d) Noon

Or

B. But to go to school in a summer morn,
O! it drives all joy away;
Under a cruel eye outworn,
The little ones spend the day,
In sighing and dismay.
Ah! then at times
I drooping sit,
And spend many an anxious hour.

(i) Name the poem and the poet.

(ii) What takes the joy away?

(a) Studies (b) Going to school

(c) Teachers (d) Summer

(iii) The term 'cruel eye' refers to

(a) parents (b) teachers

(c) seniors (d) principal

(iv) What does the speaker's posture indicate?

(a) Impatience (b) Bore

(c) Anxiety (d) All of these

(v) What does the speaker feel in school? Why does he feel so?

13. Answer the following questions in about 15-20 words. (4)

(i) How does Major Ahluwalia feel on the top of Mount Everest?

(ii) What does the poet learn when he reaches 10 thousand feet in the air?

(iii) Which part of 'The Short Monsoon Dairy' contain an poem?

(iv) Why does the boy buy the Jalebis?

14. Answer any three of the following in 30-40 words. (9)

(i) How according to Hans Wolf, football is a better way to resolve war?

(ii) What does the Ant and the Cricket tell us about humans and animals?

(iii) How does the leopard make its presence known in Mussoorie?

(iv) Why does Princess September free the little bird?

(v) How does nature create beauty all around the year? Answer with reference to the poem 'On the Grasshopper and the Cricket'.

15. Answer any one of the following in 100-150 words. (6)

A. All the character in 'This is Jody's Fawn' face a moral responsibility. Justify.

Or

B. The system of education curbs creativity, joy and imagination. Do you agree? Answer with reference to the poem 'The School Boy'.

15. Answer any one of the following in 100-150 words. (6)

A. Draw the character sketches of both Suraj and Ranji comparing and contrasting their natures.

Or

B. The Indian Education system focused on the all round growth and development of an individual. Elaborate with reference to the chapter 'The Ancient Education System in India'.